LEFT LIBERALS, THE STATE, AND POPULAR POLITICS IN WILHELMINE GERMANY

Left Liberals, the State, and Popular Politics in Wilhelmine Germany

ALASTAIR P. THOMPSON

OXFORD

UNIVERSITY PRESS

OXFORD

UNIVERSITY PRESS

Great Clarendon Street, Oxford OX2 6DP

Oxford University Press is a department of the University of Oxford.
It furthers the University's objective of excellence in research, scholarship,
and education by publishing worldwide in

Oxford New York

Athens Auckland Bangkok Bogotá Buenos Aires Calcutta
Cape Town Chennai Dar es Salaam Delhi Florence Hong Kong Istanbul
Karachi Kuala Lumpur Madrid Melbourne Mexico City Mumbai
Nairobi Paris São Paulo Shanghi Singapore Taipei Tokyo Toronto Warsaw

and associated companies in Berlin Ibadan

Oxford is a registered trade mark of Oxford University Press
in the UK and certain other countries

Published in the United States
by Oxford University Press Inc., New York

© Alastair Thompson 2000

The moral rights of the author have been asserted

Database right Oxford University Press (maker)

First published 2000

British Library Cataloguing in Publication Data
Data available

Library of Congress Cataloging in Publication Data
Data available

ISBN 0-19-820543-0

1 3 5 7 9 10 8 6 4 2

Typeset in Ehrhardt
by J&L Composition Ltd, Filey, North Yorkshire
Printed in Great Britain
on acid-free paper by
Biddles Ltd,
Guildford and King's Lynn

Preface

HISTORIANS, like liberals, tend to prize the individual. The individual example, the singular piece of evidence is still treasured even when seeking to establish a general pattern, a social context, or a political context. And most works of history have the hallmarks, at least in style and approach, of a single mind. This book is no exception. The subject chosen, the approach taken, and the judgements arrived at, all no doubt reflect to some degree my particular interests. Certainly, unlike some politicians, liberal or not, I have no hesitation in bearing sole responsibility for any imperfections. I do, however, owe a substantial debt of gratitude to a range of people and organizations. As will soon become evident to the reader, this study could not have been written without the help and professional expertise of a large number of archivists throughout Germany, and also in Poland and Britain. I would also like to thank the librarians particularly of Birkbeck College library, the British Library, the library of the Institute for European History, Mainz, Kiel University Library, the Preußische Staatsbibliothek Berlin, the John Rylands Manchester University Library, the library of the German Historical Institute London, and Durham University Library for allowing me to use their collections.

As with any historian currently working on Wilhelmine Germany I owe a general debt to my predecessors and colleagues in the field for the considerable volume of fresh investigation and critical re-examination especially evident over the last two decades. I hope and trust that Wilhelmine Germany will continue to the subject of such vigorous, but generally civilized and constructive debate. It would take too long to thank all the individuals who have given their time discuss aspects of German Liberalism with me, or helped my research in various ways. I should, however, acknowledge my most substantial debts. David Blackbourn, who supervised the project from the outset, provided the ideal combination of a free rein, astute advice, and incisive comment. Even from across the Channel, or now across the Atlantic, he has remained a generous source of encouragement.

Martin Vogt and John Breuilly have also read virtually the whole manuscript, and have offered valuable advice. In Poland, Adam Galos and Marek Czaplinski shared their knowledge of Silesian history with me. Marek also kindly agreed to provide a German translation of some Polish research. Although archival research tends to be a solitary occupation, numerous friends have provided company and encouragement, especially Erich and Katrin Kundel, Werner Köhler and Martina Reiling-Köhler, Cord Mempel, Fiona Morton, and Linfei Xu.

I must thank Helmut Goetz and the Petersen family for their permission to use the papers of Walter Goetz and Carl Petersen respectively. Annette Hohmeyer-Schücking not only allowed me to use the papers of her father Lothar Schücking, but accommodated me while I read them. Professor Gerhard Wehle generously provided copies of his transcriptions of shorthand sections in the Georg Kerschensteiner papers. I would also like to thank and acknowledge the following for their financial support: the German Academic Exchange Service, British Academy, the Institute for European History, Leverhulme Trust, the British Council, and Durham University's staff research fund. I am also grateful to the staff of the Oxford University Press. Finally, I want to thank my parents. They have helped me for longer and in more ways than anyone. The book is dedicated to them.

Durham A.T.

Contents

I. MEN, MACHINERY, AND MISSION

II. EXECUTIVE, PARTIES, AND PUBLIC OPINION: THE LEFT LIBERALS IN NATIONAL POLITICS, 1907–1914

III. LEFT LIBERALS IN LOCAL SOCIETY

List of Tables

List of Abbreviations

AA Bonn	Politisches Archiv des Auswärtigen Amtes Bonn
AA Wrocław	Archepiscopal Archive Wrocław (Archiwum Archdiecezjalne we Wrocławiu)
AW Wrocław	State Archive Wrocław (Archiwum Panstowe we Wrocławiu)
AfS	*Archiv für Sozialgeschichte*
AHR	*American Historical Review*
BA Koblenz	Bundesarchiv Koblenz
BA Berlin	Bundesarchiv Berlin
BA-MA Freiburg	Bundesarchiv-Militärarchiv Freiburg
BLPES	British Library of Political and Economic Science
CEH	*Central European History*
DKP	German Conservative Party (Deutsch-Konsersative Partei)
DVP	Deutsche Volkspartei (1868–1910)
EHQ	*European History Quarterly*
FrVg	Freisinnige Vereinigung
FrVp	Freisinnige Volkspartei
FVP	Fortschrittliche Volkspartei
GG	*Geschichte und Gesellschaft*
GLA Karlsruhe	General Landesarchiv Karlsruhe
HAS Cologne	Historisches Archiv der Stadt Köln
HSA Stuttgart	Hauptstaatsarchiv Stuttgart
IISH	International Institute of Social History
JBP	*Jenaer Beiträge zur Parteiengeschichte*
JCH	*Journal of Contemporary History*
JMH	*Journal of Modern History*
LA Schleswig	Landesarchiv Schleswig
LB Kiel	Landesbibliothek Kiel
LBI	*Leo Baeck Institute Yearbook*
NL	Nachlaß
P&P	*Past and Present*
RLAA	Reichsverein liberaler Arbeiter und Angestellte
SA	Staatsarchiv
SB Munich	Stadtbibliothek München

SPD	German Social Democratic Party (Sozialdemokratische Partei Deutschlands)
StA	Stadtarchiv
UB	Universitätsbibliothek
ZfG	*Zeitschrift für Geschichtswissenschaft*

Glossary

ALTE FRAKTIONEN	old parties (in Hamburg city politics)
BAUERNBUND	Peasant League
BEAMTE	state offical, public employee
BÜRGERMEISTER	mayor
BÜRGERVEREIN(E)	citizens' association(s)
BURGFRIEDE	civic truce (in First World War)
FRAKTION	parliamentary party, caucus
FREISINN	independent, radical, anti-clerical; political label for German (and Swiss) left liberalism
HONORATIOREN	notables
HONORATIORENPOLITIK	notable politics
HOSPITANT	associate member of parliamentary party
KARTELL	pro-Bismarck, pro-tariffs parliamentary majority (Conservatives, Free Conservatives, and National Liberals)
KREIS	basic administrative unit in Prussia (excluding large towns)
LANDRAT	district official in charge of Kreis
LANDTAG	state parliament
MACHTPOLITIK	power politics
MAGISTRAT	municipal council executive
MITTELSTAND	middle estate
MITTELSTANDSRETTER	supposed saviours of the Mittelstand
NATIONALE VERBÄNDE	nationalist associations
OBERBÜRGERMEISTER	mayor (generally of city or large town)
OBERPRÄSIDENT	provincial governor
PRIMAT DER NATIONALEN	belief in the primacy of the 'national' cause
REGIERUNGSPRÄSIDENT	district governor
SAMMLUNGSPOLITIK	politics of anti-socialist alliance
VEREIN	association, club, local party branch
VOLKSPARTEI	people's party

Introduction

For me Liberalism is no fine cloak to be worn on festive occasions, only to be left in the cupboard during the week. Rather belief in a free system and free ideas governs my whole political outlook. I cannot bring myself to be liberal in political matters only to turn a blind eye to reactionary economic and church policy. A great, high-minded people, my desire for our nation, should be free in thought and feelings in all matters: on economic issues have scorn for pettiness and the interest-broker; in religious affairs exercise toleration; and on constitutional questions bend not the knee, even before the most powerful of men. (Theodor Barth, cited by Georg Gothein, *Biographisches Jahrbuch und Deutscher Nekrolog*, 14 (1912), 346).

[A]bolition of duties on grain must not be demanded. If you do so, whatever else you promise [the peasants] will not believe you. . . . Best not to raise the subject . . . talk about cows and pigs, oxen and horses, also throw in the odd joke. That interests the people much more than a speech they can't digest. . . . And, finally, don't forget our rural population is frightfully patriotic and nationalistic. That's something which no doubt every candidate should take into account. (UB Marburg, NL Rade, A. Wedermann to Martin Rade, Colbe bei Marburg 31 Jan. 1912).

Discussing cows and pigs was not exactly the sort of energetic democratic activity Theodor Barth envisaged in his crusade for the regeneration of Liberalism. Indeed, what divided Barth, a brilliant political commentator and 'conscience of German Liberalism', from the ill-educated rural political agitator, Wedermann, sometime secretary of the local left liberal rural association in the Marburg constituency, is more readily apparent. Socially, culturally, economically they inhabited different worlds. Barth's writings were sprinkled with literary allusions and well-turned foreign phrases, Wedermann's with grammatical errors. Barth's immediate milieu was that of the highly educated, culturally sophisticated liberal bourgeoisie. He was at home, literally and metaphorically, in the wealthy Tiergarten district of Berlin.[1] Wedermann's social contacts, by contrast, centred on

---

[1] BA Berlin, NL Barth 58. For an insight into Barth as an individual and writer see Barth's own *Politische Porträts*, 2nd edn. (Berlin, 1923), and E. Feder, *Theodor Barth und der demokratische Gedanke* (Gotha, 1919). K. Wegner, *Theodor Barth und die Freisinnige Vereinigung* (Tübingen, 1969) is the best analysis of Barth and party politics.

peasants, farm labourers, and village artisans in rural Hessen. And while Barth was familiar, through travel, study, and personal contacts, with western and especially English and North American society, Wedermann's world encompassed the 180 villages inside the Marburg Reichstag constituency.

This study analyses these different worlds within Wilhelmine society. In particular, it examines the function and form of politics against these differing social backgrounds. Such an approach is familiar to British and American historians. It is central, for example, to our understanding of Victorian and Edwardian political history.[2] By contrast, its importance in the context of imperial Germany has been often overlooked. The conventional image of the Bismarckian German Empire presents a double barrier against investigating the infrastructure of Liberalism. Party politics has been judged relatively unimportant and, moreover, Liberalism was accorded only a subordinate and subsiding position amongst the political parties after the 1870s. Both contentions harbour a kernel of truth. In the national parliament, the Reichstag, and in state assemblies, German parties wielded less power than their western counterparts. Parliamentarians had extensive budgetary powers and could block or amend proposed legislation. But the Reichstag had no constitutional power to compel the Reich leadership and the representatives of the state governments in the upper house, the Bundesrat, to respond to its legislative initiatives, and was unable to make and unmake ministries. Moreover, as Hans-Ulrich Wehler has rightly emphasized, there was a marked contrast between the considerable potential lent the Reichstag by the growing need for federal funds and legislation and the limited appetite and ambition of parliamentarians to exploit this.[3] Equally, it is evident that a marked erosion in Liberal electoral support and political influence

---

[2] See e.g. the recent study E. F. Biagini, *Liberty, Retrenchment and Reform: Popular Liberalism in the Age of Gladstone, 1860–80* (Cambridge, 1992) and, esp., John Vincent's pioneering *The Formation of the British Liberal Party 1857–1868*, 2nd edn. (Hassocks, 1976). For the vast literature on Edwardian Liberalism: P. F. Clarke, *Lancashire and the New Liberalism* (Cambridge, 1971); George L. Bernstein, *Liberalism and Liberal Politics in Edwardian England* (London, 1986); and D. Tanner, *Political Change and the Labour Party 1900–1918* (Cambridge, 1990).

[3] H.-U. Wehler, *Deutsche Gesellschaftsgeschichte* (4 vols.; Munich, 1987–   ), iii, 864–6. For suggestive reflections on the *de facto* evolution of the Bismarckian constitution see T. Nipperdey, *Deutsche Geschichte 1866–1918* (2 vols.; Munich, 1990–2), ii, 471–97.

had occurred after the onset of economic depression in the mid-1870s and government's turn to the right in 1878/9.[4]

None the less, there is considerable scope for revising the customary image of imperial Germany, and prompted by a questioning of the notion of a German *Sonderweg*, or special path, historians have started to scrutinize official claims about a strong monarch, army, and administration standing above party and popular ferment.[5] This image, projected by imperial Germany's ruling institutions and embellished by the Wilhelmine academic establishment with a zeal born of belief, sycophancy, and self-interest, is indeed deceptive. It reflects not so much reality as minority ideal. German authoritarianism failed to meet the claims of strength, efficiency, and acceptability made for it; it was far more susceptible to pressure from below than its supporters publicly admitted. The very fact that the Wilhelmine governing élite was increasingly having to argue within public sphere that the wider opinion was of no account underlined the contradictions between image and reality.[6]

If views of the Wilhelmine state have been shrouded in persistent, powerful tradition, so the same is equally true for German Liberalism, which has generally been studied through ideas and individuals.[7]

[4] H. Rosenberg, 'Political and Social Consequences of the Great Depression of 1873–1896 in Central Europe', in J. J. Sheehan (ed.) *Imperial Germany* (New York, 1976), 39–60. On left liberals before 1890 see G. Seeber, *Zwischen Bebel und Bismarck: Zur Geschichte des Linksliberalismus 1871–1893* (Berlin, 1965); H.-E. Matthes, 'Die Spaltung der Nationalliberalen Partei und die Entwicklung des Linksliberalismus bis zur Auflösung der Deutsch-Freisinnigen Partei 1871–1893', Diss., Kiel University, 1953; U. Steinbrecher, *Liberale Parteiorganisation unter besonderer Berücksichtigung des Linksliberalismus* (Cologne, 1960); and U. Müller-Plantenberg, *Der Freisinn nach Bismarcks Sturz*, Diss., Berlin, 1971.

[5] D. Blackbourn and G. Eley, *The Peculiarities of German History* (Oxford, 1984); G. Bonham, *Ideology and Interests in the German State* (New York, 1991); T. Süle, *Preußische Bürokratietradition: Zur Entwicklung von Verwaltung und Beamtenschaft in Deutschland 1871–1918* (Göttingen, 1988); R. M. Halmen, *Staatstreue und Interessenvertretung: Studien zur Soziologie und Sozialgeschichte der Beamtenbewegung bis zur Novemberrevolution* (Hamburg, 1988).

[6] On state ideology see B. Faulenbach, *Ideologie des deutschen Weges* (Munich, 1980). For summary of left liberal intellectual critiques see E. Demm, *Ein Liberaler in Kaiserreich und Republik: Der politischer Weg Alfred Webers bis 1920* (Boppard am Rhein, 1990), 80–94.

[7] F. C. Sell, *Die Tragödie des deutschen Liberalismus*, 2nd edn. (Baden-Baden, 1981) is the classic account of German Liberalism as a history of (failed) ideas. Earlier, but on similar lines, is O. Klein-Hattingen, *Geschichte des deutschen Liberalismus* (2 vols.; Berlin and Schöneberg, 1911–12). The most important biographies of Wilhelmine left liberals are: W. J. Mommsen, *Max Weber and German Politics 1890–1920* (Chicago, 1984); J. J. Sheehan, *The Career of Lujo Brentano: A Study of Liberalism and Social Reform in Imperial Germany*

4 *Introduction*

Certainly these themes are valid, given Liberalism's claim to be a party of ideas, and of ideas based on individualism. This book, too, investigates ideas and individuals. Identifying those ideas and attitudes which led Wilhelmine Germans to embrace or reject left liberal politics is a constant concern, while Chapter 3 deals specifically with left liberal ideology. And prominent left liberals, like Barth, are assessed not just as figureheads but as parliamentarians (Chapter 4), campaigners (Chapter 2), and leading influences in regional and local society (Chapters 7–9). Yet to understand how left liberalism operated in party politics, its successes and failings as a political movement, requires additional perspectives.

This study reconsiders German Liberal politics in four respects. First, more insight into the mechanics of Liberal politics is needed. Historians describe nineteenth-century German Liberalism being progressively squeezed between state (*Staat*) and people (*Volk*).[8] This is undoubtedly a valuable concept. It cannot, however, replace the need for concrete examination of how these forces impacted upon Liberalism. Moreover, the image created is inevitably telescopic. Not only is Liberal decline portrayed as remorseless and relentless, but the state and popular pressure are accorded an irredeemably negative and destructive role in the history of German Liberalism in the late nineteenth and early twentieth centuries. This book aims to examine the substance of Wilhelmine Liberalism rather than discoursing on its absence. The complete party spectrum is considered: from parliamentarians and intellectual critics through local leaders and newspaper editors to party workers (*Vertrauensmänner*), members, and voters. The political setting ranges from receptions in the Reich Chancellor's palace to drinking sessions after public meetings in village pubs. (Strangely, we know almost less about the former, the inner workings of Berlin politics, than the latter.) This wide-ranging analysis of left liberal political activity will question the perceptions of Liberal

(Chicago, 1966); Wegner, *Theodor Barth*; P. Theiner, *Sozialer Liberalismus und deutsche Weltpolitik: Friedrich Naumann im wilhelminischen Deutschland (1860–1919)* (Baden-Baden, 1983); I. S. Lorenz, *Eugen Richter: Der entschiedene Liberalismus in wilhelminischer Zeit, 1871–1906* (Husum, 1981); J. Reimann, *Ernst Müller-Meiningen senior und der Linksliberalismus in seiner Zeit: Zur Biographie eines bayerischen und deutschen Politikers (1866–1944)* (Munich, 1968); Demm, *Ein Liberaler*; and A. C. Nagel, *Martin Rade—Theologe und Politiker des sozialen Liberalismus: Eine politische Biographie* (Gütersloh, 1996).

[8] J. J. Sheehan, *German Liberalism in the Nineteenth Century* (Chicago, 1978) is a masterly exposition of this theme.

decline and the straightforward vision of Liberalism as the opponent and victim of the state and popular pressure.

The second respect in which this study seeks to add to previous works on German Liberalism is regional. There can be few statements about Wilhelmine Germany less contentious than those stressing the importance of regionalism. The well-rehearsed points about recent unification, and the different traditions, constitutional diversity, and contrasting social and economic structure within the twenty-five states which formed the Kaiserreich need no further emphasis. Historians have emphasized both the importance of German Liberalism's social grassroots in shaping its values and political fate, and the need for further research in this crucial area.[9] Indeed, the left liberals have been particularly neglected. There is no full-scale analysis of regionalism comparable, for example, to Dan White's study of National Liberalism in Hessen.[10] This is perhaps understandable, for regionalism presented National Liberalism with particularly acute difficulties.[11] Moreover, the pattern reflects regional research in general. Western and southern Germany, the main National Liberals heartlands, have generally been studied far more than the north and east. As a result, existing regional studies of left liberalism are largely concentrated on its south-western strongholds, Württemberg and Frankfurt am Main.[12] However, much of left liberalism's electoral support lay in eastern rather than western districts of Germany. Along the North

[9] L. Gall and D. Langewiesche (eds.) *Liberalismus und Region: Zur Geschichte des deutschen Liberalismus im 19. Jahrhundert* (Munich, 1995); L. Gall (ed.), *Bürgertum und bürgerlich-liberale Bewegung in Mitteleuropa seit dem 18. Jahrhundert* (Historische Zeitschrift, Sonderheft 17; Munich, 1997); G. Eley, 'James Sheehan and the German Liberals: A Critical Appreciation', *CEH* 14 (1981), 273–88; R. J. Evans, *Rethinking German History* (London, 1987), 90–1.

[10] D. S. White, *The Splintered Party: National Liberalism in Hessen and the Reich, 1867–1918* (Cambridge, Mass., 1976).

[11] A. J. O'Donnell, 'National Liberalism and the Mass Politics of the German Right 1890–1907', Ph.D. thesis, Princeton University, 1973; B. Heckart, *From Bassermann to Bebel: The Grand Block's Quest for Reform in the Kaiserreich, 1900–1914* (New Haven, Conn., and London, 1974); J. Thiel, *Die Großblockpolitik der nationalliberalen Partei Badens 1905–1914* (Stuttgart, 1976); G. S. Vascik, 'Rural Politics and Sugar in Germany: A Comparative Study of the National Liberal Party in Hannover and Prussian Saxony, 1871–1914', Ph.D., University of Michigan, 1988; G. Eley, *Reshaping the German Right: Radical Nationalism and Political Change after Bismarck* (London, 1980). K. H. Pohl has analysed Saxon National Liberalism before 1914 in a series of pieces. For further references see J. Retallack, 'Society and Politics in Saxony in the Nineteenth and Twentieth Centuries: Reflections on Recent Research', *AfS* 38 (1998), 429.

[12] K. Simon, *Die Württembergischen Demokraten: Ihre Stellung und Arbeit im Parteien- und Verfassungssystem im Württemberg und im Deutschen Reich* (Stuttgart, 1970) and J. C. Hunt, *The People's Party in Württemberg and Southern Germany, 1890–1914: The Possibilities of*

German coast, for example, the significance of left liberalism in Schleswig-Holstein and Oldenburg has been acknowledged and partly studied.[13] Yet left liberalism further east along the Baltic, from Mecklenburg on to coastal Pomerania, Danzig, and Eastern Prussia has remained essentially unexplored. There are several reasons for this. Sources for these regions are scarcer and less accessible. Moreover, historians from Poland and the GDR were, for understandable reasons, more concerned with history of the oppressed, Poles and socialists, and their oppressors, the Prussian state and Junkers, than with Liberalism. Yet this neglect is certainly no reflection of actual political influence of left liberalism in these areas on the eve of the First World War. For left liberalism along the Baltic could hardly be considered a spent force at a time when it held most of the Reichstag seats, gaining votes and constituencies from the Conservatives and maintaining support against the SPD.

The left liberals were frequently a significant force within the small, and indeed miniature, states within the German Empire. All three diminutive states to the west of Hanover and Kassel—Lippe-Demold, Schaumberg-Lippe, and Waldeck-Pyrmont—were represented in the Reichstag by left liberals in 1914. In central Germany the left liberals were an important force in several of the patchwork of states which made up Thuringia. Here again left liberalism has often escaped detailed scrutiny, although Torsten Kupfer's recent study of left liberal and SPD relations in Anhalt is a welcome exception.[14] Therefore,

Democratic Politics (Stuttgart, 1975) are the fullest accounts of Württemberg left liberalism. For Frankfurt see J. Palmowski, *Urban Liberalism in Imperial Germany: Frankfurt am Main, 1866–1914* (Oxford, 1999); J. D. Rolling, 'Liberals, Socialists and City Government in Imperial Germany: The Case of Frankfurt am Main, 1900–1918', Ph.D., University of Wisconsin-Madison, 1979; R. Roth, *Stadt und Bürgertum in Frankfurt am Main: Ein besonderer Weg von der ständischen zur modernen Bürgergesellschaft 1760–1914* (Munich, 1995); and S. Wolf, *Liberalismus in Frankfurt am Main vom Ende der Freien Stadt bis zum Ersten Weltkrieg (1866–1914)* (Frankfurt am Main, 1987).

[13] For Schleswig-Holstein see, in addition to Ch. 8 below, R. Heberle, *Landbevölkerung und Nationalsozialismus: Eine soziologische Untersuchung der politischen Willensbildung in Schleswig-Holstein 1918 bis 1932* (Stuttgart, 1963); for Oldenburg see W. Günther (ed.), *Parteien und Wahlen in Oldenburg: Beiträge zur Landesgeschichte im 19. und 20. Jahrhundert* (Oldenburg, 1983).

[14] T. Kupfer, *Der Weg zum Bündnis: entschieden Liberale und Sozialdemokraten in Dessau und Anhalt im Kaiserreich* (Cologne, 1998); cf. the more general survey E. Wörfel, 'Liberalismus in den thüringischen Staaten im Kaiserreich', in Gall and Langewiesche (eds.), *Liberalismus und Region*, 217–52. M. Hettling, 'Von der Hochburg zur Wagenburg: Liberalismus in Breslau von den 1860er Jahren bis 1918', ibid. 253–76; and W. W. Hagen, *Germans, Poles and Jews: The Nationality Conflict in the Prussian East 1772–1914* (Chicago, 1980) offer rare case-studies of left liberalism in the east.

the three regional case-studies of left liberalism, in Baden, Schleswig-Holstein, and Silesia, which make up the final part of this book, add significantly to previous research. Their main purpose, however, is qualitative not quantitative. Wilhelmine politics can only be fully understood with a regional and local context. And, given the substantial differences between east and west, north and south, urban and rural, it must be assessed against varying backgrounds of confession, economic structure, and political tradition. Baden, Schleswig-Holstein, and Silesia were selected to reflect much of this variety: cities and small towns; large rural estates and small peasant holdings; Protestant and Catholic communities; areas where the left liberals were traditionally strong, and those where they had few roots.

A third sphere where a wider approach is required concerns ideas and issues. There is an inevitable temptation to focus on great causes, and particularly, given the beliefs of our age, on the issue of democratic reform. Such temptations have taken a different form in Germany than Britain. Events both before 1918 and after 1930/33 present formidable obstacles to a Whig interpretation of German history, though this has not deterred Manfred Rauh.[15] The failure to achieve parliamentary government and to reform the undemocratic three-class Prussian franchise has promoted a tendency is to look for what might have been.[16] This inclination is naturally particularly strong with respect to the Liberals, the grouping expected to force through political reform. German Liberals have often been assessed not according to what they did, but what they failed to do. Fortunately, the sweeping 'liberalism a study in failure' approach is no longer pervasive.[17] Indeed, there is even some danger of historians exaggerating those aspects of imperial Germany which were successful and 'modern'.[18] There remains, however, a residual sense in which

[15] Rauh's rather overstated theory of creeping parliamentarization is advanced uncompromisingly in *Die Parlamentarisierung des Deutschen Reiches* (Düsseldorf, 1977) and *Föderalismus und Parlamentarismus im Wilhelminischen Reich* (Düsseldorf, 1973).

[16] See e.g. D. Grosser, *Vom monarchischen Konstitutionalismus zur parlamentarischen Demokratie: Die Verfassungspolitik der deutshen Parteien im letzten Jahrzehnt des Kaiserreiches* (The Hague, 1970); and Heckart, *Bassermann*.

[17] See e.g. the rejection of all-consuming notions of failure in D. Langewiesche, *Liberalism in Germany* (Houndmills, 2000), esp. 121–85; and the introduction to K. H. Jarausch and L. E. Jones (eds.), *In Search of a Liberal Germany: Studies in the History of German Liberalism from 1789 to the Present* (New York, 1990). An older unpublished work, S. T. Robson, 'Left-Wing Liberalism in Germany, 1900–1919', D.Phil, Oxford University, 1966, also took a more favourable, perhaps too favourable, view of left liberal prospects.

[18] The articles 'looking at the bright side' (p. ix) in J. R. Dukes and J. Remak (ed.), *Another Germany: A Reconsideration of the Imperial Era* (Boulder, Colo., 1988) are a case in point.

the approach to Wilhelmine politics is condemnatory. Politics was criticized for failing to live up to the past. It was common among educated Germans in the second half of the nineteenth century, and liberals in particular, to depict a continual coarsening and decline of politics, with political ideals giving way to economic self-interest, the common good to class conflict, decorum to demagoguery.[19] Politics has also been accused, retrospectively, of failing to prepare for the future. Historians have sought explanations for the sweeping Nazi electoral support of the early 1930s in the long-term legacies of imperial politics as well as immediate economic crisis. Weimar foundered, it is argued, partly because Wilhelmine Germany had a febrile, nationalistic, and superficial form of politics rather than a stable, democratic political culture.[20]

There is substance to both sets of criticisms. Wilhelmine politics were materialistic, populist, and irresponsible. And the search for antecedents of the Nazi seizure of power is justified and important. This is the case for the particular issue of anti-Semitism. Racial anti-Semitism was being propounded by the 1880s and 1890s, and not just in the literary form of a Houston Stewart Chamberlain or Paul de Lagarde. Theodor Fritsch, venerated by the Nazis as an ideological father figure, not only published incessantly, but played an active role in countless political associations and interest groups. Besides a string of anti-Semitic and *Mittelstand* organizations Fritsch was involved in campaigns for traditional bread, garden cities, and polygamy.[21] On the mainstream right, anti-Semitism was, by 1914, a

[19] Such sentiments have been discussed by Lothar Gall on numerous occasions. See 'Liberalismus und "bürgerliche Gesellschaft": Zu Charakter und Entwicklung der bürgerlichen Bewegung in Deutschland', *Historische Zeitschrift*, 220 (1975), 324–56; . . . ich wünschte ein Bürger zu sein": Zum Selbstverständnis des deutschen Bürgertums im 19. Jahrhundert', *Historische Zeitschrift*, 245 (1987), 601–23; and *Bürgertum in Deutschland* (Berlin, 1989).

[20] See G. Eley, *From Unification to Nazism* (Boston, Mass., 1986), esp. 254–82. The fullest accounts of change and continuity in Liberal party politics after 1918 are L. E. Jones, *German Liberalism and the Dissolution of the Weimar Party System 1918–1933* (Chapel Hill, NC, 1988) and L. Albertin, *Liberalismus und Demokratie am Anfang der Weimarer Republik* (Düsseldorf, 1972).

[21] See, in the absence of a monograph on Fritsch, the material in BA Berlin, Reichslandbund personalia 136, fos. 60–91. P. Pulzer, *The Rise of Political Anti-Semitism in Germany and Austria*, 2nd edn. (London, 1988) and P. A. Massing, *Rehearsal for Destruction: A Study of Political Anti-Semitism in Imperial Germany* (New York, 1949) emphasize the spread of anti-Semitism in German society, R. S. Levy, *The Downfall of the Anti-Semitic Political Parties in Imperial Germany* (New Haven, Conn., 1975) the electoral and parliamentary failures of anti-Semite splinter parties.

widespread weapon used not just by its Agrarian League auxiliaries, but by the Conservative party (DKP) itself, which employed subsequent Nazi functionaries like Richard Kunze and Wilhelm Kube.[22] More broadly, whatever the political legacy from imperial to Weimar Germany, this inheritance patently failed to cushion politics from the destabilizing effects of economic crisis. For historians of German Liberalism, for the Wilhelmine age as well as Weimar, the question why the Protestant middle strata proved so politically volatile and susceptible to Hitler, why they deserted the Liberal parties to a greater degree than Catholics the Centre and workers the SPD, is inescapable. Recent research into the Hitler electorate has corrected the overwhelming role ascribed to Protestant lower middle classes by establishing Nazi appeal to the established middle class, workers, and Catholics. These findings do not, however, undermine the fact that the sort of people most likely to vote Liberal in 1912 were amongst those most likely to vote for the National Socialists after 1928.[23]

These approaches do raise real and important issues. But they are only part of the truth, and, as a result, can provide an incomplete and rather distorted reflection of Wilhelmine politics. Indeed, the two strands of criticism are inconsistent. While concurring on some points, notably the important and malignant role of demagogy,[24] they conflict elsewhere. Many who contended that Wilhelmine politics was not living up to the past complained about too much party politics: about parties pushing into municipal politics and involving themselves with economic groups and interests; about the advent of machine politics, and pandering to the masses. By contrast, for critics of the Wilhelmine political legacy there was not enough party politics. Not only were party politicians kept from executive responsibility, but the bourgeois parties were clinging on to an outdated form of 'notable politics' (*Honoratiorenpolitik*) refusing to embrace

---

[22] For the agitation of Kunze and Kube see Ch. 9 below. Cf. H.-J. Puhle, *Agrarische Interessenpolitik und preußischer Konservatismus im wilhelminischen Reich (1893–1914)*, 2nd edn. (Bonn, 1975); and J. N. Retallack, *Notables of the Right: The Conservative Party and Political Mobilization in Germany, 1876–1918* (Boston, Mass., 1988).

[23] T. Childers (ed.), *The Mobilisation of the Nazi Constituency 1919–1933* (London, 1986); T. Childers, *The Nazi Voter: The Social Foundations of Fascism in Germany, 1919–1933* (Chapel Hill, NC, 1983); R. Hamilton, *Who Voted for Hitler?* (Princeton, NJ, 1982); and J. W. Falter, *Hitler's Wähler* (Munich, 1991).

[24] D. Blackbourn, 'The Politics of Demagogy in Imperial Germany', *Past and Present*, 113 (1986), 152–84.

genuine mass politics and actively involve its mainly petty-bourgeois support.[25]

In reality neither interpretation fully reflects Wilhelmine politics. Despair and resignation about the state of Wilhelmine politics was neither universal nor deep-seated. This was the case even within the educated middle classes, the part of society to which such sentiments were most ascribed. Liberal intellectuals, as the discussion of nostalgia in Chapter 3 makes clear, retained, on balance, an optimistic belief in progress. And the same was true of the railway- and Zeppelin-worshipping middle classes in general.[26] Equally, the argument that the political culture of Wilhelmine Germany was peculiarly hollow should be treated with caution. Widespread references in Wilhelmine Germany, be it to aloof notable politics, to middle-class political abstinence and ignorance, or to dangerous demagogues, have been taken too much at face value. Such charges were part of the political debate. Indeed their profusion reflected the liveliness of Wilhelmine politics, and, moreover, that all sides were in fact appealing to a perceived a set of standards, of commitment, competence, and respectability. Notable politics, for example, was an accusation levelled much more at the National Liberals after the turn of the century, when the party had a mass membership, paid officials, and prolonged campaigns, than during the 1860s and 1870s when the party genuinely adhered to this mode of politics. Similarly, the sin of political inactivity was castigated all the more at a time of ever rising political agitation and electoral turn-out. The unaware, unpolitical German, *der deutsche Michel*, was multiplying in the editorial columns at the very time he was steadily disappearing in the world outside.[27]

This is not to assert that Wilhelmine politics was any model of virtue. However, it is important, first, to underline the message of recent studies, that political involvement was considerable and that

[25] The theme of notable politics is addressed in T. Nipperdey, *Die Organisation der deutschen Parteien vor 1918* (Düsseldorf, 1961), esp. 42 ff and 392–3, still an unsurpassed guide to Wilhelmine party organization, and in virtually all subsequent work on bourgeois politics. The concept is reassessed in Ch. 2 below.

[26] D. Blackbourn, 'The German Bourgeoisie: An Introduction', in D. Blackbourn and R. J. Evans (eds.), *The German Bourgeoisie: Essays on the Social History of the German Middle Class from the Late Eighteenth to the Early Twentieth Century* (London, 1991), 8–9; C. Ritter, ' "Zeppelin flieg ...": Zur Geschichte einer Erfindung', in W. Gutsche and B. Kaulisch (eds.), *Bilder aus der Kaiserzeit: historische Streiflichter 1897–1917* (Cologne, 1985), 155–64.

[27] C. Köhler, *Warum müssen wir uns politisch betätigen?* (Cologne, 1909) is typical of such admonitions.

party politics actually did mean something to the electorate.[28] Second, the frame of reference needs to be reconsidered. Geoff Eley has rightly warned against the tendency to judge nineteenth-century German Liberalism according to the standards of post-1945 social liberalism.[29] And in general there has been a greater sense of moral rectitude than political realism. Certainly, we do not need apologias for material self-interest, dishonest promises, and populist rhetoric, still less for anti-Semitism, imperialism, and chauvinism. But what is crucial is not moral condemnation, but a close understanding of the strength and shape of these forces. For all the monographs written on the Pan-German League, for example, relatively little is certain about nationalism's precise form across the political, social, and regional spectrum, and still less known about its causes.[30]

Nowhere is the tendency to analyse politics according to what we want it to be, rather than what it was, more evident than in the area of economics and material self-interest. Too often accounts echo contemporary (mainly Liberal) complaints that politics was being overtaken and debased by competing material interests. But 'pocket book' issues were an inevitable and important part of politics and need to be taken seriously. Indeed, as the later discussion demonstrates, left liberal rhetoric condemning the rise of interest politics was disingenuous. It was advanced to claim a moral superiority over opponents, but at the same time left liberals were among the most adept in harnessing material grievances to attract support. To understand Wilhelmine politics, a wide agenda of political causes and antagonisms must be examined, not just the great issues of 'national' questions, constitutional reform, and class-conflict. It is also imperative to focus not just on the static, often unreal world of written party programmes, but on the dynamics of political campaigning and decision-making, and the important realm of informal politics.

---

[28] See S. Suval, *Electoral Politics in Wilhelmine Germany* (Chapel Hill, NC, 1985); D. Blackbourn, *The Fontana History of Germany 1780–1918: The Long Nineteenth Century* (London, 1997), esp. 408–24; B. Fairbairn, *Democracy in the Undemocratic State: The German Reichstag Elections of 1898 and 1903* (Toronto, 1997); and L. E. Jones and J. Retallack (eds.), *Elections, Mass Politics and Social Change in Modern Germany: New Perspectives* (New York, 1992).   [29] Eley, 'Sheehan and German Liberals'.

[30] On the growth of nationalism in Wilhelmine Germany see Eley, *Reshaping*; R. Chickering, *We Men Who Feel Most German: A Cultural Study of the Pan-German League 1886–1914* (London, 1984); and M. S. Coetzee, *German Army League: Popular Nationalism in Wilhelmine Germany* (New York, 1990); C. Applegate, *A Nation of Provincials: The German Idea of Heimat* (Berkeley, Calif., 1990).

Finally, the history of a political party must also be comparative. It is now generally agreed that the prevailing view of Wilhelmine politics in the 1960s and 1970s was coloured by comparing it to the sort of idolized model of English politics shared by left liberal Anglophiles like Barth and Lujo Brentano.[31] Not only was Edwardian England significantly less liberal than the latter imagined, but the reputation of German left liberals' as boundless admirers of England was not always deserved. Some, like Theodor Wolff and Conrad Haußmann, looked more to France than the Anglo–Saxon countries, while Friedrich Naumann and Max Weber were ambivalent about England. Still more, like the political leaders Eugen Richter and Friedrich Payer and indeed many voters, took very little interest in things abroad.[32] It is welcome, therefore, that much recent study of the German middle classes has been within a comparative European framework.[33] There is a need for a comparative domestic as well as international setting. Much recent literature on Wilhelmine politics focuses on a single issue, election, or party. Although this has been done in the cause of greater depth, there is a danger of excessive compartmentalizing. The stance of competing groups is a permanent element in the political equation. To analyse a political party in isolation is rather like describing the function of a cog in the machine without reference to other mechanical parts. Although the social structure or political stance of a party can be described in absolute terms, it is only by comparison with rival political forces that the picture assumes its true perspective.

Of course, such an analytical framework is appropriate to a wide range of parties and political systems. However, its application to the particular case of the left liberal parties in Wilhelmine Germany merits further discussion. It has been argued that the Wilhelmine state took little account of public opinion, and, where it did, it listened to a panoply of nationalist or economic groups rather than the political

---

[31] See G. Eley, 'Liberalism, Europe, and the Bourgeoisie 1860–1914', in Blackbourn and Evans (eds.), *German Bourgeoisie*, 296–8.

[32] S.-G. Schnorr, *Liberalismus zwischen 19. und 20. Jahrhundert: Reformulierung liberaler politischer Theorie in Deutschland und England am Beispiel von Friedrich Naumann und Leonard T. Hobhouse* (Baden-Baden, 1990).

[33] On the Liberals see D. Langewiesche (ed.), *Liberalismus im 19. Jahrhundert* (Göttingen, 1988); on the middle classes more generally: J. Kocka (ed.), *Bürgertum im 19. Jahrhundert: Deutschland im europäischen Vergleich* (3 vols.; Munich, 1988); Blackbourn and Evans (eds.), *German Bourgeoisie*; H. Siegrist (ed.), *Bürgerliche Berufe: Zur Sozialgeschichte der freien und akademischen Berufe im internationalen Vergleich* (Göttingen, 1988); and W. Conze *et al.* (eds.), *Bildungsbürgertum im 19. Jahrhundert* (4 vols.; Stuttgart, 1985–92).

parties.[34] Yet the case against the importance of political parties in the Wilhelmine state underestimates two things: the influence on the executive that the budgetary powers of the Reichstag and state parliaments gave to the parties, and the ties between the political parties and the electorate. The state might, for example, have a greater direct role in the economy than elsewhere, but the political parties can be left out of the equation. There was, for example, much talk of a carve up between the bureaucracy and powerful economic interests. However, even in two of the most notorious cases, the coal and potash industries, close ties with National Liberals and Agrarian Conservatives respectively demonstrated an appreciation of the importance of party-political backing for the maintenance of economic interests. This was made even more explicit in pre-war proposals for a state petroleum monopoly. The left liberals were accused of acting as agents for the Deutsche Bank, while the Centre was said to be awash with money from American oil interests. Members on the Reichstag committee considering the question found themselves bombarded by lobbyists from all sides.[35]

The links the parties enjoyed with the electorate were reflected in increasing political mobilization. Electoral turn-out increased at each Reichstag election after 1898, until over 12 million Germans went to the polls in 1912, 85 per cent of those entitled to vote. Similarly, turn-out at state elections exceeded 70 per cent in the increasing number of states, like Bavaria, Saxony, Baden, Württemberg, Oldenburg, and Hamburg, which had introduced a direct franchise and secret ballot after the turn of the century.[36] Organizations like the Navy League and Imperial League Against Social Democracy might be enlisted locally as auxiliary forces, but the parties continued to provide the bulk of campaigning as well as the masthead.[37] Though the

[34] See e.g. H.-U. Wehler, *The German Empire 1871–1918* (Leamington Spa, 1985); H. Kaelble, *Industrielle Interessenpolitik in der Wilhelminischen Gesellschaft: Centralverband Deutscher Industrieller 1895–1914* (Berlin, 1967); Puhle, *Agrarische Interessenpolitik*; S. Mielke, *Der Hansa-Bund für Gewerbe, Handel und Industrie 1909–1914: Der gescheiterte Versuch einer antifeudalen Sammlungspolitik* (Göttingen, 1976); H.-P. Ullmann, *Der Bund der Industriellen: Organisation, Einfluß und Politik klein- und mittelbetrieblicher Industrieller im Deutschen Kaiserreich 1895–1914* (Göttingen, 1976).

[35] *Breslauer Zeitung*, 887 (17 Dec. 1912); *Jauersches Stadtblatt* (12 Apr. 1913); Gerhart Schulze-Gaevernitz to his mother, undated letter [1913], BA-MA Freiburg, NL Schulze-Gaevernitz v. 21; Vascik, 'Rural Politics and Sugar', esp. 38–102.

[36] Suval, *Electoral Politics*, esp. 17–29.

[37] See Chs. 2 and 7–9 below. A contrary view is put forward in D. Fricke, 'Der deutsche Imperialismus und die Reichstagswahlen von 1907', *ZfG* 9 3 (1961), 538–76.

campaigning influence of the Agrarian League was more substantial,
even its electoral successes west of the Elbe, where a majority of its
members lived, were modest. Where the League mounted a direct
challenge to local party tradition its success was usually partial and
short-lived. The boast of Agrarian League director Diederich Hahn
that the League would root out the National Liberal party in Hanover
has been frequently recalled. It is less often remembered that the
National Liberals were still Hanover's strongest party in both the
Reichstag and Prussian Landtag in 1914, and that Hahn had lost his
Reichstag seat in the province in 1912. In the Palatinate the Agrarian
League was more successful in damaging the National Liberals, but it
was often the Centre and SPD rather than League's Conservative
allies which profited from the conflict.[38]

The parties were unique barometers of German society. They
made up the Reichstag which, because of its franchise, electoral
turn-out, and position as the sole visible national forum, enjoyed
wide credibility as the legitimate voice of the people.[39] With few
exceptions, the same parties also sat in the state legislatures. Increasingly, even municipal government was coming within the purview of
party politics. As has been appreciated in a number of studies, the
development of Wilhelmine urban government, with its increased
range of services, did not owe all to ambitious non-political mayors
and technocrats. The role of parties and a politicized electorate must
not be overlooked.[40] Municipal politics was of particular importance
to left liberalism both in terms of ideas (discussed in Chapter 3) and
infrastructure (see Part III).

Parties represented people in different forums with distinct compe-
tences and franchises. Imbalances within the political system were
reflected in internal party life. Relations between the Reichstag and
Prussian Landtag caucuses, for example, mirrored the differences

[38] Vascik, 'Rural Politics and Sugar'; E. O. Bräunche, *Parteien und Reichstagswahlen in der
Rheinpfalz von der Reichsgründung bis zum Ausbruch des Ersten Weltkrieges 1914: Eine
regionale Partei- und wahlhistorische Untersuchung im Vorfeld der Demokratie* (Speyer, 1982).

[39] D. Blackbourn, 'New Legislatures: Germany, 1871–1914', in *Historical Research: The
Bulletin of the Institute of Historical Research*, 65 (1992), 201–14; and Nipperdey, *Deutsche
Politik 1866–1918*, ii. 491–7.

[40] F. Lenger, 'Bürgertum und Stadtverwaltung in Rheinischen Großstädten des 19.
Jahrhunderts: Zu einem vernachlässigten Aspekt bürgerlicher Herrschaft', in L. Gall (ed.),
Stadt und Bürgertum im neunzehnten Jahrhundert (Munich, 1990), 97–169; B. K. Ladd,
Urban Planning and Civic Order in Germany, 1860–1914 (Cambridge, Mass., 1990); and, par-
ticularly convincing in the context of left liberal politics, Palmowski, *Urban Liberalism*.

between the Reich and Prussia. In particular, they reflected the views of the different set of electors whose votes counted; the massed ranks of petty bourgeoisie, peasantry, and workers who held sway under the equal franchise and high turn-outs of Reichstag elections, or the most propertied and prosperous fifth of voters who controlled the first and second classes in the plutocratic three-class Prussian state franchise. However, the parties also demonstrated the interconnectedness of German politics and the challenge to formal convention. Conservatives debated agrarian tariffs in the Prussian Landtag, while the left raised the issue of the Prussian constitution or that of even more backward Mecklenburg in the Reichstag.[41] Liberal conduct in municipal government was exploited by opponents in state and national elections, while Liberals countered by bringing the debate round to education even when, as in Reichstag contests, the issue was beyond the competence of the body being elected.

Nor did many constituents share the view that party politicians were men of little standing and influence. If Wilhelmine parliamentarians had a cause for complaint, it was about being snowed under with requests, rather than being bypassed. Such was the volume of a Reichstag deputy's correspondence that some would doubtless have had secret sympathy with the remarks of Sir Hubert Ashton MP to a complaining constituent by in post-war Britain: 'Sir, I'm elected to represent Chelmsford at Westminster, not Westminster at Chelmsford.' In Wilhelmine Germany, however, precisely this double set of obligations was demanded. Constituents expected their deputies to represent them in Berlin, and, through public meetings and newspaper reports, Berlin in the constituency.[42] The parties, with the press as sounding board, connected national and local politics. They were the essential mediators between the public and the state, not just on political matters, but also a variety of social and economic issues.

What applied to the parties in general applied also to the Liberals in particular. The widespread notion that the Liberals played by the old rules of idealism and notable politics while others got on with the

---

[41] See e.g. H. Pachnicke, *Die Mecklenburgische Verfassungsfrage* (Parchim, 1907), 13–15, 35.

[42] The demands constituents placed on Reichstag deputies across all parties and regions are reflected in the correspondence in SA Hamburg, NL Carl Braband B2; BA Berlin, NL Reinhard Mumm 72–74; H. Cardauns, *Karl Trimborn: Nach seinen Briefen und Tagebüchern* (Mönchen-Gladbach, 1922); and E. von Liebert, *Aus einem bewegten Leben: Erinnerungen* (Munich, 1925).

new game of demagogy and mass politics is too simplistic. Liberal populist style was sometimes more restrained. Talking about pigs and cattle was not going to the lengths of the notorious anti-Semite Hermann Ahlwardt who reputedly promised each peasant in his constituency twice as much of everything. Equally, Liberal party organization failed to reach the standard set by the best. By 1914, the left liberals and National Liberals claimed some 240,000 and 300,000 members respectively, whilst Social Democratic membership stood at one million.[43] The financial disparity was even greater. Liberal members typically contributed a mark or less in annual dues, whereas the Social Democratic worker paid 5 marks.[44] The differences, however, were partly accounted for by circumstances. The Liberal electorate was more susceptible to a subtler form of propaganda than wild accusations and promises obviously too good to be true. Similarly, they were more accustomed to informal associations than to regimented organizations with high fixed costs. Above all, the differences were those of accomplishment rather than intent. Mediation may have been more problematic for Liberals than others, but it was also more important. Conservatives showed little enthusiasm for the *Volk*, whilst most Social Democrats were equally sceptical about the value of persuasion where the state was concerned. The Centre Party dealt with both, but from a well-established niche in parliament and the Catholic population.[45] Universal claims and commitments to *Staat* and *Volk*, and a paradoxically insecure footing in both, was a combination unique to the Liberal political parties.

Strictly speaking, there were no truly nation-wide political parties. Even in their 1870s electoral heyday, the National Liberal Party left

[43] For an introduction to the very extensive literature on the labour movement see G. A. Ritter and K. Tenfelde, *Arbeiter im Deutschen Kaiserreich 1871 bis 1914* (Bonn, 1992); A. von Saldern, *Auf dem Wege zum Arbeiter-Reformismus: Parteialltag in sozial-demokratischer Provinz* (Frankfurt, 1984); L. Abrams, *Workers' Culture in Imperial Germany: Leisure and Recreation in the Rhineland and Westphalia* (London, 1992); V. L. Lidke, *The Alternative Culture: Socialist Labor in Imperial Germany* (New York, 1985); G. A. Ritter (ed.), *Der Aufstieg der Deutschen Arbeiterbewegung* (Munich, 1990); and D. Groh, *Negative Integration und revolutionärer Attentismus: Die deutsche Sozialdemokratie am Vorabend des Ersten Weltkrieges* (Frankfurt am Main, 1975).

[44] See Nipperdey, *Organisation*; and, for the SPD, D. Fricke, *Handbuch zur Geschichte der deutschen Arbeiterbewegung 1869 bis 1917* (2 vols.; Berlin, 1987), i, esp. 220–336.

[45] On political Catholicism see H. W. Smith, *German Nationalism and Religious Conflict: Culture, Ideology, Politics, 1870–1914* (Princeton, NJ, 1995); Blackbourn, *Class, Religion and Local Politics*; W. Loth, *Katholiken im Kaiserreich: Der politische Katholizismus in der Krise des wilhelminischen Deutschlands* (Düsseldorf, 1984).

many constituencies uncontested. Only the SPD put up candidates in all 397 Reichstag seats, and that was more a statement of principle than a reflection of strong support throughout Germany.[46] However, the range of local interests represented by each of the main political parties, was considerable. In view of the mediating role played by political parties, regionalism was of major significance. It was important enough to the parties least affected, those on each end of the political spectrum, the Social Democrats and Agrarian Conservatives. For the parties in-between, less tied to a particular class, and dependent on rural and urban support, it was vital. This applied to the National Liberals, who made notably heavy weather of the problem, but also to political neighbours more adept at damage limitation. Regionalism, moreover, should not simply be equated with state boundaries. Considerable diversity existed in the medium-sized states, but especially in Prussia. Too often a monolithic image of Prussia is projected from the perspective of the East Prussian estate, an image which bore little resemblance to the lives of most Prussians.[47]

Differences in the local environment possessed a double importance for party politics. Local knowledge conveyed to voters an impression of competence and concern. Furthermore, it enabled candidates to slant their address to secure the best response. A catalogue of the social, economic, and political conditions in each part of a constituency was one of the most important weapons in the rapidly expanding private archives of politicians.[48] However, the political parties had not just to play to different local interests, but to reconcile them publicly in the national arena.

This dual role provides an important explanation of the myriad of issues generated by German politics. The lack of executive responsibility compounded this by allowing parties to attach themselves to a raft of popular demands without having to answer for the consequences. Of course, much of this political activity has been derided as trivial and inspired by sectional economic interests. And the detached and high-minded would find it hard to disagree. It is

---

[46] Fricke, *Handbuch*, ii. 737–44.

[47] This point is discussed further in the introduction to D. Blackbourn, *Populists and Patricians: Essays in Modern German History* (London, 1987).

[48] See e.g. Heinz Potthoff's files on Waldeck-Pyrmont passed on to Naumann, his successor as Reichstag deputy, or Hermann Hummel's notes on the Triberg-Hornberg Landtag seat. BA Berlin, NL Friedrich Naumann 20–2; SA Darmstadt NL Hermann Hummel, correspondence on 1909 Baden state election.

important, however, to be realistic as well as moralistic. Wilhelmine
politics was largely fuelled by economic issues, but this is true of
modern industrial states in general. Moreover, political or ideological
divisions tended to be transfused by economic issues rather than
crowded out altogether. Lloyd George's 1909 'People's Budget' and
the German tax increases of the same year differed vastly in fiscal
direction, but both were powerful examples of the inextricable links
between economics and political ideology. Even *Mittelstandspolitik*,
the appeal to petty-bourgeois purses and votes, was not pure political and economic cant: somewhere amid the sea of insincere promises lay a social ideology.[49]

Just as large economic issues were important, so too were comparatively small local changes. Politicians throughout Germany, for example, were branded the architects of the tax on train tickets or the
abolition of cheap-rate local postage.[50] The railway, as we shall see
later, provided an especially powerful local issue in state and national
elections. Voting in response to particular grievances was so
widespread that it generated its own vocabulary ranging from the
prosaic *Protestwähler* (protest voter) to the more mysterious
Waldstreusozialdemokrat (an expression coined in honour of a prosperous Badenese village which turned Social Democratic overnight
when officials put a stop to traditional exploitation of nearby wood-
lands).[51] Of course, Wilhelmine politics was more than an amalgam of
materialism and pavement politics. The confessional divide and the
associated realm of *Kulturpolitik* played a fundamental and, until
recently, insufficiently appreciated role in the political outlook of many
Germans. The difficulty of conveying the meaning of *Kulturpolitik* to
an English-speaking audience suggests its particular importance in
Germany. The literal translation, cultural politics, suggests museums
and opera but *Kulturpolitik* also meant clashes about education, artistic
freedom, and the role of church and state. For some left liberal figures, notably Karl Schrader, promoting the cause of reform Protestantism was a major calling. But even those left liberals uninterested in

---

[49] D. Blackbourn, 'The Mittelstand in German Society and Politics, 1871–1914', *Social
History*, 4 (1977), 409–33.
[50] E. Katz (ed.), *Agitationshandbuch für liberale Redner* (Berlin and Schöneberg, 1906),
83–5.
[51] F. Hoff, *Politische Zeit- und Streitfragen in demokratischer Beleuchtung: Ein Wort der
Aufklärung für die kommenden Wahlen* (Berlin, 1920), 80. Blasheim in Westphalia provided a
further vivid example. Here most peasants voted SPD in 1903 to protest against restrictions
on breeding bulls. C. Severing, *Mein Lebensweg*, (2 vols.; Cologne, 1950), i. 146.

theology and church life were acutely aware of the political potency of the Protestant/Catholic confessional divide in imperial Germany.[52] Sharp swings to the right in the 1887 and 1907 elections underlined the potential of a well-orchestrated appeal to nationalism. However, to ignore local issues and show contempt for the role played by economic interests is to neglect an important part of the political equation. A preconception that real politics was about constitutional reform and 'national' questions produces a distorted and incomplete picture. If the interrelatedness of political issues has been underplayed, the same applies to the parties themselves. It has been argued that German political parties led a relatively distinct existence. Each operated within its own social-moral milieu, while the Reichstag failed to develop a collegial spirit like that of Westminster or the French Chamber of Deputies.[53] Certainly, social ties between deputies of different parties were more characteristic of the House of Commons than the Reichstag. However, party relations should not be judged solely by the battle of words across the floor of the chamber, designed largely for outside consumption. Cross-party negotiations behind the scenes and practical co-operation in Reichstag committees often told a different story. Even a notably combative debater like the left liberal Georg Gothein got on well with deputies from all parties.[54] Certain interests were common to all deputies: the prospect of another winter election campaign, for example, met a universal groan.[55] Deputies from different parties conversed at Berlin functions given by ministers, business leaders, and society figures, or in Hans Delbrück's Wednesday circle and similar discussion groups.

The argument that parties were tied to particular social-moral milieux works best for large East Elbian agricultural estates, close-knit

---

[52] G. Hubinger, *Kulturprotestantismus und Politik: Zum Verhaltnis von Liberalismus und Protestantismus im wilhelminischen Deutschland* (Tübingen, 1994); O. Blaschke und F.-M. Kühlemann (eds.) *Religion im Kaiserreich: Milieus, Mentalitäten, Krisen* (Gütersloh, 1996); A. Müller-Dreier, *Konfession in Politik, Gesellschaft und Kultur des Kaiserreiches: Der Evangelische Bund 1886–1914* (Gütersloh, 1998).

[53] On the concept of the social-moral milieu see M. R. Lepsius, 'Parteiensystem und Sozialstruktur: Zum Problem der Demokratisierung der deutschen Gesellschaft', in G. A. Ritter (ed.), *Die deutschen Parteien vor 1918* (Cologne, 1973), 56–80, and, in modified form, K. Rohe, *Wahlen und Wählertraditionen in Deutschland* (Frankfurt, 1992), 98–121, On the perceived absence of collegial spirit in the Reichstag see J. Sheehan, 'Political Leadership in the German Reichstag, 1871–1918', *AHR* 74 2 (1968), 511–28. G. A. Ritter, *Die deutschen Parteien 1830–1914* (Göttingen, 1985) illustrates how both sets of ideas are widely accepted.

[54] BA Koblenz, NL Gothein 14, fos. 169 ff.

[55] BA Koblenz, NL Südekum, 109, fo. 22.

Catholic villages and small towns, and working-class suburbs. It is much less applicable to the many Protestant areas not dominated by aristocratic estates or tenement slums, nor does it fit the political stance of Catholic city dwellers. Each party had a natural base of support, but the areas of competition and overlap were substantial. Even the great dividing-line between the Social Democrats and the other parties was broad and regionally diffuse. Voting shifts in 1903, 1907, and 1912 underlined the existence of floating voters on both sides of the divide. In addition, many workers remained on the bourgeois side of the line, while a significant part of SPD support came from outside the working class.[56] Above all, the Liberals' natural base, the Protestant middle strata, formed the real cockpit of Wilhelmine elections, in which all the main parties except the Centre battled for support.

The growth in election run-offs and pacts tells a similar story. After fewer than fifty run-offs in the 1871 and 1874 elections, their number rose to 147 by 1890, and 190 in 1912.[57] The Wilhelmine period was increasingly an age of coalition politics. This applied particularly to the left liberals. No party was more dependent on run-off elections. In 1903 and 1912 every left liberal Reichstag deputy was returned in the second round of voting. And no party was more successful. Four out of five left liberal run-off candidates won, compared to one in two for the other non-socialist parties and fewer than one in three for the SPD.[58] Necessity rather than choice also brought the left liberals to the fore in the formation of party pacts. Electoral accommodation with the National Liberals led to a single Liberal candidate in most constituencies in 1907 and 1912. The conclusion in 1912 of a formal, national run-off pact between left liberals and Social Democrats broke new ground. Left liberal parliamentary influence was similarly dependent on coalitions, whether in an arrangement like the Bülow Bloc, the alliance of Conservative and Liberal parties which provided a government majority in the Reichstag from the 1907 election to the 1909 finance reform, or, more typically, on an informal or *ad hoc* basis. It was with good reason that a leading left liberal parliamentary

---

[56] J. Sperber, *The Kaiser's Voters: Electors and Elections in Imperial Germany* (Cambridge, 1997); R. Blank, 'Die soziale Zusammensetzung der sozialdemokratischen Wählerschaft Deutschlands', in Otto Büsch *et al.* (eds.), *Wählerbewegung in der deutschen Geschichte* (Berlin, 1978), 184–96.

[57] G. A. Ritter, with M. Niehuss, *Wahlgeschichtliches Arbeitsbuch: Materialien zur Statistik des Kaiserreichs 1871–1918* (Munich, 1980), 125.

[58] Ritter, *Die deutschen Parteien*, 46–8.

tactician Otto Fischbeck proclaimed the doctrine that understanding politics was about understanding alliances.[59] It is important, therefore, to study left liberalism in the context of party politics as a whole and of how party politics related to state and society. This breadth of approach and the range of sources employed imposes unavoidable limits on the length of period which can be analysed. I have chosen to focus the detailed investigation of left liberal politics during the last decade of Wilhelmine Germany, though viewing these years not in isolation, but as part of the period from German Unification to Nazi *Machtergreifung*. This is not to deny the need for case-studies of liberal politics for earlier periods. Nor I do not regard these years as uniquely important. The intensification of popular politics took place at different times and to differing degrees. Singling out the 1890s as the crucial decade of popular mobilization, as Geoff Eley and others have done, tends to understate what had already taken place. The pattern of rising turn-out at Reichstag elections was already firmly established. And while the mass agrarian protest against grain tariff reductions in the early 1890s marked a new stage of political mobilization in many rural districts, the process elsewhere was often already under way. Dan White for the National Liberals and James Retallack for the Conservatives both make convincing cases for the substantial impact of popular mobilization during the 1880s.[60] Nor was the pre-war decade just a continuation of the 'new politics' of the 1890s. Besides a quantitative leap in party organization and a further increase in political activity, the pre-war years also saw substantial changes in political fashion, issues, and allegiances. Whilst change in imperial Germany was often convulsive and unpredictable, mobilization is best seen as a process stretching across the whole of the period, with many of the political, economic, and social seeds sown at the outset. That said, there are strong grounds, in a study of left liberal ability to adapt to popular mobilization, to focus on the years before the First World War when mobilization was at its greatest.

These years also represented a distinctive phase in left liberal politics. It marked a change of generation and, with it, a shift in attitudes.

---

[59] Cited in Robson, 'Left-Wing Liberalism', 421.

[60] White, *Splintered Party*; J. N. Retallack, 'Reformist Conservatism and Political Mobilization: A Study of Factionalism and Movements for Reform within the German Conservative Party, 1876–1914', D.Phil., Oxford University, 1983. For a local study which also emphasizes political mobilization in the 1880s see N. Schloßmacher, *Düsseldorf im Bismarckreich: Politik und Wahlen, Parteien und Vereine* (Düsseldorf, 1985).

To associate this just with the death of Eugen Richter in 1906 is to overstate the influence wielded by one man. Nevertheless, personalization has more to be said for it here than usual. Richter did have thousands of ardent admirers (*Verehrer*)—businessmen, members of the free professions, but also sections of the petty bourgeoisie—whose views on the state, economics, and citzenship echoed those the left liberal leader propounded so remorselessly in parliament.[61] Amongst the faithful his *ABC-Buch* was a well-read bible. Richter symbolized Manchesterism, liberal political and economic orthodoxy, but also, in the left liberal splits and electoral decline of the 1890s, its fall from fashion. In the pre-war decade left liberal politicians and rank and file alike were increasingly people who had lived virtually all their lives in the unified Bismarckian state. Many of the 1912 influx of left liberal Reichstag deputies were born after 1870. They were much more positive towards nationalism, imperialism, and colonialism, but also towards social reform.[62] It was Friedrich Naumann, the most prominent of those Richterites decried as yesterday's anti-Semites and tomorrow's socialists, who succeeded Richter, not as party leader but as the popular prophet of left liberalism. It is tempting to dismiss Naumann, in the wake of Theodor Heuss's hagiography, as an object of too much admiring attention. His political ideas were usually borrowed, and his grasp of economics and history often inadequate. Nor did Naumann have a place in the inner counsels of left liberal politics. In the untypically acute words of the right-wing historian and nationalist Johannes Haller: 'He did not have influence, he wasn't even taken seriously . . . They called him the bard of the parliamentary party, allowed him to exercise his lyrical pulpit tones . . . on suitable occasions, and used his reputation as a workers' friend as an electoral *Lochvogel*.' However, Naumann's popular appeal should not be underestimated. Bebel's death in 1913 left him as perhaps the most popular and listened-to platform speaker in Germany. Moreover, Naumann was particularly attractive within three groups unmoved by Richterite left liberalism: university graduates, Protestant clergymen, and the

---

[61] See F. Rachfahl, 'Eugen Richter und der Linksliberalismus im neuen Reich', *Zeitschrift für Politik*, 5 (1912); E. Müller-Meiningen, *Parliamentarismus* (Berlin, 1926); and *Eugen Richter und der Wahlkreis Hagen-Schwelm*. The approach in Lorrenz, *Eugen Richter*, rather neglects Richter's popular appeal.

[62] For a detailed account of the left liberal switch in the Reichstag from opposition to support of the government on 'national' issues by 1906 see L. Elm, *Zwischen Fortschritt und Reaktion: Geschichte der Parteien der liberalen Bourgeoisie in Deutschland 1893–1918* (Berlin, 1968).

young in general. Second, Naumann as a party-political leader did not become a central force in left liberal politics before 1919. But the ideas he represented—political and social reform at home, imperialism abroad—undoubtedly did.[63] Along with revised attitudes on a range of issues went a new flexibility and willingness to compromise in return for a share of power. Tactical considerations were nothing new. Richter was an electoral horse-trader as well as an obstinate defender of political beliefs.[64] And later left liberals did not jettison all adherence to principle. The Centre still tended to be a more amenable negotiating partner for the executive, not only because it commanded a larger and more stable block of seats, but also because it had fewer scruples. However, with the new generation of left liberal politicians, pragmatism became ever more predominant and the capacity to compromise much greater. This reflected broader changes in the left liberal electorate. Division into three small parties, and the political impotence this implied, became increasingly unacceptable to rank-and-file left liberals. This shift in attitude was reflected both in the formation of a united left liberal party in 1910, and the search for better relations with the Reich executive.

Here two things coincided. On the one hand, left liberals increasingly identified with the Wilhelmine state and yearned for practical results after over two decades in opposition. On the other hand, the government needed a broader political consensus. The Bismarckian *Kartell* of Conservatives, Free Conservatives, and the National Liberals had no prospect of a Reichstag majority after 1890. By 1912 they totalled only 102 of the 397 Reichstag seats. And the addition of the Centre to form the 'tariff reform' majority no longer provided a reliable governmental majority by 1906. The left liberals and Reich executive were two sides in search of each other, but the process was facilitated by a convergence of social and economic interests. Both wanted a modern, successful capitalist state and derived material satisfaction from the booming economy. In addition, the greater cost-effectiveness in colonial administration, sought by Dernburg and Solf, and Bethmann Hollweg's attempt to improve Anglo-German relations were just the sort of measures to gain left liberal approval.

---

[63] BA Koblenz, NL Haller 27, 'Gesehenes, Gehörtes, Gedachtes (1865–1945)', MS 1946, III. 6.

[64] See the correspondence about electoral deals between the Centre and Richter's FrVp for the 1898 Reichstag elections in HAS Köln, NL Carl Bachem 86c.

Despite these changes, however, a crucial gap remained. True, ministers like Bethmann, Delbrück, and Solf were aware of the need to accommodate the political parties and the desirability of administrative reform. However, they preferred to keep the two problems separate, rather than contemplate the establishment of publicly accountable cabinet government. Moreover, matters before the war were not sufficiently 'inevitable' (*zwangsläufig*), as Bethmann put it, for governmental reformers to risk the Emperor's unpredictability and the opposition of unreconstructed conservatives at court and in the Prussian bureaucracy and military.[65] Left liberal politicians and voters, on the other hand, remained attached to domestic political reform. Most left liberals in Prussia were visibly patriotic and not insistent on full parliamentary rule. But they continued to voice support for electoral reform, responsible government, free assembly, and the complete rule of law. Political dissatisfaction remained as long as the sort of vague promises the government alluded to with its wartime slogan of a new course (*Neuorientierung*) had not turned into concrete action. As a result, left liberal politics reflected the contradictions of social integration and political contention in the last decade of Wilhelmine Germany.

[65] Conversation between Naumann and Bethmann at Hohenfinow after Bethmann's resignation in 1917 recalled in HLH Darmstadt, Martin Wenck, 'Wandlungen: Ein Sechziger sieht sein Leben zurück' (typescript, *c*.1927), fo. 171.

I

Men, Machinery, and Mission

I
Locating the Left Liberals

Who were the left liberals? No political grouping in Imperial Germany, anti-Semitic splinter groups apart, had a comparable history of splits and short-lived mergers (see Figure 1.1).

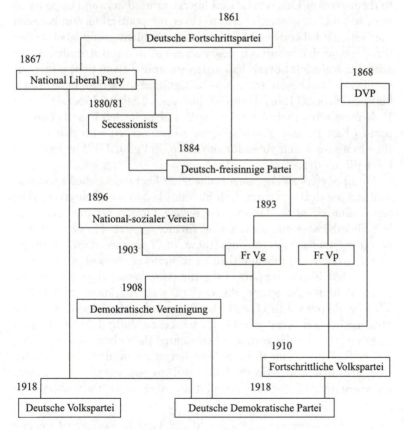

FIG. 1.1. Liberal Parties in Germany: 1861–1918

These disruptions were partially bridged by continuity of personnel and tradition. The FVP regarded itself as the 'legal successor'
(*Rechtsnachfolgerin*) of the Progressive party, whose fiftieth anniversary it celebrated in 1911.[1] Yet left liberal party politics remained
characterized by flux and division. The label 'left liberal' was itself a
product of diversity. It included North German groups who generally
called themselves *Freisinnige*. (This term is difficult to translate,
though it has a definite anti-clerical intonation. The best nineteenth-
century English equivalent is probably Radical, particularly as the latter label encompassed men who were certainly not radical in every
respect.) However, most South German left liberals, reflecting a
greater openness and attachment to radical political reform, referred
to themselves as Democrats. Left liberal, as used here and by contemporaries, was an umbrella term to cover the political terrain between
the National Liberals and SPD. It is a convenient group label, rather
than an objective or subjective assessment of political attitudes. As we
shall see, some left liberals had little substantive claim to be either left
or liberal. Moreover, there was a significant overlap in attitudes
between National Liberals and left liberals: a National Liberal voter in
Baden was often more liberal in outlook than his left liberal counterpart in East Prussia. Essentially, we are concerned with that part of
the electorate which voted for the FrVp, FrVg, or DVP in 1907 and
the FVP in 1912.

To supporters and opponents alike, left liberal described a social as
well as a political spectrum. Left liberals liked to see themselves as the
representatives of the German *Bürgertum*. Opponents countered that
left liberals were the servants of finance capital. However, it was
becoming increasingly obvious these verdicts were more claims to
moral virtue or opprobrium than an accurate assessment of the structure of left liberal support. Like the *Mittelstand*, the more people
talked about the *Bürgertum*, the less clear its definition became. But as
left liberals tended to classify the *Bürgertum* as just about everyone
untainted by aristocratic birth, ignorance, or sloth, only securing an
eighth of the popular vote seriously dented their claim to be its political embodiment. But if $1\frac{1}{2}$ million out of 12 million votes in 1912
were insufficient to allow the left liberals to pose convincingly as sole
representative of the *Bürgertum*, they were more than enough to

---

[1] *Fünfzig Jahre Fortschrittliche Volkspartei* (Berlin, 1911); *Jauersches Stadtblatt* (9 June
1911).

counter the accusation that left liberals were just the party of bankers and the stock exchange. Not only were the vast majority of left liberals not bankers, but most bankers were not left liberal.

Contemporary descriptions of the close ties between left liberal party politics and finance capital were closer to caricature than accurate characterization. Unfortunately, the caricature has become reinforced and set into stereotype. Marxist and non-Marxist historians have tended to embellish rather than correct contemporary clichés about business and party politics. Ludwig Elm's claim that, 'besides banking, commercial and industrial circles traditionally represented by the left liberals, young, rapidly advancing branches of industry, especially the electrical and chemical industries, achieved stronger influence on the party leadership', considerably overstates the extent to which these groups even supported let alone determined left liberal politics. Certainly, the specific illustrations used to make Elm's case of an 'increasing monopolistic dictat' are erroneous and unconvincing. The 1912 Mannheim party conference did not reject, but backed Gothein's motion demanding reduced grain tariffs. Naumann may have 'distanced himself from the earlier free-trade platform' but he was never a convinced free-trader in the first place. Moreover, his position owed a lot more to voters in his semi-rural constituencies than monopoly capital.[2] As we shall see, banks, commerce, and industry were not linked primarily to the left liberal parties. The electrical and chemical industries had still fewer ties. When a Lower Silesian left liberal suggested putting up Walther Rathenau in his constituency, the FVP executive committee did not know what Rathenau's political views were and did not even have sufficient contact to ask him directly. Not surprisingly, the reply to enquiries through an intermediary was that Rathenau could not accept the FVP programme as a whole.[3] It is, of course, an easy exercise to list bank directorships held by left liberal politicians.[4] The 20,000 marks annual income from a directorship of the Dresdner Bank comfortably financed the left liberal leader Friedrich Payer's full-time Berlin political career after 1912.[5] Left

---

[2] Elm, *Fortschritt*, 218; BA Berlin, NL Naumann 236, Friedrich Naumann to Jacob Rießer, 28 May 1913.
[3] BA Berlin, FVP 36, fo. 314. For Rathenau's greater sympathy for the National Liberals before the war see H. Pogge von Strandmann, *Walther Rathenau. Industrialist, Banker, Intellectual and Politician* (Oxford, 1985), 9 and 129.
[4] The table in Elm, *Fortschritt*, 217, could be added to considerably.
[5] BA Koblenz, NL Payer 44, fo. 17, Payer to wife, 17 Mar. 1916.

liberals also had a range of informal contacts with the financial establishment. The left liberal deputy for Lippe-Detmold, Adolf Neumann-Hofer, for example, when informed of plans for the state bank to merge with the Dresdner Bank, discussed alternative arrangements with Arthur von Gwinner of the Deutsche Bank.[6] But links between National Liberals and finance capital were even stronger. Jacob Rießer and most of the Hansa-Bund's national leadership were National Liberals.[7] Ernst Bassermann, chairman of the Süddeutsche Disconto-Gesellschaft and associated companies, had more business connections than his left liberal counterpart Payer.[8] The DDP treasurer Hermann Fischer, whose directorships outstripped other Weimar deputies, had been a National Liberal before 1918.[9] Franz Adickes, the archetypal 'unpolitical' National Liberal, became chairman of the Dresdner Bank after retiring as mayor of Frankfurt.[10] And although Agrarian League leaders like Wangenheim, Roesicke, and Hahn condemned involvement with finance capital, DKP as well as Free Conservative figures had banking connections. Wolfgang Kapp and Friedrich von Loebell had ties with the Deutsche Bank, and bankers played a part in establishing Conservative organizations in Altona and Hamburg in 1911–12.[11]

Banks and commerce, like all good lobbyists, attempted to influence a broad political spectrum. They did not just focus on a single minority political party. The financial sector had been associated with liberal opposition in the pre-unification period. It was a natural supporter of national unity and economic liberalization, and one of the few avenues open to dissident talent during the political reaction of the 1850s. Left liberalism was also the haven, after 1878, of those who had rallied behind the liberal politician and head of the Deutsche Bank Georg von Siemens in their opposition to Bismarckian protectionist tariffs. But by the turn of the century much of the financial establishment

---

[6] SA Detmold, NL Adolf Neumann-Hofer 5, Neumann-Hofer to Thörner, director of the Lippische Landesbank, 23 Jan. 1917.

[7] BA Berlin, FVP 36, fo. 19, comments of Karl Mommsen and Johannes Kaempf in executive committee, 10 Sept. 1910. Cf. Mielke, *Der Hansa-Bund*, 124–34 and 212–15.

[8] 'Aus Bassermanns Leben und Wirken', *Neue Badische Landeszeitung* (24 July 1917) lists ten chairmanships, one vice-chairmanship, and five directorships.

[9] Out of the eighty-seven directorships held by DDP Reichstag deputies in 1928 Fischer accounted for forty-nine. R. Lewinsohn, *Gold in der Politik* (Berlin, 1930), 99.

[10] *Schulthess' Europäische Geschichtskalender* (1912) 99.

[11] D. Stegmann, 'Linksliberale Bankiers, Kaufleute und Industrielle 1890–1900', *Tradition: Zeitschrift für Firmengeschichte und Unternehmerbiographie*, 21 (1976), 28; BA Koblenz, NL Loebell 27, fo. 69; BA Berlin, Nachlaß Conrad Freiherr von Wangenheim 7–9.

had been reconciled to tariffs. Left liberalism was again the exception rather than the rule in big business. The contrast between Georg von Siemens and his successor in the Deutsche Bank Arthur von Gwinner exemplified a broad shift in political attitudes. Siemens combined dynamic business activity with an open role in left liberal party politics. Gwinner played an equally domineering role in business and behind-the-scenes political negotiations.[12] But his political stance was far more conformist and discreet. Gwinner's preference for quiet persuasion was illustrated by his role in the 'German Baghdad Committee for Humanitarian Purposes', where he used a Deutsche Bank subsidy to prevent the committee launching public appeals.[13] Whereas Siemens had stood for popular election and had been returned to the Reichstag, Gwinner was nominated by the Emperor to the Prussian Upper House. A rural estate and his children's marriage into the Prussian landowning and military aristocracy were further indications of close ties to the political establishment.[14] The open political stage, with its increasing demands and enmities, was abandoned in favour of lobby politics. Businessmen were left with limited time after increasing business commitments, and also faced potential economic sanctions from political opponents. An Oldenburg left liberal, for example, had to resign his Landtag seat after Centre boycott threats, rather than see thirty years' work building up the Oldenburgische Landesbank ruined. Similarly, the Saxon National Liberal August Weber stood down at the 1912 election after agrarian threats.[15]

The contrast between the Wilhelmine banker, Deputy Chancellor, and later DNVP politician Karl Helfferich, a stout supporter of rule by officialdom, and his father, an enthusiastic follower of Eugen Richter, was a further illustration of the generational shift in business attitudes from left liberalism to vaguely National Liberal or Free Conservative attitudes and support for bureaucratic rule.[16] Even in the left

---

[12] Gwinner's energetic lobbying was particularly evident over plans for a petroleum monopoly in 1912/13, and the Deutsche Bank's overseas railway interests. For the latter see W. Gutsche, *Monopole, Staat und Expansion vor 1914* (Berlin, 1986), 110, 149–54, 247–8. For Siemens K. Helfferich, *Georg von Siemens: Ein Lebensbild aus Deutschlands großer Zeit* (3 vols.; Berlin, 1921–3) remains the only detailed account.

[13] BA Koblenz, NL Hans Delbrück 33, Karl Schrader to Geheimrat Dr Flügge, 7 June 1906 (copy); Flügge to committee members, 1 Feb. 1910.

[14] See BA Berlin, Reichslandbund 170, fos. 80–104, personalia Arthur von Gwinner.

[15] BA Koblenz, NL Walther Schücking 64, Max tom Dieck to Walther Schücking, 31 Dec. 1917; BA Koblenz, Kleine Erwerbung August Weber.

[16] J. G. Williamson, *Karl Helfferich 1872–1924* (Princeton, NJ, 1971), 7–8.

liberal stronghold of Frankfurt, most bankers were low-profile National Liberals.[17] If not from the pre-Unification generation, like Karl Schrader and Johannes Kaempf, the few bankers and business leaders still active in left liberal national politics tended to come from a traditional left liberal family like Karl Mommsen, or were Jewish, as with Louis Aronsohn. Even amongst German Jews left liberal big business support is easily overstated. Whilst the left liberals had some 60–70 per cent of the total Jewish vote, compared to 10–15 per cent for the National Liberals, the latter included many of the most esteemed and established, particularly in western Germany. Amongst Jewish bankers the left liberals were supported mainly by lesser lights in the eastern provinces. The leading figures in Berlin, Hamburg, and Frankfurt tended towards National Liberalism rather than left liberalism.[18]

The favourable and unfavourable contemporary stereotypes about the left liberals both fail to fit. They were not the political incarnation of the *Bürgertum*, nor were they a party-political extension of high finance and exporters.[19] Yet both descriptions were influential even though they were inaccurate. Amongst those who saw themselves as part of the *Bürgertum*, the traditional association between Liberal and *Bürgertum*, reinforced by the popular image of the Conservatives as a band of Junkers, the Centre as a combination of clericalism, Catholicism, and backwardness, and the SPD as a proletarian party, still gave an inherent advantage to the Liberal political parties. Conversely, popular association with financial capital, compounded by the party's image as a 'protection league for Jews' (*Judenschutztruppe*), blunted the left liberals' appeal to sections of the peasantry and petty bourgeoisie. Naumann, campaigning in Waldeck-Pyrmont, 'came up against the objection that Liberals were in the service of big capital in all corners'. One Waldeck left liberal even attributed the FVP's

---

[17] Rolling, 'Liberals, Socialists and City Government', 53.

[18] W. E. Mosse, *The German-Jewish Economic Élite 1820–1935: A Socio-Cultural Profile* (Oxford, 1989), 258–9; P. Pulzer, *Jews and the German State: The Political History of a Minority* (Oxford, 1992), 123–47; D. L. Augustine, *Patricians and Parvenus: Wealth and High Society in Wilhelmine Germany* (Oxford, 1994).

[19] This is not to deny that left liberal views on matters like stock-exchange controls, trade treaties, and department stores were also the position of finance capital. See e.g. *Die Freisinnige Volkspartei im Kampf für Handel und Industrie* (Berlin, 1905). But if this is the yardstick then the SPD would equally merit the label 'stock-exchange party' (*Börsenpartei*).

ambivalence towards equal women's rights to 'the far too close links of [left liberal] men with modern capitalism'.[20] There remains the need for a more detailed and accurate assessment of left liberal sociology. Two sets of figures often used to shed light on left liberal social composition—the occupations of deputies and of party conference delegates—have important limitations.[21] The deputies provide too small a sample. Moreover, deputies were untypical of the people who voted for them. This was true for every party, but was particularly striking in the case of the left liberals. No one, for example, could mistake Conrad Haußmann, a Stuttgart lawyer, for the rural and small-town inhabitants of the Schwäbisch Alp, or the Berlin-based publicist Friedrich Naumann for the petty-bourgeois citizenry of Heilbronn or the obdurate peasants of Waldeck-Pyrmont. Party conference delegates provide a larger sample. But this amounted to only 0.5 per cent of total membership, and was unrepresentative for three reasons. First, the location of the sole regular FVP national party conference in Mannheim meant that more delegates came from Southern Germany, especially Baden, and comparatively few from centres of left liberal electoral support along the North German coast and in eastern Prussia.[22] Second, there was an inherent occupational bias. Only a minority could afford the cost, in time and money, of attending a national conference, and only a few local parties were willing to subsidize less well-off delegates. Finally, party conferences were not even intended to be gatherings of the rank and file; rather they were conclaves of constituency leaders. This was reinforced by an upper limit of three delegates from each Reichstag seat for the 1912 FVP conference, and of the three left liberal parties merged in 1910 only the DVP held annual conferences open to ordinary party members.

There is, therefore, no direct way of analysing left liberal social composition: no surviving national or regional lists of party members. Moreover, judging the standing of a person by occupational title is an inexact science. The profusion of job titles for state employees, be it in education, the customs house, or on the railways, allow a ready

---

[20] BA Berlin, NL Naumann 236, Friedrich Naumann to Jacob Rießer, 28 May 1913; UB Marburg, NL Rade, Heinrich Kramer to Carl Köhler, Arolsen, 8 Oct. 1912.

[21] For the social composition of National Liberals and left liberals see Langewiesche, *Liberalism in Germany*, 129–83, and for deputies in general, H. Best, 'Elite Structure and Regime (Dis)continuity in Germany 1867–1933: The Case of Parliamentary Leadership Groups', *German History*, 8 (1990), 1–28.

[22] *Der zweite Parteitag der Fortschrittlichen Volkspartei*, 135.

assessment of social status and income, but the description *Fabrikant* (manufacturer) could be applied both to a very prosperous minority and to the numerous owners of very small concerns producing profits less regular and not very much greater than the income of skilled workers. *Kaufmann* (salesman, merchant, but often just businessman) had a similarly wide usage. Moreover, activities, particularly of deputies, often cut across categories. Georg Gothein, for example, could be classified as a retired state official, a businessman, a pressure group organizer, a writer, or a professional politician. Because we know much more about the few at the top and little about the many at the bottom it is useful to analyse left liberal social composition at four different levels: first, those prominent in national and state politics, members of the FVP business and central committees, parliamentary deputies, and provincial leaders; secondly local leaders, members of regional and local committees; third, rank-and-file party members; and fourth, much the largest category, unorganized left liberal voters.

The first group is compact and easily identifiable. Left liberal politics above district (*Bezirk*) level was in the hands of fewer than 200 people. The eighteen-man business committee was dominated by professional or semi-professional politicians with parliamentary seats. In 1910 six were current Reichstag deputies, three were Landtag deputies, and eight had double mandates. By late 1918 the respective numbers were seven, four, and six.[23] The sixty members of the central committee were supposedly elected at district level. In practice representatives were not chosen by a ballot of party members. In most cases the chairman or deputy chairman of the state, province, or district association put themselves forward and were endorsed by the regional committee or district party conference. The central committee was also weighted according to the chances of Reichstag electoral success. The small Liegnitz district in Silesia, for example, had two representatives, and the rest of the province only one. Often regional representatives were former deputies, or men who had deliberately refused the chance to enter parliament. The Silesian left liberal leader Adolf Heilberg, for instance, always refused invitations to stand in a winnable constituency. The group of businessmen who ran left liberal politics in Hagen and represented the district in the central committee also refused a Berlin parliamentary seat. Johannes Leonhart and

[23] BA Berlin, FVP 36, fo. 1; FVP 35/4, fo. 15.

Ernst Carstens, central committee representatives of Schleswig-Holstein, were both former deputies who had deliberately stood down from the Reichstag.[24] This was a small circle, and it was drawn from a correspondingly narrow social grouping. While lawyers might hold strong opinions about who had the more prestigious practice, and university academics consider themselves quite distinct from mere secondary-school 'professors', the fact remained that well over half the left liberal *Reichstag* caucus were drawn from the professional middle classes. Typically two-thirds of left liberal deputies in imperial Germany were graduates: twenty-five of forty-two left liberals returned in 1912.[25] Even deputies whose main occupation fell into another category often had strong ties to the educated middle classes. The stove manufacturer August Hoffmeister, for example, was related by marriage to the celebrated historian Theodor Mommsen. The economic specialist

Table 1.1. *Social composition of left liberal Reichstag deputies, 1907 and 1912*

	1907	1912
Lawyers	7	12
Farmers	1	6
Businessmen	11	4
Officials	11	5
Doctors	3	1
University professors	1	2
Craftsmen	2	1
School teachers	7	5
Judges	2	1
Writers	4	3
Clergymen	0	1
Publicans	0	1
TOTAL	49	42

Source: *Fränkischer Kurier* (1 March 1912).

[24] A. Heilberg, 'Erinnerungen 1858–1936', unpubl. MS, Breslau 1936, extract in M. Richarz (ed.), *Jüdisches Leben in Deutschland: Selbstzeugnisse zur Sozialgeschichte im Kaiserreich* (Stuttgart, 1979), 292; *Eugen Richter und der Wahlkreis Hagen-Schwelm*, 26–9.
[25] D. Langewiesche, 'Bildungsbürgertum und Liberalismus im 19. Jahrhundert', in J. Kocka (ed.), *Bildungsbürgertum im 19. Jahrhundert*, iv (Stuttgart, 1989), 95–121; *Der Fortschrittliche Volkspartei im neuen Reichstag* (Berlin, 1912).

Georg Gothein cited Goethe as well as trade statistics. Hugo Wendorff was a Pomeranian estate owner but, as was quickly pointed out, had little in common with his agricultural neighbours. He had a doctorate and impeccable family ties: his father was president of the state law courts and his second wife a niece of the poet Wilbrandt.[26] The elementary-school teachers in the left liberal *Fraktion* also saw themselves as members of the educated middle classes, as their repeated demands that their profession should have access to the universities and the magistracy clearly reflected.[27] If the range of occupations of left liberal deputies was restricted, their social aspirations were even more closely clustered.

Left liberal regional leaders were just as socially exclusive. Indeed, they tended to have an even higher social standing, including, as they did, successful businessmen and professionals deterred from a Berlin mandate by career and family commitments, or the rough-and-tumble of Reichstag elections. The Oldenburg left liberal leader Theodor Tantzen, for example, preferred to look after state politics and the farm. The task of representing Oldenburg in Berlin fell to the politically and socially inferior elementary-school teacher Ahlhorn, dismissed by Payer as an 'old ass', and to a Berlin-based professional politician, Albert Traeger, until his death in May 1912, and then Otto Wiemer.[28] The FVP central committee's composition reflected both the greater role of businessmen in regional organization, and the rather high social standing of left liberal regional leaders.

Left liberal regional leaders, deputies, and local party chairmen remained overwhelmingly respected and rather prosperous members of Protestant urban society. However, the wider group of left liberal political activists exhibited more democratic influences. The list of FVP Reichstag candidates in 1912 combined members of the left liberal establishment with representatives of new social groups demanding greater political representation.

The presence of 'new' and 'old' *Mittelstand* representatives and some liberal Hirsch-Duncker union leaders indicated that this level was less exclusively the preserve of the professional and business classes. Nevertheless lawyers, teachers, and journalists retained a strong presence amongst Reichstag candidates, especially those standing in winnable constituencies. They were also prominent in

---

[26] BA Koblenz, NL Gothein 14, fos. 175–81.
[27] M. Lamberti, *State, Society and the Elementary School in Imperial Germany* (New York, 1989).   [28] BA Koblenz, NL Payer 41, Payer to wife, 18 Jan. 1913.

Table 1.2. *Social composition of FVP Central Committee, 1912*

	Members	Replacements
Agriculture	2	4
Businessmen	15	13
Judges	1	1
Lawyers	12	11
Doctors	3	5
Professors	7	2
Other education	2	8
Editors/publishers	7	4
Clergymen	2	1
White collar	1	2
Deputy/councillor*	5	4
Women	1	1
Senior engineer	1	0
Archive director	1	0
Town geometer	0	1
Retired	0	1
No information	0	2
TOTAL	60	60

Source: *Der zweite Parteitag der Fortschrittlichen Volkspartei*, 142–5.
* Only listed as such where no other occupation known.

Table 1.3. *Occupations of FVP candidates: 1912 Reichstag election*

Occupation	Number	%
Agriculture	14	8.2
Workers' representatives	4	2.4
Artisans and shopkeepers	13	7.6
Merchants and manufacturers	18	10.6
White-collar staff	9	5.3
Writers and journalists	14	8.2
Doctors	3	1.8
Clergy	9	5.3
Lawyers	32	18.8
Judges	4	2.4
Elementary school teachers	17	10.0
Secondary school teachers	11	6.5
University professors	5	2.9
Municipal officials	8	4.7
Administrative officials	5	2.9
Retired state officials	4	2.4
TOTAL	170	

Source: *Breslauer Zeitung*, 20 (9 Jan. 1912).

published lists of left liberal local chairmen and secretaries.[29] But occupational similarities between the two groups masked significant differences in social standing within occupations. Education, for example, was represented largely by university professors in the central committee and by elementary-school teachers on the hustings. Lawyers in the national and regional leadership were generally more prosperous and prominent (they frequently had a 'Justizrat' or 'Geheimer Justizrat' title) than their local counterparts. Whereas the leadership group was largely drawn from the prosperous middle classes, local political activists came from a broader spectrum. The composition of the FVP Landesausschuß in Baden (Table 1.4) did not just reflect the more open society south of the Main. Artisans, and particularly members of the 'new' *Mittelstand*, also featured in North German left liberal associations. The FVP *Vorstand* in Pomerania, for example, included carpenters, small farmers, elementary-school teachers, a lathe operator and an abattoir worker, with Hanover and Württemberg following a similar pattern.[30]

Table 1.4. *Social composition FVP Landesausschuß Baden: 1914*

Occupation	Number
Agriculture	1
Businessmen	13
Management/technical	7
Artisans/shopkeepers	5
Judges/state administrators	2
Mayors/councillors	7
Lawyers/doctors/vets	8
Clergymen	2
Grammar school teachers	8
Other school teachers	5
White collar workers	7
Rail workers	2
Factory workers	2
Women	1
TOTAL	60

Source: *Badischer Landesbote* (2 July 1914).

[29] See *Vereinskalender der Deutschen freisinnigen Partei zum Handgebrauch für das Jahr 1892* (Berlin, 1892); *Vereinskalender der Freisinnigen Volkspartei für das Jahr 1894/5* (Berlin, 1894) and successive edns publ. in 1895, 1897, 1899, and 1902.
[30] BA Koblenz NL Gothein 35, fos. 30–1; *Freisinnige Zeitung* (2 May 1914); Hunt, *People's Party*, 49; and Simon, *Württembergische Demokraten*, 28–9.

Precisely how much broader the social composition of ordinary left liberal party membership was is difficult to assess. Few state officials appear to have maintained registers of left liberal members even before the 1908 Associations Law removed the authorities' right to demand the names of all party members. This casts an interesting light on state attitudes towards left liberalism. The rhetoric that labelled left liberals as *Reichsfeinde*, enemies of the state, was increasingly disregarded in practice. But the resultant absence of local membership lists hardly helps illuminate the social make-up of left liberalism. And the picture is most incomplete precisely for those years when the great majority of party members entered organized politics. Left liberal membership, like party membership generally, mushroomed between 1904 and 1914. SPD membership rose from under 400,000 in 1905 to a million in 1914, while National Liberal associations increased from 940 in 1907 and to 2,007 and a claimed membership of 283,711 in 1914. The People's Association for Catholic Germany (Volksverein für katholische Deutschland), rather than the Centre Party itself, reflected increasing popular involvement in organized political Catholicism. It grew from 322,000 members in 1903 to 805,000 in 1914. Only the disintegrating anti-Semite parties departed from the trend of rapid expansion.[31] Within left liberalism FrVg membership tripled from 3,004 in 1904/5 to 9,494 by March 1909.[32] Some 720 associations were affiliated to either the FrVp or FrVg in 1909/10: 570 to the FrVp and 150 to the FrVg.[33] The FVP had double this number by autumn 1912.[34] And by May 1914 the FVP claimed a total of 240,000 members in nineteen state associations; fourteen regional associations; eighty-three constituency associations; 1,587 local associations; 151 subassociations (*Ortsgruppen*); forty-three youth associations; two women's associations; sixty-six branches of the National League of Liberal Workers and White-Collar Staff (Reichsverein liberaler Arbeiter und Angestellter, RLAA); and thirteen other labour associations.[35] The claimed total membership was

---

[31] Fricke, *Handbuch*, i. 308; BA Berlin Deutsche Volkspartei 1, fo. 15; D. Fricke *et al.* (eds.), *Lexikon zur Parteiengeschichte: Die bürgerlichen und kleinbürgerlichen Parteien und Verbände in Deutschland 1789–1945* (4 vols.; Leipzig, 1983–6), i. 436.

[32] FrVg Vorstand, 7 Jan. 1906, BA Berlin, FVP 5, fo. 8; FrVg executive committee, 27 Mar. 1909, BA Berlin, FVP 8, fo. 2.

[33] *Die Freisinnige Volkspartei, ihr Programm und ihre Organisation* (Berlin, 1909), 18; Langewiesche, *Liberalism in Germany*, 163.

[34] *Der zweite Parteitag der Fortschrittlichen Volkspartei*, 136.

[35] Otto Wiemer to FVP central committee, cited in *Oberbadische Volkszeitung*, (18 May 1914).

no doubt inflated. The growing pressure, external and internal, to claim a large organization meant all parties, with the partial exception of the SPD, declared a membership significantly in excess of the true figure, including those who paid little or no subscriptions and optimistic estimates for those associations which failed to return membership figures. Even so left liberal membership was undoubtedly many times greater in 1914 than a decade earlier.

The social composition of party membership around the turn of the century did not, therefore, necessarily reflect the much larger membership on the eve of the war. Moreover, local associations inevitably mirrored different local environments. The National-Social Association in Munich, for example, bore the hallmarks of a university city and seat of government. Sixty of the 160 members had doctorates.[36] The membership of a Breslau FrVp district association, on the other hand, mirrored the continued predominance of small firms and artisans in the local economy. The strong presence of manufacturers, merchants, and doctors was also partly a result of the substantial proportion of Jews in these groups.[37] Finally, the relatively small number of state employees reflected the stricter attitude towards the political behaviour of public employees taken by the authorities in the east.[38]

In the south and west, by contrast, state employees had more latitude and inclination to became active in left liberal politics. A petition about political rights of state officials organized by the Nationalverein für das liberale Deutschland after the disciplining of the left liberal Bürgermeister of Husum, Lothar Schücking, in 1908 reflected the increasing involvement of public employees and the 'new' *Mittelstand* generally in left liberal politics.

Despite the absence of an extensive set of membership lists, the logical presumption is that petty-bourgeois and working-class groups provided the bulk of the increase in left liberal membership during the pre-war decade. The development of left liberal local politics in Mainz and Lissa reinforce this assumption. In Mainz established left liberal leaders blamed their removal from the FVP committee on new

[36] BA Koblenz, NL Goetz 65.

[37] *Der Greif*, 28 (16 Aug. 1910); cf. P. Pulzer, 'Die Jüdische Beteiligung in der Politik', in Werner E. Mosse (ed.), *Juden im Wilhelminischen Deutschland 1890–1914* (Tübingen, 1976), 189; and Hettling, 'Hochburg', 270 ff.

[38] For the close supervision of state employees in Silesia and their untypical rejection of left liberal politics see Ch. 9 below.

Table 1.5. *Membership of Verein Waldeck, Breslau: 1900*

Occupation	Number	%
Farmers	2	0.6
Manufacturers/owners	20	6.5
Merchants	99	32.0
Doctors/dentists	22	7.1
Pharmacists	3	1.0
Lawyers	6	1.9
Editors/journalists	8	2.6
Arts	2	0.6
School teachers	13	4.2
Secondary school teachers	2	0.6
White collar workers	19	6.1
Master artisans	44	14.2
Services/traders	19	6.1
Supervisors	10	3.2
Artisans/skilled workers	20	6.5
Rail workers	2	0.6
Workers and caretakers	6	1.9
Councillors*	2	0.6
No occupation given	10	3.2
TOTAL	290	

Source: Compiled from membership list in *Siebenter Jahresbericht (1899–1900) des Vereins 'Waldeck' in Breslau.*
* Figure excludes councillors listed under their specific occupation.

socially inferior members.[39] In the Poznanian town of Lissa the left liberal local association, a rather somnolent collection of mainly Jewish businessmen and lawyers, threatened to be transformed by an influx of new members, especially railwaymen. The shocked chairman, Justizrat Wolff, could 'not comprehend how dependent people could dare to join a [left] liberal association'.[40] The sort of direct confrontation between old leaders and new members seen in Mainz and Lissa was rare. In both towns the rebellion against autocratic local leadership was heightened by an untypical and much resented action: a local electoral pact with the Centre.[41] But the refusal to look on those with a lower social status as equal party members was widespread. Left liberal politicians frequently accused SPD bureaucrats of

[39] BA Berlin FVP 15, fos. 1–97.   [40] BA Berlin FVP 12, fo. 36.
[41] BA Berlin FVP 12, fo. 36, and FVP 15, fo. 94.

Table 1.6. *Social composition of signatories to petition on
political rights of state officials, 1908*

	Number	%
Agriculture/forestry	6	1.1
Manufacturers/rentiers	22	4.1
Merchants	81	15.1
Judicial officials	7	1.3
Retired officers	2	0.4
Clergymen	2	0.4
Lawyers	17	3.2
Doctors/dentists/pharmacists	19	3.5
Academics	12	2.2
Senior teachers	15	2.8
School teachers	72	13.4
Journalists	6	1.1
Arts	8	1.5
Services/shopkeepers	15	2.8
Technical	32	6.0
Supervisors	15	2.8
Rail/postal workers	23	4.3
White collar workers	66	12.3
Master artisans	20	3.7
Artisans/skilled workers	56	10.4
Factory workers	10	1.9
Women*	6	1.1
Others/no information	25	4.7
TOTAL	537	

Source: Compiled from original petitions and letters in NL Lothar
Schücking.
* A further eleven female signatories, mostly teachers, are listed under
their stated occupation.

expecting ordinary members just to 'pay up and shut up' (*Zahlen und
Maul halten*). But local left liberal committees were at least as guilty in
this respect. The reluctance of left liberal local parties to adopt worker
candidates was a clear manifestation of such attitudes. The prejudice
of left liberal local leaders encountered by Hans Meier in Eschwege
was typical: 'We now have a good number of workers in the party. But
I can clearly see our committee members thinking: "isn't that nice.
Even workers are going along with *us*." They just don't imagine that
workers have a sense of belonging to the Volkspartei.'[42]

[42] UB Marburg, NL Rade, Hans Meier to Martin Rade, 19 Dec. 1911.

Such attitudes hardly encouraged workers to join left liberal organizations. The failure to have a single workers' representative as a Reichstag or Prussian Landtag deputy or, before 1918, on the FVP executive committee was a constant reminder of the discrimination felt by some left liberal workers. The failure of existing FVP organizations to meet worker aspirations was also reflected in the setting up of the RLAA by Erkelenz and others in 1912 as a separate association affiliated to the FVP. However, the RLAA attracted only a minority of left liberal workers, with less than 5,000 members compared to 100,000 for the Hirsch-Duncker unions.[43] Nevertheless, the growth of left liberal membership came partly from the working class. The contribution of the petty bourgeoisie was even more significant. Not only did a wider section of the petty bourgeoisie feel attracted to left liberal politics. These recruits, particularly members of the 'new' *Mittelstand*, had more success in securing an active role in left liberal politics, as the case-studies in Chapters 7–9 underline. Even so, left liberal leaders, at national and local level, were either too prejudiced, or fearful for their own positions, to harness the full potential of new members. As Wilhelm Ohr perceptively remarked, left liberal leaders were always complaining at party conferences how few people were there to take up the liberal cause, but 'for reasons I don't understand, again and again [let] able people who want to devote themselves to it go by unnoticed, instead of putting them in positions where they can achieve something'.[44]

As a result, the role of petty-bourgeois and working-class members in left liberal associations was subordinate and often silent. Nevertheless, their numerical weight grew as party membership mushroomed. There were also some signs of established middle-class barriers to the new social groups being overcome. By 1912, for example, the Verein Waldeck was still headed by two journalists, a doctor and a businessman, but they had been joined on the committee by master carpenter Kleeberg, clockmaker Lebram, trade union secretary Köthner, and Fräulein Tondeur.[45] Similarly, the slate of left liberal candidates in municipal elections increasingly included petty-bourgeois and liberal union representatives.[46] If the typical left liberal local party continued to be led by businessmen and professionals, an increasing number of

[43] Fricke (ed.), *Lexikon*, iv. 87–9.
[44] BA Berlin, NL Wilhelm Ohr 4, fo. 28, Ohr to Fritz Crämer, Nürnberg FVP.
[45] *Breslauer Zeitung*, 759 (27 Oct. 1912).
[46] See the case-study of Kiel in Ch. 8 below.

activists and most ordinary members were artisans or white-collar and skilled workers. It is, paradoxically, rather easier to assess the social composition of left liberal voters than party members. Reichstag electoral returns are the obvious source. They provide a huge sample, largely unbiased by abstentions and electoral corruption. However, the figures must be treated with some caution because of the profusion of electoral pacts in 1912 as well as 1907. In addition, Wilhelmine voters had a keen sense of electoral arithmetic. In the cities, for example, substantial numbers voted not necessarily for the party of their choice, but for the party most likely to defeat the SPD. The following figures, therefore, somewhat exaggerate the left liberal share of the urban vote. Nor, inevitably, do they take account of substantial regional variations. Nevertheless, the figures confirm that most left liberal voters lived in towns and cities, and that the left liberal share of the vote, like that of the SPD, rose as the size of the community increased, whilst support for the right declined. Reichstag returns also underlined the Protestant bias of left liberal support.[47] However, there is a limit to what published Reichstag election statistics reveal about the social distribution of party support. State elections held under class franchises can provide useful additional information though some caution is needed in relating regional figures to the national picture.

Unfortunately, Prussian Landtag election results are only of limited use. The great majority of the electorate abstained and open voting produced notorious distortions. There were also grotesque

Table 1.7. *Percentage distribution of votes according to community size: Reichstag election 1912*

Community size	DKP	FCon	A–S	Centre	NLP	FVP	SPD
Under 2,000	17.5	4.6	4.1	20.5	12.8	8.8	19.0
2,000–10,000	5.7	2.6	2.2	19.8	15.0	12.2	35.8
Over 10,000	3.0	1.7	—	10.9	13.8	15.6	49.3
All Germany	9.2	3.0	2.5	16.4	13.6	12.3	34.8

Source: J. Bertram, *Die Wahlen zum Deutschen Reichstag vom Jahre 1912: Parteien und Verbände in der Innenpolitik des Wilhelminischen Reiches* (Düsseldorf, 1964), 188; Ritter, *Wahlgeschichtliches Arbeitsbuch*, 179.

[47] H. Nöcker, *Der preußische Reichstagswähler in Kaiserreich und Republik 1912 und 1924* (Berlin, 1987), 57, finds a higher correlation between left liberal support and size of Protestant population (Pearson product-moment correlation 0.59) than for other political parties. Cf. Sperber, *Kaiser's Voters*, 251–61.

differences between polling districts in the income needed to get into the higher voting categories. In Berlin the taxes needed to vote in the first class varied from 52 to 365,644 marks. And opponents of the Prussian franchise delighted in a polling district in the capital where the first class electorate consisted of a sausage manufacturer while the third contained several Prussian ministers, including Bülow, amongst its 270 electors. The same was true for Kiel where some workers could vote in the first class in the 121st district in 1913, whereas in the 58th district Oberbürgermeister Lindemann, Admiral Thomsen, Oberlandesgerichtspräsident Dr Kirchner, and other notables only made the third class.[48] It is more illuminating to look at state election results in Saxony and Hamburg which had much higher electoral turn-outs, secret ballots, and voting categories more closely related to social class. In addition, the Protestant population of Saxony and Hamburg allows us to look at the voting behaviour of this vital group without the confessional divisions and national minorities which complicate analysis of Prussian and Reich returns.

Though the Saxon plural voting system introduced in 1909 and the 1906 Hamburg franchise were both convoluted attempts to stave off SPD electoral success, they nevertheless provide valuable indications of the social composition of party-political support. To be enfranchised in Saxony, voters had to be males at least twenty-five years of age, to have held Saxon citizenship for two or more years, at least six months residence in polling district, and annual taxable income over 400 marks. As a result only 17.3 per cent of the population were eligible to vote, as against almost 22 per cent in Reichstag elections. Additional votes were granted essentially on the following basis: for a second vote, annual income over 1,600 marks. or ownership of two hectares of land; for a third vote income over 2,200 marks or four hectares of land; for a fourth vote income over 2,800 marks or eight hectares of land. Somewhat lower income limits applied to those in public service, with a fixed position, or who owned non-agricultural land. Only a quarter of land area (for example, two hectares for four votes) was required for wine-growers and market gardeners. In

---

[48] LA Schleswig, Oberpräsidium 301, 8118, David Waldstein to public meeting, Altona, 17 Apr. 1913; F. Hoff, *Auf zum Kampfe für das Reichstagswahlrecht in Preußen* (Berlin, 1908), 18; R. Paetau, *Konfrontation und Kooperation* (Neumünster, 1988), 160 and 483 n. 258. On Prussian Landtag elections in general see T. Kühne, *Dreiklassenwahlrecht und Wahlkultur in Preußen 1867–1914: Landtagswahlen zwischen korporativer Tradition und politischem Massenmarkt* (Düsseldorf, 1994).

addition, each voter over 50 years old was given an extra vote unless they already had four votes. Voting in Hamburg was restricted to citizens with a taxable income of at least 1200 marks. In general elections in the city voters with an income above 2,500 marks elected two-thirds of the seats and those with an income of 1,200–2,500 marks one third. Each elector had twelve votes and seats were apportioned by proportional representation. In addition, there were separate elections for 'notable' and property owners.

Saxony was not a traditional left liberal stronghold. Even the modest share of the poll in 1909 was considerably better than the left liberals had received in recent elections. Although the left liberals had made sharp gains in the Reichstag and Landtag at the beginning of the 1880s, after the National Liberals supported Bismarck's tariff policy, by the beginning of the 1890s the National Liberals had reasserted themselves as the party of the Saxony's industrial middle classes, and the Social Democrats had claimed a large share of petty-bourgeois and working-class votes. In the decade before 1909 the left liberals held only two or three seats in the Landtag.[49] The election results were also affected by the 1909 Reich finance reform. Nevertheless, the voting figures, based on a turn-out of 82.6 per cent, comparable to Reichstag contests, remain a revealing illustration of the even spread of left liberal support across different income groups. The voting system, with a bias towards landowners and those over 50, discriminated somewhat against the left liberals, who were more likely to appeal in

Table 1.8. *1909 Saxon state elections: distribution of party support according to category of voter (%)*

Party	All electors	Electors with			
		1 vote	2 votes	3 votes	4 votes
Conservatives	16.6	7.6	16.4	24.1	35.6
Anti-Semites	3.2	1.4	3.0	4.9	6.9
National Liberal	19.7	9.3	19.2	33.2	39.6
Left liberal	6.6	4.1	7.2	11.2	9.5
Social Democrat	53.8	77.6	54.1	26.5	8.3

Source: *Zeitschrift des Könglichen Sächsischen Statistischen Landesamtes*, 55 (1909), 228–43, cited in G. A. Ritter, 'Wahlrecht und die Wählerschaft der Sozialdemokratie im Königreich Sachsen 1867–1914', in Ritter (ed.), *Aufstieg der Arbeiterbewegung*, 90–1. See also the unattributed report 'Wahlrecht im Königreich Sachsen' drawn up by opponents of Prussian franchise reform in BA Koblenz, NL Richthofen, 13, fos. 146–7 (copy).

[49] Sheehan, *German Liberalism*, 227.

urban areas and to younger voters less ingrained in their party allegiance. Nevertheless, the figures clearly indicated that left liberal supporters were, on average, better situated than the great majority of
SPD voters, but occupied a lower position in the social hierarchy than
those of the other non-socialist parties.

While the Saxon figures confirm that most voters with low incomes
and status voted SPD and respectable, prosperous electors favoured
the National Liberal party and right, they caution against simply
equating the working class with the Social Democrats and the middle
strata with the other parties. Most of the 54 per cent of two-vote electors who voted for the SPD had an additional vote simply because
they were over 50. Two-thirds of electors with two votes, 143,000 out
of 213,000, qualified for an additional vote solely by age. But the SPD
was also the second most popular party even amongst three-vote electors. SPD support in the higher voting categories reflected a blurring
of economic and social boundaries. It was increasingly difficult to separate the incomes and lifestyles of skilled workers, artisans, clerks, and
lower ranked state employees. The result was that some workers had
an income sufficient for additional votes, and the SPD was also able to
extend its constituency within the petty bourgeoisie. However, even in
'Red' Saxony, the non-socialist parties had the support of almost a
fifth of one-vote electors. Party support was weighted according to
social class. But at the same time all parties, and the Liberals especially, battled for support across a broad social spectrum.

Left liberals attracted a higher level of support in Hamburg,
where they were the most popular non-socialist party. Again, however, it is the relatively even spread of left liberal support which
attracts attention. The established council caucuses on the right, the
Alte Fraktionen, were the Right, Left Centre, and the Left, the
groups responsible for passing the 1906 franchise changes. The confusing labels referred to the traditional and increasingly jettisoned
division in Hanseatic municipal politics between the Right, the commercial and social élite, and the Left, the representatives of the petty
bourgeoisie, particularly small traders and shopkeepers. While the
Left did continue to challenge the Right's monopoly of mayoral and
Senate posts in the Wilhelmine period, they no longer represented a
force for general progressive change, and in economic and cultural
matters were often more reactionary than the Right. Party labels conformed more to political reality in spring 1918 when Right became
the *Bürgerschaft* caucus of the National Liberal Party, and the

Conservative Association and some members of the dissolved Left Centre formed the 'New Hamburg Right', in co-operation with members of the Left.[50] Names apart, it was clear that all three right-wing groups drew most sustenance from electors in the higher income group while Social Democrat support came mainly from those with annual incomes under 2,500 marks. The left liberals, the bourgeois opponents of the 1906 franchise changes who had a new party, the United Liberals (*Vereinigte Liberale*) functioning from 1910 as the FVP's Hamburg organization, had support, by contrast, which was much more evenly balanced.[51] In the 1913 *Bürgerschaft* elections the left liberals had the support of 25 per cent of electors earning over 2,500 marks and 18.3 per cent of voters whose income fell between 1,200 and 2,500 marks.[52] That the left liberal share of the vote in the category over 2,500 marks rose much more sharply compared to the 1907 elections than the other categories suggests considerable numbers of left liberal voters previously earning some 1,800–2,500 marks had been taken into the higher voting category by inflation (see Tables 1.9 and 1.10). Similarly, the lower level of left liberal support in the notable elections (Table 1.10), indicated the left

Table 1.9. *Hamburg* Bürgerschaft *general elections, 1907 and 1913: share of vote (%)*

	1907		1913	
	I	II	I	II
Alte Fraktionen	66.3	17.2	61.7	17.5
Left Liberals	20.2	18.1	25.0	18.3
SPD	5.1	60.9	8.8	62.2
Anti-Semites	5.4	2.3	—	—
Hamburg Conservatives	—	—	3.9	1.6
Others	3.0	1.5	0.7	0.4
TOTAL	100	100	100	100

I Hamburg citizens with annual taxable income of above 2,500 marks.
II Hamburg citizens with annual taxable income of 1,200–2,500 marks.

[50] The *Bürgerschaft* figures in Tables 1.9 and 1.10 are based on the first electoral district. Voting in the second district, the other half of the city, took place only once under the 1906 franchise, in 1910. The results of this election were similar to those of 1913. SA Hamburg, NL Carl Braband B23, 'Statistische Übersichten: Die Ergebnisse der Wahlen zur hamburgischen *Bürgerschaft* im Jahre 1910', *Öffentlicher Anzeiger*, 103 (30 Apr. 1910, Beilage).
[51] Freie und Hansestadt Hamburg (ed.), *Jahresbericht des statistischen Amtes und Bureaus der Zentralwahlkommission für das Jahr 1912*, 71–84.
[52] J. Bolland, *Die Hambürgische Bürgerschaft in alter und neuer Zeit*, (Hamburg, 1959), 88.

Table 1.10. *Left liberal share of vote in Hamburg
elections: 1907 and 1912/13 (%)*

	1907	1912/13
Reichstag suffrage	22.5	25.3
Citizens over 2,500 marks p.a.	20.2	25.0
Citizens 1,200–2,500 marks p.a.	18.1	18.3
Notables	12.7	14.1
Property owners	9.5	9.4

liberal electorate in the higher voting category was more skewed towards those with a reasonable rather than lavish income. Of course, much about Hamburg's economy, society, and politics was as untypical as its electoral system. However, the pattern of left liberal support revealed is reasonably representative. Left liberal support was widely spread, but at its strongest in middle income groups. In Hamburg the focal point of support was low- and middle-ranking public-sector employees, white-collar workers, and the professions.[53] If the extent of this was exaggerated by local circumstances, it was nevertheless part of a general trend. The Hamburg evidence, like the Saxon electoral returns, indicated that the left liberal share of the vote tended to be somewhat greater amongst more prosperous members of the middle strata. In absolute terms, however, most Hamburg left liberal voters had only modest incomes. Around 4,800 left liberal *Bürgerschaft* voters were below and only 3,300 above the 2,500 mark income barrier in 1913. And the 'small man' was doubtless even more predominant amongst the 57,106 Hamburg FVP Reichstag voters in 1912.

Table 1.11. *Votes in Hamburg Reichstag elections: 1903–1912*

Party	1903	1907	1912
National Liberals		29,159	26,823
Left liberals		41,897	57,106
National Liberals and left liberals	54,636		
Centre	2,309	1,493	1,738
Anti-Semite	2,942	618	1,572
Social Democrat	100,112	112,930	138,360

Source: *Jahresbericht des Statistischen Amtes und Bureaus der Zentralwahlkommission
für das Jahr 1912, 82.*

[53] For left liberal cultivation of 'new' *Mittelstand* support in Hamburg-Altona see Ch. 8 below.

The same was true of left liberal popular support elsewhere. Despite the great inroads made by SPD in left liberal urban support during the 1880s and 1890s, workers still accounted for a significant part of left liberal support. Indeed, Jonathan Sperber has recently argued, on the basis of regression analysis, that Liberal suppport amongst Protestant workers was sizeable and rising after the turn of the century. A contemporary, Anton Erkelenz, estimated that half a million left liberal voters were employees, and claimed, from a rather optimistic interpretation of Reichstag election statistics, that over a third of 'workers' voted Liberal in 1912. Erkelenz probably included white-collar workers, for he opposed differentiating between *Arbeiter* and *Angestellte*.[54] A motion from Frankfurt FVP leaders urged the party to pursue social policies on behalf of the 'not inconsiderable part of the dependent strata' which 'still adhere to left liberalism'.[55] Even non-dependent left liberal voters were typically men of modest means. Robert Gyßling, leader of the left liberals in East Prussia, described artisans and small businessmen as the core of the party in his district.[56] Similarly, Dr Hegenscheidt, a Silesian *Landrat* and Free Conservative deputy, described left liberal support as coming largely from 'artisans and small and medium-sized business'. Even the rabid Conservative agitator Richard Kunze admitted, between tirades against the left liberals as a 'Jewish protection league', that they had continued support amongst artisans, small businessmen, and peasants.[57] Proposed attempts to widen the FVP's base in 1917 were aimed towards those 'occupational groups on which the party can support itself in the first instance . . . artisans, peasants, public employees and workers'.[58]

Two features emerge from this analysis of left liberal social composition. The first is the clear correlation between party and social hierarchy. The role of those with means (*Besitz*) and, more especially, education (*Bildung*) increased steadily as we proceed up the party's organizational ladder. The second is the wide, but correspondingly shallow spread of left liberal support. Left liberalism was a party of

[54] BA Koblenz, NL Erkelenz, 117, minutes of RLAA first national conference, Leipzig, 11 Aug. 1912; and *Die Volkspartei* (Apr. 1913); Sperber, *Kaiser's Voters*, 149.
[55] BA Berlin, FVP 37, Dr Ernst Cahn, Prof. Dr Heinrich Rößler, Amtsrichter Müller-Vilbel, motion to central committee, 18 Apr. 1910.
[56] BA Berlin, FVP 37, fo. 195, FVP central committee, 21 Nov. 1910.
[57] *Schlesische Freikonservative Parteikorrespondenz*, 1/6 (17 Dec. 1913); R. Kunze, *Was der deutsche Reichstagswähler wissen muß*, 2nd edn. (2 vols.; Berlin-Friedenau, 1911), ii. 49 and 57.
[58] BA Berlin, FVP 36, fo. 276, executive committee, 24 Oct. 1917.

minorities. It was embraced by a confessional minority, German Jews, and by minority causes, pacifism, feminism, and Manchesterism. More importantly here, the left liberal vote represented an aggregate of minorities from a succession of social and occupational spheres. The precise composition of these minorities defies a neat statistical answer. The main problem is to disentangle left liberal support from competing groups based primarily in the Protestant middle strata. Left liberal national and local leaders, for example, were, sociologically if not politically, very similar to counterparts in the Pan-German League. Roger Chickering's findings on Pan-German activists, the predominance of the Protestant eductated middle classes, and a particular appeal to its newer and less socially established branches, apply equally to left liberal local leaders. Unlike National Liberals, left liberal committee members were very rarely the same people who sat on Pan-German local committees (Direktor Fick in Würzburg was an exception) but they were frequently the same *sort* of people.[59] The main sociological difference between the two organizations was the lack of petty-bourgeois participation in the much smaller Pan-German League. However, the major and most complicated overlap was that between left liberal and National Liberal support. Left liberals liked to present themselves as modest men compared to socially aloof National Liberals. The left liberal economist Max Apt claimed you had to be not just a commercial councillor but a privy commercial councillor to be really at home in the National Liberals.[60] Ernst Müller-Meiningen defined National Liberal deputies as the sort of people who dined out for 5 marks while left liberals ate in the Reichstag canteen at half the price.[61] Such comments echoed an undoubted difference in average social standing between left liberal and National Liberal politicians. Moreover, the analysis of Saxon and Hamburg elections showed these differences were reproduced amongst voters. The average National Liberal had a higher social position than the average left liberal.[62] Likewise, within left liberal politics, FVP supporters tended to have a higher social position than the more radical Demokratische Vereinigung.[63] The correlation

---

[59] Chickering, *We Men Who Feel Most German*, 102–18.

[60] BA Berlin, Reichslandbund 6, fo. 136, personalia Max Apt, *Vossische Zeitung* (24 May 1923).   [61] Cited in Reimann, *Müller-Meiningen*, 10.

[62] Cf. M. Hettling, 'Bürgertum und Liberalismus im deutschen Kaiserreich', *Liberal*, 33 (1991), 63–4.

[63] *Das Freie Volk* (21 Dec. 1912); BA Berlin, FVP 37, fo. 191, central committee, 21 Oct. 1910.

between social position and political orientation should not, however, be pushed too far. The relatively high social position of left liberal national and local leaders has already been emphasized. There were, equally, many socially humble National Liberal party members and voters. Left liberals always tended to exaggerate the social status of National Liberals as part of their attack on the latter's *Honoratioren* image. Yet the National Liberals were actually more populist than the FVP in terms of organizational size, the type of constituency won, and the election of worker deputies.

There was no rigid sociological dividing line between National Liberals and left liberals. Indeed, a substantial block of voters floated between both parties. The sharp swings of electoral support between National Liberal and left liberal in 1881, 1887, 1890, and 1893 levelled out after the turn of the century. But this was done partly by electoral pacts: arrangements which tacitly acknowledged the preparedness of many voters to switch support between the National Liberals and left liberals. There remained a sizeable section of liberal voters who tended to lean to the right when 'national' issues were to the fore, and to the left when attention focused on economic grievances.[64]

The pattern of Liberal support was also influenced by continuing regional traditions. In regions like Schleswig-Holstein, Oldenburg, and Württemberg National Liberals and left liberals largely represented two different and antagonistic sections of society. National Liberals represented the establishment—in education, administration, and landownership—while left liberalism was the mouthpiece of small business, the peasantry, and white-collar workers.[65] In other areas one party was clearly predominant. In Berlin, Bremen, Alsace-Lorraine, Mecklenburg, and the eastern provinces of Prussia, most Liberal voters identified with left liberal parties, whilst the National Liberals took the great majority of Liberal votes in western Prussian provinces like Hanover, the Rhineland, and Westphalia, together with Saxony, Hessen, and Baden. School teachers tended to vote National Liberal in Göttingen and Leipzig, but left liberal in Berlin and Königsberg; master craftsmen National Liberal in Magdeburg and Bochum, but left liberal in Frankfurt and Bremen; peasants National Liberal in Hanover and the Palatinate, but left liberal in Mecklenburg and Lower Silesia. Moreover, they did so in many cases for similar

---

[64] GLA Karlsruhe, NLP Baden 179, Fuhrmann to Thorbecke, 4 Jan. 1911.
[65] Suval, *Electoral Politics*, 124.

reasons. Sometimes, therefore, the two Liberal factions represented different regions, but the same sort of people. To further complicate the picture, the left liberals also represented different people in different areas. In Hamburg the left liberals, labelled a *Beamtenpartei* by opponents, drew much support from the large reservoir of middle and lower ranking public employees, but in Württemberg and Lower Silesia they traditionally represented small businessmen, artisans, and peasants opposed to interfering and expensive big bureaucracy.

A national analysis of left liberal sociology is, therefore, no replacement for an analysis of how the party functioned in local society. Nevertheless, some universal traits in left liberal social composition are worth noting. Left liberal activists were concentrated in the free professions, market economy, and municipal government. There were hosts of lawyers, but few judicial and hardly any higher administrative civil servants. The sort of difficulties faced by a judge who was a left liberal activist were exemplified by the authorities' extensive if unavailing attempts to repress Dr Harz (Harburg) in National Liberal-dominated Hanover.[66] Education was no real exception, for it was almost a public monopoly and elementary-school teachers in urban areas came under municipal government influence. In the private sector left liberals were to be found more in competitive rather than cartellized economic activities. Amongst artisans the left liberals tended to do better amongst groups like tailors and carpenters than those like chimney sweeps which favoured tightly regulated guilds. In addition, the frequency of the description *Kaufmann* reflected some bias towards commerce rather than manufacturing.

Left liberals tended to do much better amongst the beneficiaries or by-products of modernization than its victims. It harnessed more support from engineers, managers, and clerks than from small retailers who felt threatened by department stores and consumer co-operatives.[67] Moreover, whilst the left liberals had little appeal to the higher echelons of state bureaucracy, they did considerably better amongst the rapidly increasing numbers of rail and postal workers and middle and lower ranked public employees generally. The trend towards the left

---

[66] H. Henning, *Das westdeutsche Bürgertum in der Epoche der Hochindustrialisierung 1860–1914* (Wiesbaden, 1972), i. 279–80. The markedly greater presence of state officials in National Liberal than left liberal ranks is underscored in Hettling, 'Bürgertum und Liberalismus', 64.

[67] On the latter see R. Gellately, *The Politics of Economic Despair: Shopkeepers and German Politics 1890–1914* (London, 1974).

liberals of such voters has already been discussed for Hamburg. It was also evident for Greater Berlin, along with Hamburg the largest concentration of the 'new' *Mittelstand* in Germany. In Teltow-Beeskow-Storkow-Charlottenburg left liberal support rose from 39,000 to 70,000 between 1907 and 1912, while Conservative votes fell from 52,000 to 29,000. And in neighbouring Oberbarnim a leading postal union official, Hubrich, gained enough support from the right to win the seat for the FVP.[68]

Clearly, there was a material basis to left liberal support. Left liberal political allegiance was good for careers in municipal government, but a bar to advancement in the state bureaucracy. Left liberal antipathy towards the web of import controls appealed to butchers, but not to customs officers. Left liberals won more support amongst publicans harassed by the police and state authorities than from landlords impeded by municipal building controls and health and safety regulations. However, material self-interest alone is an insufficient explanation. An important part of the left liberal electorate came from sections of society, like the free professions, for whom the implications of the parties' different economic stances were relatively slight. The left liberal share of the vote tended to rise or fall where left liberalism went with or against the grain in a wider sense.

The paucity of support for the left liberals amongst higher ranking state officials and the non-Jewish industrial and commercial élite, for example, was only partly a matter of self-interest. There may have been few left liberals amongst the élite in Conservative Prussia, where pronounced liberal views were a handicap to a high-level career in government service and to good commercial relations with the state. But the pattern was similar even in a state like Württemberg where the left liberals suffered little discrimination and were even regarded, after 1906, as a governing party. The propertied and, even more, the educated attached themselves to the *Deutsche Partei*, the Württemberg National Liberals, rather than the left liberal People's Party (*Volkspartei*).[69] The natural political alignment in these circles was

---

[68] Süle, *Preußische Bürokratietradition*; *Kieler Zeitung* (19 Jan. 1912) morning edition. Nöcker, *Der preußische Reichstagswähler*, 57, notes a weak positive correlation between left liberal support and the tertiary sector generally.

[69] This contrast is emphatically underlined in the memoirs of the left liberal Friedrich Payer and the National Liberal Gottlob Egelhaaf: G. Bradler (ed.), *Friedrich Payer (1847–1931): Autobiographische Aufzeichnungen und Dokumente* (Göppingen, 1974); G. Egelhaaf, *Lebenserinnerungen*, ed. A. Rapp (Stuttgart, 1960). See also Hunt, *People's Party*; Simon, *Württembergische Demokraten*.

National Liberal and Free Conservative; the pervading preference for calm bureaucratic rule and social exclusivity. The left liberals, by contrast, were deemed socially below the salt, dangerously radical, and too keen on popular politics. East Elbian landowners like Wendorff were, predictably, ostracized by their Junker neighbours because of their liberal views.[70] However, as the Silesian FVP chairman Adolf Heilberg recalled, left liberal local leaders suffered a similar social plight in smaller Prussian towns where 'those who were not reserve officers had no role in "society", no place at the *Stammtisch*, and were considered second class citizens'.[71] Even in Hamburg left liberal *Bürgerschaft* members like Carl Petersen and Carl Braband were boycotted by a swathe of respectable society because of their campaign against the 1906 franchise restrictions.[72]

The tone of ingrained hostility to left liberalism might have had its origins in the state bureaucracy, but it had spread to others who shared a *Stammtisch*, subscribed to the same cultural associations, or had a classical grammar-school or university education. It echoed in the Kaiser's comment to Bülow: 'the Liberals just aren't gentlemen'. This ingrained prejudice worked against the National Liberals in the court, upper bureaucracy, military, and eastern provinces, and the left liberals almost everywhere.[73] Such sentiments were not universal. It was, after all, the educated and established who led left liberalism in Berlin and in the provinces. The left liberal constituency included both younger members of the educated middle classes attracted by Naumann and venerable survivals like Felix Gilbert's great grandfather Otto-Georg Oppenheim, a judicial official conservatively correct in dress and conduct but who always voted left liberal.[74] Nevertheless, many upper middle-class Germans regarded left liberalism as offering a threat to privilege, or an equally unwelcome invitation to social martyrdom.

The Catholic community was another obvious sphere where a left liberal political allegiance represented a clear stand against

[70] BA Koblenz, NL Gothein, 33, fo. 233, Hugo Wendorff to Gothein, 22 Apr. 1914.

[71] Heilberg, 'Erinnerungen', 295.

[72] G. Schiefler, *Eine Hamburgische Kulturgeschichte 1890–1920: Betrachtungen eines Zeitgenossen*, ed. G. Ahrens, H. W. Eckardt, and R. Hauschild-Thiessen (Hamburg, 1985).

[73] Bülow to Holstein, 4 Oct. 1892, N. Rich and M. H. Fisher (eds.), *The Holstein Papers: The Memoirs, Diaries and Correspondence of Friedrich von Holstein 1837–1909* (4 vols.; Cambridge, 1955–63), iv. 266; cf. K. Riezler, *Tagebücher, Aufsätze, Dokumente*, ed. K. D. Erdmann (Göttingen, 1972), 169–70, 248, 476.

[74] F. Gilbert, *A European Past: Memoirs, 1905–1945* (New York, 1988), 10–11.

convention. Similarly, left liberal factory workers faced pressure from the Social Democratic majority, particularly where left liberal local leadership was in the hands of manufacturers. This was reflected in the shopfloor tribulations of Georg Semmelroth, a left liberal metalworker in Wetzlar. He faced hostility not just from the SPD-inclined majority of workers angered by time and motion studies, but also from supervisors suspicious about a political ally of the boss.[75] In such cases, the left liberals were supported only by a small minority prepared to stand against the tide. However, there were regions and sections of society where the prevailing mood was left liberal. In the small Silesian town where Willy Hellpach grew up, lawyers, merchants, doctors, and pharmacists were all involved in local left liberal politics.[76] In Frankfurt the left liberals were not only the largest party in the council chamber, but set the tone in a network of informal organizations from private charities to residents' associations and shooting clubs.[77] Here left liberalism, supported by tradition, was a visible force with powerful local influence.

Left liberalism also attracted a higher level of support less on its own merits, but more because it was seen as a response to an alien, but powerful section of society. In cities like Bremen, Stettin, or Berlin, it was bourgeois opposition to the socialist labour movement, in Oldenburg and Schleswig-Holstein peasant opposition to the rural hierarchy, and in eastern Prussia urban opposition to Agrarian Conservatism. Even here the left liberals did not gain the sort of numerical supremacy achieved in some polling districts by other parties. There was no left liberal equivalent of the East Elbian estate, close-knit Catholic community, or proletarian suburb. Even in traditional strongholds like Frankfurt am Main and Liegnitz the left liberals had continually to defend the upper end of their constituency against the right and the lower against Social Democratic inroads. Even in villages which had supported the left liberals for decades, there was invariably a dissenting minority. However, in these places large sections of the population identified with the left liberals. Here, at least, the party came close to its proud claim to represent the *Bürgertum*.

75 UB Marburg, NL Rade, Semmelroth to Rade, 3 Apr. 1911, 25 Feb. 1912, and 3 Apr. 1913.
76 Sheehan, *German Liberalism*, 242. For further Silesian examples see Ch. 9 below.
77 Rolling, 'Liberals, Socialists and City Government', 69ff.

2
Hard-Working *Honoratioren*: The Mechanics of Left Liberal Party Politics

The importance of organization, or more precisely the lack of it, to German Liberalism has long been recognized. Though they differ about the effectiveness of the solutions found, both Geoff Eley and Anthony O'Donnell agree that adapting the party's traditional mode of notable politics to cope with popular mobilization was the most crucial challenge facing the National Liberals after 1890.[1] Admittedly, the treatment of left liberal organization has been less extensive. Here too the general opinion is that the left liberals were not quite so ineffective as the National Liberals, but still suffered by not having the sort of powerful mass organizations which were at the disposal of the labour movement, political Catholicism, or Agrarian Conservatism.[2] Such arguments reflect a wide range of contemporary opinion. Foremost amongst prophets of organization was Naumann, who, with a characteristic allusion to railways, insisted that there were thousands in the 'waiting room' of Liberalism willing to climb aboard if an imposing express train ('großer D-Zug') came along.[3] Pre-war party politics was in part a dash for organizational growth: setting up party newspapers, establishing more *Vereine*, recruiting more members, and employing paid officials. It was also a contest to present a popular image to the electorate. 'Are we a people's party (*Volkspartei*)?' was the theme for countless public meetings across all regions and political parties. While North German deputies objected to Democrat and Southerners to Liberal or *Freisinn* in the name of the merged left

---

[1] Eley, *Reshaping*, esp. ch. 2; O'Donnell, 'National Liberalism and Mass Politics'.

[2] Sheehan, *German Liberalism*, 249–52; Langewiesche, *Liberalismus in Deutschland*, 162–4; Nipperdey, *Deutsche Geschichte 1866–1918*, ii. 526.

[3] T. Barth and F. Naumann, *Die Erneuerung des Liberalismus: Ein politischer Weckruf* (Berlin and Schöneberg, 1906), 22.

liberal party, the label *Volkspartei* was supported by both sides.[4] Even Centre grandees like Peter Spahn or the aristocratic DKP felt compelled to seek the guise of a people's party.[5] Party apparatus and popular style were matters of image and reality, fashion as well as necessity. Organization and agitation were, therefore, far from being the poor relations of Wilhelmine politics. Even critics did not deny the importance of 'machine politics'. On the contrary, they despaired precisely because these seemed to play such a large and almost inevitable role in German politics. Moreover, agitation and organization were even more important to the Liberals with their diffuse support, than to parties which could call on close class, confessional, or regional loyalties. However, although the mechanics of mobilizing mass support are important, it is necessary in some areas to depart significantly from existing interpretations. The problem lies in some general assumptions which historians share with contemporary opinion. One was that formal organization was modern and effective, and informal organization old-fashioned and inadequate. In the same way *Honoratiorenpolitik* was deemed redundant and inferior by comparison with mass politics. Another was that big was beautiful. An organization which had 100 party secretaries and 300,000 members is held to be stronger than one with only fifty officials and 200,000 members. A third is that an expanded party organization fosters greater discipline and unity. Of course, these assumptions are plausible and were often borne out by events, but this was not always the case. Moreover, they lead historians to ask how far a particular mode of organization and political style were achieved, rather than to analyse party apparatus and agitation as means to an end. In addition, the question has been slanted according to the group under discussion. The account is a tale of success if the party is the SPD or Centre, and a study in failure where the Liberals are concerned. And, just as parties are adjudged either successes or failures, so the analysis of political style revolves around two opposite poles, *Honoratiorenpolitik* and popular mass politics. The Wilhelmine reality, however, was not made up of black and white contrasts, but various shades of grey. As the following analysis of left

---

[4] HSA Stuttgart, NL Haußmann 100, draft minutes left liberal *Fraktionsgemeinschaft* meeting, 14 Dec. 1909.

[5] See, e.g. Spahn's address to the 1905 Rhineland Centre Party conference, *Das Zentrum und sein Programm* (Cologne, 1907); and for largely inept and unsuccessful Conservative attempts at populism, Retallack, *Notables*, esp. 179–207.

liberal organization and agitation seeks to demonstrate, notable politics were more flexible, energetic, and successful than the traditional stereotype of *Honoratiorenpolitik* allows. Furthermore, there were drawbacks to formal organization and an ambivalence towards mass politics amongst voters as well as politicians.

Naumann's hopes for a grand organizational edifice remained unfulfilled. It has already been noted that left liberal national and regional politics were guided by only a small number of people. The organizational apparatus at their disposal was similarly limited. Indeed, the National Liberal party headquarters was lavish by comparison. The National Liberals employed up to three national general secretaries, but the FVP had only one, Reinhold Ißberner, between 1911 and 1918. Moreover, Ißberner was not, strictly, a full-time general secretary for he repeatedly helped out on the *Freisinnige Zeitung*, also housed in the cramped FVP headquarters. A party secretary dealing mainly with party organization in Berlin and Brandenburg and three or four clerks and typists completed the employees in the Zimmerstraße. The National Liberal central office, by contrast, had a more prestigious address in the Wilhelmstraße, and some three times the ancillary staff. The six National Liberal organizational handbooks compiled by the party general secretary Hermann Kalkoff between 1907 and 1914 underscore the different sizes of National Liberal and left liberal central offices, for the FVP was unable to provide a comparable guide for regional and local leaders.[6] Even the Eastern Marches' Association, a single-issue pressure group with under half the membership of the FVP, had a considerably larger Berlin office, with staff numbers increased to twelve in 1908.[7]

Poverty was the crucial limiting factor. Left liberal hopes that the creation of a merged party would attract sufficient funds for a well equipped and staffed central headquarters were dashed. Rich benefactors preferred to give money direct to particular individuals and causes rather than a central party fund. Contributions from the local organizations were even more disappointing (Table 2.1). Local associations were supposed to contribute 10% of dues to party headquarters, but few fulfilled this. Clearly the FVP followed the FrVp, whose

---

[6] National Liberal central office records have not been preserved, but valuable fragments survive in BA Koblenz, R45 I National Liberal Party 3–4; and BA Berlin, Deutsche Volkspartei 1 and NL Bassermann.

[7] A. Galos *et al.*, *Die Hakatisten: Der Deutsche Ostmarkenverein (1894–1934): Ein Beitrag zur Geschichte des deutschen Imperialismus* (Berlin, 1966), 135–7.

Table 2.1. Verein *contributions to FVP headquarters, 1912 (marks)*

Province	Branches	Paying branches	Contribution
East Prussia	26	2	32.20
West Prussia	7	—	—
Berlin	59	11	521,30
Brandenburg	110	10	790,65
Pomerania	76	7	141,55
Posen	4	—	—
Silesia*	22	4	240,75
Prov. Saxony	44 (Halle)	10	248,15
Schleswig-Holstein	111	4	291,47
Hamburg, Lübeck			
Lower Saxony	45	Prov. Org	246,35
Oldenburg/Ostfriesland	60	1	5,50
Rhineland/Westphalia	195	10	363,50
Bergischer Verband	20	?	650,00
Hessen–Nassau	117	5	553,10
Bavaria†	91	11	323,20
Saxony	105	8	215,00
Württemberg	136	7	142,90
Baden	124	12	612,34
Hessen	134	6	56,10
Thuringia	75	6	165,65
Anhalt	3	—	—
Mecklenburg	20	4	88,10
TOTAL	1,581		5,687,91

Source: Friedrich Naumann, 'Was wir leisten', BA Berlin, FVP 37, fo. 124.
*Lower Silesia only.
†Excludes the Palatinate.

local associations had no obligation to contribute to Berlin party head-quarters in Berlin, rather than the smaller FrVg, whose local branches had been expected to pay a third of their membership dues to national headquarters.

Left liberal national organization also lagged behind competing parties in other respects. A left liberal parliamentary press bureau was discussed for years, but plans never came to fruition.[8] The SPD and Centre, by contrast, both founded party press offices before the war. Similarly, parliamentary parties increasingly engaged professional business managers. The Agrarian League loaned Josef Kaufhold to

[8] See the abortive discussions in the FVP press commission: BA Berlin, FVP 44.

the DKP Reichstag caucus, while the Prussian Centre Party engaged Maximilian Pfeiffer. Liberals, however, spurned outside assistance. In the FVP Reichstag caucus the Silesian deputy and grammar-school teacher Dr Karl Doormann bore the increasing burden of paper-work.[9] Left liberals and especially National Liberals had non-pecuniary reasons for preserving this pattern. Both were concerned to stress the autonomy and supremacy of the parliamentary party and thus raising it, as far as possible, above squabbling regional factions. But the chronic state of FVP central finances would have precluded the employment of a full-time business manager in any event.

The absence of a strong central organization had important consequences. It represented a missed opportunity for concerted mass propaganda. Issues like taxation, the Prussian franchise, or education struck a chord throughout the Reich. The same was true of reaction to the *Daily Telegraph* affair, or the series of scandals about state interference with the rights of public employees. Similarly, pamphlets on peasant politics, artisan issues, or public employees addressed particular social groupings essentially on a national basis. As the SPD and People's Association for Catholic Germany demonstrated, centrally produced mass-circulation pamphlets were effective in winning and consolidating popular support. The SPD produced 88,000,000 leaflets and brochures for the 1912 election and 47,200,000 during the next year. The People's Association distributed 22,620,000 leaflets, periodicals, and pamphlets in 1911/12, and 12,174,362 in 1912/13.[10] Left liberal party publications were slight and sporadic by comparison. They sometimes appeared too late. The calendar 'Die Scholle' produced by the Nationalverein für das liberale Deutschland, for example, was distributed so late in 1912 that few copies could be sold.[11] In addition, financial constraints meant higher cover prices and lower circulations. The failure to produce a new left liberal party handbook to succeed Richter's ageing *ABC-Buch* highlighted the shortcomings of official party propaganda.

Weak central organization also led to failures of co-ordination and direction. In Reichstag elections the most promising terrain was not the cities and large towns where most left liberal politicians and

---

[9] *Kieler Zeitung* (28 Nov. 1912).

[10] LA Schleswig 301, Oberpräsidium 2252; H. Heitzer, *Der Volksverein für das Katholische Deutschland im Kaiserreich 1890–1918* (Mainz, 1979), 319.

[11] UB Marburg, NL Rade, correspondence between Martin Rade and Verlag der Scholle, Oct. 1912 to Jan. 1913.

wealthy supporters lived, but small towns and semi-rural areas. This was underlined by the size distribution of those Reichstag constituencies held by the left liberals. It was one of the ironies of Wilhelmine politics that the most urban of the German political parties after the SPD held none of the fifty most populous Reichstag seats, but five of the eight smallest constituencies.

The blatant geographical mismatch between left liberal membership, resources, and Reichstag electoral prospects presented an obvious need to redistribute money and effort. However, the left liberal central organization lacked the material resources required. In organizational terms, the left liberals failed to address adequately the advent of a national political stage. They were not, however, alone in this. Although other parties possessed more imposing party headquarters and central party funds they too failed to exploit the full potential of national politics. Only the SPD was exemplary. It is often forgotten that the Centre largely lacked a national party apparatus. The party only agreed to set up a national committee (*Reichsausschuß*) in 1911 and this body did not meet until February 1914.[12] The National Liberal Party had great national pretensions, but was notoriously racked by regionalism.[13] Richter could point to a chronic lack of organizational substance as well as political prejudice to support his contention that the Free Conservatives were not worth the name Reichspartei. As

Table 2.2. *Ranking of FVP constituencies according to size of the electorate*

Seats with largest electorate	No. of FVP seats
1–50	0
51–100	2
101–150	9
151–200	8
201–250	4
251–300	5
301–350	7
351–397	9

Source: AA Bonn, IA Deutschland 125, 3, 26, secret report by Deputy Reich Chancellor Helfferich on the Reichstag committee considering the constitution and Prussian franchise, 23 April 1917 (copy).

[12] HAS Cologne, NL Carl Bachem 523, *Kölnische Volkszeitung* (14 Feb. 1914).
[13] White, *Splintered Party*, esp. 168–98.

for the German Conservatives, even supporters could hardly pretend the party possessed a nation-wide organization or had even decided, name notwithstanding, to be a German rather than a Prussian party.

Formal left liberal organization in the provinces was similarly slight. The FrVg was one of the first parties to emulate the SPD when it employed provincial party secretaries in 1904. However, the early lead over the other non-socialist parties was soon lost. The rapid turnover of party secretaries makes a precise figure impossible, but Naumann's claim that the FVP had at most thirty-five paid officials to deal with 1.5 million voters appears realistic.[14] This fell far behind the numbers employed by mass organizations such as the SPD, People's Association of Catholic Germany, or agrarian and ex-servicemen's leagues. In 1910 the central organizations of the Agrarian League and the People's Association of Catholic Germany employed ninety-seven and 140 respectively. Likewise the Berlin offices of the ex-service-men's league had fifty-five officials in 1907 compared to thirteen in 1895. The SPD increased regional party secretaries from sixteen in 1905/6 to fifty-one in 1913/14, and had 106 constituency party secre-taries before the war.[15] The left liberals even failed to keep pace with the National Liberals, which claimed fifty-seven party secretaries in 1912, and the DKP, which expanded its eastern organizations after the electoral defeats of the same year.[16] Most left liberal provincial and district (*Bezirk*) organizations employed only a single party secretary. The DKP, by contrast, had four or five party secretaries in most east-ern provinces by 1914. The left liberal party secretary in Branden-burg, for example, found himself outnumbered by five Conservative agitators with a party car, an unimaginable luxury for left liberal offi-cials.[17] It was also unheard of for the left liberals to have six party sec-retaries in a single constituency, as the National Liberals had in Bochum before 1912.[18] In addition, though the tendency of National Liberal and Conservative officials to term themselves general secre-taries rather than party secretaries mainly reflected an inflated sense

[14] SA Hamburg, NL Petersen L 50.

[15] BA Berlin, NL Naumann 59, 'Was andere Leisten'; H.-P. Zimmermann, *Der feste Wall gegen die rote Flut* (Neumünster, 1989), 157; and Fricke, *Handbuch*, i. p 284.

[16] *Breslauer Zeitung*, 747, 23 Oct. 1912. For the growth in DKP paid officials in the pre-war decade see Retallack, *Notables*, appendix 4, and the case-study of Silesia in Ch. 9 below.

[17] BA Berlin, FVP 27, report of party secretary Elbel, Apr. 1911.

[18] They were, however, made redundant because of the withdrawal of industrial support after the election: a powerful reminder that an expanded party organization did not necessar-ily reduce the influence of sectional interests. *Landeshuter Stadtblatt* (27 June 1912).

of self-importance, they were generally better paid than their left liberal counterparts. The latter had to make do with an annual income of
2,000–3,000 marks, when National Liberal or Conservative officials
could receive twice as much. Thorbecke, National Liberal general secretary in Baden, had a salary of 5,000 marks per annum and Richard
Kunze, the DKP's 'travelling' general secretary, boasted of an annual
income of 12,000 marks.[19] This was yet another indication of the
severe restraints imposed by a lack of money. A subsidy from central
funds, usually 1,500 marks, met only around a quarter of the annual
running costs of a provincial party secretariat. Moreover, the parlous
state of central finances prevented the party leadership from guaran-
teeing future subsidies. Attracting financial support within the areas
covered by the party secretaries proved equally difficult. The history
of the Kurhessen party secretariat based in Marburg was typical.
Though run on a shoestring budget, it was never financially secure
and was kept above water only by the efforts of Martin Rade, the
regional FVP chairman. Though city party secretariats usually
enjoyed a bigger budget, their finances were similarly strained. The
Rhineland secretariat had to 'watch every penny',[20] and sizeable
annual deficits led to the closure of the Breslau secretariat in 1912.
Even in prosperous Hamburg the treasurer had to ask leading left liberals for advance contributions to tide over the party secretariat.[21]

The finances of most left liberal local associations were equally precarious. Left liberals continually called for a more 'commercial spirit'
(*kaufmännischer Geist*) in government administration. Yet, as Naumann
noted dolefully, they failed lamentably to put principle into practice in
their own organization. Left liberal merchants and factory owners
were acutely aware of the necessity of capital accumulation in
business, but failed to recognize its importance in party politics.[22]
Very few of the 1,671 FVP *Vereine* in December 1913[23] had substantial reserves. More still had debts from the last Reichstag elections.
Genthin and Braune, two towns in the Mecklenburg district of
Jerichow, were still burdened by pre-war electoral costs in 1916. Such
indebtedness was common in those small and medium-sized towns

---

[19] GLA Karlsruhe, NLP Baden 178, Thorbecke to National Liberal executive, 23.7.1911;
Breslauer Zeitung, 467 (5 July 1912).　　　　　　　　[20] BA Berlin, FVP 24, fo. 64.
[21] SA Hamburg, NL Braband, B2, circular from treasurer of the Hamburg United Liberals (7 Jan. 1913).　　　　　　　　[22] Barth and Naumann, *Erneuerungen*, 31.
[23] BA Berlin, FVP 37, central committee, 6 Dec. 1913, fo. 83.

where left liberals had little support amongst the urban élite.[24] The pause in political activity during the war was an opportunity for financial recuperation. To the despair of the Zimmerstraße, however, many left liberal *Vereine* gave away all their reserves to the Red Cross and other charities. Of course party organization at the local rather than national or regional did not require paid staff for routine administration. Moreover, many left liberal local organizations in urban areas were well-established, with a history stretching back into the 1880s. Hagen, Richter's old constituency, provided the classic example of a dense organizational network, led by businessmen and members of the professions, which had been built up over decades.[25] In other areas the left liberals succeeded in recruiting a mass membership in the prewar period. Here Alzey-Bingen, Bamberger's old seat, led the way. After a bitterly fought by-election in 1909, the party claimed that more than three-quarters of the 8,000 left liberal voters were signed up party members.[26] However, there remained parts of the Reich without left liberal local associations and also traditional left liberal areas where party organization failed to keep pace with the times and the opposition. In summer 1912 twenty-one Reichstag constituencies in the Rhineland and Westphalia had no left liberal organizations.[27] Württemberg had numerous local associations, but many had become lethargic. Payer complained, in January 1910, about 'our often stagnating organization'.[28] Left liberal local organizations formed a patchwork pattern, encompassing associations both large and small, recent and well-established, active and dormant. However, even the larger and better organized left liberal *Vereine* lacked the material resources to fight costly Reichstag contests without outside help.

Left liberal formal organization remained comparatively slight. The 1910 party fusion patently failed to regenerate the left liberal central organization. Indeed, the real disciples of organizational machinery, the former National-Socials, found themselves squeezed out of positions in party headquarters. This was seen most demonstrably in the Richterites' successful efforts to prevent Friedrich Weinhausen taking charge of the central office although he was clearly the most

---

[24] BA Berlin, FVP 13, fo. 56.
[25] See *Die Organisation der Fortschrittlichen Volkspartei in Westfalen-Rheinland* (Hagen, 1911) in BA Berlin, FVP 19, fos. 6–18; and *Eugen Richter und der Wahlkreis Hagen-Schwelm*.
[26] *Liberale Blätter*, 4 (Feb. 1910).   [27] BA Berlin, FVP 20.
[28] BA Koblenz, NL Goetz 39, fo. 1, Friedrich Payer to Walter Goetz, 25 Jan. 1910.

qualified candidate.[29] Similarly, Naumann had to be content with a marginal role in the FVP central organization. Critics spoke justifiably of a continuation of the 'System Zimmerstraße' dominated by Richterite epigoni.[30] The way Julius Kopsch, Otto Wiemer, and Otto Fischbeck oversaw the running of party headquarters marked a clear continuity of Eugen Richter's maxim that a compact, absolutely reliable apparatus was preferable to something more extensive and ambitious, but less controllable. This Richterite desire for tight control was reflected in their anger at Hansa-Bund money for the 1912 elections being given to the left liberal banker Karl Mommsen for distribution rather than channelled through FVP headquarters.[31]

In the regions, the impact of the 1910 merger was more mixed, but rarely dramatic. In regions like East Prussia local left liberal organizations were already affiliated to just one of the left liberal parties. Here the 1910 fusion meant only a change of name. Elsewhere, the clear predominance of a particular left liberal party, like the Democrats in Württemberg, the FrVg in Bremen, and the FrVp in Silesia, was such that it forced members of the other left liberal parties into the role of compliant junior partners. Supporting DVP candidates, for example, had become almost a reflex action for Württemberg National-Socials. A draft Landtag election address reflected a subconscious unity when unintentially describing the DVP, rather than Democrats and National-Socials together, as 'the party of democratic, liberal and social progress'.[32] In areas of more evenly divided loyalty, regional or local agreements were often already in place. There was a joint left liberal state committee in Hesse, and in Schleswig-Holstein differences in party label had become almost meaningless well before 1910.[33] Attempts to poach each other's supporters proved largely unsuccessful—the National-Socials, for example, failed to wean left liberal voters in Oldenburg and Schleswig-Holstein away from their traditional party allegiance—and, as a result, rapidly declined after the 1903 Reichstag elections. In most Reichstag constituencies in the pre-war decade, the prospects of a place in the run-off elections depended not only on agreement between the left liberal parties, but on a pact with

[29] HSA Stuttgart, NL Haußmann 100, Wilhelm Cohnstaedt to Conrad Haußmann, 21 Dec. 1910.
[30] See *Mitteilungen der Hauptvereine Groß-Berlin der Fortschrittlichen Volkspartei*, 1–8 (8 Dec. 1917–1 Nov. 1918).
[31] BA Berlin FVP 36, fo. 92, executive committee, 19 July 1911.
[32] BA Koblenz, NL Walter Goetz 38, fos. 135–6.   [33] See Ch. 8 below.

the National Liberals to field a single Liberal candidate. When, as in Baden, the three left liberal parties were forced to seek electoral alliances with both Social Democrats and National Liberals, any public disagreement within left liberalism invited both ridicule and electoral oblivion.

Political necessity was, therefore, the motor of left liberal co-operation in the localities and regions as well as at national level. Outside Berlin, however, the process was fostered by better personal relations and an absence of sharp social and political differences. The differences between Richter and the Secessionists, which carried over in an attenuated form into the next generation of left liberal leaders, had few parallels in the provinces. As election campaign organizers, local leaders were keenly aware of the need for co-operation. This applied especially to municipal elections, where an agreed slate of candidates and disciplined voting were crucial to success. The differences in social status between members of the FrVp and FrVg were also more marked inside parliament than amongst local leaders and the party rank and file. In Berlin, Richter's caustic sense of humour could christen Lenzmann a 'Crown Prince court democrat' for preferring the dining circle run by the FrVg's Hermann Frese to the more humble company of his party colleagues in the FrVp.[34] But such a remark made little sense in pre-war Hamburg. There the committee members of the Verein der Freisinnigen Volkspartei chaired by a wealthy manufacturer had a similar standing to their counterparts in the Liberaler Verein.[35] Indeed, the social composition of the parties generally does little to sustain the depiction, favoured by former GDR historiography, of the FrVg as party of the upper bourgeoisie and the FrVp as the representatives of the petty bourgeoisie. If there was an appreciable difference between the two groups, it was not in social standing, but rather in the ratio of property to education, *Besitz* to *Bildung*. The former was more strongly represented in the FrVp and the latter in the FrVg, especially after the entry of most National-Social Association members into the FrVg in 1903.[36] Even here, however, the

[34] BA Koblenz, NL Gothein 14, 169 ff.

[35] See the committee lists in SA Hamburg, Akten der politischen Polizei Abt. IV, V950, and V1004.

[36] Figures for the occupations of delegates to the party conferences of the three groups in Langewiesche, *Liberalism*, table 12, 168–9, give general support to the argument at the local leadership level. For evidence of the large number of teachers amongst National-Social members see Villain, 'National-sozialer Verein'.

differences should not be exaggerated. There were still substantial numbers of lawyers and teachers in the ranks of Richter's party, and a significant presence of businessmen amongst the FrVg supporters. In the main, therefore, negotiations at regional and local level were not complicated by a sense of social superiority or inferiority, but conducted by men with a similar background as respected members of the non-Catholic middle strata. Both sides were embedded in the same local society.

It was increasingly difficult to point to major political or ideological differences between the left liberal parties. On the traditional bone of contention, military spending and the colonies, sharp differences had given way to a new consensus. This applied in parliament, where after 1906 all three left liberal parties gave consistent support to government defence and colonial bills, but equally outside. Ironically, a left liberal paper which had opposed the 1892 defence bill, and forced Barth out of the Hirschberg-Schönau constituency, invited Bülow to honour its centenary celebrations in 1912.[37]

The threatened successor to 'national' issues as a cause of dispute within left liberal ranks was the attitude to be adopted towards the SPD. Indeed, the question led, particularly from the late 1890s to 1906, to a bitter battle of words in the columns of *Die Nation* and the *Freisinnige Zeitung* between publicists and intellectuals led by Barth and Naumann on one side and Richterite party politicians on the other.[38] However, the issue largely failed to disturb inter-party relations at regional and local level. In part, this was because the dispute did not simply set one left liberal party against another. At the national level the bulk of opposition to an opening to the left was located in the FrVp, but some FrVp deputies, notably Albert Traeger, favoured an alliance of the left.[39] And some of the most vociferous opponents to 'Barthian tactics' were in the FrVg, especially in the Prussian Landtag and in Bremen, Stettin, and Danzig.[40] Similarly,

---

[37] See the account of the centenary celebrations of the *Bote aus dem Riesengebirge* in *Breslauer Zeitung*, 634 (9 Sept. 1912).

[38] Barth and Naumann, *Erneuerung des Liberalismus*; and *Die Freisinnige Volkspartei und die Barth-Demokraten* (Berlin, 1908). See also Conrad Haußmann's discussion with Barth about Richter and Haußmann's obituary of Barth in HSA Stuttgart, NL Haußmann 114.

[39] BA Berlin FVP 36, fos. 36–7, executive committee, 6. Dec. 1910; *Biographisches Jahrbuch und Deutscher Nekrolog*, 17 (1912), 144–6.

[40] BA Berlin, FVP 4, fo. 20, FrVg *Vorstand*, 15 Jan. 1905; FVP 4, fo. 24, FrVg general assembly, 12 Feb. 1905; FVP 5, fo. 27, FrVg executive committee, 15 June 1906; SA Bremen, NL Fitger 6, 50, Max Broemel to Emil Fitger 10 Jan. 1905, 11 May 1905, and 26 Jan. 1905; *Freisinnige Zeitung* (10 May 1906).

opinions in the DVP were divided over the relative merits of a pact of the left and Richter's 'two front' strategy. The party in Württemberg generally gave less support to Barth's projected left alliance than DVP leaders in Frankfurt and Baden.[41] More importantly, the realities of electoral politics imposed a discipline which generally overcame ideological differences. Even though Frankfurt was an intellectual home for the idea of a united left, the city's Reichstag and council elections inevitably came down to a contest between left liberals and SPD.[42] Nor did advocates of a left alliance spurn the votes of right-wing supporters in run-off contests against the SPD. 'A vote is a vote' was Carl Braband's riposte to Social Democratic complaints in 1907 that, while he talked about co-operating with the SPD, left liberals were being supported in run-off elections by the Imperial League Against Social Democracy.[43] The Richterites on the other side were equally opportunistic, angling for SPD support where seats were at stake. Pre-war circumstances were to lead even parliamentarians who had vociferously opposed a *rapprochement* with the SPD to advocate an alliance of the left.[44] Tactical considerations often imposed a unity of action on the ground. If local Social Democrats refused co-operation, or were the prime electoral opponents, then competition was inevitable, regardless of attitudes towards a *Großblock* in national politics. If, on the other hand, the SPD support could tip the balance between left liberal electoral success and failure, then the temptation to compromise was rarely resisted.

Such pragmatism produced a pattern of politics which appeared paradoxical and disjointed if analysed at the national level. But reflecting local circumstances could have a positive and unifying effect from the perspective of individual electors and constituency associations. Local harmony within national diversity was exemplified by left liberal attitudes towards agricultural tariffs. In the rural parts of areas like Rhinehessen, Lower Silesia, and Schleswig-Holstein left liberals gave increasingly explicit support to existing grain tariffs, while in towns and cities the party continued to demand tariff reductions. The

---

[41] HSA Stuttgart, NL Haußmann 114, Conrad Haußmann to Theodor Barth, July 1903; StA Frankfurt, NL Rößler 3, Heinrich Rößler, 'Der Zusammenschluß der Parteien und Theodor Barth', MS 1909.

[42] Rolling, 'Liberals, Socialists in City Government', esp. 105–40.

[43] SA Hamburg, NL Braband, B17. Cf. comments in a similar vein in *Berliner Tageblatt*, 658 (29 Dec. 1906).

[44] For the pragmatic acceptance of 'Barthian' politics by men like Pachnicke and Fischbeck after 1912 see Ch. 6 below.

moral and political implications of such behaviour are to be discussed elsewhere. The effect in organizational terms, however, was to create a demand and climate for merger. The permanent need to ally at elections and the repeated provincial spectacle of the different left liberal parties represented by similar looking people saying the same sort of things produced widespread grassroot incomprehension at the continuance of old party divisions. Gothein sensed 'an elemental will of the voters who refused to understand why men who ultimately agreed on all fundamentals should belong to different parties and caucuses'.[45] This was even more the case after the establishment of the Bülow Bloc and the joint left liberal caucus (*Fraktionsgemeinschaft*) in 1907. At party conferences and in correspondence perplexed supporters repeatedly challenged left liberal deputies to explain the political differences between the three left liberal parties which were delaying merger. A series of resolutions from regional associations calling for the rapid establishment of a united party were sent to FrVp and FrVg leaders in Berlin.[46]

The widespread support for left liberal merger at a regional and local level was generated against a background of *de facto* co-operation and considerable political consensus. But it also reflected the spirit of the age. The continuation of three small left liberal parties symbolized for many an absent 'will to power' (*Wille zur Macht*). This shortcoming was doubly felt. In the first instance, it ran against the general belief in Wilhelmine society in the importance of *Machtpolitik*. Secondly, and more specifically, it signalled an unwelcome further continuation of the long period of Liberal 'opposition'. That it was the detested Centre which subsequently played 'trump' in the Reichstag only sharpened Liberal supporters' appetite for a substantial share of power that had been denied since the 1870s. Such considerations evoked a response generally, but from younger left liberals in particular. For them small parties were an anachronism when everything, from states and cities to schools, steelworks, and ships, was increasing in scale and scope. Complaints in autumn 1917 about the left liberals still working 'within a small business format from a past age'[47] gave a

---

[45] *Kieler Zeitung* (5 Mar. 1910, morning edn.).

[46] See the resolution submitted by the Deutschfreisinnige Partei Schleswig-Holsteins in Apr. 1909 calling for the makeshift *Fraktionsgemeinschaft* to be replaced by a unified left liberal party within the year. BA Berlin, FVP 8, fo. 333, Freisinnige Vereinigung executive committee minutes, 21 Apr. 1909. Cf. a similar situation in Oldenburg and the wrecking tactics of the FrVp Berlin headquarters in FVP 17, fos. 41 ff.

[47] Oeser in central committee meeting 7 Oct. 1917: BA Berlin, FVP 37, fo. 11.

good reflection of attitudes forged in an age of expansion and technology. Many younger left liberals regarded disunity as the fatal flaw in their political predecessors. Only a single party presenting a united front could overcome the faults of the past. A leading Hamburg left liberal Carl Braband, born in 1870, summed up this belief in the overriding necessity of party unity:

In all question of fundamental importance a party has to act unitedly ... Much better to atone for some stupidity of the party majority where you are innocent, than to be robbed of the fruits of every action because supporters of the same standpoint can say everytime: our party is more reliable than the Progressives, because this or that Progressive has said or voted thus.[48]

There was, therefore, some substance to the claims of left liberal leaders that the 1910 fusion, unlike its forerunner in 1884, had been forged from the bottom-up rather than engineered in Berlin. Of course, the role of individual left liberal leaders cannot be discounted, at least in the timing and shape of the 1910 merger. Payer, for example, was instrumental in ensuring the creation of a single party before rather than after the 1912 Reichstag general elections.[49] In addition, the organizational and programmatic details of the merged party were thrashed out in a seemingly unending series of meetings of small groups of parliamentarians: Gothein plausibly put his catarrh down to 'the long sojourn in smoke-filled rooms because of the left liberal fusion'.[50] Nevertheless, extra-parliamentary pressure was fundamental to the 1910 fusion in a way which was not the case in previous Liberal splits and reunions, nor in the formation of the DDP and DVP at the end of 1918. The attitude of left liberal members and electors towards union left Berlin leaders with few options. Failure to agree on a single party would have exposed left liberalism to two contradictory but damaging responses: resigned political withdrawal or provinces forming united local organizations against the will of Berlin.

Against such a background, the 1910 merger met with predictably little resistance. The Demokratische Vereinigung, which remained outside the new party, had already attracted much of that minority of North German left liberalism implacably opposed to pragmatic compromise. In the South, some Democrats raised objections both to the

---

[48] SA Hamburg, NL Carl Braband B30/2, Braband to Frau Professor Wendt, 21 Nov. 1912.   [49] F. von Payer, 'Mein Lebenslauf' (typescript, Stuttgart 1932), 47.
[50] BA Koblenz, NL Gothein 25, fo. 20, Georg Gothein to Dr Georg Lattermann, 8 Mar. 1910 (copy).

programme and personalities of the new party. However, most dis-
senters, including the leading Southern radicals Ludwig Quidde,
Martin Venedey, and Oskar Muser, overcame their reluctance and
joined the new party. Only four DVP local associations defected to the
Demokratische Vereinigung in March 1910.[51] In Mecklenburg, left
liberal groups initially refused to affiliate to the merged party. Partly
this was in deference to a minority of National Liberal supporters
within the Mecklenburg organizations. More important, however,
was an emotional and sentimental attachment to regional independence. As a result the Mecklenburgers had not been officially affiliated
to either the FrVg or FrVp. However, reliance on outside finance,
pamphlets, and speakers made independence more a façade than a
reality. When the left liberal organizations in Mecklenburg were
finally persuaded before the war to affiliate to the FVP, the change was
more one of form than substance. Similarly, more material difficulties
were largely inherited. The FVP in Stettin, for example, was divided
into two warring camps. However, this was a continuation of an old
political dispute between the same fractious individuals who had led
left liberal politics in Stettin before 1910.[52] The new party also had to
deal with personal and political disputes within the Rhineland District Association which could only be stilled by the creation of two
geographically distinct district associations.[53]

In the great majority of cases, however, the continuity was one of
co-operation rather than disagreement. The frequency with which
letters from local associations to the FVP central office were written
on paper with printed headings relating to the pre-1910 parties was a
tribute to left liberal thrift. More significantly, it underlined the continuity of left liberal local organization and leadership. Admittedly,
things could not go on quite as before in localities where more than
one of the pre-1910 left liberal parties had been organized. The organizational statutes of the merged party stipulated that existing associations should be dissolved and a single new *Verein* founded. Here
again, however, continuity was the predominant characteristic. The

---

[51] *Neue Konstanzer Abendzeitung* (4 Mar. 1910).

[52] For the difficulties between the 'Freisinnige Vereinigung Ortsgruppe Stettin' and the
'Liberaler Wahlverein zu Stettin' before 1910 see SA Wolfenbüttel, NL Schrader, III. 3,
Eberhard Wolff to Friedrich Weinhausen, 26 May 1906 (copy); BA Berlin, FVP 8, fos. 41–2,
letter from FrVg executive committee, 26 Feb. 1909; BA Berlin, 36, fos. 28, 40, FVP executive committee, 14 Dec. 1910 and 10 Jan. 1912.

[53] See e.g. the discussion of the Rhineland dispute in the sitting of the executive committee on 16 July 1911, BA Berlin, FVP 36, fos. 81–7.

standard pattern was for the membership of the existing organizations to be combined and an enlarged committee containing the established local leaders to be constructed. The process, in most cases, was neither dynamic nor disruptive. A letter from Weinhausen to Conrad Haußmann, suggesting the latter 'take in hand' the creation of a single party in Württemberg, was typical of the casual path towards left liberal organizational unity in much of Germany. Indeed, as Weinhausen correctly assumed, the personal prestige of a leader like Haußmann and the established co-operation between the Democrats and Liberale Vereine in Württemberg ensured a straightforward transition to a unified party.[54] Where, as in Frankfurt am Main, the foundation of a united party was accompanied by festivities, large public meetings, and an intensive recruitment drive, the initiative came from local individuals rather than the national party.[55]

There was, therefore, both a positive and a negative side to the 1910 merger. Its major achievement, especially by comparison with 1884, was a genuinely unified structure based on consensus as well as necessity. Moreover, if it failed to produce a great organizational leap forward, the creation of a single party at least provided a more favourable framework for the continued growth in left liberal *Vereine* and party membership. The disappointment of merger was its failure to transform left liberal prospects. It was, as Barth had feared, largely organizational fusion without ideological regeneration. In addition, it made little immediate contribution to left liberal electoral success because the pre-1910 organizations and co-operation between left liberal parties had tended to be most effective precisely in those areas where parliamentary seats were at stake. Finally, merger produced a larger organization, but one which continued to function like its predecessors. The united left liberal party was less Naumann's gleaming new express and more a collection of familiar, well-travelled carriages and an old engine bearing a new nameplate.

For an analysis of the most important left liberal response to the growing demands for money, men, and effort placed on political parties in Wilhelmine Germany, a shift of focus from formal to informal organization is required. Here the role of newspapers was central. As the Social Democrat Albert Südekum correctly observed, it was the

[54] HSA Stuttgart NL Conrad Haußmann 100, Friedrich Weinhausen to Conrad Haußmann 24 Mar. 1910.
[55] HSA Stuttgart, NL Haußmann 100, Wilhelm Cohnstaedt to Conrad Haußmann, 21 Dec. 1910.

press which lent power to the party-political elbow. Südekum also had no doubt which parties drew most strength from the printed page: 'Liberalism in Germany lives exclusively from [its] press, which dominates the cities, yet pushes out a long way outside their boundaries.' By contrast, 'the reactionaries ... are virtually characterized by an absence of literary needs: they have no decent paper because they don't need one'. SPD newspapers too, Südekum admitted, were often boring. This, alongside a shortage of advertising and relatively high subscription prices, meant many SPD voters preferred left liberal or *General-Anzeiger* newspapers.[56] Südekum's analysis was rather sweeping. His insistence that there was an unbridged chasm in the Centre press between the *Kölnische Volkszeitung* and *Germania*, the two papers of national standing, and the run-of-the-mill 'prelate-press', though a good reflection of Liberal and Socialist disdain, was overstated. Catholic regional papers like the *Bayerischer Kurier* (Munich), *Schlesische Volkszeitung* (Breslau), and *Essener Volkszeitung*, though less impressive than their Liberal counterparts, had distinctly more content and refinement than the local Centre press. Similarly, it was hardly possible for Conservative newspapers to be quite so desperate and their readers so benighted as depicted. However, such stereotypes were widely believed. Südekum's judgement was echoed, for example, by the Conservative publicist Adolf Grabowsky and, of course, by Liberals of all shades.[57] Indeed, such beliefs were fundamental to Liberal claims to be the party of culture.

The direct contribution of newspapers to the workings of left liberal politics depended on real rather than reputed strength. It is difficult to divide the 4,200 newspapers in Germany on the eve of the First World War precisely into the various party-political camps. Apart from the SPD, which controlled its newspapers directly, the parties largely relied on privately owned journals. In some cases the difference was more apparent than real. Papers like the *Frankfurter Zeitung*, *Kreuzzeitung*, and *Kölnische Volkszeitung* were owned by party figures

---

[56] BA Koblenz, NL Südekum 101, fo. 169, 'Eine Politische Kulturfrage', diary entry early 1914; fos. 102 ff., 128 ff. Criticism of the party press in general and *Vorwärts* in particular was a long-standing theme of SPD party conferences: W. Sperlich, *Journalist mit Mandat: Sozialdemokratische Reichstagsabgeordnete und ihre Arbeit in der Parteipresse 1867 bis 1918* (Düsseldorf, 1983), 31 ff.

[57] *Das neue Deutschland*, 6 and 11(1914). See also *Konservative Monatsschrift* (Sept. 1907), 1158–64; and Wilhelm Kube, *Wie organisieren wir uns? Ein Beitrag für die Aufgaben der Deutschnationalen Kreisvorsitzenden und Vertrauensleute* (Breslau, 1920), 13, on the power of the left liberal press and the right's failures in this area.

in an individual capacity, and the same was true of various provincial titles. There remained, however, a sizeable section of the press where the political orientation was uncertain and dependent on individual owners or editors and on commercial considerations. And because newspapers were not obliged to disclose circulation (only the most successful tended to do so) apportioning market share between the parties is even more problematic.[58] It is therefore unrealistic to offer precise figures for the number of left liberal papers, let alone total readership. The FVP sent a membership appeal to some 130 newspapers in 1911. However, this figure undoubtedly excludes a substantial number of smaller newspapers and those which, though left liberal in general outlook, would be unlikely to provide free adverts for the FVP.[59] The best guide at national level is provided by advertising agency catalogues. At first sight these appear to contradict Südekum's assertion of Liberal press ascendancy (Table 2.3). Although the Liberal parties compared reasonably well with the other political groupings, under a quarter of the newspapers with a circulation of over 10,000 hardly amounted to Liberal dominance of the urban press.

A closer examination of the papers described as unattached (*parteilos*) reveals a different picture. Though ten of the sixteen newspapers with a circulation of over 100,000 described themselves as unattached, virtually all followed a discernible political line. Indeed, it would be difficult to find a more inappropriate description than *parteilos* for Hellmut von Gerlach's bitingly sarcastic and politically radical leaders

Table 2.3. *Stated party affiliation of German newspapers with circulation over 10,000 in 1912*

Affiliation	Number
Right-wing	28
Official	4
Centre	47
Liberal	66
SPD	34
Unattached	114

Source: Roth, *Programme der politischen Parteien*, 10.

[58] P. Roth, *Die Programme der politischen Parteien und die politische Tagespresse in Deutschland* (Halle a. S., 1913).
[59] BA Berlin FVP 36, fo. 49, executive committee minutes, 7 Feb. 1911.

in the *Welt am Montag*. Similarly, the *General-Anzeiger für Hamburg-Altona* could hardly be termed unattached when its chief editor Curt Platen was a left liberal member of the Hamburg *Bürgerschaft* and the paper acted unambiguously as a vehicle for left liberal views. Occasionally a city general advertiser (*General-Anzeiger*) leaned to the right, as with the *Berliner Lokal-Anzeiger* and *Dresdner Neueste Nachrichten*, but most favoured the Liberals. Like the 'unpolitical' German, the 'unpolitical' general advertiser was largely a myth. Admittedly, the general advertiser tended to avoid the sort of stridency likely to offend readers with differing political views. Nor did their political coverage compare in scope with that of the leading heavyweight newspapers. However, the value of the general advertiser to the political parties lay not in preaching to the converted, but in reaching and influencing a wide audience, including many waverers and uncommitted voters.

With such newspapers added in, it is certainly justified to talk of a substantial numerical preponderance of the Liberal press in urban Germany. Left liberals dominated the Berlin press led by the Ulstein and Mosse concerns. In Hamburg the three main left liberal papers, the *Hamburger Fremdenblatt*, *Neue Hamburger Zeitung*, and *General-Anzeiger*, together sold around 150,000 copies. By contrast, the socialist *Hamburger Echo* had a circulation of a little over 60,000 and the right-wing *Hamburger Nachrichten* only 20,000. The city's National Liberals, dependent on the rather unreliable support of the latter in city politics, had good reason to envy 'the unified publistic battlefront of the United Liberals'.[60] The position was similar in Stuttgart and many other cities.[61] Moreover, claims for a qualitative superiority were also well-grounded. In the *Vossische Zeitung*, *Berliner Tageblatt* in the capital and the *Frankfurter Zeitung*, *Kölner Zeitung*, and *Münchener Neueste Nachrichten* in the other major cities, the Liberal press had titles whose collective national and international reputation far outstripped that of rival political groupings. The supremacy of the Liberal press ranged widely; evident in both domestic and foreign news coverage, in the *Feuilleton* as well as the financial section. Amongst periodicals, while the intellectual gap left by *Die Nation* in 1907 remained unfilled, Naumann's *Die Hilfe* at least matched its rivals in

---

[60] *Elbwart* (1910) 50–1, 'Wahlkampf und Presse'.
[61] BA Berlin, Reichslandbund 2774, fos. 111–12, *Süddeutsche Conservative Correspondenz* (14 July 1914).

content and had a rather higher circulation.[62] Standards in the Liberal provincial press were lower and less uniform. But smaller Liberal newspapers were still, in most cases, superior to their local rivals. Naumann might complain about the calibre of left liberal provincial journalists and include better training for local journalists as a main aim of his proposed political academy (*Hochschule für Politik*). Yet inadequate though these men appeared by Berlin standards, they generally compared favourably to their right-wing and SPD counterparts. Marburg provided a telling illustration of qualitative differences in the local press. Whilst von Gerlach attracted talented outsiders like Nuschke to the left liberal *Hessische Landeszeitung*, the local right-wing paper, despite official backing, was notoriously badly edited.[63] In addition, the fact that much of the content of local papers was culled from press agencies and the major newspapers meant that Liberal superiority at the national level percolated down to the provinces.[64]

It did not necessarily follow, of course, that Liberal press predominance was turned to concrete party-political advantage. There were discernible differences of outlook within the left liberal press. However, the main problem, ironically, was not disunity, but the success of the left liberal press compared to the left liberal political parties. Unlike left liberal politicians, editors of the major left liberal newspapers felt no sense of inferiority when they compared themselves with their English counterparts. Whilst the left liberals in the Reichstag and most state parliaments had to be content with a minority, mainly oppositional role, in many cities the left liberal press had the largest circulation and considered itself the leader of public opinion. This resulted in a sense of self-importance and a certain disdain for left liberal party politics. Leading left liberal papers, whether the *Berliner Tageblatt* on the left or the *Vossische Zeitung* on the right, considered themselves the true representatives of liberal values, and had little time for the compromises and populist promises of left liberal politicians. In return, FVP leaders complained about journalists judging

[62] In Jan. 1908 the *Jungliberale Blätter* put the circulations of the leading political periodicals at: *Die Hilfe* 15,500; *Jungliberale Blätter* 14,500; *Neue Zeit* 8,200; *Sozialistische Monatshefte* 5,000; *Deutsche Stimmen* 5,000; *Grenzboten* 5,000. BA, Berlin, Reichskanzlei 1393, fo. 90.
[63] Wenck, 'Wandlungen', fo. 139.
[64] The major left liberal newspapers were not just used by left liberal provincial journals. When Philip Scheidemann worked on SPD newspapers in the 1880s and 1890s, most articles came from the *Vossische Zeitung* and parliamentary reports from the *Frankfurter Zeitung*. P. Scheidemann, *Memoirs of a Social Democrat* (2 vols.; London, 1929), i. 40.

politics from the 'comfort of the editorial office' and the unreliable and commercially motivated stance of the Berlin left liberal press.[65]

The left liberal press, therefore, did not act simply as an extension of a particular left liberal party. Even editors of small provincial papers were prepared to protest openly against decisions of the parliamentary party. The absence of blind loyalty did also bring benefits. Echoing local dissent against left liberal decisions in Berlin could cushion the political damage by directing resentment against particular deputies rather than left liberalism *per se*. Newspaper commentaries also conveyed local reaction to deputies, acting as a warning not to proceed further, or alternatively as encouragement to press ahead. The unparalleled worth of the left liberal press, however, lay in the field of agitation. It was more than a good debating point when that archetypal Junker Oldenburg-Januschau declared to a left liberal election meeting in his Elbing constituency that he need not have bothered coming because everything the speaker said had already appeared in the press.[66] Even in a rural eastern province such as West Prussia the left liberal political message was disseminated mainly by newspapers. The pattern was even more apparent in areas of established left liberal strength like Württemberg, Lower Silesia, and along the North German coast. Here a network of newspapers repeatedly brought left liberal claims and attitudes before a large readership. The electoral importance of the readership reached by the left liberal press was acknowledged in the recommendation of Ludwig Asch and Otto Hammann that 'in many cases even Generalanzeiger and left liberal organs' should be used in the government's 1907 election campaign.[67] Even the right's disparaging remark about the clamouring left liberal press (*freisinnige Lärmpresse*) was indirect testimony to the vigorous crusading spirit characteristic of left liberal newspapers.[68]

A certain editorial latitude allied to private ownership at first sight indicated a looser, less effective structure than that obtaining for SPD newspapers which were party-owned and under the control of an

---

[65] See e.g. BA Berlin, 36, fo. 93, executive committee minutes, 19 July 1911 and BA Koblenz, NL Goetz 227, Friedrich Payer to Wilhelm Heile, 30 Aug. 1912 (copy). Such complaints continued undiminished during Weimar. Frye, *Liberal Democrats*, 97.

[66] E. von Oldenburg-Januschau, *Erinnerungen* (Leipzig, 1936), 118.

[67] BA Berlin, Reichskanzlei 1794, fos. 26–32, 'Vorschläge zur Führung des Wahlkampfes durch die Regierung', Berlin, 14 Dec. 1906; cited in Fricke, 'Der deutsche Imperialismus', 552.

[68] The material in BA Berlin, Reichslandbund 2274, reflects the increasing discussion in Conservative circles about the need to counter left liberal press superiority.

elected press commission. Appearances were, however, deceptive. In reality, left liberals were keenly aware of the importance of news-papers and anxious to exploit their potential to the full. It soon came to the attention of the Silesian FrVP party secretary in 1909, for ex-ample, that the new editor of the left liberal *Oberschlesisches Tageblatt* was 'neither a journalist, nor left liberal, nor even any sort of politician' and therefore incapable of editing 'the way we want'.[69] Unlike Berlin, in the provinces virtually every left liberal journalist was expected to be a political activist. They were to be found addressing public meetings, on left liberal local committees and in a variety of civic associations. And, also unlike Berlin, provincial journalists campaigned alongside local party leaders. For example in East Prussia Dr Gustav Herzberg, the long-serving editor of the *Königsberger Hartungsche Zeitung*, worked hand in glove with Gyßling, the left liberal provincial leader.[70] Left liberal newspapermen were imbued with a crusading spirit, nowhere more so than in those outposts where left liberals had little support. Karl Kästner, who published the *Schma-Bote* in Annaberg for twenty-two years before failing eyesight forced the one-man paper to close, was typical of numerous persevering left liberal pressmen.[71] Untrammelled by party bureaucracy, left liberal editors were on aver-age better educated, more talented, and more effective politically and journalistically than their underpaid, overworked, and undervalued SPD counterparts.[72]

The press was, therefore, vital to the workings of left liberal pol-itics. It was also representative of the ability of informal organization to adapt to new challenges. The press expanded, for example, in response to greater political mobilization and social and economic change. This occurred partly through founding new newspapers, but more importantly through increased circulation and daily publication. Existing institutions had the potential to expand and become more active in response to new circumstances and increasing demands. The press was also an important example, like the branch railways and improvements in motor transport, of how the surrounding country-side could be influenced from an urban base. Finally, newspaper

---

[69] BA Berlin, FVP 18, fo. 75, Carl Müller to Carl Kundel, 16 Feb. 1909.
[70] See the obituary in *Freisinnige Zeitung* (7 Jan. 1913); and P. Listowsky (ed.), *Ein halbes Jahrhundert aus der Geschichte der Königsberger Hartungschen Zeitung Verlags-druckerei, Ges-sellschaft auf Aktien von 1872 bis 1922* (Königsberg, 1922).
[71] *Bautzener Nachrichten* (1 July 1910).
[72] On the latter see Sperlich, *Journalist, passim*.

Table 2.4. *Newspaper circulation in Wilhelmine Germany*

Year	Total no. papers	Circulation given	Circulation over 10,000	Average circulation	Papers appearing at least 6 times a week
1885	3,069	2,493	102	2,604	26.6%
1906	4,183	1,599	246	6,139	39.3%
1914	4,221	1,819	327	8,609	46.8%

Source: G. Muser, *Statistische Untersuchung über die Zeitungen Deutschlands 1885–1914* (Leipzig, 1918), 58–65.

editors and proprietors exemplified the role of energetic, well-connected individuals. What emerge are the contours of a more active and adaptable form of notable politics. We must look beyond *Honoratiorenpolitik* as a Wilhelmine term of abuse, as a rhetoric stick with which to beat the National Liberals, to the actual participation of notables in Wilhelmine politics. The role of the left liberals in this respect was particularly disingenuous. They were foremost amongst those who hurled abuse at the image of *Honoratiorenpolitik*, but also in the van of those harnessing the political potential of notables: most left liberal critics of *Honoratiorenpolitik* were, by any objective assessment, themselves *Honoratioren*. The role of notables in left liberal politics was vital in two respects. The first lay in the direct contribution of personal effort and resources, the second in the exploitation of prestige and position in local society.

The changes in *Honoratiorenpolitik* between the 1870s and the pre-war decade, but also its continued centrality, were particularly evident in the role of notables as election candidates. It was generally expected that such candidates would meet much of the campaign costs out of their own pocket, as did prosperous businessmen or, increasingly, lawyers and functionaries with business connections like Payer, Bassermann, Stresemann, and Heckscher. In Berlin the reluctance of the left liberal party hierarchy to put up teachers, officials, and other financially less well-endowed candidates was notorious. Substantial contributions were solicited not only for campaign costs, but also for the Berlin party organization and, especially, the loss-making *Freisinnige Zeitung*.[73] It was an indication of how such candidatures persisted

---

[73] See e.g. the criticism, led by the Mosse press, about the 1905 election to the Landtag of Hugo Gerschel, a generous contributor to the FrVp and provider of directorships. BA Berlin, FVP 11, fos. 16–18, 39–40. The banker Johannes Kaempf, FVP Reichstag deputy for Berlin I, was also a notable financial supporter of the *Freisinnige Zeitung*. Elm, *Fortschritt*, 19.

throughout the Wilhelmine period that the most drastic example came as late as autumn 1918 in the Berlin I Reichstag by-election. The leader of the Berlin organization Julius Kopsch was able to push through the selection of Maximilian Kempner, a lawyer whose chairmanship of the potash syndicate and other links with commerce were far more obvious than his commitment to left liberal political ideals.[74]

So blatant a manœuvre in such a centre of attention represented a serious political mistake: the damage to party reputation far outweighed the short-term benefit to party finances. The unavoidable inference was that even the left liberals' most prized constituency was up for sale. On the other hand, such candidatures were more easily accepted in many small-town and rural constituencies. Indeed, party supporters were only too pleased to adopt a candidate capable of raising the costs of a Reichstag campaign.[75] Such constituencies, obviously, did not contain the number of rich benefactors found in urban areas. Perhaps more importantly, party members in such constituencies had become more accustomed to profiting from elections rather than paying for them. Hans Meier, treasurer for the 1912 left liberal Reichstag campaign in the Hessian district of Eschwege-Schmaldkalden, complained, for example, that two decades of anti-Semite politics had so corrupted the constituency that no one would do anything without payment. With few exceptions the local left liberals looked on 'the party as a business'. The rural *Vertrauensmänner* 'who declare openly, that if we do something for the cause, then we want money for it' were at least preferable to their urban counterparts who claimed for 'every glass of beer drunk during the meeting'.[76] As a result, campaign costs soared to 42,000 marks.[77]

Certainly, Meier was correct in identifying the anti-Semites as prime perpetrators of a costly combination of paid agitators, free beer, and promises of financial gain to every interest group in the constituency. This was reflected both in the parlous state of anti-Semite

[74] BA Berlin, FVP 36, fos. 305–9, executive committee, 25 Sept. 1918; *Mitteilungen der Hauptvereine Groß-Berlin der Fortschrittlichen Volkspartei*, 7 (1 Oct. 1918).

[75] In Flensburg-Apenrade e.g. the local left liberals, having selected an Altona merchant, expected him to meet all electoral debts. BA Berlin, FVP 10, fo. 20, Hermann Leube to Nielson, 28 June 1909.

[76] UB Marburg, NL Rade, Hans Meier to Martin Rade, 19 Dec. 1911. R. Hochhuth and H.-H. Koch (eds.), *Kaisers Zeiten: Bilder einer Epoche. Aus dem Archiv der Hofphotographen Oscar und Gustav Tellgmann* (Munich, 1973) provides a vivid pictorial record of Eschwege in the imperial period.

[77] UB Marburg, NL Rade, Wilhelm Ohr to Martin Rade, 17 Feb. 1913.

party finances and the disreputable money-making schemes resorted to by anti-Semite politicians. Nevertheless, certain anti-Semite excesses aside, such intensive and expensive Reichstag campaigns were a general hallmark of mixed-confession or Protestant constituencies consisting substantially of small or medium-sized towns and peasant villages. The anti-Semites, for example, could hardly be blamed for the style and costs of campaigning in the Freiburg constituency. Yet left liberal election expenses in 1912 of almost 40,000 marks were scarcely less than those in Eschwege-Schmaldkalden, though in Freiburg there was a double compensation: the left liberals managed both to win the seat and persuade others to meet much of the campaign costs: 15,000 marks came from National Liberal sources; 10,000 marks from the FVP; 7,000 marks from the Hansa-Bund; and 2,000 marks from the candidate Schulze-Gaevernitz.[78]

The key to the intensity of campaigning in such seats lay in the openness of the possible outcome. Frequently three groups, Liberals, Social Democrats, and the right, all considered they could win. By comparison, campaigns in constituencies with a similar social structure, but an overwhelmingly Catholic population, were usually much calmer and cheaper. True, even here the days had passed when a candidate actually had to persuade the local electoral committee that he should give an address to the voters, as happened when Wilhelm Marx was elected to the Prussian House of Deputies in Neuß-Grevenbroich-Krefeld (Land) in 1899. His predecessor, von der Acht, a Cologne businessman, had represented the constituency for twenty years without speaking in Neuß, and local Centre party worthies saw no reason to break the tradition.[79] However, in such areas much of the local campaign work could still be arranged by the parish clergy and the candidate need only make a modest number of personal appearances to secure a comfortable victory. As a Badenese Democrat from St Blasien complained bitterly, the Centre had it so easy in his area that they could afford to treat it as a sort of training ground to break in young agitators.

However, cut-throat competition was not the only explanation for the pattern of electioneering in marginal semi-rural constituencies. The expectations and demands of peasant and small-town electors played an important part. These were the people Posadowsky had in

---

[78] GLA Karlsruhe, NLP Baden 181, report on Freiburg election, 19 Jan. 1912.
[79] HAS Cologne, NL Marx 5, 'Wie ich Abgeordneter wurde!'

mind when he complained, to sympathy from all sides of the Reichstag, that 'it is demanded in some constituencies that the deputy in hundreds of public meetings give each voter an individual verbal massage'.[80] Dillenburg-Oberwestwald in Hesse gives some indication of the scale of campaigning which could be reached in semi-rural seats. The left liberals had held 155 meetings by the beginning of December 1911 and planned another 100 by polling day. Similarly, in the Brandenburg marginal Züllischau-Crosson, the successful FVP candidate Bruckhoff personally addressed ninety meetings before the first round of voting, despite having to teach in Guben each morning.[81] To some extent this represented an appetite for politics as a form of entertainment. Eugen Schiffer referred specifically to villagers 'going to all the meetings as if they were theatre performances'.[82] Similarly, the regular encore, the long drinking session in the local barn or ale-house, clearly came under the heading of rustic enjoyment rather than political enlightenment. This was an essential ingredient in poltical meetings, especially in the countryside. It was also an example of *Honoratiorenpolitik* working in practice. Younger or more humble candidates were expected to down the innkeeper or wine-growers' prized brew in person. Payer, standing in Württemberg in the 1870s, was obliged to drink so much that he had good reason to be grateful that his student days were not long over. Similarly, the inhabitants of East Holstein peasant villages asked no questions during the meeting, but expected election workers to stay with them 'till deep into the night with countless glasses of grog'.[83]

Nor, as Westarp grumbled, was the rural voter willing to travel a few miles, 'but jealously insisted that the candidate seek out his own village'.[84] The resultant spectacle was one of prominent politicians more at home in a villa suburb or hunting estate being conveyed by cart or, as far as local resources and road surfaces would allow, by car to a succession of outlying villages. That the 1907 and 1912 Reichstag campaigns were conducted in the midst of winter made the scene yet more incongruous and uncomfortable. Clearly, the physical demands

[80] Cited in 'Draußen und Daheim', illustrated supplement, *Bote aus dem Riesengebirge* (17 Aug. 1913).
[81] UB Marburg, NL Rade, FVP organising committee for Dillenburg-Oberwestwald (Nassau 5) to Martin Rade, 8 Dec. 1911 and 12 Dec. 1911; *Berliner Tageblatt*, 18 (11 Jan. 1912).   [82] Bertram, *Wahlen*, 189.
[83] Bradler (ed.), *Friedrich Payer*, 41; Wenck, 'Wandlungen', fos. 113 ff.
[84] K. Westarp, *Konservative Politik im letzten Jahrzehnt des Kaiserreiches* (Berlin, 1935), i. 30.

placed on notables in such constituencies were considerable. The Silesian electoral experiences of the left liberal lawyer and regional leader Adolf Heilberg were typical:

travelling by cart or sledge for hours in wind and weather huddled in blankets, in order to spend one or two hours in badly heated halls . . . Then came a short sleep in a more or less poor provincial hotel; [and] at the break of dawn . . . the first train back to Breslau to be at court again for nine o'clock.[85]

In a by-election campaign in Waldeck in May and June 1913 Naumann at least avoided the worst of the weather. Still, there was an unmistakable sense of trepidation in his words: 'Tomorrow I'm going out onto the battlefield: 121 places!'[86]

It would be wrong, therefore, to depict energetic *Honoratiorenpolitik* as a process of untroubled adaptation. There was also the problem of attitude as well as physical strain. Many notables viewed such engagements with ill-disguised disdain. In fact, the attitude towards voters was often undeservedly harsh. In the first place, politicians were partly themselves to blame for the increased demands placed on them by constituents. Flattering peasants as the well-stream of social renewal or the *Mittelstand* as the bedrock of the nation inevitably inflated the sense of self-importance of such groups. In addition, such statements were usually accompanied by fulsome praise for the region, town, or village. Above all, there were claims of a special affinity, a unique bond between deputy and constituency. Continually told what important people they were, it was perhaps only reasonable for voters to expect a personal visit from their deputy. This was particularly so when, as in Conrad Haußmann's constituency in Balingen, it was proclaimed not just that the deputy pursued 'Balingen politics' rather than party politics drawn up in Stuttgart or Leipzig but that 'He is ours! And he remains ours!'[87]

The second point to be made is that peasant and small-town attitudes towards electoral politics were far from being as perverse and pleasure-bent as Posadowsky, Westarp, and others contended. Schiffer was correct to suggest that the applause of packed public meetings was frequently followed by disappointing voting returns, but this was by no means a response peculiar to provincial backwaters. The same

[85] Heilberg, 'Erinnerungen', 293–4.
[86] SA Hamburg, NL Petersen L50, Friedrich Naumann to Carl Petersen 28 Apr. 1913.
[87] HSA Stuttgart, NL Haußmann 104, Württemberg Landtag elections 1912, 'An die Wähler des Bezirks Balingen!'

thing happened to the Demokratische Vereinigung in Greater Berlin and Rhineland cities. And big-name politicians like Naumann and Bassermann filled city halls regardless of the local support of their own party. Nevertheless, the pattern of attendance at public meetings clearly signalled an identification with a national political process. Audiences were considerably larger immediately before Reichstag elections. Similarly, candidates, and above all deputies, attracted greater interest than mere agitators. Both were indications that peasants took their role as voters seriously. Equally, peasant and small-town voters consciously spurned Prussian Landtag elections just as much as their urban counterparts. They were not sophisticated electors possessing detailed political knowledge: straight talking and concrete references to rural life were the keys to successful village speech-making. Nevertheless, there was an undeniable association with national politics. Even the smallest provincial newspaper carried national stories and brief parliamentary excerpts. That peasants demonstrated an increasingly positive attitude towards the fleet was also evidence of a national perspective, for in parochial terms ships brought no benefits and tangible losses. In this national perspective the Reichstag enjoyed a prominent place. It debated matters of material interest, *Bauern-* and *Mittelstandspolitik* as well as the great issues of state. Moreover, it was the only national institution in which the ordinary citizen felt a genuine sense of participation.

From the voters' perspective, therefore, that the candidate should present himself personally in the village represented neither wilfulness nor an unwillingness to walk a few miles. The deputy was seen as their representative, the personal link between the immediate locality and Berlin. The fact that the deputy took the trouble to visit the village where the voter actually lived was both an act of respect and a reinforcement of the image of the deputy as the knowledgeable representative of local concerns. Although candidates frequently failed to appreciate the fact, the insistence on a personal inspection was a tribute to the perceived importance of Reichstag politics. Voters wanted to see the goods in the same way as a peasant replacing an ox or a butcher buying a carcass.

Such attitudes had important implications for the possibilities of *Honoratiorenpolitik*. On the one hand, electors demanded openness and local contact. The common touch was invaluable. Voters were offended if candidates appeared aloof either in their demeanour or by refusing to hold a local meeting. The left liberal press, adept at exploiting such sentiments, gleefully aired a letter of a voter from the Lower Silesian village of Tiefhartmannsdorf, outraged that the Conservative candidates gave just a fifteen-minute address and then disappeared rather than make themselves available for questions: 'And with such behaviour by the candidates we are expected to vote Conservative? That's some presumption I'll say. I can tell you now, the men of Tiefhartmannsdorf will not think of it.'[88] On the other hand, voters' attitudes towards parliamentarians was often wrapped in an air of mystique. Indeed, the deputy and the motor-car cavalcade was in some respects a miniature, modern equivalent of the medieval royal procession. The Centre paper *Der Greif*, for example, mockingly described Julius Kopsch descending like 'the uncrowned Prince of Löwenberg' from the steps of the Berlin *Kurswagen* to be greeted by the faithful. Similarly, in Haußmann's Balingen constituency, the Centre, Agrarians, and SPD all railed in vain against the way 'Conrad the Great' attracted the misplaced adoration of the small man.[89]

The notion that their deputy was an important man appealed to many rural and small-town inhabitants. Liebert, for example, recalled how during his Reichstag campaigns in Saxony the locals crowded round to see and hear 'the General': 'I moved from place to place—the constituency contained 11 towns and over 200 villages—every townsman and possibly every farmer wished to able to see "the General" and to hear him speak.'[90] There was more to this, however, than a search for reflected glory. Electors wanted competence; and someone capable of cutting a figure in Berlin, not just a provincial *Stammtisch* performer. Ability and respectability were unquestionable electoral assets, not handicaps. The result of these attitudes was seen most clearly in the high proportion of outside candidates returned in such constituencies. Local sentiments were still deemed strong enough for some candidates to buy into a local agriculture holding so they could describe themselves as part-time farmers. However, such pretences tended to prove counter-productive. Most voters knew a lawyer or businessman when they saw one. Moreover, it was easy for rival parties to expose the fact that the holding was only a couple of acres in joint-ownership and candidate himself was too busy at an office desk to go anywhere near it. The more successful approach was to claim

---

[88] *Bote aus dem Riesengebirge* (4 May 1913).
[89] See the newspaper clippings in HSA Stuttgart, NL Haußmann 104.
[90] Liebert, *Aus einem bewegten Leben*, 179.

that the party had of course looked for a local man, but unfortunately had been unable to find someone with all the qualities of the proposed outside candidate.[91] Providing the candidate then made a good show of acquainting himself with the area few problems arose, apart from a small number of isolated districts where localism was particularly pronounced. Similarly, candidates from the professional middle classes were well-represented not just because they were *abkömmlich* and could mobilize resources. The qualities voters wanted in a deputy— accessibility, knowledge, ability, diligence, and effectiveness—were exalted versions of what they expected from a good doctor or lawyer.

Energetic notables were, therefore, essential to the workings of popular politics in the countryside. As Otto Nuschke justifiably complained, constituencies like Waldeck lacked both the 'money and men' to generate effective local organizations and political activity.[92] Even the occasional meetings between Reichstag elections often had to be arranged and financed by the candidate himself. Naumann, for example, spent over 4,000 marks in Waldeck and 1,200 marks towards the Kurhessen party secretariat between late 1913 and summer 1916.[93] Not all rural and semi-rural constituencies were as politically desolate as Waldeck. Many rural *Vertrauensmänner* prepared to arrange a room for a public meeting, canvass neighbours, and distribute ballot papers did so out of a sense of political duty rather than for personal profit. Within the local élite—landowners, doctors, vets, teachers, manufacturers—some displayed a keen appetite for politics and accumulated a fund of knowledge by subscribing to a Berlin or major provincial paper. Such people remained a small minority. This is reinforced by the sense of cultural and political isolation which emerges repeatedly from the memoirs and letters of political enthusiasts living in provincial towns.[94] Nevertheless, such people undeniably made looking after a constituency more manageable and agreeable. A handful of politically acute contacts could provide valuable information about the general mood in the constituency, the emergence of local issues, and

---

[91] For a skilful example of this see the 1909 by-election in Alzey-Bingen: BA Berlin, FVP 9, fo. 2, *Freisinnige Wähler-Zeitung*, no. 1, meeting to put up candidate in Armsheim.

[92] UB Marburg, NL Rade, Otto Nuschke to Martin Rade, 20 Apr. 1913.

[93] UB Marburg, NL Rade, Friedrich Naumann to Martin Rade, 19 June 1916.

[94] See e.g. the experience of the Conservative Dietrich von Oertzen in Siegen, or the left liberals Martin Wenck in Marburg and Dr Johannes Rathje in Greifswald. D. von Oertzen, *Erinnerungen aus meinem Leben* (Berlin and Lichterfelde, 1914); Wenck, 'Wandlungen', fos. 137 ff; BA Koblenz, NL Gothein 43, fos. 52–3, Friedrich Weinhausen to Gothein, 16 Apr. 1909.

the activities of rival parties. Similarly, even the most worldly politician preferred to be met with naïve enthusiasm rather than cynical self-interest. This helps explain Naumann's attachment to Heilbronn, the seat he represented from 1907 to 1912: the constituency was *gemütlich* in a way which Waldeck, most obviously, was not.[95] Nevertheless, the modern, motorized campaigns run by the left liberals in Heilbronn were based less on local party men and more on outside talent, ideas, and finance.[96]

At the opposite end of the agitational scale to sprawling rural constituencies were small, prosperous inner-city districts like Berlin I, Munich I, and Leipzig I. In Munich, so Walter Goetz was assured, once a candidate was selected 'the organization did the [work]'.[97] The compactness of such constituencies reduced the need for public addresses to a minimum. Indeed, the victorious left liberal candidate in Munich I, Georg Kerschensteiner, gave only four electoral addresses during the 1912 campaign, compared to the hundred or more delivered by many of his colleagues in semi-rural seats. Nor did the distribution of ballot papers present the same difficulties: unlike many rural districts they could safely be sent by post. Similarly, election costs were generally lower, and the local wealth which could be tapped to meet them much greater: the 'parliamentary evening' held by the chairman of the left liberal election committee in Berlin I was overflowing with *Justizräte* and champagne.[98] In addition, there was a breadth to political involvement in cities and large towns which the countryside lacked. Whilst Reichstag elections represented the only realistic opportunity for political participation in much of rural and small town Prussia, the cities witnessed a wide variety of contests. Even under the three-class franchise, urban Landtag elections were often intensely fought. The point applies even more to municipal elections, as contact between municipal electors and councillors was often closer than that between voter and deputy at state or national level. Municipal elections generally took place annually rather than every five years, and councillors were more likely to live in the immediate

95 BA Koblenz, NL Payer 40, fo. 24, Payer to wife, 22 Nov. 1910; UB Marburg, NL Rade, Friedrich Naumann to Martin Rade, 23 June 1913, and 19 June 1916; T. Heuss, *Friedrich Naumann: Der Mann, das Werk, die Zeit*, 2nd edn. (Stuttgart, 1949).

96 DSB Berlin, NL Hans Delbrück, Wilhelm Cohnstaedt to Hans Delbrück, 14 Jan. 1907; T. Heuss, *Erinnerungen 1905 bis 1933* (Tübingen, 1963), 58–64; and E. Jäckh, *Der goldene Pflug: Lebensende eines Weltbürgers* (Stuttgart, 1954).

97 BA Koblenz, NL Goetz 227, letter to Goetz, 19 Jan. 1911 (author's signature illegible).

98 BA Koblenz, NL Payer 40, fo. 86, Payer to his wife, 8 Dec. 1912.

neighbourhood. Above all, the council bore a responsibility for a range of services central to the everyday life of city dwellers: electricity, gas and water supplies; abattoirs and markets; education and transport; municipal baths and public parks; housing and hygiene regulations. In addition to the council there were elections for lay members of the local church boards, or for sickness insurance boards and labour courts. The list could be extended further to chambers of trade, guilds, residents' associations, and the jungle of municipal *Vereine*, some of whose functions were certainly political in a broader sense.

City politics was, therefore, both more institutionalized and much greater in scope. Nevertheless, the role of individuals and informal groups remained considerable. Indeed, one response to the electoral threat posed by the labour movement was the search for particularly attractive candidates. Sometimes parties selected a candidate whose humble social background, and common touch (*Volkstümlichkeit*) would appeal to workers and the petty bourgeoisie. In Bremen, for example, instead of the customary rich merchant, the left liberals decided to put up a school supervisor Hinrich Hormann, a son of a level-crossing attendant who still lived in the working-class suburb of Woltmershausen.[99] Likewise Ruhr coal-owners successfully put up a miner, Karl Heckmann, as the National Liberal candidate in Bochum in 1912.[100] Just as often, however, the trail led towards a socially venerated figure: hence the unsuccessful request in 1907 to Albert Hänel to stand again in Kiel at the age of 73, or Siegmund Günther's comment in Munich in 1911 that 'only a personality of universally acknowledged importance can rescue the seat this time against the Social Democrats'.[101]

A similar pattern could be observed in the social composition of non-socialist representatives in municipal government. Trained lawyers dominated the council executive (*Magistrat*). Even those posts which did not by law require legal qualifications tended to go to the educated middle classes. Lawyers, men like Oskar Cassel in Berlin, Johannes Junck in Leipzig, Ernst Frey in Karlsruhe, and Wilhelm Freund in Breslau, were similarly to the fore as council chairmen and deputy chairmen. Amongst councillors, however, businessmen,

---

[99] Kastendiek, 'Der Liberalismus in Bremen', 128.

[100] K. Rohe, 'Die Ruhrgebietssozialdemokratie im Wilhelminischen Kaiserreich und ihr politischer und kultureller Kontext', in Ritter (ed.), *Aufstieg der Arbeiterbewegung*, 343–4.

[101] SB Munich, NL Kerschensteiner AKB, Siegfried Günther to Georg Kerschensteiner, 30 Sept. 1911.

lawyers, high-school professors, and newspaper owners were joined by journalists, teachers, artisans, railway and postal officials, and skilled workers. The traditional image of *Honoratiorenpolitik* was departed from in two ways. First, respect had to be earned. A place in local politics could not simply be claimed by virtue of a high-status occupation or membership of a prestigious society, still less by a commission in the reserve. Such lethargic snobbery produced the sort of amused contempt within broad sections of society well captured by Moritz Julius Bonn's recollection of 'High school teachers, called professors, . . . who had a reserved table in the town's best inn or its café. There they regularly met in the evenings, playing cards or dominoes, and discussing world affairs seated according to official rank.'[102] A high social position commanded much more respect when attained by ability and effort and untainted by arrogant exclusivity. Secondly, there was a mobilization amongst subordinate social groups which produced active as well as passive participation in political life. Whilst the peasants remained interested spectators, craftsmen and especially members of the 'new' *Mittelstand* joined political organizations, spoke at public meetings, and demanded places at the committee table and in elected offices. This development was partly reflected in the formation of separate *Mittelstand* parties around the turn of the century. These were mostly short-lived and relatively unsuccessful.[103] But, more importantly, there was a general growth of petty-bourgeois and skilled-worker participation in local party-political organizations and residents' associations within the mainstream of public life.[104]

---

[102] Bonn, *Wandering Scholar*, 26–7.

[103] C. Bürger, *Die politische Mittelstandsbewegung in Deutschland* (Groß-Lichterfelde, 1912). Works written in the 1970s tend to base analysis of petty-bourgeois politics too much on the words of right-wing leaders of artisan organizations, and too little on how the petty bourgeoisie actually voted. K. Saul, *Staat, Industrie, Arbeiterbewegung im Kaiserreich* (Düsseldorf, 1974); D. Stegmann, *Die Erben Bismarcks: Parteien und Verbände in der Spätphase des wilhelminischen Deutschlands* (Cologne and Bonn, 1970); S. Volkov, *The Rise of Popular AntiModernism: The Urban Master Artisans, 1873–1896* (Princeton, NJ, 1978); H. A. Winkler, *Mittelstand, Demokratie und Nationalsozialismus: Die politische Entwicklung von Handwerk und Kleinhandel in der Weimarer Republik* (Cologne, 1972). Though artisan functionaries were overwhelmingly Conservatives and protectionists, the political and economic outlook of their members (and the many artisans who were not members) was much more varied. F. Lenger, *Sozialgeschichte der deutschen Handwerker seit 1800* (Frankfurt am Main, 1988), 154–9; Blackbourn, 'Between Resignation and Volatility'.

[104] This also applied to Catholic towns and cities. See H. Lepper, 'Von Honoratiorenverein zur Parteiorganisation: Ein Beitrag zur "Demokratisierung" des Zentrums in Rheinland 1898–1906', *Rheinische Vierteljahresblätter*, 48 (1984), 238–74. For petty-bourgeois participation in left liberal local politics see Part III below.

These were trends discomforting to Prussian officialdom. There were also Liberal and Centre politicians who bemoaned the increase in deputies of a lower social class resulting from the introduction of parliamentary allowances. However, such critics were not only wrong to blame the introduction of parliamentary salaries for changes already under way, they also greatly overestimated the alterations in parliamentary social composition. Landowners and officials still dominated the DKP *Reichstagsfraktion*. Over half were estate owners (*Rittergutsbesitzer*), a proportion almost matching that in the Prussian House of Deputies.[105] Similarly, lawyers, businessmen, landowners, and academics continued to fill most positions of power within the National Liberal, left liberal, and Centre parties. Far from being swamped by minor officials, artisans, and worker representatives, the parties were more open to charges of tokenism. When, for example, master joiner August Pauli lost his Reichstag seat in 1913, opponents joked that the Conservative Reichstag caucus would have to do without a *Renommierhandwerker* for the next few years. Similarly, both National Liberal and left liberal parliamentary parties were packed with lawyers, but tended to get by with a couple of artisans, a rail or postal official, and a lone white-collar worker.[106] Equally, the *Besitz-* and *Bildungsbürgertum* remained numerically powerful in the council chamber. The Hirsch-Duncker trade union leader Karl Goldschmidt, for example, may have had a seat on the Berlin City Council, but most of his left liberal colleagues were businessmen or members of the free professions.[107]

Furthermore, the critics also exaggerated when they accused the 'small man' of a lack of vision and an addiction to pecuniary self-interest. Certainly, the history of the canal rebellion did not support the contention of men like Mirbach and Clemens von Delbrück that large landowners and officials, imbued with Prussian tradition, possessed a more moderate and wider outlook on the state than their social inferiors.[108] Admittedly, all parties contained *Mittelständler* and others whose function was to satisfy particular electorally important

---

[105] Retallack, *Notables*, 166 ff., 232–4.   [106] Sheehan, *German Liberalism*, 240–1.

[107] See the attack on the dominant left liberal clique in *Mitteilungen der Hauptvereine Groß-Berlin der Fortschrittlichen Volkspartei*, 1–8 (8 Dec. 1917–1 Nov. 1918); and BA Berlin, NL Nathan 18, fos. 1–18, esp. Paul Nathan to Hugo Preuß, 2.12.1919.

[108] BA Koblenz, NL Bülow 105, fo. 35, Mirbach to Bülow, 10 July 1913; C. von Delbrück, *Die Wirtschaftliche Mobilmachung in Deutschland 1914* (Munich, 1924), esp. 52, 57–8; H. Horn, *Der Kampf um den Bau des Mittellandkanals* (Cologne, 1964).

groups and who proved incapable of contributing much to parliamentary work. However, a significant proportion of politicians from modest social origins owed their political careers to their own intelligence and industry. Erzberger, the classic example, could be accused of many things, but never of being a 'political nobody', or not knowing how to scrutinize the budget.[109] Similarly, education, intelligence, and energy propelled Stresemann up the National Liberal political hierarchy despite modest social origins. (His father ran a pub and struggling beer business in Berlin).[110] Both were unmistakably new *Honoratioren*. The label can also be applied to a less talented, more run-of-the-mill parliamentarian like Hinrich Hormann. As Reichstag deputy for Bremen he conveyed proposals from the Norddeutscher Lloyd to ministers and officials in the same way as the wealthy tobacco merchant Hermann Frese had done before 1903. His adoption into the circle of social respectability in Bremen was further confirmed by a seat in the city parliament (*Bürgerschaft*) and membership of the Bremer Gesellschaft 1914.[111] The pattern also extends to councillors and activists not yet 'wrapped in the toga of a Reichstag deputy'.[112] Anton Erkelenz, for example, differed somewhat from the typical left liberal lawyer or businessman in his youthful exuberance as well as in his particular support for workers' interests. Nevertheless, his political activities, whether press articles, visits to England, speeches to the party conference, or belief in the importance of parliamentary politics, all fitted well enough into the framework of energetic left liberal *Honoratiorenpolitik*.

The new form of *Honoratiorenpolitik* was, therefore, far from being simply an aristocracy of merit. Indeed, the parties consciously looked

---

[109] C. Severing, *Lebensweg*, i. 329, provides a good first-hand account of Erzberger succeeding Richter as budget expert and scourge of the executive. The best general portrait of Erzberger remains K. Epstein, *Matthias Erzberger and the Dilemma of German Democracy* (Princeton, NJ, 1959).

[110] On Stresemann's family background and pre-war political and business career see K. Koszyk, *Gustav Stresemann: Der kaisertreue Demokrat* (Cologne, 1989), 19–131; D. Warren, *The Red Kingdom of Saxony: Lobbying Grounds for Gustav Stresemann* (The Hague, 1964); and K. H. Pohl, 'Die Nationalliberalen in Sachsen vor 1914', in Gall and Langewiesche (eds.), *Liberalismus und Region*, 195 ff.

[111] BA Koblenz, NL Solf 10, fos. 94–100, contains a list of members. The exalted social company kept in the Bremer Gesellschaft, 'a great number of our most respected merchants, shippers, industrialists, senators (both our mayors), academics', was underlined in a letter from its chairman Dr Bernhard Wilckens to Hans Delbrück. DSB Berlin, NL Delbrück, Wilckens to Delbrück, 20 Apr. 1916.

[112] F. Meinecke, *Straßburg Freiburg Berlin 1901–1919: Erinnerungen* (Stuttgart, 1949), 125.

for well-established men of means to head local organizations. However, even for the most successful businessman or lawyer, a career in local politics meant a considerable sacrifice of time. It also meant participation in associations recruited from a range of social classes, and a willingness to perform, as aloof government officials put it, 'amidst beer and tobacco'.[113] Finally, *Honoratiorenpolitik* was also reinvigorated by the absorption of those who would previously have been excluded because of their youth or lesser social status.

As the cast of notable politics was modified, parallel changes could be observed in the organizational setting. The *Stammtisch*, the classic location of notable politics, whilst remaining a pervasive feature of Wilhelmine society, became increasingly tainted with the image of philistinism, of *Spießbürgertum*. It was also too small a forum to accommodate the increasingly large local élites created by economic growth, expansion of higher education and continued urbanization. A social club like, for example, the Verein Erholung in Nordhausen, became a more appropriate way of bringing together the local élite. A town's museum society, historical association, or a private charity often fulfilled a similar function, and the worthy cultural or charitable cause dispersed suspicions of philistinism. It was, however, *Bürger-* and *Bezirksvereine* which had become the main forum for airing municipal issues and mobilizing support. In Hamburg, for instance, the various citizens' associations had over 20,000 members by 1911, many more than any other non-socialist organization involved in municipal politics.[114] Though membership and organizational apparatus were obviously more modest, citizens' associations were equally important outside the big cities. They were the forums in which pressing local problems were aired, be they the state of the railway station, road-widening proposals, or the introduction of modern sewerage. Such associations had a major say in the selection of non-socialist candidates at municipal elections, and they continued to monitor the actions of the council and to pester and petition both local and state authorities. Also important to the respectable citizen in German urban society were sporting, cultural, and professional groups: the bowling club and the choral society; in larger towns the theatre and the concert

---

[113] O. Hauser (ed.), *Provinz im Königreich Preußen* (Geschichte Schleswig-Holsteins, 8/1, Neumünster, 1966), 81.

[114] The growth of membership is chartered in A. Obst, *Geschichte der Hamburgischen Bürgervereine: Festschrift zur Feier des 25 jährigen Bestehens des Zentralausschusses Hamburgischer Bürgervereine am 10.6.11.* (Hamburg, 1911).

house; the teachers' and lawyers' association. The great majority were outwardly non-political: many citizens' associations had a clause in their statutes denying any connection with party politics. The inner reality, however, was becoming increasingly different. Those who played a leading role in town councils and local associations were frequently the local leaders of a political party and the organizers of Reichstag campaigns. It was no coincidence that many of the newcomers to parliamentary parties and the committees of local party associations had close links to a variety of occupational and other interest groups. The Conservative Landtag deputy and Silesian activist Max Conradt, for example, was prominent in the Cartel of Productive Estates, the Imperial Mittelstand Association (*Reichsmittelstandsvereinigung*), the Mittelstand Association in Silesia, and the Breslau chimney-sweeps' guild.[115] Felix Marquardt, the newly elected National Liberal deputy for Eisenach in 1912, was at the same time the chairman of the Leipzig Association of Commercial Clerks.[116] Even the most unlikely societies were drawn in as competing local political factions sought endorsements. Hamburg politicians joked that the rising tide of parish-pump politics (*Kirchturmspolitik*) in *Bürgerschaft* elections would end up with bowling-club-sponsored candidates and in 1910, to an amused cry of *gut Holz*, the joke came true.[117] More generally, such organizations formed a central part of the social fabric and were therefore a significant sphere of informal politics. They both supported and were supported by a local political élite. Such an élite was rarely without party-political allegiance. The particular party favoured depended on circumstances. In Aachen and Trier, where the size of the Catholic population outweighed the effect of the three-class franchise, it was the Centre which held sway. In Hanover and Karlsruhe National Liberals predominated, in Frankfurt, Königsberg, and Berlin the left liberals. In the great majority of cases, however, these groups found political expression in Germany's Liberal parties and, as Reichstag election returns in urban

[115] The Breslau journal edited by Conradt, *Mitteilungen des Deutschen Mittelstandsbundes Provinzialverband Schlesien*, gives a cross-section of his political activities. For left liberal ripostes to 'the chimney sweep at Heydebrand's table' see Ch. 9 below.

[116] And not, as O'Donnell 'National Liberalism', 57, implausibly suggests, chairman of the anti-Semitic Deutsch-nationaler Handlungsgehilfenverband. His position on the left of the National Liberal Party and the importance of white-collar support led the FVP executive committee to agree to Marquardt addressing the FVP party conference planned for Eisenach in Sept. 1914. BA Berlin FVP 21, fo. 34.

[117] *Generalanzeiger für Hamburg-Altona* (22 Jan. 1910).

areas and the composition of municipal councils reflected, the left liberals in particular.

Descriptions of a deep-seated crisis or general failure of *Honoratiorenpolitik* cannot, therefore, be accepted. Indeed, one of the main reasons for the persistence of *Honoratiorenpolitik* was that the system never broke down completely. Things tended to turn out reasonably well in the end. As Kurt Schumacher, FVP party secretary in Berlin, recalled: 'We managed with a single shorthand typist. Admittedly, we could not undertake grand moves, but we got by through all the years . . .'[118] Equally, in election after election, local parties usually managed belatedly to scrape together sufficient campaign funds, mainly from companies, individual businessmen, and economic interest groups. Indeed, such was the frenzy of left liberal campaigning in the last weeks before Reichstag elections that both Wilhelm Ohr and Anton Erkelenz came to the conclusion that the party suffered from too much rather than too little agitation.[119] Energetic *Honoratiorenpolitik* had the attraction of appearing more responsive to local society than a centralized bureaucracy. It also functioned, as Chapter 8 will demonstrate, in districts where the opposition of *Landräte* and landowners, or the absence of suitable local leaders, made formal organization impossible.

Inevitably, even a regenerated *Honoratiorenpolitik* remained more susceptible to the actions of individuals and the general political mood than the organized political machinery of the SPD or the ingrained social solidarity of political Catholicism. Nevertheless, two Reichstag by-elections gained by the left liberals in July 1914 were only confirmation of the continued potential of informal organization. In one case, Coburg, the victor Oskar Arnold was the epitome of the well-connected notable. A prominent local manufacturer, his Neustadt toy factory employed over a thousand people. He was also the long-serving President of the Coburg Landtag. Alongside positions in chambers of trade and other economic organizations, Arnold was the chairman, actual or honorary, of the Coburg veterans' association, the tourist association, the medical volunteers, the Neustadt agricultural association, and the poultry raisers' association. He was also an honorary citizen of Neustadt and honorary member of the Neustadt

[118] BA Berlin, NL Naumann 30, Schumacher to Naumann, 28 July 1919.

[119] Both, however, called for more permanent organization and greater long-term planning: BA Berlin, NL Wilhelm Ohr 14, fo. 9, Ohr to Fabrikant Hochhut, Eschwege, 18 Jan. 1912; BA Berlin, Reichslandbund, 112, fo. 82, personalia Anton Erkelenz.

shooting association, besides participating in the staple diet of left liberal community involvement: education, theatre, and the voluntary
fire-brigade. Last, but far from least, he was an arch railway enthusiast: the promoter of five lines built between 1886 and 1922, he was
accorded the ultimate accolade of a line being popularly called after
him.[120] The other victory, Labiau–Wehlau, also owed something to a
well-respected local candidate Richard Wagner, the Bürgermeister of
Tapiau. Above all, however, it showed that, even in East Prussia, left
liberal informal organization bolstered by outside finance and talent
could overturn a Conservative backed by the machinery of the Agrarian League and local Prussian administrators. Party secretaries, politicians, and, above all, outside money were drafted in to bolster the left
liberals' campaign in Labiau–Wehlau. At most 5,000 marks could be
raised in East Prussia (and that probably from Königsberg rather than
the constituency), but FVP headquarters and the Hansa-Bund each
agreed to give 15,000 marks.[121]

Paradoxically, the introduction of paid officials and the way they
were regarded tended to reinforce rather than undermine *Honoratiorenpolitik*.[122] Humdrum tasks predominated in the work of left liberal party secretaries: the growing burden of routine administration,
visiting rural *Vertrauensmänner*, addressing minor meetings, and send-
ing stories to local newspapers. They worked under the supervision of
local leaders, and were employed mainly to allow notables more scope
to meet the increasing demands of politics by freeing them from routine, time-consuming tasks. It was in line with such expectations that
most party secretaries had at most petty-bourgeois social origins. Many
had been trained as elementary-school teachers, or had been minor
union officials. Richterites, especially, took the view that party secretaries were there for routine tasks and to carry out instructions. It was
repeatedly stressed, for example, that a party secretaryship was not to

---

[120] The Steinachtbahn was popularly called the Arnoldbahn. For details of Arnold's life
see the collection of press cuttings in SA Coburg, NL Oskar Arnold 7.

[121] BA Berlin, FVP 36, fo. 206, executive committee, 6 May 1914; BA Berlin, Reichslandbund 6213, 4 ff.

[122] No single source contains extensive material on left liberal paid officials. No papers of
FVP party secretaries are available, apart from fragments of Heinrich Haupt's correspondence in Stadtarchiv Mannheim, NL Wolfhard 16, and BA Koblenz, NL Heuss 573. The
summaries of party secretary reports in BA Berlin FVP 27 are relatively uninformative. Party
secretaries were often too busy to complete monthly reports, but if they did, they were understandably inclined to exaggerate their own importance. The following analysis of left liberal
paid officials is based on an accumulation of press reports, and widely scattered references in
the FVP files and individual private papers.

be regarded as a stepping stone towards a parliamentary seat. An FVP party secretary would be sanctioned as a Reichstag candidate only 'in the most extreme emergency'.[123] Attitudes in the FrVg were rather more open. Regular party secretary conferences in Berlin allowed an exchange of information and improved co-ordination. The presence on such occasions of leaders like Barth and Naumann undoubtedly gave party secretaries a sense of worth and belonging. Indeed, a significant number of left liberal officials idolized Naumann in particular. Haupt was presented with a picture of his hero Naumann when leaving the Hamburg party secretariat, while an obituary of Martin Wenck described Naumann as the pivot around whom Wenck's life revolved.[124] FrVg party officials were consulted, not just instructed. Of course, much of this amounted ultimately to more skilful man-management rather than any shift of decision-making away from deputies and regional notables. Nevertheless, it was no coincidence that former left liberal party secretaries like Otto Nuschke, Wilhelm Heile, and Johannes Fischer, who went on later to careers in national politics, came from this section of the left liberal political spectrum.

It was characteristic that such talented party secretaries with parliamentary ambitions soon moved to better paid and more highly regarded posts, usually in the left liberal press. The long-serving left liberal party secretaries were those for whom the office represented the summit of their political career: men like Albert Kuhlmann, party secretary in Darmstadt from 1906 into the 1920s, Heinrich Haupt, party secretary in Hamburg 1904–1914 and then in Mannheim till his death in 1917, Karl Elbel in Brandenburg and Dornbluth, party secretary in Thüringen in the decade before 1918 and then in Halle. Such men were undoubtedly effective agitators and administrators. They would not otherwise have survived so long in such a precarious post. However, handicapped by a working-class background, they lacked the dynamic political talent needed to break into a higher position within the party.[125] Most party secretaries, however, left quickly,

---

[123] BA Berlin, FVP 36, fo. 26, executive committee minutes, 10 Sept. 1910.
[124] *Hamburger Fremdenblatt* (25 June 1914); *Darmstädter Zeitung* (18 Sept. 1931) in Wenck, 'Wandlungen'.
[125] See StA Mannheim, NL Wolfhard 16, correspondence between Haupt and Weinhausen, *Hamburger Fremdenblatt* (25 June 1914) and *Neue Badische Landeszeitung* (2 May 1918, evening edn., Haupt); BA Berlin, FVP 5, fo. 33, and Wenck, 'Wandlungen', fo. 222 (Kuhlmann); BA Berlin, NL Wilhelm Ohr 6, fo. 76, Ohr to Lehrer Peters, 1 July 1913, BA Berlin, FVP 36, fo. 295 (Dornbluth); and BA Berlin, FVP 36, fos. 144–5, and FVP 48, fo. 3 (Elbel).

having been found ineffective or untrustworthy. Ernst Possel's dismissal in 1914, for example, formed 'another sad chapter' in the history of left liberal party secretaries in Greifswald.[126] Similarly, in the neighbouring post of secretary for the left liberal rural workers' association in Pomerania, one secretary failed because of his accent and another had to be dismissed for calling more on various women than on farm workers, before someone reliable and effective could be found.[127]

The left liberals were far from alone in suffering misfortune. Indeed, left liberal party secretaries were generally more honest and able than average, particularly compared to National Liberal, Conservative, and anti-Semite paid officials. The Zimmerstraße referred justifiably to 'morally and politically non-housetrained' right-wing agitators, who could quickly be discredited by exposing their past history. A typical example of this was the case of Malkewitz, a deputy, and proprietor of an agrarian newspaper, whom the DKP tried to pass off as an artisan. The left liberal press gleefully recalled his past as trade union radical with the nickname 'bloody Gustav'.[128] Left liberals recruited more carefully and rejected unsolicited offers to speak in return for money. Moreover, the fact that impoverished left liberal organizations paid less than going rate meant they tended not to attract men motivated by money alone. As Wilhelm Heile commented: 'I could not work for 200 marks a month unless there was an idealistic motive.'[129] In addition, the close supervision by local party leaders made impossible the sort of repeated embezzlement suffered by Böckel and others at the hands of paid officials.[130]

Even though incidents involving left liberals were comparatively rare, the potential damage of allowing agitators for whom politics were more a source of profit than an expression of principle to speak in the party name remained considerable. A core of anti-Semite supporters were comparatively inured to disreputable behaviour, but a scandal concerning an FVP party official clashed with the claims of moral superiority regularly advanced by left liberals and undoubtedly

---

[126] BA Koblenz, NL Gothein 33, fo. 235, Hugo Wendorff to Georg Gothein, 11 June 1914.
[127] BA Berlin, FVP 53.
[128] BA Berlin, FVP 64, fo. 57, circular from general secretary Ißberner, 12 July 1912; *Bote aus dem Riesengebirge* (19 Aug. 1913). For further examples of 'Conservative turncoats' see *Breslauer Zeitung*, 8 (4 Jan. 1912).
[129] BA Berlin, FVP 7, fo. 8, Wilhelm Heile to Friedrich Weinhausen, 27 Mar. 1908.
[130] R. Mach, 'Otto Böckel und die antisemitische Bauernbewegung in Hessen 1887–1894', in *Neunhundert Jahre Geschichte der Juden in Hessen* (Wiesbaden, 1983).

lost support. Thus it was with understandable gloom that Julius Kopsch reported the effect of the 'Mattheus Affair' on the party in Thüringen. Mattheus, an FVP official in Weimar, had left his family 'unter Nacht und Nebel', accompanied by an under-age girl.[131] Whilst Kopsch's concern was certainly more for votes than values, the ingrained revulsion at having to work with a man like party secretary Jakobs felt by Georg Semmelroth, a left liberal metal-worker in Wetzlar, gives a more authentic reflection of rank-and-file attitudes. Jakobs, according to Semmelroth, possessed a blustering oratory and some administrative ability, together with an abundance of self-confidence. But he lacked any sense of taste or tact. The prospect of Jakobs' standing for election was abhorrent: 'Even if people with no greater ability than Jakobs's have been put up for election by other parties, and been returned, I must say that he lacks the moral qualifications to be a representative of the people.' For Semmelroth, the final straw was Jakobs's impending divorce on the grounds of adultery: a sad reward for Frau Jakobs, who had 'worked and gone hungry' to help her husband work up from being an apprentice mechanic, and the end of Jakobs's political career were it to become public knowledge.[132] Such views summed up the opposition to 'party secretary agitation'. Its failure lay partly in the personal inadequacy of the agitator, but even more in the entrenched attitudes of left liberal supporters. In Hesse, for example, Wilhelm Ohr found the polemical attacks of men like party secretary Bitz in Schmalkalden alienated supporters. Most skilled workers, artisans, and clerks, as well as academics and businessmen, preferred a well-argued address to crude polemic, and a proper profession to the dubious pursuit of paid agitation.[133]

There was, then, clearly still a place for *Honoratioren* in the mass politics of Wilhelmine Germany. They were capable of mobilizing resources even amongst the venal voters of Eschwege-Schmalkalden, as a letter from a Schmalkalden businessman in 1912 indicated:

I will willingly give Herr Heck leave until Reichstag polling day as far as business will allow, and . . . stand in for him myself. Here we are all making some contribution on the side, not just in free time, but also during business hours. Once again, my people have for days being writing down rolls of village voters into the night, my firm again donated 200 M. to the war-chest, I've made

---

[131] BA Berlin, FVP 36, fo. 158, executive committee, 4 Nov. 1912.
[132] UB Marburg, NL Rade, Georg Semmelroth to Martin Rade, 25 Feb. 1912.
[133] UB Marburg, NL Rade, Wilhelm Ohr to Martin Rade, 4 Mar. 1912.

horses, coaches and drivers available till polling day, likewise my brother-in-law, and, if it proves necessary, I'll also mobilize a few more sets for the last few days from the firm Nordmeyer, with which I'm connected. Also, I've the agreement of Herr Konrad Müller here, that he'll place his big *automobile* at our disposal tomorrow for Herr Brandt and on polling day. Also, I'll help myself on polling day and make available various members of my counter-staff . . . Here in the firm everything is directed towards getting rid of people like Raab and Lattmann for good.[134]

The mainstream party with the smallest and least funded formal organization, the left liberals proved capable of mounting forceful election campaigns, which even opponents recognized as being amongst the most powerful in Germany.[135] It was, however, agitation without adequate financial foundation, and without the active partic-ipation of a mass dues-paying membership. Ever-rising campaign costs were met only with a struggle during the pre-war decade, and deputies showed increasing signs of being unable to bear the physical strains the working of left liberal politics placed upon them. The war led to a further inflation of electoral costs, more physical strain, and exposed the financial weakness of the smaller left liberal provincial newspapers. It is important to give recognition to the left liberal cam-paign performance in the pre-war decades. Moreover, some of the cir-cumstances and challenges facing left liberal organization after 1918 were unforeseen products of war and revolution. Ultimately, however, Naumann and the other advocates of an SPD-style party apparatus were proved correct. The system which, with continual modifications, had served the left liberals fairly successfully from the 1880s to the outbreak of war was in no position to meet either the spiralling costs of Weimar elections or the switch from single-member constituencies to large electoral districts and that nursery of competing interests, the party list system.

[134] BA Berlin, NL Wilhelm Ohr 14, fos. 156–7, Emil Schweizer to Wilhelm Ohr, Schmalkalden, 6 Jan. 1912.
[135] Kunze, *Was der Reichstagswähler wissen muß*, ii. 28; Kastendiek, 'Liberalismus in Bremen', 150.

3

Liberal Ideals:
Faded Remnants or New Dawn?

Chapter 1 identified those who gave support to left liberal politics, and Chapter 2 examined the methods of left liberal popular politics. The intention now is to focus on left liberal ideas and attitudes. What did left liberals stand for? Not much is the usual answer.[1] Ideological decline, a continual erosion of liberal substance, lies at the centre of interpretations of left liberal failure in Germany.[2] There are two strands to the story. The first is the debasement of ideology: the glittering tenets of democracy, militia, and social harmony increasingly tarnished by monarchism, militarism, and market economics. Wilhelmine left liberals, it is argued, failed to live up to the ideals of their early nineteenth-century precursors. The second concerns the dissolution of social base. It claims left liberalism succumbed to socio-economic inevitability, not just to infections of nationalism and imperialism, or left liberal leaders' sins of omission and commission. The uneven but dynamic growth of Germany's capitalist economy fostered class division and fractured the Protestant middle strata into competing interests.[3] The result was a party which, no matter how opportunistic, was unable to command a solid block of support.

One aim of this chapter is to look more closely at the formation of this interpretation in Wilhelmine Germany itself. At one level it was, predictably, an accusation levelled by political opponents. 'There's no left liberalism in Germany any more', the right and SPD concurred,

---

[1] Sheehan, *German Liberalism*, 236.

[2] K. Wegner, 'Linksliberalismus im wilhelminischen Deutschland und in der Weimarer Republik', *Geschichte und Gesellschaft*, 4/1 (1978), 120–37.

[3] Gall, 'Liberalismus und "bürgerliche Gesellschaft"'; Sheehan, *German Liberalism*, 239–57. See also the articles by Witt, Gall, and Wolfgang Mommsen in Holl (ed.), *Liberalismus und imperialistischer Staat*.

'only a pile of seat-hungry political profiteers'.[4] The contemporary observer of Germany, William Harbutt Dawson, mirroring official Prussian distaste towards political parties, claimed the left liberals, 'who had more and more become opportunists and time-servers', were 'least excusable of all'.[5] But, intriguingly, many left liberals came to similar conclusions. Any attempt to find common bonds between left liberals must account for the contempt shown by the sort of people who read Barth's *Die Nation*, and also by some more lowly left liberals, towards Philistines ('Spießbürger', 'Philister') who, they sensed, made up the bulk of left liberal politicians and voters. Such sentiments were a recurrent theme for satirical journals like *Simplicissimus* and *Kladderadatsch*, and condemnation of bourgeois philistinism was a regular feature of left liberal private correspondence. Barth, for example, claimed to be setting out to counteract 'the political philistinism raised by Richter'.[6]

But the sense of failure and disillusion was counterbalanced by identification with bourgeois economic, social, and cultural achievements. The propertied and educated middle classes, not Prussian Junkers, held sway in German cities. They also invaded aristocratic preserves. 'Under William II', as the left liberal economist Moritz Julius Bonn put it, 'money had come in to its own.'[7] Contemporaries described the 'liberal money aristocracy' buying up rural estates and elbowing aside Conservative landowners in the Berlin social scene, at the Kiel regatta, and in the Imperial Automobile Club.[8] This was at least as much commercialization of the aristocracy as feudalization of the bourgeoisie.[9] And further down the social scale groups laid claim to economic and social advancement: petty-bourgeois families who put sons through secondary or higher education; small producers boosted by the Wilhelmine economic boom; peasants benefiting from

---

[4] *Vorwärts* (19 Mar. 1908), cited in Kunze, *Reichstagswähler*, ii. 88. Cf. *Vorwärts* (6 Jan. 1912) and *Daily Telegraph* (3 Jan. 1912).

[5] W. H. Dawson, *The German Empire 1867–1914 and the Unity Movement* (2 vols.; London, 1919), ii. 328–9.

[6] BA Berlin, NL Naumann 143, letter from Theodor Barth, 18 Jan. 1904. Equally, Wilhelm Ohr was actually rather pleased at criticism of his Nationalverein für das liberale Deutschland from all the 'Nachtwächtern und Spießbürger'. BA Berlin, NL Wilhelm Ohr 2, fo. 162, Ohr to Platzhoff, 28 July 1907.　　　　　[7] Bonn, *Wandering Scholar*, 292.

[8] *Kölnische Volkszeitung* (3 Jan. 1907); BA Berlin, Nachlaß Wangenheim, 7, fo. 57, von Grumme-Douglas to Gustav Roesicke, 9 July 1912.

[9] M. Weber, 'Wahlrecht und Demokratie in Deutschland', L. Gall and R. Koch (eds.), *Der europäische Liberalismus im 19. Jahrhundert* (4 vols.; Frankfurt am Main, 1981), ii. 305; Blackbourn and Eley, *Peculiarities*, 228–37.

tariffs and improved agricultural productivity; technicians and clerks jostling for social recognition.

There were, of course, losers as well as winners in the battle for economic sustenance and social status. Our understanding of Wilhelmine Germany is hardly advanced by transforming the tale of total left liberal political failure into an unmitigated social, cultural, and economic success story. But such aspects, and the positive attitudes they generated, need to be included in assessing left liberal outlook. This chapter seeks to assess left liberal attractions or defects not in absolute terms, but relative to other Wilhelmine parties. Ideas are assessed according to their practical impact rather than their innate quality. And negative factors—resentment towards clericalism, inherited privilege, or organized labour—are accorded as much place as positive beliefs. The search is for popular political sentiment rather than abstract principles or textual criticism of official party programmes, which were often ignored, insincere, and outdated.

The observation that party programmes provide a distorted mirror of Wilhelmine politics is based on more than the usual discrepancy between words and action.[10] The departures from formal party programmes were not just those of chance and circumstance, but of basic belief. All contained passages which a substantial cross-section had come to oppose or consider irrelevant. Ironically, it was not ignoring but attempting to honour pledges which often presented more problems. The sudden revival of a long dormant programme point generally stirred up more trouble than its silent abandonment. Hence, for example, Graf Galen's anger at the Centre's support in 1917–18 for the introduction of the Reichstag suffrage for Prussian state elections. 'When Centre party people had earlier demanded equal franchise,' the Count's revealing comment on the Centre's insincerity towards a part of its programme continued, 'there was no danger then of achieving it.'[11] SPD activists tended to take programme questions more seriously than counterparts in other Wilhelmine parties, but there were still many who attached little meaning to the final goals of the Erfurt programme, Kautsky's statement of orthodox Marxism adopted by the party in 1891. Growing pragmatism and impatience of theoretical

---

[10] W. Mommsen (ed.), *Deutsche Parteiprogramme*, 3rd edn. (Munich, 1971), and W. Treue (ed.), *Deutsche Parteiprogramme seit 1861*, 4th edn. (Göttingen, 1968) provide accessible compilations of the main party programmes.

[11] HAS Cologne, NL Carl Bachem 523, *Rheinische Zeitung* (3 Nov. 1917). Quotation by Galen emphasized in original.

with orthodoxy was typified by Ignaz Auer's response to the refusal of the land reformer Adolf Damaschke to join the SPD because he was opposed to the central regulation of production and consumption. No sane man believes in such a ideals, Auer asserted, only a few 'bloody theorists'.[12]

Were the left liberals, reputedly obsessed with pure politics and observance of principle, the exceptions to the rule? Left liberal politics retained traits of individualism. Divergence from the party line on individual issues was more likely to lead to resignation or withdrawal than elsewhere. A left liberal school teacher managed to join and leave the FrVg twice between June 1893 and July 1895.[13] The Jute manufacturer Max Bahr repeatedly declared his intention to withdraw from active left liberal politics because of disaffection on particular issues. In 1907 it was left liberal naval enthusiasm compounded by despair at middle-class political indifference; in 1917 Bahr's personal rejection of equal franchise in Prussia.[14] Left liberal intellectuals like Max Weber, Lujo Brentano, and Theodor Wolff, though fascinated by politics, placed too much importance on their own ideals and too little on the compromising demands of party discipline and mass politics to take a lasting and direct part in organized party politics.

But fastidious attachment to principle and programme were more characteristic of the educated middle classes than other social groups. Concern for programme and ideas in the DVP, for example, characterized intellectuals surrounding Leopold Sonnemann in Frankfurt more than the party's petty-bourgeois rank and file in Württemberg.[15] Similarly, the strong presence of the educated middle classes in the

---

[12] BA Berlin, Reichslandbund 8, fo. 117, personalia Ignaz Auer. Cf. *Von einem alten Parlamentarier: Bilder aus unserer Reichstagsfraktion*, 1. *Die Mitte* (Berlin and Karlshorst, 1915), 7–19. A case is made for the importance of radical intellectuals, but their growing isolation from the mainstream of the labour movement in the pre-war years is brought out in S. Pierson, *Marxist Intellectuals and the Working-Class Mentality in Germany, 1887–1912* (Cambridge, Mass., 1993), 229–55. The SPD's concentration in campaigns on actual grievances and democratic demands rather than the Erfurt programme is emphasized in Part III below.   [13] BA Berlin, FVP 1, FrVg membership declarations.
[14] SA Wolfenbüttel, NL Schrader III. 4, Max Bahr to Karl Schrader, 4 Oct. 1907; BA Berlin, FVP 26, fo. 43, Max Bahr to Reinhold Ißberner, 7 June 1917. For background see M. Bahr, *Eines Deutschen Bürgers Arbeit in Wirtschaft und Politik* (Berlin, 1926).
[15] See K. Gerteis, *Leopold Sonnemann: Ein Beitrag zur Geschichte des demokratischen Nationalstaatsgedankens in Deutschland* (Frankfurt am Main, 1970); Rolling, 'Liberals, Socialists and City Government', 54–64; Simon, *Württembergische Demokraten*; Hunt, *People's Party*.

National-Social Association encouraged a more extensive discussion of ideals and programme than in the larger left liberal groupings. Many left liberals liked to think that they represented a concern with 'the higher pursuits' and that other groups served shallow vested interests. Karl Schrader's address to an assembly of FrVg deputies and agitators in Berlin in February 1907 was a typically evocative and vigorous left liberal self-portrait as the defenders of political ideals and morality against the onslaught of economic interests.[16] Such sentiments, as we shall see, did form a significant part of left liberal self-belief for party politicians and ordinary supporters as well as high-minded intellectuals. But this creed, though widely believed, was not actually true. Neither the programme nor the conduct of the main left liberal groups justified claims to the lion's share of political ideas and idealism. When Richterites and Secessionists merged to form the Deutsch-freisinnige Partei in 1884 the programme adopted was an uneasy, vague compromise. And the parliamentary party was so dis-united that it never felt able to call a party conference to discuss ideals.[17] When the two factions divided again in 1893 the result was two parties less riven by personal and political rivalry, and more capable of internal discussion. But the split was primarily a settling of old scores, not a new beginning. Neither the FrVp nor FrVg presented an ambitious programme and fresh ideas. Secessionists in the FrVg and Richter's FrVp both preferred to have programme and ideals determined by a small circle of leaders rather than popular debate. There was also considerable scepticism at the top of left liberal pol-itics about the value of a formal programme. Notables like Heinrich Rickert and Theodor Barth felt this promoted sterile inflexibility. More important than paragraphs, they argued, were principled indi-viduals able to act in the spirit of liberalism. Rickert, leading discus-sion at the FrVg founding conference in 1893, openly declared that after thirty-six years in three political parties he no longer attached much importance to a party programme.[18] Sections were overtaken by changing circumstances, and few people paid much attention anyway. Moreover, a party's conduct could render a programme's content meaningless. Rickert referred, tellingly, to the fate of his favourite manifesto, the 1867 National Liberal programme. Though formally

---

[16] SA Wolfenbüttel, NL Schrader III. 4.   [17] *Breslauer Zeitung*, 123 (18 Feb. 1907).
[18] BA Berlin, FVP 2, *Konstituirende Generalversammlung des Wahlvereins der Liberalen: 2/3 12/1893 Berlin*, 28 ff.

retained, it stood in hopeless contradiction to the actions and attitudes of the National Liberal party after 1879. Instead, Rickert urged his audience, characteristically, to 'act like the practical English'.[19] The party had to take a position on the issues of the day, not map out dreams for the distant future.

In volume at least, the FrVp appeared more attached to formal programmes. A party programme was approved at Eisenach in 1894, and further ideals declarations were appended at subsequent party conferences.[20] However, this was hardly a genuine reflection of widespread and intense ideals debate: the composition of the FrVp conference was restricted and the press excluded.[21] Richter and his lieutenants employed the party programme less as a positive statement of belief, and more as a disciplinary code, a weapon wielded by the *Freisinnige Zeitung* to denounce internal dissent. For Richter, the defensive purpose of a programme was partly a matter of preserving ideals: opposition to naval and colonial demands or support for Manchesterite economics. Fixing them as official party orthodoxy was some barrier against a growing shift of left liberal opinion. But after his departure the party programme was put overwhelmingly to pragmatic use. The FrVp campaigning expert Julius Kopsch believed, like Rickert, that detailed programmes repelled more voters than they attracted. The party's electoral interests were best served by a programme which steered away from controversial issues and towards the lowest common denominator. Richter's successors increasingly sought to use the programme to defuse rather than define.

The results of these attitudes were evident in the programme of the merged party. The FVP programme was a dictionary of unspecific phrases: *friedlicher Ausgleich* (amicable compromise), *zeitgemäße Entwicklung* (timely evolution), *Vereinfachung und Verbesserung* (streamlining and improvement). Vague formulation apart, the 1910 programme was less a thorough reassessment and more a splitting of the difference between existing FrVp, FrVg, and DVP programmes. Again it was characteristic of the desire to avoid genuine ideals debate

[19] BA Berlin, FVP 2, *Konstituirende Generalversammlung des Wahlvereins der Liberalen: 2/3 12/1893 Berlin*, 31.

[20] See e.g. the Eisenach programme, the 1897 Nuremburg agricultural programme and the resolutions of the 1907 party conference reprinted in *Die Freisinnige Volkspartei, ihr Programm und ihre Organisation* (Berlin, 1909), 6–15.

[21] For the numbers (after 1894 barely 200) and occupations of attenders of FrVp conferences see Langewiesche, *Liberalism*, table 12b, 169.

that the programme was drafted by a small group of leaders, the 'Committee of Four' made up of Friedrich Payer, Ernst Müller-Meiningen, Otto Wiemer, and Karl Schrader. The way the programme was handled in practice was further evidence of the triumph of tactics over abstract principle. When Otto Fischbeck complained 'it's really not on, that members of the party override the letter and spirit of the programme',[22] the objection was less to the abandonment of principle, than to the concrete political damage inflicted on the party. Revealingly, Fischbeck placed FVP Landtag deputies' support for taxes on department stores in Hesse and Baden, and for franchise restrictions in Reuß, on a similar level. The former a minor infringement of ideals, but a real threat to party finances, was accorded as much importance as the latter, a blatant contradiction of the central demand in the left liberal programme calling for progressive reform of state franchises. For the Zimmerstaße the important point was not that members adhere faithfully to the party programme, but that their actions avoid embarrassment and a loss of support. Thus the FVP executive committee dismissed the suggestion of Rhineland left liberals that they take action against Richard Eickhoff because he opposed substantial parts of the FVP programme, including ministerial responsibility and labour legislation. What counted, the committee decided, was not Eickhoff's own political beliefs, but his willingness to accept *Fraktion* discipline.[23] Similarly, General Secretary Ißberner assured Max Bahr that opposition to equal franchise in Prussia was no reason to resign from the FVP: the party tolerated a variety of opinion, and the question (the FVP programme's commitment to equal franchise in state elections notwithstanding) was 'hotly disputed' within the party.[24] That left liberals would bend programme and policies according to local interests or popular mood was not merely condoned but expected. There was inherent suspicion of those who stuck to programme or principles regardless. When Fischbeck dismissed Gottfried Traub, the one Berlin left liberal deputy who clearly exceeded the boundaries of party tolerance, as 'an ideologue and bad politician', he clearly considered the two descriptions essentially synonymous.[25]

---

[22] BA Berlin, FVP 36, fo. 160, executive committee, 8 Dec. 1912.
[23] BA Berlin, FVP 36, fos. 81–9, executive committee, 16 Sept. 1911.
[24] BA Berlin, FVP 26, fos. 46–7, Ißberner to Bahr, 6 June 1917.
[25] *Liegnitzer Zeitung* (30 Oct. 1917).

The FVP national programme, therefore, betrayed few signs of regeneration, of a German New Liberalism. This applied both to its content, and the opportunistic way it was treated in practice. The party's 1912 electoral manifesto was similarly long on vague promises of a better future, and short on specific suggestions of how to get there.[26] Moreover, despite the claim to represent the cause of the state against sectional interests, demands were clearly directed towards electorally important groups like peasants, artisans, and white-collar workers. There were few indicators of a new departure which were not either clouded by vague promises, or compromised in practice. Clear signs of a changed attitudes at the national level were largely limited to two areas.

The first was a new emphasis on military and imperial strength. Left liberals could and did point to passages in earlier left liberal programmes stating the need for adequate defence. When the right claimed, for example, that Fortschrittspartei had wanted to dissolve the regular army and rely on a militia, left liberal politicians cited a part of the 1861 programme which proclaimed that 'no sacrifice will ever be too great for the honour and power of our fatherland'.[27] The 1910 programme, however, gave greater weight and prominence to the issue. In 1894 the FrVp's Eisenach programme did not mention military matters until the fifth of six paragraphs. In 1910, by contrast, the FVP programme opened with the declaration: 'the party stands for the defence and strengthening of the Reich'. It also placed more emphasis on technical modernization than on the Richterite (or Gladstonian) concern for military cost-cutting. Secondly, the 1910 programme was more positive towards social ideals and economic intervention. Paragraph six of the FVP programme advocated housing measures, collective wage agreements, arbitration offices, public labour exchanges, more social insurance, and greater rights for employee organizations. The phrase self-help appeared only once, and then as a partial remedy rather than cure-all. In both spheres emphasis was placed increasingly on the state rather than the individual. A powerful state was needed for defence and foreign ideals, while domestically a framework of state regulation and intervention

---

[26] It was perhaps some testimony to the unimpressive content of the two documents that they found a place in the SPD publication *Sünden des Freisinns* (Berlin, [late 1911]), 61–4.

[27] *Die Freisinnige Volkspartei*, 3.

was required to secure effective individual choice.[28] Left liberals were reacting to what they saw as the realities of an imperialist age and a modern industrial state. Their politics reflected not just a heightened abstract appreciation of the value of a strong state, but positive identification with some of the more modern and progressive aspects of the Wilhelmine state. The FVP programme talked as much about 'securing' and 'defending' existing rights and social structures as 'creating' and 'developing' new ones.

Left liberal policy at municipal level provides further evidence of growing support for social welfare and state intervention. Although the tendency in Reich politics was to avoid detailed programmes, and rely on intensive campaigning, personality cult, and the nurturing of constituency interests, the pre-war period increasingly saw the introduction of detailed municipal programmes. As we have seen, the traditional stereotype of non-political councillors standing and acting as individuals had long been displaced. Parts of Germany reached a further turning-point in which ideals was laid out in an explicit electoral programme rather than *Bürgerverein* meetings. The Schöneberg Liberal Municipal Programme of 1907 played a pioneering role. The programme attracted attention not just as one of earliest German non-socialist municipal programmes, but for the range and radicalism of its proposals.[29] A prelude advocating the general aims of social liberalism was followed by proposals for electoral and administrative reform, an active municipal housing and land ideals, progressive direct taxation, levies on capital gains and undeveloped land. The programme advocated educational improvements—new schools, municipal kindergartens, more reading rooms, and popular theatre—and expanded welfare services—municipal midwives, improved orphan care, women social workers—and better public transport with cheap workers' and monthly tickets. This was a document of innovative social liberalism lacking from left liberal national politics, and barely matched by progressive party programmes outside Germany. The programme was so advanced that it

---

[28] This emphasis was particularly evident in the publications of the Nationalverein für das liberale Deutschland, founded in 1907. See *Was ist liberal?* (Munich, 1910) and U. Zeller, *Der Linksliberalismus* (Munich, 1912); cf. W. Link, 'Der Nationalverein für das liberale Deutschland (1907–18)', *Politische Vierteljahresschrift*, 5 (1964), 422–44. Cf. D. Graue, 'Liberalismus als Weltanschauung', *Die Volkspartei* (Apr. 1914).

[29] For copies of the Schöneberg programme see BA Berlin, FVP 35/2, fos. 1–4; or BLPES London, Jastrow collection.

achieved the rare distinction of being retained after the 1918 revolution, with the Schöneberg DDP standing on the same programme in 1920.[30] The Schöneberg programme showed another side to left liberal politics. Its author Walter Voßburg was typical of a small but dynamic group of young left liberal academics whose bold enthusiasm for social and political reform contrasted markedly with the cautious pragmatism of the FVP national leadership. Wilhelm Constaedt, like Voßburg a youthful enthusiast of social liberalism and admirer of Naumann, agreed with Hans Delbrück's description of Richter's successors as 'weak-legged old women' (*schwachbeinige alte Weiber*).[31]

The Schöneberg programme indicated that the radical social liberalism which came to the fore in 1918–19 had a toe-hold in pre-war party politics. It became the basis for left liberal municipal programmes elsewhere. The FVP in Halle, for example, missed out some radical points, notably specific support for equal suffrage and for lifting the requirement that most councillors be property owners. It also limited the demand for free school books to children from poor families. But it copied the Schöneberg introduction and many demands word for word.[32] Similarly, discussion of a common municipal manifesto for Greater Berlin closely followed the Schöneberg programme.[33] Where the left liberals drew up municipal programmes at a regional level, as in Baden, the Palatinate, and Alsace-Lorraine, individual points were sometimes less specific to accommodate a greater range of immediate circumstances.[34] They nevertheless went in the same reforming direction.[35]

Of course the scope for realizing the Schöneberg programme in Wilhelmine Germany was strictly limited. Much of it required the consent of the Conservative-dominated Prussian parliament and executive, something unlikely for the foreseeable future. Nevertheless, it was significant not just that such ideas had traversed the divide between academic thesis and electoral programme, but that New

[30] BLPES London, Jastrow collection.
[31] DSB Berlin, NL Delbrück, Cohnstaedt to Hans Delbrück, 3 May 1908.
[32] BA Berlin, 35/2, fos. 5–6, FVP Halle, draft municipal programme.
[33] BA Berlin, FVP 50, fo. 1, draft municipal programme for Greater Berlin.
[34] See the discussions of the FVP district conferences in Ludwigshaven, 9 Jan. 1913 and 26 Apr. 1914. BA Berlin, FVP 35/2, fos. 7–8.
[35] This applied especially to the political and social reforms put forward by the 1913 Alsace municipal programme. For the complete programme see 'Für die Parteiarbeit', Beilage, *Hilfe* (Dec. 1913), iii–iv.

Liberalism generated a positive response from the electorate. The party made rapid gains in Schöneberg and achieved an absolute majority in the council chamber.[36] Municipal government was, moreover, the one area where the left liberals could implement some practical measures without tangled negotiations with other political parties and the state authorities. By contrast to the national and state legislatures, left liberals, cushioned by franchise restrictions, had an absolute majority of councillors in many cities and large towns.[37] In addition, there was often a strong left liberal presence in the council executive (*Magistrat*). Certainly Wilhelmine mayors saw their primary tasks as administrative rather than political. A common bureaucratic ethos and concern with the interests of the city meant, for example, that successive mayors of Danzig, the Conservative bureaucrat Clemens Delbrück and the left liberal parliamentarian Ehlers, conducted the office in a similar fashion.[38] The same was true in Berlin where the left liberal Martin Kirschner was succeeded in 1912 by Adolf Wermuth, the former treasury secretary of state.[39] But Wilhelmine mayors were not just technocrats. The times when men like Max Forckenbeck or Johannes Miquel could combine mayoral office with a leading role in Liberal parliamentary politics may have passed.[40] The mayoral and party roles were too onerous to carry out side by side. Conrad Haußmann's brother-in-law von Gauß, mayor of Stuttgart and also a DVP deputy in the Württemberg Landtag, claimed to be 'running himself physically into the ground'.[41] But important links remained between mayors and party politics. Some, like the mayor of Hagen, Cuno, who had succeeded Richter as the town's Reichstag member in 1906, sat as deputies, speaking in parliament mainly as specialists on municipal affairs. More often mayors played significant roles behind the scenes and within party organizations. Unlike his left liberal predecessors in Breslau, Franz Ziegler and Forckenbeck, Georg Bender shunned a high-profile role on the national stage. But he was an active proponent of left liberalism within Breslau and Silesia. Bender's chosen role was to promote practical progress in the locality

---

[36] *Hilfe* (1907), 631 and 725; V. Viergutz, *Schöneberg* (Berlin, 1988), 73.

[37] Sheehan, *German Liberalism*, table 15.7, 230.   [38] Delbrück, *Mobilmachung*, 4 ff.

[39] A. Wermuth, *Ein Beamtenleben: Erinnerungen* (Berlin, 1922), 318–20.

[40] J. Sheehan, 'Liberalism and the City in Nineteenth-Century Germany', *Past and Present*, 51 (1971), 116–37.

[41] HSA Stuttgart, NL Haußmann 116, Friedrich Payer to Conrad Haußmann, 10 Jan. 1910; *Frankfurter Zeitung* (20 Jan. 1914).

and to lend support to others as parliamentary candidates.[42] Mayors, as servants of the whole community, avoided excessively partisan behaviour. But this did not mean a position 'above politics'. Mayors were (usually) elected by and responsible to increasingly politicized councillors.[43] The left liberal and SPD council majorities in many German cities inevitably favoured the election of reform-minded mayors. This, in turn, made progressive administrative achievement in smaller municipalities a passport to prestigious positions in the major conurbations. This was the case in the election of Voigt as mayor of Frankfurt in 1912, and Geßler as mayor of Nuremberg in 1913.[44] A left liberal political background was an advantage in much of urban Germany. Mayors like Kirschner, Gauß, Bender, Geßler, Liebetrau (Gotha), Schwander (Strasburg), Dominicus (Schöneberg), and Pohlmann (Kattowitz) were either left liberal supporters or close associates. Similarly, in National Liberal strongholds like Baden and Hessen mayors like Wilckens (Baden Baden) and Dietrich (Konstanz) or Koch-Weser (Kassel) played an influential role in the National Liberal politics, and in Dresden, one of the very few cities where the right were strong, Mayor Otto Beutler was a leading member of the DKP.

The efficiency and range of municipal services which so impressed outside observers of Wilhelmine cities was not, as they sometimes imagined, the product of Prussian bureaucracy.[45] The initiative and finance were mainly local. Moreover, the leading examples usually involved left liberals. Strasburg's housing ideals, under Schwander, was considered the most advanced in Germany. Frankfurt's social services directed by the FVP Landtag deputy Karl Flesch were also widely admired.[46] The Social Democrat Südekum judged municipal health care according to the standards attained by Charlottenburg's

---

[42] See *Festgabe des Vereins für die Geschichte Schlesiens zum siebzigsten Geburtstage seines Ehrenmitglieders Oberbürgermeister a. D. Dr. phil. et med. hc. Georg Bender am 31. Dezember 1918* (Breslau, 1919).   [43] See Lenger, 'Bürgertum und Stadtverwaltung'.

[44] Rolling, 'Liberals, Socialists and City Government', 251; BA Koblenz, NL Geßler 65, fos. 132–42.

[45] Although fallible in detail—the National Liberals did not overshadow left liberals in municipal government (p. 153); it is misleading to state that a Prussian law in 1900 'shifted many average taxpayers from the third voting class into the second' (p. 190); the SPD did not have council majorities in Munich and Strasburg (p. 195)—G. Steinmetz, *Regulating the Social: The Welfare State and Local Politics in Imperial Germany* (Princeton, NJ, 1993) is a valuable case-study of the expanding role of municipal government in social welfare.

[46] BA Koblenz, NL Luppe 54, fos. 65–72, Hermann Luppe, obituary for *Stadtrat* Dr Karl Flesch, 23 Aug. 1915; cf. Palmowski, *Urban Liberalism* and Rolling, 'Liberals, Socialists and City Government', *passim*.

Liberal administration.[47] Certainly, there was substance to SPD claims that their participation in local elections had done much to sharpen the left liberal social conscience. Equally, there was a clear correlation between economic prosperity and progressive local government. It was financially much easier to provide good services in wealthy Charlottenburg than working-class Neu-Kölln.[48] Nor was municipal New Liberalism universal. Berlin was not, as Adolf Wagner suggested, 'the most reactionary city in the world', but nor was it a centrepiece of advanced municipal liberalism.[49] The city's left liberal administration had a deserved reputation for penny-pinching. Königsberg was similarly unenlightened.[50] An FVP official looked on with despair in 1918 as the city starved and froze whilst Körte, its supposedly left liberal Bürgermeister, toured Germany touting support for Fatherland party.[51] In Halle, according to Bürgermeister Rive, Richterite councillors refused even to provide municipal baths. Rive's depiction of himself as the apostle of municipal progress battling against blinkered, penny-pinching councillors should however be treated with caution. As the Halle municipal programme discussed above underlined, left liberal city councillors had themselves taken up social demands in the pre-war period.[52] Yet it was certainly the case that away from the larger towns and cities there was a greater tendency for left liberals to be more concerned about burdens on the taxpayer and property owner than providing new services. This was particularly so in the Prussian eastern provinces. Nevertheless, municipal government remains one of the few areas where Wilhelmine left liberalism had genuine claims to political glory. Like other areas of left liberal politics, however, this sphere was subject to wide regional variations.

Left liberals were, generally, far from being a collection of high-minded political idealists, detached from the real political world. Indeed, a range of contemporaries considered left liberals to be the most opportunistic exponents of vote-catching and exploiters of

---

[47] BA Koblenz, NL Südekum 152c.

[48] F. Esher, *Neukölln* (Berlin, 1988), 52; D. Schütte, *Charlottenburg* (Berlin, 1988), 52.

[49] H. Herzfeld (ed.), *Berlin und die Provinz Brandenburg im 19. und 20. Jahrhundert* (Berlin, 1968), 89–91. For a favourable comparison of Berlin and British municipal government: J. Pollard, *A Study in Municipal Government: The Corporation of Berlin*, 2nd edn. (Edinburgh, 1894).   [50] *Sünden des Freisinns*, 52–7.

[51] BA Berlin, FVP 35/0, fos. 1–4, report by East Prussian party secretary Stark, 15 Jan. 1918.

[52] R. R. Rive, *Lebenerinnerungen eines deutschen Oberbürgermeisters* (Stuttgart, 1960), 75 ff.

popular resentment. To assess how far such comments were justified
we need to look at the background of ideals-making: the set of attitudes, intellectual and popular, which influenced and informed the
conduct of left liberal deputies.

The remarkable thing about assessments of liberal downfall is not
the claims of political opponents. It is the harsh verdicts and sense of
decline expressed by left liberals themselves. Each year a small group
of politicians, ranks progressively thinned by advancing age and SPD
electoral success, gathered by Eduard Lasker's grave in Berlin to
remember what might have been.[53] Unlike England, where statues of
Wilberforce and Peel abounded, Germany had few monuments to successful reforming politicians, though Richter did manage a Berlin
statue and a tower in Hagen to mark four decades of uncompromising
toil. The many monuments in Wilhelmine Germany were erected
above all to Bismarck and the Hohenzollerns, the thwarters of liberalism.[54] The 1860s and 1870s came to be seen, in retrospect, as *the* liberal era in Germany, and the turn of the century became the age of the
liberal obituary. When Ludwig Bamberger (1899), Georg von Siemens
(1901), Rudolf Bennigsen, Heinrich Rickert, Rudolf Virchow (all
1902), Theodor Mommsen (1903), and Eugen Richter (1906) expired,
newspapers announced the death of the cause as well as the individual. By 1909 the mood was even more morbid. Obituaries for Theodor
Barth referred to beliefs already cold in the grave. Barth was, *The
Times*'s Berlin correspondent summed up, 'a conspicuous and constant defender of the doomed causes of German Radicalism and German free trade, the decline of which has been so rapid that he
practically outlived them both'.[55]

In a sense these were indeed doomed causes. There was no prospect
of the German left liberals again being, as in the early 1880s, the
largest party in the Reichstag with over 100 seats, or even regaining
the seventy-six seats held in 1890. Nor was a return to free trade a
practical possibility. Agricultural tariffs had the support of the Conservatives, Centre, and National Liberals, the 1902 majority, and an
increasing number of left liberals, together with maverick Social
Democrats. Such liberal shortcomings must indeed have been striking
to newspaper readers in England, where protectionism remained

---

[53] *Kieler Zeitung* (7 Jan. 1909, morning edn).

[54] On the profusion of Bismarck monuments, over 700 planned and 500 completed by
1914, see *Bismarck: Preußen, Deutschland und Europa* (Berlin, 1990), 472–4.

[55] *The Times* (4 June 1909).

beyond the electoral pale and the Liberals had an overwhelming Commons majority. However, too narrow a focus on German Liberalism as a weakened political force, unable and unwilling to refight the battles of the past, runs the danger of misrepresentation. That 'optimism and sincerity were both unspent' was not purely, as *The Times* correspondent had it, the product of Barth's personality, but of trends evident in German society. Barth's funeral took place in Heidelberg, in *Großblock* Baden. Had he survived till 1912, he would have seen the fulfilment of his prediction that left liberal politicians as a whole would come to accept the political arithmetic that each Social Democrat elected in place of a right wing-deputy increased left liberal influence. Similarly, cremation, the form of funeral chosen by Barth and something taken very seriously by liberals as an issue of scientific progress against hide-bound religious orthodoxy, was becoming increasingly accepted. Even in the Prussian Landtag cremation legislation had passed in 1911 by 176 votes (the FVP, National Liberals, Free Conservatives and thirty-six DKP deputies) to 155 (most of the DKP and all Centre and Polish deputies). And it was not coincidence that the left liberal stronghold of Hagen was in the forefront of Prussian towns pressing successfully for its introduction.[56] Many Conservatives, Heydebrand included, feared that the tide of political, social, and economic development might favour liberal reform in Germany.[57]

The sources of left liberal optimism lay mainly outside politics. The thoughts of many liberal intellectuals on party politics ran parallel to the obituarists. True, they were generally not quite so pessimistic. For them, liberalism was not so much in its death throes, as weakened by prolonged illness. They too, like the obituarists, tended to judge liberalism by two criteria: ability to fulfil a programme of liberal ideals and the individual worth of the leading representatives of the liberal cause.[58] For numerous left liberal figures in Wilhelmine Germany there was a distressing dichotomy between what they thought politics should be about and what political activity actually entailed. For Adolf Heilberg, the leader of the left liberals in Silesia from 1892 to 1918, politics and public life should have been the

[56] *Jauersches Stadtblatt* (20 May 1911).

[57] H. Pachnicke, *Führende Männer im alten und neuen Reich* (Berlin, n.d.), 63.

[58] For a broader exploration of the sense of living in an era of epigoni, of lesser figures, see M. Doerry, *Übergangsmenschen: Die Mentalität der Wilhelminer und die Krise des Kaiserreichs* (Weinheim, 1986).

rational triumph of great men and fine principles. The reality was different: countless election meetings, smoke-filled rooms, and unpalatable compromise: 'A great deal of "electoral politics" was practised everywhere; if not sacrificed then the great principles were more or less adapted to vote catching (*Stimmenfang*) on a grand and small scale. And this sort of politics led to cliques and favouritism (*Klüngel-Wirtschaft*) . . .'[59]

Similarly, to Ludwig Heilbrunn, the diaries of his fellow Frankfurt left liberal Carl Funck seemed to reflect a grander liberal age of the past. Again it was personality which counted: 'the best names of liberalism . . . Eugen Richter, Ludwig Bamberger, Heinrich Rickert, Freiherr von Stauffenberg, Albert Hänel, Virchow, Forckenbeck, Siemens, Schrader, Bunsen' stood in the party's ranks.[60] By contrast, when Heilbrunn succeeded Funck in 1913 as a Frankfurt Landtag deputy, he found the left liberal *Fraktion* full of second-raters politically and socially: unimaginative minor officials, elementary-school teachers, artisans, and other interest-group representatives.[61]

Self-criticism was, thus, a liberal trait. There was much justification to Friedrich Naumann's comment that liberalism was the only political force in Germany criticized as much by friends as opponents.[62] Much liberal self-criticism was undoubtedly merited. However, its underlying premiss, that politics should amount to a civilized conflict of ideals conducted by great men, was unworldly. Interest representation, use of patronage, addressing popular instincts, attempting to manipulate public opinion, these were all an inevitable part of politics in a modern, industrial society whether the political system was liberal or authoritarian. Liberal 'failures' in Germany derived to a significant extent not from a peculiar moral bankruptcy or political, economic, and social misdevelopment, but from unrealistic ideals. The marginalizing of pacifism, for example, provides an instructive insight into the nationalistic chauvinism of Wilhelmine Germany.[63] However, categorizing republicans and pacifists, men like Ludwig Quidde, Walther

---

[59] Heilberg, 'Erinnerungen', 291.

[60] L. Heilbrunn, Introduction to C. Funck, *Lebenserinnerungen* (Frankfurt am Main, 1921), 8; cf. A. Stein, *Es war alles ganz Anders: Aus der Werkstätte eines politischen Journalisten* (Frankfurt am Main, 1922), 57.

[61] StA Frankfurt, NL Heilbrunn, 'Eine Lebensskizze 1870–1936', typed MS., fo. 157.

[62] The habit was also well-ingrained. See e.g. H. Baumgarten, 'Der deutsche Liberalismus: Eine Selbstkritik', *Preussische Jahrbücher*, 18 (1866), 455–517 and 575–628.

[63] R. Chickering, *Imperial Germany and a World without War: The Peace Movement and German Society, 1892–1914* (Princeton, NJ, 1975).

Schücking, and Hellmut von Gerlach, as the only real liberals, and interpreting their marginalization as proof of the Kaiserreich's irredeemably illiberal character is more useful as a moral than a historical exercise. Pacifism admittedly attracted more support and less opposition in England, the idealized object of comparison, but even there it was a minority movement with relatively little influence. True, England had a liberal parliamentary government in the pre-war period, but it was not the counterparts of Quidde, Schücking, and Gerlach who filled the Cabinet. These were men magnetically attracted to minority causes, predestined to the role of the political outsider. They lacked both the temperament and capacity for political office-holding. Had they lived in England, France, or America, rather than Wilhelmine Germany, they might have found themselves with a seat in parliament, but would have remained in all probability critics of the political establishment without decisive influence.

Theodor Barth imagined playing the German Cobden to Caprivi's Peel. The dream, as Barth envisaged it, was cruelly dashed.[64] The analogy becomes more plausible, if the comparison is drawn with Cobden's real role in British politics, as opposed to what Barth imagined it to be. In several respects Barth was the German Cobden. Both men were forceful critics of the worldly imperfections of government and people. Few liberal condemnations of the indifference of the German *Bürgertum* matched the verbal force of Cobden's denunciation of the English as 'a servile, aristocracy-loving, lord-ridden people', mesmorized by 'armorial hocus-pocus, primogeniture, and pageantry'. Both were unceasing in the causes of free trade and international understanding. If the message was comparable, so was the political position it brought its bearer. Both men were consigned, beyond the pale of government office, to a missionary role in the press and on the podium. The message brought devoted admirers, but also mutual incomprehension between the prophets of liberal idealism and the indifferent majority.[65]

Of course, important liberal aspirations were thwarted in Germany by a reactionary political system. This applied, above all, to the Prussian state apparatus, which remained both an active opponent of reform and an impassive monument to an unfulfilled liberal political

---

[64] Wegner, *Theodor Barth*; G. Daniels, *Individium und Gemeinschaft bei Theodor Barth und Friedrich Naumann* (Hamburg, 1932), 3–61.

[65] N. Edsall, *Richard Cobden: Independent Radical* (Cambridge, Mass., 1987); W. Hinde, *Richard Cobden: A Victorian Outsider* (New Haven, Conn., 1987).

agenda. However, some of the features of German politics most dis-
liked by liberal critics were at least as prevalent in Western parliamentary and presidential systems. Significantly, it was a phrase borrowed
from America, 'machine politics', which best summed up all that
these liberal critics most despised in public life.[66] Indeed, liberal
idealists like Heilberg began to see that such features were a universal
characteristic of mass politics: 'We slowly realized . . . that [politics]
do not turn on education, on teaching and knowledge. But that irrational elements, unconscious and subconscious feelings, guide and
determine human action as much as the intellect. Maybe even more—
amongst the great mass [of people] definitely in greater measure.'[67]

This recognition led mainly to disillusion rather than pragmatic
reassessment. However, nostalgia and the note of despair about the
state of politics should not be given undue significance. It was partly
an ageing generation holding fond memories of the past. Nor should
the peculiarly strong effect of later events on retrospective accounts be
overlooked. It was an almost impossible task for left liberals writing in
the 1920s and later to provide an account of pre-war politics
uncoloured by a war of unparalleled magnitude and subsequent political, economic, and social turmoil. A sense of failure and foreboding,
for example, was the inevitable leitmotiv for the private memoirs of
Georg Gothein and Adolf Heilberg written in the 1930s. Both men
had seen their causes and values completely rejected and were subject
to political and racial persecution.[68] The post-1918 impression of disillusionment was often greater than the pre-war reality.

We should also take care with the many contemporary statements of
despair. Not surprisingly, given the fluctuations of political fortune,
there were switches of mood between pessimism and optimism. Men
like Eugen Katz and Wilhelm Ohr interspersed elegiac testimonies to
the death and futility of left liberalism with optimistic reports of
revival and regeneration.[69] For the majority of left liberal activists, if
not intellectual onlookers, hope usually triumphed over adversity.

---

[66] See e.g. the public dispute between Barth and Julius Kopsch in BA Berlin,
Reichslandbund 21, fos. 48–184, personalia Theodor Barth; or Max Weber's condemnation
of American-style machine politics in M. R. Lepsius and W. J. Mommsen (eds.), *Max Weber
Gesamtausgabe: Max Weber Briefe 1906–1908* (Tübingen, 1990), iii. 640.

[67] Heilberg, 'Erinnerungen', 290.

[68] BA Koblenz, NL Gothein 12 and 14; Heilberg, 'Erinnerungen', 289–97.

[69] See Katz's letters to Brentano in BA Koblenz, NL Brentano 32 (esp. 30 Dec. 1903,
10 May 1905, 2 Nov. 1905, 13 June 1906 and 15 Apr. 1907); and BA Berlin, NL Wilhelm
Ohr 1–6; and the correspondence between Ohr and Martin Rade in UB Marburg, NL Rade.

With both Barth and Naumann all the practical set-backs were insufficient to destroy confidence in ultimate victory. Wilhelmine left liberals retained a markedly more optimistic view of Germany's future than did the political right. This did not mean, however, that they wished to forgo the pleasure of evoking a golden past. The story of left liberal decline became a comforting memory, the artificial tale of a Liberalism 'which lives off memories, where they gather for 25th and 50th anniversaries and say: what idealists we were and what an ideal age it was!'[70] Moreover, it was perhaps a reflection of the party's innate Protestantism, but many left liberals liked to see themselves as individuals suffering for the cause. This was true not just of the educated middle class leaders, but men like Fiedler, a railway worker in Gießen, and Georg Semmelroth, a Wetzlar metal-worker.[71] Theodor Barth offered delegates to the 1897 Schleswig-Holstein party conference the prospect of blood, sweat, and tears: 'Politics . . . is no business which you can live off—definitely not if you belong to a left liberal party. You can expect no material advantages, only material sacrifices . . .'.[72] Left liberals sent each other printed postcards bearing a sombre-looking Naumann and a quotation from his *Demokratie und Kaisertum* describing politics as 'no mere Sunday pastime', but a vital, earnest national task.[73]

The extent of genuine left liberal disillusionment should not, therefore, be exaggerated. Even amongst left liberals whose earlier aspirations had been dashed, a sense of public duty sustained active political involvement. The point is illustrated most prominently by Karl Schrader's political career. Though privately pessimistic, and unfairly portrayed in the press as a relic from the Crown Prince era, Schrader's parliamentary career continued to the age of 77, a year before his death in 1913. He regularly worked a thirteen-hour day, a physical burden which caused him to collapse in the Reichstag in 1909.[74] Besides a full involvement in Reichstag debates and committees, Schrader was also responsible for the running of the FrVg until the 1910 merger. He represented the party in the 'Committee of Four',

[70] F. Naumann, 'Der Niedergang des Liberalismus', Gall and Koch (eds.), *Der europäische Liberalismus*, iv. 254.

[71] See Martin Rade's correspondence, Fiedler and Semmelroth in UB Marburg, NL Rade.

[72] LA Schleswig 301, Oberpräsidium 8087, *Kieler Zeitung* (4 Oct. 1897).

[73] 'Politik ist kein blosses Sonntagsvergnügen, sondern eine nationale Arbeit, von der Leben und Streben des Volkes abhängt.' See the collection of Naumann postcards in SA Hamburg, NL Carl Petersen L50.   [74] *Neue Konstanzer Abendzeitung* (22 Mar. 1909).

chaired executive committee meetings, supervised party headquarters in Berlin, and deputized when the general secretary was laid low by a bad back or left the capital for the summer vacation.[75] Finally, Schrader's liberal commitment extended beyond party politics to charitable and church causes.[76]

This deep attachment to politics and public life was shared by others. Supporters and opponents alike acknowledged the intensity of Theodor Barth's devotion to politics. Even his daughter's engagement was seen by Barth in a political light. Fortunately, the prospective son-in-law, 'not just a very promising academic, but also a good Democrat despite having three Prussian *Geheimräte* as uncles', accorded perfectly with left liberal values.[77] Georg Gothein was involved in discussion about the Reichstag committee on shipping duties even amidst the trauma of his wife's premature death.[78] Left liberals further down the social and political hierarchy displayed similar attitudes. The Badenese left liberal Oskar Muser, making an unexpected return to the public podium at the age of 78, conveyed to the audience not only trenchant views on education, but also 'how this man was still seized by a passion for politics (and philosophy), and with what ceaseless endeavour and vigour he continued to follow political events and intellectual developments'.[79] Amongst vital background figures who co-ordinated left liberal activity at local level, there were many like Julius Rothenberger, a retired Frankfurt bank official, 'who just lived for politics'.[80] This passion for public life cushioned left liberals against political disappointments and made them indomitable campaigners.

It is also important in understanding left liberals to realize that the dissatisfaction shown at the state of domestic politics was untypical of their attitudes towards other aspects of Wilhelmine Germany. Left liberal critics may have abhorred political machines, but they admired machinery in the workplace, whether it be the latest in technology and

---

[75] See the reports from General Secretary Weinhausen to Schrader in SA Wolfenbüttel, NL Schrader; and Weinhausen's obituary of Schrader in *Hilfe* (8 May 1913), 289.

[76] The most important of Schrader's many involvements outside party politics was as a promoter of liberal Protestantism as chairman of the Deutscher Protestantenverein. See Hubinger, *Kulturprotestantismus*; and *Lexikon*, ii. 251–7.

[77] HSA Stuttgart, NL Haußmann 114, Theodor Barth to Conrad Haußmann, 17 Apr. 1906.

[78] BA Koblenz, NL Gothein 9, Karl Schrader to Georg Gothein, 8 Feb. 1911.

[79] GLA Karlsruhe, NL Muser 5, *Frankfurter Zeitung* (27 Apr. 1930).

[80] BA Koblenz, NL Luppe 8, fo. 167.

scale in the chemical industry or the simple electric motor in the arti-san's workshop.[81] Certainly, admiration for German technological achievement was no respecter of political boundaries. The Pan-German Heinrich Claß was as wildly enthusiastic about Zeppelins as the radical democrat Richard Gaedke.[82] Nevertheless, left liberal politicians, newspapers, and supporters remained the most ardent worshippers of technology and the most unambiguous supporters of an industrial market economy. Admittedly, they saw pitfalls in eco-nomic development. No political group could be more aware of the electoral drawbacks of industrialization than left liberals who had been supplanted by the SPD in a succession of urban Reichstag seats in the 1880s and 1890s. Equally, the everyday mundane monotony of the *Mietskaserne* (barrack block tenement) was an anathema to the val-ues of liberal individualism. However, liberals in other countries showed a similar concern about the dark side of industrialization. Indeed, a theme such as physical degeneration proved more worrying to liberals in Edwardian England than in Wilhelmine Germany.[83] The writings of Friedrich Naumann, for instance, displayed a concern for urban social problems and a distaste for the uniformity and crudity of mass culture in an age of the cheap souvenir, the mass-circulation newspaper, the 'strictly realistic' false moustache, and the gradual spread of undemanding popular fare from the printed page to the sil-ver screen.[84] Nevertheless, in Naumann's optimistic world, material problems could be cured by progressive social ideals and the imper-fections of popular culture erased by education. For Naumann and others the virtues of modernity far outweighed the drawbacks. Indeed, Naumann's enthusiasm for technology spilt over from the narrowly economic to the political and social. Most important was the belief that economic and national strength were inextricably linked, but technological and mechanical allusions were to be found through-out Naumann's writings.[85]

Enthusiasm for technology and material progress prevailed even where initial indicators seemed to point in an opposite direction. The

---

[81] F. Naumann, *Werke* (6 vols.; Cologne and Opladen, 1964–9), ii. 414–19, vi. 351–451; L. Frank, *Liberalismus und Mittelstand* (Heilbronn, n.d.).

[82] H. Claß, *Wider den Strom* (Leipzig, 1932), 121–2; *Liegnitzer Anzeiger* (1 Sept. 1909, speech by Gaedke in Breslau (28 Aug. 1909).

[83] G. R. Searle, *The Quest for National Efficiency 1899–1914* (Oxford, 1971).

[84] 'Das Wachstum der Großstädte', *Die Nation* (6 Jan. 1906).

[85] Naumann, *Werke*, esp. ii. 407–39; vi. 351–451.

Badenese left liberal Hermann Hummel, for example, frequently expressed admiration for the peasant lifestyle of his grandfather. However, this was a mixture of affectation and calculated appeal to rural constituents.[86] In reality, Hummel, who moved from teaching science in a Karlsruhe secondary school to the boardroom of IG Farben, was anything but an opponent of technological advance and industrial growth.[87] Similarly, urgent demands by Max Weber and Schulze-Gaevernitz for a 'living wall of German peasants in the East' reflected a stance which was anti-Slav and anti-Junker rather than anti-industrial.[88] Doubtless, they shared the notion of the sturdy peasant as ideal fighting material, but unlike Prussian Conservatives their ideal peasant was well-educated, well-versed in modern farming methods, and economically, socially, and politically independent from large estate owners.

Pride in middle-class economic diligence was matched by admiration for bourgeois achievement in the cultural sphere. Left liberals disapproved of limits on academic freedom, anti-Semitism, duelling, and other archaic customs in German universities, but they proudly believed that German institutes of learning were at least a match for counterparts in other civilized nations (*Kulturnationen*). For them politics was letting the side down. They saw a nation scaling the summits of economic progress and scientific and artistic achievement, but languishing in the foothills of political backwardness. Politics marked the Achilles' heel of the German state in general and the liberal bourgeoisie in particular. Not only were achievements in the economy and society adjudged to have outstripped those in politics, but the actors on the political stage appeared markedly inferior. In part, this was a peculiarity of the political spotlight. Elsewhere attention was drawn to the outstanding and successful. Countless mediocre industrialists and intellectuals were ignored, while the public spotlight fell on major figures: business moguls like Krupp, Ballin, and Rathenau or Nobel-prize-winning intellectuals like Mommsen, Virchow, and Hauptmann. The political spotlight was more penetrating,

---

[86] SA Darmstadt, NL Hummel, Badenese Landtag elections, 1909 and 1913.

[87] See H. Hummel, *Vermischte politische und wirtschaftliche Aufsätze aus den letzten Jahren: (1925–32)* (Mannheim, 1935).

[88] *Breslauer Zeitung*, 213 (24 Mar. 1912); M. Weber, 'Der Nationalstaat und die Volkswirtschaftspolitik', repr. in Gall and Koch (eds.), *Der europäische Liberalismus*, iii. 195–219; Martin Riesebrodt (ed.), *Max Weber Gesamtausgabe*, i/3 (Tübingen, 1984), 926–9; BA Berlin, NL Naumann 6, fo. 26, Naumann to Hugo Erdmann, 22 Apr. 1914.

exposing the shortcomings of mediocre deputies. In part this set of attitudes led to a criticism of the government and the political system as a whole. However, it also directed criticism towards the force that had failed to fulfil its appointed role: Liberal party politics.

The terms of reference may have been unfair and elision of liberal and bourgeois theoretically unsound.[89] The credit claimed for developments and achievements outside the political arena frequently reflected faith rather than reality. There was not much about Graf Zeppelin, for example, which was liberal or bourgeois. Similarly, the view of politics was unrealistic. Little allowance was made for the fact that, as Friedrich Payer was fond of repeating, to follow a grand political scheme was far easier for political philosophers or editorial writers than for party leaders.[90] But this had little effect on the attitudes of figures like Weber, Brentano, and Dernburg. Knowledge about actual workings of mass politics had curiously little effect on the values by which they judged left liberal party politics. They continued to crave politics in the style of *Die Nation* in the age of the *General-Advertiser*.

Also left out of account were the much greater difficulties faced by liberals competing in the political rather than the economic or cultural market-place. Political parties had to go for market share. Reichstag deputies needed, at least in the run-offs, majority support amongst over 80 per cent of adult males in a constituency. Anything less meant failure. By contrast, markets elsewhere were differentiated. Unlike political parties, newspaper owners, manufacturers, and artists were not compelled to compete in the popular market. Economic competition was more akin to the municipal than the Reichstag franchise: the support of the urban well-to-do counted for far more than that of the factory worker, artisan, or small shopkeeper. It was no coincidence that the *Vossische Zeitung*, with its largely bourgeois Berlin-based readership, carried the most advertising of any German newspaper. Good money was to be made from fashionable or quality products for the prosperous minority. Left liberal Reichstag deputies in the early 1880s became known as 'The Golden Hundred and Ten', a reference to the upmarket gents outfitters in the Leipziger Straße. The politicians were unable to sustain either the quantitative or qualitative comparison. Left liberal numbers dropped to seventy-four in 1884

[89] Blackbourn and Eley, *Peculiarities*, 76–90.
[90] GLA Karlsruhe, NL Muser 8, Payer to Oskar Muser, 29 May 1910 and 20 June 1912; BA Koblenz, NL Goetz 227, Payer to Wilhelm Heile, 30 Aug. 1912 (copy).

and thirty-two in 1887, and social standing lessened as the Secessionists, the friends of the Crown Prince, drifted out of parliamentary politics. But the outfitters blossomed, as did others catering for the prosperous middle classes. This applied to cultural as well as material goods. New money in Wilhelmine Germany was almost as rapacious in its quest for modern art and drama as for old estates and titles.[91] Riches and critical acclaim, not Bohemian poverty, greeted the dramatist Gerhart Hauptmann or the artist Max Liebermann.[92]

Liberals faced much greater outside competition in the political rather than the economic and social arena. The right's resort to political weapons for economic sustenance was eloquent testimony to an inability to compete directly in the economic sphere. Moreover, the partial successes they achieved here—agricultural tariffs, stock-exchange restrictions, and *Mittelstand* legislation—were insufficient to turn the economic and social tide. Landowners had to play by the capitalist rules: to adapt to the market, to speculate on the stock exchange, to establish manufacturing on their estates, or to marry money. And even this was insufficient, in most cases, to avert relative economic decline.[93]

For left liberal economic writers the more significant challenge to capitalism came from the left. The right offered only backwardness and self-interest. Bamberger's comment, 'Facts the gentlemen opposite cannot prove, they call practice; and facts they cannot refute they call theory',[94] typified the condescension shown towards the right's attempts at economic ideals. Socialism at least offered an intellectual alternative, and the trade union movement a beguiling practical economic force. Liberal political economists took up intellectual debate with Marxist theory and investigation of the trade unions' economic and social role with enthusiasm. Nevertheless, they felt confident that prolonged expansion and increasing prosperity undermined Marxist economic theory and

---

[91] On the latter, H. Rosenberg, 'Die Pseudodemokratisierung der Rittergutsbesitzerklasse' in idem, *Machteliten und Wirtschaftskonjunkturen: Studien zur neueren deutschen Sozial- und Wirtschaftsgeschichte* (Göttingen, 1978), 83–101.

[92] E. Friedegg, *Millionen und Millionäre: Wie die Riesen- Vermögen entstehen* (Berlin and Charlottenburg, 1914), 156 and 161.

[93] Weber, 'Wahlrecht und Demokratie', 310. On German agriculture see J. A. Perkins, 'The Agricultural Revolution in Germany, 1850–1914', *Journal of European Economic History*, 10 (1981), 71–118; and 'Dualism in German Agrarian Historiography', *Comparative Studies in Society and History*, 28 (1986), 287–306.   [94] Bonn, *Wandering Scholar*, 46.

that trade union growth accompanied rather than endangered the development of the capitalist economy.[95]

The challenge in the cultural sphere appeared even weaker. The right's adamant antediluvianism was confirmed by the eclipse of any attempt, like Adolf Grabowsky's 'cultural Conservatism', to provide a modern image more acceptable to public opinion outside the East Elbian estates.[96] The cry of despair from Junker or Catholic clerics about the state of German cultural life was, to liberal ears, welcome confirmation of their own achievements. Despite restrictions, German society provided an effective framework for artistic and academic expression. The state might prevent *Simplicissimus* being read in the barracks or sold in Prussian station bookshops, but it could not suppress publication, at least in peacetime. On the contrary, ham-fisted acts of repression only filled columns and increased readership.[97] Attempts to impose more restrictions like the *Umsturzvorlage* (Anti-Revolution Bill) and *Lex Heinze* were defeated or emasculated by the Reichstag.[98] Even the Kaiser came round to the view that a relatively free press was a necessary part of modern society.[99]

The left, liberal and Social Democratic, found co-operation easier to achieve in *Kulturpolitik* than in any other area of politics; unsurprisingly, for the Social Democratic stance on cultural issues was essentially a more robust version of bourgeois liberalism. The size and number of auxiliary socialist organizations in Wilhelmine Germany was impressive, but also demonstrated the degree to which workers accepted the norms of bourgeois culture.[100] The similarities and shared cultural assumptions with corresponding bodies in non-socialist associational life were readily apparent. Despite the hue and

[95] The economic journal edited by Max Broemel, *Volkswirtschaftliche Zeitfragen*, provides a good cross-section of left liberal economic thinking. Left liberals also contributed to the voluminous debates and publications of the *Verein für Sozialpolitik*. The key figure of Lujo Brentano is assessed in Sheehan, *Career of Lujo Brentano*.

[96] Retallack, *Notables*, 184.

[97] A. T. Allen, *Satire and Society in Wilhelmine Germany: Kladderadatsch and Simplicissimus, 1890–1914* (Lexington, Mass., 1984), 3, and 41–3.

[98] E. L. Turk, 'German Liberals and the Genesis of the Association Law of 1908', in Jarausch and Jones (eds.), *In Search of a Liberal Germany*, 243–52.

[99] H. Pogge von Strandmann and I. Geiß, *Die Erforderlichkeit des Unmöglichen* (Frankfurt am Main, 1965), 39.

[100] Social Democrats showed the same 'prounced respect for scientific learning' as left liberals. H.-C. Schröder, *Sozialismus und Imperialismus: Die Auseinandersetzung der deutschen Sozialdemokratie mit dem Imperialismusproblem und der 'Weltpolitik' vor 1914*, 2nd edn. (Bonn, 1975), 183.

cry about indoctrination, the activity and organization of socialist gymnastic clubs, for example, followed much the same pattern as their bourgeois equivalents. And while the establishment of peoples' theatres (*Volksbühnen*) represented emancipation from progressive bourgeois theatre in terms of organization, their activities underlined continued artistic indebtedness and the common commitment to modernity and the importance of the arts.[101] Bourgeois society and the labour movement both looked to merit and achievement as the basis of authority. The biblical quotation 'Seest thou a man diligent in business? He shall stand before kings' was gospel to Wilhelmine left liberals, and its meritocratic implications were shared by Social Democrats.

Identification with the nation-state, market economy, artistic and scientific achievement, urban society, municipal government, and other aspects of Wilhelmine Germany was crucial to the character of left liberalism. Even the more radical and theoretically inclined of left liberals neither offered nor desired a comprehensive alternative to the Wilhelmine state. Certainly, most nineteenth-century German achievements were claimed for liberalism and the *Bürgertum*, and almost all the shortcomings laid at the Junkers' door. Nothing illustrated the left liberal view of German history better than its unreserved assessment of Stein and Hardenberg as heroic representatives of liberalism and the *Bürgertum*.[102] Yet the state remained eminently redeemable despite the links with Junkerdom. The highest cause, in left liberal eyes, was to abolish archaic privilege, set the people free, and, as a result, strengthen the state. With Bismarck, memories were too recent and the cup of illiberal measures too full for liberal canonization. Nevertheless, the creation of a strong national state against Prussian Conservative opposition was recognized as a monumental achievement. Left liberals were deeply ambivalent towards the 'bitter sweet apple' of Bismarck's work.[103] The perception of German

---

[101] In line with the argument presented here: Saldern, *Auf dem Wege zum Arbeiter-Reformismus*, 130–201; W. J. Mommsen, *Der autoritäre Nationalstaat: Verfassung, Gesellschaft und Kultur des deutschen Kaiserreiches* (Frankfurt am Main, 1990), 262 ff. By contrast, Lidtke, *The Alternative Culture*, and R. J. Evans (ed.), *Kneipengespräche im Kaiserreich: Die Stimmungsberichte der Hamburger Politischen Polizei, 1892–1914* (Reinbek, 1989) argue that revolutionary language, e.g. in song texts, reflected participants' fundamental attitudes.

[102] Portraits of the two men adorned the frontispiece of O. Klein-Hattingen, *Die Geschichte des deutschen Liberalismus* (2 vols.; Schöneberg, 1911–12).

[103] BA Koblenz, NL Payer 10, fo. 69, H. Simon, *Frankfurter Zeitung*, to Payer, 24 Mar. 1915.

success in the economic, social, and cultural areas had the effect of binding left liberals to the existing state, even though they maintained that progress had often been achieved despite rather than because of state ideals. If the state had failed to fulfil its proper role as the architect of social, economic, and cultural progress, it was at least seen as its defender. It was obvious from Reichstag election results that parliamentarization was unlikely to produce liberal government. The Hertling government in Bavaria provided a particularly unwelcome practical demonstration of liberal fears.[104] Gradual liberalization of the existing state was an increasingly attractive alternative. A genuinely non-political civil service open to talent was a more appealing prospect than one subject to party-political patronage. Similarly, liberal *Rechtsstaat* concepts included a strong element of insulation from transient parliamentary majorities and populist influence. Moreover, there were obvious problems in adopting party government in the English manner. The dream of a ministry of all the talents was hardly to be achieved from a Reichstag of bickering parties and mediocre politicians. Certainly, formal constitutional change to create a proper Reich cabinet collectively responsible to the Reichstag was desired. It would improve accountability and decision-making in the executive and induce more scrupulous and responsible behaviour on the part of the political parties. However, the value of a strong executive capable of taking decisive and, where necessary, unpopular action was appreciated, as was the ability to bring in experts from outside the political arena. This was reflected in the enthusiasm which greeted Dernburg's appointment as colonial secretary in 1906. Although ideological obeisances to the *Volk* continued, attitudes towards democracy were ambivalent and uneasy. The great problem for the left liberals about the state political machine was not that it was undemocratic, but that it was being run in the wrong way by the wrong people. If it came into hands which were modern, intelligent, and liberal rather than archaic, incompetent, and conservative, then the problems of Wilhelmine Germany could, it was thought, easily be mastered.

Left liberalism was, therefore, far removed from being a force of outright opposition. In important areas left liberals saw themselves as defenders of the status quo. Support for the existing social and

---

[104] For the alarm engendered by clerical influence in South Germany see Ch. 7 below. For the less dramatic reality see K. Möckl, *Die Prinzregentenzeit: Gesellschaft und Politik während der Ära des Prinzregenten Luitpold in Bayern* (Munich and Vienna, 1972).

economic order was consistently emphasized.[105] In foreign policy
there was little evidence of an alternative concept even before the left
liberals attracted the wartime description of the party of Bethmann
Hollweg *sans phrase*. Left liberalism was avowedly evolutionary rather
than revolutionary, and its reforming intentions were largely limited
to domestic political renewal. The essential aim was a modern political system to complement economic, social, and martial modernity.
As Regina Gottschalk has rightly emphasized: 'Not an overthrow, but
a strengthening of the existing state through modernization was the
aim of the left liberal reform movement.'[106] Liberal intellectual critics
did not greatly mind a party of generals without soldiers. It was the
dubious quality of the officer corps which they found particularly
objectionable. As Theodor Vogelstein complained, far too often the
left liberal standard-bearer was 'the parish-pump (*Bezirksverein*)
politician, the petty agitator: above all, the man just put up because,
lacking outstanding personality, he had the best chance in adverse
run-off conditions'.[107]

The description of officers without foot soldiers fitted the
National-Social Association far better than the FrVp or FVP. The
Spießbürger at the provincial *Stammtisch* was a far more representative
left liberal figure than the radical intellectual. Even the ascendancy
which the collapse of the Kaiserreich gave the radical intellectual
wing of left liberalism proved short-lived. The old organizations and
local leaders were needed to fight impending elections.[108] The liberal
academic critique, however, amounted to more than the voice of an
ineffective, naïvely idealistic minority. In important areas it represented, in a more refined and intellectually coherent form, popular left
liberal attitudes. The social circles in which Theodor Wolff moved
may have been strictly restricted, but the *Berliner Tageblatt* had a circulation of 230,000. Hellmut von Gerlach propounded a demagogic
version of the intellectual critique to the mass readership of the *Welt
am Montag* and to the peasants in the Marburg countryside. Above
all, it was Friedrich Naumann who conveyed a bowdlerized form of
liberal intellectual thinking to a mass left liberal audience.

[105] J. de Grandvilliers, *Essai sur le Libéralisme Allemand* (Paris, 1914), 345, 355.

[106] R. Gottschalk, *Die Linksliberalen zwischen Kaiserreich und Weimarer Republik: Von der
Julikrise 1917 bis zum Bruch der Weimarer Koalition im Juli 1919* (Mainz, 1969), 50.

[107] BA Koblenz, NL Brentano, 63, fo. 55, Theodor Vogelstein to August Stein, 19 Oct.
1918 (copy).

[108] Albertin, *Liberalismus*; Jones, *German Liberalism*, 15–22; Robson, 'Left Liberalism',
410 ff.

Popular receptiveness had two main causes. One was that liberals, continual references to the *Volk* notwithstanding, looked up for guidance. This was not just Prussian conditioning to authority, though it was partly that. There was widespread liberal expectation, in Gladstonian Britain as much as Wilhelmine Germany, that popular will was expressed through great men.[109] The second and more important reason was a substantial overlap between intellectual and popular attitudes. The stance of the left liberal rank and file towards German economic, technological, and cultural achievements was as positive as that of the intellectuals. The left liberal appeal was to people who thought they were capable of standing on their own feet in a modern and fair society. The craftsmen who voted left liberal in Sorau and Greifswald seconded Gothein's opinion that the only *Mittelstandspolitik* they needed were customers who appreciated good workmanship and paid in cash.[110]

Popular support for left liberal aims was evident, above all, in the cultural sphere. Petty-bourgeois and working-class left liberals as much as doctors and lawyers shared a passion for education. The prizes in a membership recruitment competition for the Reich Association of Liberal Workers and Clerks were the works of Heine and Schiller.[111] The debate about artistic and religious freedom was not confined to small intellectual groups and high-brow newspapers. Thousands attended public meetings held by the Goethe-Bund or by disciplined Protestant clergymen.[112] Such issues had the power to mobilize: Fischbeck adjudged 'cultural questions the only thing which could stir up the Prussian people', and the sustained press and public response to the action taken by the conservative church authorities, the Evangelischer Oberkirchenrat, against liberal clergymen Carl Jatho and Gottfried Traub in 1911–12 underlined Fischbeck's point.[113] Such campaigns were also a unifying force. Antipathy towards political Catholicism became an increasingly intense and central theme of left liberal politics. Though most obvious in everyday

---

[109] For the burning and rather misplaced grassroots faith in Gladstone, see Vincent, *Formation of the British Liberal Party*, 233–4.

[110] BA Koblenz, NL Gothein 14, fos. 103–4. Cf. H. Pachnicke, *Liberalismus als Kulturpolitik* (Berlin, 1907), 56–7.

[111] BA Koblenz, NL Erkelenz 117, *Mitteilungen des Reichsvereins der liberalen Arbeiter und Angestellten* (1 June 1914).

[112] H. von Bassi, *Otto Baumgarten: Ein 'moderner Theologe' im Kaiserreich und in der Weimarer Rebublik* (Frankfurt am Main, 1988), 90 ff.; DSB Berlin, NL Adolf Harnack 24 and 25; and Nagel, *Martin Rade*. [113] BA Berlin, FVP 36, fo. 297.

campaigning and press comment, increased hostility was also reflected
in the support given by the great majority of FVP deputies after 1912
to the retention of §1 of the Jesuit law, a paragraph they had previously opposed on civil rights' grounds.[114] Such virulent opposition to
political (and not just political) Catholicism might appear negative and
hysterical in retrospect, but it was a major theme which united both
left and right within left liberalism. There was almost universal agreement 'that the Centre, because of its unscrupulous mixing of religion
and politics, and because of its casual lack of principle, is not only the
most unpleasant, but the most dangerous apparition in our party life'.
These words of a Richterite journalist Scherek were echoed by the
more progressive Georg Gothein. The radical liberal Minna Cauer
equally looked on political Catholicism as a 'sickening caricature of
Christianity' and its followers as 'a dumb herd'.[115] Centre politicians
and priests were constant targets for critics, satirists, and cartoonists.
The liberal satirical journals *Kladderadatsch* and *Simplicissimus* even
published special anti-Centre compilations.[116] The partial *rapprochement* between executive and political Catholicism did nothing to
defuse *Kulturkampf* passions in society. On the contrary, the Centre
party's influential position in the Reichstag and Landtag only deepened Protestant resentment. And, given the right and the National
Liberal party's greater preparedness to co-operate with the Centre in
legislation, it allowed left liberals to present themselves as the only
true opponents of political Catholicism. The same uncompromising
appearance was repeated at local level. The Düsseldorf left liberal
Heinz Potthoff, for example, beseeched councillors to reject introducing nuns as hospital nurses claiming that this, like confessional education, 'would surrender the souls of thousands'.[117] In exploiting
anti-Catholicism left liberals touched on fears and prejudices shared
by a wide cross-section of Wilhelmine society. As the 1907 and 1912
elections exemplified, left liberals attracted support from left and

---

[114] BA Koblenz, NL Goetz 227, Wilhelm Heile to Walter Goetz, 3 Sept. 1912,
including copies of correspondence between Heile and Fischbeck, Payer, Wiemer, and
Müller-Meiningen.

[115] *Breslauer Zeitung*, 258 (13 Apr. 1912); IISH Amsterdam, NL Cauer 1, diary entry,
12 Sept. 1911.

[116] Vivid images of the extent and venom of liberal bourgeois antipathy towards the Cen-
tre and Catholic Church are conveyed in *Gegen das Zentrum!* (Munich, 1912). See also the
Simplicissimus cartoon reproduced in M. L. Anderson, 'Voter, Junker, *Landrat*, Priest: The
Old Authorities and the New Franchise in Imperial Germany', *AHR* 98 (1993), 1449.

[117] HAS Cologne, NL Marx 5, *Düsseldorfer Tageblatt* (26 Jan. 1911).

right by portraying opponents as allies of the Centre. By focusing on the common external enemy, they mitigated the impact of social and economic divisions within the left liberal electorate. Unable to define the political, economic, and social goals of the *Bürgertum* positively, left liberals fostered a common consciousness by negative means. Many identified with the left liberals as the party of Protestant middle strata because it was the most vociferous opponent of its most detested enemy. The pattern was repeated, though with less dramatic impact, with regard to arrogant Junkers, autocratic bosses of heavy industry, and unskilled, uneducated workers. Left liberals associated party-political opponents with one or more of these resented groups, and regarded their party as an expression of common antipathy.

Just as intellectual and popular left liberal attitudes towards 'Junker und Pfaffen' ran on parallel lines, so did enthusiasm for the introduction of business efficiency into public administration. In short, there was a core of issues and sentiments—education, communication, technology, independence, free competition, civic pride, nationalism, anti-feudalism, anti-clericalism—which exercised a significant appeal to left liberals in all regions and at each social level.

However, sharing popular attitudes on these issues could prove a mixed blessing for left liberalism as a political movement. A comfortable income and a secure place in the *Skatrunde*, bowling club, or choral association could lead to self-satisfaction and political apathy. The Junkers and the right had little direct and tangible part in the everyday life of most members of the urban middle strata. The more immediate threat to ascendancy in urban society, economy, and local politics came from the labour movement. As a result, defensive attitudes towards their position in society played an important part in the outlook of many left liberals. The way this was expressed often raised intellectual hackles about petty-bourgeois philistinism and reactionary behaviour. But, as we have seen, liberal intellectuals were also attached to the existing state. That this attachment appeared in a different form owed something to greater intelligence, better education, and a more cosmopolitan outlook. What must not be overlooked, however, was that the labour movement impinged on the lives of the petty bourgeoisie in a very different way than on liberal academics. The villa suburbs, first- or second-class train compartment, exclusive cultural association, and other haunts of the upper middle classes were free from any significant proletarian presence. On the other hand, it was easy for the *Kleinbürger* to feel threatened. Agitation for higher wages and boycott threats were directly hostile to the economic interests of small manufacturers, artisans, and retailers. Being surrounded by large numbers of workers was an uncomfortable feeling for those members of the petty bourgeoisie unable to live in the better parts of town. Pronounced anti-socialism was also a response from those who, unlike liberal intellectuals, had an income and education little different from skilled workers, and felt a pressing need to assert status. Petty-bourgeois anti-socialism may have had unattractive features, but it was more understandable than liberal intellectuals thought. Indeed, the question might be asked why anti-socialism was not more extensive, given the SPD's Marxist programme and mass following.

If popular and intellectual attitudes towards the SPD diverged, so did the way in which mass politics was regarded. Understandably, the small man did not agree that his views were inferior and things would be better if he had less of a say. Nevertheless, the contradictions were not as sharp as they might have been. When intellectuals railed against wretched Philistines, one of the main targets, opportunistic left liberal deputies and members of the local hierarchy, readily agreed, confident in the belief that the charge referred not to them, but to others further down the line. Sim-ilarly, machine politicians and their audience often operated with a modified version of the liberal intellectual view of politics. No one more typified the unimaginative, unprincipled left liberal tactician than Julius Kopsch. While the war threw left liberal intellectuals into spells of alternate ecstasy and agony by what they saw as momentous, unparalleled events, Kopsch as ever was calculating political and personal advantage. A visit with 'friend Wiemer' to Poland in 1915 was less a chance to witness heroic struggle and more an organized excursion, with guides, good red wine, and pretty Polish girls laid on. Kopsch was even accused of what to many left liberals was the ultimate sin: pandering to Catholicism, reputedly touring Catholic villages in his Löwenburg constituency with the greeting 'Jesus Christ be praised' and the response 'may He live in eternity' on his lips.[118] Nevertheless, when Kopsch spoke in Landeshut during the election campaign in 1912, the first half of the speech was devoted to the decline of ideals, the deplorable rise of interest politics, and the need to reassert the principle of the general good. The sizeable audience signalled its agreement.[119] But this was no anachronistic

---

[118] SA Detmold, NL Neumann-Hofer 9, Julius Kopsch to Adolf Neumann-Hofer, 11 Sept. 1915; Wenck, 'Wandlungen', fo. 173.   [119] *Landeshuter Stadtblatt* (6 Jan. 1912).

mourning of lost innocence. For Kopsch and his audience, the common good was a rhetorical stick to beat political opponents, above all the Agrarian League. That it was agrarian agitation and interests under attack, not populism and interest politics *per se*, was confirmed by the second half of the speech: a catalogue of demands, all in the material interest of the Protestant urban middle strata, reeled off and received with enthusiasm. Naturally enough, both speaker and audience maintained the fiction that such demands furthered the general good. Far from being totally opposed to populism and material interest, most left liberals operated behind a veil of ideological convenience, opposing only those aspects which adversely affected their own interests.

II

Executive, Parties, and Public Opinion:
The Left Liberals in National Politics, 1907–1914

4
Left Liberal Parliamentarians

It is helpful, before I analyse left liberal national politics in detail for the period 1907–1914 in Chapters 5 and 6, to explore a rather neglected theme: how left liberal deputies (and party politicians in general) actually functioned in Berlin. Attention has been brought by John Röhl, Isabel Hull, and others to court politics and the influence of the Emperor's entourage.[1] The diaries and correspondence of court diplomats, most notably Eulenburg, Holstein, and Lerchenfeld, have been exhumed from the archives and made available in multivolumed form.[2] But the workings of the Reichstag, and the way ministers and deputies conducted politics behind the scenes, remain under-researched.[3] Accounts of the Reichstag's changing political position have sometimes focused on a relatively unimportant question—the social composition of elected deputies[4]—rather than the more significant issue of how the Reich executive's need to secure money and legislation allowed political parties to have influence on policy and administration. Government-attempted manipulation of the political parties, press, and public opinion has been recognized and investigated, but the influence of the latter groups on ministers and

---

[1] See esp. J. C. G. Röhl, *The Kaiser and his Court: Wilhelm II and the Government of Germany* (Cambridge, 1994); J. C. G. Röhl and N. Sombart (eds.), *Kaiser Wilhelm II: New Interpretations* (Cambridge, 1982); J. C. G. Röhl, *Germany without Bismarck: The Crisis of Government in the Second Reich, 1890–1900* (London, 1967); J. C. G. Röhl (ed.), *Der Ort Kaiser Wilhelm II. in der deutschen Geschichte* (Munich, 1991); I. Hull, *The Entourage of Kaiser Wilhelm II, 1888–1918* (Cambridge, 1982), and K. A. Lerman, *The Chancellor as Courtier: Bernhard von Bülow and the Governance of Germany 1900–1909* (Cambridge, 1990).

[2] P. Eulenburg, *Philipp Eulenburgs Politische Korrespondenz*, ed. J. C. G. Röhl, iii (Boppard, 1976–83); Rich and Fisher (eds.), *Holstein Papers*; E. Deuerlein (ed.), *Briefwechsel Hertling-Lerchenfeld 1912–1917*, ii (Boppard, 1973).

[3] See Peter Molt, *Der Reichstag vor der improvisierten Revolution* (Cologne and Opladen, 1963).

[4] Sheehan, 'Political Leadership'; Heinrich Best, 'Politische Modernisierung und parlamentarische Führungsgruppen in Deutschland 1867–1918', *HSR* 13 1 (1988), 5–74; Willy Kremer, *Der soziale Aufbau der Parteien des Deutschen Reichstages von 1871–1918* (Emsdetten, 1934).

officials has been unduly discounted.[5] For the period before 1914 there has been no systematic account of the parties' use of Reichstag committees to fashion majorities and extract concessions.[6] Backstage negotiations, whether discussions with ministers or officials like Friedrich von Loebell and Arnold Wahnschaffe at the Chancellor's office, working breakfasts or ministerial dinners, have yet to receive substantial investigation.

There is, inevitably, a problem of evidence about aspects of politics which both ministers and parliamentarians preferred to keep out of the public gaze. Even in memoirs written in retirement, ministers, officials, and politicians were reluctant to discuss the inner workings of Berlin politics. Private memoirs, for example, by Loebell, Gothein, and Payer, reveal considerably more about the inner recesses of Berlin politics than published recollections of figure like Bethmann, Bülow, and Clemens von Delbrück. Also people on the fringes tended to be more forthcoming than those at the centre. Relatively junior figures like the left liberal Reichstag reporters Erich Dombrowski and Martin Wenck, and the SPD politician and journalist Friedrich Stampfer, wrote openly about the interchange between ministers, deputies, and political journalists. By contrast, the published works of government press director Otto Hammann and August Stein, the doyen of Berlin political correspondents, concealed more about their private contacts and political influence than they revealed.[7]

These gaps are exacerbated by sparsity of *Fraktion* records and official sources.[8] But despite these difficulties it is essential to acknow-

---

[5] See e.g. Volker Berghahn's books *Der Tirpitz-Plan* (Düsseldorf, 1971); *Germany and the Approach of War in 1914* (London, 1973).

[6] For illustrations of this process on individual issues see R. W. Lougee, 'The Anti-Revolution Bill of 1894 in Wilhelmine Germany', *CEH* 15 (1982), 224–40; and Rauh, *Parlamentarisierung*.

[7] BA Koblenz, NL Loebell 26 and 27; BA Koblenz, NL Gothein 12 and 14; Payer, 'Lebenslauf'; T. von Bethmann Hollweg, *Betrachtungen zum Weltkrieg* (2 vols.; Berlin, 1919–22); B. von Bülow, *Denkwürdigkeiten*, i–iv (Berlin, 1930–1); Delbrück, *Wirtschaftliche Mobilmachung*; F. Stampfer, *Erfahrungen und Erkenntnisse. Aufzeichnungen aus meinem Leben* (Cologne, 1957); J. Fischart [pseud Erich Franz Otto Dombrowski], *Das alte und das neue System* (4 vols.; Berlin, 1919–25); Wenck, 'Wandlungen'); Stein, *Es war alles ganz Anders*.

[8] For the left liberals only fragments of *Fraktion* records could be traced: brief notes of a left liberal *Fraktionsgemeinschaft* meeting on 14 Dec. 1909, and an FVP *Fraktion* meeting, 27 Sept. 1916 in HSA Stuttgart, NL Conrad Haußmann 31 and 100; and shorthand minutes of half a dozen meetings in 1916–17 in SB Munich, NL Kerschensteiner AKM 195–8. Official records of contacts between the executive and left liberal deputies in BA Berlin, Reichskanzlei 1393–5, and AA Bonn, IA Deutschland 125, are also incomplete and unrevealing.

ledge the importance (despite public condemnation of Centre-style horse-trading) of political bartering in Berlin to left liberal politics. Left liberals adhered to the image of the deputy as the voice of the people, making grand speeches from the floor of the Reichstag. But supporters as well as politicians increasingly realized that effective decision-making took place in backstage negotiations and detailed committee work.

The performance of left liberal Reichstag deputies deserves particular attention for two reasons. The first was their particular position of prestige. Even though the Landtag dealt with issues as close to the left liberal heart as education and railways, members of the Prussian House of Deputies were regarded as subordinate figures compared to Reichstag deputies. Richter, a brooding, powerful presence in Reichstag debates, rarely bothered to enter the Prussian House of Deputies, though he had been a member since 1874. Later left liberals displayed similar priorities. Some, like Georg Gothein and Franz von Liszt, abandoned the Landtag once they had been returned to the Reichstag. Others continued to be returned for both Houses, but directed their involvement were more towards the Reichstag. Indeed, the FVP *Landtagsfraktion* had to call for fewer 'double' candidatures in 1913 because members of both Houses were too busy in the Reichstag to contribute to the Landtag's work. This priotizing of the Reichstag was also true of those who were outside parliament. Oskar Tietz, for example, when attending a conference between the FVP and textile interests, was disappointed that the party delegation consisted mainly of Landtag not Reichstag deputies.[9] Secondly, it was the Reichstag parliamentary party which had both formal powers of left liberal policy-making at national level and the major role in practice of mediating between the interests of left liberal voters and the state.

The Reichstag caucus had an important integrative function. It was a forum for different economic and regional interests to be debated and alternative political proposals discussed and decided on. The result, inevitably, was not perfect reconciliation. Most left liberal deputies invested too much pride and confidence in their individual political opinions to be converted by mere weight of numbers. Georg Gothein, in his memoirs, claimed to have been an uncomfortable parliamentary colleague, willing to stand up for what he believed rather than meekly following the instructions of party leadership.[10] Gothein,

---

[9] BA Berlin, FVP 43, fo. 15, Textil-Beirat, 14 May 1918.
[10] BA Koblenz, NL Gothein 14.

with his energy, uncompromising economic and political rectitude, and, above all, forthright anti-annexationist stance during the war, presented more problems than most for a party leadership seeking practical compromise with the government and wary about offending parts of the left liberal electorate by unnecessary outspokenness. Nevertheless, Gothein's basic attitude was shared by most left liberal deputies. Ernst Müller-Meiningen was even more insistent, declaring himself dead against 'party dogmas' and 'slavish party spirit'.[11] My party right or wrong was not an acceptable principle even to those members like Payer and the Richterite epigoni who emphasized pragmatism and compromise. They still had individual views which they endeavoured to have accepted by the party as a whole.

For a group of men already convinced they knew best, parliamentary caucus meetings frequently proved a tiresome encumbrance. Payer complained to his wife about difficult and interminable party meetings which made him yearn for the sleeper back to Stuttgart. Naumann sketched drawings to ward off the tedium of prolonged, sterile debate. Individualism was not the only reason for doubting the worth of these meetings. The sessions were used by junior deputies to make up for the lack of opportunity to speak from the floor of the Reichstag, while the tendency for lengthy debate on minor points was not improved by the large number of lawyers present. It was also inevitable that caucus meetings reflected varying party traditions and the recent, rather improvised, nature of left liberal political co-operation. As Gothein commented, it was a different matter working with a less familiar group of fifty deputies than a dozen close-knit colleagues.[12] An attempt to foster social ties, such as a caucus beer evening with wives, generated 'little general enthusiasm'.[13] In addition, the *Fraktionsgemeinschaft* (joint caucus) period from 1907 till the formation of the FVP in March 1910 was a rather uneasy half-way house. All the differences between the three parties could come to the surface, but there was no formal authority to make decisions binding on all sides. Even an enthusiastic prophet of liberal unity like Naumann was forced to concede inherent difficulties: 'We want to appear in public as a unified body, without yet having actually become one. We want to demonstrate to demonstrate feelings of comradeship and fellowship even at times of political sacrifice,

---

[11] Reimann, *Müller-Meiningen*, 7.   [12] BA Koblenz, NL Gothein 27, fo. 43.
[13] BA Koblenz, NL Payer 40, fo. 21, Payer to wife, 17 Feb. 1910.

although we are all still aware that it is not long since we quarrelled amongst each other.'[14]

Besides clashes of personality, policy, and party tradition, there were also social divisions which could not be overlooked. Outside the Reichstag and party meetings, left liberal deputies tended to divide into small groups. Soon after his arrival in the capital in the 1890s, Gothein settled in the Hotel Kronprinz as part of the left liberal *Tafelrunde* presided over by Hermann Frese, the prosperous tobacco merchant and deputy for Bremen. There the small core of regulars, the Danzig deputy and future mayor Ehlers, the Lübeck lawyer and councillor Dr Goetz, estate owner Mager, and other hardy drinkers (*trunkfeste Leute*), were augmented, from time to time, by such august left liberal figures as Alexander Meyer, Karl Schrader, Theodor Barth, and the professors Albert Hänel and Ludwig von Bär.[15] A fairly distinct set of social acquaintances also formed itself around Naumann. Significantly, Naumann's immediate circle did not include long-standing and influential party leaders. His closest ties amongst left liberal parliamentarians were to Schulze-Gaevernitz, Liszt, and Kerchensteiner, all new to the Reichstag in 1912 and more prominent in the educational than political world. And the setting was no longer Tiergarten, but the less opulent and exclusive suburb of Schöneberg. The archetypal Naumannites were rising young journalists and party secretaries, Wilhelm Heile, Theodor Heuss, Otto Nuschke, Johannes Fischer, Anton Erkelenz, and Gertrud Bäumer, left liberal activists before the war, but whose entry into Reichstag politics came after 1918.

Inevitably, the notoriously intimate and sectional world of Berlin municipal politics played a significant part in the public and social lives of those left liberals based in the capital. Otto Fischbeck, Otto Wiemer, and Otto Mugdan were on the Berlin council executive (*Magistrat*); Johannes Kaempf was the president and Heinrich Dove the *Syndikus* of the capital's exclusive commercial corporation, the Älteste der Kaufmannschaft; Oskar Cassel, Karl Mommsen, and Rosenow led the various left liberal factions in the Berlin council chamber. Others were active in neighbouring Charlottenburg, Schöneberg, and Steglitz.[16] On top of this came regional and

---

[14] *Hilfe* (3 Mar. 1907), 151.   [15] BA Koblenz, NL Gothein 14, fos. 169 ff.
[16] J. Kaempf, *Reden und Aufsätze* (Berlin, 1912), introduction; BA Berlin, Reichslandbund 68, fos. 1–16; Landeshauptarchiv Potsdam, Provinz Brandenburg Rep. 30 Berlin C Tit. 94, 7064; and Tit. 95, 15441; Wermuth, *Beamtenleben*, 319 ff.

professional affinities. Payer, for instance, favoured the company of fellow Württemberg lawyers Conrad Haußmann and Theodor Liesching. In the same way, education both forged links between small numbers of individuals and erected barriers to those not similarly qualified. Indeed, friendships could be created which remained unshaken by substantial political differences. The good relations which existed between two political veterans, the left liberal Albert Traeger and the Free Conservative Kardorff, for example, were founded on common membership of a Halle student corporation.[17]

Berlin itself provided a further obstacle. The German capital was, like London, one of those places where social contact was difficult and anonymity abounded. A retreat after work to different suburbs was increasingly the order of the day, a trend strengthened by the *S-Bahn* and electric tram. Although left liberal politicians were more likely to reside in the south and west of Berlin rather than the proletarian north-east, few were close neighbours. Indeed, different addresses provided a further opportunity to pigeonhole deputies. Following the volatile Berlin housing market, the changes of fashion, and the spiralling prices, was an established passion for the status- and money-conscious middle classes. A hierarchy of hotels and neighbourhoods was etched on the mind.

A further barrier to strong social ties was the limited amount of time most deputies spent in Berlin. Of the forty-two left liberal deputies elected in 1912 over half were new to the Reichstag and only eleven had belonged to the Reichstag or Prussian Chamber of Deputies before 1903. The parliamentary careers of most left liberals were limited to one or two legislative periods, a brevity accounted for only in part by the whims of the electorate. Johannes Leonhart, the Reichstag deputy for Tondern-Husum since 1903, typified the attitude of a number of left liberal provincial leaders towards a career in national politics. An invitation to stand again in 1912 was declined despite the likelihood of victory. Men like Leonhart saw themselves more as good citizens than politicians. Public service was a part of the duty of a *Staatsbürger*. Parliamentary activity in Berlin flowed more from obligation than ambition. There was an obligation to the party, if the candidature was offered and its acceptance facilitated electoral success, to the ideal of political participation, and to the office of Reichstag deputy as 'voice of the people'. Against this was set the

[17] Eickhoff, *Politische Profile*, 27.

disruption to family life, to profession—Reichstag attendance allowances provided a fraction of the income of a successful business-man, lawyer, or doctor—and to a lifestyle embedded in local society. Berlin politics brought a heavy burden of additional work and, often enough, disappointed ideals: far from being free to pursue the general good, deputies were submerged in a sea of petitions and requests from interests and individuals 'wanting something from the state',[18] as left liberals unenthusiastically put it. Indeed, left liberal leaders repeat-edly had to resort to urgent persuasion to encourage prominent local figures to stand for national election. Naumann's letter to Kerschen-steiner was typical in its combination of moral admonition and the attempt to dispel the worst fears about Berlin politics: 'It will not be pure joy for you, but a noble task . . . With you a quite definite prac-tical ideal will enter the legislative body, not instantly triumphant, but effective nevertheless. I do not regret having sat here for five years, and nor would you. And who else then should stand if people like you do not care to?'[19] Even where the appeal to public duty succeeded, the parliamentary appetite of the genteel Reichstag deputy, unsharpened by national political ambition or a narrow devotion to politics, rarely lasted longer than one or two legislative terms. It was also the case that those left liberals who sought personal prestige from elected office were usually content with a short parliamentary career. A former deputy had most of the status and none of the burdens of those still in harness. The resultant pattern was not only one of relatively brief parliamentary careers; most deputies also spent as little of the year as possible in the capital. They were eager participants in the summer exodus of Berlin's propertied classes to mountain, coastal, and spa resorts. Karl Schrader, who dismissed the whole thing as a fad and insisted on staying at home, was very much an exception.[20] In add-ition, when the Reichstag was sitting deputies based in the provinces were keen to spend as much time at home and as little in Berlin as pos-sible. Bruno Ablaß, a Hirschberg lawyer and deputy for Hirschberg-Schönau, attended the Reichstag on forty-five days during the parliamentary session which ran from autumn 1910 to the end of 1911 and considered that sort of figure perfectly normal.[21]

[18] *Hilfe* (1914), 360.
[19] SB Munich, NL Kerschensteiner AKB, Naumann to Kerschensteiner, 28 Nov. 1911.
[20] *Hilfe* (8 May 1913), 289.
[21] BA Berlin, Reichslandbund 1, fo. 117, personalia Bruno Ablaß.

It was perhaps only natural that left liberal deputies favoured other social company and preferred home to Berlin. Nevertheless, the disparate social contacts of left liberals outside the confines of the Reichstag were significant. There was no all-consuming common cause capable of forging social as well as political unity. Indeed, some of the deputies' social attitudes sat uneasily with left liberal political ideology. Social groupings looked uncomfortably like divisions along class lines. Both snobbery and inverse snobbery played a part. Similarly, the absence, in most cases, of an absolute commitment to Berlin politics was readily understandable in human terms and against a political background in which, for liberalism, victories were hard-won and optimism severely tested. Nevertheless, it was part of an approach which tended towards undue passivity. The details of pre-war left liberal parliamentary politics will be discussed in the next two chapters. The general point to be made here, however, is that the left liberals had the potential to influence matters in the Reichstag in the last decade of the Kaiserreich. If 1890 marked the disappearance of the *Kartell* majority of Conservatives and National Liberals as well as Bismarck its architect, then the 1906 dissolution represented a further watershed in Reichstag politics: the end of the *Kartell*'s successor, the alliance of Conservatives, Centre party, and National Liberals as an informal, but relatively stable and decisive governmental majority. While the Reichstag leadership continued to serve Conservative interests wherever practical, it was the support of parties in the centre of the political spectrum which was crucial to securing Reichstag majorities for budgetary and legislative measures. The left liberals joined the Centre party and National Liberals, as one of the parties courted by the Reich leadership, and whose position had considerable political consequences. Even in December 1909 during the supposed rule of the Blue-Black Bloc of Conservatives and Centre, the prominent National Liberal Eugen Schiffer identified the left liberals as a group 'whose active co-operation in the Reichstag' was unavoidable for the Reich executive.[22] After 1914, moreover, this degree of dependence increased significantly. The war effort raised the premium on political and social unity, and the occasions on which the left liberals were pressed into service to defend the Reich leadership against the nationalist right multiplied. However, the majority of left liberal deputies

---

[22] BA Berlin, Reichskanzlei 1395, fo. 81, Schiffer to Hutten-Czapski, 19 Dec. 1909 (copy).

seemed more preoccupied with what they could not do. Rather than an ambitious striving to achieve political goals and maximize power, the dominant notes were those of caution and patience and the general tactic one of avoiding conflict and disfavour with the Reich leadership. It was Friedrich Payer's later judgement that the pre-war Reichstag lacked not the opportunity but the will to increase its own power decisively. Such an assessment was particularly applicable to the left liberal *Fraktion*, Payer included.[23]

An unheroic party in an unheroic age was an ungenerous, but reasonably fair description of the left liberal parliamentary party. Indeed, repeated references in print to left liberalism of the bloc (*Blockfreisinn*) and 'the "liberalism" of the Fraktionsgemeinschaft' conveyed just such an image to contemporaries.[24] Furthermore, the deficiencies of enterprise and ideological ardour were not just disappointments to the politically romantic and naïvely idealistic, but had significant practical political consequences. However, left liberal parliamentary activity in the last decade of the Kaiserreich was not merely a tale of shortcomings, of ineptitude, inconsequence, and insincerity. First, given the history of German liberalism, the degree of unity achieved by left liberal politicians must be considered a success. That only four left liberals voted against the language paragraph of the 1908 Imperial Law on Associations was viewed by some as a sacrifice of liberal principle. However, it was also an indication of the importance left liberals placed on unity and its corollary, compromise. The will of the majority was accepted despite the individualism of left liberal deputies. Left liberal cohesion after 1907 stood in marked contrast to the ill-fated attempts at party unity in the Deutsch-Freisinnige Partei between 1884 and 1893. It was rare for left liberals to speak or act against the party line. When, as on the 1911 Reich Insurance Code, left liberals divided, they did not do so in a spirit of hostility. The agreement to differ was accompanied by reassuring commentaries. Fundamental differences were denied and the episode presented as a matter of deputies coming to different conclusions about the balance of advantages and disadvantages contained in the Bill. The considerable stir created by the open rebellion of the liberal theologian and Landtag deputy Gottfried Traub in the second half of the war owed much to

[23] Payer, 'Lebenslauf'; SA Hamburg, NL Carl Petersen L52, Payer's address to FVP central committee, 8 June 1918.
[24] R. Breitscheid, *Der Bülowblock und der Liberalismus* (Munich, 1908); T. Barth, *Der Freisinn im Block* (Berlin, 1908).

the importance of the point of disagreement, war aims, but it also caught the attention because it had become unaccustomed behaviour for a left liberal deputy.

The most obvious fear at the time of union, that the clique of Richter's ex-lieutenants would control the merged party as they had done the FrVp, proved unfounded. This group itself was in a process of decomposition. Hermann Müller-Sagan, Richter's successor as chairman of the executive committee, and Reinhart Schmidt-Elberfeld, a particularly distrusted figure, left the Reichstag at the end of 1906 and retreated rapidly from the centre of the political stage. Müller-Sagan was implicated on a shop-lifting charge, and an attempted political comeback, when he was adopted as a candidate for his old seat of Sagan-Sprottau, was cut short by relatively early death in 1912. Schmidt-Elberfeld suffered repeated ill health and died in 1909. Another influential Richterite Robert Gyßling, the leader of the left liberals in Ostpreußen, was to die in October 1912. His role, in any case, was greater in the Prussian Landtag and party organization than in the Reichstag where he represented the usually safe SPD seat Königsberg-Stadt from 1907 to 1912.[25] Johannes Kaempf became more and more occupied with representative functions as opposed to political decision-making, particularly after his election as Reichstag president in 1912.

This left Otto Fischbeck, Otto Wiemer, and Julius Kopsch. Kopsch remained, as before, the most acute and active deputy in matters of party organization. However, despite being a long-standing member of both Houses, he never achieved a comparable importance in the Reichstag or Prussian Landtag. Otto Wiemer chaired the FVP Reichstag caucus for the first two years, but patent mediocrity proved an insuperable barrier to respect and authority. Erich Dombrowski, the *Berliner Tageblatt*'s parliamentary reporter claimed deputies, including left liberals, fled the chamber when Wiemer rose to speak.[26] His electoral defeat in January 1912, and brief absence (he was returned to the Reichstag at the Varel-Jever by-election later the same year) provided a welcome opportunity to select a more able leader. Otto Fischbeck was undoubtedly the most important and talented of the Richterites. Even the left liberal intellectuals Theodor Wolff and

---

[25] BA Berlin, Reichslandbund 170, fos. 105–16, personalia Robert Gyßling.

[26] BA Berlin, Reichslandbund Personalia 493, fo. 60. Cf. E. Wetterle, *Les Coulisses du Reichstag* (Paris, 1918), 50–1; K. Bachem, *Vorgeschichte, Geschichte und Politik der Deutschen Zentrumspartei*, i–ix (Cologne, 1927–32), vii. 52.

Willy Hellpach, who had little sympathy for Fischbeck's cautious pragmatism, came at close quarters to respect his political abilities. To Hellpach, Fischbeck was the cleverest of the Richterites and, in Wolff's view, a much more capable politician than rhetorically gifted Friedrich Naumann.[27] Fischbeck succeeded Wiemer as chairman of the parliamentary party, was intimately acquainted with and committed to Berlin politics, and also influential in organizational matters. He was, however, hardly a second Richter. He had none of his mentor's aptitude and appetite for public speaking and journalism. While Richter was the darling, or occasionally the villain, of local left liberal associations throughout the land, Fischbeck was scarcely known outside Liegnitz, where he was elected, Westphalia, where his political career began, and, of course, Berlin where he lived and worked. Platform appearances by Richter were recalled years later, but Fischbeck's public appearances were rare and unmemorable. What Fischbeck shared with Richter was political shrewdness allied to personal gruffness. The lack of a winning personality, compounded by the liability of a notoriously difficult wife, was reflected in the attitudes of parliamentary colleagues. Fischbeck earned respect for his political knowledge and ability, but little affection or devotion. Gothein, for example, valued Fischbeck for his 'cool, clear reasoning'.[28] Ill-health provided an even more significant barrier to complete authority. A nervous disorder required total rest for several months in 1912/13 and again during the war.[29]

With Fischbeck periodically disabled, the leading role in the left liberal Reichstag caucus was taken by Payer. He alone possessed the required qualifications: respect, ability, experience, robust health, and a full-time devotion to Berlin politics. Payer's emergence as the most important left liberal figure was significant in several respects. First, it indicated that left liberal unity had become more than a façade. In 1910 all national positions in the new party were apportioned in a fixed ratio to former members of the three merged parties. The elevation of Payer, the ex-leader of the smallest of the pre-merger parties with less than a fifth of the Reichstag seats, demonstrated the absence of block voting according to old party affiliations. Similarly, departing members of the executive committee were replaced by the

---

[27] C. Führ and H. G. Zier (eds.), *Hellpach-Memoiren 1925–1945* (Cologne, 1987), 14 ff.
[28] BA Koblenz, NL Gothein 12, fos. 93–4.
[29] It was poor health, according to Wermuth, which prevented Fischbeck becoming mayor of Berlin. Wermuth, *Beamtenleben*, 326.

most appropriate candidate, not necessarily someone with the same party background. David Waldstein, for example, succeeded Albert Traeger on the FVP executive committee in 1912, despite being a former member of the FrVg rather than the FrVp. The FVP was acquiring its own identity and set of interests.

Secondly, Payer's role as the most influential left liberal parliamentarian said something about the general political direction of the FVP. Payer may have belonged to its moderate wing, but he remained unmistakably a representative of South German left liberalism. He attempted unsuccessfully to have the DVP's commitment to equal suffrage for local elections included in the programme of the new party, and was instrumental in toning down the pro-Hohenzollern and anti-socialist passages of the 1912 election address to suit the non-Prussian electorate.[30] Prussians may still have formed a majority of the Reichstag party, but ideas, initiative, and influence were increasingly coming from elsewhere. This was a trend also visible in other parties and was to reach its zenith in the cabinet of Prince Max in which, ironically, the only Prussian was the Social Democrat Scheidemann. Neither Elm's account of continual leaning to the right under the auspices of the Richterite epigoni, nor the dominance of the left-wing former deputies of the FrVg and a new radical departure, which is Robson's assessment, provides an accurate analysis of the left liberal Reichstag caucus after 1910. Fusion certainly liberated deputies from Richter's old party and made it possible for them to pursue a more progressive line with the support of the South Germans and the more radical Reichstag deputies of the FrVg. On the other hand, Hermann Pachnicke, the figurehead of the FrVg right wing who had been outvoted and marginalized in the party leadership after 1903, found a central role first in the *Fraktionsgemeinschaft* and then in the FVP.[31] Pre-war political circumstances produced pragmatism combined with a turn to the left in significant areas of domestic policy. The latter trend, but also a greater enthusiasm for *Weltpolitik*, was strengthened by the 1912 intake of deputies.[32] The mechanical effect of left liberal union, however, was to increase the influence of those at the centre of

---

[30] BA Berlin, FVP 37, fos. 154–6, central committee, 12 Nov. 1911.

[31] A comparison of FrVg and FVP executive committee minutes underlines Pachnicke's changed position. BA Berlin, FVP 4, 36. Pachnicke, *Liberalismus als Kulturpolitik*, emphasizes the meekness of Pachnicke's liberal demands particularly during the Bülow Bloc.

[32] See Ch. 6 below.

the left liberal political spectrum at the expense of those from the left of the FrVg and the right of the FrVp.

Finally, the way the parliamentary party operated reflected Payer's character and position inside the party. On the one hand he lacked the machinery which had been available to Richter. There was no sizeable group of lieutenants and devotees within the *Fraktion* to carry out the leader's bidding. Nor could the columns of the *Freisinnige Zeitung* or pressure from local parties be used to secure compliance. Payer had, of necessity, to act as chairman and conciliator rather than as a leader intent on enforcing his own will. On the other hand, unlike the abrasive, uncompromising Richter, he was well suited to such a role.[33] Payer, who had kept on reasonable terms with bitterly feuding Richterites and Secessionists for over two decades, was well able to cope with lesser personal and political differences between left liberal politicians after 1910. To Richter *Dinerpolitik*, the mingling of the social and political, was something to be avoided. Payer, by contrast, was superbly adept at parlour politics, as well as having a good Swabian eye for a free lunch.[34] Richter viewed political opponents, and often enough political allies, with personal hostility. Payer possessed the valuable quality of getting on well despite differences of personality and political outlook. Payer succeeded as a party leader partly because authority was exercised lightly, but also because of a keen awareness of what was politically damaging and an ability on those occasions to act effectively, but without creating resentment. Gothein, for instance, clashed with Payer particularly during the war, but remained on respectful good terms.[35]

However, harmony within the parliamentary party was based on more than able orchestration by the leadership in general and Payer in particular. In practice the role of more senior members of the *Fraktion* was generally accepted, particularly if accompanied by aptitude and energy. Moreover, the circle of experienced parliamentarians— Payer, Fischbeck, Wiemer, Müller-Meiningen, Pachnicke, Gothein, and Haußmann—represented the spectrum of political views within the parliamentary party. References to 'party popes' (*Parteipäpste*)[36] were hardly complimentary in view of what left liberals thought about

---

[33] Payer, 'Lebenslauf', 45.
[34] See Payer's letters to his wife, BA Koblenz, NL Payer 40–5.
[35] BA Koblenz, NL Gothein 14, fo. 182; NL Payer 43.
[36] BA Koblenz, NL Erkelenz 12, fo. 53, L. Nelson to Anton Erkelenz, 7 Nov. 1918; BA Koblenz, NL Traub 7, diary, 9 June 1918.

things Roman. They were, however, the occasional expression of wounded pride rather than a sustained rejection of arrangements within the parliamentary party. Although private lives followed different paths, the frequency with which left liberals dined together at the *Fraktionstisch* in the Reichstag canteen indicated at least some collegial feeling as well as a rather Philistine parsimony and lack of culinary adventure.

As with social position, the range of political views inside the parliamentary party was smaller than that in the party outside. There was no representative of the pacifist group like Quidde and Schücking. On the right, those who were anti-socialist first and last were underrepresented. Though they could debate individual points for hours, there was agreement about the general direction German politics should take, and major themes and events in pre-war Reich politics reinforced this party consensus. The 1908 *Daily Telegraph* affair, when various remarks made by the Kaiser on a visit to England the previous year were published as an interview, creating public uproar in Germany, allowed left liberals to emphasize opposition to 'personal government', and the importance of responsible conduct of government. Similarly in the Zabern crisis of late 1913, the left liberals were part of a sweeping majority of Reichstag and public opinion which condemned a rashly led Prussian garrison which had seized police powers and begun assaulting and arresting civilians in a previously docile small Alsatian town. The incident was perfect illustration for the left liberal theme of the importance of anchoring civil rights in a fully fledged *Rechtsstaat*. On state finances left liberals were apostles of financial probity—the need to balance the books—and of a progressive Reich property tax. Strong, modern defences at sea and on land were supported by all sides of the parliamentary party. This, as well as the political exigencies of appearing reliably 'national', was behind acceptance of military bills. Even where the left liberal position was unclear or a range of views lay beneath the surface, a sense of discipline and political circumstances allowed this to be largely concealed. In foreign policy, for example, there was little evidence of a positive policy of its own, but the party could at least agree in its opposition to both the sabre-rattling chauvinism of the nationalist right and the 'dangerous' internationalism of the SPD. On the question of agrarian tariffs, deputies held differing opinions and represented divergent constituency interests. Fortunately, however, the government and most politicians were content to live with the status quo of 1902/3. Left liberals could quietly say different things to different voters or highlight a tariff like the fodder duty which worked against peasant livestock farmers as well as the urban electorate.[37] On constitutional reform the left liberals lacked a comprehensive set of concrete proposals. Indeed, left liberal deputies differed considerably over the extent and pace of constitutional reform they thought desirable. All were agreed, however, in the direction of change and could unite behind unspecific words and phrases like responsibility, accountability, 'goals of liberalism', and 'new opening'.

Equally, there was common assent that the circumstances demanded unity, and that gradual reform in league with other parties was the only practical path of political progress open to the party.[38] Payer may have complained repeatedly to his wife about disputes and difficulties within the parliamentary party, but there were also recurrent references, sometimes within days, to a unity of purpose inside the *Fraktion* which made his role much easier. In fact there were fewer personal and political differences in the left liberal than National Liberal, Centre, or Social Democratic parliamentary parties. Nothing in the left liberal *Fraktion*, for example, resembled the personal antagonisms raised by Erzberger, the clash between the 'Berlin' and 'Cologne' factions, Bavarian regionalism, the juxtaposition of agrarians and Christian trade unionists, and political attitudes ranging from the avowedly conservative to the almost democratic, all of which coexisted inside the Centre.[39] Perhaps the significant conclusion to be drawn, however, was that left liberals, unlike Centre party deputies and voters bound by things less transient than politics, needed a convergence of political stance, personal compatibility, and a conducive political environment to make a sacrifice of individualism for party discipline acceptable. If Payer's summary that 'the last, long Reichstag period' from 1912 to 1918 'had completely welded together the deputies . . . and everyone knew one another exactly' rather overstated the case, left liberal unity in the last decade of the Kaiserreich was significant. It was a concrete political achievement, which previous and subsequent disunity only highlighted.[40]

As a group, the left liberals were conscientious; it was inspiration not perspiration which was lacking. Earnestness and industry were

---

[37] See Part III below.   [38] Grosser, *Verfassungspolitik, passim.*
[39] The fullest account of the factionalism in the Centre Reichstag caucus is Loth, *Katholiken im Kaiserreich.*
[40] Payer, 'Lebenslauf', fo. 64.

respected qualities. Asquith's leisurely lifestyle would have been looked on almost as disapprovingly as his immoderate intake of alcohol. Richter's devotion to careful scrutiny of political material, above all the budget, set exacting standards which other left liberals aspired to. The strain of a deputy's life was summed up by Hermann Pachnicke:

Our work is already hard enough, perhaps the most strenuous of any. Caucus meetings which are becoming ever longer, livelier and fuller; committee sittings for many hours; and then into the chamber for eight or more hours. In addition, study of draft legislation, written material, the press, professional work, conferences with everyone wanting something from the state. We parliamentarians stand between the electorate and the majesty of the state. We are the voice of people [hear hear!]. Everything comes to us which causes a stir in the land and seeks a solution.[41]

There was, perhaps, something inherently suspicious about claims of overwork. Certainly, there was an element of special pleading in Pachnicke's conclusion that Landtag deputies be given free rail travel covering all of Prussia and for the whole of the legislative period. In fact, there was very little a deputy had to do, providing conscience, party, and constituency would allow. However, left liberal supporters expected 'representatives of the people' to speak out. There were rude comments in the left liberal press about 'parliamentary Moltkes', deputies who declined to speak. Indeed, their columns held a sarcastic celebration in 1918 to mark the twenty-fifth parliamentary anniversary of Rothger, a Silesian Conservative deputy since 1893, who had yet to make his maiden speech.[42] It was true that the burden of routine work dealt with by the Reichstag was expanding inexorably. The budget became ever larger and more complicated. Items like the navy and colonial administration, which barely needed consideration at the outset of the Kaiserreich, occupied a significant amount of time. The Reich Insurance Code was a monument to the complexity and length of modern legislation. The piles of petitions and paperwork generally continued to mount. The introduction of Reichstag attendance allowances in 1906 was partly motivated by the need to spread the burden of parliamentary work. The effect was largely illusory as the backwoodsmen encouraged to attend often lacked the competence to contribute to committee work.[43]

---

[41] Speech in Prussian Landtag, 18 May 1914: *Hilfe* (1914), 360.
[42] *Breslauer Zeitung*, 402 (11 June 1912).
[43] Stein, *Es war alles ganz Anders*, 156–8; Cardauns, *Karl Trimborn*, 109.

By contrast, the amount of new legislation introduced by the government in the pre-war years was less than overwhelming. The 1910–11 session was fairly crowded, for it was obvious that the next Reichstag would be less compliant. The period of the Bülow Bloc, however, saw plenty of slack periods. The 1911 constitution for Alsace-Lorraine was an untypical piece of legislative enterprise, and hardly one rewarded by subsequent events. Like the 1909 finance reform, so the other pieces of legislation of major political significance in the pre-war period, the 1913 defence bill and military finance bill (*Deckungsvorlage*), were brought to the Reichstag out of necessity rather than expectation. After 1912 the Reichstag majority would not accept right-wing legislation, and the party-political weakness of the nationalist right made it even more determined to resist reform. Understandably the Reich leadership, as exemplified by Delbrück's announced halt to further social legislation in early 1914, came to the conclusion that the best thing, for the time being, was to do nothing. In addition, much of the traditional fare of Reichstag controversy was lacking. The disputes about 'national issues' had dampened down and existing trade treaties ran till 1917. Far from being a climax to the expansion of parliamentary business, the Reichstag in the first half of 1914 was notably quiet and dull. 'There are barely 30 men in the Reichstag', Payer wrote to his wife, and on another occasion that he was the only FVP deputy in the chamber.[44]

In addition to the summer months, there were then plenty of periods when a deputy's presence in the Reichstag was not required. Nor, indeed, could he be held accountable for unexcused absence. When the Reichstag voted by a single-vote majority to confirm the validity of the 1912 election in Alzey-Bingen, a decision which probably cost the left liberals a seat, an attempt by a newly elected deputy to make those left liberals who had missed the vote explain their absence was considered most improper and impertinent by senior parliamentarians.[45] Nevertheless, that under-explored area of a deputy's activity, approaching the authorities on behalf of individuals and organizations, played a increasingly important and time-consuming role. There is an obvious problem of evidence with this side of politics. Payer's letters to his wife give a good impression of the amount of time taken up, and of the general importance of informal negotiation.

---

[44] BA Koblenz, NL Payer 42, fos. 20 ff., Payer to wife, 11 and 27 Feb. and 3 Mar. 1914.
[45] BA Koblenz, NL Payer 41, fo. 39, Payer to wife, 27 Feb. 1913.

The unsorted papers of Adolf Neumann-Hofer, seized by the Gestapo in 1933, provide the most dramatic account, revealing a network of dealings, frequently corrupt, with businessmen and officials. Certainly, the great majority of left liberal deputies did not, like Neumann-Hofer, go in for selling titles, or profiteering from wartime supply of artificial fertilizers. Nevertheless, all were making personal requests to ministers and officials on behalf of a wide range of interests. Carl Braband, for example, vigorously pursued Hamburg's claim to be the seat of the colonial law courts, and took up requests for compensation from Germans abroad.[46] Such activities were an inevitable reflection of the state's growing participation in economy and society, but the volume of work, particularly on Liberal parliamentarians, was compounded by political circumstances. The number of Reichstag deputies remained pegged at 397, despite the huge rise in population and political mobilization since 1871. In addition, left liberal deputies often found themselves representing more than one set of local interests. As SPD deputies were deemed unsuitable for the role, left liberals from Berlin and Hamburg, for example, acted as an advocate for their home cities as well as the semi-rural constituencies for which they were returned. As left liberal deputy for Bremen 1907–12, Hinrich Hormann was looked to by shipping interests in other ports, as well as the Bremen-based Norddeutscher Lloyd, to represent the industry.[47]

For the most influential party politicians, though a Reichstag seat was an essential base, their fields of involvement went far wider than regular parliamentary activity and looking after constituency interests. Erzberger, for example, was at the centre of a web of contacts and activity, which earned him the reputation of having a finger in every pie, a role which demanded formidable energy: 'with the most intimate knowledge of everything, thanks to a thousand informants, he terrifies the top officials (*die Geheimen Räte*)'.[48] The left liberals had no Erzberger in their ranks. Naumann, the nearest equivalent, played a similar role, but without the same ambition, unscrupulousness, and effectiveness. Georg Kerschensteiner's sympathetic portrait of Naumann drew attention to a central political failing, the lack of an inner drive for power. Naumann, the prophet of power politics was not

[46] BA Koblenz, NL Payer 40–5; SA Detmold, NL Neumann-Hofer *passim*; SA Hamburg, NL Braband B2.   [47] Kastendiek, 'Liberalismus in Bremen', 129.
[48] BA Koblenz, NL Bülow 107, fo. 180, Bassermann to Bülow, 19 Mar. 1914. Cf. Severing, *Lebensweg*, i. 329.

himself a *Machtmensch*.[49] Nevertheless, the political commitments of left liberals deputies outside the Reichstag were substantial. Requests for Reichstag deputies to speak in public were so numerous that it was impossible to fulfill more than a small proportion. After Kerschensteiner, the Munich education director, was elected in 1912, he received well over a hundred requests to speak, from Kiel to Kattowitz.[50] Inevitably, with a full-time job as well as parliamentary commitments, all but a few were turned down. The demand for Naumann was insatiable. A less well-known left liberal Jan Fegter, deputy for Norden-Emden, spoke in no less than 220 places, from entering the Reichstag at a 1908 by-election to the end of 1911.[51] The great majority of left liberal deputies were involved in local government and many continued in local office at the same time as representing a constituency in Berlin. Many Reichstag deputies also had a seat in a state parliament. The majority continued to pursue a career. Ernst Müller-Meiningen, for example, combined active political involvement in the Reichstag and Bavarian Landtag with rapid promotion in the Bavarian state justice service.[52] Most wrote press articles and pamphlets. The strains of a full political career were reflected in ill health. A significant proportion of leading left liberals suffered physical collapse and serious illness. Besides Fischbeck, this applied to Gothein, Schrader, Neumann-Hofer, Liszt, Karl Mommsen, and others. The early deaths of men like Barth, Naumann, Braband, Gyßling and both Haußmann twins testified to the physical demands of a left liberal political career. Pachnicke's account of the burden of work was, therefore, only a slightly embellished version of reality.[53]

Left liberal diligence was reflected in the parliamentary basics. Committee work was taken seriously. Important material was mastered. Naumann's passion for statistics was shared by others. Left liberal spokesmen usually possessed expert knowledge in the field allotted to them: bankers like Kaempf and Mommsen spoke on stock-exchange legislation; Dove on commercial law; Gothein, a trained mining engineer, on technical matters. Hugo Wendorff, who farmed his estate without a manager, was the *Fraktion*'s 'dung expert'.[54] If

[49] SB Munich, NL Kerschensteiner AKM 193, 'Naumann als Politiker', 23 Oct. 1918, fo. 14.   [50] SB Munich, NL Kerschensteiner letters, box 2.

[51] J. Fegter, *Reichstagsreden und sonstige politische Tätigkeit* (Leer, 1911), 62.

[52] Reimann, *Müller-Meiningen*, 13–14.

[53] Stein, *Es war alles ganz Anders*, esp. 95–103, 108–58. The particular burdens placed on leading party politicians are well caught by Cardauns, *Karl Trimborn*, 100–19.

[54] BA Berlin, FVP 48, fo. 35.

left liberal committee members lacked the required knowledge they strived conscientiously to acquire it. Schulze-Gaevernitz, for example, plunged into research on the oil industry after being put at short notice on the Reichstag committee considering a petroleum monopoly.

Indeed, subjects could be approached with an earnestness of purpose which their importance scarcely merited. It was hard, for example, to imagine anyone becoming as enthusiastic about the Cameroons economy as Carl Braband.[55] In general, left liberal members were conscientious attenders and voters when important debates and divisions took place. The vote on the validity of the Alzey-Bingen election was untypical. The performance of the parliamentary party was workmanlike in both senses of the word. It lacked sparkle and invention, but at the same time was reliable and industrious. Indeed, the more influential left liberal parliamentarians had similar characteristics to their equivalents in neighbouring parties—men like Junck, Schiffer, and von Calker for the National Liberals and Trimborn, Müller-Fulda, and Fehrenbach for the Centre. The judgement of Wilhelm Kulemann from his Reichstag experience that the Progressives had the best minds and speakers in the Reichstag did not apply to the left liberal parliamentarians in the period 1907–18 as it had done to their predecessors in the 1880s.[56]

There had been qualitative as well as quantitative decline. Naumann even compared the attitude of veteran left liberals to the 1907 *Fraktionsgemeinschaft* to the Israelites who cried when they saw the new temple, because they could still remember the older one which had been larger and more beautiful.[57] The election in 1912 of Schulze-Gaevernitz and Liszt, together with the narrow failure of Hugo Preuß, suggested some reversal in the decline in the number of academics in the Reichstag. Nevertheless their numbers remained small compared to the first decades of the Reichstag. None of the later left liberals had the same exquisite touch when addressing the Reichstag as men like Alexander Meyer and Albert Hänel. Nor was there a left liberal deputy capable of dominating a debate as Richter had done.

---

[55] Braband was particularly fervent, in deed as well as word, about Cameroon tobacco. NL Braband B14, Reichstag sitting, 30 Mar. 1914.

[56] W. Kulemann, *Politische Erinnerungen* (Berlin, 1911), 75–9. For an admiring and appropriate written monument to the passing generation of left liberal leaders see Barth, *Politische Porträts*.   [57] *Hilfe* (3 Mar. 1907), 151.

'With the best will in the world,' the usually sympathetic *Kieler Neueste Nachrichten* complained in 1906, 'the left liberal Reichstag deputies cannot be described as élite troops.'[58] Liberalism, at least according to left liberals, was the *Kulturträger* (pillar of culture) in German economic and social life, and a similar superiority was expected in the political sphere. There was a craving for a *Reichstagsfraktion*, the pinnacle of the party, composed only of first-rate men. The crucial barometer was not necessarily political: standing in business and, even more, in education weighed heavily. Ironically, some of the most admired left liberal deputies were politically naïve or ineffectual. As well as Naumann, this applied to Franz von Liszt, Schulze-Gaevernitz, and Kerschensteiner. Such sentiment ran throughout the left liberal party membership. Spontaneous applause would break out amongst the delegates the moment Theodor Mommsen, Virchow, or Hänel entered the conference hall. However, in the real world of politics, as opposed to liberal ideals, unity and discipline were more than a match for intellect and oratory.

[58] *Kieler Neueste Nachrichten* (18 Dec. 1906).

5

Left Liberals in National Politics,
1907–1912

I. THE CHANCELLOR'S NEW CLOTHES:
LEFT LIBERALS AND THE BÜLOW BLOC, 1907–1909

How did the government and left liberals, after more than two decades of dispute focused on 'national' issues, come to be fighting a nationalistic Reichstag election campaign on the same side in December 1906? And what did the resultant 'Bülow Bloc', the uneasy collection of Conservatives, anti-Semites, National Liberals, and left liberals called upon to provide a government majority, mean both for the course of German politics in general, and left liberal integrity and influence in particular?

The answer to the first question is rather harder to find with respect to the government than the left liberals. Indeed, the break with the Centre was less a collective decision and more a foray launched by the Chancellor, his office, and intimates like press director Otto Hammann. And with many of those close to the throne and executive surprised, the dissolution, predictably, took left liberal politicians completely unawares. As Conrad Haußmann told a public meeting in Heilbronn on 14 December 1906: 'this suddenness [is] at the same time proof of the uncertainty of political conditions in Berlin. There no surprise can be excluded from one day to the next.'[1] Certainly, many Germans were prepared to believe the allegation that the Centre had abused its key Reichstag position. Nevertheless, for those in high office, the argument that the Centre was in effect a government on the side (*Nebenregierung*), that its influence had become overweening, was incredible. Posadowsky, as state secretary for the interior the minister most involved in behind the scenes negotiations with

---

[1] HSA Stuttgart, NL Haußmann, 104, *Heilbronner Zeitung* (15 Dec. 1906). Cf. T. Eschenburg, *Das Kaiserreich am Scheideweg: Bassermann, Bülow und der Block*, (Berlin, 1929), 42–50.

party leaders, was a decided opponent of a break with the Centre, complaining to his subordinate Adolf Wermuth that Colonial Secretary Dernburg was 'storming in like a bull in a china shop and smashing my best pieces to bits'. Indeed, Posadowsky's continued scepticism about the Bloc and sympathy for a *rapprochement* with the Centre was used by Bülow to engineer his dismissal in June 1907.[2] Nor could the Centre's rejection of supplementary estimates for South-West Africa be termed a major act of opposition. The party was prepared to change its stance and eagerly sought to repair relations, with governmentalists like Peter Spahn and Hertling to the fore. The continued reliance on a particular party and the rise of populist influence within the Centre, symbolized powerfully if idiosyncratically by Erzberger, were causes for government concern in the longer term. Nevertheless, for the immediate future the Centre remained the most stable and flexible negotiating partner. There was no pressing reason at the end of 1906 why relations between government and Centre could not continue to be workable and mutually beneficial.

Government hostility towards Social Democracy, unlike the Centre, was unambiguous. At one level the 1907 election was clearly an attempt to isolate the SPD and reduce the party's seventy-nine seats as far as possible. However, the absence of a further programme to combat Social Democracy either by social, political, and economic reform, or by legislative repression and restriction, argues against interpreting the dissolution as the start of a systematic new anti-socialist strategy.

Alongside two essentially negative aims, it is possible to construe a third, more constructive intent. The dissolution, Bülow asserted later, was designed to make an emotional appeal 'especially in those circles and classes against which the nation can be governed in the long term only with difficulty'.[3] As a letter written in 1911 to Loebell, head of the Reich Chancellor's Office during the Bloc period, reflected, the experience of office taught that 'the monarchy must not rest just on *Ritter* and *Heilige*', the civil service needed 'freshening up', and 'agricultural and conservative interests can be maintained only with moderation, foresight and cleverness'. A policy directed against both the Centre and SPD, combined with modest reform, was seen by

---

[2] Wermuth, *Beamtenleben*, 256–58; Lerman, *Chancellor as Courtier*, 178–9; BA Berlin, NL Otto Hammann 13, fo. 15, Bülow to Hammann, 8 Mar. 1907.

[3] SA Bremen, NL Fitger 6/50, Bülow to Emil Fitger, Villa Malta, 8 Feb. 1910.

Bülow as a way of completing the integration of previously critical groups within the Wilhelmine political system.[4] In party terms this implied bringing the left liberals into the circle of 'nationally reliable' parties. More importantly, it meant giving the economically predominant urban middle classes a sense of participation in and identification with the political as well as the economic and social structure of the Wilhelmine state.

Again, this was more a matter of intuitive improvisation than of fixed purpose and firm programme. The 1906 dissolution must also, as always with Bülow, be seen in personal terms. It offered the Chancellor an opportunity to restore his authority and relations with the Emperor, eroded by events during the previous year. Alongside German isolation over Morocco and difficulties with the Centre party in the Reichstag, the Chancellor had upset the Kaiser by tendering his resignation over the Björkö treaty and supporting the removal of Podbielski as agricultural minister. Court observers ascribed waning influence to Bülow, who had collapsed in the Reichstag in April 1906 and appeared to be losing control of appointments.[5]

Yet, even if the view of a minority of historians that Bülow was a sincere, even liberal reformer and a strategist rather than tactician is generally unconvincing,[6] casting the 1906 dissolution simply in a context of court political intrigue underplays the undoubted intention to harness the popular forces of nationalism, anti-Catholicism, and anti-socialism.[7] The Chancellor hoped to enthuse the Protestant middle strata as well as the monarch, to alleviate problems of popular consent as well as of imperial mistrust and wilfulness. Such a dual aim was problematic enough in itself. In both areas, however, Bülow's solutions were essentially short-term. The problem was not immediate electoral success, but how to keep both Emperor and electorate happy afterwards. Moreover, not only was Bülow's concept of necessary, limited

---

[4] BA Koblenz, NL Loebell 7, Bülow to Loebell, Villa Malta, 10 Feb. 1911.

[5] Lerman, *Chancellor as Courtier*, 127–66.

[6] T. F. Cole's articles 'Kaiser versus Chancellor: The Crisis in Bülow's Chancellorship 1905–6', in Evans (ed.), *Society and Politics*, and 'The *Daily Telegraph* affair and its Aftermath: The Kaiser, Bülow and the Reichstag, 1908–9', in Röhl and Sombart (eds.), *Wilhelm II*, ascribe good intentions to Bülow and the Bloc which, in parts, were not shared even by Bassermann, the leader of Chancellor's contemporary fan club. 'The Eel' has also escaped with a favourable assessment of his foreign policy in P. Winzen, *Bülows Weltmachtpolitik* (Boppard, 1977).

[7] See Bülow's comments in the margins of Riezler's report on a conversation with Naumann, 25 Aug. 1907, in BA Koblenz, NL Heuss 495.

concessions imprecise, but it was not shared by much of the traditional Prussian ruling élite. There were differences and a lack of clarity from the outset which underlay the repeated uncertainty and limitations of the Bülow Bloc.

Short-term electoral gain was similarly a motive for left liberal politicians, particularly the renowned 'seat-hagglers' (*Mandatsschacher*) of the FrVp. After the left liberal electoral nadir of 1903, riding the tigers of nationalism and *furor protestanticus* promised a rise in popular support which orthodox liberalism could not deliver. Pacts between the Liberal and Conservative political parties brought the prospect of victory in otherwise hopeless urban seats. The rise in left liberal parliamentary representation from thirty-six to forty-nine seats was achieved predominantly by left liberals standing as the agreed bourgeois candidate in urban seats: Bremen, Frankfurt, Königsberg, Breslau (West), Stettin, Magdeburg, Plauen, Fürth, Hof, Halle, and Zittau were won in this way. Finally, subventions for the FrVp from the government-controlled Komitee Patria eased the perennial left liberal problem of campaign fund-raising.[8]

Left liberal participation in the Bloc elections was, however, more than an opportunistic calculation by Berlin political leaders. In the first place, the left liberal role was not just engineered from the top. There was spontaneous support for the Bloc amongst constituency committees and rank and file alike. Telegrams of obeisance sent to Bülow from left liberal victory rallies revealed the enthusiasm for the Bloc amongst ordinary voters.[9] After the run-off elections jubilant Berlin left liberals crowded around the imperial automobile returning from a scientific lecture, and greeted Wilhelm's appearance on the palace balcony with patriotic songs.[10] Secondly, the 1907 election was more a coming out than a sudden conversion. It had the effect of bringing into the open the underlying and growing left liberal support for colonies and the navy. It brought to an end the macabre practice of FrVp deputies making speeches substantially supporting the military or colonial demand under discussion, but ending, out of respect for Richterite principle, in a vote against the proposed measure.[11]

---

[8] G. D. Crothers, *The German Elections of 1907* (New York, 1941), 162–3; Elm, *Fortschritt*, 179.

[9] *Altonaer Tageblatt* (3 Feb. 1907); Elm, *Fortschritt*, 184.

[10] *Kieler Neueste Nachrichten* (7 Feb. 1907).

[11] For examples of this unconvincing attempt to look both ways at once see *Die Freisinnige Volkspartei und die deutsche Flotte* (Berlin, 1906).

Even critics of the left liberal role in the 1907 elections like Barth and von Gerlach backed a more positive left liberal attitude towards 'national' issues. The elections also brought to the surface another theme obscured by Richter's inflexibility: a desire for co-operation with the government rather than confrontation. Again, even radical Barthians agreed that left liberals had to seek a more positive role, though they denied that a Bloc policy which weakened the left at the expense of right was the way to achieve it.[12] As for the Richterites, 1907 demonstrated how far Richter's natural distrust of the executive and personal animosity for Bismarck had hidden an increasing acceptance of the fundamentals of the Wilhelmine state. The FrVp consistently displayed more 'Bloc enthusiasm' than either the FrVg or DVP. Moreover, this was a pattern which did not just reflect the younger generation of leaders: 90-year-old veteran Paul Langerhans, a founder member of the Fortschrittspartei in 1861, urged the FrVp central committee in 1909 'not to knock the Bloc'.[13]

If Richterite tradition on 'national' issues and attitudes to government was stripped away, its petty-bourgeois anti-socialism was reinforced, especially in Northern Germany. This was underscored by a new edition of Richter's pamphlet *Sozialdemokratische Zukunftsbilder* (Social Democrat Pictures of the Future) in 1907, raising the total circulation of this anti-socialist diatribe from 255,000 to 264,000.[14] However, hostility towards the Centre went both deeper and wider. The Centre was the enemy for all seasons. Left liberal machine politicians envied the Centre's key position in the Reichstag and saw the 1907 election as an opportunity to supplant it as an indispensable part of the government's majority. Even left liberal opponents of the government's election campaign, like Max Weber and Theodor Barth, hardly intended to assist the party they regarded as the prime practitioners of unprincipled horse-trading, the perpetuators of an unworthy *Trinkgeldpolitik*.[15] The perceived success and influence of the Centre since the early 1890s multiplied basic left liberal hostility towards what the party stood for. Most importantly, attacks on political Catholicism appealed to prejudice as well as belief. Antipathy towards Rome, the 'dead hand', and 'dark' forces of cultural backwardness attracted a far wider section of opinion than specific liberal

---

[12] Wegner, *Theodor Barth, passim.*   [13] *Liegnitzer Anzeiger* (19 Jan. 1909).
[14] *Fortschritt: Halbmonatsschrift für Politik, Volkswirtschaft und Marinefragen* (1907), 187.
[15] HSA Stuttgart, NL Haußmann 114, Theodor Barth to Conrad Haußmann, 1 July 1906.

economic, social, or political policies. As Max Bahr, a left liberal Jute manufacturer in Landsberg, correctly observed, it was the deep-seated Protestant bitterness against the Centre which did most to mobilize the electorate in 1907. Although this sentiment, in Bahr's view, 'had by and large precious little to do with real politics and political principles', he could not deny its hold on the left liberal electorate.[16]

The 1907 election was therefore more a catalyst than a transformation of left liberal politics. Richter himself had predicted the end of left liberal opposition to defence and colonial bills.[17] The 'Hottentot campaign' made change more rapid and complete. Similarly, a background of patriotic fervour accentuated the imperialism, nationalism, anti-socialism, and antipathy to the Centre party which were already part of the everyday attitudes of left liberal voters. However, if the 1907 election brought greater clarity to left liberal attitudes in some areas, its ambiguities were equally significant. Though the Bloc parties reached agreement in a range of constituencies, in many others the left liberals and right continued to fight each other. Most accounts of the 1907 elections have focused on the high profile of radical nationalist associations and figures like August Keim and Eduard von Liebert.[18] However, nationalism, anti-Catholicism, and anti-socialism succeeded in mobilizing voters precisely because they were not specifically 'radical nationalist recipes', but common sentiments shared by many hostile or indifferent to radical nationalist groups. Moreover, the bulk of constituency campaigning and the local and regional agreements which mattered were made by the political parties. The establishment of joint candidates in many constituencies, the key to the Bloc majority, was brought about primarily by meetings between Conservative and Liberal local leaders.

The key to Liberal–Conservative agreements was SPD strength. Inevitably, agreements were harder to reach in areas with a history of rivalry between the bourgeois parties. However, there were competing Liberal and Conservative candidates above all where the SPD was either too strong or too weak for the outcome to be affected. In the three Hamburg seats, for example, separate left liberal and National Liberal candidates were a reflection of the fact that the SPD would

---

[16] SA Wolfenbüttel, NL Schrader III. 4, Max Bahr to Karl Schrader, 4 Oct. 1907.

[17] *Freisinnige Zeitung* (30 July 1908); Elm, *Fortschritt*, 174.

[18] See Crothers, *German Elections*; Fricke, 'Der Deutsche Imperialismus'; Chickering, *We Men*; Eley, *Reshaping*.

win anyway, as well as a relationship between the two parties poisoned by changes to the local franchise. The more important and more typical areas of continued conflict were between left liberals and the right in predominantly small town and semi-rural seats, particularly in the east. In Mecklenburg and Pomerania left liberals and Conservatives continued their long-standing electoral rivalry.[19] The bourgeois parties reached agreement in Kiel and Breslau, but not in the surrounding semi-rural districts.[20] The immediate Social Democratic presence was too insubstantial to generate a common set of apprehensions, and the local cleavages represented by different non-socialist parties—rural against urban, smallholders against estate owners, authoritarianism against independence—were too deep to be papered over by national-ist rhetoric.

Although voting in the cities partly justified radical *schadenfreude*, neither a 'single reactionary mass' nor a division into Liberal–Conservative and SPD–Centre blocs was an adequate description of voting patterns. True, the damping down of the main point of difference, 'national' issues, and mutual self-interest, the pressing need for enough votes to enter the run-offs, ended traditional National Liberal–left liberal electoral rivalry in much of Germany. The two parties stood against each other in only forty-four of the 356 constituencies they contested. According to Naumann, this had led to prospects of Liberal success being endangered in only four seats.[21] However, first round co-operation between the left liberals and other non-socialist parties was essentially limited to areas of particular SPD strength: urban seats and regions like Saxony and Thuringia. Conservatives and Centre continued to support each other in parts of Southern Germany as well as the east. Even after the election there was a continued Conservative desire for some co-operation with the Centre, with some deputies wishing to support a Centre candidate for Reichstag deputy president. Only fear of

---

[19] Rohe, *Wahlen und Wählertraditionen*, 118.

[20] For the continuing battle in Schleswig-Holstein by left liberals against both National Liberals and Conservatives, and between left liberals and Conservatives in Lower Silesia see Chs. 8 and 9 below.

[21] BA Berlin, FVP 37, fo. 158, Naumann to FVP central committee, 19 Mar 1911. The figures in Sheehan, *German Liberalism*, 347 n. 6, are calculated on a different basis, exclud-ing constituencies where one Liberal party polled under 5 per cent. Nevertheless, they give a good picture of the decline in seats contested by both National Liberals and left liberals after 1890: 1890 (113); 1893 (89); 1898 (68); 1903 (47); 1907 (29); 1912 (47).

Protestant public opinion, together with Liberal insistence, brought about a 'Bloc' praesidium.[22]

Though the government and Liberals talked threateningly about a 'red–black bloc' there were only partial electoral agreements between Centre and SPD. Where the two parties co-operated it was primarily against Liberal candidates in regions like Baden, the Palatinate, and the Rhineland. Finally, SPD voters continued to give run-off support to left liberals against the right, despite the conduct of most left liberal politicians and electors.[23]

The absence of a national pattern of electoral alignments underlined the lack of a Bloc programme. On the one hand, left liberal candidates rode the tide of emotional appeal: anti-clerical resentment, anti-socialism, *Weltpolitik*, and support for 'our boys'.[24] On the other hand, they continued to put forward a programme of established liberal demands. The assault on political Catholicism was a pursuit of liberal education policy as well as prejudice. The attack on the 'international' labour movement was also a call for integration through social and political reform. Support for imperialism and nationalism was also a quest for national efficiency, predicated on modernization and meritocracy. Tactical flexibility, the evident desire for compromise, and a share of influence were accompanied by programmatic rigidity. What the left liberals sought, they insisted, were 'new paths to old goals'.[25]

Such aspirations were not at all what the Conservatives or— disingenuous left liberal suggestions notwithstanding—the government had in mind.[26] From the outset, therefore, both the Bloc parties and executive were fissured over the key question of modernization. There were those like the bulk of the DKP and most Prussian ministers who were opposed to any change. Others, like the Chancellor, Reich Chancellory officials, and moderate Conservatives saw certain concessions to the spirit of the age as unavoidable. However, the

[22] AA Wrocław, NL Neise, 3, Pfarrer Stull to Franz Josef Neise, 22 Feb. 1907; NL Neise, 4, Felix Porsch to Neise, 20 Feb 1907.

[23] See e.g. the SPD run-off support given to left liberal candidates in Schleswig-Holstein and Lower Silesia detailed in Chs. 8 and 9 below.

[24] 'Unsere kämpfenden Jungen in Afrika lassen wir nicht im Stich!', *Niederschlesischer Anzeiger* (3 Jan. 1907); cf. *Berliner Tageblatt*, 29 (17 Jan. 1907).

[25] *Freisinnige Zeitung* (30 July 1908).

[26] For examples of left liberals claiming to patriotic peasant and small-town voters that they were the 'government party' and that the Chancellor wanted more Liberals and fewer Conservatives in order to implement liberal reforms, see Elm, *Fortschritt*, 182–3.

intention, particularly in the political sphere, was to create the illusion of change in the interests of the status quo. This was supplemented, in some quarters, by a more genuine appetite for technocratic reform. Such a course was supported especially by National Liberals and, amongst ministers, by Bethmann and, more energetically, by Dernburg. Finally, a mainly left liberal minority advocated general liberalization. This was a wide spectrum of views reflecting deep political differences and, equally important, the gulf between popular and traditionalist attitudes towards government.

How far was the Bloc able to synthesize or at least suppress such obvious differences? It is useful, before turning to specific legislative measures, to examine the less obvious, but possibly more significant area of general methods. If the Bloc did not represent a serious intention to modernize substance, did it at least modernize style? At least some case can be made for this. To some extent, the 'Hottentot' campaign was a rerun of 1887 or other Bismarckian attempts at electoral manipulation. However, there was novelty in both the extent and methods of government involvement. Dernburg's electoral barnstorming and direct appeal to popular sentiment went well beyond previous norms of ministerial conduct. This appeal to populism generated some 500 direct messages of support from local parties, radical nationalist branches, Bismarck *Stammtische*, bowling clubs, and the like.[27] Similarly, Bülow's New Year's letter and other pronouncements lessened the degree of detachment implied by anonymous articles and private telegrams. Moreover, the government sought to enrol public opinion on particular matters, the 1908 Associations Law and especially the 1909 Finance Bill, and throughout the Bloc period referred back to a popular mandate it claimed from the 1907 elections. From its very foundation, imperial Germany had depended to some extent on a wider current of public opinion as well as the wishes of a small ruling class. Nevertheless, the attempt during the Bloc period to harness public sentiment against traditional resistance was more sustained than any since the 1870s.

The Bloc also witnessed revisions to the relations between the executive and political parties. Again there was nothing new about ministers and higher officials bartering with deputies. For years there had been negotiations with party figures behind the scenes. Friedrich Althoff, the *éminence grise* of Prussian higher education policy, for example,

---

[27] BA Koblenz, NL Dernburg, vol. 13.

was past master in the art of giving and receiving favours.[28] Even the left liberals, though the Bloc undoubtedly gave them improved access to 'ministerial hotels',[29] were already familiar visitors on constituency matters, or on behalf of a variety of groups and individuals. Apart from the SPD and national minorities, who were largely excluded or excluded themselves, the executive and political parties each had something important to offer the other. Deputies obviously had an interest in securing government action across a wide range of issues where no legal or parliamentary remedy was available. Conversely, whatever the limits to the Reichstag's authority, majority parliamentary support was essential for new legislation or increased national taxation. A combination of disciplined party voting in Reichstag and state parliaments, together with parliamentary budgetary powers and legislative influence, meant that informal negotiations and deliberations in committee between the executive and political parties were essential to the workings of government in Wilhelmine Germany. The Bloc, however, took the process a stage further. Grudging acceptance of the parties' importance was superseded by open acknowledgement. Whereas Lieber had once donned disguise to slip into furtive negotiation with Posadowsky, now the Chancellor took it upon himself to arrange a succession of high-profile audiences with party leaders at Nordeney in summer 1907. The schedule, carefully arranged and reported, included meetings with Bassermann (9 August), Normann (21 August), Kaempf (2 September), Payer and Schmidt-Elberfeld (7 September), Gamp (10 September), Liebermann von Sonnenberg (11 September), Schrader (13 September), and Wangenheim and Roesicke (18 September).[30] Though the Kaiser undoubtedly resented this further nail in the coffin for the convention of 'above party' government, publicly announced meetings between the Chancellor and Conservative and Liberal party leaders became a feature of the Bloc period.[31] Likewise, legislative detail, neglected by Bülow, was

---

[28] See e.g. Eickhoff's description of Althoff's famous 'Versprecherkeller'. R. Eickhoff, *Politische Profile* (Berlin, 1927), 181–95.

[29] AW Wrołcaw, Regierungspräsidium Oppeln 227, meeting Freisinniger Verein Zabrze, 26 Mar. 1909.

[30] See the Chancellor's telegrams to Hammann detailing the messages to be circulated to the press. AA Bonn IA, Deutschland 122. 4, vol. 5.

[31] In reply to Wilhelm II's objections Bülow described the discussions with party leaders as tiresome 'but necessary so that we can hold the Bloc together'. Bülow to Wilhelm II, 9 Sept. 1907, cited in Lerman, *Chancellor as Courtier*, 191. Bülow's expressions of displeasure should not be taken at face value. In fact the Chancellor found such meetings

discussed in meetings between party leaders and other ministers. The 1908 Imperial Associations Act was the result of compromises reached after numerous meetings between Bethmann and representatives of the Bloc parties. The finance reform was another marathon of executive–party discussion. Moreover, the importance of such nominally informal meetings was underlined when the government's decision to include the Centre in discussions with the Treasury State Secretary Sydow in September 1908 was taken as a signal of the Bülow Bloc's approaching end.[32]

Inevitably, the attempt to appeal more extensively to public opinion and the political parties involved making greater use of the press. The Nordeney meetings showed the importance Bülow placed on news management. Newspapers were called upon to generate popular Bloc enthusiasm, and to impress the importance of Bloc policy on Liberal and Conservative politicians. The press and government–press relations became more central to the process of government. For the Reich leadership, a favourable press was essential in maintaining a political climate conducive to the Bloc. Both left liberal and Conservative newspapers had to be encouraged to conclude that the Bloc brought more advantages than disadvantages, so that pressure was placed on the respective parliamentary parties to continue the arrangement.

The press was used in a variety of ways. Unattributed suggestions were floated either to test likely reactions in various parts of the Bloc, or, more deviously, simply to create a favourable impression without serious intent to proceed. Legislation like the 1908 Associations Act offered scope for saying different things to different newspapers: drawing the attention of liberal newspapers to progressive aspects, whilst stressing the restrictive elements to the Conservative press. There was a natural temptation for newspapers to build up a white or, in the case of the Catholic, socialist, and radical press, a black legend of the Bloc. Newspapers on all sides had a vested journalistic interest in presenting the Bloc as a dramatic new development in German politics. By exaggerating the Bloc the press did however make some contribution to its real significance. The existence of a pro- and anti-

opportunities to exercise his vanity and gift for smooth talking, enjoyable as well as essential. BA Koblenz, NL Loebell 27, fo. 12, 'Lebenserinnerungen'.

[32] HSA Stuttgart, NL Haußmann, 116, Naumann to Haußmann, 22 Sept. 1908; StA Mannheim, NL Wolfhard, FrVg executive committee minutes, 24 Sept. 1908.

Bloc press had the effect of making the Bloc more of a dividing line for both parties and public. As with its successor, the Blue-Black Bloc, the Bülow Bloc took on far more concrete and impressive form in the newspaper columns than in parliament. That Bülow's political swansong as Chancellor took the form of a newspaper interview was a blow to convention, but entirely appropriate.[33]

The Bloc, then, brought a new emphasis to relations between government, public, press, and parties. It was a more extensive and explicit arrangement than its informal predecessor, the tariff reform majority of Conservatives, Centre, and National Liberals. At the same time, it was more diverse and less subservient than the Bismarckian *Kartell.* However, the government's commitment was not wholehearted and its efforts were only partially successful. The emphasis placed on the Bloc owed much to unforeseen circumstance. Ironically, the party which most furthered the cause of parliamentary influence during the Bülow Bloc was the Centre. Though opponents, especially left liberals, attributed the Centre party's unexpected determination to be rid of Bülow to arrogance and base motives, it was this which tied the Chancellor closer than anticipated to a particular party constellation and underlined the need for a Reichstag majority. In addition, the *Daily Telegraph* affair and resultant antipathy between Kaiser and Chancellor forced Bülow into the role of the defender of responsible government. After November 1908 it was clear that the support of a Reichstag majority and public opinion were the props which kept Bülow in office.

The Bloc was shaped by circumstance as much as intention. Moreover, the bulk of Germany's and, in particular, Prussia's ruling classes remained largely impervious to the necessity for a more popular and modern style of government. The officer corps, naval as well as army, remained nests of unreconstructed conservatism.[34] Even the partial opponents of tradition were not interested in political modernization. Ludendorff was concerned only with the expansion and technological modernization of the army. Tirpitz, though assiduous in influencing politicians, public opinion, and the press in the interest of building battleships, remained indifferent or hostile to a similar approach across a wider political agenda. Rather than embracing the political

---

[33] For Bülow's interview with Eckardt, editor of the *Hamburgischer Correspondent*, see P.-C. Witt, *Die Finanzpolitik des Deutschen Reiches von 1903 bis 1913* (Hamburg, 1970), 291 ff.

[34] H. H. Herwig, *The German Naval Officer Corps: A Social and Political History 1890–1918* (Oxford, 1973).

realities, the court, paying sycophantic homage to the pretence of personal rule, continued the illusion that parties, press, and public opinion had no part to play. The refusal of the Kaiser to meet party leaders seriously weakened Bülow's efforts to enlist party support through a great show of consultation and a minimum of real concessions. The South German example demonstrated how far even sporadic and largely social meetings could improve relations between monarchs and the political parties. With small cost to personal belief and pro-National Liberal administrative practice, South German monarchs managed to win the respect of a broad spectrum of party and public opinion.[35] By contrast, Hohenzollern aloofness, rather than imparting political detachment, only emphasized in the popular mind the dynasty's attachment to the outmoded social and political attitudes of the Prussian aristocracy. At the same time it left non-Conservative politicians with an underlying grievance about a sphere of government which was out of touch and out of reach.[36]

Equally, the Bloc did little to change a similar air of condescension and contempt for political parties and public opinion displayed by many ministers and administrative officials. The objection of Breitenbach, the Prussian minister of public works, to a deputy receiving an honorary order, on the grounds of his low occupational status as a railwayman, was a small, but telling example of the persistence of blinkered attitudes. Tirpitz and a succession of Prussian ministers all wrote in support of Breitenbach's ludicrous contention that, despite the convention that deputies were offered orders not lower honours, any recognition higher than a mark of honour in silver or (preferably) bronze would be prejudicial to discipline. It was left to Delbrück to point out, as politely as possible, the political realities of the situation: even if the deputy himself did not throw such an insulting honour back in the government's face, the press certainly would.[37]

With such archaic attitudes still rife in 1913 it comes as little surprise that Bülow had only limited success in persuading ministers not to act against the grain of party and political opinion. Bülow may have discovered a typically crafty way of interesting Wilhelm II in the appointment of a liberal banker of Jewish extraction as colonial secretary: he was thinking, the Chancellor told the technologically inclined

---

[35] Bonn, *Wandering Scholar*, 194.   [36] Eschenburg, *Kaiserreich am Scheideweg*, p. xi.
[37] BA Koblenz, R43/F Reichskanzlei, 1384, fiche 7, Breitenbach memo 23 Mar. 1913 and ministerial replies.

Emperor, about a man who possessed his own automobile.[38] Never-theless, Dernburg remained a political and social outsider in bureau-cratic and court circles.[39] Though advised that a modest number of administrative posts could secure Liberal loyalty, the Chancellor was unwilling or unable to break the Conservative near monopoly of administration. The feeling of helplessness about changing the direc-tion of Prussian administration from the top was reflected in the widely reported words of a senior official figure (probably Clemens von Delbrück): 'Is liberal rule possible for us? For twenty-five years no *Landrat*, no Regierungsrat or Regierungspräsident, barely an Oberpräsident, no Amtsvorsteher, hardly a parish chairman has been confirmed in office in East Elbia who was not conservative to the bone. We find ourselves in an iron net of conservative administration and self-administration.'[40] Nor was it just political one-sidedness which generated continued resentment. It was still a typical experience for deputies dealing with the executive in Berlin, and even more, for members of the public facing provincial officials, of being looked down upon by the self-important sons of bureaucratic or estate-owning families. Certainly, the self-propagated image of the *Beamtenstaat* created some awe in non-Conservative circles. See, for example, the exaggerated respect shown towards Kurt Riezler, who had been a junior member of the National-Social Association when a student in Munich, by Naumann and Haußmann.[41] In many cases, however, this was more than offset by resentment at official high-handedness.[42] The Bloc, with its absence of administrative reform, did nothing to enhance the long-term popular acceptance of government. It only highlighted the inherent conflict in government between a minority of more flexible, forward-looking conservatives and the traditional majority bent on an unyielding maintenance of privilege and trad-ition. The divisions between government departments which had to deal with the forces created by a modern industrial society, with the Reichstag, and mass social and economic issues, and those accountable

---

[38] BA Koblenz, NL Loebell, 27, 'Erinnerungen'.

[39] W. Schiefel, *Bernhard Dernburg 1865–1937: Kolonialpolitiker und Bankier im Wilhelminischen Deutschland* (Zürich, 1976).

[40] *Liberale Korrespondenz* (22 Oct. 1910), cited in Molt, *Reichstag*, 142.

[41] BA Koblenz, NL Heuss 495, Riezler's notes of conversation with Naumann on 25 Aug. 1907; BA Koblenz, NL Goetz 65, membership list National-Social Association Munich.

[42] HSA Stuttgart, NL Haußmann 105, *Frankfurter Zeitung* (9. July 1921); Epstein, *Erzberger, passim.*

to the Prussian Landtag and primarily concerned with preserving the vested interests of small groups, became increasingly marked. Conservative references to the Reich interior ministry as 'the red office' (*das rote Amt*) revealed just how bitter such conflict had become in the pre-war period.[43] Such attacks had their roots in resentment and foreboding towards a department in the forefront of accommodating party and popular pressure. Similarly, Friedrich Wilhelm von Loebell and Arnold Wahnschaffe, both long-time DKP members, found a growing and unavoidable estrangement between Conservative intransigence and their position as leading members of the Chancellor's Office.

Of course, tensions between the Reich and Prussia, the problematic combination of the Chancellor's vast responsibilities and reliance on prestige rather than collegiate government, and the uneven and uneasy mixture of monarchical and parliamentary powers, were inherent to the Bismarckian constitution. However, such difficulties were cushioned when, as from the mid-1890s to 1906, the government could fall back on the same loose arrangement of Conservatives, Centre, and National Liberals in both the Reichstag and Prussian House of Deputies. The Bloc made the dichotomy between Reich and Prussian politics more striking. A break with the Centre in the Reich contrasted with a continued Conservative/Centre alignment in Prussia, above all on cultural issues. Public credulity was strained by ministers, not least the Chancellor, appearing to face different directions depending on which hat, Reich or Prussian, they were wearing. Moreover, the greater appeal to Protestant middle-class opinion implied by the Bloc produced winners and losers amongst government ministers. The task for departments dealing with 'national' issues was made easier. The 1907 election marked the end to government difficulties getting defence or colonial bills through the Reichstag. Oppsition to the 1908 naval bill was minimal. The 1907 electoral set-back led the SPD to emphasize its own patriotic credentials, most controversially in Gustav Noske's contributions to Reichstag military debates. The Centre's response was well caught by a declaration at the 1907 Silesian conference: 'Nevetheless we will continue to work for the Kaiser and the Reich and will not be outdone by anyone in love for the Fatherland.'[44] However, in other areas, the current of Protestant

---

[43] Delbrück, *Wirtschaftliche Mobilmachung*, 311. Delbrück referred, with black humour, to a Conservative ministerial death list with his name on it.

[44] AW Wrocław, Regierungspräsidium Oppeln 221.

middle-class opinion ran against ministerial intention. Just as the colonial office under Solf as well as Dernburg, welcomed greater Liberal participation and took a lead in consulting a range of political parties, so the Prussian agriculture and education ministers had good reason to fear popular influence and to look with dismay on Liberal, especially left liberal influence displacing that of the Centre party. The Bloc period saw a stoking up of the disharmony between Reich and Prussian politics, between the Chancellor and his deputy on the one hand and much of the Prussian state ministry on the other, which was to come to a head after 1912. The government's relations with the fourth estate were similarly problematic and lacking in consequence. To the extent that the Bloc lived by the press, it also died by it. The journalistic tendency to excess worked both ways. Just as small advances were presented as great triumphs for Bülow, so set-backs were also magnified. 'Crisis in the Bloc' became a recurrent headline. The stance of the press also reflected the fragility of the Bloc. Newspapers like the *Deutsche Tageszeitung* on the right and the *Berliner Tageblatt* on the left were sceptical from the outset. And though their hostility was untypical, the attitude of the left liberal and Conservative press towards each other, like that of the parties themselves, always bore the air of an uneasy truce.[45] The intense war of words which broke out over the finance reform during the first half of 1909 effectively reduced the Bülow Bloc to an empty shell well before the Reichstag vote on the inheritance tax in June, and demonstrated the severe limits to the government's ability to influence the press. Though Bülow and Hammann demonstrated an exquisite touch at times, their attitude was a strange contradiction of old and new. The significance of the press in a modern state and the importance of being able to influence it were recognized, but this was combined with archaic aloofness and snobbery.[46] Hammann was, ironically, a press officer who refused to have much contact with the press outside a small circle of confidants, above all August Stein and Arthur von Huhn, the Berlin correspondents of the *Frankfurter Zeitung* and *Kölnische Zeitung*. Not only was this a far too narrow basis to guide popular opinion, it was often the correspondents who influenced

---

[45] See G. Fesser, 'Zum konservativ-liberalen Bülow-Block 1907–1909', *Jenaer Beiträge zur Parteiengeschichte*, 44 (1980), 129; *Konservative Monatsschrift* (Oct. 1908), 12–25, and BA Berlin, NL Wangenheim 2i-4, correspondence Wangenheim and Roesicke, for Conservative Bloc doubts.

[46] See Bülow's instructions to his press chief in BA Berlin, NL Hammann 6–15.

officials rather than the reverse. Friedrich Holstein's acerbic comments on 'the Press trio of Hammann, Huhn and Stein' were coloured by personal animosity. However, his insinuation that they represented a close-knit circle with significant influence on the executive's conduct of Bloc policy was close to the mark, as was the suggestion that Hammann was at least as much influenced by Huhn, and especially Stein, as they were by him.[47] Equally, the Reich chancellery only considered newspapers like the *Hamburgischer Correspondent* and *Schlesische Zeitung*, high-brow, hide-bound, and with a select, largely governmental readership, good enough to have direct links. *General-Advertiser* and other mass-circulation newspapers were shunned despite having precisely the large, socially mixed and, in part, politically uncommitted readership the government needed to win over. Thus, for example, a request from the political editor of the widely read *Hamburger Fremdenblatt* for an audience with Bülow to help encourage 'that certain optimism . . . which is the conditio sine qua non of Bloc politics' was not even given the courtesy of a reply.[48]

There remained, therefore, chains of tradition which government leaders were unwilling to break. But if partial change and cosmetic improvisation rather than comprehensive renewal summed up the shifts in government style during 1907–9 such reservations are even more appropriate to the specific measures passed by the Bülow Bloc. The bang of the 1907 election campaign was followed by the whimper of a light and unconvincing legislative programme. Reichstag sessions were kept short; the House ceased sitting on 14 May 1907 and 7 May 1908, the earliest summer dissolutions since 1894, apart from the election years of 1898 and 1903.[49] And the pressing question of Reich finances was put off. The fruits of Bülow's 'mating of the conservative and liberal spirit' were so sparse that contemporaries began to mock the Bloc as an instrument capable only of 'national' melodies.[50] Parliamentary inactivity was the natural inclination of a diplomat-chancellor, who, in Loebell's phrase, 'loved a clean desk'. Unlike his

---

[47] Rich and Fisher (eds.), *Holstein Papers*, esp. iv. 415, 471, 510, 619. For an assessment of Stein's extensive contacts and behind-the-scenes influence, see Payer's review of his essays: HSA Stuttgart, NL Haußmann 105, *Frankfurter Zeitung* (9 July 1921).

[48] BA Berlin, Reichskanzlei 1393, fos. 17–23, letter from Dr Paul Raché, *Hamburger Fremdenblatt*, to Bülow, 16 Sept. 1907 and internal memos; BA Koblenz, NL Bülow 185, fos. 43–51, Verlag *Hamburger Fremdenblatt* to Bülow, 9 Oct. 1907. For the considerable electoral importance of the *Hamburger Fremdenblatt*'s readership see Ch. 8 below.

[49] A. Plate, *Handbuch für das Preußische Abgeordnetenhaus* (Berlin, 1908).

[50] Sheehan, *German Liberalism*, 262–3.

successor, Bülow was not interested in questions of internal reform and was 'barely abreast of domestic politics'.[51] However, the central reason for the legislative paucity of the Bloc was the incompatibility of its component parts. The slow pace of legislation was an uneasy compromise between Conservative resistance to change and Liberal calls for modernization. 'The two and half years of the Bloc', as Wermuth put it, 'boiled down to the attempt to keep both unwilling partners in some sort of reasonable mood.'[52]

It was no coincidence that much of 'Bloc legislation' dealt with Prussian problems under a national pretext. The 1908 Imperial Associations Law was largely about replacing the antiquated 1850 Prussian Associations Law. Reforms to the *lèse-majesté* laws were more relevant to Prussia than the South, where denigration of the Hohenzollerns was treated leniently.[53] Prussian agricultural and industrial interests were at the forefront of the battle over stock-exchange legislation. It was in Prussia that divisions between the Conservative and Liberal components of the Bülow Bloc were most implacable. The former insisted that the Bloc concerned only 'national' issues and had nothing to do with Prussian politics. In the end Prussian Conservatives brought the Bloc down rather than place a direct tax, the inheritance duty, in the hands of the Reich rather than Prussia. By contrast, Liberals demanded that the Bloc be extended to include Prussian reform. Indeed, Liberal Bloc aspirations were essentially a catalogue of Prussian rather than Reich matters. Moreover, discontent about the Conservative stranglehold on power and influence in Prussian politics was to be found in National Liberal as well as left liberal ranks. National Liberals, as Richard Witting, mayor of Posen, put it, were willing to support every 'national' demand,

but that apart, they do not want to go along with things in *Prussia* under any circumstances. They have had enough of for decades playing the role of a governmental party which has absolutely no say, and is kept distant from everything to do with the executive. Nor will they be fobbed off in any way with a few ministerial posts in the technical departments.[54]

[51] Payer, 'Lebenslauf', 45. For a detailed analysis of Bülow's lackadaisical approach to government see Lerman, *Chancellor as Courtier*, *passim*.

[52] Wermuth, *Beamtenleben*, 262.

[53] In Bavaria e.g. state legal officials took an indulgent, even sympathetic view towards Ludwig Quidde's barbed attacks on Wilhelm II. L. Quidde, *Caligula: Schriften über Militarismus und Pazifismus*, ed. Hans-Ulrich Wehler (Frankfurt am Main, 1977).

[54] BA Berlin, Reichskanzlei 1393, fos. 15–16, Witting to Kammerherr von Roell, 21 Aug. 1907, (copy).

Unfulfilled Liberal Bloc demands—reform of the three-class franchise, administrative modernization, non-confessional schooling—were all at the core of political conflict in Prussia.

The Chancellor's attempts to engineer cosmetic concessions to 'the liberal-democratic idea in Prussia'[55] managed to worry Conservatives without convincing public opinion. Bülow's sharp rejection of the Reichstag suffrage for Prussian elections in January 1908 offended left liberal sensibilities without assuaging the right. The mere suggestion of an 'organic development' of the Prussian franchise aired in the speech from the throne in autumn 1908 triggered deep Conservative disquiet. However, such a deliberately vague formula inspired little confidence amongst supporters of reform. Walking the tightrope between the conservative and liberal elements of the Bloc, Bülow discovered two unpalatable lessons. First, that even illusory reform proposals were enough to upset the DKP; and, secondly, that Liberals had appetite for real reform: 'our voters *on the ground* want at last to see *liberal deeds* to follow the liberal words'.[56] Far from lessening Liberal–Conservative differences, which seemed at least feasible at the outset, the Bloc ended up confirming and inflaming them.

Was it not, then, a serious miscalculation and blow to party prestige for left liberals to enter an arrangement which offered little more than marginal concessions and brief existence? Two considerations speak against such an interpretation. The first was the absence of an alternative. An anti-imperialist stance would have cost votes and seats. An alliance with the Centre and SPD mooted by radical liberals like Breitscheid was hardly practical. The general mood of the Protestant middle strata in January 1907 aside, political and electoral mechanics rendered such an arrangement unworkable. The proposal overstated the Centre's interest in constitutional reform and overlooked deep social antagonisms. Equally, an SPD–left liberal electoral understanding threatened a considerable loss of seats. As the SPD insisted on fighting every seat in the first round, any agreement could not help the left liberals into more run-off elections. Indeed, by offending

---

[55] Bülow's attitude was reflected in a prediction that the fall of the Bloc would lead to 'real (not imaginary) compensations to the liberal-democratic idea in Prussia'. His intentions for the Bloc were precisely the reverse: imaginary (not real) compensations. Quotation from Bülow's marginalia, 8 Apr. 1909, to Loebell's notes, 6 Apr. 1909, cited in Witt, *Finanzpolitik*, 275–6, and Retallack, 'Reformist Conservatism', 285.

[56] FrVp delegate assembly in Bezirk Hagen, 25 Aug. 1907. *Liegnitzer Anzeiger*, (30 Oct. 1907).

nationalist supporters and blocking pacts with the National Liberals and Conservatives, it could only reduce left liberal prospects in the first round. In the crucial run-off elections, any formal understanding between the left liberals and SPD was likely to alienate more votes on the right than it would attract on the left. More importantly, left liberals sensed an absence not just of alternative partners, but of an alternative political course. The classic left liberal programme, free trade and parliamentarization, not only failed to find allies in the government and other bourgeois parties. It increasingly failed to mobilize electoral support. Left liberal involvement in the Bloc was not purely tactical. It was also part of a search for a more attractive and relevant political message. As the FrVg executive committee's discussion of the political situation in 1905 reflected, left liberal prospects for the near future were distinctly unpromising. What the party needed was 'to discover a new, attractive idea'.[57] Even if left liberals, unlike Bassermannite National Liberals, did not regard the Bülow Bloc as some instrument of political or national salvation, they at least saw it as an experiment which might eventually lead to better results. They felt, as one left liberal newspaper put it, that they had nothing to lose, for left liberalism had enjoyed neither government influence nor great social respect during the last two decades.[58] Such sentiments were echoed by Friedrich Payer, who emerged during the Bloc period not just as the most experienced left liberal parliamentarian, but a leading influence in negotiations with the executive and in decision-making within the left liberal *Fraktionsgemeinschaft*: 'We must just await Bülow's deeds . . . It's possible that everything will collapse if they demand too much from us. But that would be a shame, for when will we have another prospect to fulfil liberal demands.'[59]

This brings us to the second reason for left liberal acceptance of the Bloc: modest expectations. During the first two years of the Bloc there was a continued sense that an attempt to pursue a radical policy within or without the Bloc would founder on the half-heartedness of many left liberal supporters. The 1908 Prussian Landtag elections confirmed 'with shocking clarity' the worst expectations of men like Justizrat Harz, the left liberal leader in Harburg:

---

[57] BA Berlin, FVP, 4, FrVg executive committee, 27 May 5.1905.
[58] *Kieler Neueste Nachrichten* (14 Feb. 1907).
[59] BA Berlin, NL Naumann 231, Payer to Naumann, 21 Sept. 1907.

The urban middle classes do not respond to purely political messages . . . Descriptions of our breathtaking political conditions they listen to like tales of war and battle cries in Turkey. And they go home reassured with the thought that all this just affects the Social Democrats and that's really no great pity. With them only economic questions arouse interest.[60]

The difficulty in raising an effective popular protest against the disciplining of left liberal mayor of Husum Lothar Schücking generated a similar sense of frustration.[61] Above all, left liberal deputies were reluctant to stir up the question of Prussian franchise reform. Naumann's attempt, in July 1907, for instance, to make Prussian franchise reform a precondition for continued left liberal participation in the Bloc was greeted with dark looks and embarrassed silence by most left liberal parliamentarians.[62] It was not that many left liberal voters actually supported existing Prussian electoral arrangements, but that they lacked a sense of urgency about reform. The truth of this cautious assessment of left liberal rank-and-file attitudes was reflected in the electoral failure of the Demokratische Vereinigung, the radical group formed in protest at the Bloc in general, and the language restrictions of the Reich Associations Law in particular. Only in Greater Berlin did a substantial number of radical liberals decide to join the new party.[63]

Inevitably, this indifference weakened the bargaining position of left liberal deputies. They were not, as was frequently said, generals with no troops, but leaders of an undisciplined infantry. Just as Bülow was well aware that left liberal politicians had no interest in equal voting in local elections which would destroy their own position, so he had an idea of the limits to the reform aspirations of many left liberal voters. Left liberal insistence on far-reaching demands could easily be portrayed as impractical and doctrinaire. Similarly, the flaw in the argument of Gerlach, Breitscheid, and others that the left liberals should block tax increases to force political reform was that the elec-

---

[60] BA Koblenz, NL Gothein 22, fo. 131, circular from Dr Harz, 13 June 1908.

[61] StA Mannheim, NL Wolfhard 16, correspondence between general secretary Weinhausen and Hamburg party secretary Haupt.

[62] Theiner, *Sozialer Liberalismus*, 173–5.

[63] K. Kundel, 'Zur Geschichte der Demokratischen Vereinigung von 1908 bis 1910', Diplomarbeit, Humboldt University Berlin 1984; Ludwig Elm, 'Demokratische Vereinigung 1908–1918', Fricke (ed.), *Lexikon*, 1. 496–503; M. Braumann, 'Die Entwicklung der Demokratischen Vereinigung bis zu den Reichstagswahlen 1912', unpublished TS, 1968 (copy in IISH Amsterdam).

torate would not support what it saw as extortion.[64] The attitude of most left liberal voters, and indeed the traditional party line, was that each issue should be considered on its merits.

Nevertheless, there remained a validity to Barth's argument that a Bloc including the Conservatives, the prime obstacle to Prussian change, dulled left liberal reform senses even more. As one Pomeranian left liberal leader complained in April 1909: 'How can we campaign outside with courage and conviction when our deputies relinquish our principles by compromises.'[65] The Demokratische Vereinigung and SPD continued to argue that the 'widows of Eugen Richter' were corrupted by the wiles of the Chancellor and their own vanity and pretensions to statesmanship.[66] What Philipp Scheidemann later referred to as Bülow's 'deadly charm' undoubtedly influenced left liberal deputies. The Chancellor's most ardent admirers included Richard Eickhoff, Otto Mugdan, Hermann Pachnicke, and Siegfried Heckscher: the latter two earned the nicknames 'Bloc man' and 'Bloc boy'.[67] Julius Kopsch even proclaimed a 'culture bloc' stretching from himself to von Kröcher, a notion swiftly derided by those who saw neither the left liberal 'political travelling salesman' nor the Prussian Junker as the highest representatives of German culture.[68] There was also foundation to the critical judgement that the left liberal leaders wanted above all else not to be shut out (*ausgeschaltet*) again.[69] That left liberal politicians were willing to accept a 500 million mark finance 'reform' containing 400 million marks of additional indirect taxation was a measure of how far they were prepared to compromise to keep in with the government.[70]

Such attitudes made it difficult to imagine the circumstances in which the left liberals might take the initiative and break with the Bloc. The compliant approach of many left liberal deputies certainly lasted well into 1909. After Haußmann's vigorous attack on the Bloc

---

[64] H. von Gerlach, *Die Geschichte des preußischen Wahlrechts* (Schöneberg, 1908); Breitscheid, *Bülowblock*; and Barth, *Freisinn im Block*.

[65] BA Koblenz, NL Gothein 33, fos. 192–3, Hugo Wendorff to Georg Gothein, 10 Apr. 1909.

[66] A recurrent theme in F. Mehring, *Politische Publizistik 1905 bis 1918: Gesammelte Schriften Band 15*, 2nd edn. (Berlin, 1973), 214–439.

[67] BA Koblenz, NL Loebell, 10, *Acht Uhr Abend Blatt* (2 May 1929); *Hamburger Echo* (4 Aug. 1908). [68] *Berliner Volkszeitung*, 124 (13 Apr. 1908).

[69] *Hamburger Echo* (4 Aug. 1908).

[70] HSA Stuttgart, NL Haußmann 116, Naumann to Haußmann 22.9.1908 (including copy of Naumann to Payer, 2 Sept. 1908); StA Mannheim, NL Wolfhard 16, FrVg executive committee minutes, 24 Sept. 1908.

in March, 'annoyed, perplexed and embarrassed expressions' were reported on the left liberal benches.[71] However, the influence of the Bülow enthusiasts was partially offset by deputies who distrusted the Chancellor. These included political veterans such as Schrader and Traeger and advocates of a pact of the left like Naumann, Potthoff, and Gothein. The centre of political gravity lay with tacticians like Payer and Fischbeck: certainly no opponents of the Bloc, but men who based their approach of cautious co-operation not on honeyed words, but calculated reflection of party self-interest. More importantly, after an initial electoral enthusiasm, many left liberals outside parliament remained reserved towards the Bloc. Only a small minority believed a protracted alliance with the Conservatives was either practical or desirable. The same newspaper which supported entry into the Bloc on the grounds that left liberals had little to lose summed up the scepticism towards Bülow's stated intention to marry conservatism and liberalism: 'That is to say the least a very uneven pairing. At most a marriage of convenience will come of it.'[72] Unlike in the National Liberals, there was an absence of left liberal calls for the Bloc's res-urrection after 1909. Left liberals openly described the Bloc as a trial, in contrast to the attempts of Bülow and Bassermann to pass it off as a statesmanlike concept. Naumannites argued that the Bloc was just a transitional phase on the path towards liberal unity and Liberal–Socialist 'Bloc of the future'.[73] Even the ultra-pragmatist Otto Wiemer felt compelled to reply to press criticism that the left liberals were cowering in Bülow's 'Blockhütte' (log-cabin). 'Blockhütten', the man for the extended metaphor insisted, were useful stopping-points on the climb to the political heights, 'permanent homes they are not!'[74]

FrVp leaders might admit ambivalence about the introduction of the Reichstag suffrage for Prussian state elections in private conversations with Bülow. In public they, like the Conservatives, insisted that they had no intention of altering their programme or principles. Left liberal politicians were aware of the need to attract what Bassermann

[71] HSA Stuttgart, NL Haußmann 152a, 'Haußmann's Rede', unidentified newspaper cutting, 31 Mar. 1909; cf. *Schwäbischer Merkur* (1 Apr. 1909).

[72] *Kieler Neueste Nachrichten*, (14 Feb. 1907).

[73] See e.g. Adolf Korell, public meeting in Kassel, 23 Oct. 1907, SA Darmstadt, NL Korell 61, *Neue Casseler Zeitung* (27 Oct. 1907); and *Neue Konstanzer Abendzeitung* (5 Sept. 1908).

[74] *Die Freisinnige Volkspartei und die liberalen 'Forderungen des Tages': Eine Kundgebung des freisinnigen Bürgertums im Zirkus Busch in Berlin, 15.9.1907* (Berlin, 1907), 11.

referred to disdainfully as 'the driftwood',[75] but they also had to satisfy committed left liberal supporters and local activists impatient at the pace and direction of reform. The sort of balancing act required was exemplified by a speech by Fischbeck in his Liegnitz constituency. The argument that political circumstances allowed only small steps rather than great strides was followed by a pledge 'not do anything which contradicts the liberal principles on which we have attained the confidence of our voters'.[76] But such verbal assurances had increasingly little effect as the Bloc failed to bring about significant reform. This was reflected in the succession of food metaphors bombarding Bülow, 'der Koch am Ordnungsbrei'.[77] One cartoon (reproduced on the dust jacket) depicted left liberal leaders dining at the Chancellor's table being offered, not meaty concessions, but only a dubious-looking 'Bülow herring'; at the FrVp conference a South German delegate warned Bülow that the left liberals wanted something to chew on, not just watery promises.[78]

The thin gruel of Bloc legislation was insufficient to build up a store of credit amongst the left liberal rank and file. Indeed, it became more a question of which compromise would finally generate a sufficient volume of popular resistance. Circumstances confined grassroots objections to the 1908 Associations Law to manageable proportions. Pragmatists could argue that its benefits outweighed its drawbacks. Moreover, whilst Barth, Haußmann, and others argued forcibly that the bill was a breach of liberal principle, widespread hostility towards the Poles meant many left liberals were indifferent or supportive towards a language clause aimed against them. Karl Mommsen, for example, was under pressure from his Danzig constituents to support an anti-Polish language clause.[79] The *Daily Telegraph* interview, and the disgrace and dismissal of court intimates Philipp Eulenburg and Kuno Moltke, who failed to clear themselves against accusations of homosexuality published by Maximilian Harden, undoubtedly influenced public attitudes towards the political establishment, and personal rule in particular. However, the way Bülow distanced himself from both affairs meant public reaction was largely deflected elsewhere. The issue which finally broke the patience of left liberal public opinion was finance reform.

---

[75] Cited in Sheehan, *German Liberalism*, 276.   [76] *Liegnitzer Anzeiger* (26 Nov. 1907).
    [77] AA Bonn, IA Baden 33. 2, Eisendecher to Bülow, 28 Feb. 1907 (copy).
    [78] 'Nicht bloß die Brühe, sondern auch Brocken', *Liegnitzer Anzeieger* (15 Sept. 1907).
    [79] SA Wolfenbüttel, NL Schrader III. 4, FrVg executive committee, 18 Nov. 1907.

The left liberal *Fraktionsgemeinschaft*'s decision to reverse its earlier opposition to a compromise property tax, starting on estates as low as 3,000 marks for the sake of the Bloc was greeted by disbelief and derision: 'Against this, we can safely say that the left liberal electorate has come more and more to the view that the *Fraktion* must finally remain firm for once, and must not make even further concessions to the "Bloc" moloch.'[80] What prevented left liberal deputies from being drawn into yet more compromises was a combination of Conservative intransigence and the exasperation of their own supporters. Left liberal politicians found themselves in advantageous positions through little merit of their own. Certainly, a desire to put the blame for a collapse of the Bloc on the right was part of the reason for their cautious approach. 'If the thing fails', as Karl Mommsen put it, 'the blame lies only with the Conservatives.'[81] However, the main concern, based on a misreading of public opinion, was to continue the Bloc. It was June 1909 before the normally acute Payer showed an appreciation of the considerable political possibilities of the inheritance tax.

A semi-enthusiasm for an inheritance tax is there, and if this were to be disappointed and the Clerics put back at the helm, this would place the Liberals in a most desirable position. And the Conservatives would have to carry the can, because broad groups, namely Protestant circles, who would otherwise support them, would not forgive their treachery vis à vis the Centre.[82]

However, even this assessment failed to foresee the convulsive effect the 1909 finance reform was to have on German politics.

2. FROM FINANCE REFORM TO PHILIPPI: LEFT LIBERALS AND PUBLIC PRESSURE, SUMMER 1909–JANUARY 1912

Future historians will describe the year 1909/1910 as the period when German Conservatives were wrecked. Belief in the adequacy of Conservative statesmanship, in Conservative ideas and in Conservative leadership has been shaken throughout Germany, and in the nation's centres of industry most of all.[83]

(Conrad Haußmann)

---

[80] *Liegnitzer Anzeiger* (7 Mar. 1909); cf. the discontent of local parties expressed in the FrVg Vorstand, 1–2 May 1909, BA Koblenz, NL Gothein 34, fos. 55–64.
[81] BA Koblenz, NL Gothein 34, fo. 56, Karl Mommsen to FrVg Vorstand, 1 May 1909.
[82] HSA Stuttgart, NL Haußmann, 116, Payer to Otto Wiemer, 2 June 1909 (copy).
[83] 'Die Staatskunst der Konservativen', *März* (17 June 1910), 412.

The 1909 finance reform has long been recognized as a significant event in Wilhelmine history. It was the first time a Chancellor had been forced to resign as a result of a parliamentary vote. The fact that Bülow lingered a few days longer for the sake of appearances did nothing to alter the clear and correct public perception that he had by driven out of office by the Reichstag's rejection of the inheritance tax.[84] The finance reform was also a major ingredient in the SPD's dramatic rise from forty-three to 110 seats in the Reichstag elections of January 1912.[85] And, as an intermezzo to these two spectacular acts, it produced a widely based protest movement of trade and industry, the Hansa-Bund.[86]

However, the finance reform had its greatest repercussions not in spectacular happenings on the national stage, but in popular attitudes. Though less dramatic and immediately obvious, they proved ultimately more important. Tax and price increases had always promised increased support for the left. The 1881, 1890, and 1903 elections reflected the pattern clearly enough. The movement of public opinion after 1909 was, however, of a different order: it was more pervasive and above all it was more persistent. The break from free trade at the end of the 1870s and the 1902 tariffs eventually attained sufficient public and party-political acceptance. The same was not true of the finance reform. Popular mobilization and pressure for domestic reform had not abated by 1914. Nor was ephemeral wartime enthusiasm enough to restore the credibility of Conservative tradition.

The evidence of a decisive shift in public opinion in summer 1909 is overwhelming. Left liberals like Haußmann naturally had a vested interest in proclaiming a irreparable loss of public confidence in the right and the political status quo. However, the same could hardly be said of his fellow Württemberger, Minister of State von Weizsäcker, who listened with alarm to country-inn conversations and found even industrialists cursing the government and threatening to vote SPD next time. This acute sense of deep public dissatisfaction was shared by the Centre party newspaper in provincial Württemberg town of Horb. Even the finest of public meetings were in vain, it complained,

---

[84] Witt, *Finanzpolitik*, provides a full account of Bülow's position, the troubled parliamentary passage of the finance reform, and its transformation by a Centre–Conservative majority. [85] Bertram, *Wahlen*.

[86] Although the Hansa-Bund's establishment on 12 June 1909 anticipated the Blue-Black finance reform and the organization was to continue till 1934, the peak of support lay between Bülow's resignation and the withdrawal of heavy industry in summer 1911. Mielke, *Hansa-Bund*; Claudia Hohberg, 'Hansa-Bund für Gewerbe, Handel und Industrie: 1909–1934', in Fricke (ed.), *Lexikon zur Parteiengeschichte*, iii. 91–108.

when 'even the women start to make a racket (*krakehlen*) about the finance reform and our Erzberger'.[87]

Such reactions were typical throughout Germany, not just in traditionally democratic regions like Württemberg. The Bürgermeister of Kattowitz reported continued public tension in the town: 'an unstoppable, general movement caused partly by the new taxes on small luxuries and consumer goods'.[88] The editor of the *National-Zeitung* received many letters against a pact with the Conservatives too strongly worded to be published.[89] The effect of the finance reform reverberated throughout Germany. Sharp swings to the left in the Badenese and Saxon state elections in autumn 1909 reflected an impact on public opinion both sides of the Main. In Baden the Centre party vote fell from 42.4 per cent to 29.8 per cent between 1905 and 1909. In Saxony, where the swing to the left was emphasized by a revised franchise and much increased turn-out, the SPD representation rose from one to twenty-five seats, and the Conservatives were reduced from a comfortable absolute majority to little more than a quarter of the chamber.[90] Thus, unlike the nationalist slogans of the 1907 elections, the finance reform issue made significant inroads into the Centre vote. The Centre lost the South German seats of Konstanz and Immenstadt, both with a Catholic population of over 90 per cent, to the National Liberals in 1911 by-elections. More irreversibly, it lost urban Catholics to the SPD. Social Democratic victory in Würzburg continued the Centre's retreat in South German cities, while in the Rhineland the SPD took Düsseldorf in a 1911 by-election and the prized Cologne constituency, the 'German Rome', in 1912.[91]

Agrarian strongholds proved equally vulnerable. The DKP lost four seats and over 33,000 votes in the six constituencies it had to defend between the finance reform and 1912 elections.[92] Losses included two seats in East Prussia: Lyck-Oletzko to a National Liberal/German Peasant League candidate in April 1910, and Labiau-Wehlau to a left liberal in December 1910. 'The roof's burning above the *Junkers*' heads, and constituencies are disappearing

---

[87] AA Bonn IA, Baden 36. 2, Below, Prussian envoy Stuttgart, to Bethmann, 28 Oct. 1909 (copy).
[88] AW Wrocław, Regierungspräsidium Oppeln 53, report by Bürgermeister Pohlmann, 10 Oct. 1909.
[89] AA Bonn, IA Deutschland 125. 6, Dr Doerkes-Boppard to Bethmann, 24 July 1910.
[90] Loth, *Katholiken im Kaiserreich*, 172; Sheehan, *German Liberalism*, 226–9.
[91] BA Berlin, Reichslandbund 6252.   [92] Fegter, *Reichstagsreden*, 6.

under their feet,' a left liberal paper rejoiced.[93] The reaction within Conservative ranks was scarcely less dramatic: 'in no constituency, no matter how secure it may appear, is one safe from surprises'.[94] Nor was agrarian discomfort confined to the Conservative east. Büdingen-Friedberg, the constituency of the arch-agrarian National Liberal Count Oriola, was taken by the SPD in June 1910, and Hessen National Liberals also lost ground in the 1911 state elections, mostly to the FVP and SPD.[95] The Agrarian League's campaign in favour of the finance reform was extensive, but it was not, as Witt concludes, generally successful.[96] Large numbers of peasant voters saw through its demagogic portrayal of the inheritance tax as an attack on the family.

There was, then, a radicalization of opinion throughout Germany in the wake of the finance reform, a change mirrored by Reichstag by-elections. A fairly stagnant pattern during the Bülow Bloc was transformed into a sharp swing to the left. The SPD, the main beneficiaries, made a string of gains, including largely rural constituencies like Büdingen-Friedberg, Coburg, and Usedom-Wollin. State and municipal elections followed a similar pattern. Despite restrictive franchises, the SPD held almost 9,000 seats in local government by 1911.[97] Above all, there was no let-up in everyday expressions of public protest. There was a stream of public resignations and signs of dissent within the DKP, and the anti-Semitic German Social

Table 5.1. *Reichstag by-elections, 1907–1911*

Party	Gains	Losses
Conservatives	0	4
Anti-Semites	0	3
Centre	0	3
National Liberals	5	6
Left Liberals	2	2
SPD	10	0
Welfs	1	0

Source: *Jauersches Stadtblatt* (25 Apr. 1911); Max Schwarz, *MdR: Biographisches Handbuch der Reichstage* (Hanover, 1965).

---

[93] *Neue Konstanzer Abendzeitung* (12 Dec. 1910).
[94] *Mitteilungen aus der konservativen Partei* (20 Aug. 1910) cited in Retallack, *Notables*, 189.　　　　　　　　　　　　　　　[95] *Neue Badische Landeszeitung* (18 Nov. 1911).
[96] Witt, *Finanzpolitik*, 256–9.　　　　　　[97] BA Berlin, Reichslandbund 5604, fo. 55.

Reform Party lost around half its 30,000 members by 1912.[98] Right-wing *Mittelstand* groups collapsed, or, in the case of the Deutsche Mittelstandsvereinigung led by Carl Rahardt, defected to the Hansa-Bund.[99] Within the 'new' *Mittelstand* the anti-Semitic German National Association of Commercial Clerks (*Deutschnationaler Handlungsgehilfenverband*) lost ground to its Liberal inclined rivals. While membership of the German National Association of Commercial Clerks increased by under 1,000, from 120,133 to 121,032 between 1908 and 1911, the 1858 Association of Commercial Clerks grew from 86,642 to 110,867 members and the Association of German Commercial Clerks from 81,705 to 93,843.[100] Towns and cities formed the main centres of public protest: the Hansa-Bund, for example, mobilized far more members and resources than the German Peasant League (*Deutscher Bauernbund*). The League had less than a fifth of the 250,000 individual membership of the Hansa-Bund. Nor was it financed by agriculture, but by liberal businessmen.[101] Although many of the most spectacular shifts in public opinion occurred in central Germany, in Hesse, Saxony, and Thuringia, a reaction was evident across every region and social grouping.[102]

Before turning to the consequences of such a widespread and persistent radicalization of public attitudes on German society and politics in general and the left liberals in particular, we should perhaps take a somewhat closer look at its causes. Certainly, the 500 million marks of tax increases contained in the 1909 finance reform were in themselves both noticeable and unpopular. Few families failed to feel increased duties on beer, tobacco, coffee, and tea directly. However, resentment was compounded by the past. Just as the pent-up disquiet about two decades of rash Imperial prenouncements was unleashed in the *Daily Telegraph* affair, so reaction to the finance reform was conditioned by successive rises in tariffs and indirect taxation. There was already growing public resistance to the extent and burden of indirect taxation. It was well caught by a Rostock left liberal's complaint in

---

[98] Retallack, *Notables*, 181–3; Levy, *Downfall*, 244.

[99] Mielke, *Hansa-Bund*, 102–12; Bürger, *Mittelstandsbewegung*.

[100] 6. *Sonderheft zum Reichs-Arbeitblatte: Die Verbände der Arbeitgeber, Angestellten und Arbeiter im Jahre 1911* (Berlin, 1913), 31.

[101] G. S. Vascik, 'The German Peasant League and the Limits of Rural Liberalism in Wilhelmian Germany', *CEH* 24/2 (1991), 147–75; Fricke (ed.), *Lexikon*, ii. 33, iii. 92; SA Hamburg, NL Carl Petersen L57, correspondence with Max Warburg.

[102] See the comments from Prussian officials based in central Germany in AA Bonn, IA Deutschland 125. 3, vol. 24.

1907 about Bülow's incessant Bloc homilies: 'these thoughts of the Reich Chancellor, [are] perhaps the only thing free of duty still around in our fatherland'.[103] The introduction of a tax on matches was an imposition tailor-made to foster this mood. Similarly, trade and industry rightly saw a finance reform which introduced a new tax on shareholders and raised production costs whilst rejecting an inheritance tax and maintaining the *Liebesgabe* (subsidy for spirit distilleries) as yet another occasion when they bore the burden and agriculture escaped. The finance reform was a final straw. It brought the dangerously volatile issue of fairness to the fore, and left the majority of Germans thinking things could not continue in the same way.

The force with which the finance reform was transformed from 'a technical-fiscal to a political question'[104] was further enhanced by circumstance. The fact that economics was the Achilles' heel of the traditional élite in Wilhelmine Germany was fundamental. It was their rapidly falling relative position in the Wilhelmine economy and their resort to the pork-barrel (*Staatskrippe*) which fatally undermined claims to be the pillars of the state. To the Junkers' proud boast that they were 'staatserhaltend', the reply came ever more clearly that they were not supporting the state, but that the state was supporting them.[105] The 1909 finance reform, and especially the rejection of the inheritance tax, was bound to be seen as another case of Junker tax dodging.[106] Moreover, whereas earlier economic changes like the turn to protectionism from the late 1870s and the 1902 tariffs were carried with government support and therefore covered to an extent by the authority of the state, the 1909 finance reform was passed against government wishes. The damage to Conservative parties, who had always stressed the importance of authority, that they were seen to have brought down the Chancellor should not be underestimated. Left liberal campaigners eagerly contrasted their own support for the national cause with the Conservatives' 'frondeur mentality'.[107] As Conrad Haußmann pointed out, the DKP dealt in generalities like 'order', 'loyalty to the crown', and 'authority' (*Authorität* and *Obrigkeit*),

---

[103] Witte, *Liberales und Soziales*, 156.   [104] Delbrück, *Wirtschaftliche Mobilmachung*, 51.
[105] C. Bürger, *Die Agrardemagogie in Deutschland* (Berlin, 1911).
[106] This was underlined when commentators like Hans Delbrück used the opportunity to bring up the issue of self-assessment and income-tax avoidance. BA Koblenz, NL Hans Delbrück, 11 and 12.
[107] *Landtagswahlrede von Herrn Dr. Hermann Barge, Liberaler Landtagskandidat im Wahlkreise Leipzig VI* (Leipzig, 1909), 8.

'but precisely these "ideas" contain, unless they are to appear to everyone as mere phrases to embellish the party's own lust for power, a moral obligation to governmentalism'.[108] The right's defence, in effect that they knew the interests of the state better than the government, fell down on two counts. On the immediate issue, many traditionally Conservative voters did not see a modest inheritance tax on larger estates as a threat to family or state. More generally, the bulk of the Conservative rank and file looked on open conflict with the government with much less equanimity than did Agrarian and DKP leaders. The great majority of Wilhelmine citizens looked to the Reich leadership for guidance and action. True, many were disappointed not to find a second Bismarck sitting there, but they still equated the Reich political leadership with the state. Not until the emergence of Hindenburg and Ludendorff during the war was there a real alternative focus of loyalty.

The finance reform highlighted the disparate distribution of economic and political power. It brought home to the economically dynamic and successful sections of society, the Protestant urban middle classes, industry, and commerce, not just their relative political weakness, but the practical consequences of that weakness. That message was particularly strong for two reasons. The first was a widespread sense of deception. The Bülow Bloc had been presented as an apparatus which would provide such groups with a greater political say, but they now found themselves more disregarded than ever. Unfulfilled expectations had also been raised by the promise of financial reform, rather than just tax increases. Of course this had always been an ingenuous claim by the Reich leadership. There was never any serious attempt to carry out one half of a genuine finance reform, sustained reductions in expenditure. And on the revenue side the government clearly intended to raise income by indirect taxation as far as politically possible. When the figleaf of the inheritance tax fell away, therefore, there was nothing left to suggest progressive fiscal reform and much to indicate yet more regressive taxation.

The second circumstance which lent weight to the political aspects of the finance reform was the clear and direct connection between the Reichstag party configuration and the taxes eventually adopted. No measure could do more to dispel the myth that party politics did not

---

[108] *März* (17 June 1910), 413; cf. Bülow's comments on a Loebell memorandum in Apr. 1909, Witt, *Finanzpolitik*, 275–6.

really matter and that officialdom decided everything. The message of the 1909 finance reform to the middle classes was that to alter the political balance required more than quiescence; it needed active campaigning and victory at the ballot box. Groups like the Hansa-Bund saw their role specifically in emphasizing the importance of business participation in politics and of activism generally: 'When the German citizen now wants to lie down for his summer and winter hibernation, *then the telephone must ring: here is the Hansa-Bund!*'[109] Many Germans, however, needed no encouragement. Dr Witte expressed a widely held sentiment when he declared in the wake of the finance reform: 'The *Bürgertum* has had enough of always being just the anvil.'[110]

Beyond a deep sense of 'political anger and bitterness' (*Verärgerung* and *Verbitterung*), as Bethmann put it,[111] the finance reform reinforced the most unfavourable stereotypes about the parties which passed it. That Polish and anti-Semite deputies made up a decisive part of the majority hardly placed the Blue-Black Bloc, as the finance reform majority was quickly dubbed, in the best of company in the eyes of most Germans. It was, however, the two major parties which bore the brunt of public criticism. As we have seen, the Conservatives' reputation as self-interested agrarians was combined with the charge of putting party interests above those of the state. But there was a third charge which weighed at least as heavy. The Conservatives were blamed for reversing the exclusion of the Centre: the one undoubted feature of the Bülow Bloc, and in many Protestant eyes a major achievement. The way the Centre skilfully manipulated itself backed into an influential position, at the same time burdening the nation with the finance reform, only increased the loathing felt for the party within the Protestant middle strata. Resentment was inflamed by Pius X's Encyclical of 26 March 1910, which combined commemoration of the tercentenary of the canonization of Charles Borromeo, Counter-Reformation archbishop of Milan, with renewed condemnation of Protestantism, and modernism. This was taken in non-Catholic Germany as further proof of Rome's intolerance, and its continued

---

[109] HAS Cologne, NL Carl Bachem 286, speech by Jacob Rießer to founding meeting of the Stuttgart branch of the Hansa-Bund, 12 Nov. 1909. For further examples in this vein see *Bürger Heraus! Ausgewählte Reden des Präsidenten des Hansa-Bundes Dr. Rießer* (Berlin, 1912).

[110] Witte, *Liberales und Soziales*, 194, speech at the founding of the Hansa-Bund branch in Rostock, 14 July 1909.

[111] Bethmann to Bülow, 14 July 1911, BA Koblenz, NL Bülow 64, fo. 28.

challenge to the authority of the state. Carl Bachem's assessment—
that 'anti-clericalism and antipathy against everything Catholic
dominates our political life at present, and is the key to the whole situation'[112]—though oversimplified, was only slightly exaggerated. Just
as a widespread *furor protestanticus* was the most effective force working against the SPD in 1907, so revulsion at a 'treacherous' liaison
with the Centre was the decisive reason for many former Conservative
voters rejecting the party after 1909.

Such a situation held obvious opportunities for the left liberals. The
Ultramontane stick which had been used to beat the SPD in 1907
could now be redirected with equal force against Conservatives and
anti-Semites. 'Blue-Black' behaviour conformed perfectly to long-
standing left liberal allegations. The left liberal press fed not just on
extreme outbursts like Oldenburg's 'Lieutenant and ten men' speech.
Familiensinn, the Conservatives' central defence of the 1909 finance
reform, could be made to evoke a response quite contrary to that
intended. Constant repetition of the phrase reinforced a pervasive
popular image of 'family-minded' Conservatives concerned not with
the material and moral welfare of the ordinary German families, but
the selfish interests of 25,000 Junker families. It was also an easy task
for left liberals to cite Conservative attacks on their own leadership.[113]
Similarly, anti-Semite attempts to explain away their stance on the
finance reform, or the scandals surrounding Wilhelm Schack and
Wilhelm Bruhn, were more incriminating than any condemnation
from political opponents. Schack was caught trying to involve a young
woman who had replied to his advert for a housekeeper in a triangular
sexual relationship. Bruhn was found blackmailing firms and individuals to place paid adverts in his journal *Die Wahrheit* (The Truth) by
threatening to print malicious stories.

The right, then, effectively discredited itself. Moreover, it did so
especially amongst the sort of voters the left liberals were aiming to
attract. Middle and lower ranking public employees on modest fixed
salaries were hit particularly hard by the finance reform and increased
food prices. Left liberals had already been exploiting the issue of

[112] HAS Cologne, NL Carl Bachem 286, Carl Bachem to Jacob Rießer, 16 Nov. 1909
(copy).
[113] The sort of attacks which circulated in the press during the second half of 1909 were
brought together in the National Liberal pamphlet *Konservative unter sich* (Berlin, 1909). On
the open rebellion within the DKP over the finance reform see Retallack, *Notables*, 142–5
and 181–3.

officials' salaries, arguing that the 1908 up-rating in Prussia was a product of Conservative meanness, insufficient to keep pace with inflation. Such arguments blossomed further after 1909. The inheritance tax question was an ideal opportunity for left liberals to bring home to more peasants the divergent economic interests of small and large landowners. Particularly important for the political orientation of both peasants and state officials, 1909 discredited the Conservatives' claimed monopoly on patriotism. Of all the charges levied by former Conservative allies after 1909 none was more devastating than Bülow's accusation that the party had played a 'frivolous game' (*frivoles Spiel*) with the interests of the monarchy.

Of course, the decline in deferential attitudes was part of a long-term trend, originating before the finance reform. The rapid rise of white-collar and public-sector staff associations from the 1890s reflected the way this section of society began increasingly to look on itself as a group with its own interests, and not just the obedient servants of the state or private employers. Protestant peasants, as the discussion in Chapter 2 emphasized, already showed a sense of political awareness, allied to a diversity of party allegiance. However, the shift in public opinion after the finance reform led to a sharp rise in those whose attitudes were at least partly critical. The discontent visible amongst rail and postal employees or urban elementary-school teachers spilt over into more quiescent branches of the public sector. The finance reform brought peasant protest not just in regions with a rural liberal tradition like Oldenburg, Schleswig-Holstein, and the south-west, but also in central and eastern Germany.

Certainly, change was not absolute. Whilst the left liberals made significant gains amongst state employees a minority retained a traditionalist right-wing outlook. Many peasants showed a tendency towards political obduracy. The prime example here was surely the Brandenburg district of Arnswalde, where the bulk of rural voters continued to vote anti-Semite despite a continuous chain of deception, unfulfilled pledges, and petty fraud, perpetrated first by Ahlwardt and then Bruhn. Most Protestant rural voters in regions like Saxony, Hesse, and East Elbia still supported the right in 1912. But as Huhn, the Berlin political correspondent of the *Kölnische Zeitung*, correctly identified, the crucial point was not how many seats the Conservatives lost in 1912, but 'that the current campaigning, both Liberal and Social Democratic, was penetrating ever further into the rural heartlands'. In the continuous erosion of Conservatism in the countryside Huhn saw exactly the same process at work as the shift of urban support from the Liberals to SPD during the 1880s and 1890s.[114] Although the subculture of political Catholicism, the local clergy, Catholic social organizations, peasant leagues, and the People's Association of Catholic Germany, was capable of channelling the demand for greater public participation to reinforce grassroots allegiance, the mechanics of Conservative electoral politics worked best where old ways persisted. The foundations were most secure where deferential voting was predominant; where for estate workers elections meant nothing more than a short speech of encouragement, free cigars and Schnapps, and casting a Conservative ballot paper in the estate office. A lack of political awareness—opponents called it ignorance—was the DKP's surest ally. Popular mobilization after 1909 rendered such a basis for support inoperable in all but a handful of Reichstag constituencies.

The finance reform also led to a loss of support for the right amongst the middle-class intellectual establishment. Hans Delbrück, for example, found himself surrounded by people announcing that they would never vote Conservative again. Such people were, of course, insignificant in numerical terms compared to groups like the 'new' *Mittelstand* and peasantry. It was also true that few came over immediately to the left liberal camp. Nevertheless, the Conservatives' loss of support in such quarters was a blow to party image and prestige. The right's agrarianism and anti-intellectualism, both highlighted by the finance reform, drove even the conservatively inclined Adolf Grabowsky to despair: 'the educated man longs to be able to call himself Conservative, but the word sticks in his throat when he thinks of the Conservative Party'.[115] This background resentment towards the right, and a growing perception of the inadequacies of the existing system, as well as the immediate circumstances of 1918/19, lay behind the later decision of men like Delbrück and Grabowsky to join the DDP.

In addition to opening up a substantial part of the previously right-wing electorate to the left, the finance reform also scuppered Conservative efforts to encroach on the Liberal electorate. The DKP's 'ride to the west' failed in its aim of attracting enough support to dissuade the National Liberals from organizing and putting up

---

[114] BA Koblenz, NL Bülow 108, fos. 45–9, Arthur von Huhn to Bülow, 28 Dec. 1910.
[115] *Der Tag* (22 Jan. 1911), cited in Retallack, *Notables*, 184.

candidates in the east. The chasm between the rhetoric and reality of urban Conservatism was shown by the fall of DKP support in urban areas. In many large towns the Conservatives did not even bother to stand and, where they did, support, low to start with, declined even further. As a result, in towns of over 10,000 the DKP's share of the vote was a derisory 3 per cent in 1912.[116] As the Conservative Landtag deputy and *Mittelstand* functionary Carl Rahardt admitted, even before 1909 many artisans had refused to identify themselves with *Mittelstand* organizations precisely because they were seen as agents for right-wing parties: 'They described us, perhaps not without justification, as being coattail-holders for the Conservative Party. . . . Our stand in favour of Conservatives and the Centre has rebounded bitterly on us.' After the finance reform, even those artisans who had previously supported the right frequently felt betrayed and turned their back on the DKP.[117] The finance reform also overshadowed Conservative attempts to persuade industry and commerce of its good intentions, thus reinforcing the left liberals' position as the leading non-socialist party in urban areas.

The left liberals were also well placed to exploit subsequent developments. In particular, the ill-fated 1910 bill to reform the Prussian suffrage provided ample scope for political point-scoring. The Conservatives could again be arraigned for the perverse use of parliamentary weapons against parliamentarism, and the Centre for a cynical combination of theoretical support for equal suffrage, and practical obstruction of reform. Above all, the bill allowed the left liberals to make an appeal to key groups in the electorate: 'the peasant and small businessman, the worker and artisan, the teacher and clerks', those whom the right and government 'officially branded as men with *no* culture and *no* experience of life' and 'herded by the million into the third class'.[118]

The left liberal attack on the Blue-Black Bloc, however, went beyond political calculation. The ferocity of left liberal reaction was partly conditioned by the Bülow Bloc period. For the more critical left liberal newspapers it was the opportunity to overthrow the last remaining artificial restraints of *Blockpolitik*, whilst newspapers like the *Vossische Zeitung*, which had placed some hope in the Bülow Bloc,

---

[116] G. Hohorst *et al.*, *Sozialgeschichtliches Arbeitsbuch*, ii. *Materialien zur Statistik des Kaiserreichs 1870–1914* (Munich, 1978), 179.

[117] Rahardt quoted in *Liegnitzer Anzeiger* (31 July 1909).

[118] *Breslauer Morgen-Zeitung* (8 Feb. 1910).

reacted with anger and a sharp reassessment of co-operation with the right. Above all, there was a general sense, amongst press and politicians, that the finance reform, by gathering together and showing the left liberals' prime enemies at their worst, had allowed the party a return to a central and righteous cause. Even Karl Mommsen, one of the more mild-mannered of left liberal deputies, looked forward with relish to 'a *political battle of the sharpest form* against everything reactionary', something to warm the hearts of all 'politically free thinking Germans'.[119]

The finance reform did not provide the 'new attractive idea' sought by left liberal politicians. Rather it gave a new vigour and relevance to old left liberal causes: upholding the general good against Blue-Black interest politics in both the economic and cultural spheres; and political reform to protect the public against unrepresentative parliamentary majorities, and an irresponsible court discredited by the *Daily Telegraph* affair and the Eulenburg–Moltke trials. Left liberal politics not only relied on this new public mood, it was directed by it. 'We must', as Gothein put it, 'be thoroughly radical to keep the voters with us'.[120] The strength of public opinion, especially amongst the Protestant middle strata, gave both Liberal parties little scope for manœuvre. 'Tactics alone', as the National Liberal leader Ernst Bassermann put it, 'can achieve nothing in times when the people are so aware (*mündig*).'[121] The electoral pact between National Liberals and left liberals was not itself a concession to radical public opinion. The main motive was to improve Liberal chances of getting into run-off elections. But the fact that both parties were forced to direct their campaign mainly against the right undoubtedly was.

The impact of the unprecedented strength of public opinion after 1909 on the parties and executive were acutely observed by the veteran political commentator Huhn. There was not the slightest possibility of an anti-socialist *Sammlung*. 'The left liberals will not do it, and if right-wing Liberal leaders wanted to do it, then their people would march with flag held high across to the left [liberals], or even to the Social Democrats.' Nor did Heydebrand's *Desperadopolitik* offer any solution. Force might prevail in Prussia, but such methods were impossible in the Reich 'without it coming to a chaotic end

[119] K. Mommsen, 'Zur Reichsfinanzreform', *Liegnitzer Anzeiger* (30 Apr. 1909).

[120] BA Berlin, FVP 36, fo. 93, executive committee, 19 July 1911.

[121] BA Koblenz, NL Schiffer 9, fo. 16, Bassermann to Schiffer or Stresemann, 21 May 1910 (transcription).

(*Kladderadatsch*)'. Under the circumstances Bethmann had little choice but to remain passive and hope for a miracle before the elections.[122]

The miracle failed to materialize. By November 1911 the executive had abandoned its search for a political slogan to stave off defeat, and was prepared for the worse. 'Even the Chancellor, who did not want to believe it before, reckons with 120 Social Democratic deputies or yet more.'[123] Measured against such expectations, the electoral verdict on the 1909 finance reform finally delivered in January 1912 was comparatively mild. After the first round of voting it even appeared that a Blue-Black majority might be maintained despite the agitation and public protest of the previous two and a half years. Although the SPD, left liberals, and National Liberals had together received over 61 per cent of the poll, compared with around 54 per cent in 1903 and 1907, they had only won sixty-eight of the 206 seats decided in the first round of voting.[124] The right fared somewhat better than expected partly because the swing to the left did not quite equal that seen in previous by-elections. The SPD lost Coburg and Usedom-Wollin in 1912, and the National Liberals Lyck-Oletzko and Konstanz, all seats gained in 1909–11. But this should not be interpreted as any significant weakening of popular protest. Unreformed constituency boundaries provided the most important explanation for the number of Conservative and Centre party first-round electoral successes.

If the large number of sparsely populated rural seats assisted the right in the first round, another perennial feature of Wilhelmine elections—the tendency of most Liberal voters to prefer Conservative to SPD candidates in run-off elections—threatened to sustain it through the second round. The prevention of a renewed Blue-Black majority in 1912 required not just SPD run-off support for Liberals against right-wing opponents, but Liberal backing for Social Democrats opposed by Conservative and Centre candidates. This was the situation facing the FVP in January 1912. The FVP's total of 1½ million votes was the highest yet cast for a German left liberal grouping. The 25 per cent rate of increase since 1907 matched that of the SPD. Left liberals lost support where it could not act as a vehicle of protest: in the cities where the party was the main opposition to the

---

[122] BA Koblenz, NL Bülow 108, fos. 45–9, Arthur von Huhn to Bülow, 28 Dec. 1910.

[123] BA Koblenz, NL Bülow 108, fo. 57, Huhn to Bülow, 20 Nov. 1911. For the executive's sense of powerlessness see also Delbrück, *Wirtschaftliche Mobilmachung*.

[124] Langewiesche, *Liberalism in Germany*, 126–7; Schorske, *Social Democracy*, 228.

SPD, or in Württemberg where left liberals were popularly associated with the state government. But this was compensated by sharp increases in support in semi-rural and rural districts. The seats eventually won by the FVP in 1912 underlined this pattern. The seven net losses all came in city seats. Of the forty-two FVP seats now only three were urban (Berlin I, München I, and Danzig), eighteen were mixed, and twenty-one were mainly rural. The FVP lost the East Prussian city of Königsberg to the SPD, for example, but gained three seats from the Conservatives in the surrounding districts.[125] The share of the poll won by left liberals (12.3 per cent), and the two Liberal parties together (25.9 per cent) exceeded all elections since 1893.[126] And the left as a whole had captured a far greater share of popular support than ever before. Yet all these advances threatened to turn to dust in the distribution of seats. The left liberals faced a double disappointment. The first was a reduction in the FVP's own parliamentary strength. As in 1903, left liberals had failed to secure any seats in the first round. The second was the failure to create a Liberal–SPD Reichstag majority.

The attempted remedy to both parts of the dilemma was the unprecedented FVP–SPD run-off pact. At one level the pact was a sudden, unexpected act by a handful of political leaders. On 14 January the FVP executive committee had concluded that divergent circumstances in individual constituencies and insufficient time precluded even a nation-wide slogan, let alone a national electoral pact.[127] But within two days informal soundings amongst SPD leaders by Karl Mommsen, led to negotiations between Fischbeck, Mommsen and Naumann for the FVP and Braun, Ebert, and Haase for the SPD. As a result, a national run-off pact was agreed on 17 January. The pact involved the SPD pledging run-off support in the twenty-five seats where the FVP stood against a candidate further to the right, support that many SPD voters were likely to provide in any event. More problematic were run-offs between the FVP and SPD. In eight constituencies the FVP seemed assured of victory, either because the FVP led after the first round (Danzig, Hirschberg, Reutlingen, Calw, and Lippe-Detmold) or the National Liberals could be relied upon to provide sufficient run-off support (Oldenburg I and II, Dithmarschen).

[125] BA Berlin, Reichslandbund 117, fos. 180–1.

[126] Langewiesche, *Liberalism in Germany*, 126–7.

[127] For this and the following see BA Berlin, FVP 36, fos. 109– 17, executive committee, 14, 16, and 17 Jan. 1912.

In ten more seats (Oberbarnim, Liegnitz, Querfurt-Merseburg, Apenrade, Lauenburg, Hagen, Balingen, Meiningen, Schaumburg, Nordhausen) the SPD held a first round lead which would normally be overturned by run-off support from the right for the left liberal candidate. Here the SPD agreed to stop active campaigning to compensate for right-wing abstentions as a result of an FVP declaration of support for the SPD. In all other seats, including the prestigious urban constituencies of Berlin I, and Frankfurt, party leaders agreed that the FVP–SPD battle be fought out as normal. In return, the FVP leadership published an official declaration urging its supporters not to vote for the Blue-Black parties.[128] The agreement was a measure of how both sides were determined, at the expense of political tradition and inner-party opposition, to bring about a change in Reichstag majorities. In concluding the deal party leaders were also reflecting what they took to be the predominant public mood.[129] The run-off pact was a piece of improvisation, but it was also 'the natural consequence of the whole direction of the election campaign'.[130]

The run-off pact was a culmination of the FVP's political stance since 1909 and a fact which would influence politics in the future. It had a symbolic as well as practical importance.[131] But its immediate electoral significance should not be exaggerated. Existing accounts have focused on the FVP's inability to persuade a majority of its supporters to obey the indirect instruction to support the SPD against the right.[132] But the disinclination of ordinary voters to follow national party directions was even wider than this suggests. Even amongst the minority of left liberals who supported the SPD many acted of their own volition rather than in response to instruction from above. The SPD won forty-six run-off contests in 1912—significantly

---

[128] BA Berlin, FVP 36, fo. 115. For accounts of the pact using slightly different figures see Bertram, *Wahlen*, 221–41, Schorske, *Social Democracy*, 229–34.

[129] The suggestion of a formal pact involving the SPD was first raised in the FVP executive committee by Rothschild, a local left liberal activist in Frankfurt. BA Berlin, FVP 36, fo. 109. As Fischbeck emphasized, while deals with the right might have brought immediate benefit in some seats, they 'could have been disastrous (*Verhängnisvoll*) with regard to the situation as a whole'. BA Berlin, FVP 36, fo. 119, executive committee, 7 Feb. 1912.

[130] Georg Gothein in FVP executive committee, 4 Mar. 1912. BA Berlin, FVP 36, fo. 126.

[131] The impact of the run-off pact on party politics beyond the 1912 election is analysed in Ch. 6.

[132] The best account is in Bertram, *Wahlen*, 221–41. Schorske, *Social Democracy*, 226–35, ignores the fact that many first round FVP voters were really National Liberals supporting a single Liberal candidate, and as a result overstates the failure of left liberals to back the SPD.

more than before—partly because of greater Liberal run-off support. But success was mainly a reflection of the fact that the SPD had itself managed to get closer to the 50 per cent barrier in the first round.

The FVP–SPD run-off pact was therefore more important as a reflection of sentiment and a symbol of greater agreement on the left than a mechanical instrument to direct support. Wilhelmine voters preferred to follow their own political instincts, rather than dance to the distant melody of party strategists. This tendency could be observed across the political and social spectrum, but it was least strong amongst Centre party and deferential rural voters, and most pronounced amongst Liberals and the Protestant middle strata. Many left liberals prided themselves that they voted according to their own political opinions, and derided 'disciplined' Centre party followers who had a Conservative ballot paper pushed into their hands by the priest on one occasion and an SPD ballot paper the next.[133] The fact that both left liberals and National Liberals gave considerably greater run-off support to a Social Democrat when he was opposed by a Centre party candidate rather than a Conservative or anti-Semite underlined the importance of popular sentiment rather than party stipulations.

The run-off pact was not, as one historian put it, the FVP's party political salvation.[134] The near unanimous SPD run-off support given to the FVP against the right accounted for half the forty-two seats won. However, many SPD voters would have supported a left liberal as the lesser evil in any case. As for the other twenty-one seats, the attitude of ordinary right-wing voters was more important than the run-off pact's rather ineffective 'muting clause'. Most right-wing voters did not act in response to the instructions from national leaders, or to the voting behaviour of left liberal in other seats. They made an individual choice about which candidate they preferred to represent them in their own constituency. As a result, the majority refused to follow the insinuations of DKP leaders to abstain in contests between the FVP and SPD, and continued to support a left liberal rather than a Social Democrat. In the two notable examples where Centre or Conservative voters secured SPD run-off wins over the FVP (Hagen and Nordhausen) SPD victories came not because they continued campaigning regardless of the run-off pact, but as a result

---

[133] *Breslauer Zeitung*, 14 (6 Jan. 1912).   [134] Schorske, *Social Democracy*, 231.

of intense local right-wing antipathy towards FVP generated by long-standing left liberal predominance in the district. Formal pacts had a relatively small role in FVP run-off victories. The main reason for a left liberal success rate of over 80 per cent remained the same throughout the Wilhelmine period: the party's continued appeal to individual voters as a second preference or lesser evil.

The overturning of the Blue-Black majority in the second round of voting depended on an informal and imperfect *Großblock* operated by the electorate as well as official pacts between the FVP and SPD, and the FVP and National Liberals. The process worked sufficiently to block the Conservatives and Centre, but not well enough to provide a clear Liberal–Social Democratic majority. The FVP, as the central group in a problematic alignment, had sought to ease difficulties and maximize electoral appeal by connections to both left and right. Left liberals now faced an even more demanding task: to foster a similar alignment as a positive force within the Reichstag.

6

Defending the Reich:
Left Liberals and German Politics from
January 1912 to the July Crisis 1914

> The majority of the left will come. It is as in spring when it rains
> softly and everything is not yet really in bloom.[1]

> (Friedrich Naumann)

The aftermath of the 1912 Reichstag elections offered a strange mixture of change, continuity, and confusion. There had been a striking
clear-out of sitting deputies: only 187 of the 397 deputies elected in
1907 were also returned in 1912.[2] Amidst such electoral carnage, however, party leaders remained largely unscathed. Although Hahn,
Richthofen, Roesicke, Trimborn, Stresemann, Naumann, and Wiemer
were notable casualties, their absence failed to generate far-reaching
change, especially as the latter five had all returned to the Reichstag
through by-elections by 1914. Those who paid the electoral price in
1912 were mainly the more junior and less influential parliamentarians.

Continuity amongst party leaders was more than matched by
ministers and senior officials on the other side of the political dia-
logue: 1912 lacked even the couple of sacrifices which had accompanied the Bülow Bloc. In addition, the leftward shift in the
party-political centre of gravity was insufficient to overturn the
pattern of government–Reichstag relations. As before, a 'tariff
reform majority' of Conservatives, Centre, and National Liberals
provided the only mathematically feasible majority which was sufficiently in accord with Bismarckian tradition. The Chancellor
therefore continued, as Südekum put it, to 'blow the *Sammlung*
flute with a persistence worthy of a better cause'.[3] However, the

---

[1] Speech to FVP conference in Kiel, *Kieler Zeitung*, 194 (27 Apr. 1914).
[2] *Breslauer Zeitung*, 72 (30 Jan. 1912).
[3] BA Koblenz, NL Südekum, 152c fo. 61, notes 1912.

clarion call of *Sammlung* was received no better after the 1912 elections than before, and the result was continued government without a fixed majority and set programme. This made the Centre, once again, trump. As in 1903–6 it had a potential blocking majority in combination with the Social Democrats. The only practical possibility of passing legislation against the Centre was to rely on a narrow *Großblock* majority of National Liberals, left liberals, and Social Democrats. Even though the Centre had been reduced to ninety-one seats, the least the party had ever held in the Wilhelmine period, its position as a parliamentary powerbroker was as strong as ever.

The considerable continuity of politics after 1912 can be interpreted as evidence of the inability of Reichstag parties and public opinion to bring about change and the absence of an immediate challenge to the executive. However, immobility was no indication of long-term stability. Continuity, ironically, bred confusion: the confusion of uncertain majorities and a manœuvring (*lavierend*) executive. Confusion also flowed from the very different reactions to the election results in non-socialist circles. Agrarian Conservatives, radical nationalists, and heavy industry responded with anger and dire warnings. Much of this, such as propaganda slogans about the 'red Reichstag' or 'Jewish Elections' was synthetic and cynical. Nevertheless, such groups felt a real threat to particular privileges and to their general vision of the state. By contrast, moderates like Hans Delbrück reacted with restraint. The growth in SPD support was unwelcome, but no worse than expected.[4] With left liberals and Centre party competing to support the government on 'national' issues, the new Reichstag was neither unworkable, nor a threat to German security.[5] The Centre also took a restrained view of events. Falling in with the criticism of the nationalistic right, an uncongenial partner in any case, risked further alienation amongst urban and Southern Catholics, and impaired the parliamentary party's flexibility in negotiations with the executive and other parties. Finally, most National Liberal and all left liberal newspapers claimed the new Reichstag was better in any event than its Blue-Black predecessor.

If responses ranging from the apocalyptic to the mildly enthusiastic were perplexing to the outside observer, so too was the continued

---

[4] BA Koblenz, NL Bülow 108, fo. 57, Huhn to Bülow, 20 Nov. 1911.
[5] *Preußische Jahrbücher*, 149 (1912), 103.

dichotomy between public show and private negotiations. In this respect, the two and a half years before and after the 1912 elections were mirror images. Where Liberals and Socialists had pressed for a dissolution and depicted a permanent reactionary Blue-Black majority, now Conservatives invoked the spectre of the *Großblock* and demanded new elections.

Inevitably, the study of a single party cannot bring complete clarity to such a complex situation. Nevertheless, the left liberals were affected, directly or indirectly, by all these developments, and in some cases particularly so. As later with the Fatherland party in 1917–18, so the campaigns of the pre-war nationalist right were targeted especially on the left liberal electorate. Similarly, the role-reversal from critics to defenders of the work of the Reichstag was particularly striking in the case of left liberal politicians and newspapers. Finally, study of the left liberals adds a different dimension to a period previously considered mainly from the perspective of the nationalist right or Reich executive.[6]

Only eighteen of forty-two left liberal deputies returned in 1912 had previously belonged to the Reichstag. This certainly demonstrated less stability than the Centre, where sixty-five deputies were re-elected. However, left liberal continuity compared favourably with the other non-socialist parties located primarily within the Protestant middle strata. Barely a dozen National Liberals were elected in both 1907 and 1912. The Free Conservatives and anti-Semites lost over half their parliamentary seats in 1912, each group falling below the fifteen seats needed to secure recognition as a parliamentary caucus.[7] Furthermore, the FVP *Fraktionsvorstand* elected in 1912 consisted of the experienced and established. The three chairmen Payer, Fischbeck, and Müller-Meiningen continued much as before.[8] The remaining two members, Georg Gothein and Heinrich Dove,

---

[6] F. Fischer, *War of Illusions* (London, 1975); Stegmann, *Erben Bismarcks*; Chickering, *We Men Who Feel Most German*; Eley, *Reshaping*; Saul, *Staat, Industrie und Arbeiterbewegung*; Rauh, *Parlamentarisierung*. Gustav Schmidt's articles—'Innenpolitische Blockbildungen in Deutschland am Vorabend des Ersten Weltkrieges', *Aus Politik und Zeitgeschichte*, B20/72 (1972); 'Parlamentarisierung oder "Präventative Konterrevolution"? Die deutsche Innenpolitik im Spannungsfeld konservativer Sammlungsbewegung und latenter Reformbestrebungen 1907–1914', in G. A. Ritter (ed.), *Gesellschaft, Parlament und Regierung: Zur Geschichte des Parlamentarismus in Deutschland* (Düsseldorf, 1974), 249–74—deal with the middle parties, but tend to ignore the FVP and overstate the *rapprochement* between National Liberals and the Centre. [7] *Breslauer Zeitung*, 72 (30 Jan. 1912).

[8] BA Koblenz, NL Payer 40, fos. 58 ff., Payer to his wife Alwine, 8 Feb. 1912; *Breslauer Zeitung*, 96 (8 Feb. 1912).

Reichstag deputies since 1901 and 1903 respectively, were also established figures.[9]

The new influx of left liberal deputies did not result in a marked change of political direction. Nevertheless, significant differences can be discerned. The year marked the final departure of left liberal veterans born in the 1830s and formed in the struggle for national unification. Karl Schrader and Heinrich Dohrn played little part in party politics after retiring from the Reichstag at the end of 1911 and both were to die in 1913. Albert Traeger, the final parliamentary standard-bearer of his generation, was again returned in Varel-Jever, but lived only till May 1912. Furthermore, few representatives remained from the next generation. Payer, born in 1847, felt an age-gap dividing him from the bulk of left liberal deputies: other leading left liberals were born in the late 1850s or 1860s, and new members came increasingly from those born in the 1870s. Hans Sivkovich (born 1881) was the youngst deputy in the Reichstag, and Franz Bartschat, Andreas Blunck, Carl Braband, Hermann Bruckhoff, Ludwig Haas, Siegfried Heckscher, and Georg Kerschensteiner were all born in or after 1870.

The influx of young, first-term deputies tended to make old left liberal parliamentary quarrels redundant. Belief in party unity was not only enhanced by the background of provincial co-operation discussed in Chapter 2 rather than Berlin rivalry. It also reflected an ambitious desire to get things done. An impatient pursuit of advancement characterized many younger left liberal politicians, whether it was a matter of personal career, party influence, or Germany's standing in the world. Payer observed striking differences between the attitudes of 'lively' young left liberal politicians and venerable Württemberg political tradition: 'The new people who are now advancing in the party may be everything politically and economically, but they're not Democrats.'[10]

Such differences were to the fore in the major measure of pre-war parliamentary politics, the 1913 defence bill. Whilst the sceptical Payer argued for delaying tactics and keeping calm (*zu bremsen und kaltes Blut zu bewahren*), 'the new men in the caucus' were 'very keen to agree'. Payer's caustic remark about admirers for the 'brilliant idea' of 'a plate-collection', the proposed defence levy, threw the

[9] *Kieler Zeitung* (28 Nov. 1912, evening edn.).

[10] On the keenness of the new deputies see BA Koblenz, NL Payer, 40, fos. 58 ff., Payer to Awine von Payer, 8 Feb. 1912; for the quotation, NL Payer, 41, fos. 14 ff., Payer to Alwine von Payer, 7 Mar. 1913.

differences in attitude into sharp relief.[11] The contrast between Payer, the pragmatic parliamentary tactician, and a younger left liberal generation more attracted to sweeping Naumannite ideals was similarly evident on the question of domestic reform. While left liberals like Haas, Sivkovich, and Blunck proclaimed 'the bloc of the future', an alliance of liberals and socialists, Payer saw above all the immediate practical difficulties: 'The Social Democrats have been behaving like little yobs (*Lausbuben*) since Luxemburg sharpened their conscience. And we are supposed to battle against the Centre and the right with people who are so dependent on the mood of the streets, [and] together with the National Liberals!!!'[12]

Yet generational differences were relative rather than absolute. Younger left liberal deputies were also aware of the importance of tactical considerations, and, like their elder colleagues, saw successful negotiations with the executive as the path to political progress. Payer was elected as chairman of the parliamentary party by veteran and newly elected deputies alike, and his warning—'with uncertain majorities, it is not always the smartest thing to drive the government by force into the other camp,'[13]—was universally acknowledged. In addition, pragmatic considerations and ideological enthusiasm often led by different routes to the same conclusion. The 1913 defence bill and associated taxation, for example, were supported both by convinced liberal imperialists and party tacticians. Just as machine politicians reacted to popular nationalist sentiment, so those attracted to grand political visions were forced to recognize the considerable obstacles to sweeping reforms. For Bassermann, it appeared 'attractive . . . to combine three things: defence bill on a grand scale, inheritance tax, and repeal of the Jesuit law. These policies of the Centre and Liberals, supported over the inheritance tax by the Social Democrats against Conservative opposition, would have to be linked to the implementation of franchise reform in Prussia.' However, Bassermann continued, 'these are of course fantasies which I don't believe can be realized: there is a lack of firm and clear goals in the decisive place [i.e. Bethmann], and also probably Plessen, Löwenfeld, Scholl, and their influence are still too strong for these to be achieved. Still, the inter-

---

[11] See Payer's letters to his wife in Mar. 1913: BA Koblenz, NL Payer 41, fos. 16 ff (8 Mar. 1913), 55 (6 Mar. 1913), 80 (3 Mar. 1913).

[12] BA Koblenz, NL Payer 41, fo. 124, Payer to Alwine von Payer, 29 June 1913. See also Payer, 'Lebenslauf', 46.

[13] BA Koblenz, NL Payer, 41, fos. 8 ff., Payer to Alwine von Payer, 19 Jan. 1913.

nal difficulties in Germany could become so huge that they can not be overcome by the present system.'[14]

Many left liberals agreed, though they continued to think in terms of opposing blocs of the left and right, rather than an arrangement of the middle parties embracing political Catholicism. They concurred with Bassermann's analysis on the two central points: first, the gradual breakdown of Bismarckian government, and second, that the path towards progressive change was likely to be protracted and rock-strewn, rather than swift and smooth. Though they saw themselves as the besieging force confident of eventual victory rather than the embattled garrison, a siege-mentality pervaded left liberals as well as the right.

One of the most important and conspicuous attempts to exert pressure on the government was continuing opposition to an anti-socialist alliance. Executive hopes that the election would give final vent to the resentments created by the 1909 finance reform were quickly dispelled. A 'Bethmann-Bloc' was no more likely after 1912 than before. Each time the idea of *Sammlungspolitik* was aired, left liberal politicians and newspapers were quick to deride the Chancellor as 'a preacher in the wilderness' and reject the concept as 'absolutely unacceptable'.[15] That left liberal opposition showed no sign of relenting was clear from Ernst Müller-Meiningen's comments in July 1914:

No one of us can deny that Social Democracy makes it damned difficult for progressive Liberalism to expose the corruption and hypocrisy of the slogan 'Sammlung der bürgerlichen Parteien' to the full . . . That said—fully recognising the failures and follies of Social Democracy—I am nevertheless a determined opponent of a *Sammlung* mish-mash just against Social Democracy, i.e purely negative with no clear goals. In such a policy, judging from experience, Liberalism alone would pay the price. The Centre and Conservatives would form a strong majority in such a 'Sammlungsfront'; they would set the direction . . . How will this 'Sammlung' combat Social Democracy? Through the only effective means of a sensible policy of reform across all areas of public life in the Reich and individual states? Who believes that? Or by combating unconstitutional privileges? Even less likely! How else then?[16]

Left liberals saw three good reasons for rejecting government overtures. First, 110 SPD seats in the Reichstag were not a mortal threat

---

[14] BA Koblenz, NL Bülow 107, fo. 159, Ernst Bassermann to Bülow, 12 Feb. 1913.

[15] *Breslauer Zeitung*, 474 (9 July 1912); *Badischer Landesbote*, (4 July 1914).

[16] 'Verfehlte Sammlungsrufe', *Bote aus dem Riesengebirge* (3 July 1914); cf. Böhme in *Deutscher Kurier* (14 July 1914).

to the state, nor even an obstacle to good legislation. Secondly, the Conservatives and Centre were undesirable partners. Finally, an anti-socialist *Sammlung* precluded essential political reform.

Significantly, this analysis was shared by large sections of the National Liberal party. Commenting on Müller-Meiningen's remarks, the *National-Zeitung* added: 'We can confidently take it that his views, which contain an absolutely true assessment of the party political consequences [of *Sammlungspolitik*], are shared by the overwhelming majority of Liberals.'[17] The prospect of a revived tariff-reform majority was even less appealing to the National Liberal centre-left. According to Bassermann: 'If the National Liberal Party is pulled along in the wake of Heydebrand and Erzberger, it loses every importance and any future.' Similarly, Stresemann concluded that a pact with the right would lead to National Liberal deputies joining the FVP, leaving a small, uninfluential rump whose only purpose would be 'to attract from time to time the sympathies of the educated middle classes for Blue-Black policies'.[18]

The period 1912–14 saw a continuation of the pattern of left liberal–National Liberal relations established by the fall of the Bülow Bloc. Despite the efforts of the right, the National Liberals continued mainly to seek agreement with left liberals rather than Conservatives. This was particularly so in Reichstag politics. The 1912 election had reinforced the centre-left predominance within the National Liberal *Fraktion*. However, political circumstances drew even deputies from the right of the party, notably Eugen Schiffer, towards co-operation with the left liberals. The Prussian Landtag remained an exception. Though the 1913 Prussian elections saw regional and local pacts between the two Liberal parties, the results moved the composition of the National Liberal *Landtagsfraktion* even further to the right.[19] However, the two parties continued to work together throughout Southern Germany and agreed on a single candidate in most of the thirty-seven Reichstag by-elections from 1912 to the outbreak of war. The overall trend towards closer co-operation between the two parties was underlined by the comprehensive electoral agreement reached in July 1914 for the forthcoming Saxon state elections. In this key battgleground, at the forefront of the electoral struggle with

---

[17] *Bote aus dem Riesengebirge* (3 July 1914).
[18] BA Koblenz, NL Bülow, 107, fo. 154, Bassermann to Bülow, 3 Apr. 1912; AA Bonn, NL Stresemann, 120, fos. 120–2, Stresemann to Weber, 29 Mar. 1912 (copy).
[19] Heckart, *Bassermann*, 247–50.

the SPD and vital to Conservative attempts to maintain a presence beyond rural eastern Prussia, the right's failure to break the National Liberal–FVP alliance was particularly significant.[20]

The continued adherence of the bulk of the National Liberal Party to moderate political reform and accommodation with the left liberals was of primary importance. Indeed, the battle from without and within for the soul of the National Liberal party was crucial to the direction of German domestic politics. Left liberal rejection of *Sammlungspolitik*, however, differed from that of the National Liberals in two important points. First, there was no opposition within left liberal ranks equivalent to that of the heavy-industry wing of the National Liberal party, and therefore no internal crisis about the direction of party policy. This was reflected in the harmonious meetings of the FVP central committee and the fractious sittings of its National Liberal counterpart.[21] Criticism came only from uninfluential individuals and was immediately and vigorously repulsed by the party press and leadership. Secondly, left liberal rejection of *Sammlungspolitik* embraced open co-operation with the Social Democrats. Although National Liberals did not object to SPD support against the right in Reichstag divisions or by-election run-offs, co-operation with the SPD at the national level remained informal and hidden after the rank-and-file outcry about National Liberal support for Bebel and Scheidemann in the Reichstag praesidium elections. The party refused to support Social Democrats in run-off elections against Conservative candidates. By contrast, the FVP continued the line that a Social Democratic victory was preferable to that of a Conservative, Free Conservative, anti-Semite, or Centre party candidate. Indeed, the party went further than the 1912 run-off slogan of no votes for the Blue-Black Bloc by directly instructing left liberal supporters to vote for SPD candidates. The urgency with which the Social Democrats were supported derived in large measure from the finely balanced distribution of seats within the Reichstag. Each constituency captured by the Social Democrats from the right reduced the reliance of the narrow Liberal–Social Democrat majority

---

[20] The National Liberals, as the main Liberal party in Saxony, were to contest sixty-three constituencies, the FVP twenty-eight. *Kieler Zeitung* (9 July 1914, morning edition). Sheehan, *German Liberalism*, 264, mistakenly refers to 'the Saxon elections of 1914', but the contest was scheduled for 1915, and did not take place because of the war.

[21] BA Berlin, FVP 37; Klaus-Peter Reiß, *Von Bassermann zu Stresemann: Die Sitzungen des nationalliberalen Zentralvorstandes 1912–1917* (Düsseldorf, 1967), esp. 27–31, 89–191.

on the votes of right-wing National Liberals. The FVP, SPD, and National Liberals won 197 of 397 seats in January 1912. This had risen to 202 by 1914. They could also count on some support from small groupings, especially the Bavarian Peasant League and the Danish deputy. Conversely, victories for the right against the SPD brought closer the possibility of a renewed Blue-Black majority. This keen sense for the balance of power and influence was echoed in sneering references to National Liberal 'harikari politicians' who, if they succeeded in helping the right to by-election victories, would only destroy the political leverage of their own party.[22] Nevertheless, this opening to the SPD still represented the culmination of a decisive change. Fischbeck, Wiemer, Pachnicke, and others who had been the most vehement critics of Barthian tactics now found themselves putting Barth's political arithmetic into practice.

This shift in left liberal opinion was most rapid and complete at the top. Whereas the clear majority of the left liberal *Fraktionsgemeinschaft* in 1907–9 had been either sceptical or hostile about possible co-operation with the Social Democrats, now no Reichstag deputies raised open objections and even the majority of the Prussian *Landtagsfraktion* concurred. Grassroots response was less unanimous. Left liberal supporters did not vote *en bloc* for Social Democrat candidates. The Conservatives regained the Mecklenburg seat of Jerichow from the SPD in February 1914 because large numbers of left liberal voters rejected the advice of party headquarters. However, left liberal run-off support enabled the SPD to take two Free Conservative seats, Zauch-Belzig in 1913 and Borna-Pegau in 1914. As in January 1912, the extent to which left liberal voters were prepared to support SPD candidates varied from constituency to constituency. Nevertheless, the overall trend was towards a gradual rise in grassroot acceptance rather than increased resistance. Although the unanimity with which left liberal national leaders pursued a policy of supporting the SPD against the right was cemented by immediate tactical considerations, both the context and consequences of the action went considerably wider. The policy relied on both left liberal parliamentarians, and most ordinary left liberal voters, agreeing that 'the errors of Social Democracy are damaging, but reactionary dominance would be much more damaging'.[23]

---

[22] *Hilfe*, 9 (1914), 135.
[23] Ludwig Haas speaking on 'The New Reichstag' in Karlsruhe: *Badischer Landesbote* (21 May 1912).

One of the clearest indications that the policy of run-off support for the SPD had indeed been accepted by the bulk of the left liberal electorate were FVP by-election gains after 1912. The appearance of a further swing to the left is partly deceptive. Most Liberal and SPD gains came in constituencies where the right had obtained slim majorities in 1912 by dubious means which were subsequently declared invalid at the instigation of the National Liberal, FVP, and SPD majority in the Reichstag electoral commission. Indeed, the vigour with which the committee investigated allegations of electoral malpractice after 1912 was one of the main reasons why the DKP, despite its pretended indifference towards the Reichstag, was desperate to overturn the Liberal and SPD majority.[24] Nor was the FVP's by-election performance consistent. In some by-elections where the party had no chance of victory from the start, the left liberal vote fell considerably compared to 1912. In Hamburg I, Bebel's old seat, turnout fell from 83.2 to 72.7 per cent and the FVP vote from 6,331 to 4,737. Left liberal performance was also poor in the Brandenburg seat of Zauch-Belzig where the FVP candidate Hormann, an outsider from Bremen, met with indifference from the local party.[25] Nevertheless, in the seats seriously contested by the left liberals, especially the two marginal seats, Varel-Jever and Berlin I, successfully defended and four constituencies gained in by-elections, the party was clearly able to consolidate the level of support achieved in the 1912 elections, despite accusations from the right that the run-off alliance with the SPD had been a betrayal of the *Bürgertum*. That the FVP gains came in North

Table 6.1. *Gains and losses in Reichstag by-elections, 1912–1914*

Party	Gains	Losses
Conservatives	1	4
Free Conservatives	0	2
Anti-Semites	0	1
Centre	1	0
National Liberals	2	2
Left liberal	4	0
Social Democrat	2	1

[24] See Westarp to the Conservative party conference in Mecklenburg, *Das Neue Deutschland* (13 June 1914).
[25] *Neue Hamburger Zeitung* (18 Oct. 1913); Kastendiek, 'Liberalismus in Bremen', 152.

German regions with little or no tradition of left liberal co-operation with Social Democrats (Mecklenburg, Kurhessen, Thuringia, and East Prussia) underscored the relative ineffectiveness of right-wing anti-socialist slogans.

A similar pattern could be observed in state politics. True, the 1912 Württemberg and 1913 Baden Landtag elections brought losses for the left and friction between liberals and socialists. Nevertheless, the main political divide remained that between Centre and Conservatives on the one side and Liberals and Social Democrats on the other, and continued left liberal efforts to bring together an electoral pact of National Liberals, left liberals, and Social Democrats were at least partly successful. Whilst the first-round agreement between the NLP and FVP in Saxony was directed against both left and right, it was clear that the left liberals were intending to unite with the Social Democrats against the Conservatives in the second round of voting. Left liberals insisted on a clause in the FVP–NLP agreement preventing either side from making any public run-off pacts before the first round of voting, precisely in order to facilitate a susequent SPD–FVP run-off pact. In Hesse, the resolution on the Landtag elections scheduled for autumn 1914 passed by the FVP state conference in June clearly reflected preference of co-operation with the left rather than the right, even if it did not mention the SPD by name: 'The party enters the campaign with the slogan: For the path of political and cultural progress of [Hesse], and against all those who hinder this development. Therefore, support of the Conservative parties, the Centre, the Bauernbund, the Agrarian League and the anti-Semites is excluded.'[26]

Antipathies built up over decades against the SPD and free trade unions did not simply disappear. They failed, however, to act as crystallization points for left liberal pre-war politics for two reasons: an element of self-perpetuation in the course of left liberal politics since 1909 and the relative behaviour of the SPD and nationalist right. To a considerable degree, the left liberal stance from the finance reform to the 1912 elections bound the party to a policy of practical co-operation with the SPD. Having advocated a majority of the left as an antidote to 'Blue-Black' politics, the left liberals were obliged to demonstrate that the option was workable rather than a mere recipe for confusion. In particular, the SPD-FVP run-off pact, once it had

---

[26] *Badischer Landesbote* (25 June 1914).

become public knowledge, committed left liberals to a vigorous defence of party tactics and their consequences. Against a background of right-wing charges of treason, an admission of guilt had fatal consequences. The way to assuage sceptical party supporters was not a sudden about-turn, inviting a general loss of credibility on top of alienation amongst supporters of a reformist left bloc, but to convince doubters how well the new Reichstag with 110 Social Democrats could function. The change of partners and political background notwithstanding, the left liberals advanced 'positive politics' and pragmatic reform, the same arguments put forward for participation in the Bülow Bloc, as justifications for co-operation with the SPD after 1912.

One consequence of this stance was a constant assertion of how much the Reichstag had achieved. The alterations to the standing orders of the House in May 1912, enabling the Reichstag to interpellate the executive and to bring a motion of censure against the Chancellor if not satisfied with the answers, were heralded as a significant step towards full parliamentary accountability. The election of two left liberals, Johannes Kaempf as speaker and Dove as his second deputy, in the three-man Reichstag praesidium and the absence of a Conservative were again taken as signs of changing times as well as a symbol of the growing parliamentary influence of the left in general and the left liberals in particular. The fact that further constitutional change failed to follow, and Kaempf, aged and hard of hearing, hardly shone as speaker, only led to more left liberal public insistence about the unstoppable process of change and the fruitfulness of the Reichstag's work. In the absence of major legislation after the 1913 defence bill, the left liberal effort to demonstrate the Reichtag's capacity (*Arbeitsleistung*) had to make the most of minor measures. The Reichstag, Naumann told readers in May 1914, had made adjustments to the military law code, revised payments for witnesses, and passed a new law on post office cheques.[27]

Alongside this constant playing up of the Reichstag's achievements went the portrayal of a more positive image of the SPD as an admittedly imperfect, but essential part of a reformist alliance. Left liberals continued to insist that they had no sympathy for a future socialist state and that liberal reform was the only effective barrier to the growth in SPD support. In addition, there was frequent criticism of

[27] *Hilfe*, 22 (1914), 345; cf. Julius Kopsch, 'Der zu Unrecht geschmähte Reichstag', *Coburger Tageblatt* (26 Apr. 1914).

SPD dogmatism. Müller-Meiningen's comment, 'If you were to give a prize for inept tactics in the sense of completely isolating and robbing of influence millions of voters, today's Social Democracy would win it brilliantly!', was typical.[28] However, increasingly left liberal politicians and newspapers defended co-operation with the SPD on two premisses previously advanced by a radical intellectual minority of Barthians and National-Socials. First, that co-operation brought benefits in parliament: the SPD could be relied upon to vote against all illiberal social and economic measures, and for most liberal-democratic demands. At the same time, there was no danger of a majority for specifically socialist proposals. Secondly, co-operation with the SPD furthered the essential process of integrating industrial workers into Wilhelmine society. Such arguments held out a double promise: more liberal domestic legislation and a stronger state based on greater consensus. This changed climate was well illustrated by the response to an article by Landgerichtsrat Brodauf, an FVP leader in Saxony, in the *Leipziger Abendzeitung*, which insisted that Social Democracy 'is and remains the deadly enemy of bourgeois society'. Such a claim, once a set-piece of Richterite politics, was immediately denounced by the left liberal press for setting the wrong tone. Applause came only from right-wing newspapers, though they feared, with some justification, that Brodauf represented a voice in the wilderness.[29]

By 1914, therefore, co-operation with the SPD where circumstances merited it, had, like the rejection of *Sammlungspolitik*, become a general assumption of left liberal politics. Through the 1912 run-off pact and subsequent by-election tactics, the FVP had broken the taboo against repeated alliance with the SPD in national politics. And the maintenance of left liberal support and increase in seats demonstrated widespread acceptance. For most left liberals, by 1914, run-off support for the SPD was no longer heresy, but accepted practice; for some, indeed, it was an article of faith.

The possibilities of co-operation, however, depended on Social Democratic just as much as left liberal conduct. The danger here lay not so much in voting at by-elections and in parliamentary divisions. In three of the four left liberal by-election gains after 1912 the support

---

[28] *Bote aus dem Riesengebirge*, (3 July 1914). Cf. *Berliner Tageblatt*, 37 (21 Jan. 1913); *Die Volkspartei* (Oct. 1913).

[29] See e.g. the right-wing National Liberal *Bismarckwart* (1914), 117; and SA Darmstadt, NL Korell 61, *Täglicher Anzeiger* (19 May 1914).

in the run-off of virtually every SPD voter was crucial to the FVP's success. SPD voters tended to support left liberal candidates against the right in any event, and the element of reciprocity made such support overwhelming. Similarly, left liberals and Social Democrats had for decades found themselves on the same side of the argument in many constitutional and economic debates. The question was more how far common opposition could be transformed into successful support for practical reform, and, further, whether the tone of Social Democratic political action would offend bourgeois and petty-bourgeois sensibilities. The 1912 election did not represent a meta-morphosis of the SPD, the *Mauserung* long predicted by Barthians and National-Socials. Though Ludwig Frank, Wolfgang Heine, Albert Südekum, and Eduard David were clearly amongst the most influential and active members of the SPD Reichstag caucus, the group of reformists and revisionists only totalled around thirty deputies.[30] As in the FVP, the majority for co-operation came from pragmatists rather than idealists. Moreover, radical tradition and the party's left-wing maintained a more persistent purchase on the SPD than Richterite views within the FVP. Powerful voices remained both inside and outside the SPD caucus against the principle of reformism and the practice of parliamentary co-operation.

As a result, co-operation proceeded on an *ad hoc* basis, and against the background of vocal opposition from SPD radicals. However, a formal agreement was neither appropriate to the circumstances nor in the interests of either side. For the left liberals, the important matter was how the SPD leadership and *Reichstagsfraktion* majority acted. The behaviour of the radicals or the six-man Prussian *Landtagsfraktion* could be passed off as unrepresentative, as an argument against an outright SPD majority, but not against co-operation with moderate parts of the labour movement.

'National' issues formed the most vulnerable area where the SPD stance might alienate left liberal voters. Thus, Fischbeck could report with some satisfaction to FVP central committee in December 1913 that 'the mood amongst the Social Democrats against the [defence] bill was feeble; their resistance half-hearted'.[31] More importantly, the SPD vote for the 1913 military finance legislation was a crucial

---

[30] Groh, *Negative Integration*, 319; D. K. Buse, 'Party Leadership and Mechanisms of Unity: The Crisis of German Social Democracy Reconsidered, 1910–1914', *Journal of Modern History*, 62 (1990), 477–502.

[31] BA Berlin, FVP 37, fo. 84, central committee, 7 Dec. 1913.

touchstone for left liberal claims about a workable and nationally reliable majority of the left. The narrow margin for approval within the SPD *Fraktion*, fifty two votes for and thirty-seven against, underlined, at least for those with inside knowledge, continued divisions and uncertainty. The election to fill Bebel's place in the *Fraktionsvorstand* in December 1913 further underlined the fine balance of groupings within the SPD parliamentary party. Scheidemann defeated the more radical Ledebour only at the third attempt, and by fifty votes to forty-seven.[32] Nevertheless, there was a striking similarity about the arguments and motives put forward by the majority of left liberals and Social Democrats. Both sides, determined to isolate the Conservatives as far as possible and not to allow the right to exploit nationalist sentiment, were anxious to focus the debate on taxation rather than armaments. Both stressed their support for progressive direct taxation, preferably an inheritance tax. As a result, the Reichstag budget committee transformed the Bundesrat's proposed flat-rate levy to a graduated tax rising from 0.15 to 1.5 per cent on property, and 1 per cent on incomes of 5,000–10,000, marks to 8 per cent on income over 500,000 marks.[33] This, of course, was above all a reminder of the electoral weight of the masses compared with the prosperous few. However, it also reflected a shared belief in the principle of the broadest backs bearing the greatest burden and a joint hope that middle- and upper middle-class ardour for more and more armaments would be diminished if they were called on to pay the bill. Südekum, for example, commented that the SPD caucus considered 'it could only have a beneficial effect, if the burden of the new armaments could be placed, at least to an almost fair extent, on those continually loud yelling circles who have gathered in Keim's Defence League, the Navy League and similar organizations, and pursue there a lively arms and war propaganda'. Similarly, amongst left liberals, Fischbeck referred to 'the educational value of the taxes' in making property owners more critical in the future about increased military spending.[34]

In fact, left liberals had little to fear about the SPD striking an embarrassing unpatriotic pose. This was unlikely on two counts: the

[32] E. Matthias and E. Pikart, (eds.), *Die Reichstagsfraktion der deutschen Sozialdemokratie 1898–1918*, i–ii (Düsseldorf, 1966), i 300–1 and 306–7; Witt, *Finanzpolitik*, 373–5.

[33] B. Barth, 'Die Innenpolitik des Reiches unter der Kanzlerschaft Bethman Hollwegs 1909–1914', Ph.D., Kiel 1950, 155–6.

[34] BA Koblenz, NL Südekum, 153b, fo. 26; BA Berlin, FVP 37, fo. 85, central committee, 7 Dec. 1913.

party as a whole still heeded the electoral warning of 1907, and, as in the FVP, the younger generation of Social Democrats showed increasingly patriotic leanings.[35] In addition, at least a third of SPD seats depended partly on the left liberals and *Mitläufer*. If the 1912 run-off agreement was confirmation that seats as well as votes counted for the SPD party leadership, individual deputies were equally anxious not to be unseated. Thus the SPD deputy for Eschwege-Schmalkalden could be found in 1913 touring the rural parts of the constituency and praising the army.[36] Concern for the effect on public opinion, and therefore on the party's parliamentary position, explained the depth of opposition from reformist deputies to the decision to remain seated in the Reichstag during the *Kaiserhoch*: 'The damage lies both in forcing the Liberals, particularly the National Liberals over to the right (where they are awaited with open arms) and making future run-off pacts more difficult even with the left liberals (without which we will not be able to hold or win around three dozen seats under present constituency boundaries.)'[37] Such reactions took place against a background of a general Social Democratic standstill in membership, press circulation, and electoral performance, and, in some instances, of actual reductions in support. Sixteen out of forty-five districts lost members during 1912/13, and subscriptions to the SPD press fell 12,830 to 1,478,042. Party membership increased from 970,112 to 982,850 in the nine months from 30 June 1912 to 31 March 1913, a rise of only 1.3 per cent compared to annual increases of around 15 per cent in the previous three years.[38] Though this was used by left-wing critics to condemn cautious and excessively parliamentary tactics, the response of pragmatic leaders like Ebert and Scheidemann, as well as revisionists and reformers, was to emphasize moderation and co-operation. The SPD faced an electoral ceiling of 35 to 40 per cent unless it could expand its electoral appeal amongst non-working-class groups. However, the party was unlikely to make greater inroads amongst white-collar workers, artisans, small peasants, and farm workers with radical phrases and Marxist tenets. Moreover, receding

[35] Gustav Noske's pre-war political activity demonstrated both strands emphatically. W. Wette, *Gustav Noske: Eine politische Biographie* (Düsseldorf, 1987), 65–133.
[36] BA Berlin, NL Wilhelm Ohr 14, correspondence between Ohr and Lehrer Peters.
[37] BA Koblenz, NL Südekum, 102, fo. 154, letter to SPD Verein Nuremberg, June 1914. For the opposition of other deputies, though not SPD local organizations, to the demonstration on 20 May 1914 see Groh, *Negative Integration*, 545–7.
[38] LA Schleswig 301, Oberpräsidium 2252, Übersicht 1913.

prospects of a Social Democratic Reichstag majority emphasized the need for co-operation with other parties to implement improvements and preserve existing achievements. Resistance, for example, to growing employer pressure to restrict the labour association laws depended, as trade union leaders were well aware, on the stance of Liberal and Centre deputies. Inevitably, perceptions of the necessity of outside co-operation, not just for future advance but to preserve the gains of 1912, increased the appeal of accommodation with the FVP: run-off agreements were mutually beneficial, not just an unreciprocated act of SPD generosity.

The standstill in SPD organization was welcomed by the FVP. Left liberals had long prophesised stagnation as the start of revisionist tactics. 'The moment . . . when Social Deemocracy starts to stagnate. That is the precondition for everything else' as Eugen Katz put it.[39] A Hamburg left liberal referred to a 'restorative crisis' leading to 'the breakthrough of a sense of reponsibility' shown by SPD leaders and officials.[40] An end to the rapid increase in SPD support also indicated a halt to the continuous erosion of left liberal support from the left which had begun with the failure of the workers' education associations in the 1870s and peaked during the 1890s. Moreover, it defused accusations from the right that left liberal conduct encouraged socialism by confusing the boundary between the bourgeois parties and the SPD. Certainly, such trends were too slight to alter the great discrepancy in size between the two parties. The fact that the SPD was two and half to three times larger (111 seats to forty-six seats by 1914, 4.25 million votes to 1.5 million votes in 1912) continued to make agreements between the bourgeois left and labour more difficult in Germany than in France, where the Socialists were outnumbered by Radicals even after the gains of 1914, and in Britain where Liberals overshadowed Labour numerically and ideologically. Nevertheless, the change in perception away from inexorable left liberal decline relative to the SPD and towards a position of stability was an important influence on relations between the two parties. It was recognized, by Kautsky as well as Bernstein, that the left liberals exercised an appeal to social groups, particularly the expanding 'new' *Mittelstand*, which would not simply be inherited if the SPD just waited for a couple of

---

[39] BA Koblenz, NL Brentano, 32, fo. 85, Eugen Katz to Lujo Brentano, 13 June 1906.
[40] *Hamburger Fremdenblatt* (1 Oct. 1913), Dr Ahlgrimm on 'The Politics of the Left after Jena'.

Reichstag elections.[41] Equally, the belief that the FVP's parliamentary seats were unlikely to be overrun by the SPD made leading left liberals more inclined to deal with the Social Democrats.

Perhaps the best way to summarize the shift in FVP–SPD relations after 1912 is in terms of a transfer of the norms of South German left liberal–Social Democratic relations to the level of national politics. A regular pattern of run-off agreements could be compared to the established electoral co-operation of Southern state elections, approval of the 1913 military finance legislation to votes for the state budgets in Baden, Bavaria, and Hesse. Although there was no agreement on a joint programme of action, decisions were based partly on presuppositions of each other's conduct. As in the South, private, informal contacts and personal friendships provided channels of communication. Admittedly, the actual amount of progressive legislation in no way matched that achieved in the South: the 1912 Reichstag was hardly a 'Reformreichstag', a national parallel to, say, the 1900–6 'Reformlandtag' in Württemberg. Crucially, the National Liberals remained more reticent at the national level than in the South about co-operation with the Social Democrats. Nevertheless, growth in pressure for domestic political reform was unmistakable: again a parallel to the south where monarchs, ministers, and National Liberals only acceded to suffrage reform after over a decade of pressure from a majority party coalition and public opinion.

Equally important, supporters and opponents alike sensed the tide was running in favour of a reformist left bloc. Rudolf Heinze, a right-wing National Liberal and Dresden judge, complained that: 'The pernicious politics of the *Berliner Tageblatt* and the *Frankfurter Zeitung* are attracting ever wider circles: the idea of the *Großblock* is making more and more progress.'[42] Heinze's perceptions were shared by Dr Jacobi, formerly an editor on the *Hannoverscher Courier*, on the opposite wing of the party: 'The way things lie today, and now appear to be moving, I hold the German left to be a structure of the future (*Zukunftsgebilde*), which can arise from circumstance. Even today, there are not inconsiderable parts of the National Liberal Party who

---

[41] Karl Kautsky, 'Der neue Liberalismus und der neue Mittelstand', *Vorwärts* (25 Feb. 1912); Eduard Bernstein, 'Hat der Liberalismus in Deutschland noch eine Bedeutung?' and 'Hat der Liberalismus eine Zukunft in Deutschland?', undated drafts for speeches in IISH Amsterdam, NL Bernstein, E 112.

[42] AA Bonn, NL Stresemann, 118, fos. 36–7, speech by Dr Heinze to the Nationalliberaler Reichsverein zu Dresden, 17 Apr. 1912.

regard this goal as positively desirable and try to facilitate its achievement.'[43] The isolation of dissenting minorities, whether in splinter organizations like the Altnationalliberaler Reichsverband, or in separatist meetings like that of SPD radicals at Eisenach in June 1912,[44] were by-products of the growing pressure for pragmatic reform.

The dividing lines established by the 1909 finance reform and the increased desire for domestic reform remained the basis for party politics after 1912. The roots of this continuity lay above all in the failure to satisfy widespread reform aspirations in Prussia as well as the Reich. The pattern was cemented by Conservative conduct: Conservatives, agrarians, anti-Semites, and radical nationalists became the functional equivalent, on the national stage, of the Centre in South German state politics, the common threat inducing a defensive alliance. It was soon apparent that electoral defeat, far from moderating Conservative politics, produced even more resistance to political, economic, and social reform. Such an attitude had little attraction to the majority of National Liberals keen on technocratic and educational reform, and to the introduction of a secret and direct (though not equal) franchise in Prussia, nor did the ever more unscrupulous and extreme methods adopted by DKP agitators. Here the tone was set by DKP general secretary Richard Kunze. Later known as 'Cudgel-Kunze', he was already advocating crude anti-Semitism and physical intimidation before 1914.[45] As for the left liberals, the irrevocable hostility of the right was obvious from the outset: immediately a widespread propaganda campaign tried to demonize the FVP as the ally of an international troika of socialism, Jews, and international capital; the underminer of monarchy, *Mittelstand*, and moral order. As a report from an FVP official in Lower Silesia in spring 1914 attested, Conservative agitators concentrated their attacks on the left liberals and were working to a standard pattern:

first run-off pact with the Social Democrats in the Reichstag elections of 1912 and the Prussian elections of 1913; second, the Zabern Affair: attack on the Kaiser's command powers, interference in the independence of the federal states by the property tax in the defence bill; third, position on economic

---

[43] Cited, with strong objections, by the *Altnationalliberale Reichskorrespondenz* (10 Jan. 1913). Copy in AA Bonn, NL Stresemann, 123, fo. 14.

[44] Schorske, *Social Democracy*, 217–19.

[45] 'Das neu-konservative Rezept', *Jauersches Stadtblatt* (24 Dec. 1911); BA Berlin, Reichslandbund personalia 259, fos. 102–65.

policy: reduction of tariffs, rejection of vegetable tariffs; fourth, protection of non-strikers and unemployment insurance.[46]

If Bethmann and Delbrück were the main ministerial targets of Conservative and radical nationalist accusations, the FVP was the main focus amongst political parties.

The ferocity of right-wing attacks was unquestionable. Their effectiveness was more open to doubt. Were they the last desperate thrashings of a drowning political cause, or the birth of a powerful, realigned right? The key weapon was nationalism: 'despite all gloomy occurrences', a Silesian Conservative insisted, 'a lively national pulse is going through the people, [something] the right-wing parties must exploit'.[47] Liebert, similarly, saw a silver lining in the nationalist youth movement and the 'silent, but lasting influence of the great chain of nationalist associations'.[48] The growth of the Defence League, announced at the end of 1911, but gaining momentum only after the 1912 election results, confirmed both the extreme tone and considerable resonance of pre-war right-wing nationalism.[49]

Even against a favourable background of domestic and international tension, however, radical nationalism posed problems as a political tool for the right. It offered little scope against Bassermannite National Liberals and Young Liberals who expressed more enthusiasm for armaments and imperialism than many Conservatives. Furthermore, the right was divided between genuine believers in a 'Primat der Nationalen' and those who sought to use 'national' issues to defend privileged positions within German state and society. In addition, radical nationalism pushed the Centre towards the left liberals and Social Democrats, underlining the position of Conservatives and right-wing National Liberals as a small and increasingly isolated Reichstag minority.[50] The right was forced to increasingly extreme positions in its attempt to exploit 'national' issues, for the

[46] Party secretary report, Lower Silesia, Mar. and Apr. 1914. BA Berlin, FVP 27, fo. 30.
[47] Kurt Nitschke to a gathering of right-wing *Vertrauensmänner* in Kr. Sprottau, *Schlesische Morgen-Zeitung* (18 Jan. 1914).
[48] *Schlesische Freikonservative Parteikorrespondenz*, 3 (29 Oct. 1913), 'Deutsche Helden und deutsches Epigonentum'.
[49] R. Chickering, 'Der "Deutscher Wehrverein" und die Reform der deutschen Armee 1912–1914', *Militärgeschichtliche Mitteilungen*, 25 (1979), 7–33; M. S. Coetzee, 'The Mobilization of the Right? The Deutscher Wehrverein and Political Activism in Württemberg, 1912–1914', *EHQ* 15 (1985), 431–52; and idem., *Army League*.
[50] Coetzee, *Army League*, 41–2.

majority political parties adeptly avoided presenting easy targets, while assiduously pressing their own claims to patriotism. This, in turn, allowed opponents to brand the right as dangerous, unrealistic ideologues.

Here, the left liberals had most work to do to repel right-wing charges. As 1907 had shown, Catholic voting loyalty was largely immune to radical nationalism. Similarly, attacks on self-interested big business, 'große Prozent-, Patent- und Panzerpatrioten', and deranged radical nationalists, 'die pseudopatriotischen Maulhelden', was a standard part of the Social Democratic repertoire, and one sure of a good response amongst party supporters. The 1913 Krupp armament scandal was also, naturally, well-timed grist to the mill for claims of vast financial exploitation.[51] By comparison, left liberal voters were more susceptible to nationalist demands *per se* and the individuals and groups raising them. The Navy League, for example, had always attracted some support in left liberal ranks, and generals and admirals, whose prominent role was a distinguishing feature of Defence League agitation, were figures of authority and respect for numerous FVP voters. A response more differentiated than flat rejection was required. Therefore left liberal politicians and papers sought to depict a sincere but dangerously misguided element amongst perpetual campaigners for military expansion:

They are overwhelmingly men whose sincerity and honour are beyond doubt, but they are—and that is much worse—idealists, with a rock-solid belief that they alone know what needs to be done, [and] that they are the sole guardians of the greatness and honour of the German Empire. But if this sort of patriotism happily conjures up a war, whose economic and social consequences these *Helden der Feder* (heroes of the pen) will never be able to realize, then they will let themselves be shot for 'God and Fatherland' and die in the knowledge of the serving the fatherland 'loyal to the grave' (*bis zum Tode getreu*).[52]

They were people out of touch after decades in the forces: for them the military was not a necessary evil, but the 'being and embodiment of the Nation'. Academics like Dietrich Schäfer and senior officers, though not tainted political activists like Keim and Liebert, were presented as respectable, but wrong-headed. They were also, it was argued, victims of more powerful groups moved by ulterior motives.

---

[51] BA Koblenz, NL Südekum, 153b, fo. 26; 153, fo. 15.
[52] *Breslauer Zeitung*, 306 (2 May 1912), 'Helden der Feder'.

Inevitably, the bad company included the two traditional left liberal villains, East Elbian Junkers and heavy-industry barons. Here armament agitation was presented as another chapter in a long history of reactionary and self-interested behaviour. Increasingly, however, they were joined by a third symbolic figure, that of the rabid Pan-German propagandist. To an extent this marked contempt rather than concern: Walter Goetz's recollections in March 1918 reflected typical pre-war left liberal scorn: 'Until the war we in Germany . . . did not take the Pan-Germans seriously, but had seen in them what they truly are: a political variant of the German beer-bank Philistine, just with heroic gestures and unspeakably grand words.'[53] Significantly, even some sympathizers expressed the fear that Pan-Germanism was a liability in popular politics. Max Bischoff, a right-wing businessman from Schweidnitz, bemoaning the ineffectiveness of the Free Conservative press, complained that *Die Post*, 'by its strong emphasis on Pan-German ideas . . . has offended many circles of society'. Similarly, Wilhelm Kube, DKP Silesian general secretary from 1914 to 1918, and certainly no enemy of extreme nationalism, claimed 'the Pan-Germans had been treated as free game for years by the Social Democratic and left liberal press' and deliberately lumped together with the Conservatives.[54] Left liberal politicians and newspapers, confident that the Pan-Germans had little influence on government and the broader electorate, took the opportunity to attack an easy target.

Nevertheless, the frequency of left liberal references undoubtedly owed something something to concern about the increased volume and vehemence of radical nationalist propaganda. Hellmut von Gerlach complained about 'Keimites and Keimlets' sprouting up all over, though they remained, he insisted, a tiny minority throughout German society.[55] Another radical journalist, Carl von Ossietzky, identified the impact of extreme nationalists on international relations. 'It is indeed fortunate that screaming Pan-Germans do not yet decide over war and peace. But the times are certainly past when you could let them carry on without paying serious attention. A long and difficult task lies before us to pull down the walls of mistrust erected

---

[53] *Leipziger Tageblatt* (9 Mar. 1918). Copy in BA Koblenz, NL Delbrück 44. On Goetz in general see W. V. Wiegand, *Walter Wilhelm Goetz 1867–1958: Eine biographische Studie über den Historiker, Politiker und Publizisten* (Boppard am Rhein, 1992).

[54] *Schlesische Freikonservative Korrespondenz*, 20 (15 July 1914).

[55] *Welt am Montag* (2 June 1913), cited in D. Glatzer and R. Glatzer (eds.), *Berliner Leben 1900–1914: Eine historische Reportage aus Erinnerungen und Berichten* (Berlin, 1986), ii 438.

by nationalists of all lands.'[56] Such views were shared not just by radical pacifists, but an increasingly wide spectrum of left liberal opinion.
Otto Fischbeck's call to 'support peace efforts . . . in the interest of
international understanding' was warmly applauded by the FVP central committee in the wake of the Zabern affair.[57] Hermann Pachnicke
speaking in the Prussian house of deputies, hardly a combination
sympathetic to radicalism, expressed similar sentiments:

These speachifying admirals and scribbling generals discredit our foreign
policy . . . It cannot be said long and loud enough to countries abroad: *the
German chauvinists are not the German people*, (hear, hear, from the FVP) the
'echt Preußische Leute' are not the Prussian people. (hear, hear) France has
its chauvinists, Russia its Pan-slavists, America its Jingoes, Germany its
Defence League Generals. *(calls and great commotion)*[58]

Such attitudes represented a shift in position since the second
Morocco crisis, when Eduard Bernstein complained to Ramsay
MacDonald that: 'The majority of Liberals even are quite mad[ly
jingoistic] . . . There is not one vigorous peace man amongst them.
They do nothing to clear the people's mind from the prejudices concerning England.'[59] Left liberal opposition to the nationalist right
increased during 1913–14, largely discarding the earlier differentia-
tions between honourable idealists and unscrupulous reactionaries,
between military improvements worth discussing and wild, unrealistic demands. Right-wing 'desperado' politicians were accused of
wanting to pack off workers, *Kleinbürger*, and peasants to fight a
'frischen fröhlichen Krieg' so that they could continue to deny them
their rights.[60] Greater stridency was partly a reflex reaction to the constant clamour from the right and to concern about increased international tension. Members of the FVP central committee, for example,
referred to the 'ever greater cheek' and 'mendacity' of the Defence
League, as well as expressing concern about increasing international

---

[56] *Das Freie Volk*, 4 28 (12 July 1913), 'Adjutantenritte'. Ossietzky, later editor of the
Weltbühne and a symbol of opposition to National Socialism, was at this time secretary of
the Demokratische Vereinigung in Hamburg.

[57] BA Berlin, FVP 37, fo. 85, central committee meeting, 7 Dec. 1913.

[58] Hermann Pachnicke, 'Die innere Politik Preußens', *Abgeordnetenhaus*, 18 May 1914;
printed as *Beilage* to *Hilfe*, 22 (1914).

[59] Eduard Bernstein to Ramsay MacDonald, 12 Nov. 1911, cited in H.-C. Schröder,
'Rezension: Roger Fletcher, Revisionism and Empire. Socialist Imperialism in Germany
1897–1914, London 1984', *Geschichte und Gesellschaft*, 142 (1988), 267.

[60] 'Krafteriertum in der Politik', *Badischer Landesbote* (25 June 1914).

tension and instability.[61] In addition, left liberal attempts to improve the climate of Anglo-German relations were undoubtedly encouraged by the new desire within the Reich government for a *rapprochement* with England. Having 'let the dogs bark' over Morocco, the Reich leadership were apparently keen for the doves to flutter in search of naval and colonial agreements and future neutrality. Conrad Haußmann's broadside against Tirpitz in March 1912 was launched with official encouragement.[62] A delegation of English workers in 1914 was received by Clemens von Delbrück and a host of high-ranking officials, a stark contrast to the official cold shoulder presented to previous exchange visits promoted by left liberals.[63] Policy towards England in the immediate pre-war years nurtured an unjustified left liberal confidence in the executive's determination to seek peace, just as the Agadir incident had raised false Pan-German hopes for a ruthless *Weltpolitik*.

Though many left liberal politicians held illusions about the real intentions of government foreign and military policy, they were keenly aware of the benefits in party terms of an apparent convergence between government and left liberal policy. Despite the growing resentment against Bethmann 'Soll weg' ('should go') in 'society' and amongst the DKP leadership, and the emergence of small radical right-wing minority primarily located in the *Bildungsbürgertum*, the great majority of Wilhelmine Germans continued to recognize the overarching authority of the Chancellor's Office. Agreement with the Reich government on national issues was, therefore, the best insurance against the charges of rival parties that the left liberals were enemies of the state.

The domestic political implications of militarism and nationalism were always central to left liberal thinking. Moreover, it was an awareness highlighted by the Zabern affair. The incident itself confounded left liberal expectations of legal decency. They fully shared Stresemann's sense of outrage:

In my opinion it is unprecedented since the foundation of the German Reich and an absolute outrage that a dashing young lieutenant takes it upon himself to arrest state prosecutors and senior judges peacefully going about their

---

[61] BA Berlin, FVP 37, fos. 84–5.
[62] *März* (6 Apr. 1912), 'Tirpitz'; K. Warnecke, *Der Wille zur Weltgeltung: Außenpolitik und Öffentlichkeit im Kaiserreich am Vorabend des Ersten Weltkrieges* (Düsseldorf, 1970), 169.
[63] *Hilfe* (28 May 1914). Bethmann stayed away only because of his wife's death.

business . . . These people simply do not have the slightest idea about the legal tenet that in Germany everyone is equal before the law.[64]

If the Zabern disturbances, crowned by Oberst von Reuter's acquittal and state honour, came as a rude shock to Liberal *Rechtsstaat* assumptions, the right's subsequent campaign to unseat the Chancellor was an equally uncomfortable reminder of the influence of court and military circles. Part, therefore, of a more aggressive left liberal response to right-wing nationalism was rooted in a greater, though still incomplete awareness of its pernicious effects. Part, however, stemmed from a growing confidence about the weakness of right-wing nationalism within Reich executive, party politics, and popular opinion, and its increasing vulnerability to counter-attack. Here left liberals attached a three-fold significance to the 1913 defence bill. First, it was held to strengthen the patriotic credentials of the Reichstag and political parties against radical nationalist aspersions, and buttress the FVP's claim to support whatever was necessary for the nation's security. Secondly, the DKP's rejection of the military finance legislation provided a perfect illustration for an incessant left liberal theme since the 1909 finance reform: the Conservatives were false patriots, always willing to vote for more arms providing others paid for them. A speech by Bruno Ablaß in Hirschberg was typical of left liberal attacks: '(Ablaß) sharply rejects the arrogance with which the opponent laid sole claim to the tag "national", and shows how unpatriotic and selfish they are in their whole taxation policy.'[65] Finally, left liberals used the agitation by the Defence League, Pan-German League and others following the 1913 increases for yet more men and arms to depict the right as extremists and fanatics who would never be satisfied.[66]

The 1913 defence bill and the Zabern affair were the burning issues, but other, less spectacular, events contributed to the increasingly sharp confrontation of left liberal and right-wing concepts of nationalism. Though the discredited three-class franchise ensured a low turn-out and few changes in the seats won by each party, the 1913 Prussian elections witnessed a particularly bitter exchange of

---

[64] AA Bonn, NL Stresemann, 138, Gustav Stresemann to Kommerzienrat Max Rüger, Lockwitzgrund, 11 Jan. 1914 (copy). For left liberal echoes of this sentiment see *Für Rechtsstaat und Reichseinheit: Kundgebungen der Fortschrittlichen Volkspartei* (Berlin, 1914).

[65] *Bote aus dem Riesengebirge* (16 Apr. 1913).

[66] *Freisinnige Zeitung* (17 May 1914). On the stagnation of the Defence League after passing of the 1913 army increases: Coetzee, *Army League*, 98–9 and 122–3.

accusations between left liberals and the Conservatives: DKP politicians were derided for empty claims to a monopoly on patriotism
(*Erbpächter nationaler Gesinnung*), whilst the FVP was depicted as the
servant (*Helferin* or *Dienerin*) of Social Democracy. The centenary
celebrations of 1813 provided a sounding board for rival patriotic and
nationalist claims. From the outset it was apparent that left liberals
and Conservatives held very different interpretations of 1813, and
that both reflected the present as much as the past. Already in January
1913, Conservative newspapers were condemning the left liberal press
for interpreting 1813 as a campaign 'für Freiheit und Volkswohl' (for
Freedom and the Common Good) rather than 'mit Gott für König
und Vaterland' (with God for King and Fatherland). 'But now, when
the great year of celebrations again begins under threatening clouds,'
the agrarian *Jauersches Tageblatt* insisted, 'we do not want to talk
about the Stein-Hardenberg legislation, about municipal government,
and peasant emancipation, but to sing and recite the exalted melody of
the freeing of the Fatherland from external enemies, and stand prepared to turn away new shame.'[67] For the right 1813 was a victory for
monarchical authority and Prussian military might, for the left liberals the triumph of enlightened state reform and a popular uprising of
peasants and townsfolk.

The left liberals sought to make political capital out of the centenary celebrations in two directions. On the one hand, they chided the
SPD's refusal to participate and lack of respect for Prussia's past. In
the Berlin town hall, for example, Oskar Cassel and Karl Mommsen
attacked Social Democratic objections to the city's proposed centenary
celebrations.[68] On the other hand, the 'super-patriots' of the right
were accused of sacrilegious manipulation, of seeking to further their
political aims through 'byzantine phrase-ology, fireworks and Bengal
lights, with hoch and hurrah'. 'The self-sacrificing love of fatherland
of our great grandfathers' had, left liberals insisted, nothing in common with a brand of present-day patriotism 'which satisfies itself
with cheers of hurrah, but gladly leaves the taxpaying to others'.[69]
The row generated by Gerhart Hauptmann's Breslau festival play was
symptomatic of the antagonisms raised. First the right was outraged
by the play's liberal content, then the left by the cancellation, under

---

[67] *Jauersches Tageblatt* (29 Jan. 1913), 'Freiheits- oder Befreiungskrieg!'
[68] *Bote aus dem Riesengebirge* (23 Feb. 1913).
[69] *Bote aus dem Riesengebirge* (5 Jan. and 22 June 1913).

court pressure, of the last scheduled performances.[70] Rather than fostering a united patriotic spirit, the 1913 centenary celebrations only confirmed that nationalism was a double-edged sword which could divide as well as unify, disrupt as well as consolidate.

Analyses which interpret nationalism in the pre-war period over-whelmingly as a weapon of the right are, then, rather misleading and insufficiently nuanced.[71] Certainly, contradiction and half-heartedness remained beneath the aggressive veneer of the left liberal stance on 'national' issues. This applied not to highlighting the domestic political motives of right-wing nationalists, but to the actual issues of arma-ments and international security. The long-standing ambivalence towards pacifist groups persisted despite greater verbal support for international understanding. Moreover, left liberal statements about better foreign relations were either peppered with unjustified optimism ('precisely the capitalist social system is in the position to preserve the peace'[72]) or simply intoned phrases like inter-parliamentary co-operation, international understanding, and legal arbitration without putting forward precise proposals. Such imprecision was more than a compromise between personal preference and political exigency. It reflected the deep-seated internal contradiction common to most left liberal politicians: an increasingly narrow patriotic pride set against shared cultural and economic interests; a desire for empire and national strength set against appreciation of the benefits of peace and the human and economic costs of war. This was typified by a Pachnicke speech which first stressed international understanding and the desir-ability of a 'Rechtsgemeinschaft der Kulturwelt', but then argued that Germany must possess sufficient military strength to launch a success-ful 'Blitzangriff' whenever necessary.[73]

However, the right was also, as we have seen, weighed down by con-tradictions. More importantly, right-wing nationalist agitation per-ceptibly failed as an instrument to recruit popular support. Building

[70] The fullest account is in the Silesian press, especially the *Schlesische Zeitung, Breslauer Zeitung* and *Bote aus dem Riesengebirge*, during June 1913. See also K. Stenkowitz, *Gegen Bajonett und Dividende: Die politische Krise in Deutschland am Vorabend des ersten Weltkrieges*, (Berlin, 1960).

[71] 'The nationalist slogan, tied up with an anxiously guarded status quo, remained in the hands of the political right.' Theiner, *Sozialer Liberalismus*, 307. The conclusion to Shee-han, *German Liberalism*, neglects other issues and sees Liberalism too straightforwardly as the victim of nationalism.

[72] Carl Petersen to the FVP central committee, 7 Dec. 1913: BA Berlin, FVP 37, fo. 85.

[73] *Hilfe*, 22 (1914), *Beilage*.

up the army failed to capture public imagination as naval expansion had done the decade before. Defence League individual membership began to slow down at around 78,000 in May 1913, barely a quarter of the Navy League's numerical strength. Moreover, the great majority of these were doubtless members of existing nationalist pressure groups rather than new converts.[74] The larger established nationalist associations like the Navy League and Eastern Marches' Association showed unmistakable signs of stagnating membership and inactivity. The loss of Liebert's Reichstag seat in March and the dismissal of general secretary Ludwig in May 1914 for selling honours crowned the continued downfall of the Imperial League Against Social Democracy,[75] and the Preußenbund, founded in June 1913, proved an embarrassment. Sections of the right-wing press tried to ignore the second 'Preußentag' at Halle in May 1914, and the *Schlesische Zeitung* bemoaned 'errors' and 'excesses'. By contrast, the left made fun of the Junkers and their allies behaving badly: 'the gentlemen have wrought havoc like certain clumsy beings in a china shop'.[76] The immediate prospects for other right-wing groups which made use of nationalist slogans were scarcely more encouraging. A move to enforce sharply higher minimum contributions led to rank-and-file protests in both the Agrarian League and Prussian Veterans' Association.[77] German National Commercial Clerks' Association membership continued to decline relative to its Liberal and SPD inclined rivals.[78] The claimed resurgence of the right represented, at best, only partial recovery from the losses of 1909.

The uncomfortable truth for the right was that nationalist appeals were more attractive to existing supporters than the new groups needed to stave off more electoral defeats. The Zabern affair entrenched and radicalized opinions on both sides, but created few political conversions. Significantly, the small number for whom Zabern was a significant staging post on journey from left to right came overwhelmingly from the higher echelons of the bourgeoisie.[79] The response to radical nationalist propaganda was concentrated in

[74] Coetzee, *Army League*, 97–9.   [75] *Volkswacht* (28 May 1914).

[76] Frank, *Aufsätze*, 317.

[77] *Bote aus dem Riesengebirge* (7 Jan.1914); *Bunzlauer Stadtblatt* (17 Feb. 1914).

[78] *8. Sonderheft zum Reichs-Arbeitsblatte* (Berlin, 1912), 12–13; *Hilfe* (1914), 147.

[79] See e.g. the factory owner Heinrich Freese, a long-standing left liberal and later a member of the Fatherland party, who referred in 1917 to 'das Treiben der Scheidemänner, Erzbergianer und ihrer Genossen Zabernschen Andenkens'. *Tägliche Rundschau* (19 July 1917), repr. in *Der 'Fortschritt' und die Deutsche Vaterlandspartei* (Berlin, 1918).

this section of society. This was reflected, for example, in different left liberal assessments of the effects of the 1913 centenary celebrations. Popular left liberal newspapers could be confident that 'the descendants of the true heroes of the Wars of Liberation' had not been enthused 'beyond the day itself' by 'court and military junketing'.[80] By contrast, a university group like the Deutscher Akademischer Freibund found that:

The court and military centenary celebrations, the whole empty 'national' rhetoric unleashed during these festivities . . . have strengthened that uncritical subservient movement amongst students; have pushed back the German sense of citizenship in favour of the 'echtpreußischen Untertanengeists'; and, above all, opened wide the flood gates for degrading anti-Semitic cries.[81]

Of course, it is vital not too overlook the influence of small *tonangebend* (tone-setting) groups on government decision-making in Wilhelmine Germany. Such attitudes were prevalent in South Germany as well as Prussia. In February 1913, Below, Prussian envoy in Stuttgart, reported that 'the leading Minister here' (presumably von Weizsäcker) had complained to him about 'Jewish values' 'spreading like a plague amongst the rich', and added that if 'this Jewish spirit cannot be got at by other means, then for God's sake we should not shrink back even from the radical cure of war'. And the previous week the Prussian envoy in Munich reported the Prince Regent of Bavaria saying that the state would not fear war. Certainly, the majority of left liberal politicians were insufficiently aware of both the spread and vehemence of nationalist attitudes amongst the traditional, academic, and business élites.[82] By overestimating the government's firmness of purpose and peaceful intentions they seriously underestimated the threat to peace posed by support for a preventative war, and belief in the inevitability of war: sentiments unquestionably important in the German predisposition and ultimate decision to risk war.[83] However,

---

[80] *Bote aus dem Riesengebirge* (1 Jan. 1914).

[81] BA Koblenz, NL Gothein 18, fos. 128–9, Zentrale des Deutschen Akademischen Freibundes to Georg Gothein, 19 Feb. 1914.

[82] AA Bonn, IA Deutschland, 121. 10, vol. 2, report by Below, 19 Feb. 1913.

[83] See, esp. Wolfgang J. Mommsen, 'The Topos of Inevitable War in Germany in the Decade before 1914', in Volker Berghahn and Martin Kitchen (eds.), *Germany in the Age of Total War. Essays in Honour of Francis Carsten* (London, 1981), 23–45. A German version of Mommsen's article is printed alongside other valuable contributions in Jost Dülffer and Karl Holl (eds.), *Bereit zum Krieg: Kriegsmentalität im wilhelminischen Deutschland 1890–1914* (Göttingen, 1986).

in electoral terms, the FVP's preoccupation, calculations that the voting strength of such groups was insignificant amidst a mass electorate were correct. Indeed, the educated middle classes, especially parsimoniously paid state officials, counted for little even under the plutocratic Prussian franchise.

Therefore, although left liberals undoubtedly underestimated the potential of radical nationalist groups, historians have been equally prone to overestimate their actual influence. Playing a significant agitational role on a single, albeit the most prominent, current political issue hardly justifies the conclusion, for example, that the Defence League 'dominated' German politics as a whole before the passing of the 1913 defence bill.[84] The claim more closely reflects the self-belief of Keim and his supporters than pre-war political reality.[85] Even on the right, advocates of a 'national opposition' remained a minority. Above all, the Pan-German League has been taken far too much at its own word, and persistently overvalued as an organizational force before the war.

Nationalism undoubtedly had the potential to mobilize the masses as well as an extremist intellectual minority. What was lacking, however, was a credible context. Ultimately, the roots of the continued party-political failure of right-wing nationalism were domestic. What precluded the right from significant gains in public support was its refusal to revise its domestic political image. Agrarian League leaders thwarted attempts within the DKP to make the party more acceptable to urban voters. Oertel and the *Deutsche Tageszeitung*, for example, immediately attacked the *Konservative Monatsschrift*'s view that 'Conservatism must battle in the towns and cities if it wants to survive in the long-term in rural areas', claiming such efforts were doomed to failure. Such division and pessimism was naturally seized on by the left-wing press.[86] That the DKP finally managed to hold a party conference in March 1913, the first since 1909, indicated at least some return of confidence. However, it consisted of rallying calls by Westarp, Heydebrand, and von Wedel-Piersdorf rather than serious policy discussion. Nor did the words of the leaders contain any evidence of fresh thinking: the left could dismiss the occasion as a 'festival parade

---

[84] Chickering, *We Men Who Feel Most German*, 276.

[85] For a corrective to Chickering's interpretation which goes somewhat too far in the opposite direction see Coetzee, 'Mobilization of the Right?'

[86] *Breslauer Zeitung*, 564 (13 Aug. 1912). Cf. Retallack, *Notables*, 183.

of stale old slogans (*alter Ladenhüter*), a grand, general rendez-vous with *staatserhaltend* rhetoric of every description'.[87]

Similarly, the Free Conservatives remained largely unorganized and hopelessly divided between moderate governmental grandees and radical nationalists. In the Reichstag they could no longer assemble even the fifteen deputies required for caucus recognition and representation in Reichstag committees. The three-class franchise may have spared the Free Conservatives from the same fate in the Prussian Landtag, but here too the party was largely ineffective and overshadowed by Heydebrand-led hardliners in the larger DKP. The Free Conservatives were incapable of putting together an electorally attractive combination of nationalism, imperialism, and moderate domestic reform. Otto Arendt's mournful assertion that 'The expression conservative progress is much laughed at, but right all the same' summed up the failure to get the message across.[88] Indeed, the party conference in March 1914 refused to adopt a programme of any description. Geoff Eley's assertion that there was a Free Conservative regeneration on the eve of the war overlooks not just continued electoral failure in Reichstag by-elections and state contests, but that the populist programme and organization advanced in Erich Deetjen's 1913 pamphlet *Freikonservativ! Die deutsche Mittelpartei* existed for the most part only on paper.[89]

Whereas the Reichstag majority set out to combat the right's charges about a lack of patriotism, entrenched Conservative resistance to social, economic, and political reforms positively invited the electorate to believe the left's accusation that the right was using 'national' issues to further selfish domestic interests. Moreover, most voters believed Liberal and SPD descriptions of anti-Semitism and anti-unionism as diversionary tricks designed to turn public attention away from the demands of fair taxation, popular accountability, appointment by merit, and Prussian franchise reform. The response amongst electors, preprogrammed in their hostility towards Prussian Junkers, was clear. Even the most rabid racial anti-Semitism, purveyed by DKP general secretary Richard Kunze in particular, failed to increase Conservative support at by-elections. Even East Prussian Conservatives expressed

---

[87] *Bote aus dem Riesengebirge* (15 Mar. 1913).

[88] *Schlesische Freikonservative Parteikorrespondenz*, 1 (1 Oct. 1913).

[89] Eley, *Reshaping*, 317, 324–6; Erich Deetjen, *Freikonservativ! Die deutsche Mittelpartei* (Ratibor, 1913). *Schlesische Freikonservative Parteikorrespondenz*, 12 (31 Dec. 1917) contains a regretful retrospective of the party's failure to put Deetjen's ideas into practice.

disquiet about the ethics and efficacy of Kunze's tactic of revealing a 'black spot' (that is Jewish ancestry) in opponents' backgrounds.[90] Overtly anti-Semitic initiatives like the League against Jewish Arrogance (Verband gegen die Überhebung des Judentums) attracted more derision than support.[91] The *Politisch-Anthropologische Revue*'s attempt, in October 1912, to analyse whether Reichstag deputies were 'Germanic' by looking at their pictures appeared ludicrous and laughable to Wilhelmine public opinion, even more so when only one out of eleven anti-Semite deputies was declared unimpeachably Germanic.[92] When Hennigsen, general secretary of the German Social Party, spoke in Mühlhausen in Thüringen on 'Jewry on the Victory March to World Domination' in May 1914, twenty-seven men and one woman turned up to listen.[93] The continued failure of anti-Semitism as an instrument to mobilize support was summed up by the plight of the *Staatsbürger Zeitung*, the Berlin flagship of the anti-Semitic press for fifty years. Struggling with a circulation of barely 3,000, little advertising, and ever-growing losses, it announced a cessation of publication in July 1914.[94]

Right-wing efforts to exploit economic issues showed greater potential. The Cartel of Productive Estates (*Kartell der schaffenden Stände*), announced in August 1913, appeared to deliver a politically promising right-wing alliance of agriculture, heavy industry, and proprietary *Mittelstand*. Moreover, owners and directors from more traditionally Liberal-inclined sectors of the economy showed increasing signs of moving to the right. Smaller companies and light industry were less well-placed than iron and coal barons to resist the demands of the free trade unions. They were also more affected by the economic downturn from 1913. The end of the long economic boom brought increasing conflict between capital and labour, threatening the political and electoral co-operation between left liberals and Social Democrats. Complaints against the rising costs of social legislation were not restricted to outright reactionaries, but spread across a wide range of industry and commerce. August Weber, a Saxon

---

[90] See e.g. the aftermath to defeat in Labiau-Wehlau in 1910. BA Berlin, Reichslandbund Personalia 259, fo. 164.

[91] See e.g. *Breslauer Zeitung*, 68 (27 Jan. 1912), 'Neuerweckung des Antisemitismus?'; 414 (15 June 1912), 'Sie werden wieder munter'; 825 (23 Nov. 1912), 'Der Antisemitismus der Konservativen'.   [92] *Landeshuter Stadtblatt* (15 Oct. 1912).

[93] Burkhardt Kirchner, 'Die bürgerlichen Parteien in Mühlhausen/Thüringen während der Zeit der Herausbildung der politischen Krise in Deutschland (1910–14)', Diplomarbeit, Jena University, 1964, 12.   [94] *Das Freie Volk*, 27 (4 July 1914).

banker and National Liberal politician, for instance, felt compelled to warn Stresemann that 'the advance of Social Democracy has unleashed currents I see growing daily during the course of business' which, despite the regard felt for Stresemann personally, threatened the support of many Saxon industrialists for his progressive stance.[95] The Hansa-Bund displayed increasing disenchantment with both Liberal parties. It objected to the 1913 defence levy (*Wehrbeitrag*) and capital gains tax (*Vermögenszuwachssteuer*) which bore more heavily on businessmen than on landowners and the masses. The Hansa-Bund directorate and general committee (*Gesamtausschuß*) found the defence taxes passed by the Reichstag budget commission 'unacceptable in many directions'. The parties' conduct awoke 'the embarassing and very worrying impression . . . that even from parties close to them the vital interests of commerce, trade and industry do not find the energetic defence they deserve and have a right to demand'.[96] Its industry council called for new anti-picketing laws, contradicting the stance taken by left liberals and National Liberal Reichstag deputies.

Such open disagreements were an obvious embarrassment and, above all, a threat to party finances. However, 'protection of those who want to work' (*Arbeitswilligenschutz*) was also, as a left liberal businessman insisted, a popular slogan amongst many artisans.[97] They formed a prime target group for right-wing agitation: the prominent role of artisan functionaries like Conradt, Pauli, and Wienbeck in Conservative election campaigns was no coincidence. Moreover, the development of artisan organizations indicated some swing back to the right after the revolt of 1909. While the Deutsche Mittelstandsvereinigung, affiliated to the Hansa-Bund, remained small and lost its leader Carl Rahardt to the less political post of chairman of the Berlin Handwerkskammer, many guilds and associations attached themselves to the right-wing Reichsdeutsche Mittelstandsvereinigung, set up with Agrarian League funding in 1911. Nevertheless the Reichsdeutsche Mittelstandsvereinigung's large corporate membership (640,000 in 1914) gave a false impression of the association's importance. As one of the leaders Erich Wienbeck recalled in 1920:

---

[95] AA Bonn, NL Stresemann 120, fos. 118–19, Weber to Stresemann, 28 Mar. 1912.

[96] SA Hamburg, NL Braband, B2, circular from Rießer to deputies with Hansa-Bund connections, 23 June 1913.

[97] BA Berlin, FVP 37, fo. 86, Thospann (Hanover) in FVP central committee 7 Dec. 1913.

'co-operation was loose (and) electoral influence very small; especially there was little willingness to make financial sacrifices'.[98]

There was undoubtedly a political audience for a hard line against unions and social reform. They were, however, outweighed electorally by those on the other side of the argument. Delbrück's announced halt to social legislation in early 1914 was objected to not just by the labour movement and *Kathedersozialisten*, but by groups, especially amongst the *Mittelstand*, who wanted social benefits extended to include them.[99] Similarly, the burgeoning growth of unions and associations, particularly amongst state employees and the 'new' *Mittelstand* generally, showed that the benefits of association were appreciated far beyond the labour movement. The already large associations of white-collar sales and clerical assistants expanded yet further. The pattern of growth suggested that the centre-left was continuing to gain within the 'new' *Mittelstand*. Although the Deutschnationaler Handlungsgehilfenverband emphasised its economic role and distanced itself somewhat from anti-Semitic party politics after 1909, this failed to ward off relative decline. In 1913 its membership fell from 123,092 to 122,156, while total membership of the three Liberal-inclined associations (Verband deutscher Handlungsgehilfen zu Leipzig, Verein für Handelskommis von 1858, and Verein der deutschen Kaufleute) increased from 192,877 to 203,791. Though membership of the SPD-backed Zentralverband der Handlungsgehilfen remained comparatively small at 24,809 in December 1913, it had increased by over a third during the year.[100] Amongst state employees ever more groups were following the lead of rail and postal workers in joining organizations to further their interests. By 1913 even Prussian policemen were attempting to set up a staff association, and when two Berlin policemen who had supported this initiative were transferred to East Prussia they were lauded by hundreds of cheering colleagues at the railway station.[101] A campaign against social reform and rights of

---

[98] Mielke, *Hansa-Bund*, 107–11; BA Berlin, Reichslandbund Personalia 493, fo. 116.

[99] Though following a different interpretation Gerhard Müller, *Die Gesellschaft für soziale Reform: Konzeptionen, Methoden und Wirksamkeit bürgerlicher Sozialreformer im junkerlich-bourgeoisen deutschen Imperialismus (1897/8–1914)*, Ph.D., Jena, 1982, relates the details of the pre-war debate over social policy and the wide response to the protest meeting organized by the Gesellschaft für soziale Reform in 1914.

[100] *11. Sonderheft zum Reichs-Arbeitsblatte*, 8.

[101] A. Funk, *Polizei und Rechtsstaat: Die Entwicklung des staatlichen Gewaltmonopols in Preußen 1848–1918* (Frankfurt am Main, 1986), 303. For state employees in general see Süle, *Preußische Bürokratietradition*.

association made more enemies than friends. Even if a combination of employers, landowners, and *Mittelstand* proprietors could be fused, this amounted to less in terms of Reichstag electoral arithmetic than the bulk of workers and 'new' *Mittelstand*.

In any event, the right largely failed to transfer such an alliance from rhetoric into reality. The left lost no time in challenging the moral claims of the Cartel, claiming, very plausibly, that it was more a collection of *raffende Hände* (grasping hands) than *schaffende Stände* (productive estates). More importantly, it questioned whether the agrarians were prepared to abandon 'lückenlos' tariffs and other economic demands hostile to industry and commerce. Naturally they were not, and as a result only a small minority of industrialists and financiers, like Henry Axel Bueck, Max Roetger, and Max Schinckel, were prepared to advocate Conservative support or a pact with the Agrarian League so soon after the lessons of 1909. As Hartmann von Richthofen informed Rießer who was returning after visiting America in early 1914:

The Cartel of Productive Estates has run aground. That part of the Conservative Party which was prepared to make certain economic concessions to go along with the Zentralverband (*deutscher Industrieller*) has lost out against ultra agrarianism. Thus the renewed, more strongly emphasized demand for the *lückenloser Zolltariff*, [and] Graf Schwerin's declarations at the conference of the Landwirtschaftskammer. Of course, these policies are impossible even for the most right-wing industrial magnates.[102]

Industry and agriculture remained suspicious of each other. There was no convincing, resurrected 'axis of iron and rye' and, though the Hansa-Bund may have been dissatisfied with the Liberal parties, it had nowhere else to go. Finally, the third pillar of the Cartel, the 'old' *Mittelstand*, was equally insecure. Behind the 640,000 claimed corporate membership of the Imperial German Mittelstand Association stood neither a disciplined organizational apparatus, nor a common party-political allegiance. Much of the rank-and-file ignored the Conservative politics of the functionaries and voted Liberal or even SPD.[103]

---

[102] BA Koblenz, NL Richthofen, 3, fo. 172, Richthofen to Jacob Rießer, 20 Feb. 1914 (copy). For Bueck's rather unconvincing attempt to depict the Conservatives as the 'sole reliable support' for industrial interests see H. A. Bueck, *Warum die Industrie der Rießerischen Parole 'Kampf gegen Rechts' nicht folgen soll* (Berlin, 1911).

[103] Lenger, *Sozialgeschichte der deutschen Handwerker*, 158–9.

An increased nationalist and protectionist mood remained, therefore, insufficient to break the substantial majority of popular support
enjoyed by the centre- left. Although statements by individual left liberal deputies displayed a need to accommodate such sentiments, the
party as a whole could be confident the right was isolated in national
politics—Westarp referred to DKP and Free Conservative Reichstag
deputies as the 'iron fifty four'—and its domestic policies were too
archaic and unpopular to mount a serious electoral challenge. There
were few signs in left liberal ranks of the 'political demoralization'
which some historians claim to have 'pervaded middle-class circles in
Germany by 1914'.[104] Optimism, not *Reichsverdrossenheit*, summed up
the left liberal mood in summer 1914. Internationally, left liberals
looked forward not to war, but to peace built on better Anglo-German
relations. Domestically, they sunned themselves in the double by-
election success of Coburg and Labiau-Wehlau which raised the FVP
to the third largest party in the Reichstag and basked in the belief that
domestic reform was on its way. Developments, left liberals insisted,
justified the 'optimists . . . who take the view that in the end the force
of ideas and power of a firm popular will directed towards good and
clear goals can win through everywhere'.[105] Left liberals saw Germany
in the middle of a process of reform which would be completed
'whether the government and Conservatives like it or not'.[106]

This was an assessment shared on the right, though naturally
accompanied by disapproval and disappointment:

The developments in our internal politics fill us . . . with great concern. We
see how democratization is making progress in virtually all areas of legislation
and public life and how the larger part of Liberalism is increasingly adopting
democratic demands, fighting against the right, and begging the favour of the
masses often in contradiction to its own best heritage. In all this Liberalism is
simply breaking ground for socialism.[107]

[104] White, *Splintered Party*, 1.
[105] *Bote aus dem Riesengebirge* (11 Apr. 1913), 'Der Druck der öffentlichen Meinung'.
[106] *Bote aus dem Riesengebirge* (20 July 1913), 'Entwicklungen'.
[107] Agrarian League resolution, Feb. 1913, cited in M. Eksteins, *The Limits of Reason:
The German Democratic Press and the Collapse of Weimar Democracy* (London, 1975), 9–10.

III

Left Liberals in Local Society

7
Mass Politics and Party Pacts:
Left Liberals in Baden, 1905–1914

Today . . . the sun of freedom appears to rise gradually in the south west casting its light, by and by, on the whole beloved German fatherland. And when we here in the south west have achieved freer conditions, we have achieved them also for the north Germans. . . . To those beautiful words 'Germany leads the world!' (*Deutschland in der Welt voran!*) we can add: our dear Baden, the Baden of freedom, Baden of the Großblock leads Germany.[1]

Schulze-Gaevernitz claimed to see the glowing dawn of freedom. Max Weber, another product of a North German liberal intellectual family to find an academic home in Baden, alighted on an alternative elemental metaphor: he likened his coming to Baden in the 1890s to an arrival 'in clean air'. Another liberal academic from the North, Gerhard Anschütz, recalled Tübingen and Heidelberg in similar terms.[2] Nor, as the rapturous applause greeting Schulze-Gaevernitz's speech emphasized, were these sentiments limited to liberal academics. The perception that Baden provided a possible guide for the future internal development of the Reich was widely held: a guide not only in narrowly political matters—the relationship between monarch, executive, and legislature, the political alignment of parties, the electoral franchise—but in the wider social attitudes and apparatus they implied: publicly accountable administration, cross-class consensus and free assembly and association. People in Baden had long been proud to believe they lived in a 'Musterländle', an exemplary small state, which would serve

---

[1] BA-MA Freiburg, NL Schulze-Gaevernitz v 17, 'Weltlage Wehrvorlage und Deckungsfrage', speech in Festhalle, Freiburg, 6 May 1913.
[2] AA Bonn, IA Baden 32. 9, Report by von Eisendecher, 25 Oct. 1911, on Weber's attack on Prussian Education minister, Hochschullehrertag Dresden 1911; Gerhard Anschütz, *Aus meinem Leben*, ed. Walter Pauly (Frankfurt am Main, 1993), 67–71. I thank Professor Michael John for the latter reference. Archival references are given here to Eisendecher's reports, but see also the published edn.: Hans-Jürgen Kremer (ed.), *Das Großherzogtum Baden in der politischen Berichterstattung der preußischen Gesandten 1871–1918*, i–ii (1990–2).

as an example to others.[3] Outside reactions were more mixed. Progressive opinion, led by the *Berliner Tageblatt* and *Frankfurter Zeitung*, continually referred to how much better things were politically in Baden. By contrast the Agrarian *Deutsche Tageszeitung* and Preußenbund (Prussian League) thundered against South German liberalism and latitude and a 'wine-drinking mentality' (*Weingeist*). The latter voices, though hardly tributes of praise, reflected in their increasing scale and stridency the growing perception that events in Baden had the potential to influence the direction of politics elsewhere.[4]

Just how significant the 'lessons' of Baden were for national politics has attracted debate amongst historians. Here, however, the disagreement has not been over desirability but practical potential. Some have echoed the optimism of contemporary Liberal and SPD leaders in Baden, seeing the state in the vanguard of a problematic, but persistent, national trend. It was a testing ground for co-operation between Liberals and Social Democrats, the reformist middle strata and workers, to bring about liberal domestic reform.[5] By contrast, others have argued that a *Großblock* of Liberals and Social Democrats was unsustainable even under favourable Badenese conditions, something which underlined the futility of attempting it in the Reich.[6] A second line of argument against the potential of the *Großblock*, propounded by Hans-Ulrich Wehler, downplays Southern German developments on account of the political, economic, and structural dominance of Prussia. This latter view, however, fails to give due allowance to the role of non-Prussians in national politics and pre-supposes a more homogeneous, archaic, and authoritarian pattern of political life in Prussia than was in fact the case.[7]

An important issue to be considered, therefore, is to what extent pre-war Baden offered a viable path of political reform and social integration which might have been followed more generally. The question is of particular significance to the present study, given the closeness of such a path to the left liberals' political ideals. In addition, the example of Baden provides an excellent opportunity to examine two crucial questions facing the left liberals in Wilhelmine Germany: how

---

[3] Cf. D. Herzog, *Intimacy and Exclusion: Religious Politics in Pre-Revolutionary Baden* (Princeton, NJ, 1996), 5–6.

[4] Heckart, *Bassermann*, brings out the increased national focus on Badenese politics after 1905.   [5] Ibid., 91–121 and 257–65.

[6] Jürgen Thiel, *Die Großblockpolitik der nationalliberalen Partei Badens 1905–1914* (Stuttgart, 1976), 272 and *passim*; Sheehan, *German Liberalism*, 264.

[7] See esp. the introduction to Wehler, *German Empire*.

to cope with a politicized mass electorate and the ability of a minority party to secure influence through formal and informal coalitions. In Baden, whether the turn-out in state and local elections, the size of party membership, or the tone and content of the press are taken as barometers, a greater degree of mass political mobilization was evident than in most other German states. Similarly, the strength of the National Liberal political tradition in Baden compelled the left liberals earlier than elsewhere to accept the inevitability of a minority position and the logic of political alliances. I begin, therefore, by looking at the political background before the first electoral accommodation of the *Großblock* parties in 1905, together with Badenese public life in general in the pre-war decade. Attention then turns to the political organization erected by the left liberals in Baden in the years prior to the war. The assessment of the left liberals' popular political apparatus and style leads to an analysis of the issues put forward in political campaigns. Public response to political issues and activity is then evaluated, both in terms of electoral support and the alignment of parties in Baden. Finally, left liberal attitudes to state and society are assessed alongside the degree to which the pattern of politics and society in Baden diverged from that found elsewhere in Wilhelmine Germany.

For most of the nineteenth century Baden possessed the conditions for parliamentarization comparable to those that had pertained in England: constitutional monarchs and a concordant executive and parliamentary majority drawn from the same élite, though in Baden it was more an élite of office-holders than of estate owners. Unlike Prussia, the 1860s did not force Liberals in Baden to choose between national unity and constitutional principles. Measured liberal reform continued with the support of monarch, ministers, and the Liberal majority in the second chamber. Equally, the more secular and economically modern 'kleindeutsch' form of German unity raised far fewer objections in Baden than in Württemberg and Bavaria.[8] Similarly the decade of the 1880s proved far less problematic for the National Liberals in Baden than in Germany generally. While rising popular mobilization and the crisis of liberal economics wrecked the party's pre-eminence in Reich politics, damaging defections over economic policy were largely avoided in Baden. It was the Centre, rather

---

[8] L. Gall, *Der Liberalismus als regierende Partei: Das Großherzogtum Baden zwischen Restauration und Reichsgründung* (Wiesbaden, 1968). On Badenese Liberalism before 1850 see also P. Nolte, *Gemeindebürgertum und Liberalismus in Baden, 1800–1850: Tradition–Radikalismus–Republik* (Göttingen, 1994).

than the National Liberal Party, which was riven by internal party strife in Baden during the 1880s. As a result, the National Liberals held forty-three of the sixty-three seats in the Badenese second chamber in 1885 and forty-seven seats four years later.[9]

The unbroken strength of National Liberalism meant, in turn, that left liberal groups in Baden remained largely without influence and support. From 1870 onwards the Democratic party in Baden never held more than six seats in the second chamber. The even smaller and more recently established Freisinn won at best one or two seats. From the early 1890s, however, the left liberals' potential to act as 'Zünglein an der Waage', the party able to tip the balance, became apparent. They benefited from the electoral pact formed by the Centre, Democrats, and SPD to try to force through franchise reform. These years saw the beginning of the long parliamentary careers of three prominent Democrats, Karl Heimburger, Oskar Muser, and Martin Venedey, elected in Lahr, Offenburg, and Konstanz respectively, largely by borrowed Centre party votes. They also saw the end of the National Liberal majority in the second chamber and, after over a decade of pressure from the other parties and public opinion, the agreement of the government and National Liberals to introduce a direct, equal, and secret state franchise in 1903/4.[10]

This brought an end to the comfortable arrangement of governmental National Liberalism. The same sort of ministry remained, but the governmental National Liberal majority in the second chamber was removed. Equal franchise ensured not only that the National Liberals remained in a minority, but that they became less governmental and more populist. The divergence between the executive and the mainstream of the National Liberal party in Baden was underlined by the distrust ministers felt for the National Liberal leader Edmund Rebmann, and the advocacy of different tactics and priorities.[11] Far from welcoming the *Großblock*, the executive in Baden, as elsewhere, urged a common bourgeois front against the SPD. Franchise reform, however, changed the electoral arithmetic. The key electoral question was no longer whether the National Liberal majority could be broken,

[9] Bachem, *Zentrumspartei*, iv. 391–418; Thiel, *Großblockpolitik*, 18; M. Niehuss, 'Die Stellung der Sozialdemokratie im Parteisystem Bayerns, Württembergs und Badens', in Ritter (ed.), *Aufstieg der deutschen Arbeiterbewegung*, 116–19.

[10] R. Ehrismann, *Der regierende Liberalismus in der Defensive: Verfassungspolitik im Grossherzogtum Baden 1876–1905* (Frankfurt am Main, 1993).

[11] AA Bonn, IA Baden 31. 15, Eisendecher's report, 19 Mar. 1913; IA Baden 40. 14, Eisendecher's report, 28 Sept. 1913.

but whether a majority for the Centre party could be prevented. Moreover, once the dust of the franchise battle had settled, it was inevitable that unresolved cultural issues, above all education and the relationship of church and state, would once again become the main points of contention. The political situation, Rebmann told delegates to the National Liberal state conference in 1910, was clear. Now, as half a century before, it was the battle against the Centre which dominated the political agenda in Baden.[12] Leaders of the other *Großblock* parties, the Social Democrat Wilhelm Kolb and Heimburger for the left liberals, echoed Rebmann's message. For them and their followers the Centre party represented a Jesuitical combination of cunning and fanaticism. Typically, Karl Heimburger's address to the 1909 Democrat party conference contained dire warnings about even a temporary triumph of clericalism.[13]

The importance of cultural issues in Germany as a whole and the depth of Protestant antagonism towards political Catholicism have already been emphasized. But they were put forward in Baden with particular intensity. The Centre fought each election with claims that its Liberal and SPD opponents intended a renewed and more radical *Kulturkampf*. Of course there was a tactical element to this, but it was more than a ploy to consolidate the Centre support. The fear, reinforced by history, was that the Liberals in Baden, more than elsewhere, had the energy and the influence to put their ideals into practice. The continual cry of the church in danger was met on the other side by dire warnings of the Ultramontane threat to Badenese traditions of tolerance and liberty.

The years before the war marked a high point of SPD and Liberal fears. There was the national message of the Blue-Black Bloc and the possibility of a similar majority in the Badenese Landtag was closer than ever before. A spirit of foreboding was engendered by political developments in the rest of Southern Germany: the winning of half the seats by Centre and Agrarian candidates in the 1912 Württemberg elections and, above all, the establishment of a Centre-led government in Bavaria earlier in the same year. Prussian Junkers were treated with contempt in the *Großblock* press, but the Hertling ministry in Bavaria was viewed with disquiet tinged by doom and hysteria. On cultural issues, Badenese Liberals and Social Democrats felt they had more to

---

[12] GLA Karlsruhe, NLP Baden 162, Landesversammlung 1910.
[13] *Neue Konstanzer Abendzeitung* (17 May 1909).

lose than the Prussians: non-confessional schools were already in place and Baden's three institutions of higher education were looked up to as monuments to culture and academic freedom. Moreover, because of the perception of growing geo-political isolation and the fact that Catholics made up 60 per cent of the population, they felt they were more likely to lose what they had. The image of Baden as the remaining rock of freedom in Southern Germany threatened by a surrounding black sea of clericalism was evoked by both Liberals and Social Democrats. The division between supporters and opponents of political Catholicism also had a geographical, economic, and organizational dimension. Almost all Centre seats were in rural areas, while most Liberal and SPD deputies represented urban constituencies.[14] Because the Centre drew much of its support from small-town and rural districts where, unlike large towns, the priest and parish organizations had retained their influence, the importance of the Catholic Church to Centre party was underlined, as, in turn, was their opponents' rejection of church involvement in politics. It was illegal for the clergy to use their office to influence state elections in Baden. Nevertheless, there were countless press allegations of clerical interference and regular parliamentary committee investigations and debates on the matter. Liberal and SPD complaints about the Catholic clergy's influence certainly had some foundation. But the considerable exaggeration and element of dramatic hysteria which accompanied such claims owed more to deep antipathy towards political Catholicism than to the true effectiveness of clerical influence.[15] The division of society on confessional lines was not limited to obvious organizations like the church itself, the Popular Association for Catholic Germany, and the various Catholic social and charitable organizations. An organization existed for Catholic school teachers and there was an attempt to establish a separate association for Catholic railway workers.[16] Such divisions were hardly unique to Baden. However, they jarred more with Badenese political tradition and the high premium set on assimilation. Moreover, because the social integration of

---

[14] See the figures in Theodor Wacker's pamphlets: *Der Gegenwärtige Mandatsbesitz der Linksliberalen* (Karlsruhe, 1913); and *Der Sozialdemokratische Mandatsgewinn von 1909* (Karlsruhe, 1913).

[15] M. Stadelhofer, *Der Abbau der Kulturkampfgesetzgebung im Großherzogtum Baden 1878–1918* (Mainz, 1969), 310–18; J. Schofer, *Zentrumspolitik auf dem badischen Landtag 1905/06* (Baden-Baden, 1907), 61 and 80–5; H. Hummel, *Gegen das Zentrum* (Berlin, 1911); H. Bodewig, *Geistliche Wahlbeeinflussungen in ihrer Theorie und Praxis dargestellt* (Munich, 1909). [16] *Badischer Landesbote* (7 Apr. 1914).

the labour movement had, by common consent, proceeded further than elsewhere, this only increased the extent to which cultural and confessional differences stood out and formed the political dividing line. Von Eisendecher, the Prussian envoy in Karlsruhe, was correct to conclude that many of the problems for the executive in Baden arose from 'the hatred and struggle between the Centre and National Liberals [which] have for years dominated and damaged the whole political situation here'.[17]

In the sphere of popular politics, therefore, Baden had something approaching a British two-party system. What was missing was a constitutional requirement for the executive to be drawn from the majority party grouping. As in other German states, parties and government owed no direct allegiance to each other, but governments inevitably had to come to a working compromise with majorities in legislatures, unless there was a prospect of a successful direct appeal to the electorate. In Baden tradition and prevailing ideology at court and in the ministries was less set against co-operation with political parties. In addition, unlike Prussia, state finances were invariably stretched, which inevitably tended to increase the influence of the second chamber. However, it was the clarity of the left–right division within popular politics which really made attempts to rule 'above the parties' precarious. Richard Kunze made an untypically perceptive point when he remarked that the National Liberals and Centre Party, for all their mutual public antagonism, often found themselves voting together forming the bulk of the government's majority in important Reichstag divisions.[18] In Baden, the whole political climate precluded this. The argument advanced by Naumann and others that co-operation between Liberals and SPD was easier in state parliaments than in the Reichstag, because agreement over state budgets contained cultural items and excluded military spending, was plausible in theory. But relations between National Liberals and SPD in the Prussian, Saxon, and Hesse state assemblies were hardly cordial. It was the grass root attitudes of party supporters towards each other which was crucial.

Having bowed before a Centre–Democrat–SPD majority and the pressure of public opinion over franchise reform, the government in Baden faced the prospect of having to come to a political

---

[17] AA Bonn, IA Baden 40. 12 Eisendecher to Bethmann Hollweg 20 July 1909 (copy).
[18] Kunze, *Was der Reichstagswähler wissen muß*.

accommodation with either left or right. The price of a *Großblock* majority was creeping political and social reform in a Young Liberal direction: further franchise reform in state and local elections, non-confessional education, and an expanded social policy. In the long term such a political constellation, provided it was not dependent for a majority, as after the 1913 elections, on right-wing National Liberals, led to parliamentary government. A prospective Centre-dominated Landtag majority of the right, the alternative political constellation, posed a different threat. As in the rest of Germany, the Centre showed interest in constitutional reform only where it served party interests, hence its opposition in Baden both to indirect, unequal voting which benefited the National Liberals and, in 1912 and 1914, to proportional representation which would have lessened the possibility of an out-right Centre majority.[19] Beneath the veneer of populist rhetoric, the Badenese Centre showed the same political flexibility and willingness to come to an arrangement with government which characterized the party in Reich politics.

The terrible price of a Centre majority was, however, administrative rather than legislative. Even in the era of the *Großblock* and popular political participation, the higher reaches of state administration continued to be dominated by governmental National Liberals. Inevitably, a Centre-led majority would have demanded an end to this, and the appointment of its own supporters in Catholic strongholds. The seriousness with which the National Liberals viewed the possibility of Centre party placemen in higher administrative positions was exemplified by attitude of senior party figures like Uibel, Bürklin, and Rebmann towards the Arnsperger 'scandal' in 1910. They felt obliged to defy public opinion and support the Badenese government's decision to transfer Arnsperger, an *Oberamtsmann*, for supporting a *Großblock* alliance against 'Junker und Pfaffen' rather than the official government *Sammlungspolitik*. If administrative officials were not obliged to toe the government line, the result could be *Oberamtsmänner* under Centre influence. Bavaria had shown how Landtag majorities could change, so a National Liberal administrative apparatus was regarded as a vital safeguard.[20] The Badenese state government also shared much of this suspicion of political Catholicism. Although Young Liberal, left liberal, and SPD demands on education and the

[19] AA Bonn, IA Baden 40. 14, Eisendecher's report, 6 July 1912; Baden 40, 15 Eisendecher's report, 20 May 1914.   [20] GLA Karlsruhe, NLP Baden 211, fos. 56–83.

division of church and state went further than was comfortable, the position of the right on these issues went against the grain for a government which in the 1860s had been in the forefront of the *Kulturkampf*.[21]

If Badenese government officials showed more understanding of party politics, it was for the most part the result of necessity rather than sympathy. 'Parliamentary evenings' were more natural affairs in Karlsruhe than in Berlin. Party leaders, including Social Democrats, were used to talking to each other and to ministers as a matter of course. Nor did the Badenese royal family pointedly distance itself like the Hohenzollerns from such occasions. In particular, the heir to the throne Prince Max displayed a keen interest in party politics and political issues.[22] Nevertheless, in Baden as elsewhere, the decisive step to parliamentary government came only in November 1918. The government still sought to use the veterans' associations as a political weapon against the SPD and barred socialists from administrative positions. When Rosa Luxemburg spoke in Karlsruhe in the first half of 1914, the authorities, like their Prussian counterparts, had policemen monitoring the meeting and waiting in numbers in nearby side streets.[23] Moreover, if the government was more enlightened and tolerant than in other German states, then parties and press were more populist and the degree of political mobilization and desire for reform was greater than elsewhere. The gap in perspective and priorities between ministers like Freiherr von Dusch, Freiherr von und zu Bodman, and Dr Böhm and the government organ the *Karlsruher Zeitung* on the one hand, and Edmund Rebmann, Theodor Wacker, and the *Badische Landeszeitung* and *Badischer Beobachter* on the other was considerable, and one between two groups serving different masters. The truth about politics in Baden in the pre-war decade was that ministers and higher officials shared Eisendecher's view that government was properly conducted by a small circle of officials insulated from the irrational and ill-educated forces of public opinion, whereas the parties professed support for the ideals of popular politics: the SPD and Democrats out of principle, the Centre out of instinct and self-interest, the Conservatives out of necessity, and the National Liberals because they were finally pushed into it by the electorate.

[21] J. Becker, *Liberaler Staat und Kirche in der Ära von Reichsgründung und Kulturkampf* (Mainz, 1973); Gall, *Liberalismus*.　　　[22] *Badischer Landesbote* (27 June 1914).
[23] AA Bonn, IA Baden 40. 10, extract of report by Eisendecher on conversation with Großherzog Friedrich, 1 Oct. 1905.

Although the problem of accommodation facing the government is an important and insufficiently explored theme, it is predominantly on the engines of popular politics that an examination of the role of the left liberals must focus.[24] When Dr Obkircher, Rebmann's predecessor as National Liberal leader, referred scathingly to 'a great deal of stirring it up' and 'politicians and whole parties who live off agitation', his charges were clearly levelled at the left liberals.[25] The long-serving and suffering Eisendecher was similarly appalled: 'Radical and beyond improvement', 'railway and school fanatics', 'demagogic rabble rousers' in the style of 1848, specialists in 'a most uncalled for, crude anti-Prussianism'. Badenese left liberals, he complained, spurned the constructive side of politics and were always sounding off (*führen das große Wort*) at public meetings and in the press.[26] Political agitation was always important to a traditionally oppositional party like the left liberals, but it was particularly vital in a region like Baden where the National Liberals were powerfully entrenched. Moreover, such activity satisfied an ideological craving as well as a practical need. For the left liberals in Baden, the majority of whom called and considered themselves Democrats, the motto 'Alles für das Volk und alles durch das Volk' (everything for and by the people) remained the guiding principle.[27] Not only was popular participation the alpha and omega of their political ideology, but most leading left liberals felt an almost evangelical calling to spread the word. It was a fervour of which those who had to listen to the two and a half hour long Landtag speeches of

[24] For research on Baden politics in the Wilhelmine period see F. L. Sepainter, *Die Reichstagswahlen im Großherzogtum Baden: Ein Beitrag zur Wahlgeschichte im Kaiserreich* (Frankfurt am Main, 1982); H.-J. Franzen, *Auf der Suche nach politischen Handlungsspielraum. Die Diskussion um die Strategie der Partei in den regionalen und localen Organisationen der badischen Sozialdemokratie zwischen 1890 und 1914*, i–ii (Frankfurt am Main, 1987); J. Schadt *Die sozialdemokratische Partei in Baden: Von den Anfängen bis zur Jahrhundertwende 1868–1900* (Hanover, 1971); J. Schadt and W. Schmierer (eds.), *Die SPD in Baden-Württemberg und ihre Geschichte* (Stuttgart, 1979); K. Elsässer, *Die badische Sozialdemokratie, 1890 bis 1914: Zum Zusammenhang von Bildung und Organisation* (Marburg, 1978); H.-J. Kremer (ed.), *Mit Gott für Wahrheit, Freiheit und Recht: Quellen zur Organisation und Politik der Zentrumspartei und des politischen Katholizismus in Baden 1888–1914* (Stuttgart, 1983); Ehrismann, *Liberalismus in der Defensive*; Thiel, *Großblockpolitik*; and Heckart, *Bassermann*. On officials see H.-G. Metz, *Beamtentum und Beamtenpolitik in Baden: Studien zu ihrer Geschichte vom Großherzogtum bis in die Anfangsjahre des nationalsozialistischen Herrschaftssystems* (Freiburg, 1985).

[25] GLA Karlsruhe, NLP Baden 211, fo. 76, Engerer Ausschuß, 12 Nov. 1910.

[26] See AA Bonn, IA Baden 31. 13, Eisendecher's reports, 2 May 1910 and 9 Nov. 1910; and Baden 40. 12, Eisendecher to Bethmann Hollweg, 20 July 1909 (copy).

[27] J. Schadt (ed.), *Alles für das Volk, alles durch das Volk* (Stuttgart, 1977).

Oskar Muser were only too aware.[28] Badenese left liberal ideology thoroughly approved of mass politics. The less straightforward question to be addressed here is how far the mass electorate approved of left liberal politics.

The importance the Badenese Democrats invested in the *Vormärz* period and the events of 1848 was readily apparent. The black, red, and gold flag was accorded a prominent place on many party occasions: a tradition which continued after the 1910 merger when it was no longer the official party flag. Similarly, the anniversaries of events like the March days and the shooting, conveniently by Prussians, of seventeen *Freischärler* at Kirchheimboladen in 1849 were marked with reverence. Nevertheless, such celebrations, while playing on a sense of tradition, did not mark any organizational continuity. Some families and individuals displayed an unbroken *Vormärz* Democratic tradition. The most striking example was Martin Venedey, son and spiritual heir of the 1848 Democrat Jakob Venedey. There was also a steady trickle of obituaries in the left liberal press of octogenarian 'Democrats of the old school' who had been active supporters of the cause for sixty years.[29] Such people, however, represented a tiny minority. As voting behaviour in the four decades following 1850 demonstrated, the great majority of the population did not identify themselves as part of a continuous, specifically Democratic tradition. In organizational terms it was even more the case that the left liberal groups were a product of the period after 1890. In Konstanz, for example, Democratic Popular Association (*Demokratischer Volksverein*) appeared something of a misnomer for an organization which at its outset in 1890 had the support of seven men. By its twentieth anniversary in January 1910, however, it had almost 300 members and was the second largest party in the town.[30] In Karlsruhe the FVP association founded by the three pre-existing left liberal groups in the city had 900 members in 1910 and almost 1,500 in 1913, figures which easily exceeded those in some North German cities where the left liberals were the main non-socialist party.[31] As the political report to the party conference in May 1914

---

[28] For evidence of Muser's Democatic enthusiasm and its soured aftermath after 1918 see his autobiographical 'Meine Rednerische Tätigkeit' and 'Die Tragödie der Demokratie auch ein Stück Tragödie meines Lebens', in GLA Karlsruhe, NL Oskar Muser 2 and 3.

[29] See e.g. *Badischer Landesbote* (7 Jan. 1913 and 15 June 1914), and *Oberbadische Volkszeitung* (25 Jan. 1915). [30] *Neue Konstanzer Abendzeitung* (2 Feb. 1910).

[31] *Badischer Landesbote* (16 Jan. 1913). See e.g. left liberal membership figures for Kiel given in Ch. 8 n. 102.

Table 7.1. *FVP Membership in Baden, 1910–1914*

Date	Branches	Total membership
10 Apr. 1910	67	7,956
12 Nov. 1911	98	10,335
May 1912	119	12,307
1 May 1914	138	14,357

Source: *Badischer Landesbote* (16 May 1914).

made clear, there had been a continued growth in left liberal party membership in Baden.

The prevalence of electoral pacts in Badenese politics makes an exact ratio of party members to party voters difficult to establish. Contemporary opinion was that the left liberals received somewhat more votes than they gave in electoral pacts with the National Liberals. Nevertheless the 30,000 votes cast for the left liberals in the 1913 state elections may be taken as a reasonable guide to left liberal strength. That implies that one in every two or three left liberal voters was a party member, a degree of organization three times greater than the national average. Though there was still undoubtedly a great difference in the amount of membership dues paid, there was nothing like the usual chasm in size and degree of organization between left liberals and SPD in Baden.

Left liberal party membership had, therefore, reached a significant size, particularly when its location is taken into account. There were understandably few left liberal members in safe Centre seats, but considerable numbers in Karlsruhe, Mannheim, and Lörrach, where there were marginal seats between National Liberals and the SPD, and in Konstanz, Lahr, and Offenburg where the Centre and National Liberals were closely matched. In some places majorities were so narrow that even small numbers of Democrats could influence the outcome of elections. In the Meßkirch district, for example, there were only some thirty Democrat party members in 1909, but the National

Table 7.2. *SPD Membership in Baden,*
1910–1914

Date	Branches	Membership
30 June 1910	195	15,228
30 June 1911	218	17,671
30 June 1912	233	20,207
31 Mar. 1914	215	25,494

Source: Jörg Schäder, *Im Dienst der Republik* (Stuttgart, 1977).

Liberals were rightly concerned that a Democratic splinter candidate might be enough to hand victory to the Centre.[32] In local government a similar picture emerges. The fifty-two left liberal *Vereine* which replied to a circular in 1914 claimed a total of ninety-three members of municipal and rural executives (*Stadträte* and *Gemeinderäte*) and 626 councillors. In addition there were four openly left liberal mayors.[33] The FVP was only the fourth strongest party in local government. The National Liberals and Centre were the leading forces in local elections as in national and state contests, but the SPD had made significant inroads. It had 146 executive members and 2,006 councillors in Baden by 1913.[34] Nevertheless, the left liberal presence was enough to indicate the FVP had gained a foothold in Baden, and was a significant minority party rather than a meaningless sect. The left liberals in Baden were even further than in other parts of Germany from being able to rule the political roost alone. By contrast with the period before 1890, however, they had advanced to the position of kingmaker in a significant number of districts.

The high degree of party organization was, moreover, a general feature in Baden. The Badenese National Liberal organizations had over 30,000 members by 1914, and the People's Association for a Catholic Germany had a mass and growing membership in the state.[35] The scale and openness of Badenese politics indicated its greater degree of political mobilization and the more prominent role of political parties. The signs of a more popular, 'modern' form of politics were numerous. As well as the size of party membership, the position of party organizers was significantly different from that generally seen in Wilhelmine Germany. Whereas paid party officials were commonly seen as disrespectable or fit only for humdrum administrative tasks, in Baden they were clearly men of a higher calibre and status. Of the left liberal party secretaries in Baden, two (Harzendorf and Butz) held doctorates and a third (Otto Ernst Sutter), had an engineering degree. A fourth official, Karl Dees, was able enough to be considered for the post of FVP deputy general secretary in 1918 and become a Landtag deputy in the 1920s.[36] Similarly, the National Liberal general

---

[32] *Neue Konstanze Abendzeitung* (3, 13, and 14 May 1909).

[33] *Badischer Landesbote* (16 May 1914).   [34] BA Berlin, Reichslandbund 5604, fo. 55.

[35] Thiel, *Großblockpolitik*; H.-J. Kremer, 'Der Volksverein für das Katholische Deutschland in Baden 1890–1933', *Freiburger Diözesan-Archiv*, 104 (1984), 208–80.

[36] BA Berlin FVP 36, fos. 279–80, executive committee, 11 Feb. 1918; A. Rapp (ed.), *Die badischen Landtags-Abgeordneten 1905/1929* (Karlsruhe, 1929).

secretary, the lawyer Dr Thorbecke, was a skilled political operator. His relationship with the party leader Rebmann, though not one of equals, was more that of a valued adviser than a menial subordinate. It was a measure of Thorbecke's social standing that he was able to move on to the impeccably respectable position of Bürgermeister of Singen.[37] The Centre, too, placed much importance in political organization, an attitude personified by its electoral general (*Wahlfeldmarschall*) Theodor Wacker and his protégé Dr Josef Schofer, a Landtag deputy and head of the Volksverein in Baden.[38] Amongst Badenese Conservatives the aristocratic leaders were largely figureheads. Populist agitators like the Brettan lawyer and Landtag deputy O. H. Schmidt or party secretary Wilhelm Schmidt increasingly took the lead in political campaigning.[39] This was all part of a growing recognition of the importance of party officials and the increasing scale of party organizations and activities. As the Richterite Friedrich Weill admitted in 1908, even for a small party like the FrVp in Baden it was 'no longer possible to get by without a party secretary'.[40] By the eve of the war the Centre, SPD, left liberals, and National Liberals found party secretaries indispensable not only in Karlsruhe, but in each region of Baden. The left liberals, for example, had additional party secretaries based in Mannheim in the north and Freiburg in the south. The need for tighter organization was not welcomed in all quarters. Nor was resentment towards paid officials entirely dissipated. Both were reflected in the objections of one National Liberal to the turning away of supporters lacking proper accreditation from party meetings: 'The party secretary stands there like the Archangel Michael at the gate, . . . albeit with a glowing cigar rather than a burning sword, and won't let the people in.'[41] The general feeling in both Liberal groups, however, was that to compete parties had to follow the SPD's organizational example.

An even more striking picture of politicization was provided by the press. Of the main Karlsruhe papers, the National Liberal *Badische*

---

[37] See the correspondence between Thorbecke and Rebmann in GLA Karlsruhe, NLP Baden 182–3.　　　　　　[38] Bachem, *Zentrumspartei*, viii. 98–210.

[39] On O. H. Schmidt, an unscrupulous rabble-rouser who boasted about trebling the number of court cases in his constituency and was convicted of professional misconduct, see BA Berlin, Reichslandbund personalia 417, fos. 8–15. Party secretary Schmidt's transfer to Hanover after leading the 1913 state election campaign underlined the right's failure to establish itself in Baden.　　　　　[40] *Neue Badische Landeszeitung*, 536 (16 Nov. 1908).

[41] GLA Karlsruhe, NLP Baden 211, Fabrikant Hülsmann, Engerer Ausschuß, Landesversammlung 1910, fos. 48–9.

Landeszeitung, the Centre Party's *Badischer Beobachter*, and the left liberal *Badischer Landesbote* were party papers, under the control of the party and reflecting the official Karlsruhe party line, in just the same way as the Social Democratic *Volksfreund*. Journalists on such papers were, in reality, just as much party officials as the party secretaries. Indeed, there was a considerable overlap between the two groups. Most party secretaries wrote press articles and many journalists and editors played an active part in political campaigning. This flexibility was underlined by an interchange of personnel. In 1910 Karl Dees moved from being left liberal party secretary to being editor of the *Badischer Landesbote*. Similarly, Otto Ernst Sutter became Baden correspondent for the *Frankfurter Zeitung*. In such circumstances it was to be expected that most papers would combine a forthright political stance with an aggressive popular tone.

Just as the press refused to stand aloof, above party politics, so local government became irreversibly drawn into the party-political arena. In the larger towns the last vestiges of non-party pretence had been stripped away. By 1914, newspaper reports of debates in the council chamber in Karlsruhe indicated the party allegiance of each speaker in the same way as the Reichstag reports. Each party put up its own slate of candidates for local elections, a trend further encouraged by the introduction of a form of proportional representation. (Voting in towns over 2,000 was by proportional representation within three classes, the first class being the top sixth, the second the next third, and the third the remaining half of taxpayers.[42]) In addition, as the left liberal party conference in 1914 noted, there was a growing party participation in elections to Kreis assemblies and commercial and health insurance tribunals.[43] A high turn-out in state and local elections underlined this mobilization. A poll of 80 per cent was commonplace, and in contests where the outcome was finely balanced turn-out could exceed 90 per cent. In the 1909 local elections in Tiengen, for instance, turn-out in the third class was 80 per cent and in the marginal second class 95 per cent. Voting in the securely Liberal first class then fell to 63 per cent as Centre supporters, disappointed at the narrow defeat in the second-class elections, stayed away from the polls. In a marginal Landtag seat like Offenburg more than 94 per cent of the electorate voted in the 1914 by-election.[44]

---

[42] For an outline of the 1910 local government reform and the parties' differing stances see Heckart, *Bassermann*, 116–18.   [43] *Badischer Landesbote* (16 May 1914).

[44] *Neue Konstanzer Abendzeitung* (25 May 1909); *Badischer Landesbote* (2 Mar. 1914).

The typical range of themes aired by the left liberals, apart from the political issues of the day, was well reflected in a FVP gathering in Konstanz in 1914. Gönner and Hummel stressed the need for house-to-house campaigning in town and country, Oskar Muser spoke on the history of Democracy in Baden and Martin Venedey described the growth of the Democrats in Konstanz. An evocative appeal to tradition was married to an exposition of the techniques and necessities of modern politics. The theme to engage local interest, however, was the state of Konstanz's railway station.[45] As Eisendecher correctly identified, the railway was a central and potent issue in left liberal campaigning. It presented a sea of unfulfilled wishes. Even the smallest of villages longed for a branch line. Towns, no matter how insignificant, expected express trains to stop at their station and pressed for improved connections. Countless places petitioned for a new station, better waiting rooms, underpasses, improved goods loading facilities, and the like. The correspondence between Hermann Hummel and the representives of towns along the Black Forest line in his constituency was replete with such demands.[46]

Left liberals took every opportunity to pose as champions of these demands and as the critics of bureaucratic insensitivity and mismanagement. In addition, they claimed to be the friends of railway workers, the advocates of better pay and conditions and rights of association and assembly. The FVP meeting for railway workers during the 1914 Offenburg by-election underlined both left liberal attitudes and the electoral importance of the railway vote.[47] True, many railway proposals were hopelessly uneconomic and remained unfulfilled. Moreover, all parties and politicians sought to claim credit for new branch lines, no matter how far in the past the plans had been approved, and to appear eager advocates for every new railway proposal in the constituency. Even august party leaders like Obkircher and Wacker became embroiled in the dispute over whether the sitting Centre party deputy or his National Liberal predecessor deserved the credit for the building of the Bonndorf railway.[48] But the left liberals, as a minority grouping not closely associated with the authorities, could avoid taking responsibility for shortcomings and point the finger at others for the failure of impossibly ambitious schemes. The

---

[45] *Neue Konstanzer Abendzeitung* (6 June 1914).
[46] SA Darmstadt, NL Hermann Hummel.   [47] *Badischer Landesbote* (23 Feb. 1914).
[48] T. Wacker, *Zur Politischen Lage im Reiche und in Baden* (Karlsruhe, 1909).

Neue Konstanzer Abendzeitung, for example, blamed the National Liberals and Centre party for the disappointments contained in the new rail timetable 1909. Both these parties, the left liberal newspaper alleged, were eager to prove their 'fitness to rule' (*Regierungsfähigkeit*) and as a result were damagingly lenient towards the rail authorities.[49] Yet more significant was the way the railway dovetailed into the left liberals' general political outlook. The estate owner's carriage pulled by 'luxury' horses and trailed by a cartload of liveried servants was contrasted with the *beschleunigter Personenzug* (speeded-up but supplement-free train) providing a public service. The first image was held up as the epitome of servitude and reaction, the second as the liberating triumph of technology. The railway, engine of economic progress, benefiting of businessman and commuting factory worker alike, was embraced by the left liberals as both part and progenitor of the modern state they wished to see. The programme to celebrate the fortieth anniversary of the building of the Black Forest line between Hausach and Villingen at Triberg, 6 and 7 September 1913, was infused with such attitudes.[50]

Aside from these general images, the way the railway was run gave particular impact to railway issues in Badenese politics in the pre-war decade. As in the rest of Germany the left liberals paraded themselves as the opponents of the 1906 train ticket tax passed in the Reichstag by Conservatives, Centre, and National Liberals. Indeed, left liberal exploitation of this tax was of major concern amongst delegates to the latter's national conference.[51] Aside from an increase in fourth-class travel at the expense of higher classes, the tax had little effect on such an impregnable financial milch cow as the Prussian state railways. In Baden, however, railway finances were less healthy, partly indeed because the minister responsible for the railways had bowed to the second chamber's demands for improved staff working conditions, better services, new stations, and the *Kilometerheft*, a block ticket which made travel in express and semi-fast trains appreciably cheaper.[52] Railway finances were also affected by increased wage costs and the economic downturn which reduced freight revenue in 1908. As a

[49] *Neue Konstanzer Abendzeitung* (26 Feb. 1909).

[50] SA Darmstadt, NL Hummel. For a concise, but compelling summary of popular railway enthusiasm and its association with the ideals of technical and material progress in 19th-century Germany see Blackbourn and Eley, *Peculiarities*, 185–8.

[51] AA Bonn, IA Deutschland, 125. 6, *National-Zeitung* (7 Oct. 1906).

[52] AA Bonn, IA Baden 36. 2, Eisendecher report, 11 Apr. 1910 (copy).

result the new minister sanctioned a programme of retrenchment involving cuts in services and station and track improvements. Opposition was aroused in all parties, reflected in the bitter criticism which the cuts in the 1909 summer timetable received throughout the Baden press.[53] Public indignation was widespread and sustained, particularly at the demise of the *Kilometerheft*.

The *Kilometerheft* was more than a beloved middle-class perk, it was seen as a symbol of south-west German superiority. The *Kilometerheft*, it was insisted, had fallen victim to an enforced conformity with Prussia. The intensity of the criticism of the rail authorities derived in part from the way people saw the railway as 'their' railway, and the high expectations which went with such an attitude. The passage in the 1871 constitution envisaging rail co-ordination at national level (*Reichseisenbahngemeinschaft*) was not quite the legislative dead-letter it appeared. Although never put into practice, it was a constant theme of debate and speculation in Baden. Here, as with the image of technological progress, a wider symbolic importance was attached to the railway. The ideal rail union was held to be genuinely federal, but made more efficient by scale and co-operation. The nightmare was a rail union which was in effect a takeover of the other state railways by the Prussian railways. Prussia was the object of attack, whether as the self-seeking obstacle to a national rail system or as the lurking predator waiting to swallow up the South German railways.[54] Indeed, it was the way in which the railway issue was harnessed to anti-Prussian sentiment, above all by the left liberals, which rendered it such a powerful political weapon. An unending series of events, more often minor than major, was seized on by the Liberal press to demonstrate Prussian 'tendencies' in the running of Baden's railways. The removal of the satirical journal *Simplicissimus* from station bookstalls and even the banning of smoking in restaurant cars were condemned as manifestations of Prussian authoritarianism.[55] The same forces were blamed for making people use the painfully slow *Bummelzüge* and the spectre was raised of inflicting seatless fourth-class Prussian cattle trucks ('4.Klasse Preußische Steh-Viehwagen') on the Badenese travelling public.[56]

---

[53] AA Bonn, IA Baden 40. 12 Eisendecher report, 3 Mar. 1909.
[54] H. Hummel, *Baden und die Eisenbahngemeinschaft* (Karlsruhe, 1912).
[55] *Badische Landeszeitung* (5 June 1908).
[56] *Neue Konstanzer Abendzeitung* (23 Jan 1909).

When the imperial train, bound for the Donaueschingen hunting estates, left a trail of delays and cancellations in its wake, the left liberal press was outraged. Why, they angrily demanded, should business and the travelling public be disrupted to ensure the Kaiser, not on public duty but a private pleasure trip, arrived exactly on time. It was, as usual, politically astute to direct the attack mainly at intermediate figures, in this case obsequious officials: 'We assume, must assume, that the Kaiser himself does not know how strongly the interests of public transport are affected when his absolutistic royal train, unbound by any traffic rules, rushes through Germany much more like a revolutionary vehicle.'[57] To many Germans, imbued with a sense of civic pride, the public timetable was an inviolable document. Lateness and breakdowns were a slur on the twin gods of technology and *Tüchtigkeit* (diligence), the wanton abandonment of a part of the timetable an act of sacrilege. Even the position of individual lines within the timetable book was considered a matter of pride, with the inhabitants of Konstanz, for example, demanding that the importance of their line to Offenburg merited a place in the first six tables in the public timetable.

The railway, then, was much more in public consciousness than a way of moving from A to B. The only means of relatively fast affordable travel and vital in the transport of goods in districts beyond the reach of the barge, its direct impact on individuals and communities was considerable. But, beyond that, the railway was a national institution, a symbol of civic pride, and a monument to technology. The government's rejection of the Titisee-St Blasien railway project provoked a mournful tribute to the railway as the harbinger of civilization and economic salvation: 'all inhabitants of our region [were] of a single mind. There is only one saviour from threatening ruin: . . . the railroad into our continually neglected district, a link to the rail network!'[58] The railway, because it meant so much to so many, provided the ideal practical example for the left liberals to illustrate the benefits of popular accountability over authoritarianism, a *Volksstaat* over an *Obrigkeitsstaat*. On the one side was the authoritarian railway: Prussianized, the home of petty regulations and faceless administrators. It had queues at the booking office, barriers at the platform entrance, and an underpaid, unrepresented workforce. Class conflict was

---

[57] *Neue Konstanzer Abendzeitung* (3 May 1910).
[58] *Neue Konstanzer Abendzeitung* (15 Apr. 1910).

mirrored in the exclusivity and privilege of the first-class saloon and the discomfort and slowness of fourth-class travel. On the other side was the promised vision of the people's railway: publicly accountable, run by a well-paid, well-trained staff, providing a cheap and efficient service with a progressive two-class fare structure, and investment in new lines, stations, and rolling stock.

As with the artisan programme of right-wing *Mittelstand* politicians, the political attractiveness of such a vision lay in the chord which individual elements struck within the population. 'Railway politics' did have the advantage that it appeared forward- rather than backward-looking, to be swimming with rather than against the tide of social and economic development. Nevertheless, as with *Mittelstandspolitik*, the sums did not add up. Any coherence was rhetorical and ideological rather than practical and economic. The demands for higher spending and lower fares were hardly compatible. The dishonest promise and the tendency to excess were hallmarks of railway politics and *Mittelstandsretterei* alike.[59]

Nothing quite matched the railway as a universal cause which blended the ideological and material side of politics. A close second, however, was the question of shipping duties (*Schiffahrtsabgaben*) which particularly affected towns along the upper Rhine.[60] Once again, Prussia was assailed as the villain of the piece. She was popularly portrayed as attempting to bully the other German states into making sacrifices to serve the interests of the Junkers. Moreover, the effect of such issues was cumulative, each feeding off the other and further inflaming an almost universal antagonism towards Prussia.[61] In addition to being popular in themselves, these themes had a further importance for left liberal politics. A sample of FVP votes cast in the 1914 local elections highlighted the relatively even spread of the party's support across the economic classes. The party received 6,038 votes in the first class, 6,637 in the second class, and 4,832 in the third.[62] Economic issues based on class interest were inevitably divisive: the FVP group on Karlsruhe City Council simply agreed to differ and allowed a free vote whenever such matters came to debate.[63] It

---

[59] For an acerbic commentary on the economics of the 'railway fanatics' see AA Bonn, IA Baden, 36. 2 Eisendecher, 11 July 1910 (copy).

[60] E. O. Sutter, *Wirtschaftsbilder vom Oberrhein: Reisebriefe für die 'Frankfurter Zeitung'* (Frankfurt am Main, 1912). For discussion of the issue in government and Reichstag committee see Rauh, *Parlamentarisierung*.

[61] AA Bonn, IA Baden 31. 13, Eisendecher report, 25 Jan. 1910.

[62] *Badischer Landesbote* (15 May 1914).   [63] *Badischer Landesbote* (21 July 1914).

was politically convenient as well as ideologically attractive to seek out issues, like the railway, which had an appeal across society. It was also a matter of belief and benefit to link economic and social issues with cultural and political causes. As elsewhere, this was most obviously manifested in the advocacy of education as a panacea for economic ills. In addition, the message that political modernity was fundamental to economic and technological progress was propounded unceasingly by left liberals. As the comment 'the Z[eppelin] 2 disaster would probably have been avoided if we'd had constitutional government'[64] exemplified, this was more an act of faith than a rational explanation of events. Consequently, the development of the Kaiserreich, which tended to suggest that economic modernity was not dependent on political reform, had little impact. Economic shortcomings were blamed on bureaucracy and political backwardness, growth and technological achievement ascribed to individual enterprise and the general economic virtues of the *Bürgertum*.

It was to the left liberals' advantage that such sentiments were widely shared. People did believe in the benefits of education, and in a general gospel of modernity encompassing political renewal as well as technological advance. Against such a background, it was understandable that Prussian franchise reform was an issue which attracted at least as much interest in Baden as in Prussia itself. The great majority of Liberals and Social Democrats in Baden, and indeed many Centre party voters, accepted Ludwig Frank's analysis that the Prussian franchise was the keystone that held up the arch of reaction.[65] They also shared his sense of urgency about its reform. Numerous public meetings, resolutions, and press articles insisted that reform of the three-class franchise was not an internal Prussian matter, but the most important political issue facing the whole of the Reich. The chorus of disapproval which greeted Bethmann Hollweg's 1910 franchise proposals was raised to a roar of public outrage by the Chancellor's attempted justification. Bethmann's assertion that equal franchise and direct elections introduced crudity and coarseness into public life was seen by the *Badischer Landesbote* as an unwarranted slur on Baden and Southern Germany. Its vigorous rejection of the Prussian franchise proposals exemplified the vivid, emotional anti-Prussianism of

---

[64] *Neue Konstanzer Abendzeitung* (28 Apr. 1914).
[65] For Frank's views see S. Tegel, 'Reformist Social Democrats, the Mass Strike and the Prussian Suffrage 1913', *EHQ* 17 (1987), 307–44.

Badenese left liberals: 'And it's none of our business how things are in Prussia? When it's Prussia which wants to hang electricity taxes on us, grasps after our railways and thrusts its brutal hand into our internal political life deflowering our state of justice bit by bit?!'[66]

This was a case of distance leading to disenchantment. Many people in Baden had never seen a Prussian Junker, let alone an East Elbian estate. Nevertheless, they readily believed even the most colourful of press reports about their alien and inferior way of life. There was also a constant attempt by Liberals and SPD to depict an 'alliance of darkness' between the external enemy of progress, the Junkers, and the internal threat to freedom, the Centre party. A similar appeal was to be heard in much of Germany, but it was given particular impact by the political tradition and pattern of electoral alliances in Baden. Numerous North German National Liberals found the *Großblocktaktik* incomprehensible and unforgivable. However, the way the SPD was treated in Prussia met with a similar response south of the Main. Conrad Haußmann's speech to a 1906 DVP Munich conference urging rulers to tolerate the red of the SPD to avert the people from the black fate of Centre domination echoed a widely shared sentiment in Southern Germany.[67]

The widespread anti-Prussianism and desire for reform which existed in Badenese society did not mean wholesale rejection of the values of Wilhelmine Germany. In attacking Prussian Conservatives, Badenese politicians explicitly supported the Reich and its institutions. They claimed that it was Prussian reactionaries, not liberal South Germans, who were the particularists. The National Liberals naturally took the lead in expressing nationalist sentiment. Rebmann and most Badenese National Liberals mirrored Bassermann's enthusiasm for colonial and military expansion.[68] As in other parts of the Reich, National Liberal meetings echoed to the sound of 'Deutschland, Deutschland über alles' and other patriotic melodies. But Badenese left liberals also showed an increasing identification with Bismarck's Germany. The Democrat leader Karl Heimburger

---

[66] *Badischer Landesbote* (12 and 19 Feb. 1910).

[67] 'Nicht ein starker, aber ein gerader und kluger Mann tut not, der spricht: Soll das Volk nicht schwarz sehen, so müssen Eure Majestät etwas rot sehen lernen'. *Nation* (6 Oct. 1906).

[68] AA Bonn, IA Baden 40. 14, 12 Dec. 1912, report by Eisendecher on NLP, *Parteitag*; Deutschland 122, 4, 6 Eisendecher to Bethmann Hollweg, 7 Jan. 1913; K.-P. Müller, *Politik und Gesellschaft im Krieg: Der Legitimätsverlust des Badischen Staates 1914–1918* (Stuttgart, 1988), 206.

claimed they had witnessed 'a development of the old police state to a liberal then a modern, social state', a progression he attributed to a spirit of democracy. As a result, the 'placing of the leadership of the [country's] affairs in the hands of the whole people' was seen as a strengthening, not a weakening of the Fatherland and as the next stage in a historical development rather than a conscious rejection of the existing state.[69]

Admittedly, the left liberal tone was rather different from that of the National Liberals. The visitor to a left liberal gathering was more likely to encounter a democratic than an imperialist anthem, 'Freiheit die ich meine' rather than 'Heil dir im Siegeskranz'. And while left liberals and National Liberals both saluted the Fatherland, it not clear that they had the same vision in mind. The left liberals' salutation was commonly coupled with a toast to the party, a practice which sat uneasily with the National Liberal tendency to place the Fatherland on an ideological pedestal above the worldly imperfections of party politics. Nevertheless, left liberals showed a similar tendency to eschew progressive reform on national issues and in foreign affairs. While the National Liberals urged change, but change towards a more active and aggressive imperialism, the left liberal response was, in general, uncharacteristically quiet and passive. Two main motives lay behind this stance. The first was simply lack of interest. For the large majority of left liberals, domestic political reform was the main aim, and the focus of political debate.[70] This *Primat der Innenpolitik* in left liberal ranks was magnified by a acceptance of Bismarckian unification and foreign policy. This was followed by a general endorsement, if not enthusiasm, for the foreign policy of later Chancellors. As Heimburger put it, Bismarck had erected a strong, secure house. Since unification, 'our one goal has been to fill the strong form of the German Reich with the spirit of freedom and create the conditions in which everyone can feel at home in the strong house'.[71] The left liberal calling was for interior decoration, not external alteration.

The second reason was self-interest. Not only were foreign and national issues less attractive, they were potentially more divisive. Whilst Badenese left liberals achieved an easy harmony on such issues as the suffrage, schools, and railways, differences were evident in their

---

[69] *Neue Konstanzer Abendzeitung* (19 May 1910).
[70] See the retrospective in *Badischer Landesbote* (31 Dec. 1914).
[71] *Neue Konstanzer Abendzeitung* (16 Mar. 1909).

attitudes to nationalism and imperialism. The pacifist wing of the party was relatively strong, represented most prominently by Muser and Venedey. Although there were no left liberal politicians in Baden who could be classified as being on the right of the party nationally, the sentiments expressed by some of the younger generation, those born in the 1870s, were clearly at variance with those of Muser and Venedey. Hummel, for instance, was prompted by events in Morocco to deliver a belligerent anti-French speech.[72]

Above all, national questions appeared to offer more electoral pitfalls than prospects. It was discontent over domestic politics rather than a concern about overzealousness on national issues which caused dissatisfied National Liberals to switch allegiance. Left liberal support for military bills in the Reichstag may have made it easier to attract votes from the right, but it was not the prime cause of such a switch. In addition, the desire of the left liberals to concentrate on domestic politics was reinforced by pre-war public opinion. The sharp rejection of *Sammlungspolitik* by the Badenese electorate was an indication that they too felt issues of domestic reform to be more pressing than national questions. Of the five state and national elections in Baden between 1905 and 1913, only the 1907 'Hottentot' elections involved foreign politics to a marked degree. And even here the significance proved more apparent than real as Liberals dwelt more on the Centre threat to South-West Germany than to South-West Africa. Likewise, the Liberals and SPD managed to turn the 1913 army expansion into a primarily domestic and financial issue. The focus, as in 1909, was on the Junkers' refusal to pay taxes.

In such a political climate it was understandable, as Eisendecher ruefully informed his superiors in Berlin, that *Sammlungspolitik* had little backing and the Conservative party in Baden 'few supporters, no leaders and no press'.[73] These popular attitudes, however, seem to present a paradox in analysing left liberalism in Baden. There was hardly another region in Germany where popular attitudes were more in accord with left liberal aims and political style. Opposition to authoritarianism and a desire for government in accordance with popular wishes ran throughout the electorate. Unlike Northern Germany, no party challenged the Democratic slogan of 'government for and by the people' directly: rather they claimed in various ways to

[72] AA Bonn, IA Baden 40. 12, Eisendecher 3 Nov. 1909 (copy).
[73] AA Bonn, IA Baden 31. 13 Eisendecher's report 9.11.1910.

have a better understanding of the voice of the people. Oldenburg-Januschau's rallying call 'Vox populi, vox Rindvieh' may have met an enthusiastic response from a minority in Prussia. In Baden it was a passport to political oblivion. Even after the 'Reform Landtag' of 1903–4 there was continued appetite for constitutional reform, particularly in local government. At the same time, however, there was hardly a state in the Second Empire where the left liberals gained less electoral success. Even in their strongholds in Baden the left liberals were normally only the third or fourth most popular party and perpetually gained less than a tenth of the total vote in Baden. In short, people were democratic in instinct and outlook, but did not vote Democrat.

This can partly be explained by the loyalty achieved by the two major parties in Baden. Although Catholics in some areas remained attached to a liberal political tradition and the SPD made inroads in urban areas, in much of Baden the Centre party was able to harness the Church and Catholic cultural and social organizations to produce a solid platform of support. More surprising and noteworthy was the resilience of National Liberal tradition in Baden. National Liberals were supposed to be fractious and fickle, a reputation supported by endless reports of party splits and crises and a high turnover of Reichstag seats. In Baden personal animosities and tactical disagreements were evident, but they were of a similar order to those encountered in other Badenese parties and very much a normal part of political life. Indeed, given the circumstances, it was the ability of the National Liberals in Baden to reach decisions which was more striking.[74] If the party in parliament was less likely to divide, it was the party's position in society where the differences from the national picture were most significant. National Liberals had dominated the state administrative machinery in Baden over many years. In some ways their dominance was more complete than that held by Conservatives in eastern Prussia. National Liberal administrators were less inclined to arouse public opposition and scrutiny by pointless acts of petty authoritarianism. Moreover, unlike the Prussian Conservatives, the National Liberal network was also pervasive in the cities, in the technical and financial branches of government service, and in the world of industry and commerce.

[74] For internal party debate see GLA Karlsruhe, NLP Baden, esp. 161–71, 181–8, and 213–45.

Admittedly, this position was being slowly eroded. As the *Frank-furter Zeitung* reflected, a National Liberal badge was no longer an absolute necessity for 'every half-way respectable person' who wanted a good reputation in society or to get on as a businessman or official in Baden.[75] While the make-up of senior officials in Karlsruhe and the *Amtsmänner* in the districts remained little changed, the increasing size and changing shape of the public sector led inevitably to a less traditional political and social outlook among state employees. Considerable numbers of elementary-school teachers in Baden, for example, were left liberals. The widespread protests against the disciplining of Rödel, a Mannheim *Oberlehrer* and editor of the radical *Neue Badische Schulzeitung*, showed 'strong democratic tendencies' among many elementary school teachers in Baden.[76] Nevertheless, if the National Liberals no longer had a monopoly of social standing, they still possessed a the major share. In Baden the National Liberals were still the party in which to be seen. This was more obvious in bureaucratic Karlsruhe and academic Heidelberg than in commercial centres like Mannheim or Pforzheim. However, even in the latter they still had considerable support, particularly in 'leading' circles.[77]

National Liberalism remained, then, an effective badge of respectability in government service and urban society. Alongside this, however, coexisted a popular National Liberal tradition. This was seen most clearly in parts of the Black Forest like the Donaueschingen and Engen districts. Here there were villages, including Catholic villages, where the inhabitants consistently supported National Liberal candidates in state and national elections. Such voting was far from being a search for respectability and was more an act of defiance than acquiescence. Here voting in the village or valley tended to be communal, to express common sentiment, not to seek in party label some sense of social superiority over neighbours. The National Liberals won support in such areas despite rather than because of their position in state administration. Unnecessary state controls were as

---

[75] *Frankfurter Zeitung* (22 Apr. 1907 and 23 Jan. 1911).

[76] AA Bonn, IA Baden 32. 9, Eisendecher report, 24 Dec. 1908.

[77] See the 1911 and 1914 local election returns in *Badischer Landesbote* (26 May and 16 June 1914). Continued National Liberal strength in Badenese municipal government is examined in Dieter Hein, 'Badisches Bürgertum: Soziale Struktur und kommunalpolitische Ziele im 19. Jahrhundert', in Gall (ed.), *Stadt und Bürgertum*, 65–96, esp. 95–6. For Mannheim see Gall, *Bürgertum in Deutschland*, esp. 402–34; for Karlsruhe, Heinz Schmitt (ed.), *Alltag in Karlsruhe: Vom Lebenswandel einer Stadt durch drei Jahrhunderte* (Karlsruhe, 1990), 162–228.

unwelcome to these peasants as attempts by the church to tell them how to vote. Significantly 'liberal' was a more commonly used description of their attitude and political allegiance than National Liberal. A strong degree of continuity from the *Vormärz* period was evident, particularly a pride in independence and a desire for freedom for outside interference. Both its longevity and the degree of resistance to decades of Centre agitation bore eloquent testimony to the durability of the liberal tradition in the Badisches Oberland. At least in terms of National Liberal voting figures, that tradition was on the wane. However, as with urban and governmental National Liberalism, the path of decline was gentle rather than abrupt.

The implications of this for the left liberals were obvious, for the natural source for significant growth in their popular support was the National Liberal electorate. For the left liberals there was no political vacuum to exploit, no plausible army of support from the previously uncommitted, nor an issue powerful enough to engineer a mass political conversion. Significant support could be gained only by a long-term process of attrition. Nor were the left liberals the only competitors for the National Liberal vote. The siren call of the Centre for liberal Catholics to come home 'where they belonged' was unceasing. And the revisionist stance of the Social Democrats, like that of Vollmar and the Bavarian SPD, was, in part, a conscious attempt to appeal to the small-town and rural electorate.

The other major obstacle to a left liberal breakthrough in Baden was the extent to which all the parties were playing the same political game. True, the Democrats were the specialists in anti-Prussianism. However, the SPD was equally vocal in this area and the National Liberal *Badische Landeszeitung* and the Centre Party *Badischer Beobachter* were not far behind the *Frankfurter Zeitung* and *Badischer Landesbote* in playing to anti-Prussian sentiment. Even the Conservatives attempted, albeit with limited success, to create an image distinct from that of the party of Prussian Junkers.[78] Similarly, in railway politics what the parties professed all lay in the same direction. All opposed timetable cuts and the removal of the *Kilometerheft*. Nor was all this simply a matter of presentation. Baden remained one of the few regions in Germany where those with a serious interest in liberal

---

[78] S. Wolf, *Konservatismus im liberalen Baden: Studien zur badischen Innen-, Kirchen- und Agrarpolitik sowie zur süddeutschen Parteiengeschichte 1860–1893* (Karlsruhe, 1990); Retallack, *Notables*, 204–5.

domestic reforms could feel at home in the National Liberal party. Indeed, it was the right wing of the party in Baden which felt frustrated and disregarded. Nor, despite the claims of political opponents, was the Centre party in Baden devoid of liberal tendencies. This was well illustrated by Fehrenbach's Reichstag speech on the Zabern affair and by the career of Joseph Wirth, an up-and-coming deputy on the eve of the war and the leading representative of the Centre's left wing during Weimar.[79]

As a consequence, the political terrain for the left liberals was far more congested than elsewhere. In most of Germany, for example, the left liberals were the only non-socialist party supporting the introduction of the Reichstag franchise for the Prussian Landtag elections. In Baden there was no shortage of National Liberal and Centre politicians advocating the same course. Instead of being able to exploit such an important and popular issue, left liberals were only able to secure a partial advantage by pointing out how the voting of National Liberal and Centre party deputies on franchise resolutions in the Prussian Landtag differed from the position taken by their colleagues in Baden. As with the railway and school questions, only an enthusiastic minority found the left liberals' position sufficiently distinct from that of the National Liberals to vote for them as a result. If the National Liberals and the Centre allowed the left liberals less political scope than their national position might suggest, the same applied to the SPD. The main left liberal themes for the state elections in 1909, besides the finance reform, were: consolidation and expansion of non-denominational schools; thorough reform of local government; restoration of 'previous, well-proven railway policies' and 'across the board rejection of the Prussianization and Berlinization of administration'.[80] As Eisendecher pointed out, the SPD was campaigning on just the same issues. It was clear that links between left liberals and SPD went beyond a common hostility to the Centre party. Social Democrats and left liberals often found themselves voting together in the Landtag and differing at election times more in tone and degree than in political direction. This was the pattern elsewhere, but in Baden the affinities were more apparent and the differences less marked. Moreover, unlike much of North Germany, where similarities were often studiously

[79] See the expression of affinity between Haußmann and Fehrenbach in HSA Stuttgart, NL Haußmann 114, Conrad Haußmann to Konstantin Fehrenbach, 12 Jan. 1922.

[80] AA Bonn, IA Baden 40. 12, Eisendecher, 3 Nov. 1909 (copy).

ignored by both sides, the advantages of co-operation were openly acknowledged. The attitude of a left liberal *Stadtrat* in Freiburg was typical: agreement with the SPD was often possible 'because they are just as *bürgerlich* as any other party in the council and are mostly on our side in cultural matters'.[81] Although the left liberals welcomed the 'positive contribution' of the SPD in Baden—'parliamentary cretinism' was Luxemburg's less enthusiastic description[82]—such reformist behaviour hardly made it easier for left liberals to persuade voters that they rather than the SPD offered the best avenue to domestic reform. Again, the left liberals had to look beyond Baden for targets to attack. *Vorwärts*, for example, was condemned as a byproduct of Prussian militarism (*echtes Kind preußischen Militarismus*).[83]

If ingrained party loyalties and a congested political terrain presented obstacles to left liberal progress, a third feature of Badenese politics, the rising tide of popular mass politics, was something the left liberals took in their stride and were able, at various points, to turn to their advantage. The results of city elections in 1911 and 1914 indicated that the left liberals as well as the SPD benefited from higher turn-outs. The Democratic summer festival, a mixture of song, celebration, and speeches, was a well-tried instrument which deliberately played on Baden's tradition of political freedom.[84] In Lahr, the constituency of the Democratic leader Karl Heimburger, it had become an annual event, with almost 4,000 attending the *Sommerfest* in July 1909. Festivals were used successfully to break into fresh political

Table 7.3. *Voting figures for Karlsruhe in 1914 (1911)*

	3rd class		2nd class		1st class	
FVP	708	(751)	1,048	(1,185)	612	(691)
NLP	600	(507)	1,471	(1,471)	1,329	(1,298)
SPD	4,593	(4,769)	921	(979)	71	(79)
Centre	1,156	(1,114)	1,248	(1,229)	406	(413)
Conservative	98	(124)	140	(172)	149	(205)
Spoilt papers	24	(108)	30	(46)	9	(28)
Turn-out (%)	*c.*60	(*c.*80)	60+	(75)	68	(78)

Source: *Badischer Landesbote* (26 May 1914).

[81] *Oberbadische Volkszeitung* (10 July 1914).
[82] Cited in Schorske, *Social Democracy*, 191.
[83] *Neue Konstanzer Abendzeitung* (24 Aug. 1908).
[84] O. E. Sutter, *Der festliche Gehalt der Politik: Feiert politische Volksfeste!* (Munich, 1911).

territory. In August 1909, 600 attended a Democratic *Fest* in Triberg and 500 in Gutach, a prelude to the Democrats gaining the Landtag seat in the October elections.[85] Similarly, the *Sommerfest* on the Hochberg near Freiburg, which attracted an audience of around 5,000 in June 1910, was one of the first moves in the expert campaign leading to the capture of the Freiburg Reichstag seat in 1912.[86] The great advantage of the *Fest* was its scale and impact. It deliberately attracted voters of all political hues. If successful, the *Fest* and, by extension, the party became the objects of fond memory. There was also an art to speaking on such occasions. It was essential to entertain, whilst introducing just enough politics to demonstrate the party's concern for the people of the district and the best interests of Baden.

The same people whose rhetoric served the party well on such occasions were also to be seen to good effect on more humdrum occasions throughout the campaigning season. An advantage held by the left liberals nationally, the ability and willingness of its leaders to speak in public, was particularly evident in Baden and an obvious asset in an age of popular politics. The major figures involved were secondary-school teachers like Heimburger, Hermann Hummel, and Reinhold Helbing, or lawyers like Muser, Venedey, Paul Frühauf, and Ludwig Haas.[87] Most weekends they were to be found addressing meetings and recruiting members throughout Baden. Though opponents sarcastically referred to *redegewandte Reiseapostel* (smooth-talking, travelling apostles) they were justifiably concerned at their activities. Although Badenese National Liberals like Rebmann recognized the need for such activity, left liberal public speakers were more numerous, more energetic, and frequently more skilful. Unlike the National Liberals, the left liberals were also able to draft in popular outside figures, like Conrad Haußmann and the Hessian 'peasant pastor' Adolf Korell.[88]

---

[85] SA Darmstadt, NL Hummel; Sutter, *Der festliche Gehalt der Politik*, 13–14.

[86] *Neue Konstanzer Abendzeitung* (20 July and 24 Aug. 1909 and 7 June 1910); GLA Karlsruhe, NLP Baden 181 Report on Freiburg election campaign, 19 Jan. 1912.

[87] For Heimburger's powerful personality see the account of a former pupil and later Centre politician: H. Köhler, *Lebenserinnerungen des Politikers und Staatsmannes 1879–1949* (Stuttgart, 1964). Friedrich Weill, who became FVP leader after Heimburger's mental breakdown in 1911, was, by contrast, less a public speaker, and more a negotiator behind the scenes.

[88] See e.g. Haußmann's crowded weekend schedule of political meetings during the 1909 campaign in Triberg-Hornberg-Gutach, SA Darmstadt, NL Hummel. See GLA Karlsruhe, NLP Baden 179, Paul Fuhrmann to Thorbecke, 4 Jan. 1911, for an admission that the National Liberals were unable to match the FVP's provision of outside speakers.

The Democrats' long-established populist image adapted easily to the political climate of the pre-war decade. They were quick to condemn the 'Badenese Junkers and consorts' as the 'high and mighty men in yellow boots posing as the representatives of our peasantry'.[89] Similarly, they criticized National Liberals for sins of the past. The way the National Liberal Party had conducted itself in the Badisches Oberland—not keeping in touch with the people and relying on higher officials at election time—made it easy for the Centre party agitators in the 1880s and 1890s to persuade the peasant 'that even genuine liberal men were just using him as voting fodder (*Stimmvieh*)'.[90] Although it was admitted that the new generation of National Liberal leaders were different, the image, it was argued, remained. Left liberals claimed that they were unencumbered by the past, and better placed to harness 'democratic sentiments' against the Centre.

Such press aspirations portrayed what left liberals wanted to happen, not necessarily what actually came about. However, the left liberals, like the other parties, were clearly trying hard to capture crucial peasant votes. As Hermann Hummel urged a left liberal meeting, they had to go out and make contact with the peasantry, 'for whoever has the peasants on his side also has power'.[91] The left liberals failed to make the great breakthrough amongst the peasantry the optimists hoped for. The areas of greatest rural success remained regions like Oldenburg, Schleswig-Holstein, and Mecklenburg where there was a long tradition of voting left liberal amongst the peasantry. Nevertheless, the amount of success was sufficient to suggest that the traditional political loyalties of the peasants could be broken down over time and that the left liberals could overcome the image of being the party of free trade and urban capitalism. Hummel, for one, practised what he preached by gaining and holding a semi-rural Landtag seat. In addition, the two Reichstag seats the party gained in 1912, Karlsruhe and Freiburg, were only partly urban. In both cases the capacity of the left liberals to win support amongst the peasantry in surrounding areas was important to success.[92] Partly this was a matter

---

[89] *Neue Konstanzer Abendzeitung* (24 June 1909).

[90] 'Wenn dann die Wahlzeit herannahte und die "Wahlchaise" in das Dorf einfuhr . . . der vorher so gestrenge Oberamtsmann als leutseligster Mann entstieg und jedem Bauer freundschaftlich die Hand drückte', *Neue Konstanzer Abendzeitung* (3 May 1909, cf. 24 June 1909).   [91] *Badischer Landesbote* (6 June 1914).

[92] GLA Karlsruhe, NLP Baden 181, report on Freiburg election, 19 Jan. 1912.

of presentation. Haas, the victor in Karlsruhe, found that 'our peasants show a very great interest in politics', providing you knew how to talk to them: 'in simple sentences but with ideas nevertheless'.[93] Haas was one of a new breed of *Honoratioren*, active rather than aloof, egalitarian rather than élitist in tone. They attracted the interest and respect of the rural population by being a 'name' politician and a prominent member of society. At the same time, the element of populism in their political style and their activities in the press and on the podium gave rural voters the impression that they were in touch and cared about their interests. Where this active *Honoratiorenpolitik* succeeded, local communities looked forward to a visit as an impending honour and a treat.

There was no denying the skill of a man like Haas, one of the most able and engaging of left liberal politicians. He not only overcame the social and political handicap of his Jewish religion, but tackled a series of demanding tasks: unseating a SPD deputy against the trend in 1912; acting as a civil administrator in Warsaw in the second half of the war; and serving as Interior Minister in the first government in Baden after the November Revolution.[94] Active rural politics, however, tended to be harder on the body than the mind. Most people read about political events in the papers and absorbed slogans and images, but few had a detailed knowledge of political and parliamentary developments. When Rebmann complained, from a Karlsruhe perspective, that the new left liberal deputy for Lahr county, Hink, a retired livestock investigator, had proved a disappointment, he was contradicted by a National Liberal constituency activist. Whatever Hink's limitations as a parliamentarian, he possessed the three qualities looked for in a rural area: he had been well-respected in his job, congratulated the local mayors on their birthdays, and promised everyone a railway from and to wherever they wanted.

Rural politics did, however, require an adjustment in party policy. The lessons learnt from peasant politics in pre-war Baden were still evident when Hummel addressed a DDP conference in 1926. The party needed votes and the peasants could provide them. Some sympathy could be won on issues such as land settlement and protected

---

[93] *Neue Konstanzer Abendzeitung* (11 May 1909).

[94] J. Schrag-Haas, 'Ludwig Haas: Erinnerungen an meinem Vater', *Bulletin des Leo Baeck Instituts*, 4/13 (1961), 73–93; L. Luckemeyer, 'Ludwig Haas als Reichstagsabgeordneter', in G. Schulz (ed.), *Kritische Solidarität: Betrachtungen zum Deutsch-Jüdischen Selbstverständnis* (Bremen, 1971), 119–74.

tenures. But real advance depended on the party grasping the nettle of agricultural prices. The party had to avoid feeding the peasants lectures and statistics, too much *Schulmeisterkram*, and promise more direct rewards. 'In our campaigning we mustn't be too doctrinaire, but adapt ourselves to their own mentality; why not promise them a price of 180 Mark for rye, if we think that's possible.'[95] In fact a similar line had long been followed by left liberals in rural Baden. Heimburger, Hink, and Schulze-Gaevernitz all assured peasant constituents that they supported agricultural tariffs.[96] As Hummel implied, the key question here was peasant mentality. Government statistics from 1902 demonstrated that only 12 per cent of agricultural holdings in Baden produced a significant net surplus of grain. Nevertheless, the great majority of peasants wanted the psychological security of agrarian protection and the satisfaction of good prices for their crops. They were not as quick as the economist or statistician to see that they lost all the benefit of tariffs when they had to buy fodder during the winter and dearer agricultural implements. The left liberals went along with this tide, as well as stressing their peasant ancestry and their belief in 'peasant culture'.[97] Typical was the declaration in the second chamber by the left liberal Dr Vogel:

We have been a Bauernpartei *from the beginning, and will remain so in the future*. . . . the German peasant owes his freedom to the liberal idea, and the liberals will not cease to proceed further along the path which has led to peasant emancipation and, through our system of tariffs, has made the German peasant that which he must be: a *free* and *independent* man with his own land (*auf freiem Grund und Boden*).[98]

If the other *Mittelstand* groups were smaller than the peasantry, the left liberals were nevertheless well aware of their electoral importance. Urban *Mittelstand* representatives played an increasingly active part in left liberal politics. Two left liberal artisans, cutler Vogel from Mannheim and a Karlsruhe master painter Karl Lacroix, were particularly prominent, speaking on *Handwerker* themes throughout Baden. Nor was the left liberal party slow to recognize the importance of men

---

[95] Hummel, *Aufsätze*, 20.

[96] See the discussions in the FVP agricultural commission. BA Berlin, FVP 47, fos. 17–19; FVP 48, fos. 24–36. BA Berlin, Reichslandbund 185, fo. 77, personalia Karl Heimburger.

[97] *Breslauer Zeitung*, 213 (24 Mar. 1914), 'Fortschrittliche Bauernpolitik' by Schulze-Gaevernitz.

[98] Hummel, *Fraktion*, 10 and 24; *Neue Konstanzer Abendzeitung* (9 Apr. 1910).

'whose names had a good ring'[99] in artisan circles. Vogel was made chairman of the party in Mannheim and was elected in the city as a Landtag deputy and *Stadtrat*. Lacroix was a member of the FVP Landesauschuß and of the party committee and Bürger-Ausschuß in Karlsruhe. In addition left liberals made the usual noises about reforming the tender system, making the municipalities use local independent artisans where possible, and offering support in the increasingly sharp 'struggle for existence'.[100]

The structure of the economy in Baden meant that the new middle classes formed a significantly smaller proportion of the electorate than in other areas. Clerks, sales staff, and mid-ranking government employees made up only 5.4 per cent of the workforce in Southern Germany, compared to 7.5 per cent in the Reich as a whole.[101] And the Young Liberal orientation of the National Liberal party increased competition for their votes. Nevertheless, if the local left liberal *Verein* was not led by a teacher, businessman, or master craftsman, then it was often headed by a postal or railway official. Left liberals seized on cases of state employees being disciplined for their political activities. The Schäufle, Rödel, and Arnsperger 'affairs' were used to embarrass the National Liberals and project left liberals as the defenders of political freedom in general and the rights of state employees in particular.[102] The fact that the key to success in popular politics was, as the National Liberal leader Dr Obkircher stressed, 'work, work and more work'[103] was in itself an advantage for the left liberals. The National Liberal cause was suffering because left liberal leaders like Hummel were attending railway employees' meeting, while their National Liberal counterparts stayed away.[104] Moreover, as new issues and 'scandals' surfaced, the underlying effect was invariably beneficial to the left liberals because of the affinity of their stance and public opinion.

National Liberals were aware that most left liberal campaigning sought to gain votes and seats at their expense. That there was a considerable degree of conformity of policy between the two parties only

[99] SA Darmstadt, NL Hummel, Otto Ernst Sutter, report on the Democrat Vertrauensmänner meeting for the 26th Landtag Constituency, Triberg, 13 Aug. 1909.

[100] *Neue Konstanzer Abendzeitung* (9 Apr. 1910).

[101] *Badischer Landesbote* (25 June 1914).

[102] GLA Karlsruhe, NLP Baden 211, fos. 50–83.

[103] GLA Karlsruhe, NLP Baden 162, Landesversammlung 13 Nov. 1910.

[104] GLA Karlsruhe, NLP Baden 182, Chairman of the press committee of the Verein Mittlerer Eisenbahnbeamten to Rebmann, 30 Sept. 1911.

made competition for votes more intense. Activity created further friction. National Liberals tried to block left liberal attempts to establish new *Vereine*. At the same time, the left liberals kept demanding more and more National Liberal votes and seats as the price for an electoral pact. Just as the left liberals were vigorous popular agitators, so they were ambitious, tenacious, and sometimes unscrupulous political brokers in private. No one who had tried to deal with the left liberals, Rebmann remarked with feeling, was anxious to repeat the experience for the sake of it.[105] The National Liberals were undeniably the party with more support, but that meant they had more to lose from the failure to reach an agreement. Moreover, there was the possibility that the left liberals could agree a deal with the SPD directed against the National Liberals if the two liberal parties failed to come to an agreement. For the National Liberals, dealing directly with the SPD was hardly feasible, for it implied a loss of just as many seats and even more face. An alliance with the Centre would have been even more damaging, inevitably leading to a party split and a mass defection of voters. The result was a succession of electoral pacts with the left liberals where the National Liberals gave more than they gained. They did, however, have the satisfaction of achieving the overriding strategic aim, the prevention of a Centre majority, and of beating the left liberals down from their ambitious initial demands.[106] As the *Bindeglied* (binding link) of the Bloc, the left liberals not only realized their political ideal of a reformist alliance of workers and *Bürgertum*, but secured more seats than the number of their supporters warranted. The *Großblock* was a political alignment which offered material and spiritual satisfaction. Seats like Konstanz, Offenburg, and Lahr, which the Democrats had held from the early 1890s largely with 'borrowed' Centre votes, were retained after 1905 with National Liberal assistance. The Freiburg and Karlsruhe Reichstag seats were won in 1912 even though the FVP was at best the third or fourth strongest party in the constituency. A first-round pact with the National Liberals secured second place in the poll. Subsequent victory was attained by conflicting means: in Freiburg by SPD support against the Centre party, and in Karlsruhe by Centre backing against the SPD. German Liberals may have 'owed their existence . . . to a tangled and often contradictory set of alliances with other political

---

[105] GLA Karlsruhe, NLP Baden 169, Rebmann in *Fraktionssitzung*, 23 Feb. 1912.
[106] See National Liberal–left liberal negotiations in GLA Karlsruhe, NLP Baden 201.

parties'.[107] However, the experience of the left liberals in Baden indicated that such reliance was far from debilitating. Seats like Konstanz and Offenburg never produced large majorities, but that in turn created a determined and disciplined electorate. Nor was the price of repeated electoral victory a betrayal of principle. Far from being political trimmers, the deputies for Konstanz and Offenburg, Martin Venedey and Oskar Muser, were renowned for the vigour with which they propounded the Democratic gospel.

While the bulk of Centre voters followed instructions from above, which varied with the political situation, the unanimity of support given by National Liberals and Social Democrats to left liberal candidates represented something more than an inclination to obey orders. It was a clear case of second-preference voting and reflected the degree of harmony between the left liberals' political stance and popular attitudes. The left liberals' presence also reduced the difficulties of co-operation within the *Großblock*. The presence of genuinely democratic politicians within the left liberal *Fraktion* formed a bridge to the SPD, making it easier for SPD reformists to argue for co-operation with non-socialist parties. In 1912, for example, Muser put the blame for SPD rejection of the budget on the government. The left liberals also argued for state subsidies for workers' gymnastic clubs and united with the SPD against a continuation of the Munich legation. Left liberal participation made the *Großblock* easier to square with National Liberal ideology than a straight pact with the SPD. That was essentially a matter for political sophists, but the left liberals presented a more weighty practical consideration for the National Liberals. The fact that the left liberals had established themselves as an organized force increased the political penalties of departing from a leftist course. Only a comparatively small number of National Liberal supporters might be expected to enter the SPD camp, a considerable social as well as political step. But many National Liberal leaders were convinced that a move to the right would lead to an exodus of supporters to the left liberals.

This underlines the crucial importance of public opinion. Aside from electoral arithmetic—as in Bavaria the only hope of defeating the Centre was for Liberals and SPD to unite—it was popular priorities and attitudes which dictated the electoral stance of the parties. As Rebmann told the 1910 National Liberal state conference: 'Even if

---

[107] Sheehan, *German Liberalism*, 246.

we, if the party leader, the inner committee, the whole meeting gathered here, were to decide on alliance with the Centre, one only needs to put such a resolution before the electorate to discover its fate.'[108] How far attitudes in Baden differed to those found in North Germany was vividly demonstrated in the reaction to the 1912 Reichstag presidium elections. Whilst the willingness of members of the Reichstag caucus to vote for a Social Democrat produced an apoplectic reaction amongst North German National Liberals, the response of Rechtsanwalt Kautz, party leader in Kehl, was quite different. For National Liberal voters in Kehl, it was the failure of the party in the Reichstag to carry through the *Großblock* which caused offence:

in our district the mood also of our supporters is sharply to the left and the behaviour of the Fraktion over the Presidium elections has caused widespread disaffection. If our party does not want to create lots of new members for the FVP in this district, we must put the message across . . . that the liberal principles, which were stressed over and over in the election have a reality at least for the South German National Liberal Party.[109]

Left liberals were unable to make a dramatic breakthrough in terms of electoral support in pre-war Baden. But their agitational exertions were not in vain. The *Großblock* alliance and pressure of public opinion led to more domestic reform than elsewhere. And the underlying support for left liberal aims in Badenese society came to the surface in 1918, when the majority of National Liberals chose to unite with left liberals in forming the DDP.

[108] GLA Karlsruhe, NLP Baden 162, Rebmann to Landesversammlung, 1910.
[109] GLA Karlsruhe, NLP Baden 201, Kautz to Edmund Rebmann, 9 Mar. 1912.

8

Persuading the Protestant *Mittelstand*: Left Liberalism in Schleswig-Holstein

If Wilhelmine left liberalism was being ground inexorably between left and right then Schleswig-Holstein might be expected to exemplify the process of decay. The area's liberal political and economic traditions were threatened from left and right. Altona had been an SPD stronghold since the 1880s. Kiel, which for years had elected the liberal notable Albert Hänel to the Reichstag, from 1903 returned the equally archetypal figure of trade union leader Carl Legien with an unassailable majority. The SPD also attracted support in small towns and amongst rural labourers. In 1903, 44.3 per cent of electors voted SPD in Schleswig-Holstein, the highest percentage for any Prussian province apart from Berlin itself.[1] At the same time the actions of the state authorities towards the Danish minority in North Schleswig had, in the person of Oberpräsident Köller, become a byword for Prussian authoritarianism.[2] And groups like the German Association for North Schleswig demanded a yet more repressive policy towards the Danish minority.[3] Even the relative weakness of the Conservatives in Schleswig-Holstein was deceptive, for the province's National Liberal Party often proved the functional equivalent of a right-wing party. While the two parties agreed on an electoral pact in much of Germany, left liberals and National Liberals continued to oppose each other in the 1907 and 1912 Reichstag elections. The only National Liberal support for left liberal candidates, in the Kiel and Altona Reichstag seats, was little more than symbolic. In the Landtag elections for these cities, when seats could be won, the National Liberals put up rival

---

[1] Bertram, *Wahlen*, 206–7.
[2] K. D. Sievers, *Die Köllerpolitik und ihr Echo in der deutschen Presse 1897–1901* (Neumünster, 1964).
[3] See e.g. *Nordschleswig: Verhandlungen einer Versammlung in Hamburg, 4.3.1911* (Hamburg, 1911); *Bismarckwart* (1 Jan. 1914); and LB Kiel, Cp 31 Deutscher Verein für das Nördliche Schleswig: Protokollbuch 1913–19.

candidates. The Schleswig-Holstein National Liberal leader, Anton Schifferer, declared that national held absolute predominance over liberal.[4] And the Hamburg notable Dr Rudolf Mönckeberg was even blunter in reflecting National Liberal leadership views in the region: 'we are proud to be called reactionaries, for we represent the reaction against the actions of the Social Democrats'.[5]

Was the pre-war decade therefore a prelude to the dramatic rise of Nazi support in the province in the early 1930s, reaching 51 per cent in the July 1932 election, the highest percentage of the poll in all of Germany's electoral districts?[6] The rise of Nazism in Schleswig-Holstein has, understandably, been much explored.[7] Of these studies the most suggestive on pre-1918 Schleswig-Holstein are Rudolf Heberle's books, which were based on the author's personal knowledge of the rural economy and extensive interviewing in the 1920s. Yet, even with the benefit of immediacy, Heberle found it hard to penetrate the peasants' political outlook. He noted that only a few had a clear knowledge of political events: 'what remained all the time was a radical basic attitude (*Grundhaltung*), difficult to define and springing from an unchanging social position and constant temperament'.[8] Nevertheless Heberle's findings about Liberal attitudes in Schleswig-Holstein before 1918 have been challenged—'the strength of rural liberalism has been exaggerated and the affinity of this liberalism to National Socialism somewhat understated' (Tilton); 'the questionable strength of a questionable Liberalism' (Rietzler)—although without detailed research into province in the Wilhelmine period.

Did Schleswig-Holstein, then, represent the hard North German reality as opposed to the socially and economically more equable and traditionally liberal South German states like Baden? Certainly, National Liberal attitudes were one indication of significant

---

[4] Report of 1910 regional conference in *Hamburger Nachrichten* (15 Oct. 1910).

[5] *General-Anzeiger für Hamburg-Altona* (14 Nov. 1909).

[6] J. Noakes and G. Pridham (eds.), *Nazism 1919–1945: A Documentary Reader* (4 vols.; Exeter, 1984–98), i. 83.

[7] R. Heberle, *From Democracy to Nazism: A Regional Case Study on Political Parties in Germany* (Baton Rouge, La., 1945); idem, *Landbevölkerung und Nationalsozialismus: Eine soziologische Untersuchung der politischen Willensbildung in Schleswig-Holstein 1918 bis 1932* (Stuttgart, 1963); G. Stoltenburg, *Politische Strömungen im schleswig-holsteinischen Landvolk 1918–1933* (Düsseldorf, 1962); T. A. Tilton, *Nazism, Democracy, and the Peasantry: Nazi Success and Neo-Nazi Failure in Rural Schleswig-Holstein* (Bloomington, Ind., 1975); R. Rietzler, *'Kampf in der Nordmark': Das Aufkommen des Nationalsozialismus in Schleswig-Holstein (1919–1928)* (Neumünster, 1982).   [8] Heberle, *Landbevölkerung*, 11.

difference. Attempts to change the municipal franchise in a reactionary rather than progressive direction were another. Debate about the municipal franchise in Schleswig-Holstein was rather overshadowed on the national stage by protests about restrictive franchise changes in Hamburg.[9] But Conservatives and National Liberals also attempted to introduce an unequal municipal franchise in Schleswig-Holstein, creating an important and unresolved political issue in the province. Nevertheless, as this chapter seeks to demonstrate, the pattern of pre-war politics already analysed at national level can be applied equally to the harsher environment of North Germany. Though powerful challenges existed, the left liberals, rather than being crushed, gained from both left and right in the pre-war decade. Indeed, to the *Mandatsschacher* (hagglers after seats) in the Zimmerstraße, Schleswig-Holstein was the jewel in the left liberal crown. Seven left liberal deputies were returned from the ten constituencies in 1912, more than in any other Prussian province or non-Prussian state. This represented a gain of two seats over 1907, and the summit of electoral expectations, for Kiel and Altona were beyond reach and Hadersleben had an in-built Danish majority. It was success brought about by a rise in the left liberal popular vote and, even more, by securing 'second preference' votes in the run-off elections (Table 8.1). All seven seats were won after entering the run-offs in second place: four against the SPD, two against National Liberals, and one against a Conservative.

The overall picture for the left liberals was one of substantial electoral success. The left liberals gained more votes between 1903 and 1912 than all the other parties put together, and were the only political grouping to increase their share of the poll. The SPD still dominated the popular vote. Only the unreformed constituency boundaries and run-off system prevented the party from winning most seats. Nevertheless, the SPD was unable to match its 1903 percentage of votes in 1912.[10]

There were underlying reasons for a high level of left liberal support in Schleswig-Holstein. The population was overwhelmingly Protestant (more than 90 per cent in Kiel and Altona, and over 95

[9] R. J. Evans, '"Red Wednesday" in Hamburg: Social Democrats, Police and Lumpenproletariat in the Suffrage Disturbances of 17 January 1906', *Social History*, 4 (1979), 1–31.

[10] Bertram, *Wahlen*, 206–7; R. Paetau, *Konfrontation und Kooperation: Arbeiterbewegung und bürgerliche Gesellschaft im ländlichen Schleswig-Holstein und in der Industriestadt Kiel zwischen 1900 und 1925* (Neumünster, 1988).

Table 8.1. *Votes cast in Schleswig-Holstein in main round
of Reichstag Elections, 1903 and 1912*

Party	1903		1912	
	votes	(%)	votes	(%)
Conservative	—		17,154	(5.4)
Free Conservative	23,121	(9.3)	9,401	(3.0)
Anti-Semite	10,207	(4.1)	6,029	(1.9)
Centre	1,589	(0.6)	1,311	(0.4)
National Liberal	35,347	(14.3)	44,231	(14.0)
Left liberal	46,402	(18.7)	92,117	(29.2)
Social Democrat	109,810	(44.3)	127,375	(40.4)
Others	20,801	(8.4)	17,678	(5.6)
TOTAL VOTE	248,488		315,494	

Source: Bertram, *Wahlen*, 206–7.

per cent in most rural districts).[11] Economic and social structure was
generally favourable. There were many small and medium-sized
towns, the places where left liberals tended to do best. Of the fifty-six
places classed as towns by the Schleswig-Holstein *Städte-Ordnung*,
only a dozen had a population of over 10,000. Most had between
2,000 and 7,000 inhabitants.[12] Apart from 'Counts' Corner' in East
Holstein, there were comparatively few large estates and large numbers of small and medium-sized landholdings. Particularly striking
were the number of medium-sized landholdings. Over 60 per cent of
farms were between 20 and 100 hectares in Hadersleben, Apenrade,
Sonderburg, Flensburg (Land), Schleswig, Eiderstedt, Bordesholm,
Süderdithmarschen, Steinburg and Segeberg. By contrast, in 1895
estates over 100 hectares accounted for only 16 per cent of agricultural
land in Schleswig-Holstein compared to c. 40 per cent in East Elbia.[13]
Schleswig-Holstein was in the middle of an arc from Oldenburg and
Ostfriesland to Mecklenburg and coastal Pomerania, containing the
largest area of left liberal peasant support in Wilhelmine Germany.
Towns along the North German coast had also shown a high level of
left liberal support after National Liberal backing for Bismarckian
protectionism in 1879/80. Finally, the right-wing orientation of the
Schleswig-Holstein National Liberal party may have frustrated left

---

[11] Nöcker, *Der Preußische Reichstagswähler*, 351–63.
[12] *Altonaer Tageblatt* (20 Jan. 1914).
[13] H. Zimmermann, *Wählerverhalten und Sozialstruktur im Kreis Herzogtum Lauenburg
1918–1933: Ein Kreis zwischen Obrigkeitsstaat und Demokratie* (Neumünster, 1978), 27.

liberal attempts to form alliances for national and state elections. But it also meant that, unlike in Baden, Schleswig-Holstein left liberals did not face a convincing National Liberal challenge for the support of reform-minded voters. Such conditions were not sufficiently distinct, however, to explain left liberal support by themselves. The social and economic structure in most of Schleswig-Holstein may have contrasted with parts of East Elbia, but was little different from its southern neighbour Hanover and other western provinces.[14] Hesse was equally a region of small or medium-sized towns and peasant landholding. It also had a right-leaning National Liberal party.[15] Yet neither were left liberal strongholds. It was the National Liberals, not the left liberals, who were the party of small dairy and livestock farmers in Hanover, the Palatinate, Hesse, and Baden.[16] While political tradition was an important part of the underlying appeal of Schleswig-Holstein left liberalism, it does not provide specific reasons for the rise in support during the pre-war decade. For these we require a closer investigation of the workings of politics. The focus will fall first on the left liberals' political activity: on formal and informal party organization, and then on the political issues raised in Schleswig-Holstein. In particular, there is an assessment of the links with two groups crucial to left liberal political prospects: the peasantry and petty bourgeoisie.

There has been a tendency to ascribe left liberal success in Schleswig-Holstein to organizational unity. Hänel, the symbol of left liberal continuity in Schleswig-Holstein, represented harmony and conciliation; Richter, by contrast, rancour and division. The 'Deutsch-freisinnige Partei für Schleswig-Holstein' remained intact while left liberals divided nationally. However, the suggestion that left liberals in Schleswig-Holstein succeeded in preserving unity in 1893 where other regions failed has little foundation.[17] The *Verein* lists of the Deutsch-freisinnige Partei in 1892 and the FrVp in 1894/5 revealed a clear split in the existing Schleswig-Holstein organization.[18] At the turn of the century the National-Socials threatened to divide Schleswig-Holstein left liberalism still further. The province

---

[14] O'Donnell, 'National Liberalism', 70.   [15] White, *Splintered Party*, passim.
[16] O'Donnell, 'National Liberalism', 64 ff.
[17] See e.g. Ludwig Elm, 'Freisinnige Vereinigung 1893–1910', in Fricke (ed.), *Lexikon*, ii. 683.
[18] *Vereinskalender der Deutschen freisinnigen Partei zum Handgebrauch für das Jahr 1892*, 24–5; *Vereinskalender der Freisinnigen Volkspartei für das Jahr 1894/5*, 13: 44–6.

was one of the few areas where they were able to mount a significant challenge. Adolf Pohlmann, a Dithmarschen landowner and proprietor of the *Nordischer Kurier* in Itzehoe, provided financial and press support. Adolf Damaschke and Hellmut von Gerlach launched a vigorous, if unavailing, electoral crusade in agrarian East Holstein.[19] In 1907 Schleswig-Holstein left liberal deputies still belonged to different parties: Johannes Leonhart, Ernst Carstens, and Wilhelm Spethmann sat for the FrVp, Wilhelm Struve for the FrVg, and Siegfried Heckscher, returned as a unattached Liberal, joined the FrVg as an associate (*Hospitant*).

Differences in party label were, however, increasingly academic. Leonhart and Struve, for example, were members of the same left liberal local party, the Liberal Association (*Liberaler Verein*) in Kiel. They were also personal friends, members of the same profession (both were doctors), and were similar in political outlook.[20] Schleswig-Holstein left liberals reached an agreement for the next Reichstag campaign in 1905,[21] well in advance of the national agreement at the outset of the 1907 election campaign, and FrVp leaders in Berlin had a constant task in persuading its supporters in Schleswig-Holstein against mergers and joint meetings.[22] Practical co-operation between the left liberal parties in the region had already reached such a stage that the establishment of the FVP in 1910 was seen more as an overdue act of catching up in Berlin than a fundamental political realignment in the province.[23] But this pattern, as Chapter 2 emphasized, was not unusual. True, Schleswig-Holstein left liberalism had a particularly prestigious figurehead in Hänel. The left liberal leaders in the province were also realists, temperamentally suited to compromise. There were no episodes like those which delayed merger in neighbouring Lübeck because FrVg and FrVg local leaders were not prepared to accept a chairman from the other party.[24] But again, a harmonious merger in 1910 was the left liberal experience in most regions. Left liberal formal organization in Schleswig-Holstein was not just considerably inferior to that of the SPD. It was also, relatively, much smaller than the FVP organization in Baden.[25] A third

---

[19] See Gerlach, *Von Rechts nach Links*, and Wenck 'Wandlungen'.

[20] Cf. the correspondence of both men with Georg Gothein, BA Koblenz, NL Gothein 25 and 31.   [21] *Kieler Zeitung* (3 May. 1905).

[22] For Berlin resistance to Schleswig-Holstein and other regional pressure for fusion see Ch 2 above.   [23] *Nordischer Kurier* (19 Apr. 1910).

[24] *Lübeckische Anzeigen* (24 Mar. 1910, morning edn.).   [25] See Table 7.1 above.

Table 8.2. *SPD and FVP organization in Schleswig-Holstein (1912)*

	Vereine	Members	% of voters per constituency
SPD	—	40,932	from 12.8% to 52.6%
FVP	72	10,600	from 5% to 13%

Source: *Elbwart* (1912), 234–5; *Kieler Zeitung* (19 Nov. 1912).

of FVP supporters were party members in Baden, while only one in ten was organized in Schleswig-Holstein, a figure similar to the national average. Schleswig-Holstein left liberal party organization was not exceptional. Indeed, the striking thing about Schleswig-Holstein party organization generally is how characteristic it was of national patterns.

The province exemplified the link between formal party organization and social and economic structure. The FVP and SPD both possessed the greatest degree of organization in the 6th Schleswig-Holstein constituency.[26] Hamburg's proximity increased politicization. So did the prevalence of modest to medium-sized towns like Pinneberg (population 7,000) and Elmshorn (population 15,000). Political life in these middling sized Protestant towns, as Theodor Heuss correctly pointed out, was often at its liveliest. Frequently part of marginal seats, they had a particularly high turn-out at Reichstag elections. Elmshorn-Pinneberg saw intensive campaigning in 1912. The right held some fifty meetings, the National Liberals eighty-seven, the FVP about 130, and the SPD around 150. The resulting turn-out exceeded 90 per cent.[27] In such towns local society was sufficiently large and varied for associational life to flourish, and the local economy often produced a social equilibrium, allowing both bourgeois groups and the labour movement to exist with vigour, but neither to dominate. At the same time, the size of the town and its cultural and economic institutions were not large enough to dissipate a strong sense of local identity.

Large cities, Hamburg, Altona, and Kiel, had almost as high a degree of organization, and by far the largest membership in absolute terms. The SPD, as elsewhere, led the way in mass organization in the city. It had about as many male members in Kiel as the whole of the left liberal membership in Schleswig-Holstein and some 60,000 mem-

---

[26] *Jahresbericht des Zentralvorstandes der Sozialdemokratischen Zentralvereins für den 6. Schleswig-Holsteinischen Reichstagswahlkreis von 1.7.09–30.6.10* (Ottensen, 1910); *Elmshorner Zeitung* (9 Mar. 1914).   [27] *Elbwart* (1912), 23–4.

bers and 138,000 votes in Hamburg in 1912.[28] As befitted the demands made upon it, party organization in the city developed a greater sophistication. The thirty-four left liberal associations based in Hamburg in 1912, for example, included the regional association, a district association, an umbrella organization for the city, local and suburban associations, a youth association, and a women's group. This list does not include the citizens' associations (*Bürgervereine*) affiliated to the United Liberals (the name used by the left liberals in Hamburg). Curt Platen estimated the number of people who were members of a United Liberal affiliated organization in 1913 to be 7,600, and that *c.* 10,000 other groups recognized the United Liberal programme as a basis.[29]

By contrast, formal party organization in the countryside remained sparse. Whether this was such a deplorable or significant state of affairs as Naumann and subsequent historians have contended must be questioned. In the village, where everyone knew each other, a *Vertrauensmann* could still fulfil the requirements party and local community placed on each other. For much of the year peasants did not have the leisure time to devote to politics. Nor, unlike school teachers, lawyers, and office workers, were their job skills easily applicable to party political activity. There was no town council to elect and badger, no traffic problems to complain about or building schemes to oppose. In short, although the vicissitudes of *Bauernpolitik* (peasant politics) were hard to match, this sphere of politics was characterized by promises in meetings and leaflets that something would or must be done in Berlin rather than by local action and organization. Certainly rural voters wanted election candidates to appear before them in person and many, but by no means all, found time during the long winter nights to read newspapers with interest. What, however, was the attraction of founding a political *Verein* with its membership dues and paperwork? And what was the point? If a peasant wanted to know his neighbours' opinions he could ask him in the field or the village meeting place.

The changes in party organization in Schleswig-Holstein during the pre-war decade also mirrored national patterns. An increase in the number and size of political organizations in urban areas was typical,

---

[28] LA Schleswig 301, Oberpräsidium 2252; *Jahresbericht des Statistischen Amtes und Bureaus der Zentralwahlkommission für das Jahr 1912*, 82.
[29] BA Berlin FVP, 20, fo. 21; *General-Anzeiger für Hamburg-Altona* (31 Mar. 1913).

as was the attempt to establish *Vereine* in small towns and a few large villages. This course was followed by the left liberals, National Liberals, and, to a degree, the Conservatives. The employment of full-time party secretaries was another familiar feature. The Liberaler Verein in Hamburg was the first to emulate the SPD. It appointed a full-time official in 1904. By 1909 the left liberals and National Liberals each had two party secretaries, one based in Hamburg and another in Schleswig-Holstein. The history of National Liberal general secretaries in the region underlined the party's right-wing orientation. In Hamburg the pro-Bassermann Young Liberal Paul Zimmermann lasted less than a year and was replaced by Lui Köster, a more flexible official, who condemned picketing and defended the army's conduct in Zabern. The Hamburg party line corresponded to that of the party in Prussian Landtag rather than the Reichstag. Likewise, in Schleswig-Holstein, the talented but left-leaning Johannes Rathje was replaced by Wenken, who, like Köster, conformed more to the principle 'wessen Brot ich esse, dessen Lied ich singe' (he who pays the piper calls the tune). The Conservatives were the final party in the province to see the necessity of a paid party secretary, employing Ludwig Schaper in 1912.[30]

The region also provides an excellent example of the increased politicization along party lines, and the assault of parties on uncharted, traditionally hostile areas, which characterized the pre-war period. The Conservatives had previously concentrated on Landtag elections and the large estates of East Holstein. However, the establishment of a joint Conservative and Free Conservative regional association in summer 1911 heralded efforts to establish Conservative organizations throughout the province. From a starting-point of seven associations with 175 members the association claimed forty-five associations and 4,300 members two years later in 1913.[31] The expansion of National Liberal organization followed a similar pattern. The number of associations rose from seven in 1906 to sixty-five in 1914. By then *c.* 4,500, a tenth of National Liberal voters in Schleswig-Holstein, were also party members. And the party which had not held

---

[30] Schaper was not, as K. Saul, *Staat, Industrie, Arbeiterbewegung*, 466, and Eley, *Reshaping*, 112, state, editor of a Free Conservative weekly in Kiel, but general secretary of the Schleswig-Holstein Provincial Association of the Conservatives and Free Conservatives and, as such, the editor of the Association's fortnightly journal *Nord West*.

[31] Annual report for 1912, *Nord West* (1913), 92.

any regional conferences before the late 1890s now assembled every two years.[32]

In this more intense party-political climate there was little place for associations which claimed to bring together all bourgeois or national elements. 'National electoral associations' containing Conservatives, Free Conservatives, and National Liberals, set up in parts of Holstein, were increasingly seen as outmoded. Even under favourable circumstances skilful orchestration was required to maintain bourgeois unity. In the aftermath of the 1909 finance reform, only virtual inactivity could prevent such organizations from falling apart. Both Conservatives and National Liberals competed to replace them with more effective party organizations. Similarly, the Imperial League Against Social Democracy proved worse than useless, according to the vexed *Landrat* in Pinneberg. Its initial attempts to win over Social Democrats by speaking in their meetings had soon been abandoned in favour of speaking to the converted in bourgeois meetings. Worse still, the League indirectly helped the left liberals against the National Liberals and Conservatives by stressing the threat of SPD victory in the constituency.[33]

Resistance to party politics was strongest in the Hadersleben constituency where, a Social Democratic minority apart, politics was considered a question of Germans versus Danes. Yet even here the left liberals were able to found an association in 1913.[34] All parties strove to emulate the SPD by raising membership, employing paid officials, and instituting a regular programme of political activity. The National Liberals were typical. They claimed to have increased membership by 50 per cent between the end of 1912 and May 1914, and during 1913 the party had established eighteen new *Vereine* and held almost 200 public meetings.[35] Social events—family evenings, summer excursions and festivals, visits to the new school or town hall—increasingly became features of the more energetic of local political organizations. One left liberal deputy even attempted to win the hearts of the voters through the stomachs of their wives, inviting the women of Morsum

---

[32] Figures taken from Wenken, 'Von früheren Parteitagen', in *Mitteilungen Deutsche Volkspartei Schleswig-Holstein*, 2/17 (25 Sept. 1920).

[33] *Nord West* (1913), 159–60; LA Schleswig 309, Regierungspräsidium 8530, *Landrat* Kreis Pinneberg to Regierungspräsident Schleswig, 2 Mar. 1907.

[34] LA Schleswig 301, Oberpräsidium 59, fo. 158, *Schleswiger Grenzpost*, 46 (24 Feb. 1913).   [35] *Bismarckwart* (1914), 130.

on Sylt to afternoon coffee and cakes, behaviour which, predictably, was all too much for the chauvinists of the *Hamburger Nachrichten*.[36]

Left liberal formal organization was, therefore, fairly typical. Though somewhat more dynamic than National Liberal and Conservative organizations, it nevertheless lacked the scale and efficiency of the SPD's political apparatus. Left liberals themselves were concerned about palpable gaps: the *Kieler Zeitung* referred in 1912 to 'a very disturbing lack of organization which showed itself so often during the campaign'.[37] Though the comment partly reflected how far the organization ethic had permeated the left liberal leadership, it also mirrored real shortcomings. As elsewhere, Schleswig-Holstein left liberals had to compensate by relying on informal structures.

The press, as usual, provided vital support. The party benefited, especially in the south of the province, from the strength of the Hamburg left liberal press. As the local National Liberals recognized, the influence of the left liberal Hamburg press was vital to FVP success even in rural districts: 'octopus-like, the progressive Hamburg press stretches out its tentacles into the province'.[38] Left liberal press strength was also evident outside the Elbe metropolis. While the Conservatives only had three small papers in the province,[39] many of the more substantial towns had a left liberal daily. Some, like the *Kieler Zeitung* and the *Nordischer Kurier* (published in Itzehoe), had a substantial readership beyond the immediate district. Where readers could choose between a left liberal and a radical nationalist paper, between the Hamburg left liberal dailies and the *Hamburger Nachrichten*, or the *Nordischer Kurier* and *Itzehoer Nachrichten*, a sizeable majority preferred the left liberal press. The tie between press and party was also becoming increasingly explicit. Representatives of the left liberal press were included on the committee of the Association of United Liberals in Hamburg as of right, and papers like the *Elmshorner Zeitung* openly carried the subtitle 'Organ of the FVP'. In addition, left liberal journalists were active party agitators. Curt Platen, editor of the *General-Anzeiger für Hamburg-Altona*, was the FVP campaign manager in Elmshorn-Pinneberg.[40] At a lower level, journalists were often dispatched to put the left liberal case at opponents' meetings. The fact that the right often preferred to risk low

---

[36] BA Berlin, Reichslandbund 39, fo. 6, personalia Andreas Blunck.
[37] *Kieler Zeitung* (14 Jan. 1912, evening edn.).   [38] *Elbwart* (1912), 53.
[39] *Nord West* (1913), 240.
[40] See the campaign records in SA Hamburg, NL Carl Braband B30/2.

attendance through short notice rather than allow time for a left liberal speaker to arrive from the nearest town was tribute to their effectiveness. In Lütjenburg in East Hostein, for example, the Conservatives tried to hold a meeting at short notice in January 1912. But locals managed to inform Kiel early enough for a journalist to arrive and defeat the right-wing speakers in verbal battle.[41] However, left liberal press superiority and journalist agitation was, again, no Schleswig-Holstein peculiarity. Indeed, the left liberal press was weaker than usual in parts of Schleswig. Here it was hampered by a relatively sparse German population, and particularly strong state support for the right-wing press, either directly from the 'reptile fund' (the Schleswig Oberpräsident's annual discretionary fund 'for the promotion of Germandom' was 40,000 marks from 1900; small beer compared to the money, 1,000,000 marks in 1902, given to combat the Poles in the east, but still a significant sum for a small area like North Schleswig), as with the *Apenrader Tageblatt* and the *Schleswiger Grenzpost*, or indirectly through official printing contracts.[42]

Left liberal electoral success was, however, still possible where both formal organization and press support was lacking. The Eckernförde-Schleswig constituency was won despite poor organization and the enmity of every newspaper in the constituency.[43] Crucial to the effectiveness of left liberal campaigning was the candidate. FVP success in Eckernförde-Schleswig was mainly due to David Felix Waldstein, a Jewish lawyer from Altona.[44] Victory was a tribute both to Waldstein's rhetorical skills and the automobile which carried him from meeting to meeting in the towns and villages of the area. Schleswig-Holstein provided the prime example of a more general trend: the rise of the outside, professional politician. Of the seven left liberal deputies returned in Schleswig-Holstein in 1912, six—Waldstein, Carl Braband, Heckscher, Andreas Blunck, all lawyers, Struve and the teacher Ferdinand Hoff—devoted most of their time to politics. The seventh, Hermann Leube, remained essentially a businessmen. As a result, he played a lesser political role both in Berlin and in the province. All

---

[41] *Kieler Zeitung* (20 Jan. 1912). For further examples of Conservative anxiety about facing left liberals in public debate see Ch. 9 below.

[42] See LA Schleswig 301, Oberpräsidium 2316, press subsidies; and GStA Berlin-Dahlem 90a, DI 2. 8, vol. 1.

[43] *Kieler Zeitung* (11 Jan. 1912). As a partial compensation left liberals sent voters free copies of the *Kieler Zeitung* during the last week of campaigning. *Kieler Zeitung* (9 Jan. 1912).   [44] *Kieler Zeitung* (6 Jan. 1912, evening edn.; 16 Jan. 1912, morning edn.).

seven lived in cities rather than the semi-rural constituencies where they were returned. Braband, Heckscher, and Blunck came from Hamburg, Hoff and Struve from Kiel, and Waldstein and Leube from Altona. The success of such candidatures was crucial to left liberalism. It ensured continued parliamentary careers for left liberal politicians driven out of urban constituencies by the SPD. Schleswig-Holstein also reinforced the point that unreformed constituency boundaries meant there were frequently more seats at stake in such districts than in cities and large towns. Hamburg, Kiel, and Altona represented just five Reichstag seats, compared to eight in semi-rural Schleswig-Holstein. Similarly, only two out of nineteen Schleswig-Holstein Landtag deputies were returned in Kiel and Altona. Therefore, a vital task for left liberalism in the region was to apply the resources of Hamburg left liberalism, money and manpower, to the favourable small-town, semi-rural political terrain in Schleswig-Holstein. The choice of Hamburg rather than Kiel as headquarters of the FVP regional association for Schleswig-Holstein, Hamburg, and Lübeck underlined the importance of the city to left liberalism in the region. Hamburg money also financed a Schleswig-Holstein party secretary. Von Ratenkranz may have been employed by the FrVp's Hamburg branch, but he was based in Husum-Tondern.

The main transfer of resources, however, took place informally. Better roads and the development of reasonably reliable covered-top motor cars allowed candidates to address the almost insatiable desire of villagers for local meetings. The canvassers and ballot-paper distributors, the poor bloody infantry of election campaigns, still had to slog along on foot. The horrors of a 1905 by-election campaign in Oldenburg-Plön amidst bad winter conditions were vividly reported by party secretary Heinrich Haupt: rain, snow, storms, darkness, vast bogs, and the water which flowed over the top even of shoemaker Ohle's best boots. It was a thankless task and in East Holstein in 1905 a fruitless one, for the left liberal helpers could only look on as 'the carts roaring with servants, and behind them the grand coaches with the masters', rolled up to the polling stations. Intimidation and blind obedience could not, however, hold the seat for Conservatives against the left liberals in 1907 and 1912.[45] Such discomforts did not have to

---

[45] H. Haupt, 'Aus dem Wahlkampfe um Plön-Oldenburg 9.12.1905', SA Wolfenbüttel, NL Schrader III. 2.

be faced by Hamburg lawyers like Waldstein, Braband, and Heckscher, who were able to drive out of the city to hold evening meetings in the rural constituencies.[46] The growth of prosperity, partnerships, and specialization in professional life allowed more scope for a political career. Behind many left liberal lawyers and political activists, like Carl Braband, there was a selfless partner willing to bear an extra burden of routine legal work and to deputize when political and professional commitments clashed.[47] Specialist doctors like Wilhelm Struve were better placed to open and close their practices in tune with Reichstag sessions than general practitioners.[48] Although allegations that left liberal-influenced city administrations appointed teachers on political grounds were exaggerated, they did grant leave to employees elected to public office, a significant act, for even council seats required a sympathetic employer. Whilst Julius Kopsch, nominally the head of a Berlin elementary school, was able to play the role of a full-time national politician, in Kiel engineer Gramm and telegraph official Schwartz, for example, had to turn down left liberal municipal candidatures because of the refusal of the Germania shipyards and postal authorities to allow time off work.[49] Newspapers with rising circulations and an expanding staff offered more scope for proprietor or editor to devote time to the town hall or hustings. Solicitors' offices, newspaper offices, and administrative departments of firms could be used to conduct political business on the side: to deal with a deputy's extensive correspondence, or copy the electoral roll. Experience gathered in running a school, a company's administration, or a local government department could be used outside the workplace to run a party.

This was a promising scenario for the left liberals. Some of the party's most able advocates were in a position to make a more telling political contribution. They had more resources, more time, and informal political machinery, and improved communications allowed them to invest those resources in politically favourable terrain. In Elmshorn-Pinneberg, for instance, it was a blow to left liberal hopes

---

[46] BA Berlin, Reichslandbund 47, fo. 5, personalia Carl Braband, *Leipziger Volkszeitung* (11 Jan. 1912).

[47] See the tribute to Braband's colleague in J. Nicolassen, C. Petersen, and F. Naumann, *Zur Erinnerung an Dr Carl Braband: Reden gehalten bei der Trauerfeier am 23.11.1914* (Hamburg, 1914), 20.

[48] See Struve's announcement that he was resuming his practice for skin and urinary disorders after the Reichstag's adjournment. *Kieler Neueste Nachrichten* (26 May 1907).

[49] *Kieler Neueste Nachrichten* (16 Nov. 1907 and 5 Dec. 1907).

when Ernst Carstens refused to stand for re-election in 1912. He had
the conventional assets of being the sitting member, a well-known
Elmshorn manufacturer, and a leader in local party politics, municipal
government, and associational life. However, his replacement Carl
Braband, though based in Hamburg, was able to mount an even more
extensive and effective campaign.[50] Of course there was still some
political mileage to be made out of social affinity with the local community. Struve, for example, emphasized his upbringing amongst
Schleswig-Holstein peasants.[51] Nevertheless, Heberle's argument that
left liberal reliance on outside candidates represented a serious weakness is misplaced. There was, first, no one within rural society to do
the job. Local administrators (*Amtsvorsteher*) and large landowners
were overwhelmingly National Liberals or Conservatives; internal
election reports clearly show the right-wing inclinations of the
province's *Landräte* and *Amtsvorsteher*, and the Conservative journal
Nord West claimed, in September 1913, that it was taken by almost all
local estate owners.[52] In any case, the left liberals portrayed themselves
as the upholders of the cause of independent small farmers and peasants against the depredations of unjust local administration and large
landowners. Clearly it would be politically problematic to choose a
candidate out of that same rural hierarchy. As for smaller landowners,
some had indeed represented Schleswig-Holstein constituencies for
the left liberals before the turn of the century. Their disappearance
from the Reichstag did not represent an estrangement between the left
liberals and the Schleswig-Holstein countryside, but rather the modernization of politics. It was no longer enough, as the Holstein peasant leader Thomsen had done, to make the occasional, incoherent
Reichstag speech.[53] As in Britain, a few agrarian backwoodsmen
remained as relics on the Conservative benches, but men like Oertel,
Hahn, and Heim, whose gifts for political populism were as apparent
as their affinity with the soil was dubious, were more representative of
rural politics in Wilhelmine Germany. Although their demagoguery
was slightly more restrained and they lacked the backing of powerful

---

[50] See the records of Braband's campaign in 1912 and Curt Platen's adept press management in SA Hamburg NL Carl Braband B30/2. Cf. H.-D. Loose, 'Der Wahlkampf des liberalen Reichstagskandidanten Carl Braband 1911/12' in F. Kahlenberg (ed.), *Aus der Arbeit
der Archive: Beiträge zum Archivwesen, zur Quellenkunde und zur Geschichte* (Boppard, 1989),
727–45.   [51] *Kieler Zeitung* (11 Jan. 1912).
[52] LA Schleswig 301, Oberpräsidium 809 and 811; cf. Heberle, *Democracy*.
[53] After he had spoken, Thomsen's left liberal friends had to go down to the clerks' office
to render the stenographic report intelligible. BA Koblenz, NL Gothein 14, fo. 170.

peasant leagues, the mode of politics employed by left liberals in Schleswig-Holstein, Mecklenburg, Oldenburg, Württemberg, and Lower Silesia was essentially the same.

Nor, in view of the increasing demands faced by deputies, was it surprising that businessmen like Carstens or Spethmann, an Eckernförde publisher, preferred to step aside. As Carstens reminded his successor, constituents expected prompt replies, whether to requests for tickets to the Reichstag public gallery or more urgent demands.[54] Increasingly, only the professional or (given the modest level of Reichstag attendance allowances) semi-professional politician was equal to the demands placed on Reichstag deputies. Opponents' attempts to stir up resentment against these 'outside' politicians had little success. In part such attacks lacked credibility because all parties put forward semi-professional politicians from outside the local community. The typical SPD candidate in Schleswig-Holstein was a trade union or party official from Hamburg.[55] In Plön-Oldenburg, the only Reichstag constituency they could hope to win, the Conservatives put up a Kiel *Justizrat* in 1905 and 1907 and the Brandenburg-based Agrarian League leader Gustav Roesicke in 1912. Constituents themselves saw the advantages of such candidates. Just as workers were happy to return journalists and officials, so peasants were willing to vote in lawyers and doctors. Increasingly voters did not insist on returning one of their own, men who looked and spoke like them. What they wanted were able advocates, not men no more articulate and knowledgeable than themselves.

The absence of formal organization in the countryside and reliance on outside candidates were not grave weaknesses. They were largely a natural reflection of local conditions, and typical of rural districts generally. The workings of rural politics in Wilhelmine Schleswig-Holstein cast doubt on the emphasis placed by Heberle and later historians on the absence of party organization and indigenous candidates before 1918 as an explanation for subsequent NSDAP success in the province. The explanation is further undermined by the fact that the NSDAP itself relied, like earlier parties, on demonstrative political campaigning supported by outside men and money, and on the economic position and general outlook of the local

[54] SA Hamburg NL Carl Braband B2, Ernst Carstens to Braband 31 Dec. 1912.
[55] W. H. Schröder, *Sozialdemokratische Reichstagsabgeordnete und Reichstagskandidaten 1898–1918: Biographisch-statistisches Handbuch* (Düsseldorf, 1986).

population.[56] Left liberal campaigning style was broadly acceptable. Although left liberal agitation relied as much on individuals as formal machinery, and often involved last-minute improvisation, it at least performed the basics of holding local meetings and distributing ballot papers.

The left liberals also benefited from a superior platform skills. Left liberal candidates were all competent speakers. The contribution Waldstein's public speaking ability made to victory in Schleswig-Eckernförde has already been noted. Even officials hostile to the left liberals were forced to admit that the adept public meetings of Johannes Leonhart and Ernst Carstens created a rapport with constituents in Tondern and Pinneberg, the Pinneberg *Landrat* contrasting the inability of the Free Conservative Landtag deputy Graf Moltke to communicate with voters to 'the very advantageous way Reichstag deputy Carstens has presented himself throughout the district'.[57] Left liberal candidates sought out SPD opponents, confident in their ability to defeat them in verbal battle. However, the disparity in public-speaking skills was greatest between the left liberals and right-wing opponents. Of the right-wing candidates in 1912, left liberals regarded the National Liberals Schifferer and Görck as reasonable speakers, and only Roesicke as a good orator. The others were dismissed as incapable of appearing without covering fire.[58]

The value of a good candidate, particularly to the left liberals, should not be discounted. There were always votes to be won on the margins between the SPD and left liberals and between left liberals and National Liberals. Left liberal election meetings were genuine public meetings open to all. They often contained SPD and right-wing sympathizers.[59] By contrast, National Liberals and Conservatives confined their meetings to 'national' or *bürgerlich* voters, and many bourgeois voters considered it improper to attend SPD rallies. The ability of men like Braband, Waldstein, and Hoff to out-debate SPD and right-wing opponents on such occasions attracted votes from the audience and, more importantly, readers of press reports.

---

[56] See the literature in n. 7 above.

[57] LA Schleswig 301, Oberpräsidium 808[4] (of pg 30, fn 86 if necessary), reports on 1912 campaign in Husum-Tondern; LA Schleswig, 309 Regierungspräsidium 8530, *Landrat*, Kreis Pinneberg to Regierungspräsident, Schleswig, 2 Mar. 1907.

[58] BA Berlin, FVP 27, fo. 69, report on Schleswig-Holstein political activity in Feb. 1911 by party secretary von Rautenkranz.

[59] See the election reports in SA Hamburg, NL Carl Braband B30/2.

For most voters, however, election meetings were demonstrative occasions where political loyalty was confirmed rather than created. And while Schleswig-Holstein exemplified the importance of the new breed of active *Honoratioren*, the region's left liberal politicians were no more skilful and dedicated than Badenese counterparts like Haas, Heimberger, and Hummel. To examine the particular reasons for left liberal appeal in Schleswig-Holstein we need to turn from organization and agitation to political issues.

Left liberals in Schleswig-Holstein depended on rural as well as urban voters. As voting in Lauenburg exemplified, the urban middle strata and peasantry provided vital electoral support (see Table 8.3). Before analysing urban political issues, we should address the question of why the left liberals were able to attract much more rural support than elsewhere. It has been suggested that Schleswig-Holstein small farmers and peasants voted left liberal out of economic self-interest. As livestock farmers they had to pay more for fodder as well as farm implements because of the tariffs.[60] Such an explanation seems too simplistic and at odds with the political situation in the province. If economic motives were paramount, then it might be expected that the large-scale farmers who fattened up cattle on the marsh lands would be enthusiastic left liberals, rather than National Liberals or

Table 8.3. *Party support in the Lauenburg constituency: Reichstag elections 1903–12 (%)*

	Towns			Rural parishes with no estates			Rural parishes with estates		
	1903	1907	1912	1903	1907	1912	1903	1907	1912
Right*	17.9	5.7	8.1	30.7	36.2	37.6	44.5	48.6	50.6
Liberal†	37.3	50.5	49.5	31.4	31.9	33.5	16.9	21.6	16.2
SPD	44.8	43.3	42.5	37.9	31.9	29.3	38.6	29.8	31.2

Source: Zimmermann, *Wählerverhalten*, 103–4.
* Includes votes cast for Conservative in 1903, anti-Semite (German-social) in 1907, Conservative and anti-Semite in 1912.
† Left liberal in 1903, left liberal standing as 'unattached' liberal in 1907, and FVP and National Liberal in 1912. (The National Liberal candidate in 1912 accounted for 7% of urban and 4% of rural votes.)

[60] Hans Beyer, 'Landbevölkerung und Nationalsozialismus in Schleswig-Holstein', *Zeitschrift für Agrargeschichte und Agrarsoziologie*, 12 (1964), 71, cited in Tilton, 'Nazism', 153 n. 9; cf. Stoltenburg, *Landvolk*, 8.

Conservatives. Moreover, if this was the reason for left liberal allegiance then the conduct of left liberal candidates in 1907 and 1912 is inexplicable. Most preferred to play down the demand in the party programme for a reduction in corn duties. Carl Braband's speech in Bellingen was typical: '[Braband] emphasized that he was definitely not a free-trader, but recognized every justifiable tariff.'[61] Andreas Blunck in Tondern-Husum in 1912 declared himself a convinced supporter of existing grain tariffs, a conversion undoubtedly prompted by the views of rural voters in the constituency.[62] As in Baden, most peasants evidently supported tariffs even if they were net buyers of grain.[63] A self-interested belief in free trade was not the basis for left liberalism in the countryside.

Support for agricultural tariffs did not signify, however, general opposition to the modern industrial world amongst rural producers in Schleswig-Holstein. On the contrary, discussions in the province's associations of cattle-breeders and fatteners centred on market opportunities and new techniques. Besides the latest livestock prices throughout Germany, the Schleswig-Holstein farming monthly *Die Weidewirtschaft* was filled with matters like railway freight rates and loading facilities, a new market for unfinished cattle, breeding improvements, and the effect of the centrifuge on dairy production.[64] Far from being suspicious or ignorant about markets, Schleswig-Holstein producers urged deputies to oppose measures to restrict the freedom to buy and sell.[65] Peasants who derived their income by fattening cattle and producing milk knew that town dwellers and those who worked in industry were their best customers. Small peasant holdings did not need permanent outside labour. As a result, local factories were more likely to be seen as a supplement to family income than unwelcome competition in the labour market.[66] Holstein, especially, was within easy reach of Hamburg-Altona, Kiel, and Lübeck. Rural dwellers came into contact with urban life at markets and

---

[61] SA Hamburg, NL Carl Braband, B30/2, public meeting in Bellingen, 1 Dec. 1911.

[62] As opponents noted, Blunck appeared against grain tariffs as a member of the Hamburg *Bürgerschaft*, but in favour of them when campaigning in the rural districts of Husum-Tondern. *Hamburger Nachrichten* (17 Sept. 1912).   [63] *Kieler Zeitung* (20 Jan. 1910).

[64] See surviving copies of *Die Weidewirtschaft: Zeitschrift für die Interessen des Vieh-Züchter- und Gräfer-Vereins* in NL Lothar Schücking.

[65] *Die Weidewirtschaft* (Nov. 1908).

[66] Hence the frequent complaints from rural areas about outside labour employed on canal building, dam schemes, and other public works. Fegter, *Reichstagsreden*, 63.

agricultural shows.[67] Many doubtless knew people who had migrated to the city. Often migration between rural districts and urban conurbations was an exchange of one hardship for another.[68] But upward mobility was possible, particularly for members of successful peasant families rather than rural workers. A small-town or village audience could identify with the careers of left liberal deputies like Friedrich Wolgast, Andreas Blunck, and Wilhelm Struve, brought up in small Holstein communities and educated at local schools. Wolgast, for example, was the son of a tailor in the village of Jersbek. He qualifed as an elementary-school teacher before becoming prominent in associational life and then a Landtag deputy.[69]

On the narrow economic question of agricultural tariffs, therefore, the left liberals stood at a disadvantage. But this was balanced by wider economic attitudes. As in Baden left liberals used railway issues to contrast their concern for community interests with official Prussian indifference. The question of ferry services to the islands and along the North Sea Canal provided a similar opportunity. Leonhart complained in parliament about the administration of the Kaiser Wilhelm Canal and high dues charged to the Kiel–Rendsburg ferry, whilst Tondern left liberals emphasized the work of their Landtag candidate Lothar Schücking as chairman of the nautical association.[70] Generally positive attitudes towards the market and technology created a more favourable political environment for left liberals than parts of Germany where peasants were backward-looking, isolated from the railway and urban influence, and felt exploited by the market. Successful market-orientated peasant production was also a feature of other liberal rural strongholds like the Allgäu and Oldenburg.[71] Schleswig-Holstein peasants may not have voted left liberal for immediate

---

[67] Neumünster was favoured for livestock markets (and party conferences) because its central location and railway connections facilitated the attendance of rural inhabitants from throughout the province. *Die Weidewirtschaft* (Nov. 1908); the Cattle-Breeding Association of Süderdithmarschen was not just keen on district livestock shows. It planned a display at the national agricultural show in Hamburg. *Nordischer Kurier* (30 May 1908).

[68] J. Scheffler, '"Dampdöscher", "Dagglöhner" und "Monarchen": Technischer Wandel, Arbeitsmarkt und Arbeiterschaft in der Landwirtschaft Schleswig-Holsteins 1870–1914', in R. Paetau and H. Rüdel (eds.), *Arbeiter und Arbeiterbewegung in Schleswig-Holstein im 19. und 20. Jahrhundert* (Neumünster, 1987), 179–215.

[69] *Kieler Neueste Nachrichten*, Wolgast obituary (9 June 1907). For Blunck and Struve see BA Berlin, Reichslandbund 39, fo. 8, personalia Andreas Blunck; *Kieler Zeitung* (11 Jan. 1912). [70] *Kieler Neueste Nachrichten* (14 Apr. 1907); *Nordischer Kurier* (10 Mar. 1908).

[71] D. Thränhardt, *Wahlen und politische Strukturen in Bayern 1848–1953* (Düsseldorf, 1973), 71–8; SA Oldenburg, NL Theodor Tantzen 3/33.

economic motives, but economic self-confidence and openness to modernity at least provided a framework for left liberals to exercise appeal on other issues.

If Schleswig-Holstein left liberalism did not represent support for free trade, was it a vehicle for resentment against Prussia? Certainly, the left liberals under Hänel had always presented a strong regional image. This was reflected in the retention of the name 'Deutsch-freisinnige Partei für Schleswig-Holstein' and the refusal to affiliate officially to a national left liberal party before 1910. Nor was there much of a cult of Prussian militarism and obedience in the province. However, anti-Prussianism was not a popular political issue in Schleswig-Holstein as in Baden and other southern states. Nor, unlike Hanover, was there a lingering separatist sentiment, apart from the Danish minority in North Schleswig. Regional identity in Schleswig-Holstein tended to be cultural and historical, not narrowly partisan. In any case, Schleswig-Holsteiners were becoming rarer at the head of left liberal politics. Most of the FVP regional executive and at least two of the deputies were Hamburg citizens.

'National' issues were more a potential weakness than a source of strength. The parallel with the question of agricultural protectionism was clear. By contrast to the 1870s and 1880s, there were no votes to be gained by advocating more free trade or fewer arms in the pre-war decade. The *Kieler Zeitung* admitted as much in January 1905: 'We are not Hurra-Patriots, but in the minds of voters, including left liberals, things sometimes look different than in the shibboleths of [Richter's] *ABC-Buch*.'[72] The paper argued for military budgets to be examined in the same way as they were by American Democrats and Republicans, on the basis of technical merit not party principle. This reflected an impatience with Richter's doctrinaire attitude. Above all, it was a recognition of a shift in public opinion which the party had to follow or lose support. It was deemed essential, both in rural and urban districts, that the party should show itself to be just as 'national' as the National Liberals and Conservatives and, indeed, to attack the 'failures' of the SPD in this area.

Nor were these moves purely tactical. Most left liberals elected in Schleswig-Holstein in 1912 were comparatively young and shared the attitudes of their generation. Though they might criticize poor administration in the colonies, outmoded aristocratic privilege in the

---

[72] *Kieler Zeitung* (6 Jan. 1905).

army, or the Kaiser's more rash pronouncements, they were essentially supporters of *Weltpolitik* and shared a vision of Germany as a Great Power with a colonial empire and strong armed forces. When Carl Braband repeatedly declared that his stance on military and national questions was identical to his National Liberal opponent von Brooker, this was not simply electoral tactics, but a genuine reflection of his views. Indeed, despite their electoral rivalry, the two established a close friendship. When von Brooker was killed in Belgium in 1914 it was to Braband the family turned to try to bring the corpse home.[73] Even Johannes Leonhart, a founder of the Kiel branch of the German Peace Society (*Deutsche Friedensgesellschaft*) and critic of annexations during the war, supported a strong army and effective navy. Antimilitarism can be dismissed as a reason for left liberal political allegiance or, indeed, as a force which had any significant hold in non-socialist society. Occasional references were made to left liberal success in reducing military service to two years and the need to modernize procedure and equipment: promotion on ability not social status; action against the mistreatment of soldiers: the development of submarines and aircraft.[74] No doubt these things exercised some appeal, but there was little specifically left liberal about them. National Liberals like Ernst Bassermann were at least as vocal in support of army reform and modernization.[75]

Schleswig-Holstein's 'own' national question, the issue of how to treat the Danish minority in the province, was also more a potential thorn in the flesh than a source of strength. Again, left liberals responded in accordance with the dictum that the best way to keep people happy was to give them what they wanted. The complication here, however, was that a large majority of left liberal voters in North Schleswig favoured a hard line against the Danes, whilst left liberals elsewhere, notably in Kiel and Hamburg, criticized such policies as illiberal and ineffective. At the turn of the century, when Theodor Barth castigated Prussian policy in the province as Kiel's Landtag deputy, local left liberals in Schleswig joined a procession through the town in support of Köller and his authoritarian anti-Danish measures.[76]

---

[73] SA Hamburg, NL Carl Braband B2, Braband to military authorities, 11 Nov. 1914.

[74] See the Kiel left liberal journal *Fortschritt: Halbmonatsschrift für Politik Volkswirtschaft und Marinefragen* (1907–9). Although there was criticism, based on inside information from Vice Admiral Galster, of Tirpitz's obsession with battleships, it was general enthusiasm for the navy which came through. [75] S. Förster, *Der doppelte Militarismus, passim.*

[76] Sievers, *Köllerpolitik,* 112, 118–19.

Divided views had by no means disappeared a decade later. Though not represented in the leadership, a considerable number of left liberal supporters were members of the German Association for North Schleswig.[77] This was reflected in the endorsement of the association's Rothenkrug programme by Leube as FVP candidate in Apenrade-Flensburg.[78] However, there was considerable left liberal backing for the *Verein für Deutsche Friedensarbeit in der Nordmark*, a small group founded by some Protestant clergymen in North Schleswig. The left liberals provided a platform for the *Friedensverein* in Kiel and Hamburg when Leonhart, Hoff, Haupt, and others supported the aim of assimilation through educational and cultural measures.[79] Left liberals were also prominent in yet another group, the short-lived *Verein zum Schutz der Deutschen Ehre in der Nordmark*. Founded by Friedrich Naumann's brother-in-law Martin Rade, it was conceived as a moral crusade against the injustice suffered by the Danes at the hands of the Prussian authorities.[80] Against such a background it was not surprising that a delegate to the FVP Schleswig-Holstein party conference in April 1914 described North Schleswig as a tricky question. Not only were party members divided, but the left liberals' electoral position in North Schleswig was contradictory. They relied on Danish run-off support in Tondern-Husum, but needed the nationalist right in neighbouring Apenrade-Flensburg.

That most of the Danish political leadership held the same views on many political issues as the left liberals provided further complication.[81] On the whole, however, there were more votes to be lost than gained by defending the Danes. For electoral reasons, FVP leaders and Schleswig-Holstein deputies declined to support Rade's campaign against injustice in the Nordmark.[82] Similarly, a remark said to

[77] *Apenrader Tageblatt* (22 Dec. 1913). See also the comment of Dr Hahn that his strictures were not directed at left liberals in North Schleswig because: 'that is unnecessary; they are thoroughly national'. LB Kiel, Handschrift Cp 31 Nordmark-Verein Protokolle 1913–1919, 6. Sommerhauptversammlung, 5 July 1913.

[78] LA Schleswig 301, Oberpräsidium 808², Kreis secretary Apenrade to Oberpräsident, 31 Dec. 1910; *Schleswiger Grenzpost* (23 Jan. 1912).

[79] *Kieler Zeitung* (22 Nov. 1910); *Zum Streit um die Nordmark: Zweite Hamburger Versammlung am 8. Mai 1911* (Hamburg, 1911).

[80] J.-P. Leppien, *Martin Rade und die deutsch-dänischen Beziehungen 1909–1929* (Neumünster, 1981).

[81] The Danish Reichstag deputy H. P. Hanssen had good friends amongst left liberal deputies and voted with them in most divisions. H. P. Hannsen, *Diary of a Dying Empire* (Bloomington, Ind., 1955).

[82] BA Koblenz, NL Delbrück 37, Martin Rade to Hans Delbrück, 4 Nov. 1910.

have been made by Hoff in a pub, that of the two candidates in Hadersleben he preferred the liberal-minded Dane to the Pan-German Free Conservative, had to be denied. Left liberal and Danish politicians could (and did) dine together in the Reichstag canteen, but not in Apenrade or Hadersleben. This was an issue where the left liberals had to tread carefully to avoid losing votes. On the whole they managed a fairly successful balancing act. At the 1914 regional party conference, despite calls for a more definite pro-German stance, delegates voted unanimously for a resolution supporting the present border, opposing hatred on both sides, and backing a 'calm, just and consistent policy'.[83]

These were all questions where the left liberals had essentially to act defensively. Success was measured more in terms of avoiding offence than winning support. The left liberal offensive, as measured by election meetings, concentrated on two areas: political reform and education. Schleswig-Holstein left liberals were far more insistent about the introduction of the Reichstag franchise for state elections than their counterparts in much of Prussia. It could be said, cynically, that the FVP stood to gain more from equal suffrage in Schleswig-Holstein than in other provinces. The party won seven out of ten Reichstag seats in 1912, but only three out of nineteen Landtag seats in 1913. Nor, importantly, did Schleswig-Holstein left liberals depend on a three-class franchise for their position in town and city councils: the 1869 Schleswig-Holstein municipal code gave equal voting rights to all citizens whose annual income exceeded a figure ranging from 660 to 1,500 marks.[84] However, demanding the Reichstag suffrage for Prussia was more than a pursuit of party interest. It reflected a groundswell of popular feeling. Public pressure for franchise reform was so strong in the province that even Free Conservative Landtag candidates like Dr Hahn in Hadersleben felt obliged to express support for direct and secret elections.[85]

---

[83] *Kieler Zeitung* (27 Apr. 1914).

[84] *Altonaer Tageblatt* (20 Jan. 1914) lists the income required in 1913 to vote in the fifty-six towns covered by the *Städte-Ordnung*. Generally, the greater the SPD challenge the higher the income needed to vote. In Itzehoe and Wandsbek the non-socialist parties had raised the required income to 1,500 marks, in Kiel, Altona, and Flenburg 1,200 marks. In the less industrialized north of the province and in smaller towns, where nominal wages were lower and the SPD challenge less, the figure often remained at 660 marks.

[85] Dryander, *Landrat* in Apenrade to Oberpräsident Schleswig, 29 Apr. 1908 in LA Schleswig 301, Oberpräsidium 811².

Table 8.4. *Landtag elections 1913 in Schleswig-Holstein: votes cast according to political parties*

	Votes	%
Conservative	6,749	5.7
Free Conservative	5,946	5.1
National Liberals	14,214	12.1
Left liberals	20,452	17.4
Danes	12,988	11.0
Social Democrats	47,983	40.8
Others/Unknown	9,224	7.8
Total	117,556	
Turnout	36%	

Source: *Beiträge zur historischen Statistik Schleswig-Holsteins* (Kiel, 1967), 75.

Antipathy towards the Prussian franchise was generated partly because the distorting effect of the three-class franchise was particularly striking. It was hard to find another Prussian province where Reichstag and Landtag elections produced more disparate results. Although all ten Reichstag deputies belonged to left of centre parties, the province returned two Conservatives, nine Free Conservatives, three National Liberals, three left liberals, and two Danes at the 1913 Landtag elections. The number of Free Conservative Landtag seats, in particular, showed a grotesque mismatch between popular support and parliamentary representation (see Table 8.4). Faced with 'a sort of political lottery' in which the public was 'controlled from above and pressurized from below' it was no surprise, as Waldstein put it, 'that many voters stayed at home and thought just how different things were at Reichstag elections'.[86] An abstention rate of over 80 per cent in many rural districts reflected widespread popular disillusionment with Landtag elections.[87]

If the differences between national and state elections were particularly apparent in Schleswig-Holstein, so was the contrast between urban and rural local government. The Schleswig-Holstein municipal ordinances gave towns more rights than other Prussian towns, apart from Frankfurt am Main. In addition to equal voting and a lower voting age of 21, mayors and *Stadträte* were directly elected,

[86] LA Schleswig 301, Oberpräsidium 811[8], David Waldstein to public meeting, Altona, 17 Apr. 1913.   [87] *Schleswig-Holsteinisches Wochenblatt* (10 May 1908).

and the Kaiser had no confirmation rights for non-mayoral Magistrat members. But Schleswig-Holstein peasants were denied local government representation just as much as elsewhere. Unlike urban workers who demonstrated openly, the resentment of the Schleswig-Holstein rural population at inadequate political rights was largely silent, but it was widely held. Citizens' rights in district assemblies (*Kreistage*) and rural parishes were a favourite left liberal theme because they were 'of immediate interest to individual voters and readily raised a discussion'.[88] Of course, the denial of peasant representation by a self-seeking rural élite was an issue left liberals sought to exploit throughout rural Germany.[89] But it was most effective, as in Schleswig-Holstein, against a background of greater awareness and proud independence. Peasants did not see why the *Amtsvorsteher* or large landowners should have greater voting rights, or the opportunity to see how they voted.

Education was also a key issue for the left liberals. The universal awe in which the venerable figure of Hänel was held personified a respect for *Bildung* bordering on idolatry.[90] The appeal of the slogan 'Freie Bahn dem Tüchtigen' was not limited to the educated urban middle classes within left liberal ranks. Julius Kopsch could be sure of striking a universal chord among the 300 delegates to the FVP regional party conference in 1910 when he singled out the 93-year-old party veteran Vollmacht Kriegesmann and insisted that his sons and grandsons should have the opportunity to rise as high as their abilities allowed. This opportunity, Kopsch told a believing audience, was being denied them by a caste of Junkers and hangers on who sought to corner power and positions.[91] The left liberals were the only bourgeois party able to pose convincingly as the champions of state education and upward mobility. Left liberal politicians claimed to be men who had advanced by their own efforts, unlike right-wing opponents cocooned by inherited privilege. Andreas Blunck, for example, contrasted his humble social origins with those of a National Liberal

[88] BA Berlin, FVP 27, fo. 34, party secretary von Rautenkranz, report on political activity in Schleswig-Holstein, Feb. 1914.

[89] G. Gothein's *Agrarpolitisches Handbuch* (Berlin, 1910) was a catalogue of peasant grievances against Prussian administrators and estate owners: unfair taxation; no peasant representation on Kreistage; shortages of land for peasant resettlement; damages caused by hunting.

[90] See the thunderous applause which greeted Hänel's appearance at the left liberal Schleswig-Holstein party conference in Dec. 1906. *Kieler Zeitung* (31 Dec. 1906, evening edn.).   [91] LA Schleswig 320, Steinburg 236, *Nordischer Kurier* (19 Apr. 1910).

opponent who had not only been born 'with millions', but had married money to boot.[92] And, as Ferdinand Hoff kept reminding audiences, the National Liberals had compromised over confessional education while the Conservative record was even more sullied.[93] As elsewhere, education, the positive side of left liberal cultural coin, was combined with the seductive negative side, anti-clericalism. Left liberals assailed Roesicke in 1912 for standing simultaneously in Kaiserslauten, but even more for trying to be elected there on the back of Centre party votes.[94] Left liberalism was able to use the association of Catholicism with backwardness and the smothering of individual enterprise as an effective counterpoint to its own message. It set out, through the ideals of education and personal *Tüchtigkeit*, to be a creed which underscored the self-esteem of peasants and the urban *Mittelstand* alike as capable, worthy individuals.

Constitutional reform and cultural issues were, therefore, two spheres of politics where left liberalism held a natural attraction. This was not just a matter of particular policies, but the way the electorate felt about society and their position in it. Some Schleswig-Holstein peasants and, even more, agricultural workers were attracted to the SPD, but most rejected the party. They disagreed with the SPD on 'national' issues and generally saw the party as one for the urban masses. National Liberals and Conservatives, on the other hand, were inextricably linked with the rural élite: *Landräte*, *Amtsvorsteher*, *Gutsvorsteher*, and large landowners. It was very hard for the small farmers and peasants to see these parties as their representatives when they were headed locally by the same people who lorded it over them, enforced unpopular regulations, and generally gave them no say in the running of affairs. Left liberalism addressed their sense of independence and egalitarian instincts: it played on tradition as well as promising a better future. The left liberal press and politicians, by castigating administrative high-handedness and highlighting abuses, gave vent to silent resentment. It was with understandable pleasure that villagers and small-town inhabitants looked on as smart-talking lawyers and journalists handed out a verbal drubbing to overbearing local officials and landowners. Such an audience also drew satisfaction from the belief that they possessed the virtues exalted by liberalism: independent-mindedness and the ability to stand on one's own feet.

[92] *Elbwart* (1912), 23–4.   [93] *Kieler Zeitung* (31 Dec. 1906, evening edn.).
[94] *Kieler Zeitung* (11 Jan. 1912, morning edn.).

Against such a background, left liberal espousal, not of equal incomes, but of equal voting rights and equal opportunity, of fair justice and fair administration, held an obvious appeal. Left liberalism both encouraged and fed off the belief among the peasantry and small farmers that they were just as good citizens as anyone else and deserved just as many rights.

Left liberalism's ability to present itself as a campaign for justice was important, but the ability to present such a campaign in the framework not of social revolution, but of tradition was vital. This was reflected in the arguments for voting left liberal advanced by the *Kieler Zeitung*:

[We] hold unbroken loyalty to Kaiser and Reich. We stand four-square in support of our constitutional state and social order. We are sworn enemies of playing with revolution or revolutionary posturing in empty rhetoric or powerless coups. But that makes it even more our duty and right to strive with all the will and capacity we can muster for the continual development of our state till its citizens enjoy complete freedom and the people's representative chamber has full constitutional rights.[95]

Reform was presented not as alien and sudden, but as a natural progression in tune with historical tradition. Left liberalism assiduously associated itself with 1848 and the freeing of Schleswig-Holstein from Danish rule in the 1860s. It presented freedom from Junker arrogance and unaccountable administration as a further stage in a process of liberation going back to 1848 and beyond to peasant emancipation. It was an ideology designed to appeal to a group who, though open to economic opportunities, still pursued a fairly traditional lifestyle. As in rural Württemberg, where Stuttgart lawyers like Payer and Haußmann were skilled in appealing to the traditional instincts of the honest peasantry (*gerade Leute auf der Alb*), Schleswig-Holstein left liberals nurtured rural pride and independence. Ironically, a left liberal political tradition was itself part of the social conservatism of the Schleswig-Holstein countryside.[96]

Left liberalism in the Schleswig-Holstein countryside was not free of contradictions. It claimed the high moral ground, but was willing to launch personal attacks on rival candidates at every opportunity. Von Rautenkranz's regret that the character of Justizrat Görck, the National Liberal candidate in Steinburg-Dithmarschen, 'offers few

[95] *Kieler Zeitung* (20 Dec. 1906).
[96] See the campaign material in HSA Stuttgart, NL Haußmann 104.

opportunities for attack' was revealing of left liberal methods. The party was quite prepared to get involved in slanging matches, with left liberal speakers and newspapers more than holding their own. In Plön-Oldenburg, for example, when the left liberal Dr Struve was accused of treating patients like laboratory rabbits, the left liberals responded that the Conservative, a lawyer Justizrat Bokelmann, was ignorant of the laws of custody.[97] The left liberals claimed to be a party of principle, but trimmed policies, particularly on economic and military questions, to curry electoral favour. The claim was to represent the general interest, but the rhetoric was directed towards particular groups in society. Yet where such contradictions were rooted in the electorate they were inevitable; and where they could be disguised or reconciled in voters' minds they were manageable. The existence of real division within local society did not render claims to represent the general interest obsolete. On the contrary, it underlined the attraction of such claims where, as in rural Schleswig-Holstein, much of the electorate could be persuaded that they were part of the general interest whose legitimate aspirations were being thwarted by a privileged minority. Left liberals argued that, because the bulk of small farmers and peasants represented the general interest, promises to help them with cheap supplies of fodder and tax allowances were not electoral bribes but measures to further society as a whole.[98] Equally, left liberals saw personal attacks on National Liberal or Conservative *Landräte* and estate owners not as unfair, but morally justified attacks, revealing the enemies of the general interest in a true light.[99] There was certainly irony in the exploitation of social resentment in the cause of social harmony. But the irony did not worry Schleswig-Holstein peasants, who were hearing a message which reinforced their own prejudices.

The Agrarian League's message—that the small man needed money more than rights—did not conform to the attitudes of most Schleswig-Holstein villagers. Indeed, the implicit suggestion, played on by left liberals, that peasants should sacrifice political beliefs and proud independence in return for an economic loyalty bonus, was resented. The problem for the Conservatives and National Liberals

---

[97] BA Berlin, FVP 27, fo. 75, von Rautenkranz's report for Jan. 1911; *Kieler Neueste Nachrichten* (24 Jan. and 2 Feb. 1907).

[98] See the FVP pamphlet, *Bauernpolitik statt Junkerpolitik*.

[99] See e.g. the left liberal poster 'An die Dithmarscher Männer aller Stände' in NL Lothar Schücking.

was that the population viewed their interests in social and political as well as economic terms. The left liberals sought to identify themselves with popular aspects of the state—its national character, its economic success, its strong armed forces, its monarchy, its social benefits—at the same time championing reform of the parts people did not like—unequal suffrage, unfair taxation, lack of public accountability, aristocratic privilege. The Conservatives and the National Liberals could not advocate similar reforms without destroying their own basis of existence. True, voting left liberal was an act of spiritual rather than material satisfaction. Deputies occasionally intervened successfully in Berlin on constituency matters—cases of maladministration, petitions about rail or ferry services—but were unable to bring about fundamental change. However, the very absence of reform provided a continued reason to return left liberals in protest against local injustice and national shortcomings. The left liberals made frequent declarations of the value they placed on rural support: 'The independent peasantry of Schleswig-Holstein have always been the strongest pillar of support for the left liberal party in Schleswig-Holstein. In looking after the interests of this important calling the left liberals will not allow themselves to be outdone by any other party guided by the general good'[100] The peasantry responded to such calculated admiration, not with cynicism, but continued political adherence.

If left liberalism was able to keep support from within the peasantry and small farmers, what about the urban electorate? Surely here factory workers and Social Democracy were seen as a greater threat than the local social and political élite? In any case, was not Liberalism too closely identified with the urban élite to be an appropriate vehicle of protest for the urban *Mittelstand?* What, moreover, were the implications of a greater social and economic diversity and more acute political awareness in urban areas? There were indications that the left liberals' position in the cities was being eroded. In Kiel, for example, the left liberal Liberal Association had long been the leading non-socialist political organization. In the pre-war decade, however, other local party associations were founded or rejuvenated. Young Liberal activists at last gave the National Liberals an organization at least as active in holding public meetings and campaigning as the Liberal Association. As a result Kiel National Liberals claimed to have

---

[100] *Kieler Zeitung* (20 Jan. 1910, morning edn.).

increased membership from 110 to 400 during 1907.[101] The call for renewal was a constant refrain in the annual reports of the Liberal Association, but little was done. Indeed, membership tended to decline.[102] The left liberals also lost press support. In 1907 the left liberals enjoyed a near monopoly of the Kiel daily press, apart from the modestly successful socialist *Schleswig-Holsteinische Volkszeitung*. Subsequently, however, the *Kieler Tageblatt* ceased publication and the best-selling paper in the province, the *Kieler Neueste Nachrichten*, moved closer to Bassermannite National Liberalism. Later the paper swung even further to the right, supporting the Fatherland party in 1917–18 and becoming part of Hugenberg's press empire.[103]

The Liberal Association in Kiel had lost the easy predominance it once possessed. The cause of its losses to the SPD in Reichstag and local elections was primarily economic change. The SPD owed their success in local elections before 1909 to the bulging tenements in the rapidly expanding working-class suburb of Gaarden. The SPD margin of victory here outweighed bourgeois majorities in the *Altstadt*. Almost three-quarters of Kiel's 220,000 population were born outside the city, one of the highest rates of influx in the Reich. As in Hamburg and Altona, the displacement of the left liberals from the top of the polls by a working-class party in Kiel was more an inevitable reflection of local social and economic change than a demonstration of liberal ideological bankruptcy.[104] Although defeat was not primarily of their own making, inability to defeat socialist candidates was a serious blow to the left liberals' political position. Previously, the SPD threat had consolidated left liberals' support. It was argued plausibly that a SPD victory could only be prevented by a united bourgeois front and by a left-of-centre candidate capable of winning over SPD *Mitläufer*. Such arguments were still effective, for example, in Bremen, Frankfurt,

---

[101] *Kieler Neueste Nachrichten* (8 Dec. 1907).

[102] Liberaler Verein Kiel Membership: 636 (31 Dec. 1911); 589 (31 Dec. 1912); 537 (31 Dec. 1913). *Kieler Zeitung* (19 Feb. 1913 and 27 Jan. 1914). The fall in members may be explained by the establishment of a separate Liberal workers association, which had around 100 members, or stricter collection of membership dues. Nevertheless, the figures betray a lack of new blood.

[103] LA Schleswig 301, Oberpräsidium 5817/5818, government press inquiry, summer 1926.

[104] For a thorough analysis of the importance of newcomers and industrial expansion to SPD membership and electoral support in Kiel see Paetau, *Konfrontation und Kooperation*, esp. 107–10, 141–51, and 529–34.

and Danzig. But they lost their force when SPD victory seemed inevitable. In Kiel this point had been reached by 1912 and right-wing parties were no longer prepared to vote FVP in the hope of keeping the SPD out. In addition, the mere fact of SPD victory produced calls for repressive action and criticism of the left liberals for being too soft on socialism. Kiel left liberals had used their electoral triumphs in the 1880s and 1890s to argue that only promises of reform could stem the rising tide of socialism. Now the right insisted, after Legien's victories in 1903, 1907, and 1912, that liberal ideas and methods had proved ineffective.[105]

Left liberals in Kiel lost out, therefore, to a rapidly growing working-class electorate, and the perception that they were likely losers. Moreover, there was a trend away from left liberalism within the Protestant upper middle class epitomized by the influential Ahlmann family. Wilhelm Ahlmann (1817–1910) stood alongside Hänel as a figurehead of left liberalism in Schleswig-Holstein. Barred from returning to university life because of his role in the 1848 Schleswig-Holstein government, Ahlmann established a successful banking house in Kiel. But business did not displace politics. Ahlmann was active in local government, owned the leading left liberal newspaper in Schleswig-Holstein, and was a key figure in election fund-raising. Ahlmann did not hesitate to use his wealth and prestige to further the left liberal cause. His son Ludwig Ahlmann (1859–1942) enjoyed similar respect as a banker and city council chairman. But he was first and foremost a businessman. His participation in associational life was considerable, but he preferred to avoid party politics. The Chamber of Trade was an obvious focus for his activity, and patronage of the Schleswig-Holstein Historical Association typified Ludwig Ahlmann's enthusiasm for the impeccable bourgeois cultural cause. Wilhelm Ahlmann's outlook might be described as bourgeois liberalism, Ludwig Ahlmann's as bourgeois respectability. And to be ultra-respectable one could not be a partisan left liberal. Ludwig Ahlmann was a reluctant supporter of Oberbürgermeister Fuß's plan to introduce the three-class franchise in Kiel, and, a more enthusiastic backer of a mass-meeting to call for an annexationist 'German peace' in September 1917. Both actions were

---

[105] The theme runs throughout radical nationalist newspapers, the *Hamburger Nachrichten* and *Itzehoer Nachrichten*, and the Conservative and National Liberal periodicals *Nord West* and *Elbwart* (from 1913 *Bismarckwart*).

opposed by the Liberal Association and would not have appealed to Wilhelm Ahlmann.[106] Kiel left liberalism was not, however, in a state of collapse. Even after the National Liberals and Conservatives had established active organizations and mounted serious electoral campaigns in the city, the left liberals remained the leading non-socialist party. The left liberals were able to retain the Landtag seat in 1913. Indeed, the threat from the right-wing candidate was less acute than ten years earlier.[107] Left liberals remained in the forefront of local associational life. Wilhelm Struve, for example, was Chairman of the Tenants' Association, prominent in the Doctors' Association, recited native verse in the *Plattdeutsch-Vereinigung* and addressed the *Verein der Handelscommis* on the dangers of VD and the need for a state insurance scheme for white-collar workers.[108] Johannes Leonhart was also a leading member of the Doctors' Association and the elected *Stadtrat* responsible for public health in Kiel. He was a leader of the city's cremation society, a popular Liberal cause,[109] and the anti-alcohol *Guttempler* organization.[110] The 1907 funeral service for Kiel's Landtag deputy Friedrich Wolgast was attended by a typical combination of civic dignitaries and left liberal representatives. A large number of his fellow teachers and Freemasons and members of the same regimental old boys' association accompanied the coffin.[111] There were numerous connections between local left liberals and residents' associations. Rechtsanwalt Daltrop was chairman of the left liberal district association, a member of the left liberal Schleswig-Holstein executive committee, and secretary of the Kommunalverein West-Kiel. Hoff and Leonhart were committee members of the Ost-Kiel and Kiel-Altstadt local associations respectively.[112] Such local and professional organizations were not exclusively left liberal, though some, like the teachers' association,

---

[106] H.-G. H. Kiehl, 'Albert Hänel und der Linksliberalismus im Reichstagswahlkreis Kiel-Rendsburg-Plön 1867 bis 1884', Ph.D., Kiel University, 1966; *Schleswig-Holsteinisches Biographisches Lexikon*, i (Neumünster, 1970), 24–6; *Kieler Zeitung* (3 Mar. 1909, evening edn.), *Nord West* (1917), 264.

[107] *Kieler Neueste Nachrichten* (5 Nov. 1907); Paetau, *Konfrontation und Kooperation*, 538.

[108] *Kieler Neueste Nachrichten* (12 and 28 Apr. 1907).

[109] The chairman of the Kiel Cremation Society was shipping director Stellter, the left liberal Reichstag candidate in 1907. *Kieler Zeitung* (22 Nov. 1912, evening edn.).

[110] J. Leonhart, *Die Alkohol-Frage in der Großstadt* (Hamburg, 1911).

[111] *Kieler Neueste Nachrichten* (13 June 1907).

[112] *Kieler Neueste Nachrichten* (9, 17, and 30 Apr. 1907); *Kieler Zeitung* (11 Mar. 1910, evening edn.).

were close to being so. But left liberals had a preponderant influence in many. The left liberals were still the party with which most non-socialist voters in Kiel identified. Moreover, the trend against the left liberals amongst the city's economic élite, people like Ludwig Ahlmann, should not be overstated. The defection of upper middle-class support was only partial. It was not an isolated development, but part of a wider change in social profile within Kiel left liberal politics. University academics still played a part in left liberal activities. The theologian Professor Titius was the FVP's Reichstag candidate in 1912. A branch of the Deutscher Akademischer Freibund catered for liberal enthusiasts at the university. However, by the pre-war decade, it was not Hänel's colleagues but school teachers and headmasters who ran the Liberal Association and, indeed, played a prominent role in left liberal organization throughout the province. The chairman and treasurer of the Kiel Liberal Association were teachers, as was the city's Landtag deputy from 1903 to 1918. School teachers figured prominently amongst Schleswig-Holstein and Hamburg delegates to the 1912 FVP party conference, and were singled out for their special contribution to electoral campaigning by the 1906 regional party conference.[113]

Lower middle-class figures, particularly men from the new technical and administrative occupations, came increasingly to the fore. This was reflected in the four candidates put forward by the Liberal Association for the 1907 municipal elections: machinist Herrmann, gas controller Czarnetzki, engineer Gramm, and telegraph secretary Schwartz.[114] They took their place alongside men from the free professions in left liberal committees, as speakers in political meetings, and as delegates to party conferences. The link between the left liberals and the 'new' *Mittelstand* was in one sense fortuitous: a political party in search of new support and a social grouping looking for an appropriate political vehicle. But men like Czarnetzki and Herrmann did not see themselves as sectional-interest representatives. Indeed they were among the most insistent in demanding liberal political reform. The left liberal political programme held an obvious attraction to the new middle classes. White-collar workers often had cause to resent restrictions placed on them by their superiors. Left liberal

---

[113] *Zweiter Parteitag der FVP*, 124; *Kieler Zeitung* (31 Dec. 1906, evening edn.).
[114] *Kieler Neueste Nachrichten* (13 Nov. 1907).

advocacy of full rights of association and assembly had a natural appeal. So did left liberal calls for social welfare to be extended to white-collar workers. In addition the party supported the right of officials to see files kept on them and opposed imprisonment as a possible disciplinary punishment. Those who had to live on a salary, often a modest one, also looked to the left liberals as the non-socialist party most likely to oppose increased indirect taxation and tariffs. Above all, left liberalism was the natural political allegiance for a group which, like the Schleswig-Holstein peasants, considered itself distinct from employers or government above and shopfloor workers below. Once again the left liberals, the apostles of social harmony, were the ironic beneficiaries of a sense of social division.

This change in social profile was reflected in greater left liberal concern about social policy. Even before 1890 the left liberals were not as rigidly Manchesterite as the speeches of Bamberger and Richter indicated. But by 1897 even a delegate to the SPD regional party conference in Neumünster dismissed the charge that the left liberals were advocates of unbridled *laissez-faire* capitalism as a stale electioneering slogan.[115] In the pre-war decade, though insisting on a market economy, most left liberals supported the idea of an expanding system of social support involving national and local government. Left liberals still claimed to be the guardians of taxpayers' money and the enemies of waste. In Kiel, for example, the Magistrat's 'incredible' East Asian Museum plan was opposed in 1909, and, as elsewhere, there were also numerous complaints from left liberal councillors and newspapers about budget over-runs on municipal building plans.[116] Nor was there agreement on the details of social welfare provision. Nevertheless, the basic principle was agreed and the trend towards municipal intervention was clear. This was reflected in the popularity of Friedrich Naumann who drew an audience of 2,500 when he spoke in Kiel in April 1914. The Kiel Liberal Association also sent the monthly *Volkspartei* and the *Fortschrittliches Taschenbuch* diary published by Naumann to each member.[117] Like Naumann, advocates of social liberalism in Kiel were moved both by theories of national efficiency and by a humane concern about the suffering visible in Wilhelmine society. Hermann Luppe, the left liberal deputy mayor of Frankfurt

---

[115] LA Schleswig 301, Oberpräsidium 2250, 'Proceedings of the Social Democratic Party Conference for Schleswig-Holstein, Lauenburg, Fürstentum Lübeck and Hamburg, Nemünster 5–7 Sept. 1897'. [116] *Kieler Zeitung* (13 Mar. 1909). [117] *Kieler Zeitung* (27 Apr. 1914).

who came from a respectable Kiel family, recalled his anger as a teenager in the 1890s at indifference shown by Oberbürgermeister Dr Fuß and his haughty wife towards working-class housing conditions.[118] Luppe was convinced, like a growing number of municipal left liberals, that local government had to intervene in the housing market through land policy, building regulations, and grants to housing charities. Less was achieved in Kiel, where Fuß remained in office till 1912, than in Frankfurt. However, the trend towards an expanded municipal social policy was unmistakable, as it was in Altona where the new Oberbürgermeister Schnackenburg, supported by left liberal and SPD councillors, instituted a large-scale housing programme.[119] Attempts in the council chamber by Herrmann to raise the wages of street cleaners by 40 pfennig a day and by Hoff for cheaper entrance to the new municipal baths reflected on a smaller scale a similar attitude to the less favoured in society.[120] The principle, enunciated explicitly by Gramm to a public meeting in May 1907, was 'support for the economically vulnerable'.[121]

As elsewhere, popular politics in Kiel did not take an idealized form. Fuß's contention that left liberal proposals to divide Kiel into electoral districts would further intensify parish pump politics, replacing *Kirchturmspolitik* with *Haustürpolitik*, was convincingly met by Hoff's observation that parish pump politics could not possibly get any worse than it was already.[122] Nor was left liberal formal organization able to keep pace with the rise in political mobilization. But left liberalism was not just well-placed, through prominence in associational life, to exploit parish pump sentiment. A new generation of lower middle-class spokesmen and a social liberal platform both reached out to a mass electorate. Left liberalism in Kiel was much more attuned to mass politics and the logic of equal suffrage in an industrial society in the pre-war decade than it had been in the 1880s and 1890s. To old-style notables like Fuß this was 'bourgeois demagogy' noisier even than the SPD.[123] Though some left liberals found populism a regrettable if necessary tactical response to stay above

---

[118] BA Koblenz, NL Luppe 8, 'Mein Leben war Kampf für Demokratie und Reichseinheit. Selbstbiographie des Nürnburger Oberbürgermeisters und Kämpfers gegen Bayerischen Separatismus und Nationalsozialismus', fos. 85–6.

[119] W. Stephan, *Acht Jahrzehnte erlebtes Deutschland: Ein Liberaler in vier Epochen* (Düsseldorf, 1983), 25.   [120] *Kieler Neueste Nachrichten* (27 May and 4 July 1907).

[121] *Kieler Neueste Nachrichten* (18 May 1907).

[122] *Kieler Zeitung* (3 Mar. 1909, evening edn.).   [123] Ibid.

water in the rising tide of political participation, for others popular politics was a tribute to universal education and a legitimization of left liberal demands for a *Volksstaat*. As the *Kieler Neueste Nachrichten* urged in 1907, they felt that it was time for governments to 'put the people in the saddle': 'Particularly a people which has gone through universal elementary education, [and] so often showed its patriotism, will soon show through action that it is able to ride.'[124]

For younger generations, popular politics had become an unquestioned fact of life. But left liberal attempts to attract *Mittelstand* support had to deal with conflicts of interest as well as increased politicization. As the clutch of rail, postal, or clerical staff associations reflected, the 'new' *Mittelstand* was internally divided as well as resentful towards outside groups. As a result, left liberals had to nurse the competing claims of different sections. Fortunately, left liberals, unburdened by executive responsibility, could appear impartial advocates of all sides. The left liberal journal *Fortschritt*, for example, carried a heated correspondence between Schleswig-Holstein train drivers and platform supervisors, each claiming to deserve a higher salary and status than other. The characteristic response was to insinuate that both sides had a good case, and that everyone could be satisfied if only the authorities pursued left liberal railway policies.

A clash of interests between *Beamten* on the one hand and artisans and small businessmen on the other raised a more intractable issue for a party needing support from the *Mittelstand* as a whole. By advocating state intervention and better salaries and conditions for white-collar workers, left liberals risked losing support from those who faced increased taxes and production costs. As an anonymous letter to Carl Braband put it, many small businessmen and artisans were appalled by 'liberal' politicians acting almost like over-eager lovers towards 'an exceptionally privileged group like the *Beamten* with high, fixed salaries and pensions, secure jobs, short hours, long holidays'.[125] The need to appeal to the 'new' *Mittelstand* as much as ideology prevented the FVP from matching right-wing promises to serve the specific economic interests of the 'old' *Mittelstand*.

---

[124] *Kieler Neueste Nachrichten* (5 Dec. 1907).
[125] SA Hamburg NL Carl Braband, B2, 'Liberaler Nichtbeamter' to Braband, 6 Feb. 1908.

Inevitably, sections of the 'old' *Mittelstand* were attracted by right-wing promises of material advantage. The trend towards the right and economic self-interest was particularly evident amongst landlords, whose opposition to property taxes earned them the description 'house agrarians'. Led by bank director Köster, an arch Conservative and three-class franchise enthusiast, they argued that left liberal and SPD councillors led ineluctably to tight regulations and high property taxes. Hence the blunt admission of a delegate to the 10,000-member Schleswig-Holstein house owners' association: 'if the house owners want to reduce their costs then the local franchise must be changed'.[126] But left liberals were able to limit this threat by three means. First they attacked both the motives and deeds of right-wing 'saviours of the *Mittelstand*' (*Mittelstandsretter*). Secondly, they tailored politics to different local circumstances. Thirdly, they sought to focus attention on issues other than sectional economic interest.

The methods Schleswig-Holstein left liberals used to discredit right-wing *Mittelstand* politics were familiar. As elsewhere, left liberals claimed that the way Conservatives and Centre had used their political power since the 1880s proved that their concern for the urban *Mittelstand* was purely cosmetic. The 'old' *Mittelstand*, they argued, had to pay high wages and taxes because of 'Blue-Black' economics rather than social spending and greedy public employees. Tariffs led to higher living costs and, through necessary increases in public-sector salaries, to more taxes. These, in turn, fell disproportionately on industry and commerce because the right favoured agriculture and 'the dead hand'. As usual left liberals used the 1909 finance reform to illustrate these points.

The left liberal stance towards the *Mittelstand* in Schleswig-Holstein was chameleon-like. Despite rhetoric about the general interest, left liberals were particularly adept at identifying different key groups of voters in various localities. In Kiel and Altona, where the tertiary sector accounted for over 55 per cent of the workforce, left liberal policies were directed towards white-collar workers and public employees. This trend was even more evident in Hamburg, which had Germany's highest concentration of the 'new' *Mittelstand*. Clerks, salesmen, and mid-ranking public employees made up over 20 per cent of the city's workforce compared to a national average of

7.5 per cent.[127] In smaller towns, where small businesses and craftsmen predominated over bureaucracy and white-collar workers, left liberals addressed artisan interests. In Hamburg the party supported ambitious spending projects—the proposed university was a classic example—but in towns like Elmshorn or Pinneberg left liberals remained closer to the Richterite local awkward squad. They opposed waste, criticized the Prussian authorities, and attacked the mayor for not standing up to the _Landrat_.[128] Artisans, not state employees, provided the bedrock of left liberal support in Hadersleben and the towns in Kreis Steinburg.[129]

Both the attack on right-wing economics and adaptation to local interests were important in securing support. It was, however, the third tactic of counteracting narrow sectional interests, the ability to focus attention on other issues, which was crucial. Here left liberal politics benefited from the economic boom from the late 1890s to 1913. It made artisans more inclined to accept the arguments of left liberal _Mittelstand_ experts like Johannes Wernicke that small workshops, assisted by electric machinery, could survive alongside factory production and department stores in a market economy.[130] A favourable economic climate enhanced left liberalism's appeal to pride and independence. Left liberal businessmen and artisans preferred personal diligence and fair treatment to feather-bedding. Typically, the chairman of the German Association for North Schleswig in Elmshorn was roundly condemned by a left liberal audience for trying

---

[127] _Badischer Landesbote_ (25 June 1914). For the bias of Hamburg left liberalism towards the 'new' _Mittelstand_ see 'Alter und neuer Mittelstand', _General-Anzeiger für Schleswig-Holstein_ (21 Jan. 1911).

[128] _Kieler Zeitung_ (23 Feb. 1909); SA Hamburg NL Carl Braband B2, Braband to Stadtsekretär Mosig, Giessen, 5 July 13 (copy).

[129] In Hadersleben left liberals harnessed the resentment of master craftsmen at the role of the _Beamtenverein_ in local politics. LA Schleswig 301, Oberpräsidium 59, fo. 158, _Schleswigsche Grenzpost_, 46 (24 Feb. 1913). Artisans were well-represented in left liberal membership lists for Itzehoe, Krempe, and Wilster. LA Schleswig 320, Steinburg 235 (Krempe); 236 (Itzehoe); 237 (Wilster). Significantly, left liberals were more dominant in small and medium manufacturing and commercial towns than similarly sized adminstrative centres like Schleswig and Ratzeburg. _Kieler Zeitung_ (20 Jan. 1912, morning edn.); Zimmermann _Wählerverhalten_, 84.

[130] J. Wernicke, _Kapitalismus und Mittelstandspolitik_ (Jena, 1907). See also the critique in U. Wengenroth, 'Motoren für den Kleinbetrieb: Soziale Utopien, technische Entwicklung und Absatzstrategien bei der Motorisierung des Kleingewerbes im Kaiserreich', in Wengenroth (ed.), _Prekäre Selbstständigkeit: Zur Standortbestimmung von Handwerk, Hausindustrie und Kleingewerbe im Industrialisierungsprozess_ (Stuttgart, 1989), 177–205.

to blame the failure of his business on a Danish boycott.[131] The atmosphere of expansion and optimism gave resonance to undivisive left liberal economic themes like technological progress, better transport, and more efficient postal services. Above all, economic stability and prosperity allowed peoples' attention to focus on left liberal strong suits: pure political issues and *Kulturpolitik*. Indeed the success of the Wilhelmine economy threw the frailties revealed by the Eulenburg–Moltke trials, the *Daily Telegraph* affair, Zabern and diplomatic reverses into yet starker relief.

Schleswig-Holstein urban inhabitants, like the peasants, did not see political rights as separate from and subservient to material benefits. The left liberals were again able to present themselves as the party of the small man. This applied especially to the issue of the municipal franchise reform. Left liberals posed as architects and sworn defenders of the 1869 municipal code. Seizing on remarks made by National Liberals and Conservatives that the franchise would have to be changed to provide a barrier against the SPD, left liberals argued that the political rights of the *Mittelstand* were safe only in their hands. In the 1907 Landtag by-election in Kiel left liberals warned anyone who wanted to keep his vote in the municipal elections against voting for the right-wing National Liberal candidate. There could, the left liberal press insisted, only be one choice, 'for we citizens of Kiel and Neumünster who want to keep our rights and have never been Conservative'.[132] When Fuß attempted to introduce the three-class franchise for local elections in Kiel in 1909, Hoff claimed this would give all the power to the toffs in Düsternbrook and the Beseller-Allee. Only those with an annual income over 8,000 marks, some 2,000 or 3,000 of Kiel's 21,000 voters, would form the first two classes of voters. The great majority of the *Mittelstand* would find themselves in the socialist-dominated third class, socially degraded and electorally impotent.[133]

At one level the left liberal position on the municipal franchise was disingenuous. The income barrier specified by the Hänel-inspired municipal code was originally intended to exclude much of the petty bourgeoisie. Unforeseen inflation rather than left liberal political

---

[131] *Zum Streit um die Nordmark*, 32–3. The same attitude was reflected by scathing left liberal references to anti-Semite groups changing their names as rapidly as failing businesses.   [132] *Kieler Neueste Nachrichten* (24 Oct. 1907).
[133] *Kieler Zeitung* (3 Mar. 1909).

intent enfranchised the petty bourgeoisie and skilled working class. And while left liberals rejected the division of voters into different classes, they supported the introduction of carefully drawn electoral districts designed to limit SPD chances.[134] However, neither aspect prevented the left liberals from making political capital out of the municipal suffrage issue. Voters were concerned about the present fate of the municipal code not the details of its inception. Nor did non-socialist voters object to measures directed against the SPD. For most of the petty bourgeoisie, the crucial question was not one of fairness towards the SPD, but of their own status. There was considerable *Mittelstand* sympathy for two specific arguments put forward by the left liberals in the municipal franchise debate. The first argument was that the proposals couched as measures to prevent SPD rule were really intended to create municipal government run by a small, unaccountable clique.[135] Secondly, instead of making the franchise responsible for SPD gains, Fuß and his co-conspirators should blame themselves for failing to pursue popular policies and mobilize bourgeois voters. 'The men who now want to save the fatherland in three hours', Hoff told a Liberal Association protest in March 1909, 'have done little by deed to work against the election of Social Democratic councillors.'[136] What really reinforced petty-bourgeois support for the left liberal position, however, was the belief that being placed in the third class of voters was tantamount to being publicly branded a third-class citizen.

The vision of red peril which right-wing National Liberals and Conservatives hoped would gain them support was mainly abstract. There were prolonged strikes in the Kiel shipyards, but they had little direct effect on most of the local population. The Kiel labour movement was more notable for discipline and orderliness than as a threat to public order. People like Legien were not even revolutionary in rhetoric. Even Fuß agreed that the SPD had played a constructive role in the council chamber.[137] The left liberals, however, were able to point out the immediate impact of threatened franchise changes on the voting rights and, therefore, status of the 'old' and 'new' *Mittelstand* alike. The Landtag franchise issue further reinforced the left liberals' role as guardians of status. Typically the FVP exploited

---

[134] *Sünden des Freisinns*, 50; *Kieler Zeitung* (3 Mar. 1909, evening edn.).
[135] *Kieler Zeitung* (3 Mar. 1909, evening edn.).
[136] *Kieler Zeitung* (9 Mar. 1909, morning edn.).   [137] *Sünden des Freisinns*, 51.

Bethmann-Hollweg's abortive proposal to allow 'bearers of culture' additional voting rights in Landtag elections, presenting it as an insult to most of the *Bürgertum*. It favoured paper qualifications over success in practical life, branding as uncivilized 'the peasant, master craftsman, retailer, no matter how capable'.[138] Despite the differences in social, political, and economic structure, there were underlying similarities to the appeal of left liberalism in urban and rural Schleswig-Holstein. In both cases left liberal success reflected a desire for measured domestic political reform. Most voters found National Liberal and Conservative reform pledges untrustworthy or insufficient. But for many the SPD appeared too radical, even though it tended, like the FVP, to castigate abuses and shortcomings rather than fundamentally reject the government's authority. (The SPD concentrated on immediate matters like the rise in meat prices and the finance reform. Moreover, most regional leaders were on the right of the labour movement. Frohme, the veteran deputy for Altona, could even remember being shouted down by the young orthodox Bernstein when he advocated supporting bourgeois democrats in 1882.[139]) The left liberals provided a well-supported middle way. Equally, left liberalism acted as badge of recognition for the middle strata of rural or urban society: people who felt themselves disregarded by the right and too good for the SPD. Ironically, left liberalism was both a critique and a form of social identification. Other aspects of left liberalism were also paradoxical. On the one hand, left liberals dealt in ringing emotional appeals. A vote for Hoff in 1907, it was claimed, was a vote for 'justice, education and freedom'.[140] On the other, it indulged in opportunism and personal attack. It was the self-proclaimed party of tradition, but also of technological progress. Left liberal candidates evoked memories of past Schleswig-Holstein liberal leaders and 'the great years of 1848–51' one minute, and the triumphs of the chemical industry and gross national product the next.[141]

The left liberal electorate was not hermetically sealed. It could be eroded from left and right. Conversely, left liberalism also had an attraction beyond the ranks of party supporters. SPD voters eagerly

---

[138] Waldstein to public meeting Altona, 17 Apr. 1913, LA Schleswig 301, Oberpräsidium 811[8].
[139] LA Schleswig 301, Oberpräsidium 2250, Social Democratic party conference for Schleswig-Holstein, Lauenburg, Fürstentum Lübeck and Hamburg, Nemünster, 5–7 Sept. 1897.   [140] *Kieler Neueste Nachrichten* (20 Oct. 1907).
[141] Ibid.; NL Lothar Schücking, speech by Hoff, 2 Oct. 1907.

supported left liberals in run-offs against the right even in 1907. Nor was left liberal-SPD co-operation confined to run-off pacts. In 1908 Braband managed to persuade the *Hamburger Echo* not to publish news of his dismissal as a reserve officer for writing a letter supporting a Social Democrat in a run-off election, the sort of political scandal the SPD press normally emblazoned across its columns. The main speaker at an SPD meeting in Schleswig in February 1912 praised the FVP for 'representing the people well in many ways'. In Plön SPD supporters joined the street festivities marking the centenary of the battle of Leipzig in 1913 despite the instructions of their local leaders. Even before 1914 there were signs of the SPD's widespread acceptance of the German state and willingness to co-operate with the left liberals within the existing system.[142]

The left liberals were also able to attract support from the right, even in run-off contests where the SPD had already been eliminated. When National Liberal and Agrarian League provincial leaders agreed to support each other in the run-offs against the left liberals in 1912 they found that they had made 'die Rechnung ohne den Wirt' (reckoned without the host). National Liberal voters in East Holstein supported the left liberal Struve and many Agrarian League voters in Tondern-Husum, including the candidate, decided to stay at home or vote left liberal.[143]

On the eve of the war, Schleswig-Holstein left liberals were in the enviable position of having the direct support of over a quarter of the electorate in rural and urban areas, and of having some support for their aims among most of the population. Although there was always the possibility of losing two or three marginal Reichstag seats, no political observer in 1914 could have predicted the collapse in Schleswig-Holstein left liberal support during the 1920s.

---

[142] SA Hamburg NL Braband B4; A. Hall, *Scandal, Sensation and Social Democracy: The SPD Press and Wilhelmine Germany 1890–1914* (Cambridge, 1977); LA Schleswig 309, Regierungspräsidium 12582, police report of SPD meeting Schleswig, 24 Feb. 1912; LA Schleswig 309, Regierungspräsidium 8317, von Rumohr, *Landrat* Plön to Regierungspräsident Schleswig, 10 Feb. 1914.
[143] LA Schleswig 301, Oberpräsidium 59, *Apenrader Tageblatt* (28 Jan. 1912).

9

Continuity and Change : Left Liberals in Silesian Politics and Society

Public disquiet was repeatedly voiced in Breslau, the Silesian metropolis, about being isolated and ignored. There was a fear of being seen in the west of Germany as virtually a frontier town on the Russian border. Naturally, as elsewhere, this was a prelude to familiar calls for faster and more frequent train services. The rail authorities were castigated for inadequate connections to the industrial cities in the north and west, but also for failing to open up trade to the east.[1] Similarly there were calls for more tourism, industry, and commerce, with their promise of prosperity and lower local tax rates. But it was more than that. Silesia, like Baden and Schleswig-Holstein, was to be found at a geographical extremity of imperial Germany. However, apart from a minority in northern Schleswig, there was no sense of apprehension about being close to national boundaries and distant from Berlin in either Baden or Schleswig-Holstein. The inhabitants of Baden welcomed being set apart from the Prussians, and considered their constitution, political life, and moral character distinctly superior. Even their royal family was viewed as fulfilling its role better than the Hohenzollerns. Schleswig-Holstein too, though a part of Prussia since the 1860s, retained a regional tradition and a distinct form of municipal government. Not that there were strong grounds for a sense of isolation. Schleswig-Holstein was not out of the way. Neighbouring Hamburg was Germany's major port and second city. The Kiel naval dockyards and Kaiser Wilhelm Canal were visible signs of the region's association with the navy, an institution in the forefront of national consciousness.

The citizens of Kiel had the Kaiser in their midst at least once a year, but Wilhelm rarely visited Breslau. He came when it was decided

---

[1] A. Heilberg, 'Breslaus großstädtische Entwicklung unter Georg Bender', in *Festgabe des Vereins für die Geschichte Schlesiens*, 17.

to hold army manœuvres in Silesia. Yet the activities of the Kaiser playing at soldiers and with boats were not strictly comparable. Kiel Week, though resented by courtiers and officials with no taste for sea air, was an international event and an occasion when Wilhelm's enthusiasm for technology and innovation came to the fore.[2] Army manœuvres, by contrast, were sited away from centres of civilization and industry.

Part of this unease was no doubt engendered by a sense of being on the wrong side of the east/west economic divide in Imperial Germany. This was an economic issue with a clear political aspect. Georg Gothein, who began his career in the Upper Silesia mining district, was a constant critic of Conservative moves to limit transport and industry in the east to the detriment of Silesian manufacturing firms.[3] The perceived need to seek economic opportunities elsewhere had its most evident reflection in the large Silesian community in Berlin. Perhaps more important, however, was a cultural element. Although left liberals, unlike National Liberals, generally rejected Bülow's coercive anti-Polish policies as unethical and ineffective, their cultural assumptions were not dissimilar. Most disturbing to them was not being near the frontiers of the country, but a sense of being on the edge of civilization, bordered by Czechs, Poles, and, even worse, Russians. It is against this background that the 1913 centenary celebrations in Breslau must be seen. The preparations were reported extensively in the Breslau press during 1912–13, particularly in the *Breslauer Zeitung*, the newspaper closest to the municipal leadership. The form and scale of this event were consciously intended to put the city on the map, to assert cultural and economic parity with other German cities. The centrepiece was the vast, modernist Centenary Hall built to house the event. A huge historical exhibition was assembled under the patronage of the Crown Prince, and a play commissioned from Silesia's most celebrated dramatist Gerhart Hauptmann.

Silesia was, then, a somewhat neglected part of Germany. Aside from geographical remoteness, this failure to capture much attention can be attributed in part to the region's lack of dominant or outstand-

[2] Hull, *Entourage*, 35–6; L. E. Hill, *Die Weizsäcker-Papiere 1900–1932* (Berlin, 1982), 139, entry 20 June 1912.

[3] BA Koblenz, NL Gothein 12, 'Aus meiner politischer Arbeit und mein Kampf gegen den Antisemitismus', fos. 128–32; and Gothein 46, 'Binnenschiffahrt 1903–39'.

ing characteristics. Even Upper Silesia, the focus of most attention at the time and by later historians, falls into the same category. The two main reasons for it attracting attention were the area's Polish population and its heavy industry. However, the Polish 'problem' was less acute in Silesia than in Posen and West Prussia where the Poles made up more of the population. The coal and iron and steel industries of the region, though impressive on an international scale, still lagged behind those in the Ruhr and Saarland. This was true not only of output, but of attempts to control the workforce. Stumm in Saarbrücken and Krupp and others in the Ruhr attempted to influence their workers through the carrot of paternalism and the stick of strict control on and off the shop floor. They financed extensive electoral campaigns and permanent, paid, party officials in their local constituencies.[4]

By contrast, an inner circle of Upper Silesian heavy industrialists headed by general directors Hilger, Williger, and Uthemann still insisted that elections be fought in the traditional way. In what Oppeln's Regierungs-Präsident von Schwerin derided as a loose, last-minute arrangement (*lockere Notorganisation ad hoc*) candidates were selected by a small number of industrialists shortly before polling day.[5] As Schwerin commented in a survey of electioneering in Upper Silesia, the age of patriarchal instruction, no matter how well meaning, was past. This applied 'not only to the workers . . . but also to *Mittelstand* and *Beamten* circles'.[6]

Economically, Silesia as a whole was removed from the rusticality of Hinterpommern, but not markedly advanced. Annual taxable income averaged 182.2 marks per head in Regierungsbezirk Liegnitz during 1905–7, compared to 283.7 marks in Prussia as a whole.[7] Even in Breslau, large-scale enterprises like the Linke-Hoffmann railway wagon works were rare. Small firms and craftsmen formed the backbone of the local economy. Confessionally Silesia was mixed,

---

[4] See L. Schofer, *The Formation of a Modern Labor Force: Upper Silesia, 1865–1914* (Berkeley, Calif., 1975); Suval, *Electoral Politics*, 127 and 216; T. Pierenkemper, 'Entrepreneurs in Heavy Industry: Upper Silesia and the Westphalian Ruhr region, 1852–1913', *Business History Review*, 53 (1979), 65–78; and D. P. Panzera, 'Organization, Authority and Conflict in the Ruhr Coal Mining Industry: A Case Study of the Gutehoffnungshütte, 1853–1914', Ph.D., Northwestern University 1980, 436–61.

[5] AW Wrocław, Regierungspräsidium Oppeln 223, von Schwerin, report on Deutsche Wahlvereine and 'Hüttenpartei', *c*.1911.

[6] AW Wrocław, Regierungspräsidium Oppeln 223, draft report on electioneering in Upper Silesia [*c*.1911], fos. 100–1.   [7] *Niederschlesischer Bote*, 36 (2 May 1908).

though, unlike the Reich as a whole, the proportion of Catholics increased from west to east. In Lower Silesia over 80 per cent of the population was Protestant, while Upper Silesia was overwhelmingly Catholic. This variegated pattern was reflected in the politics of Silesia during the Kaiserreich. The distress and radicalism seen in *Vormärz* Silesia was no longer evident. Certainly the anti-Semite parties spawned by economic distress and political discontent in the early 1890s never got a real hold in the province, unlike in neighbouring Saxony. Again in contrast to its more industrialized and Protestant western neighbour, Silesia was not seen by government, parties, and observers as being in the forefront of the electoral battle for or against Social Democracy. Even the pamphlet against the socialist peril produced by the Silesian DKP agitator Kurt Nitschke referred largely to developments in central Germany.[8] At least in terms of Reichstag seats won, Silesian politics were unusually constant. There existed political dividing lines which corresponded fairly closely to the administrative districts Liegnitz, Breslau, and Oppeln, or put geographically, Lower, Mid-, and Upper Silesia. In each area a single political grouping persisted as a dominant force throughout the imperial period. Lower Silesia was Liberal; before the change in economic policy in the late 1870s National Liberal, afterwards left liberal. It was the policy of the National Liberal parliamentary party which had altered, not the outlook of liberals in the Liegnitz region. Mid-Silesia, at least outside the city of Breslau and the industrialized region around Waldenburg, continued to elect Conservative estate owners and notables as their representatives. Upper Silesia remained a bastion of the aristocratic, conservative wing of the Centre party.[9]

However, if the mould of politics in Silesia was not broken, both the issues and style of politics had altered considerably. The economic, social, and confessional variety of Silesia, together with the strength of local political traditions make the province an excellent testing ground of the extent and content of 'new politics'. Unlike Baden, Schleswig-Holstein, and most of Wilhelmine Germany, Silesia was a region in which all of the major parties were serious electoral contenders, though the National Liberals were somewhat under-

---

[8] C. S. [pseud.], *Die Sozialdemokratische Hochflut und ihre Eindämmung: Ein Wort an Nationalgesinnte* (Breslau, n.d. [1903]).

[9] The essays in H. Neubach, *Parteien und Politiker in Schlesien* (Dortmund, 1988) give an overview.

represented. As elsewhere in East Elbia National Liberals had largely deferred to the Conservatives in Silesia. The drive for organizational and political independence came only in the pre-war decade. At the end of 1910 National Liberals had associations in eighteen of Silesia's thirty-five constituencies and 3,407 members. By Februrary 1912 they were organized in twenty-three constituencies with 4,893 members.[10] Moreover, the changes within Silesian politics were general in character, rather than the result of the rise of a single political movement, or sudden economic or social upheaval.

The merit of analysing the path of political change where conditions to an extent militated against it applies not only to Silesia as a whole, but Lower Silesian left liberalism in particular. The Liegnitz district was unmatched as a long-term electoral base for the left liberal parties in Germany. Even the left liberal stronghold of Württemberg could not quite match Lower Silesia as a regular provider of Reichstag seats. The Württemberg Democrats briefly lost all their seats in the 1887 *Kartell* elections. In the Liegnitz district the left liberals won nine out of the ten seats in 1881 and all ten in 1884. Subsequently between seven and nine left liberals were returned, though in 1912 the number elected dropped to five. Lower Silesia had an importance in numerical terms alone: in 1903 a third of the FrVp's twenty-one Reichstag deputies were returned in Silesia. The area was even more significant as a provider of Reichstag mandates for Berlin-based leaders of the FrVp. A stable electoral base in Lower Silesia allowed left liberal deputies to concentrate on Berlin politics, paying only occasional visits to their constituencies. Those who benefited in this way included Otto Fischbeck, Julius Kopsch, Otto Hermes, and Hermann Müller-Sagan. Indeed *Vorwärts* referred sarcastically to Müller-Berlin rather than Müller-Sagan. The task facing the left liberals in Lower Silesia was, therefore, unusually defensive. Electorally, at least, they aimed to preserve things the way they were.

This electoral continuity was mirrored in the composition of the left liberal local leadership. When 200 Glogau left liberals gathered in 1907 to celebrate renewed victory over the Conservatives, their leader Dr Gabriel was fêted for an involvement in the 'movement for freedom' lasting fifty years.[11] Born in October 1830, the son of a Glogau businessmen, Immanuel Gabriel returned to his home town after

---

[10] BA Koblenz, R45 National Liberal Party I/4, fo. 36, appendix to business committee report 1912.   [11] *Niederschlesischer Anzeiger* (10 Feb. 1907).

studying in Breslau, Berlin, and Prague, to devote himself to public life and medical practice. And although age was to prevent him from taking on the physical strain of leading another Reichstag election campaign, Dr Gabriel had no intention of retirement. In November 1913 he was still a practising doctor and reached forty years unbroken membership of the Glogau Kreistag: facts recorded with customary left liberal reverence for public service and professional life.[12] A similar, if socially more exalted, left liberal veteran was the Breslau Jew Dr Wilhelm Freund, a long-serving chairman of the city council and Silesian Law Society. By 1911, his fiftieth *Dienstjubiläum*, Freund had sat on the council for forty-one years and been its chairman for the last twenty-five. On the way he had acquired the title Geheimer Justizrat and, an award perhaps closer to the heart, the honorary citizenship of Breslau.[13]

Naturally, with the passage of time, the generation of Freund and Gabriel, well into adulthood at the time of German Unification, had largely given way to those educated in the 1870s and 1880s. However, the academic anti-Semitism and illiberalism for which this period has been noted had little obvious impact on the local left liberal leadership in Lower Silesia. This was some reflection of the fact that those who had not gone near Treitschke's lecture hall, but who had made their way in the 'University of Life', were markedly more prominent amongst Silesian left liberal local leaders than in Baden or Schleswig-Holstein. Emil Peikert, leader of the left liberals in Liegnitz town and chairman of the FVP Lower Silesian Regional Association, was a successful local businessman. The leader of the party in the Löwenberg constituency was Julius Seidel, a market gardener. The factory owner Max Endemann headed the party in Sprottau. All five delegates nominated from Sagan-Sprottau for the FVP Prussian party congress in 1917 were factory owners or directors.[14]

Of course these people are hard to assess from published lists of committee members alone. However, those Lower Silesian left liberal leaders engaged in commerce were likely to have been among the more substantial and successful of local businessmen. All parties were keen to be associated with prominent and prestigious local figures. This even applied, in a modified form, to the SPD which, like the British

---

[12] *Niederschlesischer Anzeiger* (16 Nov. 1913).
[13] *Jauersches Tageblatt* (2 May 1911); *Liegnitzer Anzeiger* (26 Jan. 1909).
[14] BA Berlin, FVP 26, fo. 53, Eugen Steinmann to FVP central office, Sagan, 6 June 1917.

Labour Party, prided itself on drawing upon the skilled and able among the workforce. There was a clear parallel in the way in which bourgeois society and the labour movement looked to merit and substance as the basis for leadership. Those unsuccessful in business lacked natural authority. They were also unlikely to have been able to spare the time required for elected office in local government and associational life which went together with local party politics. Nor did the local party press hesitate to highlight shortcomings in the business and private lives of political opponents.

Respectability, then, was a prerequisite. The left liberal local leaders in Lower Silesia were unlikely to have been men of great wealth. The region was one of small and medium-sized towns supported by commerce, craft-production, and light industry. Liegnitz town had 60,000 inhabitants, but was more an administrative than an industrial centre. Only Görlitz, with a population of 85,000 and a reputation as a prospering pensionopolis, had a substantial group of very wealthy industrialists and businessmen. However, Görlitz was one of the few Lower Silesia towns where the National Liberals had significant support and there was also a Conservative association in the town. The Görlitz left liberals, led by senior engineer Sondermann, had to be satisfied with a smaller share of business support than elsewhere in Lower Silesia.

The Lower Silesian left liberal local leader active in politics and commerce was, therefore, typically a well-respected businessman, significant politically and economically in the local community, but not in the whole region, let alone the Reich. This is confirmed by the examples of August Hoffmeister, Reichstag deputy for Glogau 1898–1912, and Hugo Wenke, Landtag deputy for Hirschberg-Schönau 1910–18, whose careers on the wider political stage allow some insight into their business activities. Hoffmeister was a conscientious stove manufacturer who built up his business in Glogau. It was still a relatively small concern, with insufficient capital to adapt to the vogue for central heating. The death of Hoffmeister's son led him to retire from Berlin politics to devote more time to running the family firm.[15] Hugo Wenke could also claim to be a member of the 'productive estates' (*schaffende Stände*). Not uncommonly for a left liberal politician, he had lived in the West, spending part of his apprenticeship in precious metal-working in Britain, France, and the Low

[15] BA Koblenz, NL Gothein 14, fo. 175.

Countries.[16] The business he established in Germany must have been successful, for it allowed him to retire early and devote himself to politics. Yet his claim to know the cares of the *Mittelstand* at first hand was not entirely spurious. His hard-earned success was more than most achieved, but it probably produced an income more comfortable than spectacular.

As left liberal local leaders can be added, alongside the businessmen, the ubiquitous lawyers, teachers, and newspapermen. In Jauer, a lawyer Kunde and a newspaper proprietor Buresch led the cause together with a retired varnisher Krause. In Hirschberg, Wenke worked alongside Paul Werth, editor of the local left liberal newspaper, and Bruno Ablaß, a lawyer and Reichstag deputy for Hirschberg-Schönau. The secretary and most active member of the FVP *Verein* in Bunzlau was a teacher named Seiffert. Whether they came from commerce or professional life this second generation of left liberal leaders had the same hallmarks of stability and endurance which characterized veterans like Gabriel and Freund. Many already held leading positions locally by the early 1890s. Sondermann, Seidel, Buresch, Ablaß, and Peikert were listed as chairmen or secretaries of Lower Silesian left liberal *Vereine* in the early 1890s.[17] Virtually all were councillors and prominent in various local associations. Bruno Ablaß, a flourishing legal practice and Reichstag seat apart, was involved in most aspects of public life in Hirschberg. He was prominent in the town council, a residents' association, the local Protestant church, the theatre association, and other cultural organizations. There was an evident contrast between Ablaß and Theodor Barth who had previously represented Hirschberg-Schönau in the Reichstag. Ablaß was, in Barth's view, a political lightweight, a man without ideas who counted for nothing in Berlin. But he counted for a great deal in Hirschberg, unlike Barth who had failed to keep in touch with the constituency.[18] Similarly, August Hoffmeister had been a councillor in Glogau 'for a lifetime' and its chairman for many years. He was a member of the Kreistag and the Sagan Chamber of Trade, as well as deputy chairman of the merchants' corporation.[19]

In a party relying on individuals, such continuity could never be absolute. The *Liegnitzer Tageblatt*, reflecting the views of its owner

---

[16] *Bote aus dem Riesengebirge* (26 Sept. 1914).　　[17] *Vereinskalender* (1892, 1894/5).
[18] BA Berlin, Reichslandbund personalia 1, fos. 111–20 (Bruno Ablaß); 21, fos. 48–184 (Theodor Barth).　　[19] *Breslauer Zeitung*, 690 (1 Oct. 1912).

Kommerzienrat Krumbhaar, shifted from an overtly left liberal stance to an outwardly non-party, but essentially National Liberal position. Justizrat Meyer in Goldberg turned his back on the Liberals to found an 'Association of the Right-wing Parties' in the district.[20] But these were limited exceptions. The way in which local leadership was transferred harmoniously and effectively from one generation to another was exemplified in Liegnitz. For most of the imperial period the leading figure was August Jungser, another Liberal veteran with over forty years of political service. After the turn of the century the chair of the constituency electoral association and the main organizational burden was passed on to Emil Peikert, with Jungser assuming the role of elder statesman. This process was repeated at the end of 1918, with Peikert handing over to his understudy, newspaper owner Reinhold Wagner, and assuming a less strenuous political role. The left liberal local leadership in Lower Silesia retained its familiar form almost regardless of national party splits and reunifications and the collapse of the Kaiserreich in 1918.

Of course the question must be raised whether this continuity was that of an unrepresentative clique, or one which reflected left liberal supporters as a whole. It is true that only the more substantial *Vereine* tended to carry out the annual committee elections prescribed by their statutes. And such elections often had a formal character, with retiring committee members being re-elected *en bloc*. However, there are convincing indications that these leaders retained the genuine confidence of Liberal supporters. Sitting town councillors were reselected by citizens' associations (*Bürgervereine*) and generally gained more votes than new candidates standing on the same slate in local elections. Above all, there were no signs of dissent within left liberal ranks during Reichstag campaigns, either in public meetings or voting returns.

These returns are, once again, the best general guide to the pattern of left liberal support. The map of electoral support corresponds, in its salient features, with that found in Schleswig-Holstein. Most urban inhabitants voted left liberal or SPD even in the smaller towns. As Table 9.1 indicates, this applied also in 1907, when the Conservatives hoped to harness national feeling to bring electoral success in urban areas. Of the above towns only in mainly Catholic Liebenthal did the FrVp and SPD fail to secure at least 70 per cent of the poll. In run-off elections between left liberals and Conservatives

[20] *Schlesische Freikonservative Parteikorrespondenz*, 16 (15 May 1914).

Table 9.1. *Voting figures in some Lower Silesian towns:*
main round of voting, Reichstag elections 1907

Town	FrVp	SPD	Conservative	Centre
Bunzlau	917	1,116	416	178
Lüben	423	330	337	13
Sagan	986	996	381	224
Sprottau	668	295	185	135
Löwenberg	556	214	212	126
Greiffenberg	368	179	44	42
Lähn	131	25	42	21
Liebenthal	34	21	21	192

Source: *Neuer Görlitzer Anzeiger* (29 Jan. 1907).

urban voters often provided a decisive margin even where they only made up a minority of the electorate. This was the case, for example, in Glogau. In 1907 the left liberals held the seat against the Conservatives by 7,126 votes to 6,384. Within the town of Glogau the left liberal candidate received 2,713 votes, his Conservative opponent only 938.[21]

The impact of the *Hottentottenwahlen* can be gauged by comparing the election results for 1903 and 1907 in Görlitz-Lauban, the most industrialized constituency. SPD voting figures followed the national trend. Most supporters remained loyal, but some who had voted SPD in protest against the 1902 tariff increases were swayed by nationalist rhetoric into the left liberal camp. SPD decline was most evident in the two county districts (*Landkreise*) where the party's vote fell by a tenth. By contrast, SPD support rose slightly between 1903 and 1907 in both Görlitz and Lauban towns. But this increase was more apparent than real. When the continuing influx of younger factory workers, the group most strongly committed to the SPD, is taken into account, probably a similar proportion of urban voters deserted the party in 1907. In Görlitz the SPD vote rose by only 400, while left liberals attracted over 2,000 new voters and former SPD supporters in addition to a thousand votes from the right. Some of the collapse of the Conservative vote in Görlitz town reflected a change in National Liberal allegiance. The local party had endorsed the Conservative candidate in 1903 and the left liberal in 1907. But this did not account for the whole decline. The fate of the Conservative Maier, the leader

[21] *Niederschlesischer Anzeiger* (7 Feb. 1907).

Table 9.2. *Votes received in main round of voting in Görlitz-Lauban: Reichstag election 1907 (1903)*

	FrVp	SPD	DKP	Centre
Stadt Görlitz	6,869 (3,622)	7,459 (7,027)	1,194 (2,829)	397 (421)
Stadt Lauban	1,443 (686)	995 (960)	172 (474)	108 (116)
Land Görlitz	4,127 (2,713)	3,468 (3,854)	2,988 (2,922)	86 (106)
Land Lauban	3,915 (2,535)	4,378 (4,730)	2,687 (2,922)	427 (425)

Source: *Neuer Görlitzer Anzeiger* (27 Jan. 1907).

of the *Mittelstandsvereinigung* in Schweidnitz, was fairly typical of right-wing *Mittelstand* candidates in the pre-war decade. Allotted unfavourable constituencies for the most part, they tended to render the seats even less winnable. This was the case even before the 1909 finance reform. Even if all the 1,200 Conservative votes in Görlitz came from the *Mittelstand*, this represented the support of only a minority. In fact it was likely that a significant part of Conservative support was recruited from retired officers and officials, for both groups were represented in the local Conservative committee, and Görlitz was well-known as a 'pensionopolis'.

The Conservative vote held up better in the countryside, where the party had the continuing support of the Agrarian League, but still declined compared to the left liberals. Moreover, it is an open question whether the League members as a whole shared the political views of the League's local leaders—invariably members of the local Conservative hierarchy.[22] Taking the rural areas of Lower Silesia as a whole, the Conservatives won more votes than the other parties. It is likely, however, that a part of the League membership, though in favour of cheap fertilizer and high crop prices, was unwilling to accept the political tutelage of Hahn and Oertel. Some 45 per cent of the working population in the constituency outside Görlitz town was employed in agriculture, but the Conservative and Centre share of the vote in the area was only 26 per cent in 1907 and 23 per cent in 1912.[23] Local left liberal newspapers, for instance, attracted a significant number of subscribers in the countryside despite the efforts of the Conservative rural hierarchy. This was particularly the case with

[22] For the intertwined relations of the DKP, Agrarian League, and large landowners in Silesia, see Jozef Pucilowski, 'Niemiecko-Konserwatywna (Deutschkonservative Partei) Na Slasku w Latach 1890–1914', Ph.D., Wrocław 1977; and BA Berlin, Nachlaß Roesicke 42, fos. 6–10, discussions for the 1898 Reichstag elections in Lower Silesia.

[23] Nöcker, *Der Preußische Reichstagswähler*, 305; *Neuer Görlitzer Anzeiger* (27 Jan. 1907).

the *Bote aus dem Riesengebirge* and, its title notwithstanding, the *Jauersches Stadtblatt*. The individual polling districts within the rural districts of Görlitz and Lauban were very varied, revealing Liberal and Conservative strongholds, and the SPD was the strongest party in some populous districts. This reflected the fact that the area was no longer simply agricultural. According to the 1907 occupational census, 38 per cent of the workforce was employed in industry and craft-production in Görlitz-Lauban excluding Görlitz town, and 16 per cent in the tertiary sector.[24] Industries had been established outside the main towns. Even in villages without factories a part of the population might travel on foot or by rail to work in the local town. Others supplied milk, vegetables, and meat for the growing numbers not working on the land. It was this economic change which underlay the fact that both left liberals and SPD outpolled the Conservatives in the *Landkreise* of Görlitz and Lauban.

The sort of people who formed the backbone of the left liberal electorate were reflected in an election address from 1907 in support of the left liberal candidate Otto Mugdan signed by over 400 voters. Property owners were well represented. They were mainly urban, though the list includes some smaller landowners—*Bauerngutsbesitzer* and *Gärtner*. The list also featured teachers and members of the free professions in the towns of Görlitz and Lauban. There were numerous master craftsmen—carpenters, tailors, and the like—together with retailers and salesmen. A variety of artisans were listed, but workers did not appear.[25] Like the lack of state employees, their absence is partly explained by the threat of intimidation. Left liberal workers were a minority, but their numbers were not so small as to be negligible. The Hirsch-Dunker trade unions were established in the area, and left liberal workers were reportedly well represented in the 1,000-strong audience at the election meeting held by Mugdan in Lauban on 4 January 1907.[26] The left liberal electorate was therefore mainly, but not exclusively, urban. With the exception of elementary-school teachers, supporters came more from the private than the public sector. They covered a considerable social span, from the educated and prosperous to craftsmen and skilled workers. The

---

[24] Nöcker, *Der Preußische Reichstagswähler*, 305.

[25] *Neuer Görlitzer Anzeiger* (24 Jan. 1907).

[26] *Neuer Görlitzer Anzeiger* (6 Jan. 1907). By 1913 the Hirsch-Dunker unions had 14 *Ortsverbände* and 135 *Vereine* in Regierungsbezirk Liegnitz. *Bote aus dem Riesengebirge* (26 Aug. 1913).

former made up the local leadership, but it was the latter who supplied the bulk of left liberal voters. In Görlitz-Lauban the left liberals were, electorally, a party of the *Mittelstand*. The same applied to Liegnitz, where right-wing attempts to persuade the towns' artisans to join the *Mittelstandsvereinigung* had attracted only nineteen men by 1907.[27]

As a seat which the SPD had the potential to gain, particularly if the non-socialist vote was split, it might have been expected that the Imperial League Against Social Democracy would play a substantial role in Görlitz-Lauban. Yet it was the political parties and the party press which bore the brunt of the campaign. The League did hold a public meeting in Görlitz before the run-off election. However the speaker Becker, whose short-lived electoral success in the SPD citadel of Offenbach allowed him to pose as a professional 'socialist-slayer' (*Sozialistentöter*), said nothing new or significant. Left liberal victory over the SPD was virtually assured when the two candidates had finished level after the first round of voting. This was confirmed not by Becker's fiery rhetoric, but by the simple statement by Oberst a.D. Reimer, the local Conservative leader, that there could be no doubt that all national-minded voters would support a left liberal against a Social Democrat in a run-off election.[28]

Indeed, the Görlitz League meeting appeared more significant in the context of 1912 than 1907. In 1912 the electoral equation for the second round of voting in Görlitz reverted to that of 1903. The SPD held a considerable lead over the left liberals and could only be denied victory if almost all the non-socialist electorate united against him. But the change in attitudes was even greater. Reimer and the Görlitz Conservative leadership urged upon their supporters what they had declared in 1907 to be unthinkable: abstention in a left liberal–SPD run-off election. As elsewhere, only a minority of DKP voters followed this instruction, but that minority was sufficient to secure SPD victory. This represented, as was seen nationally, a significant shift of political alignment. The strength of this shift was underlined in Görlitz, both by the character of the left liberal candidate Otto Mugdan, one of the most nationalistic and anti-socialist of the party's parliamentarians, and by the markedly different outcome in 1912 compared to 1903.

Broadening the analysis to include the other Lower Silesian constituencies, a similar pattern of left liberal support is revealed.

---

[27] *Breslauer Zeitung*, 25 (11 Jan. 1907).   [28] *Neuer Görlitzer Anzeiger* (3 Feb. 1907).

Crucial to left liberal electoral success was, in each case, a hold on the Protestant urban lower middle-class electorate. In most towns this, together with support from the more prosperous skilled workers, was sufficient to provide majorities in Reichstag elections and pre-eminence in local political life. Whilst the overall framework held good, local circumstances also had an impact. In the Liegnitz-Goldberg-Haynau constituency, for instance, politics in the latter two towns reflected differences in the local economy. In Haynau, a town with an expanding manufacturing industry, left liberals and Social Democrats competed for votes, with the latter capturing the council seats for the third class in the pre-war decade. This mirrored the situation in Görlitz where, despite a united list of non-socialist candidates, the Social Democrats won the third-class elections with an increasingly unassailable majority.[29] By contrast, Goldberg saw little industrial expansion. Here press and public life had a more restrained tone, and the right rather than the SPD was the main challenge to the left liberals, particularly in Landtag elections.

Social and economic structure was fundamental to voting patterns. However, political tradition and the action of prominent individuals were also of significance. Both help to explain the particular strength of the left liberals in Hirschberg. The town and its surroundings had a long-standing reputation as a stronghold of left liberalism. It was a reputation that the left liberal newspaper in Hirschberg, *Der Bote aus dem Riesengebirge*, nurtured and exemplified. It was a tradition subtly modified, but still flourishing. When the paper celebrated its centenary in 1912 it had reached a circulation of 15,000—an impressive figure for a paper based in a town of 20,000 people.[30] Allied to a strong tradition, left liberalism was assisted by an active and influential local leadership. Hirschberg was a case where tradition and activism reinforced each other. However, active individuals could also counteract tradition. The wealthy businessman privy councillor Beuchelt provides an example of how a single individual could influence party politics in the locality. His Conservative candidature and active espousal of the cause secured a much higher vote for his party in his base of Grünberg in 1907 and 1912 than in Neusalz,

[29] W. Polte, 'Die Wahlrechtskämpfe 1906/10 in Görlitz', *Beiträge zur Geschichte der Görlitzer Arbeiterbewegung*, iii (Görlitz, 1968); *Bote aus dem Riesengebirge* (5 Nov. 1913).
[30] *Bote aus dem Riesengebirge* (7 May 1913).

Freystadt, and Beuthen, the other towns in the Grünberg-Freystadt constituency.[31]

If a Conservative industrialist could produce an untypical result in an urban district, the same was true of Liberal landowners in rural parts of Lower Silesia. Gerhart Hauptmann elected the first-class *Wahlmänner* in Agnetendorf. The same was true for Liberal owner of Schloß Jeschendorf, Kreis Liegnitz, whose earnings from Breslau pushed neighbouring Conservative estate owners into the second class.[32] There were also rural small towns and villages, like Antoniwald, where the farmers maintained a proud liberal tradition. This was the place, Julius Kopsch reminded a local audience of 150 on a festival Sunday in March 1914, where he had given his first speech in the Löwenberg constituency twenty-one years before. As the election returns for 1912 confirm, it had remained a Liberal stronghold throughout the period.[33] This tradition was strongest in the Riesengebirge region where the hilly terrain favoured independent-minded livestock farmers. In the Landtag elections the left liberals were only able to achieve significant success outside the towns in the Hirschberg-Schönau constituency. Here in 1908 and 1913, although the Liberals secured their margin of victory in Hirschberg town, success was also dependent on *Wahlmänner* elected in rural districts.

The only other Lower Silesian Landtag seats actively contested by the Liberals in 1913 were those where urban *Wahlmänner* were sufficiently numerous to allow success: Görlitz-Lauban and Liegnitz-Goldberg-Haynau. In the latter constituency, the numbers of *Wahlmänner* elected were: 272 Liberal, 272 Conservative, and sixty-two Social Democrat. Of these, 204 Liberals, seventeen

Table 9.3. Wahlmänner *elected in Hirschberg-Schönau: Landtag elections 1908 and 1913*

	Liberal		Conservative		SPD	
	1908	1913	1908	1913	1908	1913
Hirschberg town	54	66	23	10	—	6
Whole constituency	197	236	189	150	5	29

Source: *Bote aus dem Riesengebirge*, 113 (17 May 1913). Liberal figures refer to left liberal candidates in 1908 and to joint left liberal and National Liberal candidates in 1913.

---

[31] See the returns for individual polling districts in *Grünberger Wochenblatt* (16 Jan. 1912).
[32] BA Koblenz, NL Gothein, 36, fo. 34, V. Z [surname illegible] to Gothein, 14 Apr. 1913).   [33] *Bote aus dem Riesengebirge* (27 Mar. 1914); *Der Greif* (23 Jan. 1912).

Conservatives, and forty-four Social Democrats were returned in Liegnitz town.[34] However, the equal franchise and, even more, the secret ballot enabled the FVP and SPD to play a more significant, if still a minority role in Reichstag elections in the rural parts of Lower Silesia. As in Görlitz-Lauban, results were extremely varied. Nevertheless, the Conservatives clearly dominated the rural hierarchy. Just as town councils, *Bürgervereine*, and *Gewerbevereine* had a Liberal complexion, so *Amtsmänner*, *Kreistage*, and *Landwirtschaftliche Kreisvereine* were overwhelmingly Conservative in make-up.[35] In Kauffung, for example, the fifty-member strong Liberal *Bürgerverein* founded in December 1912 was considered 'a sort of haven for the artisan, small businessman and the Liberal peasant, for here certainly almost all of those who set the tone and exercise influence are arch Conservatives'.[36] Formal Liberal local associations were rare in rural areas, but to be faced with a phalanx of Conservative landowners and officials was commonplace in Lower Silesian rural society. There were polling districts, usually those based on a single estate (*Gutsbezirk*), where every vote was cast for the Conservative candidate. An element of 'electoral terrorism' was obvious. Heilberg found many peasants preferred to sit by the walls at left liberal meetings rather than in front of the speaker where they could be seen by the passing rural policeman or *Amtsvorsteher*.[37] But deference and other forms of social control were just as important to Conservative rural support. The Silesian DKP was at its strongest in districts with virtually no political activity: where people voted Conservative with an unthinking acceptance, and DKP local leaders exercised silent social dominance. The party was less successful where it felt compelled to badger voters for support.[38]

Outside Lower Silesia the left liberals were of most significance in Breslau. As in most Lower Silesian towns, left liberals played a leading role in local government, the press, and associational life. However, the provincial capital was a special case. Public life in a city of half a million people was on an understandably greater scale. Here all six major political parties—DKP, Free Conservatives, Centre, National Liberals, FVP, and SPD—were able to play a significant role. There were other towns in Mid-Silesia, for example Striegau, where

---

[34] *Bote aus dem Riesengebirge* (22 May 1913).
[35] Pucilowski, 'Niemiecko-Konserwatywna', *passim*.
[36] *Bote aus dem Riesengebirge* (8 May 1913).   [37] Heilberg, 'Erinnerungen', 294.
[38] See Pucilowski, 'Niemiecko-Konserwatywna', 155–7.

the left liberals made up majorities in the council chamber. However, in Reichstag and Landtag elections it was rural areas, particularly the large estates, which held sway. Whether politically well-known, like Heydebrand, Kardorff, Richthofen, and Zedlitz, or content to leave active politics to other Conservatives, large estate-owning families continued to find success at the polls. The scope for left liberals in Upper Silesia, with its predominately Catholic and Polish population, was just as limited. Nevertheless, even here the same sort of people who formed the backbone of left liberal leadership throughout Germany were prepared to engage in political activity, despite the unfavourable circumstances. The Catholic press described the audience of the public meeting on the eve of the FVP Upper Silesian Party Conference held in Zabrze in 1910 as typical of any left liberal public meeting: 'teachers with their wives, middle ranking administrative officials from the courts, mines, and local government, radically minded businessmen, many people there out of curiosity, and a few Social Democrats'.[39] Beneath the condescension, this was a reasonably accurate social profile of those interested in left liberal politics. However, as the list of the members of FrVp Upper Silesian Regional Committee in 1907 confirms (see Table 9.4), the report underestimated the role of those from the free professions and exaggerated the number of officials.

Although they lacked mass support, observers claimed Upper Silesian left liberals exercised more influence than numbers alone suggested. According to von Schwerin, apart from the Centre, Poles, and Social Democrats, 'only left liberal, mostly Jewish circles, were

Table 9.4. *Left liberal Upper Silesian regional committee members, September 1907*

District	Member	Replacement
Kattowitz	Lawyer Reiche	Editor Losch
Gleiwitz	Legal Councillor Pohl	Teacher Galinski
Königshütte	Dr Glowalla	Foreman Hausmann
Beuthen	Dr Bloch	Lawyer Faerber
Ratibor	Foreman Noak	Dr Eisner
Zabrze	Legal Councillor Meller	Teacher Lindner
Tichau/Rybnik	Teacher Giehmann	Factory Owner Dr Haase

Source: *Liegnitzer Anzeiger*, 207 (4. Sept. 1907).

[39] *Der Greif* (5 Nov. 1910).

united politically, and therefore played a much greater role than was their due'. Alexander Pohlmann, the left liberal Bürgermeister of Kattowitz, shared the same analysis of party politics in Upper Silesia. The left liberals were active and well-organized compared to Conservatives and National Liberals, but their potential base of support was considerably narrower.[40] In towns like Kattowitz and Ratibor, the prevailing political current amongst the propertied and educated middle class was National Liberal/Free Conservative rather than the left liberalism found in Lower Silesia and Breslau. But lethargy and ineffective organization prevented these groups, often loosely grouped together in German Electoral Associations (*Deutsche Wahlvereine*), from mobilizing their potential support.[41] Von Schwerin's assessment of Upper Silesian left liberals was coloured both by 'cultural' anti-Semitism, and a need to justify his attempts to popularize and strengthen the German Electoral Associations. He therefore tended to overstate the effectiveness of Upper Silesian left liberal organizations. In Zabrze left liberal meetings only attracted small audiences.[42] In Gleiwitz the left liberals were ably led and, bolstered by the Jewish community, had some eighty of the 155 first-class municipal electors as signed-up party members by 1913.[43] Even so, their chairman, Justizrat Pohl, had to look to Lower Silesia for a realistic opportunity of a Landtag or Reichstag seat, briefly representing Liegnitz in the Reichstag before 1903, and returned by the same constituency to the Prussian Landtag in 1913 after Fischbeck had decided to concentrate on the Reichstag.

Silesia, then, displayed almost the full range of left liberal substructure to be found in Wilhelmine Germany. Left liberalism in Lower Silesia resembled that in Württemberg: long-established, fostered by tradition and environment. It was the natural political allegiance, shared both by enthusiasts and those without a strong class, religious, or ideological commitment to an alternative political party. By contrast, in much of Middle and Upper Silesian the party more closely resembled left liberalism in the Rhineland or the rural interior of provinces like Pomerania and West Prussia: a party with little sup-

---

[40] AW Wrocław, Regierungspräsidium Oppeln 223, von Schwerin to Under State Secretary Holtz, 1 Feb. 1912 (copy); Pohlmann, report on 1913 Landtag elections in Kattowitz.   [41] Ibid.

[42] See the police reports in AW Wrocław, Regierungspräsidium Oppeln 227.

[43] AW Wrocław, Regierungspräsidium Oppeln 223, *Oberschlesischer Anzeiger* (29 Nov. 1913).

port outside a small, dedicated core, working in unfavourable circumstances and without an established local tradition. Largely lacking in left liberal ranks in Silesia, however, were the lower and middle-ranking white-collar workers who formed an important part of the left liberal electorate nationally. Unlike similar organizations in much of Germany, the *Bund der Festbesoldeten* (League of Fixed Salary Employees) in Breslau endorsed Conservative/Catholic rather than left liberal candidates.[44] And the Breslau organization declined to follow the lead of branches in Berlin and elsewhere by joining the Hansa-Bund.[45] Either out of conviction or self-interest, government officials were usually Conservative or Free Conservative in political outlook. They were given markedly less political leeway in Silesia, especially Upper Silesia, than in western provinces. In open elections the authorities combed through voting returns and lists of state employees. Anyone who had voted for another candidate or abstained was likely to be disciplined. Action was taken, for example, against Kattowitz postal officials in 1908 for supporting a National Liberal candidate, an incomprehensible episode to much of Germany which caused heated exchanges in press and parliament. In the Oppeln district the letter carrier as well as the postal director had to support the approved candidate.

Nevertheless, the leaders of the left liberals in the localities had a familiar look to them. Throughout Silesia, as in Germany as a whole, lawyers, doctors, teachers, businessmen, and newspapermen were to be found running left liberal local politics. Equally, the leaders of the other political parties in Silesia reflected the national pattern. Most Conservative leaders were landowners, active or retired government officials, or retired officers. Leading National Liberals often held senior positions in state institutions—secondary schools, prisons, archives—or were well-heeled businessmen.[46] In the Breslau SPD paid officials—journalists, union organizers, and party secretaries—came to the fore. Such a pattern was familiar, and had not changed significantly over time. While no party in Silesia had as many long-serving veterans as the left liberals, political longevity was a

---

[44] *Breslauer Zeitung*, 735 (18 Oct. 1912), 'Die "unpolitischen" Festbesoldeten', and 801 (13 Nov. 1912).   [45] *Schlesische Morgen-Zeitung* (5 Jan. 1914).
[46] See the typical composition of the National Liberal committee in Hirschberg-Schönau: prison director Butter, *Oberlehrer* Dr Dreesbach, factory owner Baeumer, *Landgerichtsrat* Wieter, *Rechnungsrat* Winderlin and *Amtsvorsteher* Dittrich. *Bote aus dem Riesengebirge* (30 Nov. 1913).

hallmark across the political spectrum. Justizrat Felix Porsch, the Centre party leader, entered the Reichstag in 1881 and the Breslau City Council in 1884. He was still playing a leading role in German and Silesian politics over forty years later.[47] Paul Löbe, Reichstag President for much of the Weimar Republic, had already established himself as the leading Silesian Social Democrat in the pre-war decade. On the whole, the sort of people who led the political parties in Silesia in 1918 were similar to those in charge in the 1880s.

But this continuity, both amongst political leaders and in voting behaviour, tended to mask considerable alterations in both style and content of Silesian politics. Political leaders maintained their position only by continually responding to shifts in opinion and to new campaigning methods. Similarly, voting behaviour was not set in concrete. Although tradition was important, loyalty had continually to be maintained by present conduct and future promises. Change in Silesian politics tended to be unseen because it occurred at different times and with uneven force. Political mobilization in Breslau, parts of Lower Silesia, and the Upper Silesian heavy industrial towns began early— by the 1880s—and took on a high profile. In much of rural Mid- and Upper Silesia it occurred substantially later—often after the turn of the century and sometimes just before 1914—and attracted less outside public attention. This change in the mode of politics tended not to be accompanied by dramatic shifts in party allegiance, but it was real none the less. The retirement of the Free Conservative veteran Wilhelm Kardorff epitomized the shift in Silesian politics, even in rural Mid-Silesia, from the respectful to the rumbustious. Declaring a reluctance to stand again, Kardorff expected a show of gratitude for past service from the selection meeting and efforts to make him reconsider. What followed was a barrage of popular grievances 'and [Kardorff] had now to experience that not the slightest attempt was made' to put him up again but that 'one tactlessness followed another'.[48]

In these populist times Silesian left liberals could not simply rest on past achievement. Preserving the party's position required constant

---

[47] See A. H. Leugers-Scherzberg, *Felix Porsch 1853–1930: Politik für katholische Interessen in Kaiserreich und Republik* (Mainz, 1990); and AA Wrocław, NL Porsch, newspaper cuttings celebrating Porsch's seventieth birthday in 1923.

[48] See the account of the right-wing selection meeting at Oels, 18 Dec. 1906 in S. von Kardorff, *Wilhelm von Kardorff: Ein nationaler Parlamentarier im Zeitalter Bismarcks und Wilhelm II, 1828–1907* (Berlin, 1936), 365.

adjustment to new political and organizational challenges. The Silesian FVP had to reconcile left liberal politics both to traditional attitudes and modern social and economic pressures. East Elbian left liberals were always careful to adapt their stance to the more conservative set of social attitudes which prevailed. As a left liberal editor in West Prussia warned Lothar Schücking, there was no place in the semi-rural east for radical social liberalism: 'People in the east differ very fundamentally from those in the west: . . . the most solid left liberal belongs to the veterans' association; you must not use the word "democratic" here (it would instantly be taken as "Social Democratic"); equally, you mustn't talk about female equality etc.'[49] Such comments applied particularly to rural and small-town districts. The response of FVP speakers in the Schweidnitz-Striegau constituency to an outbreak of foot and mouth in autumn 1913 exemplified the left liberals' skilful appeal to village sentiment. Initial sympathy was secured by a heart-rending account of the shattering effect of the disease on rural harmony. Only then came the attack on the Conservative rural establishment: no one up there cared; the Agrarian League did nothing; and while the authorities ordered the blanket slaughter of peasant animals, livestock on aristocratic estates were being spared.[50] Left liberal petitions and protest meetings could not stop the spread of disease. But they presented a show of concern which brought additional political support.

As in much of rural Germany, left liberal candidates like Fischbeck, Kopsch, Liszt, and Achilles assured peasant voters that they supported existing grain tariffs. But this, as the warnings of the rural agitator Wedermann underlined, was an unfavourable issue for left liberals.[51] Conservatives simply outbid them by demanding even higher duties on grain and the introduction of vegetable tariffs, the latter aimed specifically at the large number of vegetable growers in the Liegnitz district.[52] More politically advantageous were left liberal charges that the right only looked after the rich and powerful. FVP newspapers eagerly recounted the arrogant refusal of large landowners to pay higher charges to saddlers and blacksmiths although

---

[49] NL Lothar Schücking, F. Fricke, editor *Neumärkische Zeitung* Landsberg a. W., to Lothar Schücking, 17 May 1909.
[50] 'Mitteilungen für Landwirtschaft und Haus', supplement to *Bote aus dem Riesengebirge* (29 Nov. 1913).
[51] UB Mårburg, NL Rade, A. Wedermann to Martin Rade, 31 Jan. 1912.
[52] BA Berlin, FVP 27, fo. 41, party secretary report for Lower Silesia, Dec. 1913.

Blue–Black economics had increased production and living costs.[53] Left liberals accused the right of hypocrisy over its agitation against department stores. They claimed that the Agrarian League's agricultural wholesale branch in Liegnitz was far more damaging to the *Mittelstand*.[54] Left liberals deliberately likened Conservatives to Social Democrats as people threatening one boycott after another, while only they supported freedom of trade. The DKP blamed peasant grievances on Jewish big business, but left liberals directed them against Conservative estate owners:

Have the 123 large landowners who form the bulk of the Conservative Party in the Landtag ever done anything for a stronger peasant representation in the Kreistage; ever anything to alter the *Auenrecht*, for a fair division of road-building costs, for cheaper fodder, for a radical and sweeping settlement of peasants on the vast acres of the East Elbian *latifundia*, or for other just demands of German peasants?[55]

The radicalization of rural opinion was insufficient to produce a swing in terms of seats. Conservative candidates either had too large majorities, or were kept in by borrowed Centre party votes. (The Centre's agreement to give their support to Conservative candidates in the first round was especially important in Lower Silesia. Had they fielded a separate candidate in Sagan-Sprottau, Grünberg-Freystadt, or Bunzlau-Lüben, then the FVP rather than a right-wing candidate would have entered the run-off against the SPD.) But it brought a significant change in way rural elections were fought. In Lower Silesia the already intense level of political activity in towns and large villages spread to all parts of constituencies. Bürgermeister Achilles, the FVP candidate in Sagan-Sprottau, spoke in 140 places large and small between November 1910 and polling day.[56] Heilberg found himself carted hours from the nearest railway to address a remote Lower Silesian hamlet.[57] The previously politically dormant reaches of Mid- and Upper Silesia saw unprecedented campaigning in 1911–12. The tradition of barely contested elections and inactive parliamentarians was ended. Of the half a dozen deputies elected in 1893 but yet to make a Reichstag speech eighteen years later, half were right-wing Silesians.[58] After 1912 only the DKP deputy Rothger in Ohlau

[53] See e.g. *Bote aus dem Riesengebirge* (22 Aug. 1913).
[54] BA Berlin, Reichslandbund 56, fo. 59, personalia Paul Büchtemann; *Landeshuter Stadtblatt* (6 Jan. 1912); and *Bote aus dem Riesengebirge* (22 Aug. 1913).
[55] *Bote aus dem Riesengebirge* (19 Apr. 1913).   [56] *Saganer Tageblatt* (14 Jan. 1912).
[57] Heilberg, 'Erinnerungen', 294.   [58] *Jauersches Stadtblatt* (12 Apr. 1911).

remained as reminder of the past when voters were largely indifferent to politics and the parliamentary performance of their elected representative.[59] Nothing showed the increased scale of rural electoral activity better than the campaign in Militsch, Heydebrand's Mid-Silesian constituency. Accustomed to being returned virtually unopposed, the DKP leader was taken aback by the vigorous campaign of his National Liberal opponent Schmidthals. A local independent farmer ideally placed to exploit peasant and *Mittelstand* resentment towards the rural élite and finance reform, Schmidthals overturned the traditional deferential pattern of politics by making a popular appeal directly to the voters in a succession of public meetings. Schmidthals's campaign generated an enthusiastic response which was deeply unnerving to the Conservative leader. A leaked telegram to Berlin urgently requesting help revealed his discomfiture to the public. Heydebrand was forced to speak daily or even twice a day in person, something 'he previously considered unnecessary'.[60] Opponents perhaps exaggerated when they put the cost of his uneasy victory at 150,000 marks.[61] But there was no doubt that by 1912 expensive and intensive campaigning had displaced political lethargy in all but the most isolated parts of rural Silesia.

The FVP–National Liberal 1912 electoral pact in Silesia had left National Liberal and Bauernbund candidates to fight the majority of seats in Mid- and Upper Silesia, while the FVP contested all ten Lower Silesian constituencies. But left liberals gave considerable support to candidates like Schmidthals, particularly through the press. More importantly, Schmidthals symbolized the way National Liberals in East Elbia were not just trying to win seats which they had previously left to the Conservatives unchallenged, but were doing so with the same methods and policies as the left liberals. As a result it was no surprise when Schmidthals was invited to address FVP meeting in Lower Silesia in 1913 and became a leading member of the Silesian DDP in 1918.

While left liberals took the lead in using popular ferment to break down the pattern of deferential Conservatism in the countryside, in urban districts they were the potential victims of popular mobilization. Especially after the electoral reverses of 1912, Silesian

---

[59] The fact that only six of the thirty-six deputies who had not spoken during the previous parliamentary session were re-elected in 1912 underlined the popular demand for active Reichstag deputies. *Breslauer Zeitung*, 402 (11 June 1912).

[60] *Breslauer Zeitung*, 21 (10 Jan. 1912).   [61] *Landeshuter Stadtblatt* (6 Feb. 1912).

Conservatives sought to shore up their eroding rural base by attracting more support in urban districts. Free Conservative leaders put aside traditional antipathy towards formal organization. In 1913 the provincial association appointed a paid official based in Breslau, Dr Leonhard Müller, and started a regular party periodical, the *Schlesische Freikonservative Parteikorrespondenz*, which appeared from October 1913 to August 1918. The acceptance of popular politics was neither as wholehearted or successful as the Breslau Free Conservative activist Ernst Deetjen had hoped.[62] But during 1913–14 the party succeeded in establishing local parties in Schweidnitz, Liegnitz, and Ratibor, and in raising party membership to almost 500 in Breslau.[63] The more powerful DKP showed an equal desire to win over left liberal urban *Mittelstand* support. Grützner, deputy chairman of the DKP in Silesia, urged the 1914 provincial conference 'to seek yet more contact with industry and artisans . . . we must advance on the towns!'[64] When the DKP established six party secretaries in the province during 1912–14 it based most of them in Lower Silesian towns rather than rural Mid-Silesia.[65]

The pre-war challenge to the left liberals from the left was not associated with such fluctuations. The SPD had always been active mainly in urban districts, and its organizational growth spread across a longer period. Breslau SPD membership, for example, had risen from 891 in 1900 to 10,317 in 1913/14, the steepest rise coming in 1904–6 when membership climbed from 2,260 to 7,437.[66] But the steady progress of the labour movement posed even more problems for the left liberals. As in other traditional left liberal strongholds, it was the SPD which presented the more serious threat to the FVP. As we saw in Görlitz, the SPD had established itself as the strongest party in Reichstag elections and a significant force in municipal contests. In Liegnitz too the party came to dominate third-class council seats. By 1912 the SPD reached the run-offs in seven of the ten Lower Silesian Reichstag constituencies. Left liberals recognized the planned establishment of a

---

[62] Compare the aspirations of Deetjen, *Freikonservativ*, with his actual experience in Silesia recounted in *Schlesische Freikonservative Parteikorrespondenz*, 5 (28 Nov. 1913).

[63] *Schlesische Freikonservative Parteikorrespondenz* (19 and 28 Feb. and 31 May 1914).

[64] *Schlesische Morgen-Zeitung* (21 Mar. 1914).

[65] *Schlesische Morgen-Zeitung* (18 Jan. 1914); BA Berlin, FVP 27, fo. 44, party secretary report for Lower Silesia, Mar. 1912.

[66] *Volkswacht* (17 and 18 Apr. 1914). Figures for 1913/14 exclude around 1,400 members lost by the creation of a separate Breslau Land organization, and include 2,186 women who had joined since 1908.

Liegnitz SPD newspaper in October 1912 as a measure of how far the SPD had advanced in Lower Silesia. More importantly, it gave the labour movement a powerful instrument to make further gains at the FVP's expense.[67] Even though economic and social development proceeded at a slower pace in Silesia than in western Germany, it created a dichotomy for left liberal politics. The attitude of left liberals towards modernization and industrialization was singularly positive. As Hartwig Seibt, a left liberal councillor, typically remarked: 'where industry is, there is life, there is trade. And that is what we want coming to Liegnitz.'[68] But the resulting economic pressures could undermine left liberalism's social base. Paul Löbe's upbringing in a large impoverished Liegnitz family typified the social conditions conducive to growing SPD support.[69] Although there was no general fall in real wage rates, insecurity and fluctuations caused by economic change and rationalization created additional burdens. And dismal, overcrowded accommodation appeared yet more oppressive when compared to the villas of the rich. The hand-to-mouth existence of many of Liegnitz's 60,000 inhabitants could be contrasted with the wealth of a fortunate minority. Similarly, in Hirschberg SPD agitators stirred up resentment against Bruno Ablaß by accusing him of living in a palatial villa financed by what was sneering referred to as a *Paragraphengeschäft*—trading in the law. (Ablaß replied in kind. He pointed to Bebel's Swiss villa and claimed that he had at least worked for his wealth rather than inheriting it like the SPD leader.[70]) Unlike Schleswig-Holstein where, as we saw, economic grievances could actually assist the FVP, Lower Silesian left liberalism was particularly vulnerable to divisions between capital and labour, because it relied heavily on the votes of both small businessmen and their employees.

There were doubtless still apprentice craftsmen who were more concerned about education and career prospects than wages paid during training. And company loyalty competed with class consciousness in paternalistic firms like the Landeshut textile manufacturers F. V. Grünfeld. Its fiftieth anniversary celebrations, 'a great family festival' replete with train excursion, folk-songs, fireworks, a play written by

---

[67] BA Berlin, FVP 27, fo. 44, party secretary report for Lower Silesia, Mar. 1912.
[68] *Liegnitzer Anzeiger* (6 Mar. 1909).
[69] See P. Löbe, *Der Weg war lang* (Berlin and Grunewald, 1954).
[70] BA Berlin, Reichslandbund 1, fo. 118, personalia Bruno Ablaß, *Vossische Zeitung* (15 Jan. 1907).

Table 9.5. *Distribution of taxable wealth above 6,000 marks, Liegnitz 1907*

Wealth (marks)	Taxpayers
6,000–20,000	1,168
20,000–32,000	650
32,000–52,000	516
52,000–100,000	480
100,000–200,000	244
200,000–500,000	126
500,000–1,000,000	19
1,000,000–2,000,000	5
2,000,000	4
TOTAL	3,212

Source: *Liegnitzer Anzeiger* (26 July 1907: based on *Liegnitz Ergänzungssteuer* statistics 1905–7).

an employee, and substantial donations to the pension fund and local causes, proclaimed that 'in the future, as hitherto, the boss and work-force should be as one'.[71] But clashes of economic interest inevitably surfaced. And because leading local left liberals were more likely than elsewhere to include manufacturers and small businessmen as well as lawyers, doctors, and journalists, it was more difficult for the party to take a neutral position. Tension between the Liegnitz branch of the RLAA founded by left liberal engineering workers in early 1914 and other left liberal local associations was symptomatic of disruptive effect of economic division.[72]

Left liberal predominance in town councils opened up further potential conflicts of interests. While left liberal teachers and munic-ipal employees demanded cost-of-living supplements, left liberal man-ufacturers and master craftsmen opposed local tax increases. Left liberal leaders eagerly assured both sides that they had a valid argu-ment, but the budget decisions made by left liberal councillors rarely satisfied everybody. As a tortuous press account of differences in the Hirschberg *Liberaler Bürgerverein* over the town's 1913–14 budget finally admitted, it was 'very difficult to find a just compromise between the wishes of teachers and public employees, in themselves justified, and the interests of the taxpayers'.[73] Left liberals could

---

[71] *Landeshuter Stadtblatt* (9 July 1912).
[72] BA Berlin, FVP 27, fo. 30, Lower Silesian party secretary report, Mar. and Apr. 1914.
[73] *Bote aus dem Riesengebirge* (14 Mar. 1913).

not make economic concessions to the growing number of white-collar and working-class voters without alienating small-business support.

As a result, the Lower Silesian FVP could not adopt social liberalism either in theory at elections or in practice in local government. Its defence against the SPD consisted of Richterite methods: anti-socialist campaigning and an emphasis on tradition. In some cases this was sufficient to stifle the SPD. In the 1913 Hirschberg third-class municipal elections, for example, left liberal candidates, helped by a low 30 per cent turn-out, won four times as many votes as their SPD opponents (757 against 173).[74] In Löwenberg in the same year the SPD received only twenty-four votes.[75] The sharp rise in SPD support in Lower Silesia in January 1919 could be taken as indirect evidence of the left liberals' success in retaining petty-bourgeois and skilled working-class support in parts of Lower Silesia before 1914. But once the labour movement had achieved a critical mass, attempted suppression tended to be counterproductive. When, as in Berlin, Liegnitz left liberal councillors declared the election of SPD councillors invalid, this just provided a further grievance for the SPD to exploit. Such action not only failed to reverse SPD gains—rerun elections mostly resulted in renewed SPD victory—but further embittered politics and deepened the very class division left liberals hoped to avoid. Relations between the FVP and SPD were significantly worse than in Germany generally. While the SPD usually ended up supporting left liberal candidates against Conservatives as the lesser evil, this was done with less enthusiasm and more insistence on signed undertakings than elsewhere.[76]

The pre-war period therefore presented left liberals with considerable challenges. Mere tradition was an inadequate response to widespread political ferment (*politische Gärung draußen und drinnen*[77]). By 1914 the FVP was threatened not just by the labour movement but 'the party secretary agitation of the big agrarians fuelled by massive financial resources'. The immense campaign fund raised by the Silesian DKP after 1912 to try to secure a better result in the next Reichstag election amounted to be between 600,000 and 840,000 marks.[78] The need for left liberal organizational renewal became

[74] *Bote aus dem Riesengebirge* (15 Nov. 1913).   [75] Ibid.
[76] Schorske, *Social Democracy*, 230.   [77] *Bote aus dem Riesengebirge* (10 Nov. 1913).
[78] *Bote aus dem Riesengebirge* (12 May 1914); BA Berlin, FVP 27, fo. 30, Lower Silesia party secretary, Mar. and Apr. 1914.

increasingly evident in the five years before the war. In 1909 Karl Müller, the energetic, new left liberal party secretary in Breslau, launched an ambitious attempt to reform left liberal organizational structure throughout the province. Rejecting the defence of existing party organizations in Silesia by Carl Kundel, Richter's former secretary, Müller admitted that some constituencies were in themselves well-organized, but a general framework was missing. 'We have', he added acutely, 'built up organisations far too much around individual people, but an organization without a democratic structure is a house of cards.'[79] As the organization and finance plan drawn up by Müller at the behest of the Silesian provincial association recognized, only an organization with an active, dues-paying mass membership could meet the new demands of mass politics.[80]

Müller's plans were supported by some leading left liberals, notably Adolf Heilberg, the Silesian party chairman.[81] However, its reception at the Silesian party conference in May 1909 showed that acceptance was far from universal.[82] As usual, the ninety delegates were more interested in hearing reports from deputies about national issues. Müller's plan was discussed only after four deputies had given addresses on national and state politics. In the debate leaders of the existing left liberal organizations objected that the plan was schematic and its proposed membership dues, at 2.40 marks per annum, were impossibly high. Two amendments to Müller's plan robbed it of meaning. All organized constituencies could 'keep their well-proven existing arrangements' and, 'for the time being, the level of membership dues, and the percentage or annual sum to be contributed to the regional association, party secretariat and campaign fund will be left to independent judgement according to local circumstances'.[83] As might have been foreseen, 'for the time being' meant indefinitely and few local associations judged they should or could make significant contributions to regional party funds.

But events were proving Müller correct. Fundamental reorganization rather than makeshift change was required to cope with the rising tide of popular politics. Paul Werth had opposed Müller's plans at

---

[79] BA Berlin, FVP 18, fo. 14, Karl Müller to Carl Kundel, 9 Mar. 1909.
[80] See the draft in BA Berlin, FVP 18, fos. 61–3.
[81] A. Heilberg, 'Eine ernste Mahnung' (printed circular FVP electoral association, Breslau 1914).
[82] For the following see the account of the FrVp conference at Sagan, 1 and 2 May 1909 in BA Berlin, FVP 18, fos. 55–60.   [83] BA Berlin, FVP 18, fo. 59.

Sagan. But his editorial 'What Needs to be Done' before the Lower Silesian party conference in June 1914 revealed a change of heart:

> we do not lack, especially here in Lower Silesia, a strong core of old and loyal friends, no doubt the old timeless ideals of Liberalism have struck down roots in the people of our district which cannot be ploughed up. But in many cases there has not been a sufficiently tight bond bringing together those who think alike. Our organizations still show gaps and shortcomings and the recognition that the *Bürgertum* must make material sacrifices if it does not want to be ground up in the battle between feudal aristocracy and Social Democracy is still far from being universally accepted . . . Today it is no longer enough to begin campaigning a few weeks before the election. Only where the ground has been well prepared by a campaign of propaganda lasting years, where between voters and candidates not just the loose bond of a short election campaign exists—only there is success assured.[84]

These needs for organization, agitation, and finance were echoed by a circular sent by Heilberg in 1914 to the members of the FVP Breslau electoral association. A mass organization was desirable in that it prevented decisions being made by a small number of full-time politicians cut off from the people. It was also essential now, when an organized group of ten had more say than a thousand individuals. Of the 20,000 who voted Liberal in Breslau in 1912 at least 15,000 were left liberals—all should be members, as should women. 'We all know,' Heilberg added, 'that the reality lags far behind these demands.' Equally, financial contributions remained 'vastly far behind that which could and must be given'. The FVP had to be freed from 'the necessity of going round again and again with the begging bowl to a small, little changing group of well-off party supporters'. The numerous workers and others less well-off in left liberal ranks should seek to match the 10 pfennigs a week given by Social Democrats. Party members with incomes of 3,000–10,000 marks or more should not feel that, 'from old habits', an annual contribution of a few marks was sufficient. A permanent election fund, not a last-minute scramble, was needed to finance political campaigning. All had 'to do their duty, to their party, to their state and their people, to themselves!'[85]

Such imploring was testimony to the organizational and political pressures faced by Silesian left liberals. Appeals to a sense of duty or honour, however, brought only a limited response. Altruistic donations could not match the sums raised when party organizations could

---

[84] *Bote aus dem Riesengebirge* (7 June 1914).   [85] Heilberg, 'Eine ernste Mahnung'.

appeal to more than political conscience alone (as was the case for SPD organizers at the workplace or in working-class housing blocks, and for tax-assessing *Landräte* in rural areas).[86] There was some increase in left liberal regular membership contributions. In Breslau, for example, a minimum annual contribution of 2.40 marks was enforced and appeals for the more prosperous to increase their contributions met with some response. But in Silesia, as elsewhere, it was rich individuals and firms, for whom the advocacy of left liberal councillors and parliamentarians could be advantageous, who met most of increased costs of politics. Although most individual companies, like the Hansa-Bund, insisted that political donations were used for elections rather than maintaining party organization, it was businessmen, alongside left liberal political leaders themselves, who were the main contributors to the Breslau party secretariat.[87]

The increased politicization of municipal government led in some cases to stronger left liberal organization. In parts of Silesia municipal politicization based on a struggle between left liberals and the right preceeded the SPD's arrival as a significant force in local politics. This applied particularly to Breslau where, from the 1880s, battle raged between the Liberals and the 'Freie Vereinigung' an electoral coalition of Conservative, Catholic, and *Mittelstand* groups.[88] But there was a further growth of left liberal municipal associations in the pre-war period. Nowhere was this more so than in Hirschberg. Here a *Liberaler Bürgerverein* was set up which contested local elections, and met before each council meeting, allowing its 300 members to discuss the forthcoming agenda with their elected representatives. It also offered members a series of lectures on practical themes—the use of post office cheques, debt-recovery, autogenous welding, filling in tax returns—and on education and travel. Finally, it provided organized entertainment: a summer excursion or an evening of Silesian songs and costumes.[89]

---

[86] P.-C. Witt, 'Der preußische *Landrat* als Steuerbeamter, 1891–1918: Bemerkungen zur politischen und sozialen Funktion des deutschen Beamtentums', I. Geiss and B.-J. Wendt (eds.), *Deutschland in der Weltpolitik des 19. und 20. Jahrhunderts* (Düsseldorf, 1973), 205–19.

[87] See the list of contributors to the Breslau FVP secretariat in 1910/11 and 1911/12 in BA Berlin, FVP 18, fos. 19, 33.

[88] A. Oehlke, *100 Jahre Breslauer Zeitung 1820–1920* (Breslau, 1920); Heilberg, 'Erinnerungen', 296–7; K. Nitschke, *Der Deutsch-Konservative Verein in Breslau in den politischen Bewegungen der letzten 25 Jahre* (Breslau, 1907), 1–8; *Jauersches Stadtblatt* (8 Mar. 1911); *Bote aus dem Riesengebirge* (14 Mar. 1913 and 26 Apr. 1918).

[89] See e.g. *Bote aus dem Riesengebirge* (30 Jan., 11 and 29 Oct. 1913, 13 Mar. and 28 Apr. 1914).

While left liberal membership in traditional Lower Silesian strong-holds grew gradually, some other districts showed more spectacular increases. This was particularly evident in the Schweidnitz-Striegau constituency where the FVP claimed eighteen local associations and over 1,100 members by 1914.[90] The district also had a dynamic, young left liberal candidate, Theißig, a Breslau drawing teacher and the most able member of the Breslau young left liberal association established in 1909, whose rhetorical skills humbled his aristocratic Conservative opponent von Richthofen.[91] But even in 1914, the calls for organizational renewal were not fully heeded. The Lower Silesian FVP conference in June 1914 seems, as usual, to have concerned itself more with political issues than political organization: deputies derided *Sammlung* cries from the right, castigated the reactionary Landtag, and sang the praises of the left liberal artisan programme. The Lower Silesian party secretary Mickeleit did give a few tips about campaigning, but this hardly amounted to anything fundamental.[92] The Breslau electoral association, despite Heilberg's homily on the need for strong finances, decided at the end of August not to levy subscriptions during the war. Other left liberal *Vereine* made similar decisions and often gave money from their reserves to war charities.

In terms of money and formal organization, the FVP in Silesia was far outstripped by the DKP as well as the SPD after 1912. While the Conservatives were recruiting paid officials and aimed to have one per constituency, the FVP dissolved its Breslau secretariat after the 1912 election because of financial deficits.[93] In 1914 the FVP had only one paid official in the province, Mickeleit in Liegnitz, while the DKP and SPD could each call on at least six party workers as well as Agrarian League or union officials. The press too showed disturbing trends for the left liberals. The alarm caused by the setting up of the Social Democratic *Liegnitzer Volkszeitung* has already been noted. The establishment, in 1910, of a Centre party paper in Lower Silesia, *Der Greif*, was less serious, given the relatively small Catholic population, but it was a nagging reminder of the steady erosion of left liberal sentiment within the region's Catholic minority. There were also strenuous efforts to increase the circulation of right-wing newspapers. An unprecedented number of Conservative newspapers were given

---

[90] *Bote aus dem Riesengebirge* (24 Apr. 1914).
[91] See *Bote aus dem Riesengebirge* (30 Apr. 1913); University Library Wrocław, Yb 2500, 'Verein "Jungfreisinn" Breslau'.   [92] *Bote aus dem Riesengebirge* (9. June 1914).
[93] BA Berlin, FVP 18, fos. 19, 33; FVP 27, fo. 48, party secretary report, Feb. 1912.

away in the run-up to the 1912 election. In the Jauer constituency, for example, a circular from the Conservative electoral association in September 1911 offered to deliver free copies of the Agrarian *Jauersches Tageblatt* until the end of the year.[94] The DKP also used its campaign fund to buy up existing titles or found new newspapers. The ailing left liberal *Bunzlauer Tageblatt* was taken over in January 1913. In Schweidnitz the DKP attempted to curb left liberal campaigning by offering 120,000 marks for the *Mittelschlesischer Volksfreund*.[95] Although the FVP was able to set up a replacement paper in Schweidnitz within a few weeks, left liberal papers had typically been founded in the first two decades after Unification. The party accounted for a smaller proportion of the new titles established after a comparative lull during the 1890s. (That the 1890s were a quiet period for the formation of newspapers compared to the 1870s, 1880s, and pre-war decade underlines the fact that political mobilization was spread over decades, and that the early 1890s did not form a signifi-cant watershed in Silesia.) Equally disturbing for left liberals was a tendency for some Lower Silesian newspapers, seeking to avoid alien-ating a part of a politically disparate readership, to adopt a hesitant neutrality. The *Bunzlauer Stadtblatt*, the most popular paper in Bunzlau-Lüben, followed such a policy although its owner was a left liberal.[96] In Glogau the *Niederschlesischer Anzeiger*, once the spring-board for Hermann Müller-Sagan's political career, damaged the left liberal cause first by raising quarterly subscriptions from 2 marks to

Table 9.6. *Foundation of Silesian newspapers by decade, 1871–1914*

Foundation	Party papers	All papers
1871–1880	28	53
1881–1890	13	38
1891–1900	8	26
1901–1910	22	43
1910–1914	8	16

Source: Erich Pittius, *Die politische Tagespresse Schlesiens* (Sorau, 1914), table XVII, 54, excluding newspapers founded before 1871. Only Silesian newspapers still in existence in 1914 are included. 'Party papers' have a definite party-political stance, but are not necessarily under the control of a party.

[94] *Jauersches Tageblatt* (8 Sept. 1911).   [95] *Bote aus dem Riesengebirge* (24 Apr. 1913).
[96] *Bunzlauer Stadtblatt* (7 Dec. 1918).

2.50 marks, too much for many peasant readers, and then by political trimming.[97] But the relative weakening of the left liberal press must not over-stated. The press remained a formidable left liberal weapon. Even in Breslau, Görlitz, Waldenburg, and Liegnitz, where a local SPD paper was available, many workers preferred left liberal newspapers. The Breslau SPD was still complaining in July 1914 about many workers reading the liberal-leaning *Breslauer General-Anzeiger* and the left liberal *Breslauer Morgen-Zeitung* rather than the party's *Volkswacht*. While the SPD had won 236,000 voters in Silesia in 1912, the SPD press in the province had a circulation in 1913 of less than 63,000.[98] Left liberal newspapers continued to attract larger circulations than right-wing journals, particularly in urban districts. Pittius's pre-war survey of the Silesian press found that 'even the Conservative daily papers in some larger towns like Liegnitz, Hirschberg, Oppeln, Neiße, Beuthen do not have more than 5,000 subscribers. The papers are, to a large extent, read only by those people who, because of their position or for other reasons, are compelled to subscribe.'[99]

Pre-war politics revolved increasingly around the propaganda battle between right-wing paid agitators and left-wing newspapers. Of the two forces the former was the more spectacular. The popular face of the Silesian DKP shifted dramatically. Paid demagogues rather than restrained aristocrats presented the party's case. DKP campaigning in 1911 relied heavily on two figures: Dr Kurt Nitschke and master chimney sweep Max Conradt. Nitschke, the DKP's Silesian general secretary until after the 1912 elections, had worked full-time for the party and its newspaper the *Schlesische Morgen-Zeitung* since 1898. Like Diederich Hahn, Nitschke received his schooling in right-wing politics in the Association of German Students (*Verein deutscher Studenten*) in the 1880s.[100] Conradt, as well as a DKP agitator, was a ubiquitous figure in regional and national right-wing *Mittelstand* organizations. Nor were such figures left merely to perform the drudgery of popular agitation. Nitschke was elected to the Breslau City Council and received the Red Eagle Order 4th Class from the Emperor in 1913 'for his services to the nation'.[101] Conradt was given a Mid-Silesian safe seat in the 1913 Landtag elections, a stark

---

[97] BA Koblenz, NL Gothein 21, fos. 2–3, Dr. Gabriel to Georg Gothein, 12 Feb. 1910.
[98] *Volkswacht* (29 July 1914); Fricke, *Handbuch*, i, 592–8 and ii, 739.
[99] Pittius, *Politische Tagespresse*, 50.
[100] See Nitschke's obituary in *Schlesische Morgen-Zeitung* (9 Oct. 1917).   [101] Ibid.

contrast to the forlorn urban candidacies the Conservatives usually offered artisan leaders. Such figures had become an integral part of Conservative politics. With their rise came new propaganda methods including mass rallies, racial anti-Semitism, and the 'big lie'. Conservative party conferences increasingly resembled Agrarian League rallies. Propaganda speeches replaced policy discussion, and a mass audience was brought in by special trains: 'monarchical rustics freighted in en masse' as the left liberal Breslau press put it.[102] The DKP mounted a systematic campaign of abuse, unparalleled in intensity and extent. Wild and totally unfounded charges were levied against unfortunate opponents. The National Liberal candidate in Guhrau-Steinau-Wohlau, for example, was falsely accused of being a Methodist and sectarian preacher, having sex with the maidservant, and battering his wife driving her to divorce and to an asylum.[103] The post-war careers of two of the chief DKP propagandists in the province, Wilhelm Kube and Richard Kunze, first in anti-Semitic splinter parties and then the NSDAP, underlined the general direction of DKP campaigning in pre-war Silesia.[104]

But if 1912–14 signified the advent of Nazi-style propaganda, it did not mark the beginnings of a positive response from the Protestant middle strata. Left liberal newspapers used reports of Conservative public meetings to discredit officials. Interspersed comment held up the self-important paid hacks to public ridicule.[105] They were accused, with much justification, of making a set speech throughout the district. Readers were informed of embarrassing details from the past. The DKP party secretary Berg was depicted as a political turncoat who had espoused the exact opposite of his present message when working for the Hansa-Bund. Kunze was accused of embezzlement.[106] Above all, left liberal newspapers claimed that right-wing 'mercenaries'[107] failed the vital test of respectability. Kunze was dismissed, intemperately, but not altogether unfairly, as 'a dog-like mare in the political race-track' (*eine hundesgemeine Schindmähre in der*

[102] *Breslauer Morgen-Zeitung* (22 and 29 Oct. 1911).
[103] *Breslauer Zeitung*, 551 (7 Aug. 1912).
[104] Kunze repeatedly addressed DKP meetings in his native Lower Silesia during 1912–18. Kube succeeded his mentor Nitschke as Silesian DKP general secretary before the war. *Die Freie Meinung*, 1. 1; BA Berlin, Reichslandbund personalia 259, fos. 102–65.
[105] See e.g. the scathing report on a Kunze rally in *Bote aus dem Riesengebirge* (9 Mar. 1913).   [106] *Breslauer Zeitung*, 467 (5 July 1912).
[107] *Landeshuter Stadtblatt* (6 Jan. 1912).

politischen Rennbahn).[108] These paid agititators neither toiled nor did they spin. Right-wing agitators may have been 'capable in anti-Semitism' (*tüchtig in Antisemitismus*), but not, the left liberals implied, in anything else.[109] Left liberal newspapers attacks were so effective that many DKP officials had to be moved on rapidly. Berg was hounded out of Hirschberg within a few months by the *Bote aus dem Riesengebirge*, and continued to be assailed in his new base of Löwenberg.[110] Nitschke even suffered a mental breakdown after the barracking of left liberal press and politicians during the 1912 campaign.[111] Left liberal rhetoric was less extreme than that of men like Kunze, but it was ultimately more effective because it harnessed popular prejudice. Public distaste towards disreputable paid officials did not need to be fanned; it was already present. When the *Jauersches Stadtblatt* attacked Nitschke and Conradt, its readers were already so disapprovingly aware of the two men that the paper did not even have to mention them by name. It needed only to refer to 'an ex-Pastor who quickly left his office for good reasons, and a chimney sweep who sweeps no more'.[112]

If social respectability was crucial to the left liberals' ability to repel Conservative agitation so also was political respectability. Public distaste was directed against disreputable methods as well as questionable individuals. Left liberal newspapers carried a series of reports on 'Conservative campaign morals' and 'Kunze's methods'.[113] New populist Conservative agitation was presented as another form of press-ganging to put alongside the well-known political and electoral malpractice of *Landräte* and estate owners.[114] There was talk of rural dwellers being forced to take Conservative newspapers and of 'dependent elements' (*alles, was abhängig ist*)[115] being dragged in to provide an audience for DKP agitators. Left liberal newspapers invited readers to contrast themselves as free, independent citizens with the estate workers forced to wear their master's politics as well as his livery. High-profile Conservative agitation offended the political sensibilities especially of urban inhabitants. Furthermore, growing popular commitment to free political expression and objection to

---

[108] *Jauersches Tageblatt* (14 May 1913).   [109] *Jauersches Stadtblatt* (7 Apr. 1911).
[110] *Bote aus dem Riesengebirge* (13 Dec. 1913).
[111] *Schlesische Morgen-Zeitung* (9 Oct. 1917).
[112] *Jauersches Stadtblatt* (12 May 1911).   [113] *Breslauer Zeitung*, 14 (6 Jan. 1912).
[114] 'Der Landrat als Kassierer', *Landeshuter Stadtblatt* (24 Aug. 1912).
[115] *Bote aus dem Riesengebirge* (25 Jan. 1914).

undue influence led to a series of internal communications being leaked to left liberal and SPD newspapers. A confidential memo from Kunze on agitation was sent to the *Volkswacht* and its compromising contents were repeated across the province. Kunze's politically embarrassing guide included advocating the use of heavies (*handfeste Leute*) to intimidate opponents, and suggesting that speakers write an account for the next day's newspapers before the meeting had even taken place. Kunze's advice on publicity—big posters, a dramatic title, and advance claims of a full house—led left liberals to sneer that this was just like the circus: a great fanfare followed by a pathetic old clown.[116] The flurry of libel cases which followed on from Conservative campaigning in 1912 was a further opportunity to expose Conservative machinations.[117] Left liberals represented themselves as 'a coalition of all decent people' against a party resorting to wild ravings and vilification (*Dreschpflegel- und Schimpfpartei*).[118]

The fate of Conservative campaigning demonstrated how, even in East Elbia, society was no longer amenable to authoritarian politics. If Conservative estate owners libelled opponents they were usually convicted—if local courts ignored the evidence then the verdict was overturned by appeal. And if Conservatives escaped with small fines this was no political victory. It merely provided further propaganda for the FVP and SPD. The *Breslauer Zeitung*, for example, frequently noted Conservative editors were given more lenient treatment for serious offences than SPD counterparts received for lesser offences, regularly concluding such reports with the ironic refrain: 'What was that Dr Friedberg said? "Our judicial system is spotless."'[119] The fact that state employees were prepared to act against the right, either by secret leaks or open political action, was a further symptom of the crumbling walls of Conservative authority and deference. Such trends were exemplified, as in much of Germany, by the attitude of elementary-school teachers. When Oberregierungsrat von Neese und Obischau, the official in charge of church and school matters in Lower Silesia, attempted to recruit Conservative support and warned teachers against left liberal political participation, the result was a running battle with the district's teachers.[120] Left liberal school teachers were not cowed by disciplinary threats. Rather they reported von Neese's

[116] *Jauersches Stadtblatt* (24 Dec. 1911).
[117] See e.g. *Breslauer Zeitung* (25 Apr., 8 June, 3, 5, and 13 July, 18 and 19 Sept. 1912).
[118] *Jauersches Stadtblatt* (9 May 1911).
[119] *Breslauer Zeitung*, 590 (22 Aug. 1912).   [120] *Liegnitzer Anzeiger* (2 Nov. 1909).

actions to the press, which held up the 'feudal' official to public obloquy. In the end it was von Neese not the left liberal school teachers who was removed. Although the Prussian state would not openly admit it, the transfer of von Neese to Münster, a place largely free of left liberals, was clear demonstration of the need to accommodate public opinion.

If elementary teachers could not be forced to become Conservative supporters nor could they be persuaded. The DKP pamphlet 'Teachers and Conservatism belong together' was greeted with derision. Left liberal school teachers felt the Conservatives had no respect for the social worth of teachers and schools. The real DKP attitude was: 'Wer Knecht ist, soll Knecht bleiben' (once a slave, always a slave). The school had to stand '*alongside the Church* not beneath it' as Conservatives and Centre wanted. Elementary teachers not only felt undervalued. They refused to accept an inflexible Conservative social hierarchy: 'teachers and above all young teachers must be part of the people. We lose the earth beneath our feet the moment reserve lieutenant megalomania severs contact with the people.'[121]

This underlined the essential feature of the political mobilization: it was fuelled not only by men and money, but by political issues. Although left liberals had to meet the challenges of popular politics through improvisation and individuals rather than fundamental reorganization, their position on current political issues was far closer to the Protestant middle strata than that of the political right. Manufacturers and master craftsmen were sympathetic towards Conservative calls for more authority at the workplace, but the DKP's agrarian image and memories of the finance reform were too strong for it to be accepted as the party of industry and commerce. Anti-Semitism, a prominent feature of both Centre party and DKP campaigning in the province, had a undeniable attraction. But its appeal was overwhelmingly to existing right-wing supporters. For most left liberal and SPD voters the anti-Semitism of the gutter (*Radauantisemitismus*) was further proof of the right's vulgarity.

The concept of the Blue-Black Bloc was far more firmly fixed in the minds of the Silesian public than the pattern of voting in the Reichstag in the period 1909–11 warranted. The Junkers were widely loathed. Antipathy to Junkerdom was exemplified by reaction to

---

[121] Meeting of elementary teachers in Hirschberg, 26 Apr. 1913. *Bote aus dem Riesengebirge* (30 Apr. 1913).

Oldenburg's '10 men and a lieutenant' speech: '[There is] for every man claiming even an ounce of liberal spirit only one political rallying-call from now on: *Away with the Junkers!*[122] Political Catholicism was just as unpalatable. Hostility to the Centre pervaded the urban Protestant community. The former army officer Deetjen, canvassing in Breslau for the Free Conservatives in 1913, was repeatedly faced with 'the fateful question': 'what is your position on the Centre party?' All Deetjen's efforts to explain that the SPD was a greater national threat and that this justified a tactical alliance with the Centre were in vain. Despite agreeing with the need for more colonies and a strong army, support was refused as 'we don't take the strongest possible stand against the Centre party.' Ironically, the Liberal parties were able to turn a nationalism which was basically illiberal to their advantage by tarring their opponents with the Ultramontane brush. The result was reflected by a factory director cited by Deetjen. 'Let me be satisfied with this policy. We must strike out against the Junkers and *Pfaffen*—that's the most important thing.'[123] The right was weighed down by associations with Junkers, Catholics, agrarianism, and authoritarianism. Because it lacked a popular political cause, it could not dislodge the left liberal allegiance of the Protestant middle strata.

[122] *Breslauer Morgenzeitung* (1 Feb. 1910), 'Die Fanfare des Junkers von Januschau'.
[123] *Schlesische Freikonservative Parteikorrespondenz*, 5 (28 Nov. 1913).

Conclusion

10

Victory in Defeat and Defeat in Victory: Left Liberal Politics and the First World War

> Just how much better we have it than the other peoples, who simply cannot believe in ultimate victory . . . That is precisely the shortcoming which strikes us most when reading the New Testament now: that there is not even a word about the relationship of man to his Fatherland.[1]
>
> (Wilhelm Ohr)

Contrasting the state of left liberal politics before and after the First World War has certain inherent problems. If we find left liberal party politics more vulnerable in 1918/19 than July 1914 the tendency is to blame the war as an external cause and to neglect hidden weaknesses exposed rather than created by the war. Assessing left liberal prospects in July 1914 also invites speculation about what might have been had war been avoided or ended quickly. An interpretation which ascribes left liberal decline to the war, Versailles, and economic crisis has two major shortcomings. First, it has a tendency to discount German responsibility for so-called accidents. Secondly, placing the sole explanatory burden on adverse circumstances ignores the internal factors which cushioned or strengthened the effect of external events. Any comparison between 1914 and 1918 must be careful. Nevertheless, an assessment of left liberal politics on the eve of war does more than bring together the findings of previous chapters. It is an essential starting-point for measuring the political effects of the First World War.

Judging success or failure of a political party depends significantly on perspective. Wilhelmine left liberal parties remained failures by

---

[1] BA Berlin, NL Wilhelm Ohr to Elisabeth Nelson-Scheumann, dated 1 Dec. 1915, but still unfinished 20 Dec. 1915.

comparison to the British Liberal party. They were also failures compared to the DKP, in terms of influence on government and administration, or to the SPD according to party organization and popular support. To men like Max Weber and Hugo Preuß Liberal parties were still largely a symbol of the German *Bürgertum*'s inability to extend its dominant influence in social and economic life into the political sphere. Images of decline voiced by Wilhelmine left liberals themselves may have been exaggerated and artificial.[2] But there was also genuine frustration and pessimism. Eberhard Gothein was not alone in believing that 'we [liberals] are gradually losing almost all fundamental support'.[3]

But setting the FVP's position in 1914 against the situation facing left liberals at the beginning of the pre-war decade provides a dramatically different perspective. In 1903 left liberals appeared condemned to the margins of German politics. There had been a continuous erosion of popular support and political influence. Left liberals had declined at each Reichstag election after 1890, winning only 9.3 per cent of the poll and thirty-six seats in 1903. Left liberals were divided into small parties incapable of agreeing with each other. They were isolated from other political groups. Conservatives, Centre, and National Liberals, kept together by Bülow's skilful manœuvring, provided a government majority on major issues. And the SPD provided stronger opposition while at the same time cutting into the left liberal's urban political base. Finally, with the withdrawal of Eugen Richter from active politics after 1903 left liberals lost the one figure still capable of making a impact despite falling support and political isolation. There appeared little immediate prospect of significant political influence and every likelihood of left liberals continuing to lose support to left and right.

Against this background the left liberal revival by 1914 was substantial. A rise in Reichstag support from 9.3 per cent to 12.5 per cent between 1903 and 1912 might not at first sight appear dramatic, especially as some of the shift came from party electoral pacts and an increase in the number of candidates. But, together with state elections, Reichstag returns were enough to mark a clear change of left liberal electoral fortune from continuous decline throughout the 1890s to steady recovery after 1903. Besides reversing an established pattern,

---

[2] See Ch. 3 above.
[3] BA Koblenz, NL Gothein 8, fo. 10, Eberhard Gothein to Georg Gothein, 20 Apr. 1908.

there are two other reasons for giving added significance to the left liberal electoral performance. Left liberals had to face two electoral handicaps. One was the increase in the electorate. Both Liberal parties had regularly been less successful in winning new voters than retaining traditional supporters.[4] In the light of this, the 50 per cent rise in the number of left liberal votes from under one million to one and a half million indicated a more impressive achievement than that suggested by increase in the percentage share of the poll. The second thing to take into account is that left liberal support was more exposed, politically and sociologically, to SPD growth than that of the other parties. The attitudes of left liberal voters made them more likely to succumb to the SPD, especially if, as FVP activists frequently complained, Social Democrats based their campaign not on the Erfurt Programme, but on radical liberal demands. So did the fact that left liberal voters were, on average, more likely to be Protestants, live in urban districts, and have a lower income and social standing. Left liberals continued to lose support to the SPD, albeit at a reduced rate. This implies a more considerable shift of support from the right to the left liberals, particularly after 1909, than the net increase in left liberal votes suggests.

The increase in votes was insufficient to dispel perennial concerns about the party's electoral base. It remained true, as Julius Kopsch admitted, that the left liberals, unlike the Centre and SPD, had 'no unified, solid mass of voters' behind them.[5] Left liberal electoral appeal remained largely confined to the Protestant middle strata. Similarly, though the party gained support in traditionally National Liberal areas like Hanover, Saxony, and Hesse this was insufficient to make a breakthrough in terms of seats. These continued to come largely from traditional left liberal areas.[6] However, the fact that the increase in left liberal support between 1903 and 1912 was concentrated within the Protestant middle strata increased its significance for German politics. The Protestant middle strata was not just the most contested part of the electorate. It was also the crucial element in the battle between left and right, reform and reaction. Left liberal gains were part of a considerable shift amongst Protestant *Mittelstand*

---

[4] Langewiesche, *Liberalism*, 128–36; Sheehan, *German Liberalism*, 221.

[5] BA Berlin 29, fo. 6, conference with FVP provincial leaders and party secretaries, 17 Mar. 1918.

[6] Over half the FVP Reichstag deputies in 1912 were elected in Württemberg, Schleswig-Holstein, Oldenburg, East Prussia, and Lower Silesia.

voters from Conservatives, anti-Semites, and right-wing National Liberals to reformist National Liberals and left liberals and the SPD. Left liberal recruits in the pre-war period included public-sector workers, artisans, and peasants, precisely those groups whose support the right most needed to win or maintain. As a result even the East Elbian heartlands were vulnerable. The left liberals won seats in East Prussia, Mecklenburg, and Pomerania in 1912 previously held by Conservatives without interruption since 1871.

There were, therefore, two sides to the left liberal advance. Put positively the FVP were attempting to win new support amongst the growing 'new' *Mittelstand*, and to compensate for urban losses to the SPD by taking surrounding rural constituencies. The electoral victims of modernity and social division in towns and cities, left liberals sought to turn the same forces to their own advantage in the countryside. But it was the negative achievement, the erosion of the right's electoral base and consequently its claim to represent German society, which had the most political impact. The swing to the left in the Reichstag and bourgeois society produced a constant underlying pressure for reform.

This brings us to the second change in the left liberals' political position. More significant than the rise in votes and seats *per se* was the shift in left liberal relations with the other parties and government. It was the Conservatives rather than left liberals who appeared politically isolated on the eve of war. Although the FVP held only forty-six of 397 Reichstag seats in 1914, this was enough to make it the third largest party. More significantly, it had a strategically important position in a Reichstag where the parties Bismarck had denounced as 'enemies of the Reich' (*Reichsfeinde*) held two-thirds of the seats. The 1907 election marked a change of political course on the part of the left liberals. It was the point at which advocates of positive co-operation with the Reich government and other political parties clearly triumphed over those who placed the maintenance of critical independence above other considerations. At the same time, potential negotiating partners became more amenable. Co-operation between National Liberals and left liberals was partly a question of pressing electoral self-interest. But it also signified a degree of political convergence. Left liberal support for 'national' bills lowered the major barrier between the two parties. National Liberals were also growing increasingly impatient about making incessant compromises for little return in order to maintain a right-wing governmental majority, especially as this involved association with the detested Centre. While Young Liberal enthusiasm for substantial domestic reform and Liberal unity was not taken up by the whole party, most National Liberals shared a growing appetite for an opening to the left and measured political reform. National Liberal supporters during the 1880s and 1890s, for example, were fairly indifferent towards the issue of Prussian suffrage reform. By the eve of the war only a small section advocated equal suffrage. But there was enough grassroots and leadership pressure for direct, secret elections to compel even reluctant Rhineland-Westphalian Landtag deputies (who used open voting to ensure their workforce supported the National Liberals) to vote for their introduction.

Left liberal co-operation with the SPD was more difficult. This was not because of greater political differences. As has been emphasized, left liberal and SPD stances on political reform, economic policy, and especially cultural issues provided significant scope for political co-operation. Equally, new-found left liberal sympathy for social policy removed a long-standing point of contention. The largest obstacle to FVP–SPD co-operation was the social and economic division between the labour movement and the rest of German society. For a non-socialist party to advocate political accommodation with the SPD risked serious consequences. State employees who publicly condoned support for the SPD, even if only as the lesser evil in run-off elections, were liable to disciplinary action. Businessmen who behaved similarly could be discriminated against in the awarding of state contracts. More widespread and important than state imposed sanctions, such people faced being treated as social outcasts by local respectable society. Pachnicke referred to left liberal local committee members 'paying with their whole social existence' if the party publicly associated itself with the SPD.[7] Even if the impact of an understanding with the SPD on left liberal organization is discounted, the party risked loss of support from many anti-socialist North Germans. As well as social divisions and fears, advocates of left liberal–Social Democratic co-operation had to overcome the accumulated resentment of decades of direct electoral battle for the support of urban Protestant constituencies. Finally, the fact that both sides were associated with opposite sides in the conflict of economic interest between

---

[7] Pachnicke, *Liberalismus als Kulturpolitik.*

capital and labour or, less abstractly, between employer and employee, master craftsman and apprentice, provided a further well of hostility. To be sure these difficulties were far from dispelled during the pre-war period. The left liberal response to the 1912 run-off pact showed that substantial numbers of FVP voters were not prepared to transfer support to the SPD in the second round. Nor was the move within the SPD towards pragmatic co-operation unequivocal. Political, economic, and social rivalries remained, but they were mitigated. As the FVP's social base became increasingly formed by the 'new' *Mittelstand*, left liberal attitudes to employees' rights moved closer to those of the SPD. The switch of left liberal attention at Reichstag contests away from the cities and towards semi-rural districts provided more opportunity for electoral co-operation. As FVP tacticians like Fischbeck realized, SPD rural candidatures mobilized support which could then be harnessed by the left liberals in the run-off. They were thus more useful to the FVP than an agreement to stand aside in the first round.[8] There was even a partial reduction in the social opprobrium associated with tolerance towards the SPD. The process was most obvious in Southern states like Baden. But 1903 and 1912 voting returns in Saxony and Prussia also showed a part of the middle-class electorate prepared, at least in secret, to cast 'a red ballot' and the revered left liberal academic Theodor Mommsen had publicly urged co-operation with the SPD.[9]

There was an increased appreciation on both sides of the benefits of co-operation. Ironically, the electoral battle between the left liberals and SPD in 1907 actually assisted the process. On the one hand, it reduced left liberal fears about being dominated by a larger and seemingly invincible SPD. On the other hand, it sharpened the SPD appetite for seats as well as votes, and underlined the importance of left liberal run-off votes to SPD success. Even for left liberal opponents of the Bülow Bloc like the DVP in Konstanz, the 1907 election and Liberal–Conservative bloc served one valuable function: it encouraged 'Social Democracy . . . to realize that Liberalism, joined together in an effective tactical union, is a force without which freedom and progress cannot be won.'[10] When the 1909 finance reform

---

[8] BA Berlin, FVP 36, fo. 131, executive committee, 22 May 1912.

[9] Cited in D. Fricke (ed.), *Deutsche Demokraten: Die nichtproletarischen demokratischen Kräfte in Deutschland 1830 bis 1981* (Cologne, 1981), 128.

[10] *Neue Konstanzer Abendzeitung* (5 Sept. 1908), 'Block und Zukunft'.

sharpened popular antipathy towards the Conservatives and Centre both sets of followers were more inclined to set aside differences to defeat the common enemy.

Admittedly the alignment of National Liberals, left liberals, and SPD did not have sufficient unity of purpose and a large enough Reichstag majority to give a positive direction to national politics after 1912. Apart from transforming the 1913 military finance bill (*Deckungsvorlage*), its main effect was to deter the government from introducing restrictive and contentious legislation. Nevertheless it provided a strong enough centre of political gravity to pull the Centre party away from one-sided ties with the Conservatives and towards limited co-operation with the centre-left. This emphasized the right's parliamentary isolation, even if it did nothing to foster a clear pro- gramme of action on the part of the Reichstag.

Against this background the position taken by the left liberals was of considerable importance to the Reich government. For a govern- ment without the backing of a solid Reichstag majority left liberal votes were significant in themselves. But the effect of the FVP's stance on neighbouring parties and public opinion was even more important. FVP opposition to a government measure meant the powerful left liberal press stirring up even more public resentment against the authorities. It also made National Liberal support much more difficult to obtain. National Liberal deputies were well aware that episodes like Zedlitz's 1892 school bill and Stengel's 1906 finance reform had allowed left liberals to gain votes at their expense. They were very unlikely to agree to unpopular measures unless the FVP also voted for them, for it would once again expose the National Liberal party to left liberal accusations of betraying the interests of the *Bürgertum* and acting as lapdogs to the Blue-Black Bloc: charges particularly damaging in the critical public mood after 1909.

The government, then, had sound reasons for consulting left liberal deputies and enlisting their support wherever possible. Even when left liberal votes were not needed to gain a parliamentary majority they important in securing greater public acceptance. As a result, Bethmann and Delbrück were anxious to cultivate left liberals during the so-called Blue-Black Bloc of 1909–11. When Payer blamed the unpopularity of the government in the 1912 election on the legislation of the previous two years Bethmann responded by inviting him to name a major measure which had been passed without left liberal co-operation.[11] As this exchange confirmed, both sides were disingenuous. The government was after the maximum show of public support in return for the minimum of private concessions; left liberal politicians wanted precisely the reverse. In two respects the left liberal yield in negotiations with the executive was disappointing. First, left liberals proved less ruthless and successful political horse-traders than their Centre party counterparts. They were too cautious and thus failed to make the most of the opportunity to press the government into making reforms. Secondly, despite the fact that the DKP's stance appeared increasingly hostile not just to the Reich leadership but to the interests of the Wilhelmine state, the government preferred attempted reconciliation with the right rather than to harness majority support even for those technocratic reforms which it itself identified as necessary. Yet the left liberals' ability to keep up the level of public dissatisfaction even when negotiating with the government in Berlin, together with the absence of popular measures, meant the government could not defuse pressure for reform. It could only postpone, thus encouraging even more discontent.

Left liberal electoral advance and growing influence in national politics in pre-war Germany was rooted in the party's appeal to the sentiments of the Protestant middle strata. This was partly the result of vigorous campaigning by left liberal activists and newspapers which belied the supposed ineffectiveness of *Honoratiorenpolitik*. Left liberal notables could not be confused with those members of other bourgeois parties and high officialdom whom the left liberal deputy Ferdinand Hoff dismissed as 'theorists and faint-hearts, who . . . cannot grasp the political and economic battles of our time are not always as quiet and peaceful as a birthday party in a well-brought up family'.[12] Left liberals were frequently the first to bring discernible political activity to rural districts. Adolf Neumann-Hofer, for example, held hundreds of meetings in the Lippe countryside. 'He spoke and appealed for political support where no one had spoken before.'[13]

Even the notorious Richard Kunze felt obliged to alert Conservatives to the force of left liberal campaigning. It was well known, he claimed:

[11] *Schulthess' Europäischer Geschichtskalender* (1912), 36–7.
[12] Hoff, *Auf zum Kampfe*, 16.
[13] SA Detmold, NL Max Staercke 586, obituary of Neumann-Hofer, *Lippische Landeszeitung* (21 May 1925).

that the electoral battle burns most fiercely and takes the sharpest and most evil forms where the left liberal party is fighting for a seat . . . With slogans: equal rights for all, freedom for every citizen of the state, battle against Junker and *Pfaffen* interest politics and others besides . . . and using small local incidents which promote discontent and greed they agitate against everything which represents authority, order, and institutions grounded in history.[14]

The spectacle of Kunze accusing others of unacceptable campaigning methods was macabre indeed. But his words convey an important point. Left liberal propaganda had a considerable impact not just because of the skill and energy of left liberal campaigners, but because it addressed popular issues and grievances. Left liberal politics depended for resonance and support on the attitudes of the Protestant middle strata.

This reliance has usually been seen as an explanation of the fundamental weakness of German Liberalism. It cut the Liberal parties off from large sections of the electorate: Catholics alienated by the *Kulturkampf* and continued attacks on the Catholic Church; and workers, peasants, and struggling members of the 'old' *Mittelstand* who felt victims of a liberal economic system. Moreover, the Protestant middle strata were internally fragmented. This prevented the Liberal parties from adopting a clear economic and political position. Divergent economic interests and political outlook led to negative attacks and trimming rather than a positive programme.[15] There was undoubtedly some truth in this. The social (and regional) concentration of left liberal support meant that the FVP had effectively no chance of victory in some 300 of the 397 Reichstag constituencies. We have also seen how left liberal candidates delivered contrasting messages to urban and rural audiences, and how left liberal politics varied in response to different regional attitudes and conditions. It would be difficult to quarrel with the argument that pre-war left liberal politics were guided by shifting tactical considerations rather than a wide-ranging and firmly held catalogue of political demands. Nevertheless, historians have tended to overstate the difficulties and ignore the advantages which were associated with left liberal ties with the Protestant middle strata.

The assertion that many Wilhelmine left liberal voters lacked strong positive motives and a single vision of what the party stood for

---

[14] Kunze, *Was der deutsche Reichstagswähler wissen muß*, ii. 28.
[15] For a synthesis of this interpretation see Sheehan, *German Liberalism*, 221–57.

may be true. But the charge could equally well be levied against most mass political parties. Attempting to be all things to all men is surely the rule rather than the exception in modern politics. Moreover, the fact that people voted left liberal for reasons which an outside observer might judge contradictory, unconvincing, or irrational does not mean that the voters themselves saw it that way. Before turning to the way the Protestant middle strata did in fact shape important contradictions at the centre of left liberal politics, it is important to outline unrecognized strengths and potential in the links between the *Bürgertum* and left liberal politics.

The first point to make is that the *Bürgertum* was not as politically helpless and powerless as often portrayed. It did not generally withdraw from politics with the advent of popular mobilization and mass parties. Nor could it be ignored by the government. The Bismarckian constitution was a barrier to direct political power, but it became increasingly clear that bourgeois consent was essential to government in the longer term. The strenuous if largely unavailing attempts at *Sammlungspolitik* were testimony to this. Both Bülow and Bethmann Hollweg realized that, if a reform-minded majority of the Protestant middle strata led by the left liberals agreed to co-operate with the labour movement, political change could not ultimately be resisted.

Secondly, the Protestant middle strata were less fragmented than commonly portrayed. Clashes of economic interest should not be overlooked. But they were of less overwhelming importance to political attitudes in the years of growth after the mid-1890s than they had been during the periodic crises of the 'Great Depression'. Similarly, many *Mittelstand* voters had been willing to blame the Liberal parties for economic difficulties during the 1870s and 1880s. But by the pre-war decade the liberal parliamentary legislation of the Unification period had become a distant memory. Those still in economic difficulties were more likely to react against the Conservatives and Centre who had failed to fulfil their promises to help the *Mittelstand* despite their influential position in the Reichstag and Prussian Landtag since the 1880s. Finally, it is important to remember that there were also economic themes around which the large majority of the Protestant middle strata could unite. The almost universal demand for a larger, cheaper, and more efficient railway system has been highlighted. The same applied to postal and telephone services, and many other aspects of everyday life. Technology and material progress were beliefs which united Protestant urban society; likewise an emphasis on personal diligence (*Tüchtigkeit*), respectability, and the value of honest work. In social standing, closely connected to economic position, there were also numerous internal divisions: between bourgeois and petty bourgeois; between members of state bureaucracy and the free professions; between established callings and the new technological occupations. But this went alongside identification with the *Bürgertum* as distinct group with values and interests which differed from those of arrogant Junkers, backward Catholics, or unskilled labourers.

This widespread self-image contained several elements which had a natural outlet in left liberal politics: it valued secular life, civil rights, and individual opportunity more than throne and altar orthodoxy, authoritarianism, and inherited privilege; education and science more than dogma and tradition. In these respects left liberalism exercised a positive appeal. But negative factors were at least as important in securing Protestant middle strata support. It was what left liberals stood against which attracted many to the party. In cities like Berlin, Königsberg, and Bremen they were seen as the main anti-socialist force. In both urban and rural districts left liberalism was seen as a rallying-point for anti-Junker feeling. Above all, left liberals were supported as the most uncompromising opponents of political Catholicism. Left liberal politics caught aspirations of members of the Protestant middle strata but, more importantly, it also mirrored their resentments.

It was this that lay at the heart of relative left liberal success during the pre-war period. Events strengthened both the positive and negative sides of the left liberal appeal to the Protestant middle strata. Court scandals and Wilhelm's rash public pronouncements failed to revive middle-class republicanism. But it shook belief in the Conservative concept of unfettered monarchy, and increased support for the left liberal idea of a constitutional monarchy with a publicly accountable government. Similarly, the Zabern affair lent more public urgency to the issue of *Rechtsstaatlichkeit*, the rule of law. The beginning and end of the Bülow Bloc managed to generate even greater antipathy against political Catholicism. The 1907 campaign whipped up the *furor protestanticus* to new heights, and resentment towards Centre party political influence was compounded by the party's role in defeating the inheritance tax and bringing down the Chancellor. The 1909 finance reform, the most important event in pre-war party politics, provided an ideal opportunity for left liberals to attract parts of the Protestant middle strata which had previously supported the right. It discredited right-wing claims to support *Mittelstand* economic interests. Burdened by unpopular new taxes and price increases, many were more inclined to believe left liberal claims that Conservatives and anti-Semites only protected the interests of large landowners. If the financial measures themselves were portrayed as reactionary, the readmittance of the Centre to a key position of influence was seen as wicked. Public projection of a Blue-Black Bloc allowed the FVP to redirect virulent anti-Catholicism against Conservative and anti-Semite accomplices.

The FVP won support more through the conduct of political opponents than its own actions. By contrast to British Conservative governments after 1886 which largely avoided policies which Liberal opponents could convincingly label wicked and reactionary,[16] the DKP produced a succession of statements and action which positively invited this description. Even when German Conservatives attempted to campaign west of the Elbe and in urban districts, their tone, image, and policies were totally unsuitable. The absence of a credible urban Conservatism is one of the most striking features of pre-1918 (and also pre-1945) German politics. Other competitors for the support of the Protestant middle strata also faced obstacles. In those regions where National Liberals and left liberals still put up opposing candidates, National Liberals' reputation for élitism and compromising with the right made them less attractive to public opinion radicalized by the 1909 finance reform. And the SPD, though undoubtedly the left liberals' most formidable electoral opponent, still offended the bourgeois sensibilities of many Protestant middle and lower middle-class voters.

All this suggests that left liberal politics had a more substantial and influential part in pre-war German state and society than indicated by conventional accounts of electoral failure and 'generals without an army'. But perhaps more illuminating than relative judgements about success and failure is the question of what left liberal politics represented. The prevailing image of left liberal politics is that of critical opposition. Under Richter it was reputedly the party which always said no. This even expressed itself in a popular, if not particularly amusing joke. Why did Richter remain single? Because he would never agree to say yes to anything. As we have seen, the talent to

---

[16] D. A. Hamer, *Liberal Politics in the Age of Gladstone and Rosebery* (Oxford, 1972), esp. 315–29.

oppose was still a vital element in left liberal politics. Voting left liberal remained a way of criticizing aspects of German state and society; a response against heavy-handed government, excessive clerical influence, unfair taxes, insufficient social recognition, and other grievances. However, this must be counterbalanced by the many respects in which left liberals positively identified with German state and society. As Bismarck was well aware, left liberals as a whole never had been 'enemies of the Reich' (*Reichsfeinde*). That indeed was the whole point of the accusation: to try to equate opposition to some of the Chancellor's policies with hostility towards the Reich, thus turning the identification of left liberal supporters with the German state against their own political leaders. In the decades following Unification, identification with the Reich and everyday social and economic life was intensified. As we saw in Baden, and Payer's long political career exemplified, even Southern Democrats had come to support many aspects of Wilhelmine Germany. *Hofdemokraten* (court democrats) rather than *Umstürzler* (revolutionaries) had become a more common and apposite label for Württemberg left liberals.[17]

Left liberal politics was part of the Wilhelmine state, not its opposite pole. The dissatisfaction and pressure for reform represented by pre-war left liberal politics was only partial. Increased nationalism, support for army, navy, and colonial bills, and the respect and willingness to co-operate shown towards the Reich leadership formed the other side of the coin. Positive and negative attitudes towards the political, economic, and social status quo coexisted within the Protestant middle strata and left liberal politics. As Hermann von Eckardstein noted, many Wilhelmine Germans were at the same time critical and respectful towards the *Obrigkeitsstaat*: they 'long[ed] for political freedom . . . but for freedom with official permission from on high'.[18] Left liberals advocated change partly to preserve Wilhelmine society and avert upheaval. They argued that vital task of government was that of 'preventing revolutions through timely reforms'.[19]

Such attitudes are hard to explain if left liberals were simply the victims of the state. But this was not the case. It was true, of course, that the state discriminated against left liberals in various ways. They were shunned at court, in the officers' mess, amongst certain student

---

[17] See Simon, *Württembergische Demokraten*; and Hunt, *Peoples' Party*.
[18] H. von Eckardstein, *Lebenserinnerungen und politische Denkwürdigkeiten*, i (Leipzig, 1919), 303.　　　[19] Hoff, *Politische Zeit- und Streitfragen*, 17.

associations, and in the higher ranks of government service. But even here the automatic assumption of Conservative political views was being eroded. An attempt to appeal to reserve officers to vote Conservative as matter of duty in pre-war Silesia no longer commanded general respect. As one liberal academic openly replied, how to vote was up to each individual. 'Thank God, the times may be past when it was part of good tone that every educated man, especially a reserve officer, had to count himself as part of the Conservative party, and when every convinced liberal was seen as someone whose company was to be avoided.'[20] Younger left liberal politicians and local leaders were often reserve officers and members of student corporations. And if left liberals were boycotted socially, it tended to be by small backward-looking groups, rather than the mainstream of urban political, social, and economic life. At least in the cities and larger towns, left liberals sensed more advantages than disadvantages. They influenced local government and faced relatively few constraints on economic and social opportunities. They lived according to bourgeois values of law and order, decency, and hard work. By contrast, Junker privileges and state authoritarianism were only marginal influences on everyday life of middle-class city dwellers. From this urban perspective many left liberals saw political reform as a matter of completing a process already under way, of removing feudal remains in an otherwise modern state.

We do not, to be sure, have an ideal liberal state. But today's legally based and civilized state (*Rechtsstaat und Kulturstaat*) is indeed on the way towards that highest form of which we dream . . . It is *our* state whatever its government happens to be. It will grow with us and sink with us. We serve it for our own sakes. A pure anti-liberal party state is no longer possible in Germany today, even there where a conservative or clerical majority rules amongst ministers . . . Thus the task of today's liberalism lies clearly before us: we *must* regard the modern state as *our* state; the goal of all our efforts, with whose life we bound up with to the last.[21]

Left liberals did not believe they were living 'in a post liberal age'. On the contrary, most identified deeply with a state and society they believed to be moving irrevocably towards the twin goals of 'a strong German Reich, [and] a free German people'.[22]

---

[20] *Hilfe* (1913), 366.
[21] W. Goetz, 'Der Liberalismus und der Staat', *Hilfe* (1914), 40.
[22] Franz von Liszt cited in *Breslauer Zeitung*, 74 (30 Jan. 1912).

The war inevitably wrought deep-seated changes in left liberal attitudes and social base. Unparalleled mass warfare presented left liberal politics not just with massive, cumulative economic and social dislocation, but an uncomfortable new range of political priorities. Initially, some left liberals, optimistic, like others, of swift German victory, saw the war as an interlude in party politics to be followed by a resumption of the usual domestic political agenda. Left liberal journals like *Das Freie Volk* and *Badischer Landesbote* announced they were suspending publication during the war, but would return with the recommencement of real, that is, domestic politics.[23] But while many left liberal local parties drifted into inactivity or became preoccupied with war charities, party leaders became uncomfortably aware of the political effects of a supposedly 'unpolitical' war.

The change for left liberals was made greater because war came unexpectedly. Like most of the leading actors, many left liberal politicians were abroad at the height of the July crisis. This was because they were oblivious to the danger of war, rather than seeking to allay suspicion. The most unfortunate, Bruno Ablaß, was detained in Russia until November 1914.[24] Even Naumann, whose speeches and writings regularly included a reflection on what would happen 'in the event of war' (*im Ernstfall*), was taken aback. Increasingly, such references had become supporting arguments for military strength and social integration rather than concrete anticipation of war. Certainly, left liberals, like others, were uneasy about international instability and Germany's increased isolation. Indeed, having Britain and France in a potentially hostile alliance distressed left liberal deputies on general cultural and political grounds, as well as the military threat posed in league with Russia. Despite increasing susceptibility to nationalism, navalism, and imperialism, it was still a common left liberal sentiment that a union of progressive, advanced nations against backward forces represented the natural order of things. However, as successive foreign policy crises passed without the threat of war becoming reality most left liberals believed less in the inevitability of war than the capacity for last-minute compromise.

Pre-war left liberalism had concentrated almost exclusively on domestic politics. The intention was to reform aspects of Bismarckian internal policy, whilst preserving the external walls of skilful

---

[23] *Das Freie Volk* (8 Aug. 1914); *Badischer Landesbote* (31 Dec. 1914).
[24] *Freisinnige Zeitung* (10 May 1916).

diplomacy and strong armed forces. Indeed, where left liberals criticized foreign, colonial, and defence policy, this was largely an extension of domestic policy. Technical backwardness in the armed forces;
aristocratic privilege in the diplomatic corps, guards regiments, and
colonial administration; shortcomings of military justice and the legal
position of the army in the state; the absence of genuine universal
conscription—these were all part of the primarily domestic cause, the
creation of a modern, efficient, even-handed *Volksstaat*. Moreover,
this echoed a 'Primat der Innenpolitik' amongst the electorate as a
whole. The 1909 finance reform had had a far greater and more sustained impact on pre-war politics and public opinion than matters like
the Morocco crises and Anglo-German naval rivalry. The *Daily
Telegraph* and Zabern affairs both had foreign political implications,
but it was the domestic aspects which were the focus of public and
parliamentary attention. People cared more about the price of pork,
milk, or beer than the state of the Balkans.[25] Railway politics, in the
public mind, was about new lines, good connections, improved station
facilities, cheaper fares, and freight rates, not military mobilization.

Although belief in the inevitability of war is central to the analysis
of the July crisis and Germany's prime responsibility for the outbreak
of world war,[26] such sentiments were more prevalent at court and in
the upper reaches of state bureaucracy and military, than in German
society as a whole. Radical nationalist propaganda exercised some
pressure on the Reich leadership and, more significantly, conditioned
the view of Germany from abroad. But, as we have seen, it played only
a subordinate role in mass politics. There is no evidence that most
ordinary members of the veterans' associations or Navy League
actively expected and 'longed for' war like Heinrich Claß. With the
onset of war, Pan-Germanism was transformed from the fervent
creed of a small minority to a widespread belief. Nor in the transfer to
a wider audience were characteristic passion, and voluble verbal
radicalism dissipated. One could hardly sit in a Berlin pub, Ludwig
Haas complained in 1917, without being harangued by a Pan-
German.[27] As the prominent left liberal opponent of radical national-

[25] The importance of the debate over prices, especially food prices is rightly stressed by
C. Nonn, *Verbraucherprotest und Parteiensystem im wilhelminischen Deutschland* (Düsseldorf,
1996). However, Nonn's arguments that this issue led to the setting aside of Liberal–
Centre differences and the supplanting of the finance reform as a major issue cannot be
sustained.   [26] Mommsen, 'Topos of Inevitable War'.
[27] *Bote aus dem Riesengebirge* (9 Oct. 1917).

ism Ludwig Quidde noted, Pan-Germans had made noisy and far-reaching demands before 1914, 'but none of the men who led German policy belonged to them, and in the larger public they were not taken at all seriously'. War-psychosis made them a much more powerful and most dangerous force in the four and a half years after the outbreak of hostilities.[28]

The war aims question and the greater public emphasis on foreign policy and military affairs generally posed a double threat to left liberal politics. First it gave the nationalist right the powerful popular cause it had failed to find during the pre-war period. And in Hindenburg, Ludendorff, and Tirpitz it found the popular figure-heads it had lacked since Bismarck.[29] Annexationist demands met with a positive response from a wide section of society, and especially the Protestant middle strata.[30] The rhetoric of total victory and military and economic domination not only tapped accumulated reserves of nationalism, imperialism, and attachment to power politics. It also fed off wartime uncertainty. Amongst the believers, the vision of new land and money from reparations was grasped even firmer amidst economic misery; assurances of certain and total victory were held on to even more passionately as the fighting continued and casualties mounted. The right offered clear and easy solutions—unrestricted submarine warfare, even determination alone—to the problem of German victory.

The second set of difficulties concerned the left liberals' own response. War aims divided the party.[31] FVP politicians took up different positions. Some, led by Ernst Müller-Meiningen and Gottfried Traub, supported the Pan-German programme of annexations, while

---

[28] BA Koblenz, NL Quidde 82, 'Das andere wahre Deutschland', 4–5.

[29] A telegram from the National Liberal Association in Cologne publicly proclaiming that Germany had produced three great men, Bismarck, Hindenburg, and Tirpitz, was a prime example of the new-found enthusiasm. BA Koblenz, R 1/9, Holtzendorff report to Ballin 420, 6 June 1916.

[30] F. Fischer, *Germany's Aims in the First World War* (London, 1967) tends to downplay differences of degree amongst annexationists, and the effect of fluctuations in Germany's military and economic position on support for large-scale annexationists. But it remains the most compelling account of widespread support for territorial aggrandizement in German society. For the particularly strong support for annexations amongst the educated Protestant middle classes see K. Schwabe, *Wissenschaft und Kriegsmoral: Die deutschen Hochschullehrer und die politische Grundfrage des Ersten Weltkrieges* (Göttingen, 1969).

[31] For differing FVP attitudes towards annexations see Robson, 'Left-Wing Liberalism', 114 ff.; Gottschalk, *Linksliberalen*, 14 ff.; H. Hagenlücke, *Deutsche Vaterlandspartei: Die nationale Rechte am Ende des Kaiserreiches* (Düsseldorf, 1997), 304–12.

a minority headed by Georg Gothein were opposed to any annexations in Europe. The majority in-between favoured varying degrees of annexations. Some supported annexations in the east, but opposed them in the west.[32] Many, including Payer and Fischbeck, were opportunists, adjusting annexationist demands according to the military outlook. Others advocated particular concepts. Naumann's pursuit of 'Mitteleuropa', a Central European union, though rejected by FVP deputies, was the most elaborate and well-known.[33]

At the parliamentary and leadership level these differences, though substantial, remained relatively well contained. Despite private differences FVP Reichstag deputies maintained a united public position on the question of unrestricted submarine warfare. Heckscher was the only FVP deputy to vote against the Reichstag Peace Resolution. At other times Payer and Fischbeck avoided damaging arguments by preventing discussion about war aims at caucus meetings.[34] Left liberal tacticians were also keen to present annexations as a matter for military experts rather than party politicians. This was partly a realization that annexations depended on military victory. There was no point, as Fischbeck put it, in dividing up the lion's skin without having slain the lion ('unsinnig, das Löwenfell zu verteilen, ehe man den Löwen hat'[35]). But it was also an attempt to cover over internal divisions by diverting responsibility on to others. As in the pre-war period, left liberal deputies were anxious to avoid a damaging show of disunity on 'national' issues. Although the lack of a clear position on war aims offended deputies on both wings of the party, Gottfried Traub was the only FVP parliamentarian to give full public vent to these disagreements.[36]

However, the ambiguous, opportunistic stance of FVP deputies on war aims created serious and less manageable disaffection at lower levels within the party. Two elements which had allowed left liberal

---

[32] This was particularly the case with many left liberal intellectuals like Lujo Brentano and Theodor Wolff. Their appetite for East European territory was not, however, as great as E. A. Menze, 'War Aims and the Liberal Conscience: Lujo Brentano and Annexationism during the First World War', *CEH* 17 (1984), 140–59 suggests. The primary concern was to weaken Russia rather than expand Germany.

[33] H. C. Meyer, *'Mitteleuropa' in German Thought and Action 1815–1945* (The Hague, 1955); Theiner, *Sozialer Liberalismus*.

[34] BA Koblenz, NL Gothein 20, fos. 64–5, Otto Fischbeck to Georg Gothein, 8 May 1915.

[35] BA Koblenz, NL Gothein 20, fo. 36, Otto Fischbeck to Georg Gothein, 14 Sept. 1914.

[36] BA Berlin, FVP 37, fo. 5, FVP central committee, 6 Oct. 1917.

leaders to overcome potential vulnerability on 'national' issues before the war no longer applied. First, foreign and military questions moved to the centre of public interest. Many more people believed in a 'Primat der Nationalen' after the July crisis than in the preceding years. Secondly, attitudes towards the respective role of the Reich leadership and political parties shifted. Before 1914 only a minority of radical nationalists had challenged the notion that parties demonstrated their 'national reliability' simply by supporting the government military bills and colonial policy. But as popular dissatisfaction about the Chancellor's failure to provide a quick Bismarckian victory or even a clear lead swelled, association with the policies of the Reich leadership increasingly became a political liability. Left liberal support for the Reich government during the 1907 election or over the 1913 army expansion had bolstered the party's appeal to the nationalistic Protestant middle strata. But when the FVP supported Bethmann's opposition to unrestricted submarine warfare and an open programme of annexations, it alienated many provincial leaders and rank-and-file supporters. As Payer noted in March 1916, the parliamentary party had managed to unite against the campaign for unrestrictive submarine warfare, but 'a great part of our party comrades here [in Berlin], and probably also in the provinces, has been totally caught and blindly participates in the hue and cry'.[37] Above all the Reichstag Peace Resolution unleashed a tide of protest from large sections of the left liberal electorate during the second half of 1917. Again, as Naumann noted, the Peace Resolution caused few problems within the parliamentary party, but met 'very strong negative responses from the provinces . . . principally from educated and industrial circles'.[38]

Nationalist passions, sharpened by the war, posed a major threat to left liberal politics. Throughout Germany many left liberal opponents of the Peace Resolution were attracted to the Fatherland party: a dangerous rival precisely because, as Hermann Cohn the left liberal leader in Anhalt admitted, it said openly what many left liberals thought.[39] In towns like Bremen and Mühlhausen (in Thuringia), the existing

---

[37] BA Koblenz, NL Payer 44, fos. 19–20, Payer to wife, 17 Mar. 1916.
[38] Friedrich Naumann to Heinrich Rößler, 1 July 1917, cited in Theiner, *Sozialer Liberalismus*, 270.
[39] BA Berlin, FVP 29, fo. 15, conference with provincial leaders and party secretaries, 17 Mar. 1918.

FVP leadership went over to the new party. More commonly, a significant section of ordinary FVP members deserted.[40] Even long-standing left liberal leaders were attracted to the arguments put forward by right-wing nationalists. The former deputy August Hoffmeister, for example, agreed with right-wing critics that the Reichstag Peace Resolution would be taken as a sign of weakness, and was unnecessary because Germany had gained land.[41] Yet more pernicious than the direct demands for annexations and unrelenting prosecution of the war was the advancement of the Jew as universal scapegoat. The passage in the Peace Resolution rejecting 'forced' annexations was capable of wide interpretation. Annexationist FVP deputies were to claim that the Treaty of Brest-Litovsk was consistent with the July Resolution. Ablaß even argued that the Peace Resolution had been a masterly diplomatic preparation for Brest-Litovsk and the Ukraine treaty.[42] As the German western offensive was halted and food rations reduced even further during 1918, support for fighting on regardless dwindled. Increasing war-weariness was exemplified by the reaction of the man on the Munich trolley car to a peal of bells: 'Another victory . . . I'd rather have 1lb of butter.'[43] But the resentment against Jews intensified, whether as war-profiteers, shirkers, or a sinister international force working against Germany.[44] Such sentiments reached the centre of left liberal politics. Even an advocate of radical social liberalism like Heinz Potthoff complained to Gothein, chairman of the Defence League Against Anti-Semitism, that many Jews had desk jobs and reputations as shirkers.[45] Similarly, Naumann had to make strenuous efforts to persuade the Leipzig grammar-school teacher Hermann Barge, a close personal and political friend, that German policy was not guided by international Jewry. In other instances his persuasions were unsuccessful. Besides the well-known examples of Traub and Max Maurenbrecher, many less prominent Naumannites like W. Schaefer, a Stettin *Oberlehrer* and *Hilfe* reader for ten years, defected to nationalist and anti-Semitic groups during

---

[40] BA Berlin, FVP 28, fos. 1–10, party secretary conference, 17 Nov. 1917.

[41] BA Koblenz, NL Gothein 22, fo. 240, August Hoffmeister to Georg Gothein, 18 July 1917.   [42] *Löwenberger Zeitung* (20 June 1918).

[43] Bonn, *Wandering Scholar*, 198.

[44] E. Zechlin, *Die deutsche Politik und die Juden im ersten Weltkrieg* (Göttingen, 1969).

[45] BA Koblenz, NL Gothein 54, fos. 9–10, Heinz Potthoff to Georg Gothein, 1 Sept. 1916. Ironically, Potthoff also requested Gothein to use his influence to secure an administrative position away from the front.

the war.[46] Most importantly, Jews increasingly displaced Junkers and *Pfaffen* as hate-figures within the Protestant middle strata electorate on which left liberal politics depended. They could pose as the opponents of Junkerdom and political Catholicism (though co-operation with the Centre during the war and in the Weimar Coalition was to compromise the latter appeal), but left liberals were totally unsuited to the demands of a new adversarial role: the opponents of international Jewry.

If the main danger was a mass defection of nationalistic voters to the right, the damage the FVP's position on war aims did to radical liberal activists must not be overlooked. They, like the ardent nationalists, became increasingly alienated by FVP passivity and attempts to hide behind the government. As Martin Rade reported in 1916, the conduct of FVP parliamentarians during the war had disillusioned left liberal leaders in Marburg. 'Our party has not taken a leading position either in internal or external matters. . . . The dilatory, purely mediatory path of our party policy has been unable to attract. And it is hard to think how resolute annexationists can combine fruitfully with determined pacifists: Traub with Schücking and Quidde.'[47] L. Nelson, another radical liberal intellectual, was even more critical. 'What does the FVP still mean today? Why bother keep trying to stir it up? It had totally failed during the war . . . The Liberals have swung here and there according to the military constellation.'[48]

Left liberal inability to deal with 'national' issues after 1914 was compounded by adverse circumstances. The rift between left liberal leaders and its electoral base was widened by problems of communication. FVP deputies, like the Reich leadership, were frequently unable to defend their position without damaging the war effort. The main reasons for opposition to annexations, particularly during the second half of the war, were an unfavourable military balance and the increasing danger of economic collapse in Germany and Austria. Yet neither left liberals nor the government could talk openly about the military weaknesses which ruled out an annexationist peace or the rising danger of crippling strikes in hunger-ridden towns and cities. Similarly, on the question of unrestricted submarine warfare the facts

---

[46] BA Berlin, NL Naumann 11, Friedrich Naumann to H. Barge, Leipzig, 29 Jan. 1918 (copy); BA Koblenz, NL Goetz 64, W. Schaefer to Walter Goetz, 10 Feb. 1918; cf. NL Goetz 64, Karl Graf von Bothmer to Walter Goetz, 11 Feb. 1918.
[47] UB Marburg, NL Rade, Martin Rade to FVP Berlin headquarters, 9 Feb. 1916 (copy).
[48] BA Koblenz, NL Erkelenz 12, fo. 52, L. Nelson to Anton Erkelenz, 7 Nov. 1918.

completely justified the left liberal caucus's actions. The FVP deputies Leonhart, Struve, and Gothein had been right before 1914 when they argued the military case for building submarines rather than battleships. Left liberals were also correct to emphasize the threat posed to Germany by American entry into the war. Finally, they were right to conclude that Germany had too few submarines, and the Allies had too much shipbuilding capacity for Britain to be compelled to seek peace. Yet none of this could be aired in public without undermining national confidence. As a result Tirpitz, who had been wrong on every military and foreign-policy point, won the domestic propaganda victory, at least within the Protestant middle classes.[49]

Left liberal deputies therefore had only a limited scope in justifying their actions to the public. In the domestic politics of pre-war Germany the left liberals had been vigorous and effective campaigners. During the war they were hampered by considerations of national interest and a sense of responsibility. Perhaps most important was a change in the prime left liberal weapon: the press. Before the war newspapers had brought left liberal attitudes to a wide section of society. They had shaped resentment against 'Junker und Pfaffen' and channelled public pressure for reform. But during the First World War the press as a whole became primarily a medium for official war propaganda. War reports in left liberal newspapers generally fed the same false optimism and blind patriotism as more right-wing journals. This was partly, of course, the product of government news management and district military censors. But it was also a question of the attitudes of left liberal newspapers themselves. Radical contemporaries complained that only the *Berliner Tageblatt* and *Frankfurter Zeitung* showed a continued interest in left liberal values. Other left liberal newspapers took the Kaiser's declaration 'ich sehe keine Parteien mehr' as a cue to abandon the party pursuits in favour of the 'national interest'. In practice this meant putting aside specific left liberal demands and cultivating patriotic fervour and state loyalty. The increase in circulation of the *Hamburger Fremdenblatt* from 70,000 to over 140,000 during the war, for example, did nothing to further left liberal politics. For the paper decided to reject 'party narrowness' and dedicate itself to 'Hamburg's international trade and the international

---

[49] DSB Berlin, NL Delbrück, Wilhelm Struve to Hans Delbrück, 12 Feb. 1927; BA Koblenz, NL Gothein 31, fos. 257–65, Gothein 39, 510 ff.

standing of the German Reich'.[50] The tendency for left liberal news-papers to focus on the Fatherland rather than the party had surfaced briefly during the Bülow Bloc. After 1914 the trait became widespread and persistent.

The left liberal press was also seriously weakened by wartime eco-nomics, particularly the sharp decline in commercial advertising. War shortages removed the need to advertise goods and services, the main source of revenue for left liberal newspapers. Right-wing official newspapers (*Amtliche Kreisblätter*) which carried public notices, and SPD newspapers relying mainly on subscriptions faced less serious losses. Advertising revenue for the left liberal *Neuer Alb-Bote* in Ebingen, for example, fell from 37,000 to 20,000 marks in 1914–15, reducing net profits from 15,000–19,500 marks in pre-war years to 1,391.50 marks in 1915.[51] A shortage of skilled labour and rapid rises in the cost of newsprint and ink placed further pressure on newspaper finances.[52] As a result, a significant number of left liberal newspapers ceased publication. While precise figures are not available, the percentage of left liberal papers which folded or were sold was undoubtedly greater than the overall fall of 15–20 per cent in the number of newspapers between 1914 and 1917.[53]

This was particularly the case in regions where left liberalism was less established. In Baden, for example, the *Badischer Landesbote* (Karlsruhe), *Oberbadische Volkszeitung* (Freiburg), and *Neue Konstanzer Abendzeitung* had all ceased publication by 1916, leaving the *Neue Badische Landeszeitung* in Mannheim as the only left liberal newspaper in a large Badenese town. In such areas the finances of left liberal newspapers had been stretched even before 1914. The same applied to many left liberal newspapers in the FVP's semi-rural constituencies. The *Tageblatt für Vorpommern* in Greifswald, for example, was important in keeping support from artisans, peasants, and workers. But it was given no municipal and state advertising, and did not have the sort of readers who attracted private advertisers or could afford a high cover price. It required continual subsidies from wealthy individuals and especially Georg Gothein, the Reichstag

[50] *Hamburg vor 90 Jahren: Zum neunzigjährigen Bestehen des Hamburger Fremdenblattes, 1828–1918* (Hamburg, 1918), 26–7.

[51] HSA Stuttgart, NL Haußmann 105, J. Beck, Genossenschaftsdruckerei Ebingen, to Conrad Haußmann, 22 Feb. 1916.   [52] Oehlke, *100 Jahre Breslauer Zeitung*, 291–315.

[53] For a general survey of the changing pattern of the press during the war, see Muser, *Statistische Untersuchung*, 164–73.

deputy for the district. Such papers had been run for political rather than commercial reasons. The war turned meagre profits or bearable losses into large, unsustainable deficits.

While left liberal newspapers were closing, the war also saw a sustained attempt by the right to counteract its traditional weakness in the press. The basis of Hugenburg's press empire was laid during the war. While the war rendered the traditional left liberal pattern of a small number of moderately rich individuals sustaining newspapers inoperable, it sharpened heavy industry's appreciation of press influence and made newspapers easier to obtain. Naumann, always aware of the importance of the press, reported with alarm how the right was buying up small and medium-sized newspapers and seriously weakening the left liberal provincial press.[54]

The left liberals' diminished capacity to influence the public through the press was the central aspect of a general disruption in the dissemination of left liberal politics. The other main left liberal channel of communication, the public meeting, was tightly controlled. Public discussion of political themes was prohibited for much of the war. This brought two disadvantages. The first was simply a question of bias. The military authorities tended to allow meetings which promoted Conservatism and right-wing nationalism under the guise of general patriotism, but ban or restrict left liberal or SPD public meetings.[55] The second was the fact that left liberals had depended particularly on an open, competitive public stage. The FVP conveyed its message in a free press, in Reichstag elections, and in open public meetings. The war prevented left liberal politics from operating where it was most effective. At the same time it increased the political influence of the right-wing establishment and minority groups. While the press was censored, officers and *Oberlehrer* provided a stream of right-wing propaganda in the armed forces and schools. While organized mass politics was suspended, members of the *Bildungsbürgertum* spread annexationist agitation through petitions, informal meetings, and word of mouth. Indeed, it was precisely the absence of mass elections and free press comment which gave added influence to articulate minorities and economic interest groups. The main victim of this process was the Reich leadership. As Carl Petersen put it: 'the

---

[54] Theiner, *Sozialer Liberalismus*, 272.

[55] BA Koblenz, NL Gothein 38, 'Zensur im 1. Weltkrieg'. DSB Berlin, NL Delbrück, Max Weber to editor, *Frankfurter Zeitung* (27 June 1917) (copy).

Chancellor, especially when he is a sensitive man like Bethmann Hollweg, is irritated and tortured by all sorts of groups and small bands in the population, of whom no one knows how much is behind them'.[56] But the left liberals were also victims.

The war faced left liberal politics with divisive, uncomfortable issues. It hampered left liberal communication and campaigning. But there was a third major adverse effect on left liberal politics: the economic and social impact of the war on the left liberals' electoral base. Although pre-war left liberalism had been a vehicle for certain social and economic grievances—resentment towards arrogant notables, or discontent from public-sector employees over living standards—it also operated against a general background of economic confidence and the pride of individuals about their position in local society. Such conditions reduced insecurity and preoccupation with immediate economic survival while encouraging belief in the liberal secular doctrine of material, cultural, and political progress. For many left liberals security and optimism were shattered by the war. The effects of the war in terms of death, injury, malnutrition, and impoverishment were felt by society as a whole. But economic misery was particularly acute for the urban petty bourgeoisie, the section of society which accounted for a major part of left liberal support. White-collar workers were laid off at the outbreak of war and suffered cuts in real wages of around a third during 1914–15.[57] Throughout the war there was a drastic erosion of 'new' *Mittelstand* incomes in absolute terms and relative to manual workers.[58]

As a recent study of Hamburg in the decade after 1914 confirms, much of the relative impoverishment of *Mittelstand* groups took place during the war. Post-war inflation was more a prolonging, than a deepening, of economic hardship and insecurity.[59] The war also brought great disruption to small producers. Those still able to provide goods for sale or exchange found a ready market. But a half of artisans had been called up by 1917 and around a third of workshops had been closed.[60] Finally, the concentration of left liberal support in towns and cities also meant they were located in the areas where the crisis of food supply was at its deepest. Even parliamentarians did not

[56] SA Hamburg, NL Carl Petersen L50, Petersen to Naumann, 26 Sept. 1916 (copy).
[57] J. Kocka, *Facing Total War: German Society 1914–1918* (Leamington Spa, 1984), 85.
[58] Ibid. 84–90.
[59] P. J. Lyth, *Inflation and the Merchant Economy: the Hamburg Mittelstand, 1914–24* (Oxford, 1990), 182.   [60] Kocka, *Facing Total War*, 102, 104–6.

escape its crushing effects. Georg Gothein lost 30lb, a fifth of his weight.[61] Naumann, who insisted on adhering to official food rations, was described by Minna Cauer as a physical and mental ruin.[62] Those members of urban society without contacts with rural districts or money to buy on the black market faced grim, unrelenting malnutrition throughout the second half of the war.

For left liberals this high level of actual suffering was compounded by the destruction of a general vision of society. The change from initial exultation through stoical determination to ultimate despair between August 1914 and 1917/18 is most easily traced in left liberal intellectuals like Weber and Schulze-Gaevernitz.[63] At first they saw the war as the manifestation of their belief in underlying German unity and social cohesion. In particular, the labour movement's support for the war effort was taken as justifying left liberal views of politics and society. The reaction of Fritz Kestner, a Jewish treasury official and friend of Schulze-Gaevernitz, was typical. 'And now above all the Reichstag and the 111 Social Democrats. That is really one of the greatest days in German history and I am boundlessly joyful about it.'[64] But by 1917/18 such observers feared the destruction, not the consolidation, of German society. The impression made by Naumann on Ludwig Heilbrunn after a party meeting in April 1917 typified the despair which repeatedly surfaced in the second half of the war. 'Every word echoed the grief of the patriot who sees his Fatherland at the edge of the abyss.'[65] Hardship replaced prosperity. State control and the black market replaced fair and open trading. Confusion and anxiety replaced order and confidence in everyday life. Rather than fulfilling aspirations of a civilizing mission in the Russian east, the war threatened internal revolution.

The war brought a sense of crisis to many left liberals, not just about political aims, but the whole fabric of German society. As early as November 1914 Loebell noted 'that in total contrast to the peaceful press', the population was 'going through a deep process of fermentation'.[66] Reports from FVP provincial leaders and party secretaries

---

[61] BA Koblenz, NL Gothein 14, fo. 308.

[62] IISH Amsterdam, NL Cauer 1, diary entry, 12 Nov. 1914.

[63] Mommsen, *Max Weber*; BA-MA Freiburg, NL Schulze-Gaevernitz v. 12, 15–22, and 28.

[64] BA-MA Freiburg, NL Schulze-Gaevernitz v. 22, war letters of Dr Fritz Kestner, 5 Aug. 1914.   [65] Heilbrunn, 'Lebenserinnerungen', 187.

[66] Loebell, report to the Emperor, 1 Nov. 1914, cited in BA Koblenz, NL Goetz 36, 358 ff.

provided similar observations of social upheaval.[67] But the left liberal leadership largely failed to respond to these developments. This was partly a matter of entrenched attitudes. When Ludwig Heilbrunn attempted, in April 1917, to awaken FVP Reichstag and Landtag deputies to the prospects of social collapse he 'came up against unexpected incomprehension . . . a complete cluelessness towards the threatening dangers. Domestic politics seemed to be the most important thing to the gentlemen: electoral franchise and electoral tactics the a[lpha] and o[mega].'[68] Oskar Cassel blithely asserted the loyalty of all classes and Karl Mommsen provided a rationale for passivity: 'Social Democratic peace demonstrations just strengthen foreign countries. Liberalism must support Bethmann to the hilt.'[69] More importantly, left liberal politics was not just unwilling, but unable to meet political challenges reshaped by the war.

There is, then, 'much to be said for the view', as Michael John has concluded, 'that German liberalism—as a theory and a set of political practices—failed because of the intolerable strains arising out of the First World War'.[70] Yet the concluding phase of the war also witnessed the apparent high-water mark of left liberal success. On the eve of the November Revolution and the outset of the Weimar Republic left liberals held leading positions in Reich and state government. Southern Democrats had a strong presence in the Reich cabinet of Prince Max. The Saxon FVP leader Oskar Günther was appointed Minister-President of his state in October 1918; as were Hugo Wendorff in Mecklenburg, Theodor Liesching in Württemberg, Theodor Tantzen in Oldenburg, and Adolf Neumann-Hofer in Lippe-Detmold during the final days of the Kaiserreich. In Hamburg the left liberals J. H. Garrels and Carl Petersen became senators. The five and a half million votes (18.6 per cent) received by the left liberals in January 1919 represented much of the Protestant middle strata.

How is this paradox explained? Part of the answer lay in the FVP's continued capacity to mediate with other parties, and between the executive and party politics. The *Burgfriede* (civil truce) and need to keep together a broad and heterogeneous Reichstag majority prevented left liberals from projecting an alliance, like the *Großblock*, which had a strong emotional appeal to part of the electorate. The

---

[67] BA Berlin, FVP 28 and 29.   [68] Heilbrunn, 'Lebenserinnerungen', 185.

[69] Ibid. 185–6.

[70] M. John, *Politics and the Law in Late Nineteenth-Century Germany: The Origins of the Civil Code* (Oxford, 1989), 257.

message, inevitably, was one of compromise and necessary sacrifice. But within Berlin politics, in contrast to the sphere of popular politics, the FVP became even more central and influential in forming policy and alliances. Left liberal efforts to encourage the SPD to play a practical role in German politics, which had been a feature of the pre-1914 periods, increased in volume and importance. Left liberals played a vital intermediary role between the SPD majority leaders and the Wilhelmine establishment. The Reich leadership frequently turned to FVP deputies to persuade the SPD to support its policies.[71] In return, SPD leaders like Ebert and Scheidemann, unwilling to enter government themselves in 1917/18, wanted indirect representation through executive positions for FVP deputies. Nor was the left liberal role as a bridge between the SPD and Wilhelmine society confined to politics. When Holtzendorff, a director and Berlin representative of the Hamburg America Line, belatedly sought contacts with the SPD in October 1918, it was Naumann and Jäckh who arranged a meeting with Ebert.[72]

Left liberal Reichstag deputies also rediscovered the similarities between themselves and Centre party counterparts on 'national' and constitutional questions. Pre-war hostility and the continued differences on cultural issues meant co-operation with the Centre did not generate popular resonance and was largely limited to the Reichstag. Moreover, internal divisions within both parties limited the scope for action.[73] While Bethmann Hollweg was right to say that, with the Peace Resolution, 'for the first time a Reichstag majority has formed with the intention to act', he was also justified in adding that no one could foresee how long the majority would last.[74] Nevertheless, the FVP continued to function, as Julius Kopsch put it, 'as the centre-point for forming a majority'.[75] Left liberals also enjoyed increasingly close relations with the executive. Similarities in the attitude towards war aims and the mutual dependence between Bethmann and the FVP

---

[71] See e.g. the private meetings between Payer and SPD politicians described in BA Koblenz, NL Payer 43, fos. 18 ff., letter to wife, 20 Aug. 1915; 43, fo. 55, letter to wife, 8 Dec. 1915; 44, fo. 4, letter to wife, 12 Jan. 1916.

[72] BA Koblenz, R 1/16, report 962, 29 Oct. 1918.

[73] For opposition to the Peace Resolution within the Centre Party see HAS Cologne, NL Carl Bachem 523. By autumn 1918 the relative influence of leading figures and the party's position on a range of issues was so unclear 'that no one can say what will now become of the Centre Party'. AA Wrocław, NL Porsch IV, 16. 9, Carl Bachem to Porsch, 30 Sept. 1918.

[74] DSB Berlin, NL Delbrück, Bethmann Hollweg to Hans Delbrück, 8 Sept. 1917.

[75] BA Berlin, FVP 29, fo. 8.

have already been noted. The FVP leader Payer was also regarded as a major link between the executive and Reichstag majorities, though his appointment as Vice Chancellor in 1917 tended to lessen rather than strengthen his ability to perform this role. A coming together between left liberals and officials also took place at a slightly less elevated level. Left liberal politicians, editors, and businessmen were enthusiastic supporters of the Deutsche Gesellschaft 1914, intended as meeting place for prominent members of German public life of all political hues.[76] Prussian envoys revised their distaste for the left liberals in the light of FVP attitudes towards the war. Eisendecher, for instance, praised the restraint and responsibility of leading left liberals in contrast to the extreme and disruptive Pan-Germans.[77] In Munich the Prussian ambassador contrasted a Tirpitz speech which drew a large crowd but had a superficial impact, with more convincing arguments against annexations put forward by Georg Gothein.[78]

It was, therefore, the FVP's role as a mediator more than its own ideas and popular support which explained much of the party's influence. This was particularly the case in the circumstances of autumn 1918. The party was seen by a section of the Wilhelmine establishment as the last chance to preserve social order. But not only was the decision to accede to bourgeois reform too late, it was only accepted by a minority of the establishment. Ernst von Weizsäcker, for example, witnessed the incomprehension shown by most OHL officers, still two-thirds 'gut preußisch Konservativ', towards Payer's attempts to outline the crushing necessity of domestic reforms.[79] The FVP was also seen by SPD moderates as a vehicle for averting chaos. But once in leading positions left liberals were powerless. The narrowness of their support was exposed. Above all, they had no means to deal with the massive economic, social, and military problems which had prompted their appointment. It was a poisoned chalice which the Wilhelmine military and political establishment handed the left liberals in October 1918.

[76] B. Sösemann, 'Politische Kommunikation im "Reichsbelagerungszustand"—Programm, Struktur und Wirkungen des Klubs "Deutsche Gesellschaft 1914"', in M. Bobrowsky and W. R. Lagenbucher (eds.), *Wege zur Kommunikationsgeschichte* (Munich, 1987), 630–49.
[77] AA Bonn, IA Baden 31. 15, 8 Nov. 1917 and 28 Oct. 1918.
[78] AA Bonn, IA Deutschland 122. 9, vol. 5, Prussian ambassador, Munich, 19 Nov. 1917.
[79] Hill (ed.), *Weizsäcker-Papiere*, diary and letter to father, 25 Aug. 1918, 277–8.

The full extent of the damage to left liberal politics was not immediately apparent. In some respects left liberals had been the initial beneficiaries of wartime social and economic dislocation. The controlled war economy might be interpreted as further departure from liberal economics. Its privations increased the attraction of liberal free trade.[80] Although war aims provided a powerful rival cause, support for left liberal demands for domestic reforms also increased during the war. Helfferich concluded, from discussions with the political parties in March/April 1917, that only FVP and SPD united in favour of parliamentary government, and 'that the introduction of a parliamentary system will [therefore not] be needed for domestic political reasons for the foreseeable future'.[81] Yet even this represented an increase in the level of support since 1914. During 1918 an increasing number of National Liberals and Centre party politicians saw parliamentary accountability, if not a full Western parliamentary system, as inevitable. Similarly, support for the introduction of equal franchise in Prussia had become far more urgent by 1917/18 than in 1914. Only a small minority of National Liberals were prepared to contemplate equal Prussian franchise before the war, but a large majority voted for its introduction at a special party conference in autumn 1917. Likewise by 1917 men like Holtzendorff and Siegfried Kardorff supported equal franchise as the only alternative to domestic unrest.

The right's inability to address domestic reform aspirations remained a crucial barrier to popular support. The equivocation of the Fatherland party on domestic reform proved no more attractive than the DKP's intransigence. Fischbeck claimed, in October 1917, that the many left liberals who had been attracted to the Fatherland party were 'melting away like snow under the sun. The realization that they wanted to cheat the people of their franchise is getting through more and more.'[82] This was rather premature. But the left liberal argument that the Fatherland party was a cover for domestic reactionaries persuaded many FVP defectors to return to the party during the course of 1918.[83]

---

[80] R. Bessel, 'State and Society in Germany in the Aftermath of the First World War', in W. R. Lee and E. Rosenhaft (eds.), *The State and Social Change in Germany, 1880–1980* (New York, 1990), 214.

[81] AA Bonn, IA Deutschland 125. 3, vol. 26, secret report by Helfferich to ministers, 23 Apr. 1917 (copy).　　　　　[82] *Liegnitzer Zeitung* (30 Oct. 1917).

[83] The Fatherland party's rapid political decline after the failure of the German military offensive in spring 1918 was reflected in a collapse of party finances. GStA Berlin-Dahlem, NL Wolfgang Kapp 519; cf. Hagenlücke, *Deutsche Vaterlandspartei*, 372–85.

The resumption of contested by-elections in early 1918 supported commentators who observed 'a powerful move to the left throughout all circles'.[84] Bautzen-Kamenz had been the only seat in Saxony that the right had managed to preserve intact from the Social Democratic electoral onslaught in 1903 and 1912. But the SPD won the seat from a Conservative/Fatherland candidate in 1918 with FVP run-off support.[85] Groups outside the educated middle classes did not show the same zeal for widespread annexations. In the wake of professorial protests, for instance, peasants from the Kaiserstuhl wrote to assure Schulze-Gaevernitz that they supported his advocacy of a negotiated peace.[86] While workers were not immune to the nationalist mood of 1914 and the lure of annexations, even in 1914–15 right-wing SPD deputies encountered rank-and-file opposition to the war. Sharpened by the material privations of 1917–18, workers' yearnings for peace far outweighed desires for territorial aggrandizement.[87]

Left liberal support in the National Assembly elections therefore represented a radicalization of sections of society during the war, as well as an attempt by conservative-minded voters to stave off social disorder. In the short term wartime resentments damaged the right-wing Wilhelmine establishment more than the left liberals. Only after 1919 did a different picture emerge. In rural Schleswig-Holstein, for example, economic restrictions placed on farmers and peasants brought a flood of resentment against the government and those associated with it.[88] In summer 1918 the *Bauernverein des Nordens* (Northern Peasants' Association) was established in a revolt against the Agrarian League and turned to left liberal deputies for advice.[89] The transparent inadequacies of the existing system, the egalitarian rhetoric which surrounded the war effort, and government promises of a *Neuorientierung* (new opening) all added weight to left liberal claims.

However, the peasants' anger was not only directed at state inspectors and aristocrats with their *Luxuspferde* (luxury horses). Economic

---

[84] BA Koblenz, NL Brentano 11, fo. 250, Moritz J. Bonn to Lujo Brentano, 12 July 1917.

[85] *Volkswacht* (15 Jan. 1918).

[86] BA-MA Freiburg NL Schulze-Gaevernitz v 16. On the weakness of the Fatherland party in Baden outside the educated middle classes, see Müller, *Politik und Gesellschaft im Krieg*, 199–209.

[87] BA Berlin, NL Heine 2; BA-MA Freiburg, NL Schulze-Gaevernitz v 19, Wilhelm Kolb to Schulze-Gaevernitz, 20 Aug. 1915; Fricke, *Arbeiterbewegung*, i. 368–408.

[88] For the catalogue of rural complaints see Hoff, *Abgrund, passim*.

[89] See *Nord West* (1918) for Conservative disquiet about this development.

difficulty and shortages rekindled anti-capitalist and anti-Semitic sentiment. It was no longer possible, as it had been before the war, for a man like Waldstein, the epitome of the articulate, urban Jew, to traverse the Schleswig-Holstein countryside attracting support for himself and his political message: people wanted a different sort of man and a different sort of rhetoric. The name of the *Schleswig-Holstein Bauern und Landarbeiterdemokratie* (Schleswig-Holstein Peasant and Rural Labour Democracy), the continuation of the *Bauernverein des Nordens*, still reflected a spirit of egalitarianism and reform. The group's deputies elected in 1919 also continued a link with the left liberals joining the DDP as *Hospitanten*. By 1921 however, the signs of disaffection were obvious. A leader Iverson claimed the Landespartei, as the party had been renamed, represented 'green democracy' as opposed to the 'golden democracy' of the DDP and proceeded to espouse the familiar canon of *Mittelstandspolitik*.[90]

The war and its aftermath rendered much of the left liberals' appeal obsolete. The Junkers no longer presented themselves as a campaign slogan and, as the Weimar school settlement made painfully clear, the left liberals were having to compromise with the *Pfaffen*. The programme of political reform had been exhausted, indeed exceeded, and, with the Centre as part of the governing majority, the party could not deliver most of its *Kulturpolitik*. In addition, the enormity of the war's impact on people's lives inevitably diminished the left liberals' ability to capitalize on loyalty and regional tradition. With the social and economic equilibrium upset, why should the political equilibrium have remained stable? By the 1920s few electors looked back to the 1860s let alone 1848. In any case, it was no longer political reform which was at a premium, but economic stability. In the 1920s, nostalgia for pre-war prosperity and national grandeur was as readily understandable as the irrelevance to the great majority of the ideals of 1848.

[90] Tilton, 'Nazism', 15.

Bibliography

ARCHIVE SOURCES

Bundesarchiv Berlin

07.01 Reichskanzlei RK 1394–6
60 Vo 3 Fortschrittliche Volkspartei
Nachlaß Carl Aldenhoven
Nachlaß Theodor Barth
Nachlaß Max Broemel
Nachlaß Paul Nathan
Nachlaß Friedrich Naumann
Nachlaß Julie Ohr
Nachlaß Wilhelm Ohr

Bundesarchiv Koblenz

R43 F Reichskanzlei
R45 Nationalliberale Partei
R1/1–16 Reports Director Holtzendorff to Ballin, 1914–18
Nachlaß Moritz Julius Bonn
Nachlaß Lujo Brentano
Nachlaß Bernhard von Bülow
Nachlaß Hans Delbrück
Nachlaß Bernhard Dernburg
Nachlaß Anton Erkelenz
Nachlaß Matthias Erzberger
Nachlaß Ernst Franke
Nachlaß Otto Geßler
Nachlaß Walter Goetz
Nachlaß Georg Gothein
Nachlaß Johannes Haller
Nachlaß Georg von Hertling
Nachlaß Theodor Heuss
Nachlaß Wilhelm Külz
Nachlaß Friedrich-Wilhelm von Loebell
Nachlaß Hermann Luppe
Nachlaß Friedrich von Payer
Nachlaß Ludwig Quidde

Nachlaß Hartmann Freiherr von Richthofen
Nachlaß Eugen Schiffer
Nachlaß Walther Schücking
Nachlaß Wilhelm Solf
Nachlaß Edmund Max Stengel
Nachlaß Gustav Stolper
Nachlaß Albert Südekum
Nachlaß Gottfried Traub
Nachlaß Hans Wehberg
Nachlaß Theodor Wolff
Kleine Erwerbung Theobald von Bethmann Hollweg
Kleine Erwerbung Adolf Damaschke
Kleine Erwerbung Bernhard Falk
Kleine Erwerbung Conrad Haußmann
Kleine Erwerbung Eugen Richter
Kleine Erwerbung Richard Roesicke
Kleine Erwerbung Paul Rohrbach
Kleine Erwerbung Anton Schifferer
Kleine Erwerbung Ernst Troeltsch
Kleine Erwerbung August Weber

Bundesarchiv-Militärarchiv Freiburg

Nachlaß Gerhart von Schulze-Gaevernitz

Amsterdam, International Institute of Social History

Nachlaß Eduard Bernstein
Nachlaß Otto Braun
Nachlaß Rudolf Breitscheid
Nachlaß Minna Cauer
Nachlaß Wolfgang Heine
Nachlaß Carl Herz
Nachlaß Karl Kautsky
Nachlaß Georg von Vollmar

Bonn, Politisches Archiv des Auswärtigen Amtes

IA Deutschland
Nachlaß Gustav Stresemann

Berlin, Deutsche Staatsbibliothek

Nachlaß Hans Delbrück
Nachlaß Adolf von Harnack

Berlin-Dahlem, Geheimes Staatsarchiv

Nachlaß Otto Braun

Nachlaß Friedrich Meinecke
Nachlaß Alexander Dominicus

Bremen, Staatsarchiv
Nachlaß Emil Fitger
Verband Bremischer Bürgervereine

Coburg, Staatsarchiv
Nachlaß Oskar Arnold

Darmstadt, Staatsarchiv
Nachlaß Hermann Hummel
Nachlaß Adolf Korell

Detmold, Staatsarchiv
Nachlaß Adolf Neumann-Hofer
Nachlaß Max Staerke

Düsseldorf, Hauptstaatsarchiv
RMV 17-4 Fortschrittliche Volkspartei
Edinburgh University Library
Charles Sarolea Papers

Frankfurt am Main, Stadtarchiv
Nachlaß Ludwig Heilbrunn
Nachlaß Fritz and Heinrich Rößler

Hamburg, Staatsarchiv
Nachlaß Carl Braband
Nachlaß Carl Petersen

Karlsruhe, Generallandesarchiv
Akten der Nationalliberalen Partei Badens
Nachlaß Oskar Muser
Nachlaß Willy Hellpach

Kiel, Landesbibliothek
Cp 31 Deutscher Verein für das Nördliche Schleswig: Protokollbuch
1913–19

Köln, Historisches Archiv der Stadt
Nachlaß Carl Bachem
Nachlaß Wilhelm Marx

London, British Library of Political and Economic Science
Ignaz Jastrow Collection
Stadtarchiv Mannheim
Nachlaß Jean Wolfhard

Marburg, Universitätsbibliothek
Nachlaß Martin Rade

München, Stadtbibliothek
Nachlaß Georg Kerschensteiner
Oldenburg, Staatsarchiv
Memoirs Wilhelm Ahlhorn
Nachlaß Theodor Tantzen

Oxford, Bodleian Library
James Bryce Papers

Schleswig, Landesarchiv
301 Oberpräsidium
309 Regierungspräsidium
320 Steinburg
384 Politische Parteien

Stuttgart, Hauptstaatsarchiv
Nachlaß Conrad Haußmann

Wolfenbüttel, Staatsarchiv
Nachlaß Karl Schrader

Wrocławiu, Archiwum Archidiecezjalne we (Archepiscopal Archive Wrocław)
Nachlaß Adolf Kardinal Bertram
Nachlaß Georg Kardinal Kopp
Nachlaß Franz Josef Neise
Nachlaß Felix Porsch

Wrocławiu, Archiwum Panstwowe we (State Archive Wrocław)
Regierungspräsidium Oppeln

UNPUBLISHED SOURCES IN PRIVATE HANDS

Nachlaß Lothar Schücking (in the possession of Dr. Annette Hohmeyer-Schücking, Detmold)

PRINTED SOURCES

Newspapers and Journals: Collections

Bundesarchiv Berlin
Reichslandbund Press Archive

Bundesarchiv Koblenz
Zeitgeschichtliche Sammlung 1

Hamburg, Staatsarchiv
Akten der Politischen Polizei Abt. IV, V950, V1004.

Schleswig, Landesarchiv
301/59–61, Literary Bureau Oberpräsidium Schleswig

Wrocław, University Library
Yb 2500, Contemporary Collection on Breslau Politics

Left Liberal National Dailies

Berliner Tageblatt
Frankfurter Zeitung
Freisinnige Zeitung
Vossische Zeitung

Left Liberal Political Periodicals

Fortschritt: Halbmonatsschrift für Politik Volkswirtschaft und Marinefragen
(Kiel)
Der Fortschritt: Halbmonatsschrift der Fortschrittlichen Volkspartei für
Niedersachsen
Liberale Blätter (Kassel)
Das Freie Volk
Die Hilfe
Das März
Mitteilungen der Hauptvereine Groß-Berlin der Fortschrittlichen Volkspartei
Mitteilungen für Vertrauensmänner der FVP
Die Nation
Die Volkspartei

Other Political Periodicals

Die Alldeutschen Blätter

Das neue Deutschland

Baden: Regional and Local Press

Badische Landeszeitung
Badische Presse
Badischer Beobachter
Badischer Landesbote
Neue Badische Landeszeitung
Neue Konstanzer Abendzeitung
Oberbadische Volkszeitung
Volksfreund

Schleswig-Holstein: Regional and Local Press

Altonaer Tageblatt
Apenrader Tageblatt
Der Elbwart (from 1913 *Der Bismarckwart*)
Elmshorner Nachrichten
Elmshorner Zeitung
General-Anzeiger für Hamburg-Altona
Hamburger Echo
Hamburger Fremdenblatt
Hamburger Nachrichten
Hamburgischer Correspondent
Husumer Nachrichten
Itzehoer Nachrichten
Kieler Zeitung
Kieler Neueste Nachrichten
Lübecker Nachrichten und Eisenbahn Zeitung
Lübeckische Anzeigen
Neue Hamburger Zeitung
Nördischer Kurier (Itzehoe)
Nord West
Schleswigsche Grenzpost
Schleswig-Holsteinische Landespost
Schleswig-Holsteinisches Wochenblatt
Die Weidewirtschaft

Silesia: Regional and Local Press

Bote an dem Katzenbach (Goldberg)
Bote aus dem Riesengebirge (Hirschberg)
Breslau. Freie Wochenschrift

Breslauer General-Anzeiger
Breslauer Morgenzeitung
Breslauer Zeitung
Der Bürger- und Hausfreund (Löwenberg)
Bunzlauer Stadtblatt
Bunzlauer Tageblatt
Die Freie Meinung (Breslau)
Der Greif (Greiffenberg)
Grünberger Wochenblatt
Haynauer Stadtblatt
Jauersches Stadtblatt
Jauersches Tageblatt
Landeshuter Stadtblatt
Laubaner Tageblatt
Liegnitzer Anzeiger
Liegnitzer Tageblatt
Liegnitzer Zeitung
Löwenberger Zeitung
Mitteilungen des Deutschen Mittelstandsbundes Provinzialverband Schlesien
Neue Niederschlsische Zeitung (Glogau)
Neuer Görlitzer Anzeiger
Niederschlesischer Anzeiger (Glogau)
Niederschlesischer Bote (Freystädter Wochenblatt)
Saganer Tageblatt
Schlesische Freikonservative Parteikorrespondenz
Schlesische Gebirgs-Zeitung (Hirschberg)
Schlesische Morgen-Zeitung
Schlesische Volkszeitung
Schlesische Zeitung
Schweidnitzer Zeitung
Schönauer Anzeiger
Sprottauer Wochenblatt
Volkswacht

CONTEMPORARY BOOKS AND PAMPHLETS, MEMOIRS

Albrecht, Joachim, and Warneken, Bernd Jürgen (eds.), *Als die Deutschen demonstrieren lernten: Das Kulturmuster 'friedlicke straßendemonstration' im preußischen Wahlkampf 1908–1910* (Tübingen, 1986).

Außerordentlicher Delegiertentag des Wahlvereins der Liberalen zu Berlin am 3. und 4. Juli 1909 (Berlin, 1909).

Barth, Theodor, *Amerikanische Eindrücke: Eine impressionistische Schilderung amerikanischer Zustände in Briefen* (Berlin, 1907).

—— *Der Freisinn im Block* (Berlin, 1908).

—— and Naumann, Friedrich, *Die Erneuerung des Liberalismus: Ein politischer Weckruf* (Berlin and Schöneberg, 1906).

Behnke, Werner, *Ein Wort für das preußische Landtagswahlrecht* (Halle a S., 1907).

Beiträge zur historischen Statistik Schleswig-Holsteins (Kiel, 1967).

Bericht über die Tätigkeit der Fortschrittlichen Volkspartei im Preußischen Abgeordnetenhause in der 22.Legislationsperiode (Berlin, 1914).

Bethmann Hollweg, Theobald von, *Betrachtungen zum Weltkrieg* (2 vols.; Berlin, 1919–22).

Bonn, Moritz J., *Wandering Scholar* (London, 1949).

Born, K. E. and Rassow, Peter, *Akten zur staatlichen Sozialpolitik in Deutschland 1890–1914* (Wiesbaden, 1966).

Bradler, Günther (ed.), *Friedrich Payer (1847–1931): Autobiographische Aufzeichnungen und Dokumente* (Göppingen, 1974).

Brandt, Peter, and Rürup, Reinhard (eds.), *Arbeiter-Soldaten- und Volksräte in Baden 1918/19* (Düsseldorf, 1980).

Breitscheid, Rudolph, *Der Bülowblock und der Liberalismus* (Munich, 1908).

Brentano, Lujo, *Mein Leben im Kampf um die soziale Entwicklung Deutschlands* (Jena, 1931).

Breslauer Statistik, 32–4 (1912–14).

Bueck, Henry Axel, *Weshalb die Industrie der Rießer'schen Parole 'Kampf gegen Rechts' nicht folgen soll* (Berlin, 1911).

Cardauns, Hermann, *Karl Trimborn: Nach seinen Briefen und Tagebüchern* (Mönchen-Gladbach, 1922).

Claß, Heinrich, *Wider den Strom* (Leipzig, 1932).

C. S. [pseud. Kurt Nitschke], *Die Sozialdemokratische Hochflut und ihre Eindämmung: Ein Wort an Nationalgesinnte* (Breslau, n.d. [1903]).

Damaschke, Adolf, Zeitenwende, *Aus meinem Leben* (2 vols.; Leipzig, 1925).

Das Deutsche Eisenbahnwesen der Gegenwart (2 vols.; Berlin, 1911).

Deetjen, Ernst, *Freikonservativ! Die nationale Mittelpartei* (Breslau, 1913).

Delbrück, Clemens von, *Die Wirtschaftliche Mobilmachung in Deutschland 1914* (Munich, 1924).

Der 'Fortschritt' und die Deutsche Vaterlandspartei (Berlin, 1918).

Der Freisinnige im Jahre 1899: Geschichte der Freisinnigen Partei, deren Grundsätze, deren Stellung mit Notizbuch und Kalender (Breslau, [1898]).

Der Hauptausschuß des Deutschen Reichstags 1915–1918, ed. Reinhard Schiffers and Manfred Koch with Hans Boldt (4 vols.; Düsseldorf, 1985).

Der Interfraktionelle Ausschuß 1917/18, ed. Erich Matthias with Rudolf Morsey (2 vols.; Düsseldorf, 1959).

Der Liberalismus und die Arbeiter (Berlin, 1906).

Der sechste Parteitag der Freisinningen Volkspartei, Wiesbaden 23. bis 25. September 1905, ed. Otto Wiemer (Berlin, 1905).

Der zweite Parteitag der Fortschrittlichen Volkspartei zu Mannheim, 5.–7. Oktober 1912 (Berlin, 1912).

Dewitz, Hermann von, *Von Bismarck bis Bethmann: Innenpolitischer Rückblick eines Konservativen* (Berlin, 1918).

Die Fortschrittliche Volkspartei im Reichstage 1907–1911, ed. H. G. Erdmannsdörffer (Berlin, 1911).

Die Fortschrittliche Volkspartei im neuen Reichstag (Berlin, 1912).

Die Freisinnige Volkspartei, ihr Programm und ihre Organisation (Berlin, 1909).

Die Freisinnige Volkspartei im Kampf für Handel und Industrie (Berlin, 1905).

Die Freisinnige Volkspartei und die Barth-Demokraten (Berlin, 1908).

Die Freisinnige Volkspartei und die deutsche Flotte (Berlin, 1906).

Die Freisinnige Volkspartei und die liberalen 'Forderungen des Tages' (Eine Kundgebung des freisinnigen Bürgertums im Zirkus Busch in Berlin, 15.9.1907) (Berlin, 1907).

Die Freisinnige Volkspartei und die Reichssteuerpolitik (Berlin, 1910).

Die Nationalliberale Partei und die Wahlreform: Rede des Abgeordneten Dr Krause gehalten auf dem Delegiertentage der Nationalliberalen Partei in Magdeburg am 26. April 1908 (Berlin, 1908).

Die politische Neuorientierung und die Fortschrittliche Volkspartei (Berlin, 1917).

Die Regierung des Prinzen Max von Baden, ed. Erich Matthias and Rudolf Morsey (Düsseldorf, 1962).

Die Vereinigten Liberalen in der Hamburger 'Bürgerschaft' 1907–1910 (Hamburg, 1910).

Die Vereinigten Liberalen in der Hamburger Bürgerschaft 1910–1912 (Hamburg, 1912).

Dix, Arthur, *Blockpolitik: Ihre innere Logik, ihre Vorgeschichte, und ihre Aussichten* (Berlin, 1908).

Dritter Delegiertentag des Wahlvereins der Liberalen zu Frankfurt/M. am 21. und 22. April 1908 (Berlin, 1908).

Eckardstein, Hermann von, *Lebenserinnerungen und Politische Denkwürdigkeiten* (3 vols.; Leipzig, 1919–21).

Eickhoff, Richard, *Die Freisinnige Volkspartei im Reichstag (Vortrag gehalten in Mühlhausen i Th. 12/1/01)* (Berlin, 1901).

—— *Politische Profile. Erinnerungen aus vier Jahrzehnten* (Berlin, 1927).

Eigenbrodt, August, *Berliner Tageblatt und Frankfurter Zeitung und nationale Fragen, 1887–1914*, 6th edn. (Berlin and Schöneberg, 1917).

Einem, Karl von, *Ein Armeeführer erlebt den Weltkrieg* (Leipzig, 1938).

—— *Erinnerungen eines Soldaten 1853–1933* (Leipzig, 1933).

Eisenhart, Wolfgang, *Liberal und konservativ: Ein Kampf um deutsche Ideale in der Politik*, 2nd edn. (Naumberg a. S., 1911).

Erster Delegiertentag des Wahlvereins der Liberalen zu Berlin am 17. und 18. Februar 1906 (Berlin, 1906).

Erster Parteitag der Fortschrittlichen Volkspartei zu Berlin am 6. März 1910 (Berlin, 1910).

Eugen Richter und der Wahlkreis Hagen-Schwelm (Hagen, 1966).

Eulenburg, Philipp, *Philipp Eulenburgs Politische Korrespondenz*, ed. John C. G. Röhl, iii. (Boppard, 1983).

Eyck, Erich, *Auf Deutschlands Politischem Forum: Deutsche Parlamentarier und Studien zur neuesten deutschen Geschichte* (Erlenbach and Zürich, 1963).

Fegter, Jan, *Materialienversammlung für Liberale im Wahlkampf* (Leer, 1911).

—— *Reichstagsreden und sonstige politische Tätigkeit unseres Reichstagsabgeordneten Jan Fegter* (Norden, 1911).

Festgabe des Vereins für die Geschichte Schlesiens zumsiebzigsten Geburtstage seines Ehrenmitglieders Oberbürgermeister a. D. Dr. phil. et med. hc. Georg Bender am 31. Dezember 1918 (Breslau, 1919).

Fischart Johannes [pseud Erich Franz Otto Dombrowski], *Das alte und das neue System* (4 vols.; Berlin, 1919-25).

Fortschrittliches Merkbüchlein (Berlin, 1913).

Frank, Ludwig, *Aufsätze, Reden und Briefe* (Berlin, n.d.).

Freie und Hansestadt Hamburg (ed.), *Jahresbericht des statistischen Amtes und Bureaus der Zentralwahlkommission für das Jahr 1912* (Hamburg, 1913).

Freisinniges Liederbuch (Varel, 1901).

Frymann, Daniel [pseud. Heinrich Claß], *Wenn ich der Kaiser wär': Politische Wahrheiten und Notwendigkeiten* (Leipzig, 1912).

Fuch, Walther P. (ed.), *Großherzogtum Friedrich I von Baden und die Reichspolitik 1871-1907* (4 vols.; Stuttgart, 1980).

Funck, Carl, *Lebenserinnerungen* (Frankfurt am Main, 1921).

Fünfter (letzter) Delegiertentag des Wahlvereins der Liberalen zu Berlin am 5. März 1910 (Berlin, 1910).

Gall, Lothar, and Koch, Rainer (eds.), *Der europäische Liberalismus im 19. Jahrhundert* (4 vols.; Frankfurt am Main, 1981).

Gerlach, Hellmut von, *Die Geschichte des preußischen Wahlrechts* (Berlin and Schöneberg, 1908).

—— *Erinnerungen eines Junkers* (Berlin, 1924).

—— *Von rechts nach links* (Zürich, 1937).

Gothein, Georg, *Liberalismus und Sozialdemokratie* (Schöneberg, 1904).

—— *Agrarpolitisches Handbuch* (Berlin, 1910/11).

Grandvilliers, Jean de, *Essai sur le libéralisme allemand* (Paris, 1914).

Grotewald, Christian, *Die Parteien des Deutschen Reichstags* (Leipzig, 1908).

Haas, Ludwig, *Die Einigung des Liberalismus und der Demokratie* (Frankfurt am Main, 1905).

Hamburg vor 90 Jahren: Zum neunzigjährigen Bestehen des Hamburger Fremdenblattes, 1828-1918 (Hamburg, 1918).

Handbuch der sozialdemokratischen Parteitage von 1910 bis 1913 (Munich, 1917; repr. Leipzig, 1974).

Handbuch für die Preußischen Landtagswahlen (Berlin and Schöneberg, [1913]).

Hannsen, H. P., *Diary of a Dying Empire* (Bloomington, 1955).

Harms, Paul, *Unter den Auserwählten: Eine Erzählung von Parliamentarien und Journalisten aus der Kaiserzeit* (Leipzig, 1925).

Haußmann, Conrad, *Das Arbeitsprogramm der Fortschrittlichen Volkspartei* (Berlin, 1911).

—— *Schlaglichter, Reichstagsbriefe und Aufzeichnungen von Conrad Haußmann*, ed. Ulrich Zeller, (Frankfurt am Main, 1924).

Heilberg, Adolf, 'Erinnerungen 1858–1936', unpubl. MS, Breslau 1936, extract in Monika Richarz (ed.), *Jüdisches Leben in Deutschland: Selbstzeugnisse zur Sozialgeschichte im Kaiserreich* (Stuttgart, 1979), 289–97.

—— *Eine ernste Mahnung* [Breslau, 1914].

Hellpach, Willy, *Wirken im Wirren: Lebenserinnerungen* (2 vols.; Hamburg, 1948–49).

Hesse, Fritz, *Von der Residenz zur Bauhausstadt* (Bad Pyrmont, 1963).

Heuss, Theodor, *Erinnerungen 1905 bis 1933* (Tübingen, 1963).

Hill, Leonidas E. (ed.), *Die Weizsäcker-Papiere 1900–1932* (Berlin, 1982).

Hoff, Ferdinand, *Auf zum Kampfe für das Reichstagswahlrecht in Preußen* (Berlin, 1908).

—— *Am Abgrund vorüber* (Berlin, 1919).

—— *Politische Zeit- und Streitfragen in demokratischer Beleuchtung: Ein Wort der Aufklärung für die kommenden Wahlen* (Berlin, 1920).

Hohorst, G., Kocka, J., and Ritter, G. A. (eds.), *Sozialgeschichtliches Arbeitsbuch*, ii. *Materialien zur Statistik des Kaiserreichs 1870–1914* (Munich, 1978).

Honigsheim, Paul, *On Max Weber* (Michigan, 1968).

Hummel, Hermann, *Die Volksparteiliche Fraktion im Landtag des Jahres 1911/12: Ein politisches Handbuch* (Mannheim and Leipzig, 1912).

—— *Vermischte politische und wirtschaftliche Aufsätze aus den letzten Jahren: (1925–32)* (Mannheim, 1935).

—— *Baden und die Eisenbahngemeinschaft* (Karlsruhe, 1912).

Ißberner, Reinhart, *Demokratisches ABC-Buch* (Berlin, 1920).

—— *Wie die Deutschnationalen regieren!* (Berlin, 1926).

Jahresbericht des Zentral vorstandes der Sozialdemokratischen Zentralvereins für den 6. Schleswig-Holsteinischen Reichstagswahlkreis von 1.7.09–30.6.10 (Ottensen, 1910).

Jahresberichte des Sozialdemokratischen Vereins Breslau (Breslau, 1906–14).

Kaempf, Johannes, *Reden und Aufsätze* (Berlin, 1912).

Kalkhoff, H., *Die Vertretung der Parteien im Reichstage 1871–1912 in graphischer Darstellung* (Berlin, 1912).

Kardorff, Siegfried von, *Wilhelm von Kardorff: Ein nationaler Parlamentarier im Zeitalter Bismarcks und Wilhelm II, 1828–1907* (Berlin, 1936).

Keim, August, *Erlebtes und Erstrebtes: Lebenserinnerungen* (Hanover, 1925).

Klein-Hattingen, Oskar, *Geschichte des deutschen Liberalismus* (2 vols.; Berlin and Schöneberg, 1911–12).

Köhler, Heinrich, *Lebenserinnerungen des Politikers und Staatsmannes 1879–1949* (Stuttgart, 1964).

Konservatives Handbuch, 4th edn. (Berlin, 1911).

Kremer, Hans-Jürgen (ed.), *Mit Gott für Wahrheit, Freiheit und Recht: Quellen zur Organisation und Politik der Zentrumspartei und des politischen Katholizismus in Baden 1888–1914* (Stuttgart, 1983).

Kube, Wilhelm, *Unsere Kriegsziele* (Breslau, 1917).

—— *Wie organisieren wir uns? Ein Beitrag für die Aufgaben der Deutschnationalen Kreisvorsitzenden und Vertrauensleute* (Breslau, 1920).

Kulemann, Wilhelm, *Politische Erinnerungen* (Berlin, 1911).

Kunze, Richard, *Was der deutsche Reichstagswähler wissen muß*, 2nd edn. (2 vols.; Berlin and Friedenau, 1911).

Kürschners Deutscher Reichstag (Stuttgart and Berlin, 1907–18).

Leonhart, Johannes, *Die Alkohol-Frage in der Großstadt* (Hamburg, 1911).

Lerchenfeld Koefering, Graf Hugo, *Erinnerungen und Denkwürdigkeiten 1843 bis 1925* (Berlin, 1935).

Liebert, Eduard von, *Aus einem bewegten Leben: Erinnerungen* (Munich, 1925).

Lieder zur Feier der Wahl des demokratischen Abgeordneten für den Landtag Herrn Rechtsanwalt Venedey. Konstanz am 2. 10. 1891 [Konstanz, 1891].

Lindemann, Hugo, *Die städtische Regie* (Berlin, 1907).

Lippmann, Leo, *Mein Leben und meine Amtliche Tätigkeit* (Hamburg, 1964).

Löbe, Paul, *Der Weg war lang* (Berlin and Grunewald, 1954).

Marx, Hugo, *Werdegang eines jüdischen Staatsanwalts und Richters in Baden (1892–1933)* (Villingen, 1965).

Matthias, Erich and Pikart, Eberhard (eds.), *Die Reichstagsfraktion der deutschen Sozialdemokratie 1898–1918* (2 vols.; Düsseldorf, 1966).

Meinecke, Friedrich, *Straßburg Freiburg Berlin 1901–1919: Erinnerungen* (Stuttgart, 1949).

Mommsen, Wilhelm (ed.), *Deutsche Parteiprogramme*, 3rd edn. (Munich, 1971).

Morré, H., *Das Schwabenalter des Deutschen Parlaments* (Berlin, 1909).

Müller-Meiningen, Ernst, *Die Feldgrauen und wir zu Hause* (Berlin, 1918).

—— *Parliamentarismus* (Berlin, 1926).

Muser, Gerhard, *Statistische Untersuchung über die Zeitungen Deutschlands 1885–1914* (Leipzig, 1918).

Muser, Oskar, *Die Agrarfrage und die Stellung der Demokratie zu derselben* (Karlsruhe, 1895).

—— *Der Ultramontanismus und das Zentrum* (Lahr, 1907).

—— *Demokratie und Block: 'Doktrinismus' und 'Realpolitik'* (Berlin, 1908).

—— *Sind die Fortschrittliche Volksparteiler 'Religionsfeinde' und 'Kulturkämpfer'?* (Villingen, 1912).

—— *Die Stellung der Frau zum Staat und im Staat. Frauenstimmrecht* (Karlsruhe, 1913).

Naumann, Friedrich, *Ausstellungsbriefe* (Berlin, 1909).

—— *Werke* (6 vols.; Cologne and Opladen, 1964–74).

Nestriepke, Siegfried, *Die Demokratische Vereinigung: Was wir sind und was wir wollen* (Bonn, [1910]).

Nitschke, Kurt, *Der Deutsch-Konservative Verein in Breslau in den politischen Bewegungen der letzten 25 Jahre* (Breslau, 1907).

Nordschleswig: Verhandlungen einer Versammlung in Hamburg, 4.3.1911 (Hamburg, 1911).

Obst, Arthur, *Geschichte der Hamburgischen Bürgervereine: Festschrift zur Feier des 25 jährigen Bestehens des Zentralausschusses Hamburgischer Bürgervereine am 10.6.11* (Hamburg, 1911).

Oehlke, Alfred, *100 Jahre Breslauer Zeitung 1820–1920* (Breslau, 1920).

Oertzen, Dietrich von, *Erinnerungen aus meinem Leben* (Berlin and Lichtenfelde, 1914).

Oldenburg-Januschau, Elard von, *Erinnerungen* (Leipzig, 1936).

Pachnicke, Hermann, *Liberalismus als Kulturpolitik* (Berlin, 1907).

—— *Die Mecklenburgische Verfassungsfrage* (Parchim, 1907).

—— *Führende Männer im alten und neuen Reich* (Berlin, 1930).

Payer, Friedrich, *Von Bethmann Hollweg bis Ebert: Erinnerungen und Bilder* (Frankfurt am Main, 1923).

Peus, Heinrich, *Dissident und Offizier: Eine wichtige Reichstagsdebatte zu Gunsten der Gewissensfreiheit (2 u. 3 Nov 1916)* (Munich, 1917).

Pittius, Erich, *Die politische Tagespresse Schlesiens* (Sorau, 1914).

Plate, R. (ed.), *Handbuch für das Preußische Abgeordnetenhaus* (Berlin, 1908).

Politisches Handbuch der Nationalliberalen Partei Deutschlands (Berlin, 1907).

Potthoff, Heinz, *Beamte, Privatangestellte und Fortschrittliche Volkspartei!* (Berlin, 1910).

Preuß, Hugo, *Die Entwicklung des deutschen Städtewesens* (Leipzig, 1906).

—— *Das deutsche Volk und die Politik* (Jena, 1916).

—— *Obrigkeitsstaat und großdeutscher Gedanke* (Jena, 1916).

Quidde, Ludwig, *Caligula: Schriften über Militarismus und Pazifismus*, ed. Hans-Ulrich Wehler (Frankfurt am Main, 1977).

—— *Der deutsche Pazifismus während des Weltkrieges 1914–8*, ed. Karl Holl (Boppard am Rhein, 1979).

R M 8 Mai 1913: Herrn Rudolf Mosse überreicht die Redaktion zum siebzigsten Geburtstage 8 Mai 1913 diese Grüsse seiner Freunde und Mitarbeiter [Berlin, 1913].

Rapp, Alfred, *Die badischen Landtagsabgeordneten 1905–1929 mit Bibliographie und Statistiken zur Geschichte des badischen Landtags* (Karlsruhe, 1929).

Rebmann, Eduard, Gothein, Eberhard, and Jagemann, Eingen von (eds.), *Das Großherzogtum Baden in allgemeiner, wirtschaftlicher und staatlicher Hinsicht dargestellt* (Karlsruhe, 1912).

Rehbein, Franz, *Das Leben eines Landarbeiters* (Jena, 1911; repr. Darmstadt, 1973).

Reiß, Klaus-Peter (ed.), *Von Bassermann zu Stresemann: Die Sitzungen des nationalliberalen Zentralvorstandes 1912–1917* (Düsseldorf, 1967).

Rich, Norman, and Fisher, M. H. (eds.), *The Holstein Papers: The Memoirs, Diaries and Correspondence of Friedrich von Holstein 1837–1909* (4 vols.; Cambridge, 1955–63).

Riezler, Kurt, *Tagebücher, Aufsätze, Dokumente*, ed. Karl Dietrich Erdmann (Göttingen, 1972).

Ritter, Gerhard A. with Niehuss, Merith, *Wahlgeschichtliches Arbeitsbuch: Materialien zur Statistik des Kaiserreichs 1871–1918* (Munich, 1980).

Roth, Paul, *Die Programme der politischen Parteien und die politische Tagespresse in Deutschland* (Halle a. S., 1913).

Sarason D. (ed.), *Das Jahr 1913: Ein Gesamtbild der Kulturentwicklung* (Leipzig and Berlin, 1913).

Schacht, Hjalmar, *76 Jahre meines Lebens* (Bad Wörishofen, 1953).

Schadt, Jörg (ed.), *Alles für das Volk, alles durch das Volk* (Stuttgart, 1977).

Scheidemann, Philip, *Memoirs of a Social Democrat* (2 vols.; London, 1929).

Schiefler, Gustav, *Eine Hamburgische Kulturgeschichte 1890–1920: Betrachtungen eines Zeitgenossen*, ed. Gerhard Ahrens, Hans Wilhelm Eckardt, and Renate Hauschild-Thiessen (Hamburg, 1985).

Schofer, Josef, *Großblock-Bilanz: Zeitgemäße politische Erinnerungen* (Freiburg, 1913).

Schrag-Haas, Judith, 'Ludwig Haas. Erinnerungen an meinem Vater', *Bulletin des Leo Baeck Instituts*, 4/13 (1961), 73–93.

Schücking, Lothar Engelbert, *Die Reaktion in der inneren Verwaltung Preußens* (Berlin and Schöneberg, 1908).

—— *Die Mißregierung der Konservativen unter Kaiser Wilhelm II* (Munich, 1909).

—— *Demokratische Betrachtungen* (Munich, 1909).

—— *Das Elend der preußischen Verwaltung* (Munich, 1911).

Schulthess' Europäischer Geschichtskalender, 47–59 *(1907–1918)* (Munich, 1908–22).

Sösemann, Bernd (ed.), *Theodor Wolff: Tagebücher 1914–1919* (2 vols.; Boppard, 1984).

Sieveking, Heinrich, *Erinnerungen 1871–1914*, ed. Gerhard Ahrens (Hamburg, 1977).

Stampfer, Friedrich, *Erfahrungen und Erkenntnisse. Aufzeichnungen aus meinem Leben* (Cologne, 1957).

Stegemann, Hermann, *Erinnerungen aus meinem Leben und aus meiner Zeit* (Stuttgart, 1929).

Stens, Hermann, *Demokratische Richtlinien in der öffentlichen Selbstverwaltung: Ein demokratisches Kommunalprogramm* (Lüdenscheid i. W, n.d.).

Stephan, Werner, *Acht Jahrzehnte erlebtes Deutschland: Ein Liberaler in vier Epochen* (Düsseldorf, 1983).

Stillich, Oscar, *Die politischen Parteien in Deutschland*, i. *Die Konservativen* (Leipzig, 1908).

—— *Die politischen Parteien in Deutschland*, ii. *Der Liberalismus* (Leipzig, 1911).

Sünden des Freisinns: Material zur Bekämpfung der Fortschrittlichen Volkspartei (Berlin, 1911).

Thimme, Friedrich (ed.), *Vom inneren Frieden des deutschen Volkes* (Leipzig, 1916).

Treue, Wolfgang (ed.), *Deutsche Parteiprogramme seit 1861*, 4th edn. (Göttingen, 1968).

Vereinskalender der Deutschen freisinnigen Partei zum Handgebrauch für das Jahr 1892 (Berlin, 1892).

Vereinskalender der Freisinnigen Volkspartei (Berlin, 1894–1901).

Vollmar, Georg, *Reden und Schriften zur Reformpolitik*, ed. Willy Albrecht (Berlin and Bonn, 1977).

Wacker, Theodor, *Zur Politischen Lage im Reiche und in Baden* (Karlsruhe, 1909).

—— *Der Gegenwärtige Mandatsbesitz der Linksliberalen* (Karlsruhe, 1913).

—— *Der Sozialdemokratische Mandatsgewinn von 1909* (Karlsruhe, 1913).

Weber, Marianne, *Max Weber: A Biography*, tr. and ed. Harry Zorn (New York, 1975).

Weber, Max, *Gesammelte Politische Schriften* (Tübingen, 1921).

Wehberg, Hans, *Als Pazifist im Weltkrieg* (Leipzig, n.d.).

Weiß, John Gustav, *Lebenserinnerungen eines badischen Kommunalpolitikers* (Stuttgart, 1981).

Wenck, Martin, *Die Geschichte der Nationalsozialen 1895–1903* (Berlin, 1905).

—— *Handbuch für liberale Politik* (Schöneberg bei Berlin, 1911).

Wer ist's? Wer ist wer?, ed. Hermann A. L. Degener (Leipzig, 1911–1922).

Westarp, Kuno Graf, *Konservative Politik im letzten Jahrzehnt des Kaiserreiches* (2 vols.; Berlin, 1935).

Witte, Friedrich Carl, *Liberales und Soziales* (Leipzig, 1911).

Zum Streit um die Nordmark: Zweite Hamburger Versammlung am 8. Mai 1911 (Hamburg, 1911).

Zweiter Delegiertentag des Wahlvereins der Liberalen zu Berlin am 6. und 7. April 1907 (Berlin, 1907).

SELECTED SECONDARY LITERATURE

Abrams, Lynn, *Workers' Culture in Imperial Germany: Leisure and Recreation in the Rhineland and Westphalia* (London, 1992).

Albertin, Lothar, *Liberalismus und Demokratie am Anfang der Weimarer Republik* (Düsseldorf, 1972).

—— and Link, Werner (eds.), *Politische Parteien auf dem Weg zur parlamentarischen Demokratie in Deutschland* (Düsseldorf, 1981).

Allen, Ann Taylor, *Satire and Society in Wilhelmine Germany: Kladderadatsch and Simplicissimus, 1890–1914* (Lexington, Mass., 1984).

Anderson, Margaret Lavinia, *Windthorst: A Political Biography* (Oxford, 1981).

—— 'Voter, Junker, *Landrat*, Priest: The Old Authorities and the New Franchise in Imperial Germany', *AHR* 98 (1993), 1448–74.

Applegate, Celia, *A Nation of Provincials: The German Idea of Heimat* (Berkeley, Calif., 1990).

Berghahn, Volker R., *Der Tirpitz-Plan* (Düsseldorf, 1971).

—— *Imperial Germany, 1871–1914: Economy, Society, Culture and Politics* (Providence, RI, 1994).

Bermbach, Udo, *Vorformen parlamentarischer Kabinettsbildung in Deutschland* (Cologne and Opladen, 1967).

Bertram, Jürgen, *Die Wahlen zum Deutschen Reichstag vom Jahre 1912: Parteien und Verbände in der Innenpolitik des Wilhelminischen Reiches* (Düsseldorf, 1964).

Blackbourn, David, *Class, Religion and Local Politics in Wilhelmine Germany: The Centre Party in Württemberg before 1914* (London and New Haven, Conn., 1980).

—— *Populists and Patricians. Essays in Modern German History* (London, 1987).

—— *The Fontana History of Germany 1780–1918: The Long Nineteenth Century* (London, 1997)

—— and Eley, Geoff, *The Peculiarities of German History* (Oxford, 1984).

—— and Evans, Richard J. (eds.), *The German Bourgeoisie: Essays on the Social History of the German Middle Class from the Late Eighteenth to the Early Twentieth Century* (London, 1991).

Böhme, Helmut, and Kallenberg, Fritz (eds.), *Deutschland und der Erste Weltkrieg* (Darmstadt, 1987).

Bräunche, Ernst Otto, *Parteien und Reichstagswahlen in der Rheinpfalz von der Reichsgründung bis zum Ausbruch des Ersten Weltkrieges 1914: Eine regionale Partei- und wahlhistorische Untersuchung im Vorfeld der Demokratie* (Speyer, 1982).

Bruch, Rüdiger vom, *Wissenschaft, Politik und öffentliche Meinung: Gelehrtenpolitik im Wilhelminischen Deutschland (1890–1914)* (Husum, 1980).

Büsch, Otto, Neugebauer-Wölk, Monika, and Wölk, Wolfgang (eds.), *Wählerbewegung in der deutschen Geschichte* (Berlin, 1978).

Büttner, Ursula, 'Vereinigte Liberale und Deutsche Demokraten in Hamburg 1906–30', *Zeitschrift des Vereins für Hamburgische Geschichte*, 63 (1977),1-34.

Chickering, Roger, *Imperial Germany and a World without War: The Peace Movement and German Society, 1892–1914* (Princeton, NJ, 1975).

—— *We Men Who Feel Most German: A Cultural Study of the Pan-German League 1886–1914* (London, 1984).

—— *Imperial Germany: A Historiographical Companion* (Westport, Conn., 1996).

—— *Imperial Germany and the Great War, 1914–1918* (Cambridge, 1998).

Childers, T. (ed.), *The Mobilisation of the Nazi Constituency 1919–1933* (London, 1986).

Cocks, Geoffrey, and Jarausch, Konrad H. (eds.), *German Professions, 1800–1950* (New York, 1990).

Coetzee, Marilyn S., *The German Army League: Popular Nationalism in Wilhelmine Germany* (New York, 1990).

Conze, Werner, Kocka, Jürgen, Koselleck, Reinhart, and Lepsius, M. Rainer (eds.), *Bildungsbürgertum im 19. Jahrhundert* (4 vols.; Stuttgart, 1985–92).

Crew, David F., *Town in the Ruhr: A Social History of Bochum 1860–1914* (New York, 1979).

Crothers, George C., *The German Elections of 1907* (New York, 1941).

Dahrendorf, Ralf, *Society and Democracy in Germany* (New York, 1969).

Dann, Otto (ed.), *Vereinswesen und bürgerliche Gesellschaft in Deutschland* (Munich, 1984).

Das deutsche Judentum und der Liberalismus: German Jewry and Liberalism (Sankt Augustin, 1986).

Düding, Dieter, *Der Nationalsoziale Verein 1896–1903: Der gescheiterte Versuch einer politischen Synthese von Nationalismus, Sozialismus und Liberalismus* (Munich and Vienna, 1972).

Dülffer, Jost, and Holl, Karl (eds.), *Bereit zum Krieg: Kriegsmentalität im wilhelminischen Deutschland 1890–1914* (Göttingen, 1986).

Eley, Geoff, *Reshaping the German Right: Change after Bismarck* (London, 1980).

—— *From Unification to Nazism* (Boston, Mass., 1986).

Elm, Ludwig, *Zwischen Fortschritt und Reaktion. Geschichte der Parteien der liberalen Bourgeoisie in Deutschland 1893–1918* (Berlin, 1968).

Epstein, Klaus, *Matthias Erzberger and the Dilemma of German Democracy* (Princeton, NJ., 1959).

Evans, Richard J., *The Feminist Movement in Germany 1894–1933* (London, 1976).

—— *Death in Hamburg: Society and Politics in the Cholera Years 1830–1910* (Oxford, 1987).

Eyck, Erich, *Das persönliche Regiment Wilhelms II: Politische Geschichte des deutschen Kaiserreichs von 1890–1914* (Erlenbach and Zürich, 1948).

Fairbairn, Brett, *Democracy in the Undemocratic State: The German Reichstag Elections of 1898 and 1903* (Toronto, 1997).

Feder, Ernst, *Theodor Barth und der demokratische Gedanke* (Gotha, 1919).

—— *Politik und Humanität. Paul Nathan: ein Lebensbild* (Berlin, 1929).

Fesser, Gerd, 'Von der "Zuchthausvorlage" zum Reichsvereinsgesetz: Staatsorgane, bürgerliche Parteien und Vereinsgesetzgebung im Deutschen Reich 1899–1906', *Jahrbuch für Geschichte*, 28 (1983), 107–32.

—— 'Zu den Auswirkungen des Reichsvereinsgesetzes 1908–1914', *ZfG* 33 (1985), 117–28.

Fischer, Fritz, *Germany's Aims in the First World War* (London, 1967)

—— *War of Illusions: German Politics from 1911 to 1914* (London, 1976).

—— *Bündnis der Eliten: Zur Kontinuität der Machtstrukturen in Deutschland 1871-1945* (Düsseldorf, 1979).

Fischer, Ilse, *Industrialisierung, sozialer Konflikt und politische Willensbildung in der Stadtgemeinde* (Augsburg, 1977).

Förster, Stig, *Der doppelte Militarismus: Die deutsche Heeresrüstungspolitik zwischen Status-quo-Sicherung und Aggression 1890–1913* (Stuttgart, 1985).

Frevert, Ute (ed.), *Bürgerinnen und Bürger: Geschlechterverhältnisse im 19. Jahrhundert* (Göttingen, 1988).

—— *Men of Honour: A Social and Cultural History of the Duel* (Cambridge, Mass., 1995).

Fricke, Dieter (ed.), *Deutsche Demokraten: Die nichtproletarischen demokratischen Kräfte in Deutschland 1830 bis 1945* (Cologne, 1981).

—— *et al.* (eds.), *Lexikon zur Parteiengeschichte. Die bürgerlichen und kleinbürgerlichen Parteien und Verbände in Deutschland 1789–1945* (4 vols.; Leipzig, 1983–6).

Gall, Lothar (ed.), *Liberalismus* (Cologne, 1976).

—— *Bürgertum in Deutschland* (Berlin, 1989).

—— (ed.), *Stadt und Bürgertum im neunzehnten Jahrhundert* (Munich, 1990).

—— and Langewiesche, Dieter (eds.) *Liberalismus und Region: Zur Geschichte des deutschen Liberalismus im 19. Jahrhundert* (Munich, 1995).

—— (ed.), *Bürgertum und bürgerlich-liberale Bewegung in Mitteleuropa seit dem 18. Jahrhundert* (Historische Zeitschrift, Sonderheft 17, Munich, 1997).

Galos, Adam, Gentzen, Felix Heinrich, and Jakókczyk, Witold, *Die Hakatisten: Der Deutsche Ostmarkenverein (1894–1934). Ein Beitrag zur Geschichte des deutschen Imperialismus* (Berlin, 1966).

Geiss, Immanuel, and Wendt, Bernd-Jürgen (eds.), *Deutschland in der Weltpolitik des 19. und 20. Jahrhunderts* (Düsseldorf, 1973).

Gilg, Peter, *Die Erneuerung des demokratischen Denkens im Wilhelminischen Deutschland* (Wiesbaden, 1965).

Gottschalk, Regina, *Die Linksliberalen zwischen Kaiserreich und Weimarer Republik: Von der Julikrise 1917 bis zum Bruch der Weimarer Koalition im Juli 1919* (Mainz, 1969).

Groh, Dieter, *Negative Integration und revolutionärer Attentismus: Die deutsche Sozialdemokratie am Vorabend des Ersten Weltkrieges* (Frankfurt am Main, 1975).

Grosser, Dieter, *Vom monarchischen Konstitutionalismus zur parlamentarischen Demokratie: Die Verfassungspolitik der deutshen Parteien im letzten Jahrzehnt des Kaiserreiches* (The Hague, 1970).

Günther, Wolfgang (ed.), *Parteien und Wahlen in Oldenburg: Beiträge zur Landesgeschichte im 19. und 20. Jahrhundert* (Oldenburg, 1983).

Hagen, William W., *Germans, Poles and Jews: The Nationality Conflict in the Prussian East 1772–1914* (Chicago, 1980).

Hamel, Iris, *Der Deutschnationale Handlungsgehilfen-Verband 1893–1933* (Frankfurt am Main, 1967).

Harris, James F., *A Study in the Theory and Practice of German Liberalism: Eduard Lasker, 1829–1884* (Lanham, Md., 1984).

Heberle, Rudolf, *From Democracy to Nazism: A Regional Case Study on Political Parties in Germany* (Baton Rouge, La., 1945).

—— *Landbevölkerung und Nationalsozialismus: Eine soziologische Untersuchung der politischen Willensbildung in Schleswig-Holstein 1918 bis 1932* (Stuttgart, 1963).

Heckart, Beverly, *From Bassermann to Bebel: The Grand Block's Quest for Reform in the Kaiserreich, 1900–1914* (New Haven, Conn., 1974).

Heuss, Theodor, *Friedrich Naumann: Der Mann, das Werk, die Zeit*, 2nd edn. (Stuttgart, 1949).

Hiery, Hermann, *Reichstagswahlen im Reichsland: Ein Beitrag zur Landesgeschichte von Elsaß-Lothringen und zur Wahlgeschichte des Deutschen Reiches 1871–1918* (Düsseldorf, 1986).

Holl, Karl, and List, Günther (eds.), *Liberalismus und imperialistischer Staat: Der Imperialismus als Problem liberaler Parteien in Deutschland 1890-1914* (Göttingen, 1975).

—— Aldenhoff, Rita, Trautmann, Günter, and Vörlander, Hans (eds.), *Sozialer Liberalismus* (Göttingen, 1986).

Hubinger, Gangolf, *Kulturprotestantismus und Politik: Zum Verhaltnis von Liberalismus und Protestantismus im wilhelminischen Deutschland* (Tübingen, 1994).

Huerkamp, Claudia, *Der Aufstieg der Ärzte im 19. Jahrhundert: Vom gelehrten Stand zum professionellen Experten* (Göttingen, 1985).

Hull, Isabel, *The Entourage of Kaiser Wilhelm II, 1888–1918* (Cambridge, 1982).

Hunt, James C., *The People's Party in Württemberg and Southern Germany, 1890–1914: The Possibilities of Democratic Politics* (Stuttgart, 1975).

Jarausch, Konrad H., *Students, Society and Politics in Imperial Germany: The Rise of Academic Illiberalism* (Princeton, NJ., 1982).
—— and Jones, Larry E. (eds.), *In Search of a Liberal Germany: Studies in the History of German Liberalism from 1789 to the Present* (New York, 1990).

Jefferies, Matthew, *Politics and Culture in Wilhelmine Germany: The Case of Industrial Architecture* (Oxford, 1996).

Jeserich, Kurt G. A. *et al.* (eds.), *Deutsche Verfassungsgeschichte*, iii (Stuttgart, 1984).

John, Hartmut, *Das Reserveoffizierkorps im Deutschen Kaiserreich 1890–1914: Ein sozialgeschichtlicher Beitrag zur Untersuchung der gesellschaftlichen Militarisierung im Wilhelminischen Deutschland* (Frankfurt am Main, 1981).

John, Michael, *Politics and the Law in Late Nineteenth-Century Germany: The Origins of the Civil Code* (Oxford, 1989).

Jones, Larry E., *German Liberalism and the Dissolution of the Weimar Party System 1918–1933* (Chapel Hill, NC, 1988).

—— and Retallack, James (eds.), *Elections, Mass Politics and Social Change in Modern Germany: New Perspectives* (New York, 1992).

—— and —— (eds.), *Between Reform, Reaction and Resistance: Studies in the History of German Conservatism from 1789 to 1945* (Providence, RI, 1993).

Kaelble, Hartmut, *Industrielle Interessenpolitik in der Wilhelminischen Gesellschaft. Centralverband Deutscher Industrieller 1895–1914* (Berlin, 1967).

Kampe, Norbert, *Studenten und 'Judenfrage' im Deutschen Kaiserreich* (Göttingen, 1988).

Kastendiek, Hermann, *Der Liberalismus in Bremen*, diss., Kiel University, 1952.

Kehr, Eckart, *Battleship Building and Party Politics in Germany, 1894–1901* (Chicago, 1973).

—— *Economic Interest, Militarism, and Foreign Policy*, ed. Gordon A. Craig (Berkeley, Calif., 1977).

Kennedy, Paul, *The Rise of Anglo-German Antagonism 1860–1914* (London, 1980).

—— and Nicholls, Anthony (eds.), *Nationalist and Racialist Movements in Britain and Germany before 1914* (London, 1981).

Koch, Walter, *Volk und Staatsführung vor dem Weltkriege* (Stuttgart, 1935).

Kocka, Jürgen, *Die Angestellten in der deutschen Geschichte* (Göttingen, 1981).

—— *Facing Total War: German Society 1914–1918* (Leamington Spa, 1984).

—— (ed.), *Arbeiter und Bürger im 19. Jahrhundert* (Munich, 1986).

—— (ed.), *Bürger und Bürgerlichkeit im 19. Jahrhundert* (Göttingen, 1987).

—— (ed.), *Bürgertum im 19. Jahrhundert: Deutschland im internationalen Vergleich* (3 vols.; Munich, 1988).

Koshar, Rudy, *Social Life, Local Politics, and Nazism: Marburg, 1880–1933* (Chapel Hill, NC, 1986).

Kroboth, Rudolf, *Die Finanzpolitik des Deutschen Reiches während der Reichskanzlerschaft Bethmann Hollwegs und die Geld- und Kapitalmarktverhältnisse: (1909–1913/14)* (Frankfurt am Main, 1986).

Krüger, Dieter, *Nationalökonomen im wilhelminischen Deutschland* (Göttingen, 1983).

Kühne, Thomas, *Dreiklassenwahlrecht und Wahlkultur in Preußen 1867–1914: Landtagswahlen zwischen korporativer Tradition und politischem Massenmarkt* (Düsseldorf, 1994).

Kupfer, Torsten, *Der Weg zum Bündnis: entschieden Liberale und Sozialdemokraten in Dessau und Anhalt im Kaiserreich* (Cologne, 1998).

Ladd, Brian K., *Urban Planning and Civic Order in Germany, 1860–1914* (Cambridge, Mass., 1990).

Lamberti, Marjorie, *Jewish Activism in Imperial Germany* (New Haven, Conn., 1978).

—— *State, Society and the Elementary School in Imperial Germany* (New York, 1989).

Langewiesche, Dieter (ed.), *Liberalismus im 19. Jahrhundert* (Göttingen, 1988).

—— *Liberalism in Germany* (Houndsmill, 2000).

Lee, William R., and Rosenhaft, Eve (eds.), *The State and Social Change in Germany, 1880–1980* (New York, 1990).

Lenger, Friedrich, *Sozialgeschichte der deutschen Handwerker seit 1800* (Frankfurt am Main, 1988).

Lepsius, M. Rainer, 'Parteiensystem und Sozialstruktur: zum Problem der Demokratisierung der deutschen Gesellschaft', in Gerhard A. Ritter (ed.), *Die deutsche Parteien vor 1918* (Cologne, 1973), 56–80.

Lerman, Katherine A., *The Chancellor as Courtier: Bernhard von Bülow and the Governance of Germany 1900–1909* (Cambridge, 1990).

Levy, Richard S., *The Downfall of the Anti-Semitic Political Parties in Imperial Germany* (New Haven, Conn., 1975).

Lidtke, Vernon L., *The Alternative Culture. Socialist Labor in Imperial Germany* (New York and Oxford, 1985).

Link, Werner, 'Der Nationalverein für das liberale Deutschland (1907–18)', *Politische Vierteljahresschrift*, 5 (1964), 422–44.

Lorenz, Ina Susanne, *Eugen Richter: Der entschiedene Liberalismus in wilhelminischer Zeit, 1871–1906* (Husum, 1981).

Loth, Wilfried, *Katholiken im Kaiserreich: Der politische Katholizismus in der Krise des wilhelminischen Deutschlands* (Düsseldorf, 1984).

Luckemeyer, Ludwig, *Kasseler Liberale in zwei Jahrhunderten* (Kassel, 1979).

—— *Liberale in Hessen: 1848-1980* (Frankfurt am Main, 1980).

—— *Wilhelm Heile 1881–1981: Föderativer liberaler Rebell in DDP und FDP und erster liberaler Vorkämpfer Europas in Deutshland* (Korbach, 1981).

Mielke, Siegfried, *Der Hansa-Bund für Gewerbe, Handel und Industrie 1909–1914: Der gescheiterte Versuch einer antifeudalen Sammlungspolitik* (Göttingen, 1976).

Milatz, Alfred, 'Die linksliberalen Parteien und Gruppen in den Reichstagswahlen 1871–1912', *AfS* (1972), 273–92.

Möckl, Karl, *Die Prinzregentenzeit: Gesellschaft und Politik während der Ära des Prinzregenten Luitpold in Bayern* (Munich and Vienna, 1972).

Moeller, Robert G. (ed.), *Peasants and Lords in Modern Germany: Recent Studies in Agricultural History* (Boston, Mass., 1986).

Mogk, Walter, *Paul Rohrbach und das 'Größere Deutschland'* (Munich, 1972).

Molt, Peter, *Der Reichstag vor der improvisierten Revolution* (Cologne and Opladen, 1963).

Mommsen, Wolfgang J., 'Domestic Factors in German foreign policy before 1914', *CEH* 6 (1973), 3–43.

—— 'The Topos of Inevitable War in Germany in the Decade before 1914', in Volker Berghahn and Martin Kitchen (eds.), *Germany in the Age of Total War: Essays in Honour of Francis Carsten* (London, 1981), 23–45.

—— *Max Weber and German Politics 1890–1920* (Chicago, 1984).

—— *Burgerstolz und Weltmachtstreben: Deutschland unter Wilhelm II., 1890 bis 1918* (Berlin, 1995).

—— and Osterhammel, Jürgen (eds.), *Max Weber and his Contemporaries* (London, 1987).

Mosse, Werner E., and Paucker, Arnold (eds.), *Deutsches Judentum in Krieg und Revolution 1916–1923* (Tübingen, 1971).

—— (eds.), *Juden im Wilhelminischen Deutschland 1890–1914* (Tübingen, 1976).

Nipperdey, Thomas, *Die Organisation der deutschen Parteien vor 1918* (Düsseldorf, 1961).

—— *Deutsche Geschichte 1866–1918* (2 vols.; Munich, 1990–92).

Nöcker, Horst, *Der preußische Reichstagswähler in Kaiserreich und Republik 1912 und 1924* (Berlin, 1987).

O'Donnell, Anthony J., 'National Liberalism and the Mass Politics of the German Right 1890–1907', Ph.D. thesis, Princeton University, 1973.

Ostfeld, Hermann, *Die Haltung der Reichstagsfraktion der Fortschrittlichen Volkspartei zu den Annexions- und Friedensfragen in den Jahren 1914 bis 1918*, Diss.,Würzburg University, 1934.

Paetau, Reiner, and Rüdel, Holgar (eds.), *Arbeiter und Arbeiterbewegung in Schleswig-Holstein im 19. und 20. Jahrhundert* (Neumünster, 1987).

Palmowski, Jan, *Urban Liberalism in Imperial Germany: Frankfurt am Main, 1866–1914* (Oxford, 1999).

Patemann, Reinhard, *Der Kampf um die preußische Wahlreform im Ersten Weltkrieg* (Düsseldorf, 1964).

Pogge von Strandmann, Hartmut (ed.), *Walther Rathenau as Industrialist, Banker, Intellectual and Politician* (Oxford, 1985).

—— and Geiß, Immanuel, *Die Erforderlichkeit des Unmöglichen* (Frankfurt am Main, 1965).

Puhle, Hans-Jürgen, *Agrarische Interessenpolitik und preußischer Konservatismus im wilhelminischen Reich (1893–1914)*, 2nd edn. (Bonn, 1975).

Pulzer, Peter, *The Rise of Political Anti-Semitism in Germany and Austria*, 2nd edn. (London, 1988).

Rauh, Manfred, *Föderalismus und Parlamentarismus im Wilhelminischen Reich* (Düsseldorf, 1973).

—— *Die Parlamentarisierung des Deutschen Reiches* (Düsseldorf, 1977).

Reimann, Joachim, *Ernst Müller-Meiningen senior und der Linksliberalismus in seiner Zeit: Zur Biographie eines bayerischen und deutschen Politikers (1866–1944)* (Munich, 1968).

Retallack, James N., 'Conservatives contra Chancellor: Official Responses to the Spectre of Conservative Demagoguery, from Bismarck to Bülow', *Canadian Journal of History*, 20 (1985), 203–36.

—— *Notables of the Right: the Conservative Party and Political Mobilization in Germany, 1876–1918* (Boston, Mass., 1988).

Ritter, Gerhard A., *Die deutschen Parteien 1830–1914* (Göttingen, 1985).

—— and Tenfelde, Klaus, *Arbeiter im Deutschen Kaiserreich 1871 bis 1914* (Bonn, 1992).

Robson, Stuart T., 'Left-Wing Liberalism in Germany, 1900–1919', D.Phil., Oxford University, 1966.

Rohe, Karl, *Wahlen und Wählertraditionen in Deutschland* (Frankfurt, 1992).

Röhl, John C. G., *Germany without Bismarck: The Crisis of Government in the Second Reich, 1890–1900* (London, 1967).

—— *The Kaiser and his Court: Wilhelm II and the Government of Germany* (Cambridge, 1994).

Rolling, John D., 'Liberals, Socialists and City Government in Imperial Germany: The Case of Frankfurt am Main, 1900–1918', Ph.D., University of Wisconsin-Madison, 1979.

Saul, Klaus, 'Der "Deutsche Kriegerbund". Zur innenpolitischen Funktion eines "nationalen" Verbandes im kaiserlichen Deutshland', *Militärgeschichtliche Mitteilungen*, 2 (1969), 95–160.

—— *Staat, Industrie, Arbeiterbewegung im Kaiserreich* (Düsseldorf, 1974).

Schmädeke, Jürgen, *Wählerbewegung im Wilhelminischen Deutschland* (2 vols.; Berlin, 1995).

Schmidt, Gustav, 'Innenpolitische Blockbildungen am Vorabend des Ersten Weltkrieges', *Aus Politik und Zeitgeschichte*, B20 (1972), 3–32.

—— 'Liberalismus und soziale Reform: Der deutsche und der britische Fall, 1890–1914', *Tel Aviv'er Jahrbuch für Deutsche Geschichte*, 16 (1987), 212–38.

Schoenbaum, David, *Zabern 1913: Consensus Politics in Imperial Germany* (London, 1982).

Schorske, Carl E., *German Social Democracy, 1905–1917: The Devolopment of the Great Schism* (Cambridge, Mass., 1955; repr. 1983).

Schulte, Franz Gerrit, *Der Publizist Hellmut von Gerlach (1866–1935): Welt und Werk eines Demokraten und Pazifisten* (Munich, 1988).

Seeber, Gustav, *Zwischen Bebel und Bismarck: Zur Geschichte des Linksliberalismus in Deutschland 1871–1893* (Berlin, 1965).

Sell, Friedrich C., *Die Tragödie des deutschen Liberalismus*, 2nd edn. (Baden-Baden, 1981).

Sheehan, James J., *The Career of Lujo Brentano: A Study of Liberalism and Social Reform in Imperial Germany* (Chicago and London, 1966).

—— *German Liberalism in the Nineteenth Century* (Chicago, 1978).

Simon, Klaus, *Die Württembergischen Demokraten: Ihre Stellung und Arbeit im Parteien- und Verfassungssystem imWürttemberg und im Deutschen Reich* (Stuttgart, 1970).

Smith, Helmut Walser, *German Nationalism and Religious Conflict: Culture, Ideology, Politics, 1870-1914* (Princeton, NJ., 1995).

Stegmann, Dirk, *Die Erben Bismarcks. Parteien und Verbände in der Spätphase des wilhelminischen Deutschlands* (Cologne and Bonn, 1970).

—— 'Linksliberale Bankiers, Kaufleute und Industrielle 1890–1900', *Tradition. Zeitschrift für Firmengeschichte und Unternehmerbiographie*, 21 (1976), 4–36.

Steinmetz, George, *Regulating the Social: The Welfare State and Local Politics in Imperial Germany* (Princeton, NJ., 1993).

Struve, Walter, *Elites against Democracy: Leadership Ideals in Bourgeois Political Thought in Germany, 1890-1933* (Princeton, NJ., 1973).

Süle, Tibor, *Preußische Bürokratietradition: Zur Entwicklung von Verwaltung und Beamtenschaft in Deutschland 1871–1918* (Göttingen, 1988).

Suval, Stanley, *Electoral Politics in Wilhelmine Germany* (Chapel Hill, NC., 1985).

Thiel, Jürgen, *Die Großblockpolitik der nationalliberalen Partei Badens 1905–1914* (Stuttgart, 1976).

Thieme, Hartwig, *Nationaler Liberalismus in der Krise: Die nationalliberale Fraktion des Preußischen Abgeordnetenhauses 1914–1918* (Boppard, 1963).

Theiner, Peter, *Sozialer Liberalismus und deutsche Weltpolitik: Friedrich Naumann im Wilhelminischen Deutschland (1860–1919)* (Baden-Baden, 1983).

Toury, Jakob, *Die politischen Orientierung der Juden in Deutschland: Von Jena bis Weimar* (Tübingen, 1966).

Ullmann, Hans-Peter, *Der Bund der Industriellen. Organisation, Einfluß und Politik klein- und mittelbetrieblicher Industrieller im Deutschen Kaiserreich 1895–1914* (Göttingen, 1976).

—— *Interessenverbände in Deutschland* (Frankfurt am Main, 1988).

Ullrich, Volker, *Die Hamburger Arbeiterbewegung vom Vorabend des ersten Weltkrieges bis zur Revolution 1918/19* (2 vols.; Hamburg, 1976).

—— *Die nervöse Großmacht: Aufstieg und Untergang des deutschen Kaiserreichs* (Frankfurt am Main, 1997).

Warnecke, Klaus, *Der Wille zur Weltgeltung: Außenpolitik und Öffentlichkeit im Kaiserreich am Vorabend des Ersten Weltkrieges* (Düsseldorf, 1970).

Weber, Marie-Lise, *Ludwig Bamberger: Ideologie statt Realpolitik* (Wiesbaden, 1987).

Wegner, Konstanze, *Theodor Barth und die Freisinnige Vereinigung* (Tübingen, 1969).

Wehler, Hans-Ulrich, *The German Empire 1871–1918* (Leamington Spa, 1985).

—— *Deutsche Gesellschaftsgeschichte*, iii (Munich, 1995).

White, Dan S., *The Splintered Party. National Liberalism in Hessen and the Reich, 1867–1918* (Cambridge, Mass., 1976).

Winkler, Heinrich August, *Liberalismus und Antiliberalismus: Studien zur politischen Sozialgeschichte des 19. und 20. Jahrhunderts* (Göttingen, 1979).

Winkler, Jürgen R., *Sozialstruktur, politische Traditionen und Liberalismus: Eine empirische Langsschnittstudie zur Wahlentwicklung in Deutschland, 1871–1933* (Opladen, 1995).

Witt, Peter-Christian, *Die Finanzpolitik des Deutschen Reiches von 1903 bis 1913* (Hamburg, 1970).

Wolf, Siegbert, *Liberalismus in Frankfurt am Main vom Ende der Freien Stadt bis zum Ersten Weltkrieg (1866–1914)* (Frankfurt am Main, 1987).

Wölk, Monika, *Der preußische Volksschulabsolvent als Reichstagswähler 1871–1912* (Berlin, 1980).

Zang, Gert (ed.), *Provinzialisierung einer Region. Regionale Unterentwicklung und liberale Politik in der Stadt und im Kreis Konstanz im 19. Jahrhundert* (Frankfurt am Main, 1978).

Index